# STATISTICAL PACKAGE FOR THE SOCIAL SCIENCES

**NORMAN NIE**
Department of Political Science
and
National Opinion Research Center
University of Chicago


**DALE H. BENT**
Faculty of Business Administration
The University of Alberta


**C. HADLAI HULL**
Computation Center
University of Chicago

# SPSS

## STATISTICAL PACKAGE FOR THE SOCIAL SCIENCES

**McGRAW-HILL BOOK COMPANY**
New York
San Francisco
St. Louis
Düsseldorf
London
Mexico
Panama
Sydney
Toronto

This book was set in Press Roman by the S. P. Miller Company, and printed and bound by Edwards Brothers, Inc. The designer was Janet Bollow; the drawings were done by Mark Schroeder. The editor was Richard F. Dojny. Charles A. Goehring supervised production.

**STATISTICAL PACKAGE FOR THE SOCIAL SCIENCES**

Printed in the United States of America.

Library of Congress catalog card number: 75-119826

90   EBEB   79876543

**ISBN 07-046530-4**

TO OUR WIVES
CAROL, PENNY, AND SUE

# PREFACE

*Statistical Package for the Social Sciences* (SPSS), a system of computer programs described in the present volume, represents the culmination of several years of systems design, programming, and documentation on the part of the authors and others. In these introductory remarks, it seems appropriate to describe the reasons why this work was undertaken and to outline the philosophy which guided the development of SPSS.

The development of SPSS was evolutionary. The initial design of SPSS was begun by Dale Bent and Norman Nie in June of 1965, while we were both graduate students at Stanford University. The impetus for its development was our continuous frustration in attempting to serve the research and teaching needs of the faculty and graduate students of the Political Science department and the Institute for Political Studies. During the academic year 1964–1965 we attempted to import a library of data analysis programs which would serve the needs of the department and the institute. While this piecemeal library met some of our most elementary needs, research and teaching which required data analysis was still a very frustrating business.

Each of the programs had its own concepts and syntax, and we consequently spent an intolerable amount of time teaching users how to operate many different single-purpose programs which were so distinct that almost no transfer learning took place. The programs were written in many different languages, and consequently, when a problem was encountered in one of them, it was exceedingly difficult to examine the program code to locate the bug. Further, we quickly found that social science data analysis was in practice four-fifths file editing and data handling and only in small part actual statistical analysis. While statistical programs abounded, we were constantly forced to write many ad hoc programs to edit files, recode and transform variables, as well as accomplish a large number of other routine file liaison and housekeeping chores. Finally, we discovered that the prevailing level of documentation was poor. Many writeups, if they existed at all, were cryptic to the point of obscurity. There appeared to be a general tendency to prepare program documentation for data-analysis programs in the fashion one encounters in the mathematical literature, and this was simply inadequate for the average social science user. In short, after a year's experience with a piecemeal program library, we felt that we were in only slightly better circumstances than when we had begun, and in fact, it often seemed to us that we had simply increased the level of frustration by announcing the availability of programs which could not be efficiently taught, easily utilized, or sufficiently supported.

The training, background, and interest of the typical social scientist aggravates the problem, for he has not thus far gained the technical grasp of computer usage to perform the data-analysis tasks required by his research. Given the number of skills that he is currently required to master, his abdication in this highly technical area may, we feel, be both justifiable and rational. We became convinced from our experience that special provisions had to be made for the social science community in order to simplify the process of data analysis so that the social science researcher himself could gain control over the day-to-day manipulation and analysis of his data.

As a result of our frustration, as well as our experience, we began to design an integrated system of programs that addressed itself to these needs. In the early period, we placed a great deal of emphasis on defining procedures that would automate the routine tasks of data processing and around which a series of statistical programs could be built. We felt that existing stand-alone programs, as well as previous statistical packages (such as the widely used BMD system), had established the feasibility of implementing generalized statistical programs, but what had not been successfully accomplished was the production of an integrated system of such programs embedded in a series of common procedures for the management and handling of complex data files. Accordingly, a set of conventions for such a system of programs was defined and coding was initiated for the IBM 7090 computer then in use at Stanford University. The code was developed in piecemeal fashion and eventually hardened into a system which became the forerunner of the present SPSS.

We were sufficiently encouraged by the results we had obtained with the 7090 programs to begin to make plans for the expansion and conversion of the system to the IBM 360, which arrived at Stanford in the summer of 1967. It was at this point that Hadlai Hull joined the project and began the arduous process of converting our semioperational concepts into a working system, a task which the original two authors feel he superbly accomplished.

Conversion of the 7090 prototype system was facilitated by the exclusive use of Fortran in the 7090 program and the fact that much of the macrologic of the system could be directly transferred to the 360. In fact OS/360 provided increased speed and core, which immediately alleviated many of the problems that plagued us on the 7090. A decision was made to fix the capabilities of the system at the level documented in the present volume, and arrangements were made for the dissemination of the program and documentation to those who wished to use the package. During this period Northwestern University has proceeded with the conversion of SPSS to CDC 6000—series equipment and an operational CDC version of SPSS should be generally available by the time this volume is in print. (Appendix G is a special guide to SPSS for CDC users.)

We are aware that the current system has a great number of deficiencies, but we believe it meets a majority of the social science data-analysis needs in a way that has not been previously possible. Further, SPSS is an open-ended system, and we are hopeful that we and others will continue to improve, add to, and modify the existing version of the system. To facilitate the ability of others to add a wider variety of statistical procedures to SPSS, a technical or programmer's guide had been included in Appendix H. Because of the design of SPSS, all future programs incorporated into the system can take complete advantage of the capabilities for file maintenance and data handling which currently exist in the package, and we fully hope that this will be an incentive to those contemplating the addition of other statistical programs.

In the rapidly changing area of computer technology, any designer of software must concern himself with the expected term of usefulness of the programs he has created. We have tried to take a number of steps to lengthen the life expectancy of the SPSS system. First, the language selected to write the programs was Fortran IV, one of the few languages in use today with any claim to universality. Second, the system was developed on the IBM 360 and translated to CDC 6000—series equipment; these two computers represent an overwhelming proportion of all university resident machines in North America. The use of Fortran IV and a firm base in these two third-generation machines should facilitate the conversion of SPSS to fourth-generation machines which should be appearing soon.

Time-sharing systems are, of course, becoming generally available throughout the United States and elsewhere. This raises the possibility of interactive or conversational programs for statistical analysis. SPSS is not a conversational system. The 7090 version was designed for conventional batch processing, and the present 360 and CDC versions operate in the same fashion. At Stanford, we have had a great deal of success running SPSS from remote terminals controlled by the WYLBUR text editing and remote batch-entry system. SPSS in this environment still operates as a batch program, but the text editor and remote batch-entry and retrieval capabilities permit the user to perpare and enter all his jobs from the terminal and to print back small jobs on his terminal.

The authors have had the opportunity to examine and in some instances use true conversational statistical systems, such as APL STATPACK at the University of Alberta and IMPRESS at Dartmouth. Each of these systems is truly elegant and a great pleasure to use, but in our experience we have not encountered any conversational data-analysis system which has the kind of data-handling capabilities, both in terms of volume and flexibility, which SPSS possesses. We are convinced that such systems will emerge in the near future; they await only slightly larger and faster machines and the emergence of a more feasible remote device for the display of large amounts of output. When these conversational system emerge, they will have a major impact on the way in which the social scientist engages in social research. And we therefore anxiously await the pending obsolescence of our own system.

For the present, however, we feel that SPSS presents the social scientist with a useful working language for data analysis. We hope that the capabilities of SPSS will act as a minimum benchmark for the designers of new and better languages for social research. Finally, we hope that the users of SPSS will find that it provides them with a substantial increase in the ease and flexibility with which they can approach their day-to-day use of the computer.

## ACKNOWLEDGEMENTS

The authors of the SPSS system would like to express their appreciation to the Department of Political Science and the Institute of Political Studies at Stanford University for their vital support in the development of the SPSS system. We would wish in particular to acknowledge our indebtedness to Professor Sidney Verba, Director of the Cross-National Program on Political and Social Change, for the generous support he gave us. Without this support the SPSS system could not have been completed. We would also like to thank Professors Heinz Eulau and Kenneth Prewitt of the City Council Research Project, who also made financial contributions to SPSS, as did the Department of Political Science at Stanford. Special thanks must also be given to William C. Mitchell, who designed the multiple-regression program and wrote the chapter describing it. A similar debt is owed to Professor Jae-On Kim, who helped with the design of the factor-analysis program and prepared the write-up for it.

The development of SPSS was greatly aided by support of the Stanford Computation Center in the programming and checkout of the IBM 7090 version. Lissner Computer Services of Mountain View, California, was also instrumental in supporting the programming of this version. The User Services group of the University of Alberta Computation Center was also most helpful in providing assistance in a variety of ways. We are indebted to the Vogelback Computing Center at Northwestern University for taking on the job of converting SPSS to CDC 6000–series equipment, particularly to Larry Young, who carried out the conversion, and Ben Mittman and Loraine Borman, who supervised the project and marshalled the resources required to support it. SPSS is currently being supported by the joint efforts of the National Opinion Research Center of the University of Chicago, the University of Chicago Computation Center, and the Volgelback Computing Center at Northwestern University. The generosity of these institutions permits us to continue to maintain SPSS for the user community and to engage in some developmental work.

Grateful acknowledgment is given to the secretarial efforts of Carol Nie, who typed and edited several drafts of the SPSS manual. Wendy Bohle also made a major contribution in editing the first draft of the manual and putting together several of the appendixes. Susan Hansen prepared several example runs and helped edit the write-up for subprogram PARTIAL CORR.

Sincere thanks, too, are due to Carol Bayha of the Institute of Political Studies and Patrick Bova of NORC, both of whom have (at different times) handled a large amount of the administrative work and have taken care of the distribution of the system and the manuals. Peter Webster was also of considerable help in the day-to-day preparation of the text. The efforts of Jarvis Rich in helping to transfer the SPSS project from Stanford to NORC at the University of Chicago should be mentioned. Dashirudden Amhed, Andrew Ellis, Professor Edward Feigenbaum, Ichiro Miyake, and G. Bingham Powell were kind enough to give us their support and advice at numerous points in the development of SPSS. Finally, the students of the Institute of Political Studies at Stanford, by their regular use of the developmental versions of SPSS, provided us with the kind of day-to-day feedback which resulted in a better system.

A system like SPSS is, of course, never developed in a vacuum, and we would like to acknowledge the contributions made to our general thinking by several previous systems: Data Text, developed at Harvard University, and BMD, developed at the University of California at Los Angeles, were especially significant. The factor-analysis subprogram was adapted from an existing program developed at the University of Alberta, Edmonton, Canada. The Guttman scale subprogram borrowed heavily from an existing program at Stanford University, originally designed by Professor Ronald Anderson, currently at the University of Minnesota. The output format and some of the table statistics used in subprobrams CROSSTABS and FASTABS were directly borrowed from the Data Text system developed by A. Couch and others at Harvard. While we wish to acknowledge our great indebtedness to those who developed these programs, we alone are responsible for whatever errors or mistakes are present in our implementation of them.

Norman H. Nie

Dale H. Bent

C. Hadlai Hull

# CONTENTS

PREFACE                                                                    vii

## 1
## THE SPSS SYSTEM: AN OVERVIEW                                              1

**1.1** THE PURPOSES OF A STATISTICAL PACKAGE OF PROGRAMS        2

**1.2** STATISTICAL PROCEDURES IN SPSS        3

1.2.1  One-way frequency distributions, measures of central tendency and dispersion        3
1.2.2  Table displays of relationships between two or more variables        4
1.2.3  Bivariate correlation analysis        4
1.2.4  Multivariate correlation and regression        5
1.2.5  Guttman scaling and factor analysis        5

**1.3** FEATURES OF SPSS        7

1.3.1  Sequencing calculations        7
1.3.2  Entering and processing data        7
1.3.3  Subfiles        12
1.3.4  Missing data        12

xi

1.3.5 Recoding data   12
1.3.6 Variable transformations   12
1.3.7 Sampling, selecting, and weighting data   13
1.3.8 Retrieval of data from the system   13
1.3.9 Output of results from the system   14

**1.4** SUGGESTIONS FOR THE USE OF THIS TEXT   14


**2**
**THE ORGANIZATION AND CODING OF DATA FOR INPUT
INTO THE SPSS SYSTEM**   **15**

**2.1** THE CASE AS THE UNIT OF ANALYSIS   15
**2.2** CODING CONVENTIONS FOR DATA   16

2.2.1 Variables and variable types   16
2.2.2 Coding missing values   16
2.2.3 Organizing data for input   16

2.2.3.1 Organizing data in fixed-column format   17
2.2.3.2 Organizing data in free-field format   17
2.2.3.3 Assigning case- and card-identification numbers   18

**2.3** SUBFILES: THEIR FUNCTION AND STRUCTURE   19

2.3.1 Using subfiles   19
2.3.2 Subfile structure   19

**2.4** RECORDING DATA ON MACHINE-READABLE MEDIA   21
**2.5** LIMITATIONS ON INPUT DATA   21


**3**
**SPSS CONTROL CARDS**   **22**

**3.1** CONTROL-CARD PREPARATION: GENERAL FORMAT AND CONVENTIONS   23

3.1.1 The control field   23
3.1.2 The specification field   23

3.1.2.1 Names   23
3.1.2.2 Values   24
3.1.2.3 Keywords   24
3.1.2.4 Labels   24
3.1.2.5 Delimiters   24
3.1.2.6 Operators   25

3.1.3 Summary of general rules for control-card preparation   25

**3.2** NOTATION USED IN PRESENTING CONTROL-CARD FORMATS   26


**4**
**DEFINING AN SPSS FILE: THE DATA-DEFINITION CARDS**   **27**

**4.1** THE FILE NAME CARD   28
**4.2** THE VARIABLE LIST CARD   28
**4.3** THE SUBFILE LIST CARD   30
**4.4** THE # OF CASES CARD   30

**4.5**   THE INPUT MEDIUM CARD    31

**4.6**   THE INPUT FORMAT CARD    32

    4.6.1  Fixed- or free-field format    32

    4.6.2  The format list for data in fixed-column format    33

    4.6.3  The format elements    33

        4.6.3.1  A-type variables    33

        4.6.3.2  F-type variables    33

        4.6.3.3  Skipping card columns with the X    34

        4.6.3.4  Skipping cards with the /    34

    4.6.4  The variable list and the format list    35

**4.7**   THE MISSING VALUES CARD    36

**4.8**   THE VALUE LABELS CARD    37

**4.9**   THE PRINT FORMATS CARD    39

**4.10**  THE VAR LABELS CARD    40

**4.11**  RULES GOVERNING THE ORDER OF THE DATA-DEFINITION CARDS    40


**5**

**CONTROLLING THE CALCULATIONS:**
**THE TASK-DEFINITION CARDS**       **42**

**5.1** THE PROCEDURE CARDS    42

**5.2** THE OPTIONS CARD    43

**5.3** THE STATISTICS CARD    43

**5.4** THE READ INPUT DATA CARD    44

**5.5** THE PROCESS SBFILES CARD    44


**6**

**THE RUN CARDS**       **47**

**6.1** THE RUN NAME CARD    47

**6.2** THE FINISH CARD    48

**6.3** THE KEYPUNCH CARD    48

**6.4** THE PRINT BACK CARD    48

**6.5** THE COMMENT CARD    48

**6.6** THE DOCUMENT CARD    49

**6.7** THE DUMP CARD    49

**6.8** THE NUMBERED CARD    50


**7**

**GENERATING AND PROCESSING SPSS FILES:**
**CARD ORDER AND DECK SETUP**       **51**

**7.1** PROCESSING FROM CARDS, BCD TAPES, OR BCD DISK FILES:
CARD ORDER AND DECK SETUP    51

**7.2** GENERATING AND RETAINING SPSS SYSTEM FILES:
THE SAVE FILE CARD    55

**7.3** PROCESSING DATA FROM SPSS SYSTEM FILES    57

    7.3.1  The GET FILE card    57

    7.3.2  Deck setup and card order for processing data from SPSS system files    57

    7.3.3  Modifying or adding to data-defining information during processing runs
          from SPSS system files    58


**8**

**RECODING AND VARIABLE TRANSFORMATION:
THE DATA-MODIFICATION CARDS**    **60**

**8.1** RECODING VARIABLES: THE RECODE CARD    61

    8.1.1  Temporary versus permanent Recoding: the *RECODE card    64

    8.1.2  Example usages and deck setup for the RECODE and *RECODE cards    64

    8.1.3  Limitations on the number of recodes    65

**8.2** VARIABLE TRANSFORMATIONS: THE COMPUTE AND IF CARDS    66

    8.2.1  Computing variables by means of arithmetic expressions:
          the COMPUTE card    66

        8.2.1.1  Constructing arithmetic expressions on the COMPUTE card    67

        8.2.1.2  Example usages of the COMPUTE card    68

    8.2.2  Variable transformations with conditional assignments: the IF card    70

    8.2.3  Starred [*] and nonstarred versions of RECODE, COMPUTE, and IF cards:
          temporary versus permanent data modification    73

    8.2.4  Data definition for variable transformations: data-definition cards
          for newly generated or modified variables    74

        8.2.4.1  Defining missing values for transformed variables    74

        8.2.4.2  Initialization of transformed variables    74

        8.2.4.3  Inserting other data-defining information for transformed variables    75

**8.3** LIMITATIONS ON THE COMPUTE AND IF CARDS    75

**8.4** DECK SETUP AND CARD ORDER FOR DATA-MODIFICATION CARDS    76


**9**

**THE DATA-SELECTION CARDS**    **78**

**9.1** GENERATING A RANDOM SAMPLE FROM A FILE:
THE SAMPLE AND *SAMPLE CARDS    78

**9.2** SELECTING CASES FROM A FILE: THE SELECT IF
AND *SELECT IF CARDS    79

**9.3** WEIGHTING CASES IN A FILE: THE WEIGHT AND *WEIGHT CARDS    79

**9.4** DECK SETUP AND CARD ORDER FOR DATA-SELECTION CARDS    81


**10**

**ALTERING DATA IN AN SPSS SYSTEM FILE:
THE FILE-MODIFICATION CARDS**    **84**

**10.1** DELETING AND RETAINING VARIABLES: THE DELETE VARS
AND KEEP VARS CARDS    85

**10.2** ADDING VARIABLES TO AN EXISTING SPSS SYSTEM FILE:
THE ADD VARIABLES CARD    86

**10.3** DELETING SUBFILES WITH THE DELETE SUBFILES CARD    88

**10.4** ADDING SUBFILES TO A SYSTEM FILE: THE ADD SUBFILES CARD    89

**10.5** OUTPUT OF DATA ONTO BCD FILES: THE WRITE CASES CARD    90

    10.5.1  The variable list for the WRITE CASES card    91

    10.5.2  The format list for the WRITE CASES card    91

    10.5.3  A note on writing cases from weighted files    93

    10.5.4  Example deck setup and card order for the WRITE CASES procedure    94


## 11
## DESCRIPTIVE STATISTICS AND ONE-WAY
## FREQUENCY DISTRIBUTIONS    96

**11.1** SUBPROGRAM CONDESCRIPTIVE: DESCRIPTIVE STATISTICS
FOR CONTINUOUS VARIABLES    97

    11.1.1  The CONDESCRIPTIVE procedure card    97

    11.1.2  Options available for subprogram CONDESCRIPTIVE    98

    11.1.3  Statistics available with subprogram CONDESCRIPTIVE    98

    11.1.4  Program limitations for subprogram CONDESCRIPTIVE    99

    11.1.5  Examples of the use of subprogram CONDESCRIPTIVE    99

**11.2** SUBPROGRAM CODEBOOK: ONE-WAY FREQUENCY DISTRIBUTIONS,
HISTOGRAMS, AND RELATED STATISTICS IN CODEBOOK FORMAT    102

    11.2.1  The CODEBOOK procedure card    103

    11.2.2  Options available for subprogram CODEBOOK    103

    11.2.3  Statistics available for subprogram CODEBOOK    104

    11.2.4  Program limitations for subprogram CODEBOOK    104

    11.2.5  Example deck setups for using subprogram CODEBOOK    105

**11.3** SUBPROGRAM MARGINALS: ONE-WAY FREQUENCY DISTRIBUTIONS
AND RELATED STATISTICS    109

    11.3.1  The MARGINALS procedure card    109

    11.3.2  Options available for subprogram MARGINALS    110

    11.3.3  Statistics available for subprogram MARGINALS    110

    11.3.4  Program limitations for subprogram MARGINALS    111

    11.3.5  Example deck setup using subprogram MARGINALS    111


## 12
## TABLE DISPLAYS OF RELATIONSHIPS BETWEEN TWO
## OR MORE VARIABLES: CROSSTABULATION
## AND DESCRIPTIONS OF SUBPOPULATIONS    115

**12.1** AN INTRODUCTION TO CROSSTABULATION    116

**12.2** SUBPROGRAM CROSSTABS: TWO-WAY TO n-WAY CROSSTABULATION
TABLES AND RELATED STATISTICS    118

    12.2.1  The CROSSTABS procedure card    119

    12.2.2  Printed output from subprogram CROSSTABS    121

        12.2.2.1  A note on value labels for CROSSTABS    123

    12.2.3  Options available for subprogram CROSSTABS: The OPTIONS card    124

    12.2.4  Statistics available for subprogram CROSSTABS: The STATISTICS card    125

    12.2.5  Program limitations for subprogram CROSSTABS    125

12.2.6 Example deck setups for subprogram CROSSTABS    126

**12.3** SUBPROGRAM FASTABS: TWO-WAY TO n-WAY CROSSTABULATION TABLES AND RELATED STATISTICS FOR INTEGER VARIABLES    129

12.3.1 The FASTABS procedure card    129
12.3.2 Printed output from subprogram FASTABS    132
12.3.3 Options available for subprogram FASTABS: The OPTIONS card    132
12.3.4 Statistics available for subprogram FASTABS: The STATISTICS card    132
12.3.5 Program limitations for subprogram FASTABS    133
12.3.6 Example deck setup and output for subprogram FASTABS    134

**12.4** SUBPROGRAM BREAKDOWN: DESCRIPTION OF SUBPOPULATIONS    134

12.4.1 The BREAKDOWN procedure card    137
12.4.2 Options available for subprogram BREAKDOWN: The OPTIONS card    139
12.4.3 Statistics for subprogram BREAKDOWN    139
12.4.4 Program limitations for subprogram BREAKDOWN    140
12.4.5 Example deck setup for subprogram BREAKDOWN    140


**13**
**BIVARIATE CORRELATION ANALYSIS: PEARSON AND RANK-ORDER CORRELATION**    **143**

**13.1** INTRODUCTION TO CORRELATION ANALYSIS    143
**13.2** SUBPROGRAM PEARSON CORR: PEARSON PRODUCT-MOMENT CORRELATION COEFFICIENTS    145

13.2.1 The PEARSON CORR procedure card    146
13.2.2 Options available for subprogram PEARSON CORR    148
13.2.3 Statistics available for subprogram PEARSON CORR    150
13.2.4 Program limitations for subprogram PEARSON CORR    150
13.2.5 Sample deck setup and output for subprogram PEARSON CORR    151

**13.3** SUBPROGRAM NONPAR CORR: SPEARMAN AND/OR KENDALL RANK-ORDER CORRELATION COEFFICIENTS    153

13.3.1 The NONPAR CORR procedure card    155
13.3.2 Options available for subprogram NONPAR CORR    155
13.3.3 Statistics available for subprogram NONPAR CORR    155
13.3.4 Program limitations for subprogram NONPAR CORR    155
13.3.5 Sample deck setup and output for subprogram NONPAR CORR    156


**14**
**PARTIAL CORRELATION: SUBPROGRAM PARTIAL CORR**    **157**

**14.1** INTRODUCTION TO PARTIAL-CORRELATION ANALYSIS    158
**14.2** THE PARTIAL CORR PROCEDURE CARD    161

14.2.1 The correlation list    162
14.2.2 The control list    162
14.2.3 The order value(s)    163

**14.3** SPECIAL CONVENTIONS FOR MATRIX INPUT FOR SUBPROGRAM PARTIAL CORR    164

14.3.1 Requirements on the form and format for correlational matrices    164
14.3.2 Conventions and control cards required to enter matrices    164

**14.4** OPTIONS AVAILABLE FOR SUBPROGRAM PARTIAL CORR     166
**14.5** STATISTICS AVAILABLE FOR SUBPROGRAM PARTIAL CORR     168
**14.6** PROGRAM LIMITATIONS FOR SUBPROGRAM PARTIAL CORR     169
**14.7** EXAMPLE DECK SETUPS FOR SUBPROGRAM PARTIAL CORR     169


**15**
**MULTIPLE-REGRESSION ANALYSIS: SUBPROGRAM REGRESSION     174**

**15.1** INTRODUCTION TO MULTIPLE-REGRESSION ANALYSIS     175

  15.1.1  An example     175
  15.1.2  Mathematical description of multiple regression     179
  15.1.3  Stepwise multiple regression     180
  15.1.4  Computational methods     181

**15.2** THE REGRESSION PROCEDURE CARD     181

  15.2.1  The VARIABLES list     181
  15.2.2  The REGRESSION list     182

**15.3** SPECIAL CONVENTIONS FOR MATRIX INPUT
FOR SUBPROGRAM REGRESSION     184
**15.4** PRINTED OUTPUT FROM SUBPROGRAM REGRESSION     185
**15.5** OPTIONS AVAILABLE FOR SUBPROGRAM REGRESSION     187
**15.6** STATISTICS AVAILABLE FOR SUBPROGRAM REGRESSION     188
**15.7** PROGRAM LIMITATIONS OF SUBPROGRAM REGRESSION     188
**15.8** EXAMPLE DECK SETUPS AND OUTPUT FOR SUBPROGRAM REGRESSION     189


**16**
**SCALOGRAM ANALYSIS: SUBPROGRAM GUTTMAN SCALE     196**

**16.1** AN INTRODUCTION TO GUTTMAN SCALE ANALYSIS     197

  16.1.1  Evaluating Guttman scales     199
  16.1.2  Building Guttman scales     201

**16.2** THE GUTTMAN SCALE PROCEDURE CARD     203
**16.3** OPTIONS AVAILABLE FOR SUBPROGRAM GUTTMAN SCALE     204
**16.4** STATISTICS AVAILABLE FOR SUBPROGRAM GUTTMAN SCALE     205
**16.5** LIMITATIONS OF SUBPROGRAM GUTTMAN SCALE     205
**16.6** SAMPLE DECK SETUP AND OUTPUT FOR SUBPROGRAM
GUTTMAN SCALE     205


**17**
**FACTOR ANALYSIS     208**

**17.1** INTRODUCTION TO FACTOR ANALYSIS     209

  17.1.1  Meaning of essential tables and statistics in factor-analysis output     213

**17.2** METHODS OF FACTORING AVAILABLE IN SUBPROGRAM FACTOR     218

  17.2.1  Principal factoring without iteration: PA1     218
  17.2.2  Principal factoring with iteration: PA2     219
  17.2.3  The remaining methods of factoring     220
    17.2.3.1  Rao's canonical factoring: RAO     220

17.2.3.2 Alpha factoring: ALPHA     220

17.2.3.3 Image factoring: IMAGE     221

**17.3**    METHODS OF ROTATION AVAILABLE IN SUBPROGRAM FACTOR     221

17.3.1 Orthogonal rotation: QUARTIMAX     223

17.3.2 Orthogonal rotation: VARIMAX     224

17.3.3 Orthogonal rotation: EQUIMAX     224

17.3.4 Oblique rotation: OBLIQUE     224

17.3.5 Graphical presentation of rotated orthogonal factors     225

**17.4**    BUILDING COMPOSITE INDICES WITH A FACTOR-SCORE COEFFICIENT (OR FACTOR ESTIMATE) MATRIX     226

**17.5**    THE FACTOR PROCEDURE CARD     227

17.5.1 The VARIABLES= list     227

17.5.1.1 The variable list for the input of matrices     228

17.5.2 Selection of factoring methods: By the TYPE= keyword     228

17.5.3 Altering the diagonal of the correlation matrix by means of the diagonal value list     228

17.5.4 Controlling the factoring process: The NFACTORS, MINEIGEN, ITERATE, and STOPFACT parameters     229

17.5.4.1 Controlling the number of factors with the NFACTORS parameter     229

17.5.4.2 Controlling the number of factors with the MINEIGEN parameter     229

17.5.4.3 Controlling the number of iterations with the ITERATE parameter     230

17.5.4.4 Controlling the number of iterations with the STOPFACT parameter     230

17.5.5 Selecting the method of rotation with the ROTATE parameter     231

17.5.5.1 Controlling oblique rotation with the DELTA parameter     231

17.5.6 Summary of the format of the FACTOR procedure card     231

**17.6**    SPECIAL CONVENTION FOR MATRIX INPUT AND OUTPUT FOR SUBPROGRAM FACTOR     233

17.6.1 Control cards required to enter matrices     234

17.6.1.1 Input of correlation matrix     234

17.6.1.2 Input of the factor matrix     234

17.6.2 Output of correlation and factor matrices     235

**17.7**    OPTIONS AVAILABLE IN SUBPROGRAM FACTOR     235

**17.8**    STATISTICS AVAILABLE FOR SUBPROGRAM FACTOR     237

**17.9**    PROGRAM LIMITATIONS FOR SUBPROGRAM FACTOR     238

**17.10** EXAMPLE DECK SETUPS FOR SUBPROGRAM FACTOR     238

**APPENDIXES**

**A**
**SPSS ERROR MESSAGES**      **245**

**B**
**SUMMARY OF SPSS CONTROL CARDS: FUNCTIONS,**
**STATUS, FORMATS, AND POSITION IN CARD DECK**      **251**

**C**
**SPSS SYNTAX**      **267**

**D**
**REFERENCE FOR STATISTICAL FORMULAS**      **272**
**D.1** STATISTICS EMPLOYED IN SUBPROGRAMS CONDESCRIPTIVE,
CODEBOOK, AND MARGINALS    272
**D.2** STATISTICS AVAILABLE FOR SUBPROGRAMS
CROSSTABS AND FASTABS    275

**E**
**GLOSSARY OF TECHNICAL TERMS**      **279**

**F**
**OS 360 JOB CONTROL LANGUAGE (JCL) FOR THE SPSS SYSTEM**
**AT THE STANFORD INSTALLATION**      **289**
**F.1** BASIC JCL CARDS ALWAYS REQUIRED WHEN
OPERATING THE SPSS SYSTEM    290
**F.2** ALTERING THE SPACE PARAMETER FOR THE ALLOCATION OF CORE    291
**F.3** DETERMINING THE REQUIRED JCL    293
**F.4** JCL REQUIRED FOR BCD INPUT FILES: FT08    294
**F.5** JCL REQUIRED FOR THE OUTPUT SYSTEM FILE: FT04    297
**F.6** JCL REQUIRED FOR INPUT SYSTEM FILES: FT03    301
**F.7** JCL REQUIRED FOR BCD OUTPUT FILES: FT09    303

**G**
**THE CDC 6000-SERIES VERSION OF SPSS**      **307**
**G.1** DEFINING AN SPSS FILE: THE DATA-DEFINITION CARDS    308
**G.2** SPECIAL-PURPOSE RUN CARDS    308
**G.3** GENERATING AND PROCESSING SPSS FILES: RETAINING FILES    309
**G.4** THE FILE-MODIFICATION CARDS    309
**G.5** NORTHWESTERN UNIVERSITY CDC 6400 ENVIRONMENT    310

**H**
**A PROGRAMMER'S GUIDE TO SPSS**     **315**

**H.1** SYSTEM FLOW AND LOGIC    316
**H.2** SPECIFIC SUBPROGRAM LOGIC    321
**H.3** INCORPORATION OF A NEW SUBPROGRAM IN SPSS    328


**I**
**LISTING OF CASES AND DATA-DEFINITION CARDS**
**FOR EXAMPLE FILES**     **333**

**I.1** FILE COMSTUDY    333
**I.2** FILE ORGSTUDY    335


**SPSS INSTALLATIONS**     **341**

# STATISTICAL PACKAGE FOR THE SOCIAL SCIENCES

# 1
# THE SPSS SYSTEM: AN OVERVIEW

The *Statistical Package for the Social Sciences* (SPSS) is an integrated system of computer programs for the analysis of social science data. The system has been designed to provide the social scientist with a unified and comprehensive package enabling him to perform many different types of data analysis in a simple and convenient manner. SPSS allows a great deal of flexibility in the format of data. It provides the user with a comprehensive set of procedures for data transformation and file manipulation, and it offers the researcher a large number of statistical routines commonly used in the social sciences.

In addition to the usual descriptive statistics, simple frequency distributions, and crosstabulations, SPSS contains procedures for simple correlation (for both ordinal and interval data), partial correlation, multiple regression, factor analysis, and Guttman scaling. The data-management facilities can be used to modify a file of data permanently and can also be used in conjunction with any of the statistical procedures. These facilities enable the user to generate variable transformations, to recode variables, sample, select, or weight specified cases, and to add to or alter the data or the file-defining information. SPSS enables the social scientist to perform his analysis through the use of natural-language control statements and requires no programming experience on the part of the user. This text is a complete instructional guide to SPSS and is written in such a way as to make the system easily accessible to users with no prior computer experience.

In this introductory chapter we attempt to describe in broad terms the general capabilities of the SPSS system. Section 1.1 presents a brief introduction to data analysis on electronic computers. Section 1.2 and its subsections describe the various statistical procedures available in the SPSS system. An introduction to the general features and operation of the SPSS system is presented along with several examples in Section 1.3. The attention of the reader is drawn especially to Section 1.4 where suggestions for the use of this text are given for persons with greater or lesser experience with the use of computers for data analysis.

## 1.1   THE PURPOSES OF A STATISTICAL PACKAGE OF PROGRAMS

Computers are extremely useful for the routine processing of large quantities of data. Indeed, the need for large-scale processing led directly to the development of the computer. Such processing includes the classification, sorting, storing, and retrieval of data which have been presented to the computer in a suitable coded form. These routine tasks, termed *data processing* constitute the most important use of computers at present.

Of course, because of their capability for carrying out arithmetic operations at high speed, computers are also widely used to carry out lengthy mathematical calculations. When such calculations are performed upon data for the purpose of analysis, the term *data analysis* is often used. Data analysis combines data processing with mathematical or statistical manipulation. The results are numbers which summarize the information contained in the original data.

Data analysis constitutes an important part of the activity in any empirical science. In the social sciences in particular, where the amount of data required to describe a phenomenon adequately is very large, data analysis is a vital means of reducing problems to manageable size.

A common distinction made in computer jargon is between business-type applications and scientific-type applications. Business applications typically require large amounts of input and output data and a small amount of calculation, while scientific applications typically involve relatively small amounts of input and output data and large amounts of calculation. If one accepts this distinction, then data analysis, particularly in the context of the social sciences, lies somewhere between these two extremes.

Analysis of social science data often involves the repeated, routine application of a number of procedures. When a computer is used, it is necessary to detail for the computer the exact sequence of steps to be followed at each stage in the procedure. Such a sequence of steps is referred to as a *program*. Once a program is prepared, the program may be applied to many different sets of data with minor external adjustments which can be made by the user with program control cards. Computer centers maintain libraries of prepared programs which one may use to carry out one or another standard procedure.

If the user is seriously engaged in data analysis, he will probably find that he has repeated recourse to a variety of procedures. Having subjected his data to processing with one program, he may wish to use the output data from that program for input to another. A long chain of such tasks may be required. It then becomes important that the output data from one program be compatible with the input data for another. If one is using various programs, and if they operate in vastly different ways, one must master the details of many programs, and the possibility of error and confusion increases.

A *system of programs* is a set of programs which performs a related set of procedures and which shares a common set of conventions regarding the way in which the set manipulates data. If well designed, the system permits the user to execute a sequence of tasks with a minimum of manual intervention, data handling, and so forth. The SPSS system is such a set of related programs for the manipulation and statistical analysis of many types of data with a particular emphasis on the needs of the social sciences. Subsequently, we will refer to the programs of the system as *subprograms*. Once the user has entered his raw data into the system, he can instruct the computer to carry out a variety of related tasks in any sequence the circumstances dictate. It is not necessary for the user to reenter his data at any time, since the system will store and retrieve the appropriate data when required.

While an attempt has been made to include in the SPSS system a number of the most commonly used procedures in social science data analysis, it is possible to retrieve data from the system so that it can be used for some other program. Also, SPSS itself can be extended to include procedures which have not already been provided.

SPSS provides a set of common conventions for using its various subprograms. This set of conventions constitutes a simplified language corresponding closely to the natural language a social scientist might use to describe the procedures he wishes to perform on his data.

## 1.2 STATISTICAL PROCEDURES IN SPSS

The purpose of any process of data analysis is to condense information contained in a body of data into a form which can be easily comprehended and interpreted. Sometimes this process is simply used to describe a body of empirical data, but it is far more common for social science data analysis to involve a search for meaningful patterns of relationships among sets of variables, that is, a means to build and test empirical social theory. The numbers which are computed from the data during the process of analysis are termed *statistics,* and there are a wide variety of statistical procedures available in the social sciences.

SPSS contains many of the most common statistical procedures employed by social scientists, but it is by no means exhaustive of the many useful procedures which have been invented for social research or which have come from other fields to the social sciences. The choice of statistical procedures in SPSS has been determined by our examination of the amount of use they receive in day-to-day statistical analysis and of course by the exigencies of time and resources.

There is no unique method for classifying the different types of statistical procedures included in SPSS. One distinction is between parametric and nonparametric statistics. Nonparametric statistical procedures require few assumptions about the distribution or level of measurement of the variables and many of these techniques may be applied to nominal and ordinal data which do not have well established metrics. The parametric procedures, on the other hand, require more stringent assumptions concerning the distribution of the data (usually an assumption of normality), and they are designed by and large for data with an interval metric. While the statistical procedures in SPSS can be cataloged according to this rubric (e.g., Spearman versus Pearson correlation; n-dimensional crosstabulation versus partial correlation and multiple regression; Guttman scaling versus factor analysis; etc.), these assumptions are so often violated (often with justifiable reasons) during the process of data analysis as to make the distinction of questionable utility.

Perhaps the best means of cataloging the statistical procedures available in SPSS is according to the function they usually (but not always) perform in the process of data analysis. In presenting these statistical procedures, we will start with those that the researcher often begins with and then proceed through the various types of procedures according to increasing level of complexity and sophistication. No single research endeavor would normally employ all or even a large number of these procedures, but it will often be the case that at least one procedure from each of the groups will be employed at some point during the analysis.

### 1.2.1 ONE-WAY FREQUENCY DISTRIBUTIONS, MEASURES OF CENTRAL TENDENCY AND DISPERSION

In most types of social science research, the first task of data analysis is to examine the characteristics of the distribution of each of the independent and dependent variables under investigation. SPSS contains three statistical procedures for this purpose: CONDESCRIPTIVE is designed for use with interval scale variables which assume a large number of values, and the two routines CODEBOOK and MARGINALS are designed for use with variables which assume only a limited number of values. An example of the type of variable for which CONDESCRIPTIVE would be appropriate would be income measured in dollars, which can assume a continuum of values. CODEBOOK and MARGINALS would be applicable to a measure of income when the information has been grouped (such as $0–$3000, $3001–$5000, $5001–$10,000, $10,001 + ). The latter two procedures can also produce descriptive frequency distributions for nominal variables, such as religious affiliation, race, or political-party affiliation.

All three subprograms, CONDESCRIPTIVE, CODEBOOK, MARGINALS, can produce statistics such as the mean, mode, minimum, maximum, standard deviation, and range, at the user's discretion. CODEBOOK will, in addition, produce rather elaborate tables with appropriate labeling, showing the values of the variable which occurred in the data, the frequency with which each value occurred, the relative frequency, and the relative frequency when adjusted for the occurrence of certain values which signify *missing* cases. CODEBOOK will also optionally produce a histogram plot of the frequency distributions for easy visualization of the information just mentioned. In short, CODEBOOK provides the investigator with the information he would normally compile initially to determine what sort of data he has. The information generated by CODEBOOK provides a reference which the investigator will consult frequently as the study proceeds.

MARGINALS produces similar information to CODEBOOK with the exception of histograms, but in a more condensed and unlabeled format. The user may prefer to use MARGINALS if the output from CODEBOOK proves too voluminous for his purposes.

### 1.2.2    TABLE DISPLAYS OF RELATIONSHIPS BETWEEN TWO OR MORE VARIABLES

After the researcher understands the characteristics of each of his variables, he normally begins to investigate sets of relationships. One or more procedures for examining relationships will be selected depending upon the characteristics of the variables and the purposes of the researcher. He may choose correlation analysis or some form of table display such as those discussed in this section.

SPSS contains two procedures, CROSSTABS and FASTABS, which permit the user to compile two-way to n-way crosstabulations of variables and to compute a variety of nonparametric statistics based on these tables. CROSSTABS produces a sequence of two-way tables showing along the vertical dimension the values of one variable and along the horizontal dimension the values of a second variable. In the body of the table occur the frequency counts of the number of occasions in which the two variables took each possible combination of values. These frequency counts can be expressed as a percentage of the row total, column total, the table total, or any combination thereof. The statistics available to measure the degree of association of the two variables based on the distribution of frequency counts in the table include chi-square, Cramer's V, Kendall's tau B and C, the gamma statistic, and Somer's D. For n-way crosstabulations, a sequence of such two-way tables are produced, one for each two-dimensional subsection of the n-dimensional table.

FASTABS produces similar output to the procedure CROSSTABS, but operates significantly faster on data which are numeric only, as opposed to data which contain nominal alphabetic categories.[1]

Another technique for examining the relationship between two or more variables in a table format is provided by the BREAKDOWN procedure. This procedure, which requires that the dependent variable be at least ordinal in scale, compiles the means, standard deviations, and variances of a criterion or dependent variable for each desired subgroup in a sample or population. In many respects this operation is analogous to crosstabulations of the type produced by CROSSTABS and FASTABS, only in this case, each mean and standard deviation summarizes the distribution of a complete row or column of a crosstabulation table. Also in this case, the means, etc., of each group within groups are available on a single table, and the user may enter up to six variables into a single BREAKDOWN table.

### 1.2.3    BIVARIATE CORRELATION ANALYSIS

Correlation analysis provides the researcher with a technique for measuring the linear relationship between two variables and produces a single summary statistic describing the strength of the association; this statistic is known as the *correlation coefficient*. SPSS has two programs for computing correlations. PEARSON CORR produces zero-order or product-moment correlation coefficients which are best suited for normally distributed data with an interval scale. NONPAR CORR enables the user to compute either Spearman or Kendall rank-order correlation coefficients or both. Both of these procedures can produce correlations

---

[1]The user should read Chap. 12 before deciding which procedure to use.

for selected pairs or lists of variables as well as complete matrices of coefficients. The output from PEARSON CORR and NONPAR CORR is similar and provides the correlation coefficient, the number of observations upon which the correlation was based, and the level of statistical significance of the coefficient. In addition each procedure provides for the output of correlation matrices for input into further statistical computations.

### 1.2.4   MULTIVARIATE CORRELATION AND REGRESSION

Partial correlation and multiple regression permit the user to accomplish a wide variety of types of analysis to explain and predict relationships among his variables when he feels that the variables meet the minimum assumptions of distribution and scale required by these statistical techniques.

Partial correlation provides a single measure of association (the partial-correlation coefficient) describing the linear relationship between two variables while adjusting or controlling for the effects of one or more additional variables. In this respect, partial correlation is analogous to n-dimensional crosstabulation for continuous and interval variables. First- to nth-order partial-correlation coefficients can be obtained for any set of variables with the PARTIAL CORR procedure. This program can operate on raw data or from matrices of simple correlation coefficients produced by a previous run of PEARSON CORR or NONPAR CORR. The matrices can, of course, also be manually prepared or can be output from a program not in the SPSS system.

Up to five orders of partials can be simultaneously computed for any set of variables, and the user has total control over the orders and the partials to be computed. Output from this procedure includes the partial-correlation coefficients, their level of statistical significance, and the number of cases upon which each partial was based. The zero-order correlations and the means and standard deviations of the variables may also be obtained. The user may also optionally request the output of correlation matrices for further computation.

Multiple regression is an extension of the bivariate correlation coefficient to multivariate analysis. Multiple regression allows the researcher to study the linear relationship between a set of independent variables and a dependent variable while taking into account the interrelationships among the independent variables. The basic goal of multiple regression is to produce a linear combination of independent variables which will correlate as highly as possible with the dependent variable. This linear combination can then be used to "predict" values of the dependent variable, and the importance of each of the independent variables in that prediction can be assessed.

A variety of multiple-regression calculations can be accomplished with the use of the procedure REGRESSION. This subprogram, like PARTIAL CORR, can operate on raw data or a matrix of correlation coefficients, either prepared by the user or obtained from a previous run of one of the correlation procedures. The user can perform the regression upon a fixed number of variables or, using a stepwise technique, allow the variables to be introduced into the computation sequentially, depending upon their explanatory power. REGRESSION allows the user to also perform a regression procedure midway between these two extremes; he can allow the program to choose the order of introduction of the variables from a certain set, then force certain other variables into the calculation, then proceed stepwise for a period, and so forth. This flexibility, together with the ability of SPSS to transform variables, allows the user to handle most multiple-regression applications with relative ease. Output from the program includes a listing of the variables included in the regression at each stage, the coefficients in the regression equation, their standard error, and the significance level of the coefficients. Residuals and multiple R are also computed at each stage. When the program operates upon raw data, the user can also obtain the correlation matrix which is computed as the basis of the regression.

### 1.2.5   GUTTMAN SCALING AND FACTOR ANALYSIS

All the statistical procedures previously discussed (with the exception of those used to examine the characteristic of individual variables) represent different methods for examining, explaining, and predicting the relationship between one or more independent variables and a dependent variable. In this section we discuss two procedures contained in SPSS for locating underlying continuums or variable sets from a larger group of variables.

Guttman scale analysis is a means of analyzing the underlying operating characteristics of three or more items in order to determine if their interrelationships meet several special properties which define an acceptable Guttman scale. Guttman scales must first be unidimensional; that is, the component items must all measure movement toward or away from some single underlying object. In addition, Guttman scales must be cumulative, and it is this property which differentiates Guttman scales from most other unidimensional indexes. A cumulative scale requires that the component items be conceptually and operationally ordered by degree of difficulty and that respondents who reply positively to a difficult item will therefore reply positively to less difficult items and vice versa.

The SPSS GUTTMAN SCALE procedure provides the researcher with a method for determining the degree to which given sets of items conform to these two required properties. This procedure enables the researcher simultaneously to test up to 50 separate Guttman scales on a single task. The scales are computed by the Goodenough technique. Each item to be included in a scale may have up to three cutting points, and on an individual scale the item is computed for all possible combinations of cutting points specified. The order of the items may be automatically determined by the subprogram according to the proportion of the respondents who "fail" or "reject" the items. Alternatively the user may fix the order of the items himself.

In addition to the basic table giving the frequencies, errors, and scale types, the user may request a number of statistics which will aid him in evaluating the scales. Included in the available statistics are: (1) the coefficient of reproducibility, (2) the minimum marginal reproducibility, (3) the percent improvement, and (4) the coefficient of scalability. All these statistics help the user determine the quality of the scale. Interitem correlations and part-whole correlations may also be requested.

Factor analysis is a much more generalized procedure for locating and defining dimensional space among a relatively large group of variables. Because of the generality of factor analysis, it is difficult to present a capsule description of its functions and applications. The major use of factor analysis by social scientists is to locate a smaller number of valid dimensions, clusters, or factors contained in a larger set of independent items or variables. And viewed from the other side, factor analysis can help determine the degree to which a given variable or several variables are part of a common underlying phenomena. A large number of tests for manual dexterity, for example, might be given to a group of subjects, and their scores on all of these tests might then be entered into a factor analysis to attempt to determine if manual dexterity has more than one identifiable dimension, component, or factor. Perhaps one might then find that there were three factors (such as speed, accuracy, and endurance) which are differentially measured by the various tests. This not only would provide a richer definition of manual dexterity, but would also enable one to know what proportions of speed, accuracy, and endurance are being measured when one of these tests is administered.

Factor analysis is performed by the SPSS procedure FACTOR. As with PARTIAL CORR and REGRESSION, the procedure can begin with either raw data or with a correlation matrix. In this case the user may also input a factor matrix. The methods of factoring which are available are principal-component factoring with or without iteration, alpha factoring, Rao's canonical factoring, and image factoring. The factoring procedure can be controlled by specifying the number of iterations to be performed, if applicable, the number of factors to be extracted, if applicable, or the minimum value of an eigenvalue for which a factor will be extracted. Following the factor-extraction phase, rotations may be performed. The types of rotations which may be used are varimax, equimax, quartimax, and a few oblique rotations. FACTOR does not require that the factoring phase always be performed; the user can start by reading in a correlation matrix, communalities, a factor matrix, and immediately proceed to rotations. Similarly, the procedure can be terminated after the factoring phase, thus omitting rotations, or it can be terminated after some rotations have been performed and restarted for further rotations at a later time. The necessary information will automatically be generated by FACTOR to implement these restart procedures.

We have described the principal statistical procedures available within the SPSS system. It is important to realize, however, that these procedures can be executed in any sequence, or repetitively, in the course of a single run or session with the computer. Thus the user may elect to perform some crosstabulations, do a multiple regression, and then do some correlations upon the same file of data in a single run. Also, the procedures described share the general capabilities of SPSS for file handling, variable manipulation, and so forth, so that they constitute a sequence of steps available to the user in any order that makes sense in the context of his problem. In the following section we discuss some of the general capabilities of SPSS which are available in conjunction with any statistical procedure the user may specify.

## 1.3 FEATURES OF SPSS

In this section we present a summary of the salient capabilities of SPSS, together with examples. In subsequent chapters all these features and how to cause the SPSS system to execute them are discussed in greater detail. For the moment our purpose is to give the user an overview of how the system operates, and to inform him of what he can and cannot accomplish with it.

### 1.3.1 SEQUENCING CALCULATIONS

SPSS is driven through its various functions by a sequence of *control cards*[1] which the user must prepare. The process is pictured in Fig. 1.1. There is a control program in SPSS whose sole function is to read control cards, decode them, and cause the appropriate function called for by the control card to be executed. The control program causes the function to be performed by passing control to the appropriate subprogram which then performs the function and passes control back to the control program, which then reads another control card, and so forth. This calculation sequence is carried out automatically by SPSS, and the details of how the control program and subprograms operate need be of no concern to the user. The important thing for the user to realize is that he must arrange the control cards he prepares in the appropriate sequence to cause the system to perform actions in the order he intends.

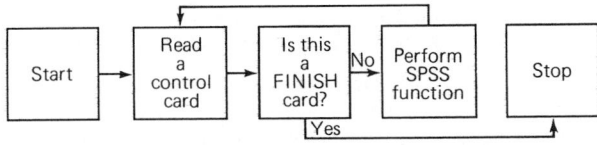

**FIG. 1.1**  Program sequencing in SPSS.

The control cards themselves must be prepared in a particular format so that they are recognizable to the system. There are over 55 different types of control cards in all, and the rules for preparing these cards are discussed in detail in subsequent chapters. An attempt has been made to define the format of the control cards so that they correspond closely to the way the user thinks about the problem at hand, and the information entered on these cards consists of a quasi-natural language for the description of data-analysis procedures. *In order to use SPSS, it is necessary for the user to learn this language.* This is not as formidable a task as it may sound, since an attempt has been made to define the control cards in such a way that all control cards have similar formats and a minimum of rules is imposed on the user. The user is free to choose names and labels that are natural to the problem at hand.

### 1.3.2 ENTERING AND PROCESSING DATA

Data may be entered into SPSS in a variety of ways. The simplest and perhaps most common way is to punch the data on cards and to enter these cards along with the SPSS control cards which instruct the system on the processing of the data. Some of the SPSS control cards define and describe the data while other types cause specific calculations to be executed. Data is organized within the SPSS system in units called *files*. A file consists of the user's data along

[1]Throughout this text, the word *card* is taken to refer to an 80-character record recognizable by the computer. In addition to implying the usual meaning (80-column IBM-card format) *card* may refer to card-image records entered via a remote terminal, etc.

with associated information (entered on SPSS control cards) describing and defining the data. Once entered, any such file may be permanently stored for future processing as an *SPSS system file* on tape, disk, or other input/output medium.

In Example 1.1, we show the data and the control cards that the user would have to prepare in order to begin to analyze the data from a hypothetical study of the political-party preference of 20 college professors. In this example, the data has been punched on 20 cards (one corresponding to the data record of each professor) and is placed in the card deck directly following the READ INPUT DATA card. The data has been prepared in fixed-column format so that each item of information for each professor is entered in precisely the same position on his data record. In this example, the faculty member's name occupies the first eight card columns of every case. His party preference occupies column 10, and so forth.

**EXAMPLE 1.1**   Control cards and data used to enter data, perform a crosstabulation, and save a file of 20 cases and 5 variables

```
                1                    16
                RUN NAME             DEFINE,CROSSTABULATE, AND THEN SAVE AN SPSS SYSTEM FILE
              ⎧ FILE NAME            FACSTUDY,SURVEY OF FACULTY PARTY PREFERENCES
              │ VARIABLE LIST        PROF,PARTYPRF,AGE,SEX,RELIGION
              │ INPUT FORMAT         FIXED (A8,1X,A1,1X,F2.0,1X,A1,1X,F1.0)
              │ PRINT FORMATS        PARTYPRF,SEX(A)/AGE,RELIGION(O)
              │ # OF CASES           20
              │ INPUT MEDIUM         CARD
   Data       │ VAR LABELS           PROF,FACULTY MEMBER'S NAME/
 definition   ⎨                      PARTYPRF,POLITICAL PARTY PREFERENCE/
   cards      │                      AGE,AGE IN YEARS/
              │ VALUE LABELS         PARTYPRF ('C')CONSERVATIVE('L')LIBERAL('S')SOCIAL CREDIT
              │                               ('N')NEW DEMOCRAT('R')NOT GIVEN/
              │                      SEX ('M')MALE('F')FEMALE/
              ⎩                      RELIGION (1)PROTESTANT(2)CATHOLIC(3)JEWISH(4)OTHER
                MISSING VALUES       PARTYPRF('R')/AGE(0)
   Task       ⎧ CROSSTABS            SEX BY PARTYPRF
 definition   ⎨ OPTIONS              3,5
   cards      ⎩ STATISTICS           1,3
                READ INPUT DATA
              ⎧ JONES    C 43 M 1
              │ SMITH    N 26 M 1
              │ OSGOODE  L 35 F 2
              │ MCFEE    R 50 M 1
              │ ALLISON  N 61 F 2
              │ SCHULTZ  L 31 F 3
              │ KLINE    L 45 F 3
              │ BENSON   C 56 M 1
              │ RICHARDS S 37 F 2
   Data       │ AITKEN   N 45 M 4
  records     ⎨ MACKAY   S 30 M 2
              │ SCHWARTZ S 44 M 1
              │ YATES    N  0 F 2
              │ MIMER    C 38 M 1
              │ ALVEREZ  L  0 F 2
              │ SAWCHUK  L 35 M 1
              │ FLYNN    C 42 M 2
              │ BATES    N 36 F 4
              │ NEMOY    L 29 M 4
              ⎩ HALLER   L 39 F 3
                SAVE FILE
                FINISH
```

The data-definition control cards which provide the system with information describing the data required for processing are enclosed within a bracket and so designated. The first of these cards, the FILE NAME card, simply names the set of data for future reference. The user may also provide an extended label for the data on this card if he so desires. On the VARIABLE LIST card the user names each of the variables in his file of data. These variable names selected by the user become permanently associated with the corresponding variables in the file, and all future processing is accomplished by reference to these names. The type of the variables and their location on the data records is specified on the INPUT FORMAT card[1] and

---

[1] Readers familiar with Fortran will recognize that the format specifications of the INPUT FORMAT card are a subset of the Fortran format list.

the number of cases (professors in this instance) is indicated on the # OF CASES card. The fact that the data are to be entered on cards is indicated on the INPUT MEDIUM control card. If the data were being entered into the system from some other input medium, the INPUT MEDIUM card would have specified a keyword other than CARD (TAPE or DISK, for example). If this were the case, the 20 data cards would not have appeared in the deck as shown in Example 1.1. The PRINT FORMATS card specifies the printing format of the variables and is required only when there are variables in the file which contain nonnumeric characters.

These six control cards are always required when defining an SPSS file. The following four types of cards provide SPSS with additional information which is frequently used during processing. These cards are optional, however, and need only be prepared if the user wishes to take advantage of certain features available within SPSS. The MISSING VALUES card enables the user to designate up to three values for each variable in his file to be treated as missing. These values are specially treated during analysis, and each statistical program has a number of user-selected options for processing missing values. Given the frequency of missing data in social science research, this card is almost always prepared, although its formal status is optional. The optional VAR LABELS cards permit the user to associate an extended label with any or all the variables in the file. These labels are automatically printed on all tables and reports where applicable. The VALUE LABELS cards serve an identical function for the individual values of the variables and are also optional.

The data-definition cards need be prepared and entered only once, and the information on them can be permanently saved along with the data as an SPSS system file. The SAVE FILE control card directly following the last data card causes one of these specially formated system files to be created on an output medium of the user's choice. Once a system file has been retained, the information initially entered on these cards is automatically passed from the file to the system along with the data whenever processing is desired. System files may be created for storage during any processing run by inserting a SAVE FILE card in the control-card deck. Thus a special run to generate the file is not required. Furthermore, while SPSS system files are permanent, they are not immutable, and updated files may be created on any subsequent run.

While there are many advantages (which are discussed later) to generating system files, the user may continue to input his data directly from cards or from any type of BCD file[1], and submit the control cards required to define the data on each processing run as is the case with most statistical programs. The control cards required to process the data from cards, BCD tape, or DISK files are identical (in kind and number) to those required to create a file for storage as an SPSS system file. In the latter case, the user simply inserts a SAVE FILE control card before the FINISH card.

While one need define a file of data only once, a new set of calculations or tasks will be defined on each processing run. The SPSS system is instructed in the execution of the statistical computations by means of a set of *task-definition* cards. The task defined in Example 1.1 calls for a single table to be computed (using subprogram CROSSTABS) crosstabulating sex by party preference. The CROSSTABS procedure card activates the crosstabulation subprogram, and the OPTIONS and STATISTICS card provides the CROSSTABS subprograms with additional detailed specifications for building the tables. The OPTIONS card enables the user to control the direction of the percentaging of the table, the processing of missing values, and the printing of labels, etc. The desired table statistics, in this case chi-square and the contingency coefficient, are selected by number on the STATISTICS card. Figure 1.2 presents a reproduction of the printed output which was computed for this run.

The remaining four SPSS control cards in Example 1.1 serve simple but special functions in the system. The RUN NAME card, which may contain any message of the user's choice, identifies the run, and the message contained on it is printed back on the top of each page of printed output generated by the run (see Fig. 1.2). The READ INPUT DATA card informs the

---

[1]For those unfamiliar with the terminology, BCD stands for Binary Coded Decimal and corresponds to the recording scheme normally used to punch data onto cards. The BCD recording scheme is one in which a single card column is used to represent a single digit or character. Other recording schemes such as column binary or the binary representation used in SPSS system files cannot be directly input to SPSS.

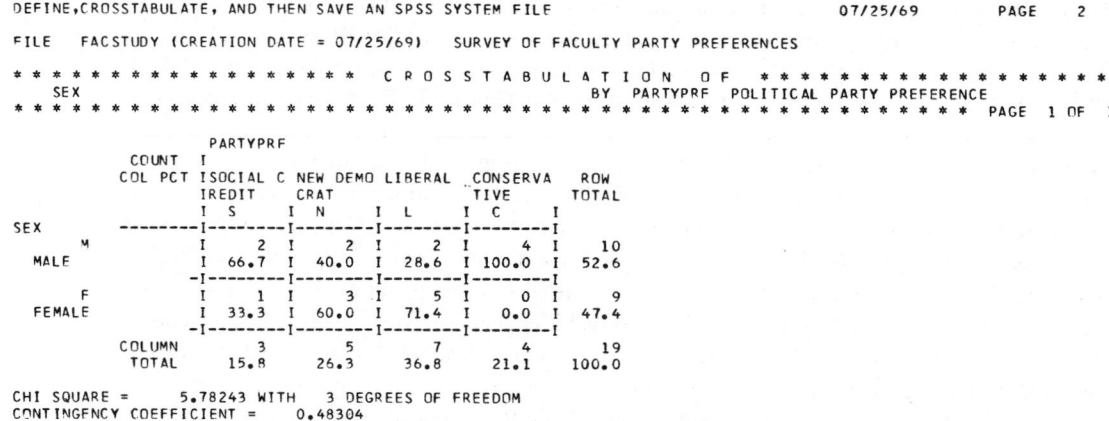

```
FILE   FACSTUDY (CREATION DATE = 07/25/69)    SURVEY OF FACULTY PARTY PREFERENCES

* * * * * * * * * * * * * * * *   C R O S S T A B U L A T I O N   O F   * * * * * * * * * * * * * * * * * *
      SEX                                            BY PARTYPRF   POLITICAL PARTY PREFERENCE
* * * * * * * * * * * * * * * * * * * * * * * * * * * * * * * * * * * * * * * * * * * * * PAGE  1 OF  1

                        PARTYPRF
                 COUNT  I
                 COL PCT ISOCIAL C NEW DEMO LIBERAL  CONSERVA   ROW
                         IREDIT    CRAT              TIVE       TOTAL
                         I   S    I   N    I   L    I   C    I
        SEX      --------I--------I--------I--------I--------I
              M          I    2   I    2   I    2   I    4   I    10
         MALE           I  66.7  I  40.0  I  28.6  I 100.0  I  52.6
                 -I--------I--------I--------I--------I
              F          I    1   I    3   I    5   I    0   I     9
        FEMALE          I  33.3  I  60.0  I  71.4  I   0.0  I  47.4
                 -I--------I--------I--------I--------I
                 COLUMN       3        5        7        4       19
                 TOTAL     15.8     26.3     36.8     21.1    100.0

CHI SQUARE =       5.78243 WITH   3 DEGREES OF FREEDOM
CONTINGENCY COEFFICIENT =      0.48304
```

**FIG. 1.2**    The crosstabulation table produced by the example run 1.1.

system that the user has finished defining the file and the first statistical task and is ready to begin to read the data into the computer. The SAVE FILE card which has been previously mentioned causes the file to be permanently saved as an SPSS system file, and the FINISH card simply informs SPSS that the current run or session is completed.

The example we have presented shows how to enter raw data into the SPSS system and retain it for future processing while performing a calculation. On any subsequent run the user can retrieve this file automatically, and the variable names, formats, labels, etc., which were originally entered by the data-definition cards are passed from the file, along with the data, whenever processing is desired. Beyond the obvious advantages of automatically storing and retrieving what may be large amounts of complicated file-defining information, the processing speed from these system files is significantly faster than that achieved with BCD files. Savings of up to 60 percent have been observed on comparable runs.[1] The conversion of the data from BCD to internal or SPSS system file representation also greatly facilitates the user's ability to recode variables and generate new scales and indexes through variable transformations without having to concern himself with card and column locations of the new or recoded variables.

In the following respect, the files are permanent, but not immutable. The data or any of the documenting information may be added to, deleted, or altered at the user's will, and a new or updated file may be retained. Additional variables can be added to the file as well as additional cases; labels may be added or altered; new variables or scales can be created from existing ones, and documenting messages may be saved in the file. In short, the system file becomes a permanent self-documenting entity, and the user need only remember the name of the file and the order of the variables in it. Even this information, if forgotten, can be retrieved automatically.

The most important aspect of system files is the potential effect they can have (if properly utilized) on the way in which the researcher interacts with his data during his day-to-day analyses. With a complicated data file, it will take a considerable amount of time to prepare and debug the initial run which defines the file. However, once this has been accomplished, massive runs taking a long time to plan and prepare need not and probably should not be made. With a system file, the researcher can begin to explore particular themes and hypotheses, submitting frequent runs requiring little card preparation, and thus the likelihood of control-card errors is minimized.

Now that we have saved the example file called FACSTUDY, a run exploring the relationship between religion and party preference, controlling for the effects of sex, can be made with the control cards of Example 1.2. The GET FILE card (the only control card which has not been previously introduced) causes all the data and required information from the file named on the card to be read into the computer.

[1]Of course, the proportion of processing time devoted to reading the data is to some degree dependent upon the number of cases contained in the file, as well as the number and type of computations being performed; therefore, the 60 percent figure will not always be achieved.

**EXAMPLE 1.2**   Control cards required to produce crosstabulations from SPSS system file saved on the previous run

```
1                 16
RUN NAME          FIRST EXAMPLE PROCESSING FROM A SYSTEM FILE
GET FILE          FACSTUDY
CROSSTABS         RELIGION BY PARTYPRF BY SEX
OPTIONS           3,5
STATISTICS        1,2,3
FINISH
```

As shown in Fig. 1.3 the output from this run is two completely labeled subtables displaying the relationship between religion and party preference for male and female faculty members. Comparable runs using many different types of statistical procedures could be made as the analysis progresses.

Each of the control cards discussed above, as well as many other cards which perform a variety of different functions in the system, are presented in great detail in the following chapters, and the reader should not be at all concerned if he feels that he only partially understands the procedures and functions already discussed. The sole purpose of this introductory section is to provide the user with a brief overview of the capabilities of SPSS. File handling and other general capabilities of SPSS are briefly described in the following sections.

```
FIRST EXAMPLE PROCESSING FROM A SYSTEM FILE                          07/25/69      PAGE    4

FILE   FACSTUDY (CREATION DATE = 07/25/69)   SURVEY OF FACULTY PARTY PREFERENCES

* * * * * * * * * * * * * * * * * *  C R O S S T A B U L A T I O N  O F  * * * * * * * * * * * * * *.* * * *
    RELIGION                                          BY  PARTYPRF  POLITICAL PARTY PREFERENCE
CONTROLLING FOR..
    SEX                                               VALUE = M            MALE
* * * * * * * * * * * * * * * * * * * * * * * * * * * * * * * * * * * * * * * * * * * * * * * PAGE  1 OF  1

                  PARTYPRF
          COUNT  I
          COL PCT ISOCIAL C NEW DEMO LIBERAL  CONSERVA  ROW
                 IREDIT    CRAT            TIVE     TOTAL
                 I   S   I   N   I  L    I  C    I
RELIGION  --------I--------I--------I--------I--------I
            1.  I     1 I     1 I     1 I     3 I     6
  PROTESTANT   I  50.0 I  50.0 I  50.0 I  75.0 I  60.0
              -I--------I--------I--------I--------I
            2.  I     1 I     0 I     0 I     1 I     2
  CATHOLIC    I  50.0 I   0.0 I   0.0 I  25.0 I  20.0
              -I--------I--------I--------I--------I
            4.  I     0 I     1 I     1 I     0 I     2
  OTHER       I   0.0 I  50.0 I  50.0 I   0.0 I  20.0
              -I--------I--------I--------I--------I
          COLUMN      2       2       2       4      10
          TOTAL    20.0    20.0    20.0    40.0   100.0

CHI SQUARE =      5.00000 WITH   6 DEGREES OF FREEDOM
CRAMER'S V =      0.50000
CONTINGENCY COEFFICIENT =      0.57735


FIRST EXAMPLE PROCESSING FROM A SYSTEM FILE                          07/25/69      PAGE    5

FILE   FACSTUDY (CREATION DATE = 07/25/69)   SURVEY OF FACULTY PARTY PREFERENCES

* * * * * * * * * * * * * * * * * *  C R O S S T A B U L A T I O N  O F  * * * * * * * * * * * * * * * * * *
    RELIGION                                          BY  PARTYPRF  POLITICAL PARTY PREFERENCE
CONTROLLING FOR..
    SEX                                               VALUE = F            FEMALE
* * * * * * * * * * * * * * * * * * * * * * * * * * * * * * * * * * * * * * * * * * * * * * * PAGE  1 OF  1

                  PARTYPRF
          COUNT  I
          COL PCT ISOCIAL C NEW DEMO LIBERAL   ROW
                 IREDIT    CRAT           TOTAL
                 I   S   I   N   I  L    I
RELIGION  --------I--------I--------I--------I
            2.  I     1 I     2 I     2 I     5
  CATHOLIC    I 100.0 I  66.7 I  40.0 I  55.6
              -I--------I--------I--------I
            3.  I     0 I     0 I     3 I     3
  JEWISH      I   0.0 I   0.0 I  60.0 I  33.3
              -I--------I--------I--------I
            4.  I     0 I     1 I     0 I     1
  OTHER       I   0.0 I  33.3 I   0.0 I  11.1
              -I--------I--------I--------I
          COLUMN      1       3       5       9
          TOTAL    11.1    33.3    55.6   100.0

CHI SQUARE =      5.04000 WITH   4 DEGREES OF FREEDOM
CRAMER'S V =      0.52915
CONTINGENCY COEFFICIENT =      0.59914
```

**FIG. 1.3**   The crosstabulation tables produced by example run 1.2.

### 1.3.3 SUBFILES

Data entered into the SPSS system may be substructured into groups called *subfiles.* Subfiles may be sampling points such as cities; they may be national samples in crossnational survey research; they may consist of data from different time trials or experimental treatments. Subfiles, then, have all of the characteristics usually associated with like samples in statistical analysis. In the SPSS system, they can be used as control variables for those statistical subprograms calculating like-sample test statistics. The subfile structure may also be used for more general types of comparative analysis whenever the researcher has two or more like samples. The same relationship, for example, can be examined simultaneously in each of the subfiles.

Once the subfile structure has been created, individual subfiles may be selected for processing, combinations of subfiles may be processed together, or the subfile structure may be ignored altogether—in which case, the data is treated as a unified file. The user controls the manner in which the subfiles are processed in each individual task.

### 1.3.4 MISSING DATA

It is a common occurrence in social science research to find that for one reason or another it has been impossible to obtain a complete set of data for every case in the file. Such a situation would occur if a respondent refused or neglected to answer a question on a questionnaire or if the response was not entered correctly on the data sheets. SPSS has a number of features for processing such missing data. Each variable may have up to three values which are designated as *missing.* The choice of these values is totally a matter of the user's discretion, and is used to designate the reason why proper data has not been obtained. For example, the user may elect to use the code 0 for *not determined,* 1 for *refused to answer,* and 2 for *didn't know.* These missing-data indicators may be defined with the use of a MISSING VALUES control card and retained with the other information in a SPSS system file. Each of the statistical subprograms contains a number of options for processing missing data, and the user may select among these options according to what he thinks are the best assumptions for his analysis in the particular situation.

### 1.3.5 RECODING DATA

In order to organize his data for analysis, the user first determines which *variables* he wishes to deal with. The term variable means a certain attribute which can be determined or measured, and it must be carefully distinguished from the term *variable value* (or *value*) which means the value determined or measured for a variable in a particular case. After listing his variables, the user next decides how he wishes the values of each variable to be coded. When the data is to be processed with the computer, the way in which this coding system is devised can make a great deal of difference in the ease with which the user can cause the computer to carry out the computations he desires.

Frequently the coding system the user has used to record his data is not the most convenient one for use in all parts of his analysis. A provision has been made in SPSS for the user to change his coding system *after* entering the data in its original form into the system. The values of any or all the variables can be changed at the user's will by means of the RECODE process. Selected values of variables may be replaced with new values, and continuous variables may be classified into discrete categories. The RECODE process can be used to temporarily alter the values of the variables in conjunction with a run of a particular statistical subprogram, or it may be used to effect a permanent recoding of the variables in the file.

### 1.3.6 VARIABLE TRANSFORMATIONS

A wide variety of variable transformations can be accomplished in SPSS by means of simplified Fortran-like statements constructed by the user. The allowable types of transformation are of two types: conditional or unconditional. The unconditional transformations, defined by COMPUTE control cards, cause a new variable to be constructed from the values of other variables. For example, the control card

```
1           16
COMPUTE     A=B+C
```

causes a new variable, named A, to be defined. The values of this new variable are determined by adding together the values of the existing variables B and C. Conditional transformations are defined by the IF card. The IF card enables the user to test if a certain condition is true; if it is true, a transformation is performed. Thus the control card

```
1          16
IF         (D EQ 1) A=B+C
```

causes SPSS to examine the values of the variable D. If for a particular case the variable D assumes the value 1, a new value for variable A is computed by adding together the values of variables B and C.

Transformations can be used to normalize or in some other way alter the distribution of variables as well as to construct scales or indices from two or more existing variables in a file. The transformation process, like the recoding process, can be used to create a permanent file of transformed variables or may be used to create temporary variable modifications during a given run of SPSS.

### 1.3.7 SAMPLING, SELECTING, AND WEIGHTING DATA

A random sample of the cases in a file may be obtained, specific cases may be selected for processing, and the cases in the file may be weighted. The user is able to specify all the conditions and criteria for accomplishing sampling, selecting, and weighting during any processing run. As with recoding and variable transformations, sampling, selecting, and weighting may be done in conjunction with a particular computation, or a new file of sampled, selected, or weighted cases may be obtained.

### 1.3.8 RETRIEVAL OF DATA FROM THE SYSTEM

All data input into the SPSS system, as well as recoded variables, new variables created by transformations, and file changes accomplished by sampling, weighting, and/or selection, may be punched on cards or written in BCD form on a device of the user's choice. The cards or the BCD data files can then be directly input into the user's own programs or to other statistical packages. The user has complete control over the selection of variables to be output and their formats, as well as control over the selection of cases to be output.

This feature enables the user to utilize the file management, data modification, and statistical capabilities of SPSS without becoming a prisoner of the system.

The SPSS correlation programs permit the user to output correlation matrices in BCD form on cards, tape, or direct-access files. All the SPSS multivariate routines using correlation coefficients allow the user to input correlation matrices as well as raw data. In addition to saving the user machine time by bypassing the initial correlation step of these multivariate techniques, the *matrix-input* feature allows matrices generated by the user's own program or by other statistical packages to be input into SPSS subprograms while *matrix output* allows for convenient usage of matrices by non-SPSS programs as well as by those in the package.

While SPSS is not designed primarily as an information retrieval language, some of the features available in it allow SPSS to be used for this purpose. When using the system in this way, the user would create an SPSS system file to be saved. On a subsequent run, a WRITE CASES control card may be used to output selected variables from this file. In this run, the user can use the selection features of the system to reject certain cases. These selection features are perfectly general because the rejection can be based on any criteria relating to the values of one or more variables, and the system possesses the ability to simultaneously evaluate the existence of more than one logical condition or combination of conditions. For example, the following control card would cause only those cases to be selected for which the value of variable A is less than 10, and the variable SEX has the value 'MALE'.

```
1          16
SELECT IF  ((A LT 10)AND(SEX EQ 'MALE'))
```

### 1.3.9 OUTPUT OF RESULTS FROM THE SYSTEM

Since in this general discussion of SPSS and its features we have mainly concerned ourselves with problems of entering information into the computer, the user may well wonder how he obtains output from the system as well. For the most part, printout is automatically provided so the user need not concern himself with how SPSS accomplishes this. Generally, output occurs when the user calls for a particular statistical procedure to be performed upon a file of data. The system then causes the calculations to be made and produces a printed report containing these results on the line printer or other output device. The level of detail these reports contain depends upon the level of detail the user has provided when defining his file.

For example, the user may have defined a variable with the name POLPREF when he furnished the data file for a particular run. When POLPREF is defined, the user has the option of also defining an extended label for POLPREF, as well as extended labels for the various values which POLPREF can assume. If these labels are present, they will automatically appear on the output reports. If they are not present, no labeling information appears. The user decides in each case whether it is worth the trouble to enter additional information to make his output data more legible.

There are some subprograms (such as the crosstabulation subprogram CROSSTABS) which allow the user a good deal of latitude in specifying the level of detail the printout contains. The user may elect to use an OPTIONS control card to cause a subprogram to produce the report he desires. These options are discussed in those sections specifying the rules for using various subprograms.

## 1.4 SUGGESTIONS FOR THE USE OF THIS TEXT

The present volume constitutes documentation for the use of the SPSS system. The authors have attempted to make the book as useful as possible to a wide variety of readers. There is some discussion which will be of interest mainly to computer specialists, and experienced users may wish to skip the more elementary parts.

Chapters 2 to 10 deal with general functions of the system and should be read in some detail by all users. In particular, we urge the reader to pay particular attention to Chaps. 2 to 4. Chapters 11 to 17 deal with particular statistical subprograms and will be consulted by users as required. Examples 11.1 and 11.3 are of special interest, since they typify the first run that a user will make with SPSS.

Appendix A contains a complete listing of all SPSS control-card error messages, and we are sure that even the casual user will have an opportunity to become familiar with it. The summary of control-card formats, functions, and positions in Appendix B will probably be quite useful to the user as he gains experience with the system and becomes less reliant on the verbal descriptions in the text. Appendix C contains the formal definition (in Backus normal form notation) of the SPSS language. A summary of the formulas used in the computations of various statistical procedures can be found in Appendix D, and a glossary of technical terms appears in Appendix E. Appendix F deals with the necessary JCL (Job Control Language) cards required to use SPSS on the IBM 360; the user will have a need to refer to it repeatedly. Appendix G contains similar information for the CDC version of SPSS as well as a description of a number of the special features of the CDC program; all CDC users should read it carefully before attempting to perform SPSS runs. Appendix H is a technical or programmer's guide to SPSS and has detailed information concerning the logic of the program flow, as well as instructions for adding additional statistical programs to SPSS. In Appendix I the user will find the data cards and data-definition cards for two files used to produce most of the example runs presented in the text. You may wish to have these cards punched so that you can experiment with the various procedures in SPSS as you learn the system.

# 2
# THE ORGANIZATION AND CODING OF DATA
# FOR INPUT INTO THE SPSS SYSTEM

Data which is to be entered into the SPSS system consists of observations or *cases* which may be substructured, if the user desires, into two or more like groups termed *subfiles*.

## 2.1   THE CASE AS THE UNIT OF ANALYSIS

A *case* is the basic unit of analysis for which measurements have been obtained. In social science research, a case is often an individual respondent in a sample survey or a subject of an experiment; however, a case may be a larger unit such as a city, nation, or institution. Occasionally a case is a more abstract unit such as an experimental condition or a time trial.

Each unit or case is composed of values for one or more measurements that have been taken. These measurements are termed *variables,* and each case within a study will have one value for each of the variables. In a hypothetical survey study, the case of John Doe might contain his sex, race, income, level of education, and party preference. For this study then, the cases of every other respondent interviewed would contain the same variables, i.e., sex, race, income, level of education, and party preference. Furthermore, the order of the variables within each case must be the same.

## 2.2    CODING CONVENTIONS FOR DATA

The measurements collected in a study (survey or otherwise) must usually be coded so that they can be punched into cards (or other machine-readable medium) before any analysis can be accomplished. As a rule, the variables are recorded so that each case occupies one or more 80 column IBM punched cards. Because it would be very cumbersome to actually punch onto the cards the names of the respondents or the alphabetic name of their race or the political parties they prefer, a coding scheme which equates numeric or alphabetic characters to each value of the variables is usually instituted.[1]

### 2.2.1    VARIABLES AND VARIABLE TYPES

Variables can be coded into one of two types for input into the SPSS system: numeric or alphanumeric. *Numeric variables* are variables which have been coded so that they take values which are single- or multiple-digit integers or numbers containing decimal points. *Alphanumeric variables* are variables which may assume one or more values that are not numerics; i.e., they are either letters or special characters. The distinction between alphanumeric and numeric variables is important because these two types of variables are processed differently in the computer. Numeric variables are considered as a special set of variables which can be mathematically manipulated as cardinal values. The user may input either alphanumeric or numeric variables into the SPSS system; however, mathematical operations may not be executed on alphanumeric variables. For example, marginals and crosstabulations may be computed for either alphanumeric or numeric variables, but means and standard deviations can be computed only for numeric variables.

Section 4.6 (The INPUT FORMAT Card) explains how the user informs the system as to the type of variable, and the individual subprogram write-ups indicate whether alphanumeric variables may be processed by them. If the user is working with data that presently contain alphanumeric variables and wishes to analyze this data with procedures requiring numeric variables, he may recode the values of these variables by means of the RECODE card (see Sec. 8.1).

### 2.2.2    CODING MISSING VALUES

Quite often in social science research, the measurement of a variable has not been obtained for every case. In survey research, this is often because respondents refuse to answer certain questions or respond with "don't know," or it is occasionally due to interviewer omission. In analysis using aggregate data, where cases are cities, nations, or institutions, certain pieces of information may not be available for every unit. For these reasons, SPSS includes a number of processing options for handling variables for which some of the cases do not have a valid measurement.

Each variable input into the SPSS system may possess from one to three values which are designated as missing. The user may select any values he desires. However, numeric variables may only possess missing values which are also numeric. Each variable may have a different set of values which are designated as missing. The user will, however, save considerable control-card preparation in the definition of missing values if a consistent set of values is used for all variables. See Sec. 4.7 (The MISSING VALUES Card), which explains how missing values are defined for the system.

### 2.2.3    ORGANIZING DATA FOR INPUT

The SPSS system offers the user two alternate ways of organizing the variables on the cards: fixed-column format and free-field format.

---

[1] A number of books on research methodology in the social sciences discuss and demonstrate the construction of coding schemes. See, for example, Herbert H. Hyman, "Survey Design and Analysis: Principles, Cases and Procedures," Free Press, New York, 1957, or Kenneth Janda, "Data Processing: Applications to Political Research," Northwestern University Press, Evanston, Ill. 1965. The user *must* note, however, that the multipunching coding techniques suggested for counter-sorter analysis by some texts *may not* be used for data to be input into SPSS. We further stongly urge that the user employ only numeric values for coding data.

**2.2.3.1    Organizing data in fixed-column format**

In fixed-column format, the values of each of the variables are located in the same columns or data fields in every case. A case may be made up of more than one card, and when this is true, the *same column* refers to the same column on that particular card of the case. For example, if John Doe's age is punched in columns 6 and 7 on the third card of his case, the age of every other respondent in the study would also occupy columns 6 and 7 of the third card of their cases. Other variables would, of course, be found in columns 6 and 7 of other cards in the cases.

| | | | | | | | | |
|---|---|---|---|---|---|---|---|---|
| CASE 1 | 001 | 36.2 | 4 | 9 | 17.3 | YES | NO | 11.3 | OFTEN |
| CASE 2 | 002 | 45.4 | 7 | 8 | 25.9 | NO | YES | 11.3 | SELDOM |
| CASE 3 | 003 | 71.6 | 4 | 3 | 96.2 | YES | NO | 12.1 | NEVER |

(a)

| | | | | | | |
|---|---|---|---|---|---|---|
| CASE 1 | 0011 | D | 19.01 | 4 | 11 | YES |
| | 0012 | F | 37.38 | 7 | 18 | YES |
| CASE 2 | 0021 | A | 14.73 | 3 | 07 | NO |
| | 0022 | R | 29.24 | 7 | 32 | NO |
| CASE 3 | 0031 | R | 43.27 | 7 | 41 | NO |
| | 0032 | A | 82.91 | 8 | 23 | NO |

(b)

| | | | | | |
|---|---|---|---|---|---|
| CASE 1 | 0011 | 31.9 | 4.2 | A | NO |
| | 0012 | 88.2 | 9.7 | C | YES |
| | 0013 | 47.7 | 5.1 | A | YES |
| | 0014 | 03.1 | 5.0 | A | YES |
| CASE 2 | 0021 | 38.1 | 9.0 | C | NO |
| | 0022 | 23.6 | 4.7 | A | YES |
| | 0023 | 18.9 | 3.9 | A | NO |
| | 0024 | 27.8 | 8.3 | C | YES |
| CASE 3 | 0031 | 34.6 | 5.6 | C | NO |
| | 0032 | 14.9 | 6.2 | C | YES |
| | 0033 | 11.7 | 4.4 | A | NO |
| | 0034 | 21.5 | 7.9 | C | YES |

(c)

**FIG. 2.1**    Fixed-column format. (*a*) One card per case; (*b*) two cards per case; (*c*) four cards per case.

Figure 2.1 demonstrates three examples of cases organized in fixed-column format. In the first example, there is one card per case; in the second example, there are two cards per case; and in the third example, there are four cards per case. A case may continue from one physical card to another, and there is no fixed limit to the number of cards a case may contain. However, no variable value may be continued from one card of a case to another; each value must be wholly contained on a single card. The cards constituting each of the cases must be in the same sequence (because the *variable order* in each case must be the same), but the cases themselves need not necessarily be sequenced.

**2.2.3.2    Organizing data in free-field format**

The SPSS system also allows the user to organize his cases in free-field format. In free-field format, there need be no correspondence between the columns occupied by the same variables on successive cases as long as the *sequence* of the variables remains constant from one case to the next. Furthermore, unlike fixed-column data, two or more cases may occupy the same physical card so that the cases constitute a continuous string of variable values. *The value of each variable appearing on a case must be separated by one or more blanks and/or commas,* for

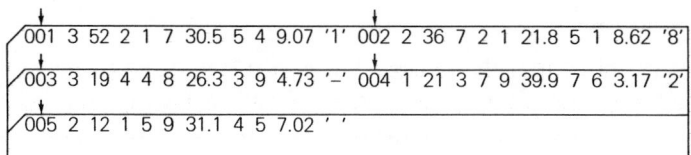

**FIG. 2.2**    Free-field format.

| CASE | VARIABLE | | | | | | | | | |
|------|---|---|---|---|---|---|---|---|---|---|
|      | 1 | 2 | 3 | 4 | 5 | 6 | 7 | 8 | 9 | 10 |
| 001 | 3 | 52 | 2 | 1 | 7 | 30.5 | 5 | 4 | 9.07 | '1' |
| 002 | 2 | 36 | 7 | 2 | 1 | 21.8 | 5 | 1 | 8.62 | '&' |
| 003 | 3 | 19 | 4 | 4 | 8 | 26.3 | 3 | 9 | 4.73 | '-' |
| 004 | 1 | 21 | 3 | 7 | 9 | 39.9 | 7 | 6 | 3.17 | '2' |
| 005 | 2 | 12 | 1 | 5 | 9 | 31.1 | 4 | 5 | 7.02 | ' ' |

**FIG. 2.3**    Tabular presentation of data of Fig. 2.2.

this is how the system determines where the value of one variable ends and that of the next begins. Like data organized in fixed-column format, the value of any variable *may not* be split between two physical cards. If there is not enough room to complete the value on one card, the remaining columns should be left blank and the value punched on the following card.

Alphanumeric variables coded in free-field format must be enclosed within single quotation marks. The variable value A must be punched 'A'. Similarly, the value B would be represented as 'B', & as '&', etc. Those variables which have been coded to take both numeric and alphanumeric values must be treated as alphanumeric variables, *and all their values must be enclosed in single quotation marks*. A variable which takes the values 1, 2, 3, 4, 5, &, and − would be represented on cases in free-field format as '1', '2', '3', '4', '5', '&', and '−'. Figure 2.2 illustrates data organized in free-field format. Each of the five cases has one value for each of the 10 variables. In addition, each case has a case-identification number. The arrows indicate the beginning of each case. The three cards in Fig. 2.2 will produce the values shown in Fig. 2.3 for the 10 variables for five successive cases. Note that the values of the tenth variable are always treated as alphabetic values even though the values of the first and fourth cases denote numerals. The second value for the tenth variable ['&'] is the representation for a 12-punch on the IBM 360. On some other computers (the 1401 and 7090 in particular), this physical punch is assigned the graphic '+'. Users of SPSS should use care in equating the correct graphic with this punch. The last value for the tenth variable [' '] is a representation of the blank or space. Note further that, as in the cases of variables 6 and 9, numeric values in free-field format may have a decimal point and, as in the case of the third value of variable 4, may have a preceding minus sign. Numeric values may *not* be preceded by a plus sign ['+'] or an ampersand ['&']. The absence of a minus sign indicates a positive number.

### 2.2.3.3    Assigning case- and card-identification numbers

In addition to the values of the variables, the researcher may wish to record identifying numbers on each card of every case. Commonly, all cards in a case will have a case-identification number as well as an additional number identifying each card within the case. SPSS does not recognize such numbers in a manner different from any other variable. However, the user may find it beneficial to have these identification fields since they will facilitate reordering dropped card decks and permit reference back to the original data source if any doubt should apply to the accuracy of the punched cards. Further, the user may manipulate these identification numbers as any other variable when processing the data. Irrespective of user-coded identification numbers, SPSS itself assigns a unique sequence number to each case within a subfile. This identification number is automatically present whenever a file is processed

**FIG. 2.4**  Assigning case- and card-sequence numbers.

and may be accessed by referring to the variable named SEQNUM. This also means that the variable SEQNUM and its values (1 to the number of cases) may be used as any other variable in the processing of the data. Case- and card-identification numbers may be punched at any place on the card. However, for convenience, they are usually placed in adjacent fields at the beginning or end of the card. Figure 2.4 demonstrates how they might be assigned.

## 2.3  SUBFILES: THEIR FUNCTION AND STRUCTURE

Quite often in social science research the researcher has data which can be best analyzed by grouping the cases into two or more groups or sets. In the SPSS system, these groups are termed *subfiles*. Subfiles may be comparative samples from a survey study; that is, they may be similar interviews taken in different communities, nations, colleges, etc. Subfiles may also be groups of cases from a single sample which have been divided according to the values of some critical variable. In a study of racial prejudice, for example, each of the subfiles might contain the cases of respondents of a different race. In other instances, subfiles might be composed of cases from different time trials or experimental treatments.

### 2.3.1  USING SUBFILES

The subfile structure enables the user to perform several different types of analysis. First, the subfile structure may be used to examine or test the distribution or central tendency of variables in different subfiles. Second, the researcher may be interested in comparisons of the relationships between variables in different subfiles. In this case, the subfile structure enables the user to automatically generate the same crosstabulation, correlation, or even the same Guttman scale for each of the subfiles in his file. In either of these types of analysis, the user may wish to do some calculations in which the subfiles are processed separately and to do others where all of the subfiles are processed together as a single (unified) file. Furthermore, particular subfiles or groups of subfiles may be singled out for special types of analysis. Once the subfile structure has been created, any of these subfile-processing modes may be exercised during any processing run. The subfile-processing modes are effected by means of a control card, the PROCESS SBFILES card, which is discussed in detail along with each of the subfile-processing modes in Sec. 5.5.

### 2.3.2  SUBFILE STRUCTURE

All subfiles within a file must contain the same variables, and the variables must be in the same format. However, the number of cases in each of the subfiles may vary, and coding differences can exist as long as these differences do not affect the type of the variables or their location on the cases.

The cases of each of the subfiles must be grouped together so that all the cases to be contained in the first subfile would be first in the data deck, those in second subfile next, and so on. The cards in each case are ordered in exactly the same way that they would be if there

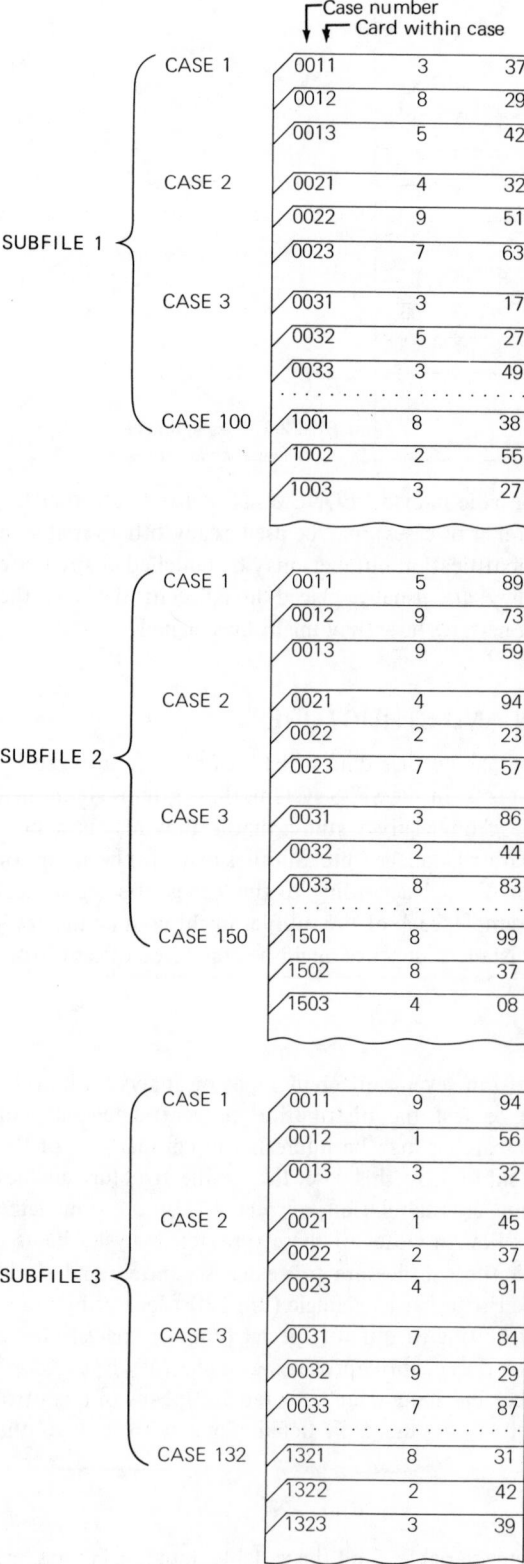

**FIG. 2.5**   Organization of cases into subfiles.

were no subfile structure. The maximum number of subfiles which may be contained in a single file is 100.

Figure 2.5 illustrates the organization of the cases in a file with a subfile structure. Notice that each subfile does not necessarily have to contain the same number of cases. In this example, the first subfile contains 100 cases, the second subfile 150 cases, and the third subfile 132 cases. The way in which the subfile structure is defined and entered into a file is explained in Secs. 4.3 and 5.5.

## 2.4    RECORDING DATA ON MACHINE-READABLE MEDIA

Once the data has been coded and punched, it may be input into SPSS directly from punched cards. Alternately, it may be copied onto a tape, disk file, or other direct-access device. The SPSS system can input data from any machine-readable device or medium which can be legitimately defined vis-à-vis the operating system's job control language (see Appendix F, Job Control Language, for instructions on defining those files). Furthermore, the data need not be in card-image records (i.e., it may reside on records which are longer or shorter that 80-column records). It must, however, be recorded in the normal BCD representation.

## 2.5    LIMITATIONS ON INPUT DATA

There is no programmed limit to the number of cases which can be entered into an SPSS file. In practice, however, the upper limit is to some degree fixed by the amount of direct access (i.e., disk, data cell, and/or drum) storage available for scratch purposes at any given computer installation. The storage requirements for SPSS files are four bytes per variable for each case in the file. If there is any question as to whether a file will be too large to be entered into the system, the user should consult with the systems-programming group at his installation. If there is insufficient direct-access storage, scratch tapes can be used, although they are somewhat more costly in terms of machine time. Irrespective of the number of cases in a file, no more than 500 variables may be entered into an SPSS file, and no file can contain more than 100 subfiles.

# 3
# SPSS CONTROL CARDS

As in most systems of prepared programs, the user controls the processing of his data by means of control cards. Control cards perform many functions in the SPSS system. Some of the cards define and describe the data as it is entered into the system; others allow the user to control the operation of the statistical subprogram being used; yet others enable the user to recode and transform the data in his file.

Although each control card in the SPSS system has a unique function, all the cards share a common format, and information is entered onto them in a similar manner. The conventions employed in constructing SPSS control cards constitute a simple language which enables the user to provide the system with the information required to process his data and to instruct the system how he wishes it processed.

The control-card language is a very simplified quasi-natural language consisting of names, values, special words, and rules governing punctuation and spacing.

The user should pay particular attention to this section, which defines the SPSS control-card language as well as the general rules and conventions to be used in constructing these control cards. These general rules and conventions are *not* included in the descriptions of the individual card types, except where some particular problem calls attention to one of them. The user will find a summary section of general rules in Sec. 3.1.3.

## 3.1   CONTROL-CARD PREPARATION: GENERAL FORMAT AND CONVENTIONS

All SPSS control cards have two portions: (1) *a control field* which occupies card columns 1 to 15 and contains the *control word* or words which identify the card to both the user and the system; and (2) *the specification field* occupying card columns 16 to 80 of that and all subsequent cards necessary to complete the specifications and containing the parameters and arguments required by the particular control card being used.

### 3.1.1   THE CONTROL FIELD

Each control card is identified by a unique control word or set of control words. These control words inform the system as to the type of specifications that will follow so that the proper procedures can be called up to read, interpret, and act upon the information on that card.

The control field is always punched in card columns 1 to 15 and left justified (i.e., always beginning in column 1). The control words that occupy this field are of variable length, but never exceed 15 characters. The spelling and spacing of control words must conform to the samples presented in the text. Each SPSS control card including its control word(s) is discussed in detail in the following sections, and a summary list of all control cards, their functions, and format, can be found in Appendix B. Control-card syntax definitions appear in Appendix C. The following are a few examples of some of the control fields which are used in the SPSS system:

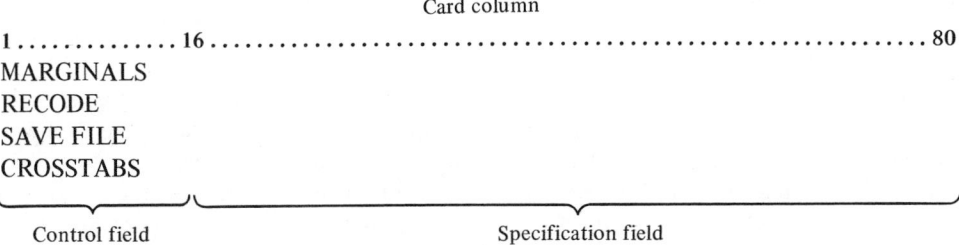

Card column

```
1 . . . . . . . . . . . . 16 . . . . . . . . . . . . . . . . . . . . . . . . . . . . . . . . . . . . . . . . . . . . . . . . . . . . . . . . . . . 80
MARGINALS
RECODE
SAVE FILE
CROSSTABS
```

Control field                              Specification field

### 3.1.2   THE SPECIFICATION FIELD

In the specification field occupying card columns 16 to 80, the user supplies the system with the parameters, labels, and/or instructions required to perform the function indicated by the control word. The specifications may be the name of a file, variable names or labels, recoding specifications, or missing-data indicators, as well as many other types of information. Specification fields are constructed out of combinations of six elements: *names, values, keywords, labels, delimiters* and *operators*. These six elements which make up the specifications do not have to be entered onto the card in any fixed columns. *All specifications may be punched free field* as long as they do not occupy card columns 1 to 15. The specifications may continue from one physical card to the next as long as columns 1 to 15 of all subsequent cards used to complete the specification are left blank.

#### 3.1.2.1   Names

Names are mnemonics supplied by the user and are used whenever he wishes to refer to (1) his file, (2) the variables contained in his file, and/or (3) the subfiles of his file (if any). A *file name* is used whenever the user wishes to gain access to the file for processing. *Variable names* are employed whenever the user wishes to utilize a variable in a computation, etc.

Names, whether they be variable names, names of subfiles, or file names, are limited to eight characters in length, and the first character must be an *alphabetic letter*. Names may be composed of letters and/or numbers, but special characters may not be used. (*Special characters* are defined as all graphics which are not letters or numbers on the IBM keypunch. This includes all punctuation marks.) Names must be made up of adjacent characters; that is, they may not contain embedded blanks. Furthermore, individual names must be contained on a single punched card; i.e., a name begun on one card may not be continued onto a succeeding card.

### 3.1.2.2    Values

Various numeric and/or alphabetic values are regularly entered as elements in the specification field. The values most commonly entered onto SPSS control cards are values of the variables in the file. However, values may also be numeric quantities to be utilized in variable transformations, or they may be other more specialized values such as the number of cases in a file or subfile or the percentage base to be used in sampling a file.

Values, like all other elements in the specification field, must be composed of contiguous characters; i.e., they may not contain blanks. Individual values, like names, must be contained on a single punched card.

Numeric values may be either integers or decimal numbers, and left zeros may be punched or deleted. Thus the values 01, 098.6, and 0.432 and the values 1, 98.6, and .432 are equivalent. Alphabetic values, *and this includes all the values of alphanumeric variables* must be enclosed in apostrophes or single quotation marks. The values of variables which have been coded so that some of their values are numbers while others are letters or special characters must be considered alphanumeric and their values enclosed in single quotation marks whenever they are referred to on an SPSS control card. This is necessary because the computer stores variables by type, and the internal representation of the numeric integer 1 is completely different from the internal representation of the alphanumeric character '1'. For example, if the values of an alphanumeric variable were 1, 2, 3, 4, 5, +, −, they would appear on the specification field as '1', '2', '3', '4', '5', '+', '−'. Other aspects of variable types are described in Secs. 2.2 and 4.6. It should also be noted that alphanumeric variables can be easily recoded into numeric variables—a procedure we highly recommend (see Sec. 8.1).

### 3.1.2.3    Keywords

Keywords are preset configurations of alphabetic characters which have a special meaning in the SPSS system. Some of these keywords, such as TO and THRU, when used in conjunction with names and values, cause action to be taken on an inclusive list of values or names such as values 1 THRU 10 or variables AGE TO SEX. Other keywords such as BY and WITH are used to inform the system that a computation involving a relationship between certain variables is desired. For example, correlate AGE WITH INCOME or crosstabulate PARTY BY VOTE. A number of other keywords are employed in constructing variable transformations. These keywords, such as EQ (equal to), LT (less than), or AND, OR, and NOT, are used as *logical and relational operators.*

Because individual keywords have specific meanings within a given context, they are described in detail along with the control cards upon which they appear. As general rules, however, keywords must be punched exactly as described in the text and, like names and values, individual keywords must not contain embedded blanks or be split between two cards.

### 3.1.2.4    Labels

The SPSS system has a large number of labeling options. Files, variables, and variable values may be given extended labels which, when present, appear automatically on printed output. Labels may contain any valid graphic available in the IBM 360 character set, with one or two label-specific exceptions. An entire label is considered a single element and is printed just as it is punched on the control cards. Unlike any of the other elements in the specifications, individual labels may be continued from one punched card to the next. Each of the various types of labels has a different maximum length which is given in the detailed specifications of the control cards on which it appears.

### 3.1.2.5    Delimiters

Individual names, values, keywords, and labels appearing in the specification field *must be separated from one another by delimiters.* Delimiters are of two types—common and special.

The two *common delimiters* (the *blank* and the *comma*) are always used to separate elements unless one of the special delimiters is required. The blank and the comma are equivalent and may be used interchangeably, and additional blanks and/or commas may be inserted between elements to improve readability.

There are three *special delimiters*: the left parenthesis [ ( ], the right parenthesis [ ) ], and the slash [/]. The left and right parentheses are always used in conjunction, and their most common usage is that of setting off a list of values, while the slash is often used to separate groups of names. These three special delimiters are used only when the specific format of a control card calls for their use. The MISSING VALUES card, for example, requires that the missing values be enclosed in parentheses and that the missing values which apply to one variable be set off from the next variable name by a slash. The card has the following format:

```
1                16
MISSING VALUES  variable name (values)/variable name (values) . . .
```

A sample MISSING VALUES card might appear as follows:

```
1                16
MISSING VALUES  INCOME (0,8,9)/RACE (3)
```

Special delimiters need not be separated from other elements by common delimiters; i.e., blanks and/or commas are not required to further separate delimiters from each other or from other elements. They may, however, be inserted around the special delimiters to improve readability, if the user so desires. The use of individual special delimiters is discussed in detail in the sections describing the control cards on which they are required.

### 3.1.2.6  Operators

A few of the SPSS control cards require the user to use mathematical operators when constructing the specifications. These operators are used mostly on the control cards which specify variable transformations. Because of the more specialized nature of these operators, they will not be discussed at length here. A full discussion of their use can be found in Sec. 8.2. The five mathematical operators and their graphics are: addition [+], subtraction [−], multiplication [*], division [/], and equals [=]. Note that the graphic used to signify division [/] is the same as one of the special delimiters. This should not cause any confusion, because they are never used in both contexts on the same control card. It should also be noted that operators, unlike names, values, keywords, and labels, need not be set off from other elements by delimiters.

### 3.1.3  SUMMARY OF GENERAL RULES FOR CONTROL-CARD PREPARATION

1.  *Control words* must be spelled and spaced correctly.
2.  *Names* have a maximum length of eight characters, the first of which must be alphabetic.
3.  *Names* must be composed of letters and/or numbers. No special characters may be used.
4.  *Values* may be composed of integers, decimal numbers, or alphabetic characters which include letters and special characters.
5.  *Alphanumeric values* as well as all values of *alphanumeric variables* must be enclosed in single quotation marks when they appear on control cards.
6.  *Keywords* must be spelled and spaced exactly as presented in the text.
7.  *Labels* may be composed of any valid characters. They may not, however, exceed their maximum specified length.
8.  *Individual names, keywords, and values* must consist of contiguous characters. That is, they may have no embedded delimiters.
9.  *Individual names, keywords, and values* must be contained on a single punched card. They may not begin on one card and be continued on a second. *Labels* can, however, be split between cards.
10. *Names, keywords, values, and labels* must be separated from one another by delimiters.
11. *Common delimiters* (i.e., blanks and/or commas) are used to separate names, values, keywords, and labels unless one of the special delimiters (i.e., parentheses or slashes) is specified.
12. Additional *common delimiters* may be inserted between names, values, keywords, labels, special delimiters, and operators to improve readability.
13. If the specification field requires more than one control card, it may be continued on columns 16 to 80 of succeeding cards. Columns 1 to 15 of these succeeding cards must, however, be left blank.

Additional rules governing the construction of individual control cards are to be found under the detailed description of the SPSS cards beginning in Sec. 4.1. The general rules listed above are demonstrated by the following two example RECODE cards:[1]

```
1                16
RECODE           AGE,, SEX RACE TO PARTY (0 2 THRU 5 = 1) (1=2)

RECODE           AGE SEXRACE TO PARTY (02 THRU 5=1) (1=2)
```

The sample RECODE cards presented above are employed to recode the values of variables in the file. The first of these two RECODE cards is correct. Each variable name is separated by at least one blank and/or comma. The values and keywords are also separated from other elements by blanks except where special delimiters are employed. Note that special delimiters may or may not be separated from other elements by blanks. The second RECODE card is incorrect and demonstrates some common violations of the rules. The variable name AGE begins before column 16 and hence is in the control field; this would cause an error message and termination of the run. Next the variable names SEX and RACE have no delimiter between them, so it is impossible for the system to recognize them as separate names. The intended values 0 and 2 have no common delimiters between them and hence would be recognized as the single value 02. Each violation of the rules for specification fields, except the last, is fatal. That is, each would cause the run to be terminated. The last type of error is of the most costly variety, as it is syntactically correct, but conveys the wrong meaning. The result is that 2's to 5's would be recoded to 1, while 0's would remain untouched, thus wasting computer time and perhaps rendering the output meaningless.

At each stage of processing, the SPSS system checks the syntax and order of all control cards for errors. If an error is encountered, an error number is printed below the offending control card. The remaining control cards of that processing step are also checked for further errors. The run is then terminated with the message, ERROR(S) IN CONTROL CARD(S) PRECLUDES FURTHER PROCESSING. The user may then locate the error number(s) in the error-message list in Appendix A, and the diagnostic information there should enable him to correct the control card(s).

## 3.2   NOTATION USED IN PRESENTING CONTROL-CARD FORMATS

Before proceeding to the detailed description of the first group of SPSS control cards, a few words are in order concerning the notation used in presenting the card format.

*Fields presented in brackets* [ ] are optional, and the user may omit the bracketed elements if he wishes. Bracketed elements will usually be labels.

*Brace marks* { } are used to denote fields which can take one or more types of element, name, list, or keyword. For example,

$$
\left\{
\begin{array}{c}
\text{CARD} \\
\text{or} \\
\text{TAPE} \\
\text{or} \\
\text{DISK} \\
\text{or} \\
\text{OTHER}
\end{array}
\right\}
\quad \text{or} \quad
\left\{
\begin{array}{c}
\text{variable name} \\
\text{or} \\
\text{variable list}
\end{array}
\right\}
$$

*Keywords and control words* are presented in FULL CAPITALS, and whenever the user encounters elements in full capitals, they should be copied just as they are presented.

*Fields presented in lowercase* are to be replaced by the user with the proper elements. If, for example, the user encounters the field (value list), he should insert the desired value list within the parentheses.

The *special delimiters* [(, ), and /] are presented where they should appear in the specification field. The common delimiters, however, are not always presented.

---

[1]The second card is an incorrect control card, for demonstration only.

# 4
# DEFINING AN SPSS FILE: THE DATA-DEFINITION CARDS

Data is manipulated in the SPSS system in groups called *files.* A file must contain the following information defining and describing the data:

1.  A file name.
2.  A variable list (defining the variables to be entered into the file)
3.  The subfile structure of the file (if any)
4.  The number of data cases in the file
5.  The input medium used to enter the data
6.  An input-format statement (identifying the structure of the cases and the location of the variables on them)

In addition, a file may contain any or all of the following optional information:

7.  Missing-data values (identifying variable values to be treated as missing data)
8.  Extended variable labels
9.  Variable value labels
10. Variable printing formats

This information is entered into SPSS by means of the *data-definition* control cards, and together with the data cases, constitutes a complete file. This file may, if the user desires, be permanently retained as an SPSS *system file*. Thereafter, this information is automatically passed to the system along with the data whenever processing is desired. Alternatively, the data-definition cards can be submitted along with the data at the time of each processing run. The creation of system files and the explanation of the file-processing procedures and options is discussed in Chaps. 7 and 8.

## 4.1    THE FILE NAME CARD

A *file name* identifies each SPSS system file and is used whenever reference to that file is required. A FILE NAME card is required for any file which is to be stored as a system file. The card is optional, however, if the user does not wish to have the file retained for future processing.

The FILE NAME card consists of the control words FILE NAME followed by a file name of the user's choice. The file name may be up to eight characters in length, and the first character must be an alphabetic letter. All the rules concerning the construction and use of names must be followed (see Secs. 3.1.2.1 and 3.1.3). The file name may be followed by an optional *file label* of up to 64 characters in length. Both the file name and the file label may be stored with the system file and will appear on all printed output generated from that file. The general structure of the FILE NAME card is

```
1                   16
FILE NAME           file name [file label]
```

The following two examples illustrate the structure of the FILE NAME card. The first contains the optional file label while the second contains only the required file name.

```
1                16
FILE NAME        STUDY1   THIS IS AN EXAMPLE FILE LABEL FOR FILE STUDY1

FILE NAME        STUDY2
```

## 4.2    THE VARIABLE LIST CARD

Each variable in an SPSS file is referred to by a unique *variable name*. Like all other names used on SPSS control cards, they have a maximum length of eight characters, the first of which must be an alphabetic letter. Furthermore, all of the other general rules and conventions governing the construction of names must be followed (see Secs. 3.1.2.1 and 3.1.3).

All processing of data is accomplished by reference to these variable names which may be permanently stored with the data in a system file. The name given to any variable is arbitrary, but must be unique in terms of the variables named in that file.[1] To fully exploit the utility of this convention, the user should select mnemonics which suggest the nature of the variable being named. For example, suppose that the variables being used in a particular study are age, sex, income, occupation, and level of education. For these variables, the user might elect to use the mnemonics AGE, SEX, INCOME, OCCUP, and EDUCAT. These variables would be entered into the file by the following VARIABLE LIST card which begins with the control words VARIABLE LIST in columns 1 to 15.

```
1                16
VARIABLE LIST    AGE, SEX, INCOME, OCCUP, EDUCAT
```

The VARIABLE LIST control card causes these variable names to be entered into the system and associated with the proper variables on the cases. In this example, each data case would consist of five values, the first of which would be assumed to be the respondent's age, the second his or her sex, etc. *Therefore, the order of the variable names must be the same as the order of the variables on the cases.* That is, the system matches the name with the variable in the corresponding order. A maximum of 500 variables may be defined for any given file.

The variable-naming convention can become tedious in cases where a large number of

---

[1]The three pre-defined variable names, SEQNUM, CASWGT, and SUBFIL, cannot be employed as variable names. This is also true of the following 20 *keywords*: TO, WITH, BY, SQRT, EXP, LN, SIN, COS, ATAN, RND, LG10, GE, LE, GT, LT, EQ, NE, AND, OR and NOT.

variables must be declared. In these cases an alternate procedure can be employed which requires much less card preparation. This convention identifies variables by means of variable-sequence numbers, and a large string of variables can be defined by the following type of inclusive variable list,

VARxxx TO VARyyy

where xxx and yyy are both three-digit numbers, and where yyy *must be greater than* xxx. The prefix VAR must directly precede each of the three-digit numbers; i.e., there must be no delimiter between it and the number. The keyword TO is placed between the two variable numbers and must be separated from each of them by one or more common delimiters.

Using this inclusive-naming convention, the variables VAR001, VAR002, VAR-003, . . . , VAR100 would all be defined by the following VARIABLE LIST card:

```
1               16
VARIABLE LIST   VAR001 TO VAR100
```

The implied intervening variable names (in this case VAR002 to VAR099) will be automatically generated by the system and associated with the proper variables in the same way that the alphabetic mnemonics are. It is clear that this notation results in a considerable economy when a large number of variables must be declared. However, the mnemonic quality of the variable names is lost.

These two naming conventions may be freely intermixed on the VARIABLE LIST card, producing a variable list for the file which contains some alphabetically named variables and some variable names of the VARxxx type. Table 4.1 gives an example of such a variable-list array as it is stored in the file. Remember that the order of the variable names must correspond to the order of the variables on the cases.

```
1               16
VARIABLE LIST   GEORGE MOXIE, TOM, VAR001 TO VAR004 SAM MARY
                ROBERT, VAR005 TO VAR007, JUDY JACK
```

**TABLE 4.1**   Definition of a variable list by the use of the VARIABLE LIST card

| Position of variable on cases | Corresponding variable name | Position of variable on cases | Corresponding variable name |
|---|---|---|---|
| 001 | GEORGE | 009 | MARY |
| 002 | MOXIE | 010 | ROBERT |
| 003 | TOM | 011 | VAR005 |
| 004 | VAR001 | 012 | VAR006 |
| 005 | VAR002 | 013 | VAR007 |
| 006 | VAR003 | 014 | JUDY |
| 007 | VAR004 | 015 | JACK |
| 008 | SAM | | |

*Summary of Rules and Conventions for the VARIABLE LIST Card*

1. The control word is VARIABLE LIST.
2. The variable list consists of mnemonic variable names and/or inclusive variable-sequence numbers of the type VARxxx TO VARyyy.
3. In the preparation of the inclusive variable-sequence numbers of the VARxxx TO VARyyy type, xxx and yyy must be three-digit numbers, and yyy must always be greater than xxx. The three-digit numbers xxx and yyy must directly follow the prefix VAR (i.e., there must be no delimiter between them). The keyword TO between them must be preceded and succeeded by one or more common delimiters.
4. All rules and conventions governing the use of names on SPSS control cards must be applied (see Secs. 3.1.2.1 and 3.1.3).

5. No variable name or inclusive number may be declared twice. Each variable in a file must be given a unique name or sequence number.
6. The sequence of the variable names and inclusive variable numbers must correspond exactly to the sequence of the variables on the data cases.
7. No more than 500 variable names may be defined for any file.
8. In addition, all the general rules and conventions governing the preparation of SPSS control cards must be followed (see Sec. 3.1 and the summary list of rules in Sec. 3.1.3).

## 4.3 THE SUBFILE LIST CARD

The cases of any file may be substructed into between 2 and 100 groups termed *subfiles*. Subfiles may be like samples from a comparative survey study, or they may be groups of cases from a single sample which has been divided along the values of some critical variable. In either case, the user will want to refer to Sec. 2.3 if he wishes to organize his data into subfiles for input to the SPSS system.

The SUBFILE LIST card informs the system as to the name of each of the subfiles being entered into the file. *Of course the* SUBFILE LIST *card is used only when a file has a subfile structure.* When processing the file, the subfiles are referred to by the subfile name entered on this card. The subfile names constitute a special variable named SUBFIL, and each subfile name becomes a value of that variable. The appropriate subfile name is automatically written on each case of each subfile as the cases are read into the system, and the special variable name SUBFIL is added to the variable list. This means that SUBFIL and its values (i.e., each of the subfile names) may be used in the analysis of the data just as any other variable entered on the VARIABLE LIST card. Furthermore, the system also provides a number of subfile-processing options which enable the user to control the way in which the subfiles are processed on any given task. Section 5.5 (The PROCESS SBFILES Card) explains in detail the subfile-processing modes.

The SUBFILE LIST card is similar in structure to the VARIABLE LIST card, and contains the control words SUBFILE LIST followed by the names of the subfiles that are being entered into the file. The name given to any subfile is arbitrary, *but the first four characters of each subfile name must be unique* in terms of the subfiles being entered into that particular file. The user must also conform to all the rules and conventions governing the construction and use of names on SPSS control cards. The user may wish to refer to Sec. 3.1.2.1 and 3.1.3 for these rules and conventions.

Subfile names *must* be entered onto the SUBFILE LIST card *in precisely the same sequence* as that of the subfiles themselves as they are to be entered into the system. This means that the first subfile name appearing on the SUBFILE LIST card will be associated with the first subfile entered, the second subfile name with the second subfile entered, and so forth. See Sec. 2.3 on organizing data cases into subfiles, and Sec. 4.4 and Chap. 7 for further examples of the deck and control-card setup for files with a subfile structure.

The following example illustrates the SUBFILE LIST card for a hypothetical comparative survey study of state legislators in eight states in which the legislatures from each state will be entered as a subfile. The abbreviation or mnenomics used to represent the name of each of the states is, of course, arbitrary, and the user might well have selected others.

```
1                16
SUBFILE LIST    TENN, NY, CALIF, MO, ILL, MASS, PENN, NCAROL
```

## 4.4 THE # OF CASES CARD

The # OF CASES card simply informs the system of the number of cases in the user's file. When the file has a subfile structure, the # OF CASES card provides the system with the number of cases in each of the subfiles rather than the number in the entire file. When the file *has no subfile structure,* the format of the card is as follows:

```
1                16
# OF CASES        number of cases in the file
```

The control words # OF CASES are followed by the actual number of cases. If, for example, the user had a file containing 1,008 cases, the # OF CASES card would appear as

```
1                16
# OF CASES        1008
```

*If the file has no subfile structure* and if the data resides on a medium *other than cards* (i.e., on a tape, disk, or another direct-access device), the user does not have to know the exact number of cases in the file. In this instance, a special version of the # OF CASES card may be prepared in which the control words # OF CASES are followed by the keyword ESTIMATED. This keyword is then followed by the number of cases the user estimates to be in his file. *It is critical that the user select a number that is equal to or greater than the number of cases actually in the file,* for the system will not read more cases than estimated. It will, however, accept fewer cases. In short, estimate high; it makes no difference how high. The format of the # OF CASES card when using this special estimating procedure is

```
1                16
# OF CASES        ESTIMATED number of cases estimated in the file
```

An example of the use of this convention is

```
1                16
# OF CASES        ESTIMATED     10000
```

*When the file has a subfile structure,* the number of cases in each of the subfiles is entered onto the card in the specification field. These numbers must be entered in precisely the same order in which the subfile names were entered on the SUBFILE LIST card (see Sec. 4.3). In turn, the actual cases composing each of the subfiles must also be in an identical sequence when input into the system (see Sec. 2.3 on organizing cases into subfiles).

The general format of the # OF CASES card, when a file has a subfile structure, is as follows:

```
1                16
# OF CASES        number of cases in first subfile, number of cases in second subfile,
                  number of cases in third subfile . . . number of cases in last subfile
```

Suppose, for example, that a user had a file composed of five comparable survey samples of political attitudes from five nations, the first of which was from the United States and had 970 cases, the second from the United Kingdom with 963 cases, the third from Germany with 955 cases, the fourth from Italy with 995 cases, and the fifth from Mexico with 1,295 cases. The SUBFILE LIST card together with the # OF CASES card would appear as follows. Note, however, that the subfile names are selected by the user, and other mnemonics could have been chosen.

```
1                16
SUBFILE LIST      US,   UK,  GERMANY,  ITALY,  MEXICO
                  ↓     ↓      ↓          ↓       ↓
# OF CASES        970, 963,   955,      955,   1295
```

## 4.5   THE INPUT MEDIUM CARD

The INPUT MEDIUM card serves the purpose of informing the SPSS system of the type of input *medium* from which the user's data will be entered into the system. The control words INPUT MEDIUM are followed by one of four control words depending upon the location of the user's data. The keyword CARD is used when the user's data is being entered on cards along with his SPSS control cards. The keyword TAPE is used when the user's data resides on a BCD tape; the keyword DISK when his data resides on a BCD disk file; or the keyword OTHER when the data to be input is on a data cell or some other exotic device available at the user's installation. The general format of the INPUT MEDIUM card is then

```
1                16
INPUT MEDIUM    ⎡ CARD  ⎤
                ⎢  or   ⎥
                ⎢ TAPE  ⎥
                ⎨  or   ⎬
                ⎢ DISK  ⎥
                ⎢  or   ⎥
                ⎣ OTHER ⎦
```

When the user's data is being entered from cards, the data cases along with the SPSS control cards are input together from the card reader. And it is the keyword **CARD** which informs the system that it is to expect the data cases to follow the appropriate control cards.

When the data is being entered from a medium other than cards (i.e., when **TAPE, DISK**, or **OTHER** is the keyword encountered on the **INPUT MEDIUM** card), the keyword informs the system of the appropriate medium from which the data is to be read for processing. In this instance, the SPSS control cards are read from a card reader (or from a remote terminal) while the data is read from a tape, disk, etc.

Whenever data is being entered from a medium other than cards, the user must prepare a JCL (Job Control Language) card indicating the exact location and nature of this data file. In the IBM 360 version of SPSS, this card is termed the FT08 card. On the FT08 JCL card (and its continuation), the user supplies the computer's *operating system* (not the SPSS system) with information such as the exact location of his file (e.g., the reel number of the tape, or the volume number of the disk on which the file is located, and the blocking factor which should be used to read the file).

We have attempted to make the preparation of these JCL cards as painless as possible for the user. Appendix F has detailed instructions for the preparation of these cards at the Stanford installation. Users at other IBM 360 installations will find this appendix useful, but should consult with the appropriate personnel at their installation before attempting to use the SPSS system. Instructions for preparing a similar card for the CDC version of SPSS are in Appendix G.

## 4.6　THE INPUT FORMAT CARD

Three further types of information describing the data are required before a file may be input to the SPSS system: (1) the organization of the data cases, that is, whether they are organized in fixed-column or free-field format; (2) the type of variables, that is, whether they are numeric or alphanumeric variables; and (3) the card and column location of the variables. These three types of information are entered on the **INPUT FORMAT** card. The control field containing the control words **INPUT FORMAT** is followed by the organization of the cases which is the first element in the specification field.

### 4.6.1　FIXED- OR FREE-FIELD FORMAT

In data organized in *fixed-column* format, the values of each of the variables are located on the same card and in the same column(s) of every case. However, for data organized in *free-field* format, there need be no correspondence between the card columns occupied by the same variable on successive cases as long as the sequence of the variables remains constant from one case to the next. Section 2.2 and its subsections give detailed specifications for organizing and coding data in both fixed- and free-field format.

The first element entered onto the specification field of the **INPUT FORMAT** card will be one of two keywords, **FIXED** or **FREEFIELD**, depending upon whether the user's data is organized in fixed- or free-field format. The keywords must be spelled out and spaced properly. The general format of the **INPUT FORMAT** card up to this point is then

```
1                16
INPUT FORMAT    ⎡ FIXED     ⎤
                ⎨    or     ⎬
                ⎣ FREEFIELD ⎦
```

### 4.6.2   THE FORMAT LIST FOR DATA IN FIXED-COLUMN FORMAT[1]

When data is in fixed-column format, the keyword FIXED is followed by a *format list* giving the type and location of the variables on the cases. *A format list is not entered when data is organized in free-field format.* When data is in free-field format, the system automatically determines the type and location of the variables, because the values of all alphanumeric variables are set off by single quotation marks and all variable values are separated by one or more common delimiters.

The format list provides the system with a set of instructions for reading the user's data. The data may be on cards or on card-image tape. The format list tells the system the type of each variable, that is, whether it is numeric or alphanumeric, and also informs the system of the card and column location of each of the variables.

The format list consists of a series of elements enclosed in parentheses. The left parenthesis indicates the beginning of the format list, and the right parenthesis indicates the end of the list. The format list directly follows the keyword FIXED and may be continued in columns 16 to 80 of succeeding cards if it cannot be completed on the remainder of the initial card. The format list is read from left to right, so the type and location of the first variable that the user has entered on his VARIABLE LIST card will be the first variable specified on the format list.

There are four format elements, and each of these elements must be separated by a *single comma*, and one or more blanks may be added to improve legibility. The first of these elements deals with the variable types.

### 4.6.3   THE FORMAT ELEMENTS

Alphanumeric variables are variables that take at least one value which is either an alphabetic letter or a special character; that is, they are variables which are not totally composed of numbers even though they may have some numerically coded values.

#### 4.6.3.1   A-type variables

The format element indicating that a variable is alphanumeric takes the form of $Aw$, where $w$ is the column width of the variable. If, for example, the user had a single-column alphanumeric variable to be entered onto the format list, it would appear as A1; an alphanumeric variable occupying four columns would be written as A4, etc.

When the user has two or more *adjacent* alphanumeric variables of the same column width (by adjacent, we mean not separated by blanks or other variables), they may be simultaneously declared by preceding the A with the number of adjacent variables of the same width. Thus the general format of the alphanumeric typing element is $nAw$, where $n$ is the number of adjacent variables of the same column width, where $A$ indicates that the variables are of the alphanumeric type, and where $w$ is the column width of the variables. When there is only one variable to be defined, $n$ may be omitted and is then assumed to be equal to 1. The following are some examples of how the alpha typing elements are constructed:

1. 50A1          50 adjacent single-column alphanumeric variables

2. A5 or 1A5     a single alphanumeric variable, five columns in width

3. 30A2          30 adjacent alphanumeric variables occupying two columns each

#### 4.6.3.2   F-type variables

Numeric variables are variables which are totally composed of numeric values. These values may be either integers or decimal numbers. The element indicating that a variable is numeric is $Fw.d$, where $F$ indicates that the variable is numeric, $w$ indicates the column width of the variable *(including the sign and decimal point if punched)*, and $d$ is the number of digits or columns to the right of the decimal point. F1.0 would, for example, define a single-column numeric

---

[1]The construction of format lists follows the conventions for construction of a Fortran IV format list as described in IBM Form C28-6516. The format lists appearing on INPUT FORMAT cards are read in by SPSS and used as *variable-format lists*. Users familiar with Fortran IV may wish to skip the following sections. Note, however, that only F- and A-type variables are recognized by SPSS.

variable in which the decimal point had not been punched. F2.0, on the other hand, could either be a single-column integer variable in which the decimal had been punched or a two-column integer variable in which the decimal had not been punched. If a decimal point is actually punched on the data card, its position takes priority over the number specified by $d$. The following examples illustrate the rules and conventions used in defining numeric variables.

| Format element | Value appearing on data card | Value read and stored |
|---|---|---|
| F3.0 | 100 | 100 |
| F3.1 | 100 | 10. 0 |
| F3.1 | .10 | 0. 10 |
| F3.1 | 010 | 01. 0 |
| F3.2 | 1. 0 | 1. 00 |

As with the alphanumeric typing element, two or more adjacent variables may be simultaneously defined if they are of the same column width and have the same number of digits to the right of the decimal. Thus 50 adjacent single-column numeric variables would be defined as 50F1.0.

### 4.6.3.3 Skipping card columns with the X

The element $n$X enables the user to skip blanks or undesired columns on his data cards. The alphabetic character X directs the system to skip the number of columns specified in $n$. Thus, if the user wished to skip nine columns, the element 9X would accomplish this.

### 4.6.3.4 Skipping cards with the /

The / instructs the system to go immediately to the next card. When a slash is the first element in a format list, it will cause the first card of each case to be skipped. When it is the last element in the format list, it will cause the last card of each case to be skipped. When it is encountered in the middle of a format list, it instructs the system to stop reading variables from the card it had been reading and proceed directly to the next card. // would instruct the system to go to the card after the next. /// would instruct the system to skip to the third card following the one which it had been reading at the time, and so forth. If there are j cards per case, there should be j — 1 slashes in the format list.

Each complete element on the format list must be separated by one, and only one, comma. Blanks can be inserted between elements to improve readability. The slash [/], however, acts as its own delimiter and need not be set off from other elements by commas. The format list is keypunched beginning with a left parenthesis and ending with a right parenthesis.

### EXAMPLE 4.1

```
1                    16
INPUT FORMAT    FIXED (10X,5F1.0,2X,3A2,12X,45F1.0/10X,25A1,2X,F3.0)
```

The above format will instruct the system to enter the data from each case as follows:

1. Skip the first 10 columns of the first card of each case.
2. Read 5 single-column numeric variables.
3. Skip 2 columns.
4. Read 3 two-column alphanumeric variables.
5. Skip 12 columns.
6. Read 45 single-column numeric variables.
7. Go to the second card of the case.
8. Skip the first 10 columns of that card.
9. Read 25 single-column alphanumeric variables.
10. Skip 2 columns.
11. Read one 3-column numeric variable.
12. Repeat 1 to 11 for each data case in the file.

**EXAMPLE 4.2**

```
1                16
INPUT FORMAT     FIXED (5X,2F6.0,A1,3X,F7.3//10X,23A1/F5.0,2X,A1)
```

1.  Skip the first 5 columns of the first card of each case.
2.  Read 2 numeric variables each 6 columns in length with 0 places to the right of the decimal point.
3.  Read 1 single-column alphanumeric variable.
4.  Skip 3 columns.
5.  Read 1 numeric variable 7 columns in width with 3 digits to the right of the decimal.
6.  Skip the second card and begin reading on the third card of each case.
7.  Skip the first 10 columns of the third card of each case.
8.  Read 23 single-column alphanumeric variables.
9.  Go to the fourth card of each case.
10. Read one 5-column numeric variable from the first 5 columns of the fourth card of each case.
11. Skip 2 columns.
12. Read 1 single-column alphanumeric variable.
13. Repeat 1 to 12 for each case.

### 4.6.4   THE VARIABLE LIST AND THE FORMAT LIST

A word is in order concerning the relationship between the variable list and the format list. Both the variable list defined by a **VARIABLE LIST** card and the format list defined on the **INPUT FORMAT** card are read (by the system) from left to right, so that the first variable named in the variable list is paired with the first variable defined on the format list, the second-named variable with the second variable on the format list, and so forth until each variable named is paired with a data field on the cases. The following figure demonstrates this pairing procedure when data is in fixed-column format. When data is in free-field format, the SPSS system assumes that the first value it encounters is to be paired with the first variable named on the variable list, assuming that there will be one value for each variable per case, and that those values will be in the same sequential order as the variable names on the variable list.

```
1                16
VARIABLE LIST    AGE,INCOME,SEX,RACE,EDUCATN,OCCUPATN,VAR001 TO VAR034,
                 VOTE56,VOTE60,VOTE64

INPUT FORMAT     FIXED (2F1.0,3X,2A1,1F1.0,5X,F1.0/10X,34F1.0,3F1.0)
```

Table 4.2 indicates the exact card and columns and their associated variable names as defined on the above VARIABLE LIST card and INPUT FORMAT card.

**TABLE 4.2   Correspondence between variable lists and format lists**

| Variable name | Variable type | Card location | Column location |
|---|---|---|---|
| AGE | F | 1 | 1 |
| INCOME | F | 1 | 2 |
| SEX | A | 1 | 6 |
| RACE | A | 1 | 7 |
| EDUCATN | F | 1 | 8 |
| OCCUPATN | F | 1 | 14 |
| VAR001 TO VAR034 | F | 2 | 11 to 44 |
| VOTE56 | F | 2 | 45 |
| VOTE60 | F | 2 | 46 |
| VOTE64 | F | 2 | 47 |

The data-definition cards thus far described provide the system with the minimum information required to define a file. In addition, the following types of optional information may be specified and retained with the file if the user so desires.

## 4.7    THE MISSING VALUES CARD

Very often in social science research some of the cases in a file do not have complete information for every variable. For this reason, the SPSS system enables the user to specify *missing values* for each of the variables, so that files containing cases with incomplete data may still be conveniently processed.

The user may specify up to three missing values for each variable in the file, and he may select any values he desires within the specifications described in Sec. 2.2.2. If, for example, the user had a file composed of three variables—AGE, INCOME, and SEX—and some cases were missing information on one or more of these variables, he might select the following values to be designated as missing. SEX would probably require one missing value [0] for those cases in which the interviewer had forgotten to report the respondent's sex. For the variables INCOME and AGE, the researcher might desire to preserve more detailed information about why the cases were missing. In this instance, he might choose the value 8 for those respondents who refused to answer, 9 for those who said they don't know, and 0 for those cases in which the interviewer had seemingly forgotten to ascertain the respondent's age or income.

When a file containing missing data is processed, the values which have been designated as missing are checked against the values on each case as it is processed. When a missing value is encountered on a case, it may be treated in a number of different ways, depending upon the statistical procedure being used and the missing-data options selected by the user. Although each procedure contains at least two options for handling missing data, the options vary in kind and number depending upon the nature of the calculations being performed. Detailed descriptions of the missing-data options available in any procedure are to be found in the individual subprogram write-ups beginning in Chap. 11.

Values to be designated as missing are defined by the MISSING VALUES card and may be stored with the data cases and all other data defining information in an SPSS system file. The MISSING VALUES card contains the control words MISSING VALUES followed by the variable name or list of variable names for which one to three missing values are to be declared. The variable name or list of variable names is in turn followed by the missing value or values which are to apply to those variables. These missing values must be enclosed within a set of parentheses. Another variable name or list of variable names may then follow this list of values; however, a slash must be placed (as a delimiter) between the missing-values list and the second variable name or list of variable names. This second list of variable names is again followed by the missing value or values which are to apply to these variables. This process can be repeated until all of the desired missing values have been defined. The general format of the MISSING VALUES card is then

```
1                      16
MISSING VALUES    { variable name  (missing values)/ }  { variable name  (missing values) }
                  {         or                       }  {         or                      }
                  { variable list                    }  { variable list                   }
```

The variables named on the MISSING VALUES card must be variables which have been previously defined. In most cases, these will be variables which have been defined on the VARIABLE LIST card. However, new variables may be defined by means of variable transformations, and these variables may also take missing values. The declaration of missing values for variables created by variable transformation is identical to that used in defining missing values for all variables. It is, however, described in detail in Sec. 8.2.4 which explains the general procedures for entering data-definition cards for variables generated by variable transformations.

When two or more variables in a file are to take the same missing values, a list of variable names can be entered onto the MISSING VALUES card. This list of variable names will cause the same missing values to be declared for each of these variables, thus reducing the amount of card preparation. The list of variable names is entered onto the MISSING VALUES card by one of two notations depending upon the sequential location of the variables on the cases.

Where three or more *adjacent* variables are to take the same missing values, the variable names may be entered onto the card by a notation of the following type:

VARX TO VARY

where both VARX and VARY are variables which have been previously defined, and where VARX precedes VARY on the actual data case, and where all variables between VARX and VARY are to take the same missing values. As usual, the keyword TO must be separated from VARX and VARY by one or more common delimiters. This notation enables the user to simultaneously define missing values for large numbers of adjacent variables.

When two or more *nonadjacent* variables are to take the same missing values, the variable names are entered onto the missing values card in the following manner:

VARA, VARC, VARF, VARN

where variables VARA, VARC, VARF, and VARN are variables which have been previously defined and are to take the same missing values. As usual, all the conventions governing the use of variable names on SPSS control cards must be followed. These two notations may be freely intermixed producing a list of variable names of the following type:

VARA TO VARE, VARK, VARP, VARR, VART TO VARZ

A variable name or any of the above types of lists of variable names is followed by the missing value or values (up to three) to be associated with the variables. The missing value or values are enclosed within parentheses and must be separated from one another by one or more common delimiters.[1] For example, (9) or (0,9,3) or ('−', '9') or (7.0 3.7,1.3)

The missing value(s) will then be followed by a slash [/] which is, in turn, followed by another variable name or list of variable names and the associated missing values in precisely the same format as before. This can be repeated (i.e., variable list, missing values, slash; variable list, missing values, slash; etc.) until all the desired missing values have been defined.

The following sample MISSING VALUES card demonstrates the general format of the card and the types of variable lists which can be used. The first missing values apply to a single variable, AGE, the second set to an adjacent group of variables from VOTE48 to VOTE66, the third to a list of nonadjacent variables, INCOME, EDUCATION, SEX, and SES, and the fourth to a large group of variables some of which are adjacent and others of which are not.

```
1               16
MISSING VALUES  AGE(0,9)/VOTE48 TO VOTE66(4,7,8)/INCOME,EDUCATN,SEX,
                SES(-1,0)/VAR001 TO VAR022,SCALE1,SCALE7,SCALE12 TO
                SCALE15,ITEM1,POLPART,ORGMEMBR,OCCUPATN TO PROPERTY
                (10,12)
```

Note that the specification field continues from one physical card to the next until all the missing values have been defined. As many cards as required may be used so long as card columns 1 to 15 of all subsequent cards after the first (which contains the control words) are left blank, and no more than 250 elements (names, values, and special delimiters) appear on a single MISSING VALUES card and its continuations. Remember, however, that individual elements may not be split between two cards (see Sec. 3.1.3). Note also that common delimiters may be inserted between the special delimiters (i.e., the left and right parentheses and the slash) and other elements to improve readability. However, they are *not required*.

## 4.8    THE VALUE LABELS CARD

It is possible to associate a label with each value of any or all the variables in a file. Whenever present, these *value labels* automatically appear on the printed output. Such labels may be particularly helpful and attractive in documenting output from simple and crosstabulated frequency distributions.

Value labels are entered on the VALUE LABELS card, and like all other data-defining information, once prepared they may be stored with the data in an SPSS system file. The control field contains the control words VALUE LABELS followed by the variable name or list of variable names for which a set of value labels are to be defined. The variable name or list of

[1]The user must remember to enclose the missing values of alphanumeric variables in single quotation marks.

variable names is followed by a value enclosed in parentheses and a label of up to 20 characters in length. The next value and its label follows. This is repeated until all the value labels desired for the variable(s) have been defined. A second, third, fourth, etc., set of value labels can be defined by ending the first set with a slash, entering the next variable name or names and repeating the procedure over again for the new variable(s). The general format of the card is as follows:

VALUE LABEL $\left\{ \begin{array}{c} \text{variable name} \\ \text{or} \\ \text{variable list} \end{array} \right\}$ $(value_1)$ $label_1$ $(value_2)$ $label_2$ $(value_3)$ $label_3$ ... $(value_n)$ $label_n/$

$\left\{ \begin{array}{c} \text{variable name} \\ \text{or} \\ \text{variable list} \end{array} \right\}$ $(value_1)$ $label_1$ $(value_2)$ $label_2$ $(value_3)$ $label_3$ ... $(value_n)$ $label_n$

Variable names are entered in a manner identical to that used in the MISSING VALUES card. The same labels may be assigned to the same values or a number of different variables. This may be particularly useful when the user has a number of variables which share the same coding schemes and when the values have identical interpretations. Value labels for a number of Lickert scale items, for example (all coded from *agree strongly* to *disagree strongly*), could be simultaneously defined by using a variable list, thus reducing card preparation.

Where there are several adjacent variables whose values will take the same labels, the variable names may be entered onto the card by a notation of the following type:

VARX TO VARY

where both VARX and VARY are variable names which have previously been defined and where VARX is assumed to precede VARY in the variable list. This convention allows the user to simultaneously define labels for the values of each of the named variables on the variable list from VARX to VARY. (Of course, this convention can only be used for values of these variables which are to take the same label.)

When two or more nonadjacent variables in a file take the same value labels, they are entered onto the VALUE LABEL card in the following manner:

VARA, VARC, VARF, VARN

where variables VARA, VARC, VARF, and VARN are variable names which have previously been defined. This convention allows the user to declare the same value labels for each of the variables entered onto the card. These two naming notations may be freely intermixed, producing a list of variables of the following type:

VARA TO VARD, VARF, VARG, VARK, VARN TO VARR, VARZ

The variable name or list of names is followed by a single value enclosed within parentheses. Each value of the variable may be given a label, or selected values may be given labels. The value is followed by a label of up to 20[†] characters in length. The label may be composed of any of the valid characters in the IBM 360 character set with the exceptions of the slash [/], the left parenthesis [ ( ], and the right parenthesis [ ) ] which, because of their function as delimiters, may not be used. Value labels are reported on output exactly as they are spaced and spelled. The user should prepare and enter them exactly as he wishes them to appear on his output. Each value label is followed by the next value for which a label is to be defined. The last value label defined for a variable or list of variables may be followed by a slash [/], if value labels for other variables are to be defined on that card. The next variable name or names follows the slash and then their values and value labels in exactly the same manner as before.

---

[†]When preparing value labels for variables which will be processed through subprograms CROSSTABS and/or FASTABS, the user should note that only the first 16 characters of the value labels are printed. Furthermore, the value labels for column variables are printed on two lines. The first line contains the first eight characters, the following line, the second eight characters; characters 17 to 20 are ignored.

The following sample VALUE LABELS card demonstrates how this card should be prepared:

```
1               16
VALUE LABELS    INCOME (1) UNDER $1000 (2) $1000-1999 (3) $2000-3999
                (4) $4000-5999 (5) $6000-7999 (6) $8000-9999 (7)
                $10000-14999 (8) $15000 AND OVER (9) REFUSED TO ANSWER (0)
                DON'T KNOW/ITEM1 TO ITEM10 (5) AGREE STRONGLY (4) AGREE (3)
                NEUTRAL (2) DISAGREE (1) DISAGREE STRONGLY (9) REFUSED TO ANSWER
                (0) DON'T KNOW/EDUCATN (1) NO EDUCATN (2) PRIMARY OR LESS (3)
                SOME SECONDARY (4) GRAD SECONDARY (5) SOME COLLEGE (6) COLLEGE
                GRAD OR MORE
```

Note that the specification field continues from one physical card to the next until all the desired value labels have been defined. As many cards as required may be used as long as card columns 1 to 15 of all subsequent cards after the first (which contains the control words) are left blank. Also, labels, unlike any of the other types of elements, may be split between two physical cards. The user will eliminate internal blanks from labels beginning on one card and continuing on the next by entering the label up to the eightieth column and beginning immediately in the sixteenth column of the next card (see Sec. 3.1.2.4 on labels and the preceding footnote). Note, further, that common delimiters (i.e., blanks and commas) may be inserted between special delimiters (i.e., the left and right parenthesis and the slash) and other elements to improve readability. However, they are *not required*. A variable name may be referenced *only once* on a VALUE LABELS card on a given computer run. All other rules and conventions governing spacing and construction must be followed (see Sec. 3.1.3).

## 4.9   THE PRINT FORMATS CARD

When any of the variables in a file are input as alphanumeric variables, a PRINT FORMATS card is required to indicate this. The PRINT FORMATS card may also be optionally used to control the number of digits to the right of the decimal point when reporting the values of numeric variables on output from SPSS statistical subprograms. When PRINT FORMATS cards are not used, two digits to the right of the decimal point are automatically printed. For example, if a numeric variable takes the values 1, 2, 3, 4, 5, and 9, the values, when printed on the output from an SPSS statistical procedure, will normally be printed 1.00, 2.00, 3.00, 4.00, 5.00, and 9.00. The user may either extend or suppress the number of digits to the right of the decimal by specifying the number of desired digits on the PRINT FORMATS cards.[1] These printing formats are only relevant when using those SPSS programs which report the variable values such as MARGINALS, CROSSTABS, or BREAKDOWN. Even then, they become important only if the user is concerned about the aesthetic appearance of his printed tables.

The control card used to control the printing formats contains the control words PRINT FORMATS followed by a list of variable names for which one printing format is to be used. The variable list is in turn followed by an integer value enclosed in parentheses or, if the variables are alphanumeric, by an A enclosed in parentheses [(A)]. This integer value will be the number of digits to the right of the decimal point to be printed on the output. This value may in turn be followed by a slash [/] and another list of variable names and their associated printing format. The general format of the card would be as follows:

```
1               16
PRINT FORMATS ⎧ variable name ⎫    (value)/    ⎧ variable name ⎫         (value)
              ⎨      or        ⎬              ⎨      or        ⎬
              ⎩ variable list  ⎭              ⎩ variable list  ⎭
```

The variable names are entered onto the card in exactly the same manner as on the MISSING VALUES and VALUE LABELS cards (see Secs. 4.7 and 4.8). The list of variable names may be a single variable name; or it may be an inclusive list of variable names of the VARX TO VARY type when a string of adjacent variables are being entered; or it may be of the VARE, VARG, VARH, . . . , VARN type when a set of nonadjacent variables is being entered. As is usual, the latter two types of lists may be freely intermixed. Variables named on the PRINT FORMATS

---

[1]Note that a maximum of five digits can be printed to the right of the decimal point.

card must have been previously defined, and of course, all the other general rules governing variable names also apply (see Sec. 3.1.3).

The number of digits to be printed to the right of the decimal point follows the list of variables to which it is to apply and is enclosed in parentheses. If the number of digits to be printed is zero, then it would be entered as (0); if it were one, then (1); three, then (3). If different groups of numeric variables are to have different printing formats, this value is followed by a slash [/]. The slash is in turn followed by a new list of variables and their associated printing format. This process can be repeated until all the desired printing formats have been defined. The following sample PRINT FORMATS card demonstrates the proper construction of the card.

```
1                16
PRINT FORMATS    AGE,INCOME,SEX (0)/FACTOR1 TO FACTOR33 (A)/SCORE1 TO SCORE5 (2)
```

The variable lists and their associated printing formats may be continued from card to card. As many cards as required may be used so long as card columns 1 to 15 of all subsequent cards after the first (which contains the control field) are left blank. Remember, though, that individual elements must be contained on a single card. Common delimiters (i.e., blanks and commas) may be inserted between special delimiters (i.e., the left and right parentheses and the slash) and other elements to improve readability.

## 4.10   THE VAR LABELS CARD

The SPSS system permits the user to associate an extended variable label with any or all the variables in his file. Whenever a variable having one of these extended labels is used in a calculation, the label is printed on the output from that calculation. This enables the user to permanently and fully document his tables and other calculations. The variable labels, like all other information entered on the data-definition cards, may be permanently stored with the data as an SPSS system file.

The cards used to enter these extended variable labels contain the control words VAR LABEL followed by a *single variable name.* The variable name is then followed by a label of up to 40 characters in length. A slash follows the label which is in turn succeeded by a second variable name and its associated label. This order of variable name, variable label, slash is repeated until all the desired variable labels have been defined. The general format of the VAR LABELS card is then

```
1                16
VAR LABELS       variable name, variable label/variable name, variable
                 label/ . . . /variable name, variable label
```

A variable label may apply to only one variable, and a variable must have been previously defined before a label can be assigned to it. The order in which variables are assigned labels is not important. The variable labels may be up to 40 characters in length and may contain any of the valid characters in the IBM 360 character set with the exception of the /, the (, and the ). The specifications on the VAR LABELS card may continue from one physical card to the next until all the desired labels have been defined. Card columns 1 to 15 of all but the first card must, however, remain blank. Variable labels like all other labels need not be contained on a single card. The following is an example of a VAR LABELS card:

```
1                16
VAR LABELS       INCOME,YEARLY FAMILY INCOME/VOTE64,PRESIDENTIAL VOTE IN
                 1964/SCALE1,THE FIRST POLITICAL PARTICIPATION SCALE/
                 SCALE6,GUTTMAN SCALE OF NEGRO ATTITUDES
```

## 4.11   RULES GOVERNING THE ORDER
## OF THE DATA-DEFINITION CARDS

All the data-definition cards have now been defined. Table 4.3 lists the control fields for all the data-definition cards. Once these cards have been prepared, the SPSS system can obtain all the necessary and any optional information to be used in processing the data. The internal order or sequence of most of the data-definition cards is quite free, and with the exception of the following four rules, the cards may be placed in any order the user desires. The four rules of card order which must always be applied to the data-definition cards are as follows:

1.  All the data-definition cards are grouped together as one block or set of control cards in the control-card deck. The location or sequence of the combined group of data-definition cards within the overall control-card deck is discussed in Sec. 7.1 after various other control cards have been defined.

2.  The FILE NAME card must always be the first data-definition card when it is used. See Sec. 4.1 for discussions concerning when the FILE NAME card should be used.

3.  The VARIABLE LIST card directly follows the FILE NAME card. When a FILE NAME card is not used, the VARIABLE LIST card becomes the first data-definition card.

4.  When a file contains a subfile structure, the SUBFILE LIST card directly follows the VARIABLE LIST card. A SUBFILE LIST card is, of course, only used when a file contains subfiles.

**TABLE 4.3     Table of data-definition card control fields**

| | |
|---|---|
| FILE NAME | INPUT FORMAT |
| VARIABLE LIST | MISSING VALUES |
| SUBFILE LIST | VALUE LABELS |
| # OF CASES | PRINT FORMATS |
| INPUT MEDIUM | VAR LABELS |

# 5
# CONTROLLING THE CALCULATIONS: THE TASK-DEFINITION CARDS

Once the data-definition cards have been prepared, the user is ready to proceed to the construction of those control cards required to obtain the specific calculations he desires. This group of SPSS control cards are termed *task-definition* cards.

Whereas the data-definition cards define the structure and contents of the data, the task-definition cards activate, define, and control the calculations to be performed on the data. Thus while the data-definition cards need not be changed from one computer run to another, the user will be constantly preparing new task-definition cards as he proceeds through each of the steps of his data analysis.

## 5.1 THE PROCEDURE CARDS

The individual procedures which actually perform the calculations on the data are *subprograms* of the SPSS system. These subprograms are selected and activated upon request from the user by means of the *procedure cards*. Each subprogram has a corresponding procedure card, and each of these cards consists of one or more unique control words which identify the subprogram to both the user and the system. The crosstabulation subprogram, for example, is called and activated by a procedure card containing the control word CROSSTABS, the Guttman scale subprogram by a card containing the control word GUTTMAN, and so forth. The control words are followed by the variables to be entered into the calculations as well as the parameters and arguments required to successfully complete the desired computations.

When the system encounters one of the procedure cards, it causes the desired subprogram to be activated, and the information on the specification field interpreted so that the procedure can be correctly executed on the user's data. The following procedure card would, for example, cause the crosstabulation subprogram to be executed and two tables to be generated—one for the variables RACE and INCOME and another for SEX and IQ. (This assumes, of course, that a file containing these variables has been properly defined.)

```
1          16
CROSSTABS  RACE BY INCOME/SEX BY IQ
```

Although all the procedure cards have a similar format, each of the subprograms is activated by a unique set of control words, and the variable names and other specifications are entered onto the individual procedure cards under different notations depending on the nature of the calculations performed. Because of these differences, the detailed instructions for the preparation of each of the procedure cards is described in the individual subprogram write-ups beginning in Chap. 11. A list of all SPSS procedure-card control words appears in Table 5.1.

## 5.2 THE OPTIONS CARD

The OPTIONS card provides the system with further information to be used in controlling a calculation which has been activated by a procedure card. The OPTIONS card enables the user to choose among available subprogram options so that the calculations are performed on his data in the exact manner he desires. For example, each of the subprograms contains several optional methods for processing missing data, and the user chooses among these by means of the OPTIONS card. The OPTIONS card also carries various types of information which are of a more subprogram-specific nature. For example, the OPTIONS card which is used in conjunction with the CROSSTABS subprogram enables the user to have his tables percentaged by columns, by rows, or in both directions.[1]

The OPTIONS card contains the control word OPTIONS followed by a specification field which consists of a list of integer numbers that indicate the options desired within a given subprogram. Each of the options is identified and selected by a unique number. However, the options available as well as their corresponding numbers vary from one subprogram to the next, and for this reason, the specific options available and their corresponding numbers are presented in the individual subprogram write-ups. The general format of the OPTIONS card is

```
1          16
OPTIONS    option number list
```

An example OPTIONS card might appear as follows, where each of the numbers on the OPTIONS card activates one of the available subprogram options:

```
1          16
OPTIONS    1,2,5,7
```

The OPTIONS card and the STATISTICS card which follows are unlike any of the other SPSS control cards insofar as they must be completed on one physical card. The specifications *may not* be continued in columns 16 to 80 of succeeding cards. This should not constrict the user, however, since the number of options and statistics can always be easily placed in columns 16 to 80 of the card. The OPTIONS card must directly follow the procedure card to which it applies.

## 5.3 THE STATISTICS CARD

The STATISTICS card is similar in structure and function to the OPTIONS card. This card enables the user to select among a number of available statistics to accompany the calculations and to be reported on the output. For example, the subprogram CONDESCRIPTIVE (Descriptive Statistics for Continuous Data) allows the user to have any or all the following statistics

---

[1] Every subprogram has a set of default options. If all the default options are desired, the user can usually skip the preparation of the OPTIONS card.

computed for the variables in the file: mean, standard deviation, variance, skewness, kurtosis, minimum, maximum, and range. Each of the above statistics has an assigned number, and the user may select among these available statistics by this number. The user may have *all* the available statistics for a given subprogram reported by following the control word STATISTICS with the keyword ALL instead of the number list. Of course, the statistics available vary from subprogram to subprogram so that here again the detailed description of the STATISTICS card which is used with each of the subprograms is given in the individual subprogram write-ups.[1] The general format of STATISTICS cards is

1                16

STATISTICS     $\left\{ \begin{array}{c} \text{number list} \\ \text{or} \\ \text{ALL} \end{array} \right\}$

An example STATISTICS card might appear as follows:

```
1                16
STATISTICS       2,4,5,7,9
```

The STATISTICS card is placed directly behind the OPTIONS card in the control-card deck. The STATISTICS card, like the OPTIONS card, must be completed in one physical card. Here again, the statistics are never so great in number that they cannot easily be contained in columns 16 to 80 of the STATISTICS card.

## 5.4 THE READ INPUT DATA CARD

The READ INPUT DATA card instructs the system to begin reading the input data. This card directly follows the STATISTICS card of the *first* group of task-definition cards. When the user is entering his data from cards, the data cards themselves follow the READ INPUT DATA card. This card contains the control words READ INPUT DATA in columns 1 to 15 and has no specification field. This card is used only when processing directly from cards or from an external BCD data set on tape or disk and is not used when processing from an SPSS system file.[2]

## 5.5 THE PROCESS SBFILES CARD

When the cases in a file are substructured into subfiles, the system must be informed as to how the user wishes the subfiles to be processed during any given task. Once the subfile structure has been organized and defined (see Secs. 2.3 and 4.3), the subfiles may be processed by a number of different processing modes, and the user controls these modes on each calculation by means of the PROCESS SBFILES card. The subfile-processing modes selected will, of course, depend upon the type of analysis being done. In many instances, the researcher is interested in comparing the distribution of some variable or in comparing the relationship between two or more variables from one subfile to another. In other circumstances, he may wish to single out individual subfiles or combinations of subfiles for special types of analysis, and at certain times in the analysis, the researcher may wish to perform calculations on the entire file, in which case the subfile structure is to be totally ignored. The following subfile-processing options are available to the user:

1.  The subfiles in the file may be processed so that the same calculation is independently performed on each subfile.
2.  A particular subfile or subset of the subfiles may be selected for processing so that the calculation is performed independently for only those subfiles selected. In this instance, all other subfiles are ignored.

---

[1] When *no* statistics are desired, the user can usually delete the STATISTICS card.

[2] Several of the multivariate subprograms allow the user to enter matrices as well as raw data. When a matrix is to be read, the READ INPUT DATA card is replaced by a READ MATRIX card (see Secs. 14.3, 15.3, and 17.3).

3. A number of subfiles may be combined into larger groups of cases which are then processed as if the combined groups were independent subfiles.

4. The subfile structure may be totally ignored so that all the cases in the file are processed as one group without a subfile structure.

The desired subfile processing mode is selected on a card containing the control words **PROCESS SBFILES**. The names of the subfiles to be processed are entered onto the specification field, and these names must be subfile names which have been previously defined for the file by a SUBFILE LIST card. The subfile names must be spelled exactly as they were defined on the SUBFILE LIST card. The names of the subfiles to be processed are entered onto the PROCESS SBFILES card, so that subfiles to be processed independently are delineated by right and left parentheses. When several subfiles are to be combined and treated as one group of cases, the names of the subfiles to be combined are enclosed by right and left parentheses. Two special conventions exist to minimize card preparation when the first and fourth subfile-processing options are employed. First, when the user wishes each of the subfiles in his file to be processed independently so that the same calculations are performed on each of them, he may enter the keyword EACH on the specification field of the card rather than enter the entire list of subfiles. When the user wishes the subfile structure to be ignored so that all the cases in the file are processed as one large file without a subfile structure, the user may enter the keyword ALL onto the specification field rather than having to enclose all the subfile names in a set of parentheses.

The conventions used on the PROCESS SBFILES card are perhaps best explained by illustration. The following examples would direct the processing of subfiles in a hypothetical file containing five subfile names: SUB1, SUB2, SUB3, SUB4 and SUB5.

1. If the user of this hypothetical file wished to have each of the subfiles processed so that the same calculations would be performed for each of the subfiles independently, the PROCESS SBFILES card would appear as follows:

```
1              16
PROCESS SBFILESEACH
```

2. If the user wished to perform a calculation independently on only SUB3 and SUB5, the PROCESS SBFILES card would appear as:

```
1              16
PROCESS SBFILES(SUB1) (SUB5)
```

3. If the user wished to combine SUB1 and SUB3, and SUB2, SUB4, and SUB5 to achieve two independent calculations—one for subfiles 1 and 3 and one for subfiles 2, 4, and 5—the PROCESS SBFILES card would be prepared in the following manner:[1]

```
1              16
PROCESS SBFILES(SUB1 ,SUB3) (SUB2, SUB4, SUB5)
```

4. Subfile-processing options 2 and 3 may be used jointly so that the calculations would be performed on some individual subfiles as well as on one or more combined groups of subfiles. If, for example, the user wished to process subfiles 1 and 2 independently and group 3, 4, and 5 as a combined subfile, the PROCESS SBFILES card would appear as follows:

```
1              16
PROCESS SBFILES(SUB1) (SUB2) (SUB3, SUB4, SUB5)
```

5. When the user desires to process his file so that subfile structure is totally ignored (i.e., treating all the subfiles as a unified file), the PROCESS SBFILES card would appear as follows:

```
1              16
PROCESS SBFILESALL
```

The PROCESS SBFILES card is inserted into the control-card deck directly in front of the first procedure card. The subfile-processing mode enacted by this card will remain in effect *for the entire run or until a new* PROCESS SBFILES *card is encountered.* When the user is

---

[1]The PROCESS SBFILES card cannot request the processing of any one subfile more than once.

making runs in which more than one set of calculations is to be performed, an additional PROCESS SBFILES card *need not be prepared* unless the user wishes to change the subfile-processing mode for these additional calculations. When the user wishes to change the subfile-processing mode, a new PROCESS SBFILES card must be inserted directly in front of the procedure card to which the new processing mode is to apply. The user should then note that the new subfile-processing mode would remain in effect for all of the following calculations unless yet another PROCESS SBFILES card is encountered. In essence, this means that the user may control and alter the subfile-processing mode each time a subprogram is called during a computer run. However, card preparation has been minimized by retaining the same subfile-processing mode until a new PROCESS SBFILES card is encountered.

Table 5.1 presents a summary of the control fields for all of the task-definition cards which are utilized in the SPSS procedure cards—each of which calls and activates one of the twelve statistical processing routines. The next three control fields in the table correspond to the SPSS control cards that provide these statistical subprograms with more detailed information on how the user wishes the calculations carried out. The final control field for the READ INPUT DATA card informs the system that user has completed the definition of both his data file and his first analysis task and is ready to begin reading the file.

**TABLE 5.1**  Table of task-definition card-control fields

| 1 | 16 |
|---|---|
| CONDESCRIPTIVE | |
| MARGINALS | |
| CODEBOOK | |
| CROSSTABS | |
| FASTABS | |
| BREAKDOWN | Procedure card |
| PEARSON CORR | control words |
| NONPAR CORR | |
| PARTIAL CORR | |
| REGRESSION | |
| FACTOR | |
| GUTTMAN SCALE | |
| OPTIONS | Control words for |
| STATISTICS | task-definition cards |
| PROCESS SBFILES | to be used |
| READ INPUT DATA | with procedure cards |

# 6
# THE RUN CARDS

Eight specific control cards are included under the category of *run cards*. A listing of the control fields for the run cards is shown in Table 6.1. The RUN NAME and FINISH cards are used at the beginning and termination of a complete processing run, respectively. It should be remembered that a processing run may involve calculations from more than one subprogram.

## 6.1    THE RUN NAME CARD

The RUN NAME card identifies the current computer run, and the user-supplied label which follows the control words RUN NAME is printed at the top of each page of output generated on that run. The label may be up to 64 characters in length and may contain *any* of the valid characters in the IBM 360 character set. The card has the following format:

```
1                 16
RUN NAME          label
```

An example RUN NAME card might be

```
1                 16
RUN NAME          THIS IS AN EXAMPLE RUN LABEL
```

The RUN NAME card is optional. If it is not used, blanks will appear in its place at the top of each page of printout. The RUN NAME card is the very first card in the control-card deck.

## 6.2   THE FINISH CARD

The FINISH card terminates the processing for the current run and switches control from the SPSS system back to the installation's monitoring system. A FINISH card is always required, and it must be the last card in the control-card deck. Its format is as follows:

```
1                16
FINISH
```

## 6.3   THE KEYPUNCH CARD

The SPSS system assumes that control cards have been punched with an IBM 029 keypunch. If the cards have been punched with an IBM 026 keypunch, a KEYPUNCH card must be placed in front of the RUN NAME card to inform the system of this fact. The format of the KEYPUNCH card is:

```
1                16
KEYPUNCH         026
```

If the user punches his control cards on an IBM 026 keypunch, the 029 graphic & (ampersand) should be multipunched as 12,0; and the 029 graphic # (the pound sign) should be multipunched as 11,0. The user must be aware that the KEYPUNCH card does not affect the reading of his data cases.

## 6.4   THE PRINT BACK CARD

The SPSS system automatically prints back all the user's control cards on the output. If for some reason it is desirable to have the printing back of the control cards *suppressed,* the following card should be used:

```
1                16
PRINT BACK       NO
```

The PRINT BACK card precedes the RUN NAME card and follows the KEYPUNCH card, if used.

## 6.5   THE COMMENT CARD

The COMMENT card serves the very simple function of enabling the user to place comments anywhere in his control-card deck. The information on these cards serves no function in the processing of the data, but is printed back along with the other control cards on the output listing. In short, they enable the user to make notes for himself which will appear in the order and at the location in the control-card deck where they were placed.

The COMMENT card contains the control word COMMENT followed by any message or comment which can be punched from valid characters in the character set. The comment may continue from one physical card to another, in which case columns 1 to 15 of successive continuation cards are left blank. The user may enter as many COMMENT cards as he desires on a given run, and the cards may be placed anywhere in the control-card deck. The general format of the COMMENT card is as follows:

```
1                16
COMMENT          any comment
```

Some examples of the use of the COMMENT card are:

```
1               16
COMMENT         THE FOLLOWING CARDS DEFINE THE NEW VARIABLE SES

COMMENT         SELECT ONLY WHITE REPUBLICANS ON THIS RUN - MISSING DATA CASES
                HAVE BEEN EXCLUDED FOR THIS SUBGROUP

COMMENT         NOTE CHANGE IN SUBFILE PROCESSING MODE HERE
```

## 6.6   THE DOCUMENT CARD

The DOCUMENT card enables the user to retain, as a permanent part of his SPSS system file, any documenting information he desires. The specifications used to recode variables, copies of the control cards used in generating variable transformations, notations on the procedures used to select, sample, or weight the cases in the file, are but a few examples of the types of information the user may desire to permanently retain by means of the DOCUMENT card. The information entered on the DOCUMENT card may be retrieved on any processing run by means of the DUMP card described in Sec. 6.7.

The DOCUMENT card contains the control word DOCUMENT followed (beginning in column 16, as always) by any message the user desires and which is expressable in the character set. There is no limit on the length of the message, and the text may continue from one physical card to the next. As usual columns 1 to 15 of all continuation cards must be left blank. However, *only one DOCUMENT card may be used on any processing run.* The DOCUMENT card may be placed anywhere in the control-card deck following the GET FILE card and before the first procedure card. If the file is saved at the conclusion of the processing run, the information on the DOCUMENT card becomes a permanent part of the SPSS system file which is saved. The general format of the DOCUMENT card is as follows:

```
1               16
DOCUMENT        any message of the user's choice
```

An example of the use of the DOCUMENT card is as follows:

```
1         16
DOCUMENT  THE CONTINUOUS VARIABLE INCOME WAS RECODED ACCORDING TO THE
          FOLLOWING RULE: $0 THRU $3000 BECAME 1; $3001 THRU $6000 - 2;
          $6001 THRU $10000 - 3; OVER $10000 - 4.  THE VALUES 99998
          (DON'T KNOW) AND 99999 (REFUSED TO ANSWER) HAVE BEEN RECODED
          TO 9.
          A NEW VARIABLE REALINC WAS CREATED BY THE FOLLOWING SERIES
          OF IF CARDS:
          IF (INCOME-(FAMSIZE*600) LE 3000) REALINC = 1
          IF (INCOME-(FAMSIZE*600) GT 3000 AND INCOME-(FAMSIZE*600)
              LE 600) REALINC = 2
          IF (INCOME-(FAMSIZE*600) GT 6000) REALINC = 3
```

The penalty for retaining documenting information is actually quite small. The exact penalty will vary according to the medium upon which the system file is retained; however, in one test in which the system file was stored on a tape recorded at 800 BPI, the run time increased 1 second for every 750 cards of documenting information saved.

The value of the DOCUMENT card may become more evident after the user has read Sec. 6.7 and Chap. 8 on recoding and variable transformations.

## 6.7   THE DUMP CARD

There may be times when the user wishes to examine the data-defining information for his SPSS file, particularly when he has forgotten the name of a variable, a subfile, or the missing values associated with the variables. He may request the listing of this information to be reported on his output by means of the following card:

```
1               16
DUMP            keyword(s)
```

where one or more of the following keywords is placed in the specification field: (1) VARLIST, a listing of all variables in the file (in their existing order) including those created by transformations; (2) VARINFO, the print formats and missing values for each variable in the file; (3) SUBDIRECTORY, the number of cases in each of the subfiles and the name of each subfile in the file; (4) LABELS, all labels associated with the file; and (5) DOCUMENT, all information entered in specification fields of DOCUMENT cards used on previous runs. The DUMP card, which is a procedure card, may be placed anywhere in the deck following the GET FILE card when processing from a system file or after all data-definition cards when processing from BCD files. The user should be aware, however, that the information which he has requested will be reported at that particular point in the output. He should also take care when requesting VARLIST to place the DUMP card after any variable transformations on the run if he wishes to have the new variables included in the listing.

## 6.8   THE NUMBERED CARD

SPSS normally assumes that the user has punched the specification-field information through column 80 or has simply left some extra common delimiters (e.g., blanks) at the end of his control cards. However, with the NUMBERED card, the user may use columns 73 to 80 of each of his control cards for sequencing or identifying information.

If the user places the control card NUMBERED at the beginning of the control-card deck, SPSS will ignore columns 73 to 80 of all control cards and their continuation. The user may then punch any information he desires in these fields. When the user has large control-card decks, sequencing information placed in these fields will permit easy referencing of cards and ordering of dropped decks. The NUMBERED card has the following simple format:

| 1 | 16 |
|---|----|
| NUMBERED | YES |

Table 6.1 presents the control fields for the eight run cards described in this chapter.

**TABLE 6.1    Control fields for SPSS run cards**

| 1 | 16 |
|---|----|
| RUN NAME | |
| FINISH | |
| KEYPUNCH | |
| PRINT BACK | |
| COMMENT | |
| DOCUMENT | |
| DUMP | |
| NUMBERED | |

# 7
# GENERATING AND PROCESSING SPSS FILES:
# CARD ORDER AND DECK SETUP

A sufficient number of cards have now been defined so that we can begin to demonstrate how the data may be processed, the desired calculations obtained, and if the user so desires, the data and the information contained on the data-definition cards saved as an SPSS system file. The first part of this chapter explains the card order and control-card deck setup to be used whenever the user inputs his data from cards or any type of BCD data file (e.g., tape, disk file, etc.). The second part explains how the data and the information contained on the data-definition cards may be saved as an SPSS system file at the conclusion of any processing run by means of the SAVE FILE control card. The third portion of this chapter describes and explains the control cards and the deck setup to be used when processing from an SPSS system file.

## 7.1  PROCESSING FROM CARDS, BCD TAPES, OR BCD DISK FILES: CARD ORDER AND DECK SETUP

An initial file-generating run enables the user to obtain the first set of desired calculations while saving the file at the conclusion of the run. When a file is retained as an SPSS system file, the variable names, and their formats, as well as all the information entered on the data-definition cards, are permanently stored with the data. With the exception of the SAVE FILE control

**TABLE 7.1    Control-card order for running with BCD data files.**

| CARD STATUS | CONTROL FIELD | REMARKS | |
|---|---|---|---|
| Optional | RUN NAME | | |
| Conditional | FILE NAME | Required if an SPSS system file is to be generated. | Data definition cards |
| Required | VARIABLE LIST | | |
| Conditional | SUBFILE LIST | Required if there is a subfile structure. | |
| Required | INPUT MEDIUM | | |
| Required | # OF CASES | The order of these cards is arbitrary. | |
| Required | INPUT FORMAT | | |
| Optional | MISSING VALUES | | |
| Optional | VAR LABELS | | |
| Optional | VALUE LABELS | | |
| Conditional | PRINT FORMATS | Required for 'A' type variables, otherwise optional. | |
| Conditional | PROCESS SBFILES | Used only for files with subfiles. | Task definition cards for first task |
| Required | PROCEDURE CARD † | | |
| Optional | OPTIONS | | |
| Optional | STATISTICS | | |
| Required | READ INPUT DATA | | |

(Cards containing the data for cases appear here when the data is being input from cards.)

(The next set of task definition cards appears here if desired.)

| | PROCESS SBFILES | | Task definition cards for subsequent tasks |
|---|---|---|---|
| | PROCEDURE CARD † | | |
| | OPTIONS | | |
| | STATISTICS | | |
| Required | FINISH | | |

†To be replaced by the desired procedure card such as CROSSTABS, REGRESSION, MARGINALS, etc.

card (which causes the SPSS system to create and save an SPSS system file), the initial file-generating run is identical to any processing run where the data is to be read from either cards, BCD disk file, etc.

Table 7.1 presents the rules of card order *when processing from cards or external* BCD *files.* All these SPSS control cards have one of the following three statuses: They are either (1) always required, (2) optional, or (3) conditionally required (that is, required when and only when some special feature of the system is utilized, such as subfile processing or saving files).

In addition, most of the cards belong to one of two groups: (1) data-definition cards or (2) task-definition cards (see Table 7.1).

The data-definition cards are all grouped together and are placed immediately after the optional RUN NAME card if it is used. The FILE NAME card is the first data-definition card, and when used, it is directly followed by the VARIABLE LIST card. The SUBFILE LIST card, which is required only when the file has a subfile structure, follows. The next six data-definition cards in Table 7.1 (i.e., INPUT MEDIUM to PRINT FORMATS) can be placed in any order which the user desires. However, they must as a group follow the VARIABLE LIST card when the file has no subfile structure and the SUBFILE LIST card when the file is grouped into subfiles. This group of data-definition cards is followed by the PROCESS SBFILES card when the file contains subfiles and by a procedure card when the file has no subfile structure. The procedure card, which of course will contain different control words depending upon what subprogram is being called, is followed by the OPTIONS and STATISTICS card in that order.

The READ INPUT DATA card directly follows the STATISTICS card, and when the user is inputting data from cards, the data cases directly follow the READ INPUT DATA card. When this is true, the last data case is followed by either a new set of task-definition cards or by a FINISH card. If the user's data is being input from a BCD tape or disk file (which is, of course, indicated on the INPUT MEDIUM card), the READ INPUT DATA card is followed by the FINISH card when only one statistical task is to be activated on the run or by a second set of task-definition cards when more than one task is to be executed during the run.

Theoretically, there is no limit on the number of tasks that can be performed during a given run. Each task will, however, require a set of task-definition cards, and *when data is being input directly from cards, the data itself follows the* READ INPUT DATA *card of the first set of task-definition cards.*

The following examples illustrate the deck setup required by the SPSS system for executing various types of tasks with files of differing structure.

Example 7.1 demonstrates the *minimum* cards required to perform a single task (in this case MARGINALS) on a file containing no subfile structure and being input from cards.

**EXAMPLE 7.1**

```
1               16
VARIABLE LIST   AGE,SEX,RACE,INCOME,EDUCATN
INPUT MEDIUM    CARD
# OF CASES      10
INPUT FORMAT    FIXED (5X,F2.0,2F1.0,F7.0,1X,F1.0)
MARGINALS       AGE TO EDUCATN
OPTIONS         3,4
STATISTICS      ALL
READ INPUT DATA
     3011    9000 2
     3113    7500 1
     4022    8300 2
     2713   12500 5
     5411   13250 4
     3512   10150 5
     2523    9500 3
     5011   17500 3
     4211    8500 1
     3222    9500 2
FINISH
```

Example 7.2 illustrates the deck setup for a file with no subfile structure using all the optional data-definition cards. Note that in this case, the data is organized in free-field rather than in fixed-column format (see Sec. 4.6 on the INPUT FORMAT card). Observe that the data cases follow the READ INPUT DATA card pertaining to the crosstabulations and precede the PEARSON CORR procedure card. The optional cards are preceded by a check [ √ ]. The beginning of each of the free-field data cases is indicated by an arrow [↓]. The output from this run would include both crosstabulations and Pearson correlation coefficients.

Example 7.3 illustrates the deck setup for a file containing three subfiles being entered from cards. Note that two tasks are to be performed by this run and that the subfile-processing mode has been changed between the first and second task. If there were no PROCESS SBFILES card preceding the PEARSON CORR card, the initial subfile-processing mode would have remained in effect for that task also. Observe also that the subfiles themselves are entered in precisely the same order as indicated on the subfile list and also that the number of cases in each of the subfiles is entered onto the # OF CASES card in the same sequence.

Example 7.4 indicates the deck setup used when data is being entered from BCD tape. This example illustrates the *minimum* number of cards required to have marginals computed for all the variables in our sample file. Note that when data is being entered from tape, disk, etc., and there is only one task, the READ INPUT DATA card is followed by the FINISH card.[1]

**EXAMPLE 7.2**

```
   1                16
√ RUN NAME          SAMPLE RUN OF THE SPSS SYSTEM
√ FILE NAME         EXAMPLE2,THIS IS THE FILE LABEL FOR FILE EXAMPLE2
  VARIABLE LIST     AGE,SEX,RACE,INCOME,EDUCATN
  INPUT MEDIUM      CARD
  # OF CASES        10
  INPUT FORMAT      FREEFIELD
√ MISSING VALUES    AGE TO RACE (0,8,9)/INCOME (7)/EDUCATN (0)
√ VAR LABELS        AGE,AGE OF THE RESPONDENT/SEX,SEX OF THE RESPONDENT/INCOME,
                    YEARLY FAMILY INCOME IN DOLLARS/EDUCATN,EDUCATN OF
                    HEAD OF HOUSEHOLD
√ VALUE LABELS      SEX(1)MALE(2)FEMALE(3)NOT ASCERTAINED/RACE(1)WHITE(2)NEGRO(3)
                    ORIENTAL(4)OTHER(9)NOT ASCERTAINED/EDUCATN(1)NONE(2)PRIMARY OR
                    LESS(3)SOME SECONDARY(4)SECONDARY GRADUATE(5)SOME COLLEGE(6)
                    COLLEGE GRADUATE(7)GRAD SCHOOL(8)OTHER(9)DON'T KNOW(0)NOT
                    ASCERTAINED
√ PRINT FORMATS     AGE TO EDUCATN(0)
  CROSSTABS         RACE BY INCOME BY EDUCATN/INCOME BY RACE BY SEX
  OPTIONS           1,3
  STATISTICS        1,4,6
  READ INPUT DATA
   ↓    ↓        ↓        ↓            ↓           ↓            ↓
  74 1 2 8999 7 64 2 1 7463 4 24 3 1 5000 6 41 3 1 4756 2 87 1 2 2746 3
   ↓    ↓        ↓        ↓            ↓           ↓            ↓
  55 2 4 8468 5 57 2 3 9999 7 25 3 4 5472 1 37 2 3 2757 4 28 1 1 7000 1

  PEARSON CORR      AGE TO EDUCATN WITH SEX TO INCOME
  OPTIONS           1,3
  FINISH
```

**EXAMPLE 7.3**

```
   1                16
  RUN NAME          SAMPLE RUN OF THE SPSS SYSTEM
  FILE NAME         EXAMPLE3,THIS IS THE FILE LABEL FOR FILE EXAMPLE3
  VARIABLE LIST     AGE,SEX,RACE,INCOME,EDUCATN
  SUBFILE LIST      CITYA,CITYB,CITYC
  INPUT MEDIUM      CARD
  # OF CASES        3 3 4
  INPUT FORMAT      FIXED (5X,F2.0,2F1.0,F7.0,1X,F1.0)
  MISSING VALUES    AGE TO RACE (0,8,9)/INCOME(7)/EDUCATN(0)
  VAR LABELS        AGE,AGE OF THE RESPONDENT/SEX,SEX OF THE RESPONDENT/INCOME,
                    YEARLY FAMILY INCOME IN DOLLARS/EDUCATN,EDUCATN OF HEAD
                    OF HOUSEHOLD
  VALUE LABELS      SEX(1)MALE(2)FEMALE(3)NOT ASCERTAINED/RACE(1)WHITE(2)NEGRO(3)
                    ORIENTAL(4)OTHER(9)NOT ASCERTAINED/EDUCATN(1)NONE(2)PRIMARY OR
                    LESS(3)SOME SECONDARY(4)SECONDARY GRADUATE(5)SOME COLLEGE(6)
                    COLLEGE GRADUATE(7)GRAD SCHOOL(8)OTHER(9)DON'T KNOW(0)NOT
                    ASCERTAINED
  PRINT FORMATS     AGE TO EDUCATN(0)
  PROCESS SBFILESEACH
  NONPAR CORR       AGE TO EDUCATN WITH AGE TO EDUCATN
  OPTIONS           1,3
  STATISTICS        1,2
  READ INPUT DATA
       7412    8999 7 ⎫
       6421    7463 4 ⎬ Subfile CITYA
       2431    5000 6 ⎭
       4134    4756 2 ⎫
       8712    2746 3 ⎬ Subfile CITYB
       5524    8468 5 ⎭
       5723    9999 7 ⎫
       2534    5472 1 ⎬ Subfile CITYC
       3723    2757 4 ⎭
       2811    7000 1
  PROCESS SBFILES(CITYA,CITYB)(CITYC)
  PEARSON CORR      RACE WITH INCOME
  OPTIONS           1,3
  STATISTICS        1,2
  FINISH
```

[1] In this case (as well as in all instances when the INPUT MEDIUM card specifies an input medium other than CARD) JCL (Job Control Language) cards for the BCD input file termed FT08 must be prepared. Section 4.5 discussed this point at greater length and Appendix F presents instructions for the preparation of these as well as all JCL cards.

**EXAMPLE 7.4**

```
1               16
FILE NAME       EXAMPLE5,THIS IS THE FILE LABEL FOR FILE EXAMPLE5
VARIABLE LIST   AGE,SEX,RACE,INCOME,EDUCATN
INPUT MEDIUM    TAPE
# OF CASES      10
INPUT FORMAT    FIXED (5X,F2.0,2F1.0,F7.0,1X,F1.0)
MARGINALS       AGE TO EDUCATN
OPTIONS         1,3,5
STATISTICS      ALL
READ INPUT DATA
FINISH
```

Example 7.5 illustrates the deck setup for a file being entered from a BCD disk file containing a subfile structure.[1] The output from this run would include marginals and selected crosstabulations. Note that the absence of a PROCESS SBFILES card preceding the CROSS-TABS card will mean that the same subfile-processing mode will be used on both tasks.

**EXAMPLE 7.5**

```
1               16
RUN NAME        SAMPLE RUN OF THE SPSS SYSTEM
FILE NAME       EXAMPLE6,THIS IS THE FILE LABEL FOR FILE EXAMPLE6
VARIABLE LIST   AGE,SEX,RACE,INCOME,EDUCATN
SUBFILE LIST    CITYA,CITYB,CITYC
INPUT MEDIUM    DISK
# OF CASES      34,57,62
INPUT FORMAT    FIXED (5X,F2.0,2F1.0,F7.0,1X,F1.0)
MISSING VALUES  AGE TO RACE (0,8,9)/INCOME(7)/EDUCATN(0)
VAR LABELS      AGE,AGE OF THE RESPONDENT/SEX,SEX OF THE RESPONDENT/INCOME,
                YEARLY FAMILY INCOME IN DOLLARS/EDUCATN,EDUCATN OF HEAD
                OF HOUSEHOLD
VALUE LABELS    SEX(1)MALE(2)FEMALE(3)NOT ASCERTAINED/RACE(1)WHITE(2)NEGRO(3)
                ORIENTAL(4)OTHER(9)NOT ASCERTAINED/EDUCATN(1)NONE(2)PRIMARY OR
                LESS(3)SOME SECONDARY(4)SECONDARY GRADUATE(5)SOME COLLEGE(6)
                COLLEGE GRADUATE(7)GRAD SCHOOL(8)OTHER(9)DON'T KNOW(0)NOT
                ASCERTAINED
PRINT FORMATS   AGE TO EDUCATN(0)
PROCESS SBFILESEACH
MARGINALS       AGE TO EDUCATN
OPTIONS         1,2,5
STATISTICS      2,4,6
READ INPUT DATA
CROSSTABS       RACE BY INCOME BY EDUCATN
OPTIONS         1,4
STATISTICS      ALL
FINISH
```

## 7.2 GENERATING AND RETAINING SPSS SYSTEM FILES: THE SAVE FILE CARD

The cases as well as all the file-defining information entered on the data-definition cards may be retained as an SPSS system file (on a medium of the user's choice) at the conclusion of any processing run by means of the SAVE FILE control card.[2] These SPSS files are stored in binary form and blocked for maximum processing efficiency. An SPSS file has two portions: the first contains all the information describing and defining the data entered on the data-definition cards; the second portion contains the data cases themselves. Figure 7.1 presents a diagram of the general structure of an SPSS system file with a subfile structure. The SAVE FILE card causes the file which is presently being processed to be saved in the form of an SPSS system file at the conclusion of the run. The card contains only the control words SAVE FILE and requires no further specifications. Its format is always as follows:

```
1               16
SAVE FILE
```

[1] See footnote immediately above and Appendix F for instructions on preparing JCL cards for BCD input files residing on disk.
[2] SPSS system files may be saved on tape, disk, or other direct-access devices. When the user wishes to save an SPSS system file, JCL cards for the output system file (termed FT04) must be prepared. Appendix F presents detailed instructions for the preparation of these cards.

```
┌─────────────────────────────────────────────────────────┐
│ File-defining information:  file name and label;        │
│ variable names, labels, and formats; variable           │
│ values and value labels; missing data indicators.       │
└─────────────────────────────────────────────────────────┘
```

| Variable → | First | Second | · · · | Last |
|------------|-------|--------|-------|------|
| First subfile | First case | | | |
| | Second case | | · · · | |
| | · · · | | | · · · |
| | Last case | | | |
| Second subfile | First case | | | |
| | Second case | | · · · | |
| | · · · | | | · · · |
| | Last case | | | |
| · · · | · · · | · · · | · · · | |
| Last subfile | First case | | | |
| | Second case | | · · · | |
| | · · · | | | · · · |
| | Last case | | | |

**FIG. 7.1**   SPSS system file structure.

The SAVE FILE card is inserted into the control-card deck directly in front of the FINISH card and may be employed during any processing run so that a separate file-generating run is not required. Example 7.6 illustrates a file-generating run and the position of the SAVE FILE card. This run will cause a complete set of marginals to be produced, as well as the creation and retention of an SPSS system file.

**EXAMPLE 7.6**

```
1                       16
RUN NAME        THIS EXAMPLE RUN DEMONSTRATES HOW A SYSTEM FILE MAY BE CREATED
FILE NAME       STUDYA
VARIABLE LIST   AGE,SEX,RACE,INCOME,EDUCATN
INPUT MEDIUM    CARD
# OF CASES      10
INPUT FORMAT    FIXED (5X,F2.0,2F1.0,F7.0,1X,F1.0)
MISSING VALUES  AGE TO RACE (0,8,9)/INCOME(7)/EDUCATN(0)
VAR LABELS      AGE,AGE OF THE RESPONDENT/SEX,SEX OF THE RESPONDENT/INCOME,
                YEARLY FAMILY INCOME IN DOLLARS/EDUCATN,EDUCATN OF HEAD
                OF HOUSEHOLD
VALUE LABELS    SEX(1)MALE(2)FEMALE(3)NOT ASCERTAINED/RACE(1)WHITE(2)NEGRO(3)
                ORIENTAL(4)OTHER(9)NOT ASCERTAINED/EDUCATN(1)NONE(2)PRIMARY OR
                LESS(3)SOME SECONDARY(4)SECONDARY GRADUATE(5)SOME COLLEGE(6)
                COLLEGE GRADUATE(7)GRAD SCHOOL(8)OTHER(9)DON'T KNOW(0)NOT
                ASCERTAINED
PRINT FORMATS   AGE TO EDUCATN(0)
CROSSTABS       RACE BY INCOME BY EDUCATN/INCOME BY RACE BY SEX
OPTIONS         1,3,7
STATISTICS      1,4,6
READ INPUT DATA
    7412    8999 7
    6421    7463 4
    2431    5000 6
    4131    4756 2
    8712    2746 3
    5524    8468 5
    5723    9999 7
    2534    5472 1
    3723    2757 4
    2811    7000 1
MARGINALS       AGE TO EDUCATN
OPTIONS         1,3
STATISTICS      ALL
→SAVE FILE
FINISH
```

## 7.3 PROCESSING DATA FROM SPSS SYSTEM FILES

Once an SPSS system file has been generated and retained (in the manner described in Sec. 7.2), the data as well as the information describing it is automatically accessed on all subsequent processing runs by means of the GET FILE control card.[1] However, neither the data nor the documenting information within an SPSS system file is unalterable, for labels and missing values may be altered, variable transformations and recoding may be accomplished, and new variables as well as additional cases may be added to an SPSS system file. In short, processing from an SPSS system file means that the user need only concern himself with defining the task, for the file has already been defined. The following sections are devoted to describing the capabilities of the SPSS system file.

### 7.3.1 THE GET FILE CARD

Whenever the user wishes to access an SPSS file which has been previously retained, he does so by means of the GET FILE control card. The GET FILE card causes the file to be positioned for processing and causes all the associated data-defining information to be passed to the programs. The card contains the control words GET FILE followed by the name of the file that the user wishes to process. The file name used, of course, must be the name of a file which has been previously generated and retained (by means of a SAVE FILE card), and the name must be spelled in the same way as it was on the FILE NAME card used to define it. The general format of the GET FILE card is then as follows:

```
1                16
GET FILE         file name
```

For example, to retrieve the sample file that was saved in the previous section, the following GET FILE card would be used:

```
1                16
GET FILE         STUDYA
```

The GET FILE card directly follows the RUN NAME card and is, in essence, the first command or instruction given to the SPSS system whenever a user wishes to process an SPSS system file. The GET FILE card is then followed by the task-definition cards.

### 7.3.2 DECK SETUP AND CARD ORDER FOR PROCESSING DATA FROM SPSS SYSTEM FILES

The following examples illustrate the control-card deck setup and card order used when processing data from SPSS system files. The examples in this section illustrate the deck setup only for those functions and control cards thus far defined in the text. The control-card deck setup when recoding and executing variable transformations, or when selecting, sampling, or weighting a file, are described and illustrated in the following sections.

Example 7.7 demonstrates the deck setup that would be used to retrieve a file named STUDYB and to have a selected set of crosstabulation tables produced.

### EXAMPLE 7.7

```
1                16
RUN NAME         EXAMPLE OF A RUN FROM AN SPSS SYSTEM FILE
GET FILE         STUDYB
CROSSTABS        AGE BY INCOME BY SEX/RACE BY VAR001 TO VAR010
OPTIONS          1,3,4,5
STATISTICS       1,2,6
FINISH
```

Example 7.8 illustrates the deck setup for a file named STUDYC which contains four subfiles. Output from this run will include marginals for all variables and a selected matrix of Spearman correlation coefficients. Note that the same subfile-processing mode will be in effect for both the marginal frequencies and the Spearman correlation coefficients. If the user had

---

[1]When processing SPSS system files which have been retained on type, disk, etc., JCL cards for the input system file (termed FT03) must be prepared. Appendix F gives detailed instruction for the preparation of these cards.

wished to alter the subfile-processing mode, a second PROCESS SBFILES card would have been inserted before the NONPAR CORR procedure card.

**EXAMPLE 7.8**

```
1               16
RUN NAME        MARGINALS AND SELECTED SPEARMAN CORRELATIONS FOR FILE STUDYB
GET FILE        STUDYB
PROCESS SBFILESEACH
MARGINALS       ALL
OPTIONS         1,3
STATISTICS      ALL
NONPAR CORR     AGE TO INCOME WITH AGE TO INCOME
OPTIONS         1
STATISTICS      2,3,5
FINISH
```

### 7.3.3    MODIFYING OR ADDING TO DATA-DEFINING INFORMATION DURING PROCESSING RUNS FROM SPSS SYSTEM FILES

The user may add to or change any of the following types of data-defining information in an existing SPSS system file:

1.   The file name and label
2.   Missing values
3.   Value labels
4.   Variable labels
5.   Print formats

Changes in or additions to any of the above types of information can be accomplished during any processing run by simply entering the desired modifications on their appropriate data-definition cards and then saving the "updated" file at the conclusion of that run by means of the SAVE FILE card.[1]

New data-defining information or data-defining information which is to alter or replace existing information is entered on the same kinds of data-definition cards and in exactly the same manner as is used to initially define the data in a file. The user must be aware, however, when making such modifications, that the information entered on the new data-definition cards completely replaces the existing piece of parallel information. This means that the user can modify only by replacement. For example, the user *cannot* add to an existing variable label, but must enter a totally new variable label for that variable if he wishes to modify it. This does not mean, however, that the user would have to enter new variable labels for all variables in order to change one; nor would the replacement of a variable's extended label in any way affect any of the other information describing that variable, such as its missing values, value labels, or print format.

The following specific rules govern the modification of existing data-defining information:

1.   A new FILE NAME card will cause the name of the file to be changed and the old optional file label to be deleted. The latter occurs even if a new extended file label is not prepared.
2.   Individual VALUE LABELS may be replaced without affecting the other value labels associated with that variable; i.e., each value label is an independent entity.
3.   The PRINT FORMATS and VAR LABELS associated with each variable are also considered independent entities and can each be replaced without affecting the PRINT FORMATS or VAR LABELS of other variables in the file.
4.   Individual missing values associated with given variables are *not independent entities*, but are treated as a group. This means that the insertion of a new MISSING VALUES card (for a variable or a group of variables) causes all of the existing missing values for the variables

---

[1]Note that when the user inputs one system file and outputs a new or updated system file, JCL cards for both input and output files must be prepared. Instructions for preparing JCL cards FT03 and FT04 appear in Appendix F.

named on the card to be deleted and the missing values to be entered on the card defined in their place. If, for example, a variable had the missing values 8 and 9 associated with it, and the user wished to add 0 to the missing values list, he would be required to submit a MISSING VALUES card defining 8, 9, and 0 as the missing values to be associated with that variable.

The user may delete all missing values for a variable through the use of a MISSING VALUES card which contains an empty set of parentheses [( )] following a variable name or variable list. Its format is therefore

1                          16
MISSING VALUES $\left\{ \begin{array}{c} \text{variable name} \\ \text{or} \\ \text{variable list} \end{array} \right\}$   ( )

These data-definition cards may be entered into the control-card deck in any internal order the user desires. *They must, however, be placed after the* GET FILE *card and before the first set of task-definition cards.*

If the user wishes the additions or modifications to the data-defining information to be permanently retained, a new or updated SPSS system file must be created. This is accomplished by inserting a SAVE FILE card directly before the FINISH card.

*If the user does not insert a* SAVE FILE *card,* the additions or modifications will be in effect for all tasks on that run, but will not in any way alter the form of the existing system file and hence will not affect future runs.[1] This gives the user the added capability of temporarily modifying the data-defining information for a particular run.

Normally the deck setup for changing or adding to the data-defining information in a file would be as follows:

RUN NAME
GET FILE
$\left\{ \begin{array}{c} \text{data-} \\ \text{definition} \\ \text{cards} \end{array} \right\}$
$\left\{ \begin{array}{c} \text{task-} \\ \text{definition} \\ \text{cards} \end{array} \right\}$
SAVE FILE
FINISH

Example 7.9 illustrates a processing run in which the user is either adding to or altering some of his data-defining information. The crosstabulations produced on this run will be affected by these changes. Note also that the file is being saved at the conclusion of the run and that it will be saved under a new file name.[2]

**EXAMPLE 7.9**

```
1               16
RUN NAME        UPDATE FILE1 AND DO CROSSTABS AND SAVE FILE UNDER NAME FILE2
GET FILE        FILE1
MISSING VALUES  AGE TO VARC19(0,8,9)
VAR LABELS      ITEM3,VOTE IN 66 CONGRESSIONAL ELECTION
VAR LABELS      ITEM4,VOTE IN 68 CONGRESSIONAL ELECTION
VALUE LABELS    ITEM3,ITEM4(1)DEMOCRAT(2)REPUBLICAN(3)DIDN'T VOTE (4)
                TOO YOUNG TO VOTE
FILE NAME       FILE2 UPDATED ELECTION STUDY FILE JAN. 25, 1969
PROCESS SBFILES(NEGRO)(WHITE)
CROSSTABS       ITEM3 TO ITEM4 BY AGE TO VARC19
OPTIONS         1,3
STATISTICS      1,5
SAVE FILE
FINISH
```

[1]In this case a JCL card for an output system file (FT04) need *not* be prepared.
[2]The user must, in this case, be sure to remember to prepare the JCL cards for the output system file FT04 (see Appendix F.5).

# 8
# RECODING AND VARIABLE TRANSFORMATION:
# THE DATA-MODIFICATION CARDS

Situations often arise during the analysis of social science data which require the researcher to modify or transform some variable or variables in his file. For example, the researcher may desire to construct a composite *index* or *scale* generated from several existing variables, or he may find it necessary to recode the values of one or more of the variables for a particular type of analysis. At some time during the analysis, the user may wish to classify a continuous variable into a smaller number of discrete categories so that it can be used in conjunction with one of the frequency-distribution subprograms, perhaps in a crosstabulation. There may also be instances in which the researcher wants to normalize or in some way alter the shape or distribution of one or more variables by replacing the raw values with Z *scores, log transformations,* or with values arrived at by some other type of function.

The SPSS system provides the user with the capability of generating an almost unlimited variety of recodes and variable transformations. Furthermore, recoding and transformations may be employed for temporary use in conjunction with a specific set of calculations, or they may be used in order to effect more permanent changes such as the creation of a file of recoded or transformed cases. Files containing these permanent changes may be saved as SPSS system files, or they may be punched on cards or written in BCD form on tape, disk, etc., for input into programs outside of the SPSS system by means of the WRITE CASES procedure (see Sec. 10.5). The temporary as well as the permanent data modifications are effected by means of the same control cards, and the alternate conventions used to achieve temporary or permanent changes are discussed after the structure and function of the cards have been defined.

There are two general purpose *data-modification cards*—the COMPUTE and IF cards—which enable the user to construct a variety of variable transformations through the preparation of simplified Fortran-type statements. There is also the special purpose RECODE card which provides the user with an economical method of changing and replacing the values of variables in his file.

## 8.1    RECODING VARIABLES: THE RECODE CARD

The RECODE card enables the user to recode any or all the variables in his file so that one, some, or all of the values of the variables are replaced by a new value or set of values. Any type of variable—nominal, ordinal, or interval, alphanumeric or numeric—may be recoded by means of this card. Variables containing alphanumeric characters may be recoded into numeric variables, and continuous variables may be grouped into discrete categories. In short, the user may replace any value or set of values by a new value of his choice.

The RECODE card contains the control word RECODE followed by a variable name or list of variable names for which one set of recoding specifications are to apply. The variable name or list of variable names is in turn followed by the recoding specifications.

The RECODE card, like most other SPSS cards, may be continued on successive cards if the entire statement cannot be completed on one physical card. When this is the case, columns 1 to 15 of succeeding cards are left blank, and the rest of the statement is entered in columns 16 to 80 of as many cards as required.

When more than one variable is to be recoded by the same set of recoding specifications, the list of variables is entered onto the RECODE card using the same notation that is used on the MISSING VALUES card, the VALUE LABELS card, and the PRINT FORMATS card (see Sec. 4.7). Adjacent and nonadjacent variables which are to be recoded with the same list of recode specifications may be entered onto the RECODE card by the following familiar types of notation:

VARA TO VARE        VARG, VARQ, VARW        VARA TO VARE, VARL, VARP, VARO

The recoding instructions are entered onto the RECODE card by a series of parenthetical specifications like

(value list=new value)

where the value list is one or more of the present values which the user wishes to have replaced by the new value on the right side of the equal sign. There are two types of alternative or combined notations which can be used to enter the values that are to be replaced by the single value which will appear on the right side of the equal sign. First, a single value may be replaced by a new value in the form of

(x=1)

where x is the present value and 1 is the value to which all x's are to be recoded. Second, a group or set of values may be replaced by a single value by the following type of recoding expression:

(4,7,9=1)

In this case, all three of these values, 4, 7, and 9, will be replaced by 1. The user should note that the three values must be separated from each other by one or more common delimiters. Third, when the user wishes to replace a series of numeric values by a single value, as is often desired when converting a continuous variable into discrete categories, he may use a notation of the following type:

(32 THRU 64=1)

where the keyword THRU indicates that all values between and inclusive of 32 and 64 will be replaced by the value 1. Note that both values must be separated from the keyword THRU by one or more common delimiters. Any of these notations may be combined to produce a list of values to be replaced by the new value at the right of the equal sign. For example,

(1,5,22,37 THRU 68=2)

When using recoding statements of the type described above, the user may convert multiple-column variables into variables which contain values that are single-column integers or vice versa without concerning himself with the number of columns occupied by the variable, for this is automatically taken care of for him. Also, when the user converts all the values of an alphanumeric variable to numeric ones, he may then perform arithmetic calculations on it. However, whenever the user is entering the values of alphanumeric variables onto the RECODE card, be they on the left or right side of the equal sign, they must be enclosed in apostrophes or single quotation marks. For example,

('X','Y', 'B','5'='A')

The above statement would cause the alphanumeric value 'A' to replace the alphanumeric values of 'X','Y', 'B', and '5'. The following two examples illustrate how an alphanumeric variable may be converted to a numeric one:

('X','Y','B','5'=1)('2'=2)('3'=3)('4'=4)('9'=9)          or          ('NJ'=1),('NY'=2),('LA','SF'=3)

A special alphanumeric to numeric recoding procedure also exists which provides for the conversion of alphanumeric variables into numeric variables. Following a variable name or variable list with the keyword CONVERT enclosed in left and right parentheses—i.e., (CONVERT)—will cause the alphanumeric characters '0' to '9' to be converted to their numeric equivalents 0 to 9; the 360 graphic '&' and its 7090/1401 equivalent, the '+', to be recoded to the numeric value 12; all minuses ['−'] to be recoded to the numeric value 11; and blanks as well as all other alphabetic characters converted to a numeric value of 13. This special recoding procedure is particularly useful for handling data coded for counter-sorter analysis where the '+' (& on the 360) and '−' zone punches were frequently used. The following two recode statements, the first using the general type of recode specifications and the second the special (CONVERT) procedure, will give the same recoded values for variables VARA TO VARC.

```
1               16
RECODE          VARA TO VARC ('0'=0)('1'=1)('2'=2)('3'=3)('4'=4)('5'=5)
                ('6'=6)('7'=7)('8'=8)('9'=9)('-'=11)('&'=12)('  '=13)

RECODE          VARA TO VARC (CONVERT)
```

The recode (CONVERT) specification can be used to convert alphanumeric variables composed of two or more adjacent alphanumeric characters, but it involves a slightly more complicated procedure requiring two steps rather than one. The user employs the general (value = value) type of recode statement to assign desired numeric values to all the combinations of characters which contain one or more nonnumeric characters; then the remaining values are converted to numerics with the (CONVERT) procedure.

The process is not as complicated as it sounds and can perhaps be best explained by a concrete example. Suppose a user wished to convert a three-character alphanumeric variable called OCCUCODE (occupational code). Let us assume that this variable is composed of the numeric values 000 through 999 plus the eight alphanumeric character strings: '−−−', '−−&', '−&−', ' −−', '−99', '&&&', '   ', '&99'. This variable could be converted to a numeric variable by the following set of recode statements:

```
1               16
RECODE          OCCUCODE ('---' = 1000)('--&' = 1001)('-&-' = 1002)(' --' =
                1003)('-99' = 1004)('&&&' = 1005)('   ' = 1006)('&99' = 1007)
                (CONVERT)
```

The eight combinations of alphanumeric characters would first be converted to numeric values ranging from 1000 to 1007. Then the (CONVERT) specification would cause all of the remaining values, those from 0 to 999, to be converted to numerics. The variable OCCUCODE would then have been totally converted to a numeric-type variable with values ranging from 0 to 1007. The user must remember to insert a new PRINT FORMATS card for variables being recoded from alphanumeric to numeric if he has previously entered print formats for them.

Two other keywords, LOWEST and HIGHEST, may also be used on the RECODE card and are of considerable convenience when recoding continuous numeric variables into discrete categories. The keyword LOWEST is used as a substitute for the lowest value which appears for a given variable, and HIGHEST is similarly used as a substitute for the highest value taken by a variable. When either or both of these values are not known or easily accessible to the researcher, the insertion of these two keywords will enable him to recode a variable without having complete information concerning its minimum and maximum.[1] An example of this use is

```
1               16
RECODE          VAR001 (LOWEST THRU 25=1)(26 THRU 50=2)(51 THRU HIGHEST=3)
```

The above types of recoding statements constitute the building blocks of the RECODE card. A number of these parenthesized recoding statements may follow the variable name or list of variable names to which they apply, so that all the desired recodes for that variable may be performed. The general format of the RECODE card is then

```
1               16
RECODE
```

$$\begin{Bmatrix} \text{variable name} \\ \text{or} \\ \text{variable list} \end{Bmatrix} \begin{Bmatrix} \text{(value list=value)} \\ \text{or} \\ \text{(CONVERT)} \end{Bmatrix} \cdots \begin{Bmatrix} \text{(value list=value)/} \\ \text{or} \\ \text{(CONVERT)} \end{Bmatrix}$$

$$\begin{Bmatrix} \text{variable name} \\ \text{or} \\ \text{variable list} \end{Bmatrix} \begin{Bmatrix} \text{(value list=value) } \dots \\ \text{or} \\ \text{(CONVERT)} \end{Bmatrix}$$

Note that as on most SPSS control cards, the recode instructions applying to a variable or list of variables may be followed by a slash, and a new variable or list of variables followed by its RECODE statements may then be placed after the slash. It is important to remember that RECODE specification lists are cumulative so that it is possible to recode a recoded variable. The following example RECODE statements may help clarify the conventions used in constructing RECODE cards.

```
1               16
RECODE          RACE ('W'=1)('N'=2)('S','O'=3)
```

This example RECODE card would cause the values of the alphanumeric variable RACE to be recoded into numeric values where 'W' (white) will now equal 1, 'N' (Negro) will equal 2, and 'O' (Oriental) and 'S' (Spanish) will equal 3. The special delimiters, i.e., the right parenthesis, the left parenthesis, the equal sign, and the slash, need not be separated from other elements by common delimiters. The user may, however, insert blanks and commas at his discretion in order to improve readability without affecting the meaning or syntax of the RECODE statement.

The following RECODE card would cause the continuous variables named ITEM1, ITEM2, ITEM3, and ITEM4 to be recoded so that they would be categorized into five discrete groups. A second two-digit alphanumeric variable, OCCUPATN, will also be recoded so that the alpha character strings will be converted to numbers and then the entire variable converted from alphanumeric to numeric.

```
1               16
RECODE          ITEM1 TO ITEM4 (LOWEST THRU 20 = 1)(21 THRU 30 = 2)(31 THRU 40 =
                3)(41 THRU 50 = 4)(51 THRU 99 = 5)/OCCUPATN ('&&' = 100)('&-' =
                101)('-&' = 102)('--' = 103)('  ' = 104)('-9' = 105)(CONVERT)
```

[1]The user should overlap the categories of variables (to be recoded) containing mixed numbers when using the THRU convention. When categories are overlapped values are recoded into the first category in which they will fit. (15.32 THRU 18.15=1) (18.15 THRU HIGHEST=2) will cause all numbers up to and including 18.15 to be recoded into 1. This overlapping is necessary because the internal representation of decimal fractions often contain more significant digits than their external BCD representations.

### 8.1.1    TEMPORARY VERSUS PERMANENT RECODING: THE *RECODE CARD

Recoding may be executed so that the values residing on the cases themselves are altered and a file containing recoded variables is saved as an SPSS system file. Alternatively, the user may generate recodes which are to apply only to a specific task.

An asterisk [*] preceding the control word RECODE—to produce the control word *RECODE—signifies that the recodes generated by that card will apply only to the following task. When the user does not precede the control word RECODE with an *, all the tasks following that RECODE card will be executed with the recode statements in force. In the latter case, the user may, if he wishes, retain the recoded file at the conclusion of the run by means of the SAVE FILE control card. If the SAVE FILE card is not inserted, the file will retain the exact content that it had preceding that run.[1]

The RECODE cards are inserted into the control deck directly preceding the first set of task-definition cards. The *RECODE cards are placed directly in front of the single task to which they apply. The relative position of the RECODE card in terms of the other data-modification cards, as well as the data-selection cards, will be discussed in following sections.

### 8.1.2    EXAMPLE USAGES AND DECK SETUP FOR THE RECODE AND *RECODE CARDS

The following two examples illustrate the use of the RECODE and *RECODE cards. The first, Example 8.1, illustrates the use of both the RECODE and the *RECODE cards when they are being used in a run where data are being entered from cards or BCD input files. In this case the BCD input file resides on an external tape.

This run would cause marginals to be computed for variables AGE to EDUCATN and the file to be retained at the conclusion of the run. The permanent recode of the variable AGE would actually replace the original values in the data. The temporary recode of the variable INCOME would apply to the marginals computed on that variable, but the original five-digit values would be retained when the file is saved at the conclusion of the run. *Note that when both temporary and permanent recodes are used together on the same task, the permanent* RECODE *cards must precede the temporary ones.*

**EXAMPLE 8.1**

```
1                   16
RUN NAME            ILLUSTRATION OF THE USE OF THE RECODE CARDS
FILE NAME           EXAMPLE1,THIS IS THE FILE LABEL FOR FILE EXAMPLE1
VARIABLE LIST       AGE,SEX,RACE,INCOME,EDUCATN
INPUT MEDIUM        TAPE
# OF CASES          10
INPUT FORMAT        FIXED (5X,F2.0,2F1.0,F7.0,1X,F1.0)
RECODE              AGE (LOWEST THRU 15=1)(16 THRU 21=2)(22 THRU 29=3)
                    (30 THRU 35=4)(36 THRU 49=5)(50 THRU 65=6)(66 THRU
                    HIGHEST=7)
*RECODE             INCOME (0 THRU 1999=1)(2000 THRU 2999=2)(3000 THRU 3999=3)
                    (4000 THRU 6999=4)(7000 THRU 11999=5)(12000 THRU 25000=6)
MARGINALS           AGE TO EDUCATN
OPTIONS             1,4
STATISTICS          ALL
READ INPUT DATA
SAVE FILE
FINISH
```

Example 8.2 illustrates the use of the RECODE cards when processing from an SPSS system file and demonstrates how the users may enter data-definition cards which are to apply to the recoded variables. The user should be aware, however, that data-definition cards associated with temporary transformations will remain in effect for all following tasks on that run. Note also that the special (CONVERT) procedure is also being employed on this run.

In the example, two variables from the existing file called STUDYX are to be permanently recoded. The missing values, value labels, print formats, and variable labels which now define these recoded variables have been inserted and will replace the existing data-defining information on the new system file. A second task, the calculation of Pearson correlation coefficients,

---

[1]The user must remember to prepare the required JCL cards for file FT04 whenever a new or updated system file is to be retained. See Appendix F.5 for detailed specifications.

is also being executed on this run. Note here that some variables have been temporarily recoded for the particular task, but that this will in no way affect the cases in the updated file, which is being saved at the conclusion of the run. Furthermore, had the user wished to define another task following the Pearson correlations, the temporary recodes defined for the PEARSON CORR task *would not* have remained in effect.

**EXAMPLE 8.2**

```
1               16
RUN NAME        ILLUSTRATION OF USE OF RECODE CARD PROCESSING FROM AN SPSS FILE
GET FILE        STUDYX
RECODE          SCALE1 (15 THRU 26=1)('A','B','C'=4)/INCOME (1000 THRU 6000=1)
                (6001 THRU 25000=2)(1,4,88 THRU 99=0)/ITEM1 TO ITEM4 (CONVERT)
MISSING VALUES  SCALE1(4)/INCOME(0)
VALUE LABELS    INCOME (1) LESS THAN 6000 (2) GREATER THAN 6000 (0) NO
                INFORMATION
VAR LABELS      INCOME, RECODED VARIABLE NOW HAVING VALUES 0,1,2/SCALE1,
                RECODED TO 1-4
PRINT FORMATS   SCALE (0)
CROSSTABS       SCALE1 BY INCOME BY VAR001 TO VAR007
OPTIONS         1,2,3
STATISTICS      1,7
*RECODE         VAR001 TO VAR007 (5=1)(4=2)(2=4)
PEARSON CORR    VAR001 TO VAR007 WITH VAR002 TO VAR006
OPTIONS         1,3
STATISTICS      ALL
SAVE FILE
FINISH
```

### 8.1.3  LIMITATIONS ON THE NUMBER OF RECODES

The following rather complicated set of parameters constitutes the limitations on the RECODE and *RECODE cards which together may precede a given procedure card. If the user exceeds any of these limitations, an error message number will be printed following the processing of the card which has caused one of the limits to be exceeded. Diagnostic messages corresponding to these message numbers appear in Appendix B.

No more than 250 words may appear on a given RECODE or *RECODE card. A [*] RECODE card is defined by the control word [*] RECODE and all specifications following it no matter how many physical cards are involved. Each of the following is counted as a single word: variable name, keyword, individual value, left parenthesis, right parenthesis, and equal sign. The following RECODE card, for example, contains 24 words:

```
1               16
RECODE          ITEM1 TO ITEM9 (0 THRU 21=1)(22 THRU 88=2)(96,98,99=3)
```

This limitation can be easily avoided by breaking long RECODE cards into two or more separate cards. None of the following limitations may be exceeded by the group of RECODE and *RECODE cards which precede a given procedure card.

1.  The number of individual values to the left of the = sign (*excluding* those of the A THRU N variety) plus the number of individual variable lists must not exceed the value 200. In other words, each variable list (be it a single name or a list of the VARA TO VARN type or of the VARA, VARB TO VARX, VARZ type) is counted as one, and each value to the left of the = sign is counted as one. The sum of these numbers cannot exceed 200.
2.  The number of times an A THRU N-type recode specification appears plus the number of times the keyword (CONVERT) appears plus the number of variable lists cannot exceed 200. Each time the keyword (CONVERT) appears (no matter how many variables it applies to), it is counted as one. Each time a recode specification of the A THRU N type appears (no matter how many variables it applies to), it is counted as one. The sum of the resulting three numbers cannot exceed 200.
3.  No more than 140 variables can be recoded at a time.

All three of the above limits are independent; they may all be at their maximum values without exceeding the recode limitations.

## 8.2    VARIABLE TRANSFORMATIONS: THE COMPUTE AND IF CARDS

The SPSS system provides the user with two general-purpose transformation cards—the COMPUTE and the IF card—which enable him to construct his own variable transformations by means of arithmetic and logical expressions. These cards contain specifications which are simplified Fortran-type statements. As in the case of the RECODE card, the user may generate temporary transformations for use with a single task, or he may wish to permanently transform or add to the variables in his file.[1] The conventions used to distinguish between the temporary and permanent transformation cards are discussed after the general function and format of the COMPUTE and IF cards have been presented.

### 8.2.1    COMPUTING VARIABLES BY MEANS OF ARITHMETIC EXPRESSIONS: THE COMPUTE CARD

In many circumstances, the researcher may want to compute a new variable which is an arithmetic function of one or more of the variables presently in his file. The new variable may be computed by adding, subtracting, dividing, multiplying, or in some other way operating on one or more variables and/or constants. These types of variable transformations are defined on the COMPUTE transformation card by means of a simplified Fortran-style statement which closely resembles a conventional arithmetic formula. The general format of the COMPUTE card is as follows:

```
1               16
COMPUTE         computed variable=arithmetic expression
```

The control word COMPUTE is followed by the name of the computed variable, and the arithmetic expression which is to be used to compute that variable is placed to the right of the equal sign. Thus, whenever a case is processed, the expression to the right of the equal sign is computed for that case, and the value produced becomes the value for that case for the computed variable indicated at the left of the equal sign. The computed variable is the only element which may be placed to the left of the equal sign. This variable may be either a previously defined variable or a totally new variable. In the first case, the newly computed value replaces the original value of that variable. In the second case, a new variable is defined for the file containing the value determined by the arithmetic expression to the right of the equal sign. This new variable is then added to the variable list and becomes the last variable in the file. The result of the arithmetic expression to the right of the equal sign becomes the value of the variable entered to the left of the equal sign. These arithmetic expressions can be simple or complex. They are usually composed, in part, of the names of existing variables. They may also contain arithmetic operators, preexisting mathematical functions, and numeric constants, all of which may be used to create the values of the new variable.

Perhaps the simplest transformation is

VARB=VARA

where VARA is a variable which presently exists in the file and VARB is the new or modified variable. This simple expression will be commonly used when the researcher wishes to recode a variable and at the same time maintain its original values in the file. The arithmetic expression may involve two or more variable names which are connected by operators, as in the following transformation:

VARX=VARA + VARB + VARC

In this instance, a new variable, VARX, is created which is the sum of the values of VARA, VARB, and VARC. This will mean that each case in the file will contain a new value associated with a variable named VARX, and that variable will contain a value which is equal to the sum of the values on that case of variables VARA, VARB, and VARC. For example, to create a new variable called Socio-Economic Status, or SES, from the existing variables INCOME, EDUCATN and OCCUPATN, one might desire to add the values of the latter three variables together. If this were the case, the following COMPUTE card would be prepared:

---

[1]The user must remember to prepare an FT04 JCL card if he wishes a permanent file containing the recodes to be saved (see Appendix F).

```
1               16
COMPUTE         SES=EDUCATN+INCOME+OCCUPTAN
```

where EDUCATN, INCOME, and OCCUPATN are variables which already exist in the file and where SES is the new or modified variable.

When the SPSS system encounters this card, the following procedure takes place for each case in the file: The value of the variable EDUCATN for that particular case is added to the value of the variable INCOME, and their sum is added to the value of the variable OCCUPATN; this total is then associated with the new variable SES and becomes the last variable on the variable list for the file. Thus, if a case were to contain a value of 4 for EDUCATN, a value of 6 for INCOME, and a value of 3 for OCCUPATN, a value of 13 would be associated with the new variable SES. In this manner, a value is computed for the new variable for each case in the file.

Numeric constants may also be introduced into the arithmetic expression:

VARX=(VARA + VARB + VARC)/3

In this case, VARX would be set equal to the sum of the values of VARA, VARB, and VARC divided by 3. This expression also introduces the use of the parenthesis which instructs the system as to the order in which the operations are to be performed. In this case, the user is instructing the system to perform the additions before the division. The following section presents the rules and conventions to be used in constructing arithmetic expressions in a relatively systematic manner. Section 8.2.1.2 demonstrates some of the potential uses of the COMPUTE card.

### 8.2.1.1 Constructing arithmetic expressions on the COMPUTE card

Each variable, as well as any constant used in the expression, may be connected to another variable or constant by one (but only one) of the following arithmetic operators. The following table lists the graphic, its meaning, and an example of the use of each of the arithmetic operators:

| Graphic | Meaning | Example |
|---------|---------|---------|
| / | Division | VARX=VARA/VARB |
| * | Multiplication | VARX=VARA*VARB |
| + | Addition | VARX=VARA+VARB |
| — | Subtraction | VARX=VARA—VARB |
| ** | Exponentiation | VARX=VARA**2 |

In addition to these standard arithmetic operators, any of the variables or constants used in the expression may also be acted upon by one of the following prepared or packaged functions:

| Mnemonic | Meaning | Example |
|----------|---------|---------|
| SQRT | Square root | VARX=SQRT(VARA) |
| LN | Natural or Naperian logarithm | VARX=LN(VARA) |
| LGI0 | Base 10 logarithm | VARX=LGI0(VARA) |
| EXP | Exponential ($e^{arg}$) | VARX=EXP(VARA+VARC) |
| SIN | Sine[†] | VARX=SIN(VARA + VARB) |
| COS | Cosine[†] | VARX=COS(VARA) |
| ATAN | Arctangent[†] | VARX=ATAN(VARA) |
| RND | Round result to whole number | VARX=RND(VARA + VARC/6) |

[†]Argument is in radians.

In order to make use of the above functions, it is necessary to follow the mnemonic of the function with an expression entirely enclosed in parentheses. The parenthesized expression may be the name of a single variable, or it may be a more complex expression containing one or more variable names and/or constants.

The COMPUTE card, like most other SPSS cards, may be continued on successive cards if the entire statement cannot be completed on one physical card. When this is the case, columns 1 to 15 of succeeding cards are left blank, and the rest of the statement is completed in columns 16 to 80 of as many cards as are needed.

The COMPUTE control card, unlike many other SPSS cards, may contain no more than one transformation though a transformation may take more than one physical card to complete. Each new statement must begin with the word COMPUTE starting in column one of the control field. For these reasons *it is incorrect to use a card like the following:*[1]

```
1               16
COMPUTE         NEWVAR=VARA*VARB        FIRSTVAR=NEWVAR/VARC        VARO38=FIRSTVAR
                /(VARC29-1)
```

The use of this card would cause the run to be terminated and an error message to be reported.

When generating variable transformations by means of the COMPUTE card, the user need not concern himself with the amount of space (i.e., the number of digits) to be taken up by the results of the transformation, since space is automatically provided by the system. The user should remember that if the calculated variables are intended for crosstabulations and other such procedures, there should be a reasonable number of categories for convenience. He has at his disposal the RND function, which will convert mixed (i.e., numbers excluding decimal fractions) to whole numbers before the values are actually output onto the cases.

The operators, the variable names, as well as the above packaged functions, may be used together to construct any arithmetic expression the user desires as long as that expression conforms to the following conventions.

*Summary of Conventions for Creating Arithmetic Expressions*

1.  No two operators may appear contiguously. Thus the expression VARX=VARA**+6 is incorrect. However, the expression VARX=(VARA**2)+(6) is quite valid.
2.  An operator may never be assumed present. The expression (VARA)(VARB) is incorrect and must be written VARA*VARB or (VARA)*(VARB).
3.  Right and left parentheses must be used to indicate the order in which the operations are to be performed. Thus, if the user wished to have VARX set equal to the value of 2 more than VARC times the value of VARA, he would write VARX=VARA* (VARC+2).
4.  When the order of the operations is not completely specified by parentheses, the operations are performed in the following order:
    (*a*)  All prepackaged functions are performed first.
    (*b*)  Exponentiation is performed second.
    (*c*)  All multiplications and divisions are performed next.
    (*d*)  Addition and subtraction are performed last.
5.  Within this order of operations unspecified by parentheses, operations of equal precedence are performed from left to right. Thus, if there are two divisions or a division and a multiplication, whose order has not been specified by parentheses, the left-most operation will be performed first, and the right-most operation will be performed last within that level of precedence. Thus the expression VARX/1/2 would result in the following operations: VARX would first be divided by 1, then that quotient would be divided by two. This would result in a value equal to exactly one-half of VARX. If the expression were written VARX/(1/2), the sequence of operations and the result would be very different. In this instance, VARX would be divided by the quotient resulting from dividing 1 by 2. The resulting value would be twice the value of VARX.
6.  Each of the arithmetic operators as well as the right and left parentheses serve as their own delimiters. Therefore, no common delimiters (i.e., blanks or commas) are required to separate these elements from each other or from other elements on the list. As usual, however, common delimiters may be inserted whenever desired to improve readability without affecting the meaning or syntax of the expressions on the COMPUTE card.

### 8.2.1.2  Example usages of the COMPUTE card

The following examples demonstrate the types of variable transformations which may be effected by means of the COMPUTE card. The first example illustrates the construction of a simple

---

[1]Note that this is an incorrect control card, for demonstration only.

additive scale or index in which a number of items are simply added together to create the index. This type of index or scale is often built from Lickert-type items where each of the contributing items is identically coded and contains the same categories.

```
1               16
COMPUTE         SCALE1=QUESTN1+QUESTN2+QUESTN3
```

The second example illustrates the construction of a similar additive scale, but here each of the variables being used to compute the scale has a different number of categories. In such cases, the user might wish to divide each variable by the number of categories it contains, so that each variable will be equally weighted in the overall scale score. The results of this transformation (i.e., the value of SES) will be rounded to the nearest whole number.

```
1               16
COMPUTE         SES=RND((INCCME/8 + (OCCUPATN/7 + EDUCATN/4)))
```

The next COMPUTE card demonstrates the construction of an additive scale of a more complicated nature. Here each variable used in constructing the scale is not only adjusted for the number of categories it contains, but is also multiplied by a unique constant so that each variable contributes differentially to the overall scale score. This type of procedure is common in building indices based on factor loadings or from part-whole correlations.

```
1               16
COMPUTE         SES =  ((INCOME/8)*(.76)) + (OCCUPATN/7*.65)+(EDUCATN/4*.55)
```

Note that in this example the component expression INCOME/8 is fully enclosed by parentheses while the following component expressions OCCUPATN/7 and EDUCATN/4 are not. In this case, either type of construct produces the same result, for multiplication and division have the same precedence in the syntax hierarchy and are therefore executed in left to right order when parentheses do not fully specify the order of the operations. See rules 5 and 6 in Sec. 8.2.1.1.

The following card gives an example of how the distribution of a variable may be altered by using one of the packaged functions. In this example, each case in the file will be given a value for variable SES2 which is equivalent to the square root of its value on variable SES.

```
1               16
COMPUTE         SES2=SQRT(SES)
```

Often the user may wish to construct a function which is not available as a packaged function. One of the most common functions used to standardize the distribution of a variable is the Z score transformation. The formula for the Z transformation is

$$Z = \frac{X - \overline{X}}{sd}$$

where X equals the value on the case of the variable being normalized; $\overline{X}$ equals the mean of that variable; and sd is the standard deviation of that variable. For the variable SES, if $\overline{X}$ equals 50 and sd equals 10, then the following expression would produce standardized scores for a new variable called SESZ.

```
1               16
COMPUTE         SESZ=(SES-50)/10
```

The next example COMPUTE card illustrates how a new variable may be computed which has the effect of other variables (which may be statistically related to it) subtracted out.

```
1               16
COMPUTE         SUBVAR=AVAR-CVAR
```

While these examples demonstrate some of the common usages to which the COMPUTE card may be put, the number and variety of variable transformations which can be accomplished by this card is virtually unlimited.

The final example COMPUTE card illustrates how a COMPUTE card combined with a RECODE card can be used to enable the user to recode a variable while also maintaining the variable in its initial or untransformed form.

```
1               16
COMPUTE         INCOMER=INCOME
RECODE          INCOMER (0 THRU 1999=1)(2000 THRU 4999=2)(5000 THRU 8999=3)
                (9000 THRU 14999=4)(15000 THRU 275000=5)
```

In this example, the continuous variable INCOME is first set equal to a new variable, INCOMER. Now two identical variables exist. Next, the new variable INCOMER is recoded into five discrete categories, so that the user has the variable INCOME in two forms: INCOME, which contains the original continuous values, and INCOMER, which consists of a single-digit value ranging from 1 to 5. Note that the effects of all data-modification cards are cumulative. That is computations on one card affecting a given variable may be used in later cards for further computations. In this case a RECODE is based on the results of a COMPUTE.

### 8.2.2 VARIABLE TRANSFORMATIONS WITH CONDITIONAL ASSIGNMENTS: THE IF CARD

The IF card permits the researcher to generate variable transformations in the same manner as does the COMPUTE card. However, it provides the additional facility of performing these transformations contingent upon logical conditions which can be specified by the user. Thus, the IF card enables the user to define new variables or to alter the values of existing variables by specifying logical expressions and contingencies as well as arithmetic expressions. The general format of the IF card is

```
1                   16
IF                  (logical expression) computed variable=arithmetic expression
```

The following sample demonstrates how the IF card may be used to create a new variable, in this case a classificatory variable called INTELGNC, by dividing IQSCORE by AGE. The new variable will take on values between 1 and 4, depending upon the size of the quotient.

```
1                16
IF               (IQSCORE/AGE LE 100) INTELGNC=1
IF               (IQSCORE/AGE GT 100 AND IQSCORE/AGE LE 115) INTELGNC=2
IF               (IQSCORF/AGE GT 115 AND IQSCORE/AGE LE 130) INTELGNC=3
IF               (IQSCORE/AGE GT 130) INTELGNC=4
```

Whenever a case is processed, the logical expression (which is always written in parentheses) is evaluated, substituting the value of the variables for the variable names for that case. As with the COMPUTE card, the computed variable may be either an existing variable or may be newly defined on the IF card. If the logical expression is true, the assignment is performed as indicated, that is the following transformation is performed. If it is false, the computed variable retains its previous value.

The arithmetic expression which appears to the right of the equal sign may be a variable name, a constant, or a full arithmetic expression which contains variable names, constants, and arithmetic operators; all rules concerning arithmetic expressions which are defined for the COMPUTE card must be used in constructing these expressions. The computed variable may be a variable which has been defined on the variable list or on previous transformations; it may also, however, be a new variable which is to be computed and added to the end of the variable list in a manner which is identical to that described for the COMPUTE card. Thus, the sole difference between the IF and COMPUTE cards lies in the logical expression which precedes the computed variable on the IF card.

A *logical expression* consists of one or more sets of relations. A *relation*, in turn, is composed of an algebraic comparison of two quantities. A relation is formed by joining two arithmetic expressions with a relational operator. Its form is then

(arithmetic expression 1) relational operator (arithmetic expression 2)

An arithmetic expression may be composed of variable names, constants, and arithmetic operators, and one of these expressions must contain at least one previously defined variable. Furthermore, no undefined variable may be used in the expression. See Sec. 8.2.1.2 for a more detailed discussion of arithmetic expressions.

The two arithmetic expressions must be linked by one and only one of the six relational operators. The following table indicates the relation, keyword, and definition of each of these operators:

| Relation | Keyword | Definition |
|---|---|---|
| Greater than or equal to | GE | If expression 1 is greater than or equal to expression 2, then the value of the relation is true; otherwise it is false. |
| Less than or equal to | LE | If expression 1 is less than or equal to expression 2, the value of the relation is true. |
| Greater than | GT | If expression 1 is greater than expression 2, the value of the relation is true. |
| Less than | LT | If expression 1 is less than expression 2, the value of the relation is true. |
| Equal to | EQ | If expression 1 is exactly equal to expression 2, the value of the relation is true. |
| Not equal to | NE | If expression 1 is not exactly equal to expression 2, the value of the relation is true. |

The six relational operators are keywords, and as such, must be spelled correctly and separated from the arithmetic expressions by one or more common delimiters. Some examples of relations follow.

VARA EQ 1

In this simple case, VARA is the first arithmetic expression, 1 is the second, and EQ is the relational operator indicating equality. This relation will be evaluated as true when and only when VARA has a value of precisely 1. A more complex relation might be

VARA*VARB GT 2* (VARC−1)

In this case, the first arithmetic expression consists of multiplying VARA by VARB; the second expression is twice the value of VARC−1; and the relational operator is GT, which indicates that for the relation to be evaluated as true, the value of the first expression must be greater than that of the second. To relate this example to the IF card, the researcher might wish, for example, to create a new variable from these three variables, which will take three values: if the first expression is greater than the second, 1; if the first is equal to the second, 2; and if the first is less than the second, 3. This could be accomplished by the use of the following three IF cards:

```
1               16
IF              (VARA*VARB GT 2*(VARC-1)) NEWVAR=1
IF              (VARA*VARB EQ 2*(VARC-1)) NEWVAR=2
IF              (VARA*VARB LT 2*(VARC-1)) NEWVAR=3
```

While a logical expression can consist of a single relation, it can also consist of several relations joined to each other by *logical operators,* which may be either AND or OR. When this is the case, a logical expression has the following format:

(relation   logical operator   relation)

Both AND and OR are keywords and must be separated from other elements by one or more common delimiters. They must also conform to all other rules governing the use of keywords. AND and OR are used to combine relations, and while no more than one logical operator may be used to combine two relations, many relations may be combined into a larger logical expression by means of their use. No matter how many relations are used to build a logical expression, the result of the evaluation of this expression must be a single value—true or false. Logical operators combine the values of relations according to the following rules:

1.   AND—the resulting logical expression will have the value *true* if and only if the relations directly preceding and following the operator have the value *true*.
2.   OR—the resulting logical expression will be *true* if either of the constituent expressions has the value *true*.

The following example demonstrates these rules:

```
1                    16
IF                   (VARA GT VARB AND VARA GT VARC) VARD=1
IF                   (VARA GT VARB OR VARA GT VARC) VARD=1
```

The first IF card will cause VARD to be set equal to 1 if and only if VARA is greater than VARB *and* VARA is greater than VARC. If either of these conditions is not satisfied, VARD will not be set equal to 1. The second card will cause VARD to be set equal to 1 if VARA is greater than *either* VARB or VARC, or if it is greater than both. That is, for the second card only one of the relations need be satisfied to obtain a value of true.

When arithmetic operators are present in logical expressions, functions are performed first; exponentiation, division, and multiplication next; and addition and subtraction last. When two operators of the same precedence level are present in one expression, the operations will be performed from left to right. The logical operators in an expression are evaluated from left to right unless parentheses are used to alter the order of operation. Relational operators are evaluated *before* logical operators and *after* arithmetic operators. The following example illustrates how parentheses may be used to alter the meaning of a logical expression. More detailed rules governing the construction of arithmetic expressions and the use of parentheses can be found in Sec. 8.2.1.2.

```
1                    16
IF                   (VARA EQ 9 OR (VARA GT 0 AND VARA LT 5)) VARD = 1
IF                   (VARA EQ 9 OR VARA GT 0 AND VARA LT 5) VARD = 1
```

The first card will cause VARD to be set equal to 1 when VARA lies between 0 and 5 or when VARA equals 9. In the second card VARD will be set equal to 1 when VARA is equal to 9 and less than 5, or greater than 0 and less than 5. Both of these statements are syntactically correct; their operational meanings, however, are quite different. The user should remember that the operation specified by the innermost set of parentheses will be performed first and that the next operation to be performed will be that which is indicated by the next most inner set of parentheses until all operations within internal parentheses have been performed. The operations within any given level of parentheses are executed according to the usual precedence order (i.e., first functions, then exponentiation, then division and multiplication, and last, addition and subtraction). When there are two operations present which have the same level of precedence within a parenthesized expression, the operations will be performed from left to right.

One more keyword is available for use in logical expressions—NOT. This keyword can precede any logical expression and has the effect of reversing the value of that expression (i.e., if the expression were considered true, its value would be reversed to false and vice versa). For example,

```
1                    16
IF                   (NOT(VARA GT 4 AND VARA LT 7)) VARD = 1
```

The use of the NOT before the expression will cause VARD to be assigned the value 1 when VARA does not lie between 4 and 7. If the NOT were omitted, as in

```
1                    16
IF                   (VARA GT 4 AND VARA LT 7) VARD = 1
```

then VARD would be assigned the value 1 only when VARA is between the values of 4 and 7.

The IF card, like most other SPSS cards, may be continued on successive cards if the entire statement cannot be completed on one physical card. When this is the case, columns 1 to 15 of succeeding cards are left blank, and the rest of the statement is printed in columns 16 to 80 of as many cards as are needed.

The IF control card, unlike many other SPSS cards, may contain no more than one statement per IF on a physical card, though a statement may take more than one physical card to complete. Each new statement must begin with the word IF starting in column one of the control field. For this reason *it is incorrect to use a card like the following:*

```
1            16
IF           (VARA GT VARB) VARC = 1  /  (VARA LT VARB) VARC = 2
```

The use of this card would cause the run to be terminated and an error message to be reported.

When generating variable transformations by means of the IF card, the user need not concern himself with the amount of space (i.e., the number of digits) to be taken up by the results of the transformation, since space is automatically provided by the system. The user should remember that if the variables are intended for crosstabulations and other such procedures, there should be a reasonable number of categories for convenience when working with future calculations. He has at his disposal the RND function which will convert mixed numbers to integer numbers before the values are actually output onto the cases.

The following example illustrates how the IF card can be used to create a scale or index which is created by prespecified contingencies on the values of other variables in the file.

```
1            16
IF           (MNINCOME GE 5000 AND PERCNEGR GE 50) CITYTYPE=1
IF           (MNINCOME GE 5000 AND PERCNEGR LT 50) CITYTYPE=2
IF           (MNINCOME LT 5000 AND PERCNEGR LT 50) CITYTYPE=3
IF           (MNINCOME LT 5000 AND PERCNEGR GE 50) CITYTYPE=4
```

In this example a variable called CITYTYPE is being created which is based on a city's mean level of income and its percentage of Negro population. Four types of cities emerge: one in which the income level is greater than or equal to $5000, and the percentage of Negro population is greater than or equal to 50; one in which income is greater than or equal to $5000, and the percentage of Negroes is less than 50; one in which income is less than $5000, and the percentage of Negroes is less than 50; and one in which income is less than $5000, and the percentage of Negroes is greater than or equal to 50.

The next example illustrates how arithmetic operators within a logical expression can be used to create a new variable which adjusts for the effects of another variable. In this case, a new variable called REALINC (real income) is created by first multiplying family size by 600 and subtracting that product from income, and then assigning it to one of three categories, (1) low, (2) medium, (3) high, depending upon the amount of actual income left after adjusting for family size.

```
1            16
IF           (INCOME-(FAMSIZE*600) LE 3000) REALINC=1
IF           (INCOME-(FAMSIZE*600) GT 3000 AND INCOME-(FAMSIZE*600)
             LE 6000) REALINC=2
IF           (INCOME-(FAMSIZE*600) GT 6000) REALINC=3
```

Note that the parentheses around FAMSIZE*600 are not required, as multiplication always takes precedence over subtraction. However, had something other than division or multiplication been required as an operator, the parentheses would have been necessary.

### 8.2.3  STARRED [*] AND NONSTARRED VERSIONS OF RECODE, COMPUTE, AND IF CARDS: TEMPORARY VERSUS PERMANENT DATA MODIFICATION

Each of the three data-modification cards described above can be used to generate either temporary or permanent data modifications. Each of the cards—RECODE, COMPUTE, and IF—has a starred [*] and nonstarred version. The starred versions direct the system to carry out temporary modifications that will only affect the task which they directly precede. The nonstarred versions will affect all tasks on the run and therefore must precede the first set of task-definition cards. Furthermore, the insertion of a SAVE FILE card before the FINISH card, when permanent modifications are being made, will create a new SPSS system file which will contain all modifications generated on that run as well as that portion of the data from the original file that has not been modified. This SAVE FILE card enables the user to save a new file in which the newly generated, transformed, or recoded variables are actually inserted into the file with each case containing its appropriate values for these variables.[1] Recodes and transformations of existing variables replace the existing values for these variables. Newly generated variables are inserted in the file being saved in the order in which they were created, following the last existing variable. If the user wishes to have a data modification stay in effect through the entire set of tasks on a given run but does not wish to generate a new file, he can use a permanent (nonstarred) data-modification card and simply omit the SAVE FILE card at the end of the run.

### 8.2.4 DATA DEFINITION FOR VARIABLE TRANSFORMATIONS: DATA-DEFINITION CARDS FOR NEWLY GENERATED OR MODIFIED VARIABLES

The RECODE card causes the values of existing variables to be altered, while both the IF and COMPUTE cards can introduce new variables. Missing values, value labels, and print formats can be provided for variables that are altered or created by a permanent variable transformation. The following sections indicate how data-definition cards can be created for these variables.

#### 8.2.4.1 Defining missing values for transformed variables

Any variable which has a value assigned to it by means of a COMPUTE or IF statement, as well as any variable modified by a RECODE, may have a set of missing values associated with it. To inform the system of the missing values for any given variable, the user must prepare a MISSING VALUES card. The format of this card is identical to the MISSING VALUES card described in Sec. 4.7. These MISSING VALUES cards should be placed after the data modification cards and before the procedure card to which they apply. In the case of a temporary transformation (*COMPUTE, *IF, or *RECODE), the user should be aware that declarations of missing values will remain in effect after the next procedure; consequently, the user may find it necessary to redeclare the normal missing values for the variables in question.

#### 8.2.4.2 Initialization of transformed variables

A problem can arise when a variable is created through a transformation, especially an IF or a *IF. The problem is that the value of the variable is undefined until a transformation assigns one. In the case of a series of IF or *IF statements, it is possible that no value will be assigned. In order to provide consistent results for those cases in which the user's transformations assign no value, the SPSS system "initializes" each variable which is created through transformations. The process of initialization consists of assigning a specific value to each such variable before applying any of the transformations. This initialization process is performed for each case. The value used for initialization is the first missing value declared for the specific variable. If the user has declared no missing values for a given variable, this variable will be initialized to whatever value a constant known as TMISS had at the time the variable was declared. Note that the applicable value of TMISS is the one this constant had at the point of declaration rather than at the time of initialization. Until the user provides a different value, TMISS is set to zero. If the user wishes to alter the value of TMISS, he enters a TMISS card of format

```
1                         16
TMISS                     value
```

where the value in the specification field is the value to which TMISS should be set. The TMISS card may be entered at any position in the card deck before or during the data-modification cards, so that TMISS can be different for different sets of transformations.

A proper understanding of the SPSS initialization procedure is very useful in answering the following two questions:

1.  Why are 50 percent of the cases for this table missing?

---

[1]If a system file is to be retained, the user must remember to prepare an FT04 JCL card for his output system file (see Appendix F).

2.  How can the (stupid) system report that 50 percent of the cases result in a value of zero for this variable when I never assign zero as a value?

In both cases, the answer is likely to be that the logic of the user's IF or *IF statements is such that no value was assigned to the variable in question.

In one sense, the TMISS constant is a default value; that is, it exists because the system may encounter a case which does not satisfy the logical expression(s). In another sense it may be used as a specific value, as in the following IF card:

```
1                 16
TMISS             9
IF                (VARA NE 9 AND VARB NE 9)VARC = VARA*VARB
```

In this example, the user is specifying the conditions under which cases will take the value 9 for VARC. But note that if the system encounters a case where both VARA and VARB equal 3, that the value computed for VARC will also be 9, and as such will take the same value as cases which do not satisfy the logical expression. The user can avoid this kind of problem through careful selection of the value for TMISS.

Note that the initialization procedure applies only to variables which are created as the result of transformations and specifically does not apply to variables which already exist in the user's file. In the latter case, the existing value is not altered prior to applying the transformation.

### 8.2.4.3   Inserting other data-defining information for transformed variables

A new file name, variable labels, value labels, and print formats may also be defined for transformed variables in the same manner and on the same cards as are used when creating any SPSS file or when altering data-defining information for any SPSS variable (see the sections on the use and alteration of data-definition cards). These new cards, along with the new MISSING VALUES card, directly follow the variable transformations to which they are to apply, and may be placed in any internal order; however, they (unlike the MISSING VALUES card) *must* precede the first set of task-definition cards, as must all permanent data-modification cards. All data-defining information will be retained if a new file is created by means of the SAVE FILE card. These cards may not be used with temporary transformations.

Example 8.3 illustrates the deck setup, including data-definition cards, for processing from an existing SPSS system file and creating an updated file to be saved under a new name at the end of the run.

**EXAMPLE 8.3**

```
1                 16
GET FILE          EXAMPLEA
FILE NAME         UPDATEA,UPDATED FILE FOR EXAMPLEA
IF                (INCOME-(FAMSIZE*600) LE 3000) REALINC=1
IF                ((INCOME-(FAMSIZE*600) GT 3000) AND
                  (INCOME-(FAMSIZE*600) LE 6000)) REALINC=2
IF                (INCOME-(FAMSIZE*600) GT 6000) REALINC =3
VAR LABELS        REALINC,REAL INCOME CONTROLLED FOR FAMSIZE
VALUE LABELS      REALINC (1)UNDER $3000 (2)$3000 TO $6000 (3) OVER $6000
                  (9) DATA MISSING
PRINT FORMAT      REALINC (0)
CROSSTABS         REALINC BY RACE
OPTIONS           1,5
STATISTICS        ALL
SAVE FILE
FINISH
```

## 8.3   LIMITATIONS ON THE COMPUTE AND IF CARDS

If either or both of the following limitations on COMPUTE and IF cards are exceeded, an error message number will be printed at the point at which the limitation(s) was violated. The syntax of the remainder of the control cards of that processing step will be checked and the run terminated. The limitations apply jointly to all permanent and temporary COMPUTE, IF, and

SELECT IF cards which apply in a given statistical procedure. [The SELECT IF card, which is used to specify logical conditions for the selection of cases for processing, has not yet been explained; however, its format is almost identical to the IF card, and it is processed and evaluated by the same SPSS processing routines; for this reason, it must be included in establishing the limitations. The number and size of SELECT IF statements are usually quite small and will therefore seldom add much toward overflowing the limitations. Nevertheless, the SELECT IF cards are included in the limitations (see Sec. 9.2.).]

1. The sum of all operators on COMPUTE, IF, and SELECT IF statements (temporary and permanent) which precede a given task (procedure card) must not exceed 1,000.
   (a) Each use of the logical operators (EQ, NE, GT, LT, LE, and GE) counts as one operator.
   (b) Each use of one of the relational operators (AND, OR, and NOT) counts as one operator.
   (c) Each use of one of the arithmetic operators [**, *, +, −, /] counts as one operator.
2. The sum of the number of RECODE card plus COMPUTE statements plus 2 times the number of IF or SELECT IF statements must not exceed the value 250. Each RECODE card or COMPUTE statement is counted as 1; each IF or SELECT IF statement is counted as 2; and the sum of these values for all statements (temporary and/or permanent) preceding any individual task must not exceed the value 250.

## 8.4     DECK SETUP AND CARD ORDER FOR DATA-MODIFICATION CARDS

The following rules govern the placement and order of data-modification cards in the SPSS control-card deck. Permanent data-modification cards must be placed after the initial data-definition cards and before the first set of task-definition cards whenever processing is from cards or a BCD tape. When processing from a system file, the permanent data-modification cards must follow the GET FILE card and appear before the first set of task-definition cards. All data-definition cards applying to variables created or altered by permanent COMPUTE, IF, and/or RECODE cards should follow the actual transformation statements but must precede the first set of task-definition cards. Temporary or starred (*) data-modification cards may be placed before any set of task-definition cards. However, if both temporary and permanent data-modification cards are used before the first task or procedure, the permanent cards *must* precede the temporary ones. Therefore, permanent and temporary transformation statements, be they COMPUTE's, IF's, or RECODE's, may not be interleaved in the control-card deck, and the former must always come before the latter.

Within these limitations COMPUTE, IF, and RECODE statements either temporary or permanent may appear in any order the user desires. The effects of all data-modification statements are cumulative. This means that a COMPUTE card altering the values of an existing variable or creating a vew variable will be in effect from that point on for all other COMPUTE, IF, or RECODE cards which may utilize that variable. A new variable, for example, may be created by means of a COMPUTE statement. A set of logical conditions may be applied to that variable by means of one or more IF cards, and this new variable may then be recoded by the insertion of a RECODE card. Similarly, the values of an existing variable may be modified by a RECODE card, and a new variable may then be constructed with either COMPUTE or IF statements employing the recoded values of the variable. It is important to remember two points: first, all data-modification cards are executed in the order of their appearance, and second, all data-modification cards are cumulative in effect. The permanent data-modification cards are cumulative in another respect—they affect the computations of all tasks on a given run, and if a SAVE FILE card is inserted and a new or updated file is generated, the results of these computations are then permanently recorded in the file. The deck setup in Example 8.4 for a run input on BCD tape includes both permanent and temporary modification cards, as well as the data-definition cards defining the transformations. Note that the permanently transformed variables will be saved at the end of the run. The temporary transformed variables will of course not be retained.

**EXAMPLE 8.4**

```
1                16
RUN NAME         EXAMPLE DECK SETUP FOR DATA MODIFICATION CARDS
FILE NAME        TESTFILE
VARIABLE LIST    VAR001 TO VAR010
INPUT MEDIUM     TAPE
# OF CASES       150
INPUT FORMAT     FIXED (10F2.0)
MISSING VALUES   VAR001 TO VAR010 (0,9)
VALUE LABELS     VAR001 (1) 1 THRU 10 (2) 11 THRU 20 (3) 21 THRU 30 (4) 31
                 THRU 40 (5) 41 THRU 99/VAR002 (1) 1 THRU 10 (2) 11 THRU 20
                 (3) 21 THRU 30 (4) 31 THRU 40 (5) 41 THRU 99/VAR003 (1) YES
                 (2) NO/VAR004 (1) MALE (2) FEMALE/VAR005 (1) UNDER ONE YEAR
                 (2) 1 TO 5 YEARS (3) OVER 5 YEARS/VAR006 (1) 0 THRU 5 (2)
                 6 THRU 10 (3) 11 THRU 25 (4) 26 THRU 50 (5) 51 THRU 99/VAR007
                 (1) NONE (2) ONE OR MORE/VAR008 (1) OWN (2) RENT (3) OTHER/
                 VAR009 (1) YES (2) NO/VAR010 (1) YES (2) NO
PRINT FORMATS    VAR001 TO VAR010 (0)
COMPUTE          NEWVAR = VAR001/VAR002
IF               (NEWVAR GT 0 AND NEWVAR LT 1) NEWVAR=VAR002/VAR001
RECODE           NEWVAR (1 THRU 4.99=1)(4.99 THRU 9.99=2)(9.99 THRU 99=3)
*RECODE          VAR006 (0 THRU 10=1)(11 THRU 99=2)
MISSING VALUES   NEWVAR(0)
VAR LABELS       NEWVAR,CONTINGENT INVERTED VARIABLE
VALUE LABELS     NEWVAR (1) LOW (2) MEDIUM (3) HIGH
CROSSTABS        NEWVAR BY VAR006
OPTIONS          1,4,5
STATISTICS       ALL
READ INPUT DATA
SAVE FILE
FINISH
```

Example 8.5 illustrates deck setup when processing from an SPSS system file and saving the updated file at the conclusion of the run.

**EXAMPLE 8.5**

```
1                16
GET FILE         TESTFILE
COMPUTE          NEWVAR=VAR001/VAR002
IF               (NEWVAR GT 0 AND NEWVAR LT 1) NEWVAR=VAR002/VAR001
RECODE           NEWVAR (1 THRU 4.99=1)(4.99 THRU 9.99=2)(9.99 THRU 999=3)
*RECODE          VAR006 (0 THRU 10=1)(11 THRU 99=2)
MISSING VALUES   NEWVAR(0)
VAR LABELS       NEWVAR,CONTINGENT INVERTED VARIABLE
VALUE LABELS     NEWVAR (1) LOW (2) MEDIUM (3) HIGH
NONPAR CORR      VAR001 TO VAR005 WITH VAR006 TO NEWVAR
OPTIONS          1
STATISTICS       ALL
SAVE FILE
FINISH
```

# 9
# THE DATA-SELECTION CARDS

Many instances arise in social science research where the user wishes to effect the selection of cases from his file. There may be times in dealing with large files when the researcher wishes to draw a random sample of his cases in order to save expensive machine time; or he may wish to weight certain portions of the sample to estimate population parameters; or he may wish to select some specified subgroup of his sample for analysis. The three *data-selection cards* SAMPLE, SELECT IF, and WEIGHT provide the SPSS system with the capability of sampling, weighting, and selecting cases from the user's file. Each card exists in both a permanent form and a temporary, or starred, form (SAMPLE, *SAMPLE; SELECT IF, *SELECT IF; and WEIGHT, *WEIGHT). They provide the user with the ability to create permanent files of sampled, selected, or weighted cases and to temporarily effect these changes for use with some particular subprogram within the system.

## 9.1   GENERATING A RANDOM SAMPLE FROM A FILE: THE SAMPLE AND *SAMPLE CARDS

The SAMPLE card provides a means for taking a random sample from a file for processing. It is useful when the researcher is presented with a file of such size that a smaller random sample of the file may still produce statistically significant results at far less cost. Its general format is

| 1 | 16 |
|---|---|
| SAMPLE | factor |

where factor is a decimal number less than 1.0 which indicates the percentage of the file which the researcher wants to analyze. For instance, a factor of 0.10 would result in a 10 percent or 1 in 10 sample of the entire file:

```
1            16
SAMPLE       0.10
```

    When a nonstarred or permanent SAMPLE card is being used, the user may generate an SPSS system file containing only the sampled cases by inserting a SAVE FILE card at the end of the run. The permanent SAMPLE card must precede the first set of task-definition cards and is in effect for the entire run, while the *SAMPLE card may precede any set of task-definition cards, but will apply only to that specific task. The sampling procedure used by SPSS is set up in such a way that a different random sample will be selected each time the user requests a sample by means of a SAMPLE or *SAMPLE card. For a complete discussion on the order of the SAMPLE and *SAMPLE cards in the deck, see Sec. 9.4 on deck setup.

## 9.2   SELECTING CASES FROM A FILE: THE SELECT IF AND *SELECT IF CARDS

The SELECT IF card provides the facility for processing only those cases for which certain criteria are met. For instance, the researcher can select only those respondents to a questionnaire who gave their race as Negro, and he must bypass all other cases. The SELECT IF card resembles the IF card; its general format is

| 1 | 16 |
|---|---|
| SELECT IF | (logical expression) |

The logical expression appearing in the specification field is constructed in the manner described in Sec. 8.2.2. and is enclosed in parentheses. an example is

```
1            16
SELECT IF    (RACE EQ 2 OR RACE EQ 4)
```

This card would result in the selection of only those cases in which the value of the variable RACE is either 2 or 4. A somewhat more complex example is

```
1            16
SELECT IF    ((RACE EQ 2 OR RACE EQ 4) AND AGE-LRES GT 20)
```

This card would select all cases in which the variable RACE has a value of 2 or 4 and in which the difference between age and length of residence (variable LRES) is greater than 20.

    When a nonstarred SELECT IF card is being used, the user may generate an SPSS system file containing only the selected cases by inserting a SAVE FILE card at the end of the run. Such a permanent SELECT IF card must precede the first set of task-definition cards and will remain in effect for the entire run, while the *SELECT IF card may precede any set of task-definition cards, but will apply only to that specific task. For a complete discussion on the order of the SELECT IF and *SELECT IF cards in the deck, see Sec. 9.4 on deck setup.

## 9.3   WEIGHTING CASES IN A FILE: THE WEIGHT AND *WEIGHT CARDS

If the researcher is confronted with a sample which requires weighting (i.e., one in which some substratum of the population has been over- or undersampled), he may wish to use the SPSS weighting process to be able to estimate population parameters. The weighting procedure allows each individual case to be considered or *weighted* more or less heavily than other cases. Specifically, a researcher can have a mixed number associated with each case, indicating how much weight is to be given that case when it is processed by a statistical procedure.

The weighting is accomplished by defining a variable which has a value for each case equal to the weighting factor required for a case containing its attributes. In some instances, researchers precode this weighting factor onto each case as part of preparing the data for analysis. Alternatively, a weighting variable can be generated by means of a series of COMPUTE and IF cards allocating the proper weights for each type of case or respondent. The actual weighting is accomplished by a card containing the control word WEIGHT followed by the name of the variable which contains the weighting information. When the cases are processed, the value of that variable determines how heavily that case will be considered or weighted for any given table or statistical procedure. The format of the WEIGHT card is then as follows:

```
1                  16
WEIGHT             variable name
```

This WEIGHT card format is used where the variable name in the specification field refers to a variable which has as its value the weight of the specific case. Normally, the researcher will not have this variable precoded and, therefore, must define the weighting variable and the weighting conditions by means of a series of COMPUTE and IF statements. The following example demonstrates the creation of such a weighting variable as well as the WEIGHT card which would have the weighting actually executed.

Suppose that a researcher had conducted a study of Negro housing conditions in a given state. Let us further suppose that because of his research focus and limited resources, he designed a sample in which he heavily undersampled urban whites and to a lesser degree undersampled rural whites. This type of sample is often drawn when one desires to do intensive analysis of some subpopulation, in this case Negroes, and to use other segments, e.g. whites, as only control groups.

Situations may emerge in the course of analysis, however, when the researcher wishes to estimate population parameters or to establish relationships requiring population parameters. Let us assume that the sample has been drawn so that each urban white must be weighted 2.5 times and each rural white 1.5 times for the sample to estimate the real population parameters. Let us further assume that a variable called RACE has been defined and coded so that Negroes have the value 1 and whites 2, and that another variable called TOWNSIZE has also been defined, so that citizens living in rural areas are coded 1 on the variable, while those in urban areas are coded 2. In order to define a weighting variable and actually weight the file, the following cards would be required:

```
1              16
IF             (RACE EQ 1) WTFACTOR = 1
IF             (RACE EQ 2 AND TOWNSIZE EQ 1) WTFACTOR = 1.5
IF             (RACE EQ 2 AND TOWNSIZE EQ 2) WTFACTOR = 2.5
WEIGHT         WTFACTOR
```

Note that in this case, all Negroes will be counted as the base weighting factor of 1. Rural whites will be weighted by a factor of 1.5, while urban whites will be weighted by a factor of 2.5. The choice of the name of the weighting factor (in this case WTFACTOR) is totally arbitrary, and the user may select any variable name as long as it follows the rules and conventions of variable names for SPSS.

The weighting is accomplished by means of fractional counters, so that any weighting factor may be used which can be expressed in terms of a decimal number, a whole number, or a whole number plus a decimal number. The weight given to a case determines the extent to which it adds to the totals being collected. In crosstabulations, for example, a case containing the weight of 1.67 will result in 1.67 being added to the total number of respondents considered in building the table and in 1.67 being added to the total number of respondents who occur in a specific cell of that table. To facilitate legibility, all counts are rounded to the nearest whole number before being reported on tables. For the sake of accuracy, however, all statistics which are not dependent upon whole numbers are calculated on the basis of the accumulated fractional numbers. Owing to the mechanics of rounding, the reported number of respondents may vary from one statistical procedure to another. The extent of this *rounding error* is exceedingly small and has been observed to amount to a difference of a single case in a file of 3,000 original cases.

Weighting may be done either permanently by means of the WEIGHT card or temporarily (in conjunction with a specific statistical procedure) by the *WEIGHT card. As usual, the format of these two cards is identical.

When a nonstarred WEIGHT card is being used, the user may generate a permanent SPSS system file containing the case weights by inserting a SAVE FILE card at the conclusion of the run. The permanent WEIGHT card must precede the first set of task-definition cards and will remain in effect for the entire run, while the *WEIGHT card may precede any set of task-definition cards, but will apply only to that specific task. The WEIGHT card should appear after all permanent data-modification cards, and the *WEIGHT card follows all of the temporary data-modification cards. A more complete discussion on the card order and deck setup of the WEIGHT and *WEIGHT cards appears in Sec. 9.4.

System files which have been weighted automatically report all statistics and cases based on the weighting factors assigned by the user. This is accomplished by means of a permanent and automatic variable called CASWGT which is automatically generated whenever permanent weighting is requested. This variable, like SEQNUM and SUBFIL, is available for the user to use. It should, however, never be *permanently* altered, for the results may be disastrous. If the user wishes to process an unweighted system file after permanent weightings have been assigned, a sequence of cards of the following type will suppress the weighting of the file for a given run:

```
1              16
COMPUTE        DUMMYVAR = 1.0
WEIGHT         DUMMYVAR
```

Note also that the weights can be temporarily suppressed for a given task by the use of the same cards as above where both the COMPUTE and the WEIGHT cards would be of the starred [*] rather than the permanent type.

The user should further be aware that weighting is noncumulative. New weights may be assigned to a file that is already weighted, and this results in replacing the existing weights and *not* by multiplying existing weights by new weights.

There are some procedures which cannot operate on fractional cases. For instance, nonparametric correlations, as well as writing out BCD cases, require integral weights. In these instances, an alternative weighting procedure is used. This weighting procedure involves reproducing the case as many times as the whole number in the weight indicates and reproducing some fraction of cases of this type with the probability equal to the size of the fraction. For example, if the weight of a particular type of case is specified as 2.5, all such cases will be included twice, and approximately 50 percent of these types of cases will be included an additional time. The write-ups of the individual procedures which use this alternative method of weighting contain further information concerning this procedure.

## 9.4 DECK SETUP AND CARD ORDER FOR DATA-SELECTION CARDS

As a group, the data-selection cards have the following order if used simultaneously: SAMPLE, SELECT IF, and WEIGHT. The cards are evaluated so that a random sample can be drawn, further selected cases can be drawn from this sample, and specified weights can be given to these sampled and selected cases. The user may *not* permanently select and then sample or weight and then select or sample on the same processing run. The starred data-selection cards have the exact same precedence order, but must follow all permanent data-selection cards; therefore, it is possible to do a permanent weighting and a temporary sample or selection on the same run.

The temporary selection cards may precede any set of task-definition cards, while all permanent selection cards must precede the first set of task-definition cards.

When data-selection cards and data-modification cards are used in the same run, the order of precedence shown in Table 9.1 must be used in inserting the cards into the control-card deck. Any combination of temporary or permanent versions of these cards may be used as long as the rules of order are not violated. These rules of order or precedence should be viewed as rankings in which no card of a lower rank may precede a card of higher rank.

**TABLE 9.1    Order or rank of data-selection and data-modification cards**

| Card type | Rank |
|-----------|------|
| SAMPLE | 1 (highest rank) |
| SELECT IF | 2 |
| RECODE | 2 |
| COMPUTE | 2 |
| IF | 2 |
| WEIGHT | 3 |
| *SAMPLE | 4 |
| *SELECT IF | 5 |
| *RECODE | 5 |
| *COMPUTE | 5 |
| *IF | 5 |
| *WEIGHT | 6 (lowest rank) |

Examples 9.1. and 9.2 demonstrate the position of each of the data-selection cards, as well as that of the data-modification cards, first for a run in which data is being entered from cards or BCD tape, and second, for a run processed from a previously existing SPSS file.

**EXAMPLE 9.1**

```
1               16
RUN NAME        EXAMPLE DECK SETUP FOR DATA SELECTION CARDS
FILE NAME       TESTFILE
VARIABLE LIST   VAR001 TO VAR010
SUBFILE LIST    SBFILEA,SBFILEB,SBFILEC
INPUT MEDIUM    DISK
INPUT FORMAT    FIXED (8X,10F1.0)
# OF CASES      150 220 139
MISSING VALUES  VAR001 TO VAR010 (0,9)
VALUE LABELS    VAR001,VAR002 (1) 1 THRU 10 (2) 11 THRU 20 (3) 21 THRU 30
                (4) 31 THRU 40 (5) 41 THRU 99 (9) DON'T KNOW (0) NO ANSWER/
                VAR003 (1) YES (2) NO (9) DON'T KNOW (0) NO ANSWER/VAR004 (1)
                MALE (2) FEMALE (9)DON'T KNOW (0) NO ANSWER/VAR005 (1) UNDER ONE
                YEAR (2) 1 TO 5 YEARS (3) OVER 5 YEARS (9) DON'T KNOW (0) NO
                ANSWER/VAR006 (1) 0 THRU 5 (2) 6 THRU 10 (3) 11 THRU 25 (4) 26
                THRU 50 (5)51 THRU 99 (9) DON'T KNOW (0) NO ANSWER/VAR007 (1)
                NONE (2) ONE OR MORE (9) DON'T KNOW (0) NO ANSWER/VAR008 (1) OWN
                (2)RENT (3) OTHER (9) DON'T KNOW (0) NO ANSWER/ VAR009,VAR010
                (1) YES (2) NO (9) DON'T KNOW (0) NO ANSWER
PRINT FORMATS   VAR001 TO VAR010 (0)
SAMPLE          0.10
COMPUTE         NEWVAR=VAR001/VAR002
IF              (NEWVAR GT 0 AND NEWVAR LT 1) NEWVAR=VAR002/VAR001
SELECT IF       (VAR004 EQ 1 AND VAR005 EQ 3)
COMPUTE         WTFACTOR=1
IF              (VAR008 EQ 2) WTFACTOR=1.20
WEIGHT          WTFACTOR
RECODE          NEWVAR (1 THRU 4.99=1)(4.99 THRU 9.99=2)(9.99 THRU 99=3)
MISSING VALUES  NEWVAR (0)
VAR LABELS      NEWVAR,CONTINGENT INVERTED VARIABLE
VALUE LABELS    NEWVAR (1) LOW (2) MEDIUM (3) HIGH
PROCESS SBFILESALL
CROSSTABS       NEWVAR BY VAR006
OPTIONS         1,4,5
STATISTICS      ALL
READ INPUT DATA
*SAMPLE         0.50
*COMPUTE        WTFACTOR2=1
*IF             (VAR007 EQ 2) WTFACTOR=1.4
*WEIGHT         WTFACTOR
PROCESS SBFILESALL
NONPAR CORR     VAR001 TO VAR007 WITH VAR006 TO NEWVAR
OPTIONS         1
STATISTICS      ALL
SAVE FILE
FINISH
```

**EXAMPLE 9.2**

```
1               16
GET FILE        TESTFILE
SAMPLE          0.10
COMPUTE         NEWVAR=VAR001/VAR002
IF              (VAR008 EQ 2) WTFACTOR=1.20
WEIGHT          WTFACTOR
FILE NAME       UPDATE
MISSING VALUES  NEWVAR (0)
VAR LABELS      NEWVAR,CONTINGENT INVERTED VARIABLE
VALUE LABELS    NEWVAR (1) LOW (2) MEDIUM (3) HIGH
PROCESS SBFILESALL
CROSSTABS       NEWVAR BY VAR006
OPTIONS         1,4,5
STATISTICS      ALL
*SAMPLE         0.50
*COMPUTE        WTFACTR2=1
*IF             (VAR007 EQ 2) WTFACTR2=1.4
*WEIGHT         WTFACTR2
PROCESS SBFILESALL
NONPAR CORR     VAR001 TO VAR007 WITH VAR006 TO NEWVAR
OPTIONS         1
STATISTICS      ALL
SAVE FILE
FINISH
```

# 10
# ALTERING DATA IN AN SPSS SYSTEM FILE:
# THE FILE-MODIFICATION CARDS

The *data-modification cards* enable the user to modify the data in his file based on the existing variables and the existing values associated with the variables. The *data-selection cards* permit the user to select from or differentially weight the cases in his file. The *file-modification cards* described in this chapter permit the user to actually add data to or delete data from an existing SPSS system file. These file-modification cards provide the user with the capability of performing the following file updating and maintenance functions:

1. Adding variables which may be input from cards or any other BCD medium, such as tape or disk, to an existing SPSS system file.
2. Adding cases to an existing SPSS system file by means of adding one or more subfiles which may also be input from cards or other BCD media.
3. Deleting or retaining selected variables from an SPSS system file.
4. Deleting or retaining specific subfiles from an SPSS system file containing a larger number of subfiles.
5. Outputting some or all of the variables contained in an SPSS system file in BCD form onto cards, tape, disk, etc., for input into other programs.

## 10.1    DELETING AND RETAINING VARIABLES: THE DELETE VARS AND KEEP VARS CARDS

Situations often arise during data analysis where the researcher wishes to intensively analyze some subset of variables in his file. Furthermore, experimentation with index constructions through variable transformations may also cause files to grow, containing far more variables than the researcher is presently utilizing.

Whenever these or other circumstances cause the user to desire a system file which contains only some subset of variables in his present file, a new or updated system file may be retained containing only those variables he presently desires for analysis.[1]

A system file consisting of some subset of the variables from a larger file can be obtained by utilizing either the DELETE VARS or KEEP VARS card in conjunction with the SAVE FILE card. The DELETE VARS card contains the control words DELETE VARS followed by a variable name or a list of variable names that the user wishes deleted from his file. The format of the DELETE VARS card is

```
1                16
DELETE VARS      ⎧ variable name ⎫
                 ⎨      or        ⎬
                 ⎩ variable list  ⎭
```

where the variable list is the list of variables to be deleted when the new file is saved. This variable list may contain individual variable names, lists of variable names implied by the usual TO convention or a mixture of the two types of conventions. As usual, the variable list may continue from one physical card to the next as long as columns 1 to 15 of all cards following the first are left blank. Remember, no individual variable name may be split between two physical cards. If there is insufficient space to complete a variable name on a given card, the remainder of the card should be left blank and the variable name should begin in column 16 of a new card. The following DELETE VARS card would cause variables AGE, INCOME, VAR001 to VAR010, and EDUCATN to be deleted when a new file is saved. All other variables in the file will remain in the new or updated file in their original sequence.

```
1                16
DELETE VARS      AGE,INCOME,VAR001 TO VAR010,EDUCATN
```

The KEEP VARS card is closely associated with the DELETE VARS card and serves the exact same function. In this instance, however, the control words KEEP VARS are followed by a list of variables which the user wishes retained in his new or updated file. Those variables not appearing on the list of variables to be kept will be deleted when the new file is saved. The KEEP VARS card has exactly the same format as the DELETE VARS card and exists only to minimize control-card preparation when it is easier for the user to list the variables he desires to retain rather than those he wishes to delete. The format of the KEEP VARS card is

```
1                16
KEEP VARS        ⎧ variable name ⎫
                 ⎨      or        ⎬
                 ⎩ variable list  ⎭
```

It is important to note that all variables which are in the existing file are available throughout the run on which a DELETE VARS or KEEP VARS card is present. In the case of both of these cards, implicit or explicit attempts to delete the three implicit variables (SEQNUM, SUBFIL, and CASWGT) will be disregarded.

The DELETE VARS or KEEP VARS card (whichever is being used) is placed immediately before the SAVE FILE card. It is also a good practice to insert a FILE NAME card giving a new file name and label to the updated file.

---

[1]Creation of files with a smaller number of variables in them will often result in considerable saving in the minimum machine time required to process a system file.

Example 10.1 illustrates the deck setup and card order for a run using the DELETE VARS card. Note that data-selection cards, data-modification cards, and new data-definition cards may be used as usual when employing a DELETE VARS or KEEP VARS card. Note also that the CROSSTABS card, as well as the COMPUTE and SELECT IF card, makes reference to several variables which appear on the DELETE VARS card; as previously indicated, *all* variables existing in the initial file are available for the entire run.

**EXAMPLE 10.1**

```
1                16
RUN NAME         SAVING A NEW SYSTEM FILE - DELETING SOME VARIABLES
GET FILE         EXAMPLE1
FILE NAME        NEWEX1,NEW FILE DELETING VARIABLES FROM FILE EXAMPLE1
COMPUTE          NEWVAR = (VARA + SCALE1)/FACTOR6
SELECT IF        (SEX EQ 1)
MISSING VALUES   NEWVAR(0)
VAR LABELS       NEWVAR,NEW COMPOSITE VARIABLE
CROSSTABS        AGE,SEX BY VARA TO NEWVAR
DELETE VARS      AGE,SEX,SCALE1 TO SCALE8,FACTOR6
SAVE FILE
FINISH
```

## 10.2　ADDING VARIABLES TO AN EXISTING SPSS SYSTEM FILE: THE ADD VARIABLES CARD

Occasionally the situation arises when the researcher wishes to add new variables to an existing SPSS system file. It may be that he wishes to merge two independent files of data gathered on the same units of analysis; e.g., the voting records of countries in the United Nations with aggregate data on their population characteristics. Or the researcher may have accidentally ignored a variable when an SPSS system file was generated and now finds that he wants this variable included in a new system file.

Whatever the reason, new variables may be added to the existing variables in a file by means of the **ADD VARIABLES** card whenever *all* of the following conditions are met:

1.　There must be a one-to-one correspondence between the number and order of cases in the system file, and the number and order of the cases carrying the variables to be added. This means that there must be exactly the same number of cases, and the cases must be in exactly the same sequential order as they were when the initial system file was generated.
2.　If the system file has a subfile structure, the number, order, and size of each of the subfiles, as well as the cases written in them, must be in total agreement in the two files.
3.　The sum of the number of variables to be added and the number of variables already in the system file must not exceed 500.

If all the above conditions have been met, the user may add variables to an existing file and save a new updated SPSS system file containing the variables from the previous system file plus the variables being added. The variables are added by means of a card containing the control words **ADD VARIABLES** followed by a list of variable names to be added to the card. The general format of the **ADD VARIABLES** card is

```
1                16
ADD VARIABLES    variable list
```

The conventions for entering variable names on this card correspond *precisely* to the conventions used on the VARIABLE LIST card, which is used to initially define variables being entered into the file (see Sec. 4.2 and particularly the summary rules at the end of that section). The user should be particularly careful to make sure that he does not violate the following conventions:

1.　Variables being added must have names which are not only unique vis-à-vis each other, but unique in terms of the variables already in the file.
2.　The user must take care to ensure that the sequence of the variable names on the ADD VARIABLES card corresponds to the order of the variables on the cases.

3. All other rules and conventions concerning the spelling, spacing of variable names, and the continuation of variable lists onto more than one physical card (spelled out in Sec. 4.2) must be followed.

The ADD VARIABLES card directly follows the GET FILE card. The following data-definition cards must appear on all runs on which the user is adding variables and should be inserted directly behind the ADD VARIABLES card:

1. An INPUT MEDIUM card specifies the medium on which the new variables are to be found. This card is prepared in exactly the same manner as described in Sec. 4.5 and, as indicated there, the data may be entered from cards, BCD tape, BCD disk files, etc.[1]
2. An INPUT FORMAT card containing the input format specification for the *new* variables is needed. This card is to be prepared exactly as described in Sec. 4.6.
3. A READ INPUT DATA card must be prepared also and is inserted into the control-card deck directly after the first procedure card and its associated OPTIONS and STATISTICS cards. This is one of the very few instances where a READ INPUT DATA card is required on a run using an SPSS system file.

The INPUT FORMAT card may, if the user desires, be followed by MISSING VALUES cards (Sec. 4.7), VAR LABELS cards (Sec. 4.10), VALUE LABELS cards (Sec. 4.8), and PRINT FORMATS cards (Sec. 4.9). As usual, PRINT FORMATS cards are optional for numeric variables but are required for alphanumeric variables which are not immediately converted. All of the data-definition cards are prepared in a manner identical to that presented in the cross-reference sections above.

Notice that a # OF CASES card and the SUBFILE LIST card *are specifically not to be prepared,* since the subfile structure and the number of cases are available in the file and *must be identical* to the information contained there.

Data modification and/or data selection can be accomplished on runs in which the user is adding variables as long as there is initially a one-to-one correspondence between the cases in the system file and those being input. Data modifications and data selections must therefore be performed after the new variables being added have been defined. Thus, *all cards accomplishing data modification or data selection must be placed after the data-definition cards defining the variables being added.*

The most critical problem encountered in adding variables and generating a new system file is ensuring that the variables are being added to the right cases. It was for reasons such as this that we strongly suggested that users include a case-identification number as one of the variables in any system file (see Sec. 2.2.3.3). If the user has a case-identification number defined as a variable in the file as well as one coded on the cases carrying the variables to be added, it is an easy matter to perform a comparison to ensure that the new variables are being added to the proper cases. If this information does not exist, the user can achieve a less powerful check by reentering some variable (under a new name, of course) which already exists in the file and performing a comparison between the two variables. The more likely such a variable is to assign a unique value to each case, the better the check will be. If neither of these procedures is possible, the user should be very sure he knows the exact order of the cases when the system file was initially created before attempting to add variables.

When the user has case-identification numbers defined in the present system file and on the cases carrying the variables to be added, the following set of IF cards will produce a check if the user enters this variable into CODEBOOK, MARGINALS, CROSSTABS, or FASTABS on the run creating the new system file. Similar cards would be used to check duplicate variables.

```
1               16
*IF             (CASEID EQ NEWID) CHECKVAR = 1
*IF             (CASEID NE NEWID) CHECKVAR = -1
MARGINALS       CHECKVAR
```

---

[1]If the INPUT MEDIUM specifies a medium other than CARD, the user must be sure to prepare JCL cards for the BCD input file FT08 (see Appendix F as well as Sec. 4.5).

In the example above, CASEID is the variable name for the case-identification number in the system file; NEWID is the variable name given to the case-identification number of the cases carrying the variables to be added. A temporary transformation is executed setting a temporary variable CHECKVAR equal to 1 when the two case IDS are equal and to −1 when they are not equal. If the frequency distribution requested by the MARGINALS card reveals that all cases have a value of 1 for variable CHECKVAR, the user has assurance that the variables were added to the right cases. If there is any case which contains a value of −1 for variable CHECKVAR, then the user knows that at least one case is out of sequence, contains the wrong identification number, etc.

Example 10.2 demonstrates the deck setup when adding cases to a file. Note that several of the variables that are being added are immediately used to generate a set of marginal frequencies. Note also that several alphanumeric variables that have been added are being converted to numeric variables and the cases are being assigned weights before the new file is saved. Further, the suggested check is being performed and the redundant case-identification variable is being deleted. The file is also being saved under a new name—a practice we highly recommend.

The JCL required for this run would be somewhat complicated. JCL cards must be prepared for the input system file FT03 on which present variables reside; JCL cards would also be required for the input BCD file FT08 which is, in this case, a tape containing the variables to be added. JCL must also be prepared for the output system file FT04 which will be the new system file containing all of the variables.

**EXAMPLE 10.2**

```
1                 16
RUN NAME          EXAMPLE RUN ADDING VARIABLES FROM BCD TAPE
GET FILE          STUDYA
ADD VARIABLES     NEWCASID,INCOME2,LOCVOTE,NMEM,NACT,VAR006 TO VAR029
INPUT MEDIUM      TAPE
INPUT FORMAT      FIXED (F3.0,1X,4F1.0,24A1)
FILE NAME         STUDYA2,SECOND VERSION OF STUDYA WITH ALL VARIABLES
VAR LABELS        INCOME2,SUPPLEMENTAL INCOME/LOCVOTE,VOTE IN LAST LOCAL
                  ELECTION/NMEM,NUMBER OF ORGANIZATION MEMBERSHIPS/
                  NACT,NUMBER OF ACTIVE MEMBERSHIPS
RECODE            VAR006 TO VAR029 (CONVERT)
VALUE LABELS      VAR006 TO VAR029 (1) AGREE STRONGLY (2) AGREE (3) NEUTRAL
                  (4) DISAGREE (5) DISAGREE STRONGLY
MISSING VALUES    INCOME2(0)/LOCVOTE,NMEM,NACT(8,9)/VAR006 TO VAR029(11,12)
COMPUTE           WGTVAR = 1.0
IF                (RACE EQ 2) WGTVAR = 1.67
WEIGHT            WGTVAR
*IF               (CASEID EQ NEWCASID) CHECKVAR = 1
*IF               (CASEID NE NEWCASID) CHECKVAR = -1
MARGINALS         CHECKVAR,INCOME2 TO VAR029
STATISTICS        ALL
READ INPUT DATA
DELETE VARS       NEWCASID
SAVE FILE
FINISH
```

## 10.3   DELETING SUBFILES WITH THE DELETE SUBFILES CARD

The user may delete one or more of the subfiles in an existing system file and generate a new file containing fewer subfiles by means of the DELETE SUBFILES card. The control words DELETE SUBFILES are followed by a list of the subfile names that the user wishes deleted from his file. This list may be composed of one or more individual subfile names and may also contain lists of the following type:

subfile name 1 TO subfile name 2

where three or more contiguous subfiles are to be deleted. Here subfile name 1 and subfile name 2 must be subfiles which exist in a system file, where subfile 1 precedes subfile 2 in the file. The general format of the DELETE SUBFILES card is then

```
1                    16
DELETE SUBFILES      subfile list
```

All references in the file to subfiles named on this card will be permanently deleted if the user saves a new system file at the conclusion of the run by entering a SAVE FILE card in his control-card deck.[1] The DELETE SUBFILES card is placed directly following the GET FILE card. It may not be used on runs in which the user is adding or deleting variables from his file. The deleted subfiles are not present or available for any statistical procedure to be analyzed on the run in which the subfiles are being expunged.

We urge the user to alter the name of his file by entering a FILE NAME card following the DELETE SUBFILES card as we always do whenever a modified file is being retained.

## 10.4  ADDING SUBFILES TO A SYSTEM FILE: THE ADD SUBFILES CARD

The user may add cases to an existing SPSS system file by adding one or more subfiles to an existing file. The user may not, however, add cases to an existing subfile or directly to a file which does not have a subfile structure without considering the added cases as an independent subfile. Subfiles are added to an existing file by means of the ADD SUBFILES card. The control words ADD SUBFILES are followed by a list of subfile names to be added. The general format of the card is

```
1                    16
ADD SUBFILES         subfile list
```

where the subfile list is a list of the new subfiles to be added. The subfile names on this list must appear in the order in which they are to be input to the file. The subfile names may not exceed eight characters in length and the first character must be alphabetic. Also, the first four characters of subfile names (unlike any other name used in SPSS) must be unique in terms of the subfiles in a given file. In the case of adding subfiles, this means that the first four characters of the subfile names must be unique in terms of the subfiles already in the file as well as unique to all subfiles being added.

The new subfiles must contain the same variables in the same order as the subfiles presently in the file. The variables must also correspond in type (numeric or alphanumeric). This means, for example, that variables which are numeric variables in the file must also be typed as numeric on the subfiles being added. If any variables have been created using variables transformations, these variables must be present in the subfiles being added. Here, however, the transformed variables may be dummied in by locating them in blank columns. The desired transformations can then be executed on the adding subfiles run. Remember, transformed variables are placed at the end of the file in the order in which they were created.

The ADD SUBFILES card directly follows the GET FILE card. In addition to the ADD SUBFILES card, a run which adds subfiles must have the following file-definition cards:

1. An INPUT MEDIUM card specifying the medium on which the *new* subfiles are to be found
2. An INPUT FORMAT card containing the input format specifications for all the variables
3. A # OF CASES card which specifies the number of cases in each of the *new* subfiles

There must also be a READ INPUT DATA card immediately following the first statistical-procedure card and its associated OPTIONS and STATISTICS cards. It is permissible to both delete (or keep) and add variables or to both delete and add subfiles in a single run. It is not possible, however, to change the number of variables and the number of subfiles in a single run.

If the user is adding one or more subfiles to a file without a subfile structure, the existing cases are considered the first subfile which is assigned a subfile name equivalent to the file name. Example 10.3 illustrates the deck setup and card order used to add subfiles to an existing

---

[1]The user must remember to prepare JCL for an output system file FT04 (see Appendix F).

file. The JCL cards for the output system file FT04 must be prepared, and if the subfiles being added reside on a medium other than cards, JCL for the BCD input file FT08 must also be entered. See Appendix F which contains detailed instructions for the preparation of all JCL cards.

**EXAMPLE 10.3**

```
1               16
RUN NAME        ADDING SUBFILES TO AN EXISTING FILE
GET FILE        STUDYA
ADD SUBFILES    INDIA,JAPAN,NIGERIA
# OF CASES      1004,1236,1527
INPUT MEDIUM    TAPE
INPUT FORMAT    FIXED (F4.0,12X,46F1.0)
PROCESS SBFILESEACH
CODEBOOK        ALL
STATISTICS      1,3,5
READ INPUT DATA
SAVE FILE
FINISH
```

## 10.5   OUTPUT OF DATA ONTO BCD FILES: THE WRITE CASES CARD

While SPSS system files have a number of distinct advantages for the user (which are discussed throughout the text) they have one serious shortcoming; they cannot be read by any analysis program outside of the SPSS system. While the SPSS system tries to encompass the most frequently used statistical procedures, the authors are well aware that many researchers will find it necessary to utilize their own programs or other statistical packages from time to time. The WRITE CASES procedure makes it possible for the user to retain SPSS system files, utilize any or all of the data-modification and data-selection capabilities of SPSS, and at the same time maintain access to his data in a form readable by all data-processing programs.

Specifically, the WRITE CASES procedure enables the user to have any or all parts of his data punched on cards, or written on tape, disk, or another medium of his choosing, in BCD form. The user has control over the selection of variables and cases to be output as well as control over the output format in which the data is to be written. The results of any data modifications (those executed on the WRITE CASES run as well as those previously performed), such as COMPUTEs, RECODEs, etc., may be output, and all of the data-selection features may also be used to produce a BCD file of sampled, weighted, or selected cases. Input to the WRITE CASES procedure may be either an existing SPSS system file or a normal BCD data file residing on cards, tape, etc.

WRITE CASES is therefore a procedure which can serve at least two important functions for the user: (1) it can be utilized to output any part or all of the data from an existing SPSS system file so that the data may be input to other programs; and (2) it can be used in conjunction with a BCD input data file so that the recoding, variable transformation, and/or the data-selection capabilities of SPSS may be utilized to create a new modified BCD output file.

From the point of view of the user, WRITE CASES resembles a statistical procedure more than a file-maintenance routine. This is true for several reasons. First, the placement of the WRITE CASES card in the control-card deck corresponds precisely to the location of the procedure cards associated with SPSS statistical subprograms. Second, any temporary data modifications or data selections in effect at the time the WRITE CASES card is encountered will affect the data being output just as permanent data-modification and data-selection cards affect SPSS system files. Third, the WRITE CASES procedure card may appear as the first, second, . . . , last task of a given run in a manner similar to all the statistical procedures.

The WRITE CASES procedure is activated by a card containing the control words WRITE CASES followed by a parenthesized Fortran IV format list and a variable list containing the variables to be output. The general format of the WRITE CASES card is then as follows:

1                16
WRITE CASES       (format list) variable list

Though the format list of the WRITE CASES card appears first, some logical issues cause us to discuss the variable list first; a discussion of the format list then follows.

### 10.5.1 THE VARIABLE LIST FOR THE WRITE CASES CARD

The variable list for the WRITE CASES card is similar to all variable lists used on SPSS control cards. Any variable which has been previously defined (on a VARIABLE LIST card, in an existing SPSS system file, or by means of a variable transformation) may appear on the variable list of the WRITE CASES card. The usual conventions concerning the definition of adjacent and nonadjacent variables apply so that a complex variable list utilizing both conventions may be prepared or a list using only the adjacent or the nonadjacent convention may be entered. The serialized form of the variable list may then be as follows:

VARA TO VARE, VARK, VARP, VARR, VART TO VARZ

The variables named on the WRITE CASES card may appear in any order irrespective of their previous location in a system file or on a variable list. The order in which they appear determines the sequence of the variables on the cases being output. A given variable or list of variables in the file may be output as many times as the user desires. If the user wishes to have a variable output more than once, he simply repeats the variable name as many times as required, entering the name at each place in the variable list where it is to appear on the cases being written or punched. This capability is particularly useful for assigning case-identification numbers to each card of a case when there will be more than one card per case.

Along these lines, the user should be aware that two of the automatic variables, SEQNUM and SUBFIL, are available to him and may be used as variables to be output on the BCD file being punched or written. The automatic variable CASWGT is *not available* and should never appear on the WRITE CASES card. Section 9.3 discusses the writing of weighted files. SEQNUM is a case-identification number automatically assigned to each case as it is read into the SPSS system. When a file has no subfile structure, each case has a unique sequence number assigned in ascending order. The first case is assigned sequence number 1 and the sequence number of the last case will be equal to the number of cases in the file. When the file has a subfile structure, each case within a subfile is assigned a unique sequence number in ascending order, with the first case of each subfile being assigned the case number 1 and the last case having a sequence number equal to the number of cases in the subfile. The first four characters of the subfile name, as entered on the SUBFILE LIST card, are automatically recorded on each case in the subfile when the file is read into the system. The variable SUBFIL exists whenever a file has a subfile structure. If the user wishes, the variables SEQNUM and SUBFIL can be used jointly to produce a unique identification for each case in any file with a subfile structure. Furthermore, even when the user has some other variable which identifies each case, he may wish to output a subfile identification onto the cases being written or punched. If some form of subfile identification based on variable SUBFIL is desired, we suggest equating a new variable to SUBFIL (by means of a COMPUTE card) and then recoding the new variable to numeric values. For example,

```
1                16
COMPUTE          SUBID = SUBFIL
RECODE           SUBID ('US' =1)('UK' =2)('ITAL' =3)('GERM' =4)('MEX' =5)
```

The variable SUBFIL itself, like SEQNUM and CASEWGT, cannot be recoded.

### 10.5.2 THE FORMAT LIST FOR THE WRITE CASES CARD

The Fortran-type format list to be prepared for the WRITE CASES card enables the user to control the location of the variables being output on cards or other BCD medium. When the output medium is cards, card-image tape, or disk, the format list enables the user to control the card and column location of each of the variables to be output. When the user is writing BCD cases which are not card image (i.e., where the length of the record is to be other than 80), the format list enables him to control the field location of the variables in a similar manner.

The format list for the WRITE CASES card is similar in structure to the format list used to input the user's data on the INPUT FORMAT card. Any users unfamiliar with Fortran IV format lists should carefully read through Secs. 4.6.2 to 4.6.4 before attempting to prepare the format list for the WRITE CASES card for the basic elements of format lists not discussed in detail here.

The format list provides the system with a set of instructions for writing the user's data. The list consists of a series of elements enclosed in parentheses. The left parenthesis indicates the beginning of the format list and the right parenthesis the end of the list. The list may be continued from one physical card to another until completed, but columns 1 to 15 must be left blank on all continuation cards. As with the input format list, only *A* (alphanumeric) and *F* (numeric) format elements can be used. The type of element (*A* or *F*) used for a given variable must correspond to the type of the variable. In other words, alphanumeric variables must be written under A-type elements and numeric variables under F-type elements (again see Secs. 4.6.2 to 4.6.4). Variables converted from alphanumeric to numeric variables on the WRITE CASES run by means of RECODEs, COMPUTEs, or IFs can be output as numeric variables. The format list is read from left to right as is the variable list. Each variable named or implied in the list is paired with the format element in the corresponding sequential position. The utilization of the X element to produce blank columns or fields and the / element to skip to a new card is identical to that described for the INPUT FORMAT card.[1]

One difference between the input format list and the format list applying to the WRITE CASES card pertains to the way in which decimal numbers are handled. The reader will recall that, on input, decimal points existing in fields subject to F-type format elements override the assumed decimal point derived from the format specification itself. On output, no decimal points are written on the cases. This means that the total field width should be calculated without counting the decimal point. If, for example, an F-type variable with a maximum value of 999.99 and a minimum value of 0.00 were to be output, a format specification of F5.2 would be used. This would cause the maximum value to be output as '99999' (in the designated fields) and the minimum value to be written as '      0'. The minimum value 0 would be right justified and the leading four columns would be left blank. In the case of negative numbers, a minus sign [−] will be written to the left of the most significant digit and will occupy one of the columns provided for in the format specification. If, for example, the user wished to output a variable which has a maximum value of 999.99 and a minimum value of −999.99, he would use a format specification of F6.2. In this case the maximum value would be printed (in the field specified) as '  99999' and the minimum value as '−99999'. Under this format the value 0 would appear on the output cases as '      0'; the value of −3 would be written as '   −300'; the value −.3 as '    −30', etc. The fact that decimal points are not punched should cause the user no pain, for any program which reads formated numeric data should enable the user to read the decimal point back into the data at the time of input.

Variables with decimal numbers may also be truncated by F-type format elements. If, for example, the user had created a variable with a COMPUTE statement in which division was involved, SPSS automatically supplied a resultant value with seven significant digits. While this provision is free when the data resides in an SPSS system file (because the size of values is of no consequence when the data is stored in internal representation), the user would normally not desire such a cumbersome variable to be written or punched in BCD form. In this instance, the user determines how much accuracy he desires and prepares a format specification accordingly. If the user has a variable with two digits to the left of the decimal point and five digits to the right of the decimal point and wishes only the whole number to be output, a format element of F2.0 would be prepared. This would cause truncation to occur at the whole numbers. If two significant digits were desired, the element F4.2 would be used. The rounding of decimal numbers before output is automatically accomplished by the WRITE CASES procedure. The size of the whole number (i.e., the portion of any value to the left of the decimal point) cannot be truncated or altered by the format specification itself. A field longer than the values may be specified, in which case the values are right justified and written or punched with leading blanks. If a specification is prepared *which is smaller* (i.e., shorter) than the maximum value taken by a variable, all values of that variable which are greater than the specification permits will be written or punched as a series of asterisks [***], a result which is unfortunate, to say the least. Therefore, whenever the user is in doubt as to the size of maximum positive value or the minimum negative value associated with a given variable, he should estimate safely high, for

---

[1] On the IBM 360, all values are stored in full words. Numeric values are in short precision floating point and alphabetic values in their internal representation, with trailing blanks (hexadecimal 40) as necessary. The highly knowledgeable user may wish to save time by using the output specification A4 for both numeric and alphabetic data to obtain the internal representation.

a few wasted card columns are far less costly than useless data sprinkled with asterisks.

Two additional specification elements not available in input format lists may be included in the output format on the WRITE CASES card. Both of these elements provide the user with the capability of recording information which is to remain constant in each case to be output. The first of these constants is the *Hollerith constant*. The form of the Hollerith constant is *nHc*, where *n* is an integer describing the length of the constant, *H* is a fixed character (like *F* or *A*) indicating that a constant will follow, and *c* is a constant of length *n* composed of any combination of valid characters found in the IBM 360 character set. The specification element 6H0123 X describes a constant field containing six characters 0123 X which will be written or punched at the indicated point on each case being output. The second additional element is the alphanumeric constant. This constant resembles all of the alphanumeric constants used in SPSS in that it is a string of one or more characters enclosed by apostrophes or single quotation marks. The characters enclosed within the apostrophes may be any valid IBM 360 character with the exception of the apostrophe itself. The function of the alphanumeric constant is the same as that of the Hollerith constant, i.e., recording a constant set of information on each case being output. The Hollerith constant 6H123 X and the alphanumeric constant '123 X' are equivalent. The major utility of these constant elements in the context of the WRITE CASES procedure is the capability they give the user in placing identifying information on files being output. If, for example, the user were punching a series of analysis decks and wished to identify each of them, the alphanumeric or Hollerith constant could be used. These constants are perhaps most useful for providing card-of-case indentification numbers when card-image cases which contain more than one card per case are being output.

In the following example, the WRITE CASES card demonstrates some of the features and conventions which are used in having cards punched or BCD tape or disk files written by means of this procedure.

```
1                16
WRITE CASES      (F1.0,F4.0,'1',4X,F7.2,2A1/,F1.0,F4.0,'2',2F2.0)
                 SUBID,SEQNUM,INCOME TO SEX,SUBID,SEQNUM,EDUC,LRES
```

Assuming that the variable SUBFIL had been assigned and recoded to a single column numeric variable SUBID as illustrated above, the subfile identification would appear in the first column of each card of every case. The case-identification number (SEQNUM) will be placed in the second to fifth columns of each card of every case. In the first card of every case this sequence number will be followed by the constant 1 indicating that this is the first card of the case. The second card of each case will contain a 2 in the corresponding column (column 6), signifying it is the second card of the case. This type of elaborate identification procedure may not be absolutely necessary if the user outputs data onto tape or disk files, but it is mandatory if the user is producing punched cards. In the latter instance, it represents the minimum amount of information required to get a dropped (or otherwise mis-sequenced) card deck back into its proper sequence.

In addition to this card- and case-identifying information, the above example indicates that the first card of each case will include a seven-digit field (two positions to the right of the assumed decimal point) containing the value of the variable INCOME, and two single-column alphanumeric fields containing the values of the variables RACE and SEX. Notice that the 4X specification will cause four blank columns to be placed between the card code alphanumeric constant and the variable INCOME. The information on the second card of each case will include (in addition to the identifying information) 2 two-column fields containing the values of the variables EDUC and LRES.

### 10.5.3   A NOTE ON WRITING CASES FROM WEIGHTED FILES

If the user wishes to output the cases from a file which has been weighted (see Sec. 9.3), he may output either a weighted file or an unweighted file containing a variable indicating the weight to be given to each case. (This weight can then be used in conjunction with other programs to achieve a properly weighted file.) Because it is technically impossible to write fractional cases, the weighting procedure utilized by the WRITE CASES procedure differs from the procedure normally used. In this case the weighted file is produced by the following procedure. The weight for each case is considered to be composed of two portions—a whole number and a fraction. When the case is written, it will appear in the output file a number of times equal to the whole number portion of its weight. In addition, a random selection procedure is used to determine whether an additional copy of the case will appear. The probability that the case will be produced again is equal to the fractional portion of its weight.

This procedure will be automatically followed whenever a file which has been weighted is to be punched or written unless the user suppresses the weighting in the following manner:

```
1                16
*COMPUTE         DUMMYWGT = 1.0
*COMPUTE         WGTVAR = CASWGT
*WEIGHT          DUMMYWGT
```

This sequence of cards will cause each case in the file to be written or punched one time. A new variable called WGTVAR has been created containing the proper weighting factor for each case. If this variable is included on the WRITE CASES card, the user will have a permanent and usable record of the weighting factor to be applied to each case. If for some reason the user does not wish to retain the weights in any form at all, the second COMPUTE statement may be deleted. The variables DUMMYWGT and WGTVAR can be any variable names the user desires; the variable CASWGT is, of course, the automatic variable containing the proper weight for each case. This variable *may not* be used on the WRITE CASES card.

### 10.5.4 EXAMPLE DECK SETUP AND CARD ORDER FOR THE WRITE CASES PROCEDURE

As previously indicated, the user may have the cases punched on cards or written on tape, disk, or any other BCD medium available at his installation. The user specifies the desired medium as well as the specific output device on JCL card FT09 which is discussed in detail in Appendix F. The user should note that this is the same logical unit used to output correlation matrices when they are requested. Therefore, the user should be quite cautious about requesting punched correlation matrices on runs in which he is also using the WRITE CASES procedure. These two features can be used on the same run, but the two files will be output one behind the other so that the user must then have a means of separating the cases from the correlation matrices. If they are being output on a medium other than cards, this may be a nontrivial matter.

The following two example runs indicate the deck setup and card order to be used when utilizing the WRITE CASES procedure. Example 10.4 demonstrates a run from an SPSS system file in which a selected group of the variables in the file are being output. Note further that the WRITE CASES procedure is being called twice, causing two passes through the data; only white respondents are being selected and output on the first task and only Negroes on the second. Because the two WRITE CASES cards are otherwise identical and because the WRITE CASES procedure enables the user to write one file behind another, the two WRITE CASES tasks will in actuality produce a new file of selected variables in which all white respondents are grouped together at the beginning of the file, followed by the Negro respondents. Finally, notice that a new variable is being generated by means of a COMPUTE statement. This new variable is available for both WRITE CASES tasks because a permanent (nonstarred) COMPUTE is being used.

### EXAMPLE 10.4

```
1                16
RUN NAME         WRITE CASES TWICE CREATING A FILE SORTED BY RACE
GET FILE         STUDYX
COMPUTE          POLPART = VOTE60 + VOTE64 + LOCVOTE + CONTACTL + CONTACTN
*SELECT IF       (RACE EQ 'W')
WRITE CASES      (F3.0,1X,A1,9F1.0,1X,F1.0,5F2.0) SEQNUM,RACE TO AGE
                 WIFEOCC,POLEFF,DOMLIB,FORNPOL,POLPART
*SELECT IF       (RACE EQ 'N')
WRITE CASES      (F3.0,1X,A1.9F1.0,1X,F1.0,5F2.0) SEQNUM,RACE TO AGE,
                 WIFEOCC,POLEFF,DOMLIB,FORNPOL,POLPART
FINISH
```

Example 10.5 demonstrates the utilization of the WRITE CASES procedure (and the SPSS system, for that matter) for a user who is solely interested in the recoding and variable-transformation capability of the SPSS system. Here data is being read into the SPSS system from cards with a minimum of data definition. A number of variables are being recoded; several indexes are being constructed, and a new file of cases containing the recoded and transformed variables are being punched out on cards. Note that the data are also being consolidated from three cards per case at input to two cards at output, and alphanumeric constants are being used to record card-sequence numbers on each card of the cases.

**EXAMPLE 10.5**

```
1                 16
RUN NAME          DO RECODES AND COMPUTES AND PUNCH NEW CARDS
VARIABLE LIST     CASEID, VAR001 TO VAR112
INPUT MEDIUM      CARD
# OF CASES        1312
INPUT FORMAT      FIXED (F4.0,4X,60F1.0,/,10X,40A1,/,10X,12F1.0)
*COMPUTE          VAR113 = VAR101 + VAR012 + VAR013 + VAR014
*COMPUTE          VAR114 = (VAR105 + VAR106 + VAR107)/3 + 1
*RECODE           VAR061 TO VAR100  ('0'=0)('1'=1)('2'=2)('3'=3)
                  ('4'=4)('5'=5)('8'=8)('-'=9)(' '=7)
WRITE CASES       (F4.0,'1',75F1.0,/,F4.0,'2',37F1.0,F2.0,F4.2) CASEID,
                  VAR001 TO VAR075,CASEID,VAR076 TO VAR114
READ INPUT DATA
FINISH
```

# 11
# DESCRIPTIVE STATISTICS AND ONE-WAY FREQUENCY DISTRIBUTIONS

In most types of social science research, the first task of data analysis is to determine an appropriate method of measuring the relationship of each of the independent and dependent variables under investigation. Different statistical measures which can be used are appropriate to data measured in various ways. Therefore, before the researcher proceeds to examine the relationships between variables, he usually must have some idea of the basic characteristics of their distribution and variability. This is almost as true for nonparametric or distribution-free statistical analysis as it is for the parametric variety.

When the researcher is dealing with more or less continuous variables which are not classified into a relatively small number of categories, he must usually rely on certain types of summary statistics to reveal the underlying characteristics of the distribution of the variables. The mean, for example, gives him a measure of central tendency; standard deviation and variance tell him about the variability and dispersion of the variable; and measures such as skewness and kurtosis enable him to more precisely understand the shape of its distribution. SPSS subprogram CONDESCRIPTIVE provides the user with the capability of obtaining these and other descriptive statistics for variables which are more or less continuous. (Appendix D contains a brief description of the statistics available in CONDESCRIPTIVE.)

When the researcher is investigating variables which are classificatory (that is, are measured in terms of a limited number of discrete categories or values), he may wish to examine the number or frequency of cases which fall into each category of the variable. If, for example, the researcher were engaged in a study of the determinates of party preference in the United States, he would certainly wish to examine the one-way frequency distributions of his sample along the dependent variable. This would involve examining the raw and relative frequency of those respondents in the sample who claimed they were (1) Democrats, (2) Republicans, (3) Independents, and (4) members of other minor parties. Indeed, one of the ways in which one verifies the validity of a sample as well as that of a questionnaire is to determine the degree to which the distributions in the sample approximate the known national distributions. While most researchers (when using classificatory variables such as those produced by survey research) usually wish to examine the one-way frequency distributions or marginals of variables visually, summary statistics such as those used in studying continuous variables may also be used to give a more precise description of the characteristics of the variables.

The SPSS system provides the user with two subprograms for the display of one-way frequency distributions as well as support statistics. These two subprograms, CODEBOOK and MARGINALS, differ only in that the former produces more elaborate tables with more complete labeling while the latter has a more compact format for variables taking a large number of values.

## 11.1 SUBPROGRAM CONDESCRIPTIVE: DESCRIPTIVE STATISTICS FOR CONTINUOUS VARIABLES

The subprogram to compute descriptive statistics for continuous data, CONDESCRIPTIVE, enables the user to compute any one, combination of, or all of the following descriptive statistics for any or all of his variables: mean, standard error, standard deviation, variance, kurtosis, skewness, range, minimum, and maximum.

All statistics computed by this subprogram assume that the variables for which they are computed are numerically coded, at least ordinal in scale, and more or less continuous. There is no fixed point at which a classificatory variable becomes a continuous one, and this is clearly a decision which the researcher himself must make.

As with all SPSS subprograms, sampling, selecting, and weighting, as well as recoding and variable transformations, may be temporarily or permanently effected while using subprogram CONDESCRIPTIVE.

### 11.1.1 THE CONDESCRIPTIVE PROCEDURE CARD

The calculation of descriptive statistics for continuous data is initiated by a procedure card containing the control word CONDESCRIPTIVE. The control word is followed by a list of the variables for which the user wishes to have one or more of the descriptive statistics computed. The variables are entered onto the card by the following conventions:

1.  When descriptive statistics are to be computed for three or more *adjacent* variables, the user may enter the variable names onto the card by a notation of the following type:

    VARX TO VARY

    where both VARX and VARY are variables which have been previously defined in the file, and where VARX precedes VARY in sequence on the data cases. This type of notation will cause the desired descriptive statistics to be computed on all variables in the file between and including VARX and VARY. The variable names must be separated from the keyword TO by one or more common delimiters.

2.  When the user wishes to compute continuous descriptive statistics on two or more *non-adjacent* variables, the variable names are entered onto the card in the following manner:

    VARA,VARC,VARF,VARN

    where VARA, VARC, VARF, and VARN are variables which have been previously defined. This notation will cause descriptive statistics to be computed for variables VARA,

VARC, VARF, and VARN. These two notations may be freely intermixed producing a list of variable names of the following type:

VARA TO VARE, VARK,VARP,VARR,VARI TO VARZ

As usual, all the conventions governing the use of variable names on SPSS control cards must be followed (see Sec. 3.1.2.1 and 3.1.3). If the user wishes to have continuous descriptive statistics computed for *all* of the variables in the file, he may simply enter the keyword ALL onto the CONDESCRIPTIVE card. The general format of the CONDESCRIPTIVE card is then as follows:

```
1                    16
CONDESCRIPTIVE  ⎧ variable list ⎫
                ⎨      or       ⎬
                ⎩ ALL          ⎭
```

The following sample CONDESCRIPTIVE card would cause the desired statistics to be computed for each of the variables listed on the card, as well as all intervening variables implied between INCOME and SESINDEX.

```
1               16
CONDESCRIPTIVE INCOME TO SESINDEX,SCALE1,SCALE3,ORGMEMBS,FAMSIZE
```

### 11.1.2   OPTIONS AVAILABLE FOR SUBPROGRAM CONDESCRIPTIVE

The CONDESCRIPTIVE card is followed by an OPTIONS card which informs the CONDESCRIPTIVE subprogram of the processing options desired by the user (see Sec. 5.2). The OPTIONS card contains the control word OPTIONS followed by a selection among the following option numbers:

*Option* 1.   Causes the system to include all cases in the computation of the statistics regardless of whether values were previously defined as missing. If option 1 is not exercised, the system deletes cases which have values defined as missing from the computations, so that the statistics computed for a given variable will be based only on cases which take values that have not been defined as missing.

*Option* 2.   Used to suppress the printing of extended variable labels which are normally reported on the output from this program and hence slightly increases the processing speed of this program.

The general format of the OPTIONS card is then

```
1               16
OPTIONS         number list
```

The OPTIONS card may be deleted for this subprogram; that is, the user need not prepare it. If it is not prepared, the following default options will be in effect:

Option *a.*   Missing values will be excluded from the computations (i.e., default of option 1 will be in effect).

Option *b.*   The extended-variable labels will be printed whenever present.

### 11.1.3   STATISTICS AVAILABLE WITH SUBPROGRAM CONDESCRIPTIVE

The user may select among the nine available statistics by number on the STATISTICS card which follows the OPTIONS card when it is used or the CONDESCRIPTIVE card when the default options are selected. The STATISTICS card contains the control word STATISTICS, followed by a list of the numbers corresponding to the statistics desired. Table 11.1 gives the statistics and their corresponding numbers. When the number is placed in the specification field, that statistic will be computed for all variables named on the CONDESCRIPTIVE card.

---

**TABLE 11.1 Correspondence between statistics and numbers in subprogram CONDESCRIPTIVE**

| | | | |
|---|---|---|---|
| 1 | Mean | 8 | Skewness |
| 2 | Standard error | 9 | Range |
| 5 | Standard deviation | 10 | Minimum |
| 6 | Variance | 11 | Maximum |
| 7 | Kurtosis | | |

---

If the user wishes all statistics, the number list may be replaced by the keyword ALL, beginning in column 16, so the following card will cause all statistics to be printed:

```
1            16
STATISTICS   ALL
```

The general format of the STATISTICS card is as follows:

```
1            16
STATISTICS   ⎰ number list ⎱
             ⎱     or      ⎰
             ⎱   ALL       ⎰
```

The following example STATISTICS card would cause mean, variance, and standard deviation to be produced for all variables named on the CONDESCRIPTIVE card.

```
1            16
STATISTICS   1,6,5
```

A description of the available statistics is given in Appendix D.

### 11.1.4 PROGRAM LIMITATIONS FOR SUBPROGRAM CONDESCRIPTIVE

The following limitations apply to the 360 version of CONDESCRIPTIVE:

*Limitation* 1.   No more than 500 variables may be used.

*Limitation* 2.   No more than 250 variable names and/or keywords may be referenced on a CONDESCRIPTIVE card. Names used with the TO convention count as only three toward this total regardless of the number of variables implicitly referenced in between the two variables.

### 11.1.5 EXAMPLES OF THE USE OF SUBPROGRAM CONDESCRIPTIVE

Example 11.1 demonstrates the use of subprogram CONDESCRIPTIVE in a run where the user entered file-defining information and cases from cards, computed descriptive statistics for the variables in the file, and saved the file at the conclusion of the run as an SPSS system file for subsequent use. Since this example is typical of the first run a user would make in a study using SPSS, we describe it in some detail.

In this case the user has prepared on cards all of the necessary information to describe his file to the system. The FILE NAME card gives the file name as COMSTUDY and associates with it an extended label to be printed back on subsequent output. The VARIABLE LIST card defines 22 variables named COMC001 through PARTROLE. The VAR LABELS card associates extended labels with these variable names, and the VALUE LABELS card associates labels with particular values of each variable. For example, variable HRSWORK takes the values 1 to 9. For this variable, the values 7, 8, 9 are identified as "missing" by the MISSING VALUES card, and referring once again to the VALUE LABELS card, we see that these values denote MISSING, INAPPLICABLE, and NA (for Not Ascertained), respectively.

The PRINT FORMATS card informs the system how many digits after the decimal place to print if the values of each variable are printed. For the variable HRSWORK the number of decimal places is zero, since the variable assumes only integer values. For the variable MEDSCH, the median number of school years for population over 25, one digit appears after the decimal point. This is consistent with the specification for variable MEDSCH (MEDSCH is the third variable) on the INPUT FORMAT card, since it is read with format F4.1.

The number of cases to be read is 64, and as we see from the INPUT MEDIUM and INPUT FORMAT cards, each case is punched on a separate data card. These data cards are inserted in the deck following the READ INPUT DATA card. For a complete listing of the data cards see Appendix I.

All the cards in the deck preceding the CONDESCRIPTIVE card constitute file-defining information with the exception of the RUN NAME card, which merely gives a label to be printed at the top of each page of SPSS output produced by the run. Once this file-defining information has been specified, we are able to execute a run of subprogram CONDESCRIPTIVE. In this case the CONDESCRIPTIVE card causes the system to produce descriptive statistic tables (18 tables in all) for all of the variables MEDFINC to PARTROLE. All of the available statistics are

**EXAMPLE 11.1**  The control cards required to define and save file COMSTUDY and to produce a run of subprogram CONDESCRIPTIVE

```
1                16
RUN NAME         CONDESCRIPTIVE RUN USING DATA PUNCHED ON CARDS,SAVE A SYSTEM FILE
FILE NAME        COMSTUDY,STUDY OF AMERICAN SMALL COMMUNITIES
VARIABLE LIST    COMCO01,CARDNO1,MEDSCH,MEDFINC,PTGOHS,PTAGRI,PTMANU,PTTERTRY,
                 POP60,POPLAT,PTCHNG,SPISOL,WHTCOLAR,LIFE,TIME,NEWSWEEK,READDIG,
                 HRSWORK,GOVSELCT,CONELECT,PARTISAN,PARTROLE
VAR LABELS       COMCO01,COMMUNITY CODE/
                 CARDNO1,CARD NUMBER/
                 MEDSCH,MEDIAN SCHOOL YEARS FOR POPULATION OVER 25/
                 MEDFINC,MEDIAN FAMILY INCOME/
                 PTGOHS,PERCENT TOTAL UNITS GOOD HOUSING/
                 PTAGRI,PERCENT LABOR IN AGRICULTURE-FOREST-FISHING/
                 PTTERTRY,PERCENT LABOR IN TERTIARY INDUSTRY/
                 POP60,TOTAL POPULATION IN 1960/
                 POPLAT,TOTAL POPULATION LATEST ESTIMATE/
                 PTCHNG,PERCENT POPULATION CHANGE 1960-66/
                 SPISOL,DEGREE OF SPATIAL ISOLATION/
                 WHTCOLAR,PERCENT CIVILIAN LABOR IN WHITE COLLAR OCCUPATIONS/
                 LIFE,LIFE MAGAZINE SALES PER 1000 POPULATION/
                 TIME,TIME MAGAZINE SALES PER 1000 POPULATION/
                 NEWSWEEK,NEWSWEEK SALES PER 1000 POPULATION/
                 READDIG,READERS DIGEST SALES PER 1000 POPULATION/
                 HRSWORK,WORKING HOURS PER WEEK HEAD OF GOVERNMENT/
                 GOVSELCT,METHOD OF SELECTING HEAD OF GOVERNMENT/
                 CONELECT,ELECTION OF HEAD OF GOVERNMENT CONTESTED/
                 PARTISAN,ELECTION HEAD LEGALLY PARTISAN/
                 PARTROLE,ACTUAL ROLE OF PARTIES ELEC HEAD
VALUE LABELS     HRSWORK (1) LESS THAN 5 HRS (2) 6-10 HRS (3) 11-20 HRS
                 (4) 21-30 HRS (5) 31-40 HRS (6) OVER 40 HRS
                 (7) MISSING (8) INAPPLICABLE (9) NA/
                 GOVSELCT (1) DIRECT ELECTION (2) ELECT LOCAL BOARD
                 (3) APPOINTED BY HIGHER ATH (4) OTHER (8) NO LOCAL HEAD
                 (9) NA (0) MISSING/
                 CONELECT (1) ALWAYS CONTESTED (2) USUALLY CONTESTED
                 (3) OCCASIONALLY CONTEST (4) NEVER CONTESTED
                 (8) APPOINTED (9) NA (0) MISSING/
                 PARTISAN (1) NONPARTSN BY LAW (2) PARTISAN
                 (8) NO LOCAL GOVT HEAD (9) NA (0) MISSING/
                 PARTROLE (1) RUN WITH PART LABEL (2) NO LABEL BUT AFFIL
                 (3) TOTALLY NONPARTSN (8) NO GOVT HEAD (9) NA (0) MISSING
MISSING VALUES   HRSWORK (7,8,9)/GOVSELCT TO PARTROLE (8,9,0)
PRINT FORMATS    COMCO01,CARDNO1,MEDFINC,POP60,POPLAT,SPISOL,LIFE TO PARTROLE(0),
                 MEDSCH,PTGOHS TO PTTERTRY,PTCHNG,WHTCOLAR(1)
INPUT MEDIUM     CARD
INPUT FORMAT     FIXED (F3.0,F2.0,F4.1,F5.0,4F4.1,2F7.0,F5.1,F2.0,F4.1,4F3.0,
                 5F1.0)
# OF CASES       64
CONDESCRIPTIVE MEDFINC TO PARTROLE
STATISTICS       ALL
READ INPUT DATA
 22 1  86 5097 217 720  33 247   8350      0   0 4 170  0  0  0  005020
 41 1  86 2757 557 613 151 168    417      0   010 168  0  0  0  006080
   •
   •
   •   DATA CARDS FOR FILE COMSTUDY (SEE APPENDIX I)
   •
   •
932 1   0    0   0   0   0   0  49845      0   0 3   0  0  0  0  005060
951 1 118 6390 788   9 277 515  37987  38600  16 6 489 65 30 15  005060
SAVE FILE
FINISH
```

calculated. Notice that no OPTIONS card follows the CONDESCRIPTIVE card; therefore full labels will be printed, and missing values are excluded from the computations.

Page 5 of the output listing is reproduced in Fig. 11.1. It contains the tables produced for variables WHTCOLAR, LIFE, and TIME. The run label appears at the top of the page together with the file name and label. The variable name and label appears at the top of each table of statistics, and at the bottom appear counts of the number of valid and missing observations. The other pages of output have a format similar to page 5.

```
CONDESCRIPTIVE RUN USING DATA PUNCHED ON CARDS,SAVE A SYSTEM FIL          07/25/69      PAGE    5

FILE   COMSTUDY (CREATION DATE = 07/25/69)    STUDY OF AMERICAN SMALL COMMUNITIES


VARIABLE  WHTCOLAR    PERCENT CIVILIAN LABOR IN WHITE COLLAR

MEAN          39.559          STD ERROR      1.692          STD DEV       13.539

VARIANCE     183.311          KURTOSIS       0.650          SKEWNESS      -0.487

RANGE         65.800          MINIMUM        0.0            MAXIMUM       65.800

VALID   OBSERVATIONS -      64
MISSING OBSERVATIONS -       0

- - - - - - - - - - - - - - - - - - - - - - - - - - - - - - - - - - - - - - - - - -


VARIABLE  LIFE       LIFE MAGAZINE SALES PER 1000 POPULATION

MEAN          36.781          STD ERROR      6.481          STD DEV       51.847

VARIANCE    2688.078          KURTOSIS      18.070          SKEWNESS       3.515

RANGE        347.000          MINIMUM        0.0            MAXIMUM      347.000

VALID   OBSERVATIONS -      64
MISSING OBSERVATIONS -       0

- - - - - - - - - - - - - - - - - - - - - - - - - - - - - - - - - - - - - - - - - -


VARIABLE  TIME       TIME MAGAZINE SALES PER 1000 POPULATION

MEAN          15.406          STD ERROR      2.137          STD DEV       17.092

VARIANCE     292.150          KURTOSIS       2.264          SKEWNESS       1.414

RANGE         81.000          MINIMUM        0.0            MAXIMUM       81.000

VALID   OBSERVATIONS -      64
MISSING OBSERVATIONS -       0
```

**FIG. 11.1**    Sample page of output from subprogram CONDESCRIPTIVE.

The SAVE FILE card, immediately following the card of the last case, causes all of the cases and file-defining information to be saved as an SPSS system file. The device which was used to write this information is specified by the user by inserting an FT04 JCL card in the set of JCL cards which would precede the cards reproduced in Example 11.1. Finally, the FINISH card indicates to the system that the last task is complete.

Example 11.2 illustrates a run of subprogram CONDESCRIPTIVE using an SPSS system file. Such a system file could have been created by the run discussed above. In this case, all necessary file-defining information and cases have already been saved, and it is only necessary for the user to insert a GET FILE card with the appropriate file name, in this case COM-STUDY, in the deck to retrieve it. (The device upon which the file is stored is specified by an FT03 card in the JCL cards which accompany this run; see Appendix F.)

The CONDESCRIPTIVE card causes a statistical table to be produced for the variables

**EXAMPLE 11.2**

```
1                16
RUN NAME         CONDESCRIPTIVE RUN FROM A SYSTEM FILE
GET FILE         COMSTUDY
CONDESCRIPTIVE   PTGOHS TO PTMANU
STATISTICS       1,2, ,7,8,9
FINISH
```

```
CONDESCRIPTIVE RUN FROM A SYSTEM FILE                                    07/25/69      PAGE  2.
FILE   COMSTUDY (CREATION DATE = 07/25/69)    STUDY OF AMERICAN SMALL COMMUNITIES


VARIABLE  PTGOHS     PERCENT TOTAL UNITS GOOD HOUSING

MEAN          66.942              STD ERROR      3.532         KURTOSIS      0.938

SKEWNESS      -1.371              RANGE         99.500

VALID   OBSERVATIONS -      64
MISSING OBSERVATIONS -       0

- - - - - - - - - - - - - - - - - - - - - - - - - - - - - - - - - - - - - - - - - - - - - -


VARIABLE  PTAGRI     PERCENT LABOR IN AGRICULTURE-FOREST-FISH

MEAN          11.520              STD ERROR      2.060         KURTOSIS      2.544

SKEWNESS       1.750              RANGE         72.000

VALID   OBSERVATIONS -      64
MISSING OBSERVATIONS -       0

- - - - - - - - - - - - - - - - - - - - - - - - - - - - - - - - - - - - - - - - - - - - - -


VARIABLE  PTMANU

MEAN          24.700              STD ERROR      1.956         KURTOSIS      -0.971

SKEWNESS       0.157              RANGE         58.500

VALID   OBSERVATIONS -      64
MISSING OBSERVATIONS -       0
```

**FIG. 11.2** Sample page of output from subprogram CONDESCRIPTIVE.

PTGOHS to PTMANU in file COMSTUDY. Referring back to Example 11.1, we see that three consecutive variables in the variable list are referenced, PTGOHS, PTAGRI, and PTMANU. For each variable, statistics numbered 1, 2, 7, 8, and 9, that is, mean, standard error, kurtosis, skewness, and range are calculated. Full labeling and exclusion of missing values from computations is exercised since no OPTIONS card appears. The output tables from Example 11.2 are reproduced in Fig. 11.2.

## 11.2 SUBPROGRAM CODEBOOK: ONE-WAY FREQUENCY DISTRIBUTIONS, HISTOGRAMS, AND RELATED STATISTICS IN CODEBOOK FORMAT

Subprogram CODEBOOK computes and presents tables containing (1) simple frequencies, (2) relative frequencies with missing values included, (3) adjusted relative frequencies with missing values excluded, and (4) cumulative adjusted frequencies for categorical data. Optionally, the user may request histograms which supplement the tables with bar graph representations of relative frequency distributions. The tables are printed in codebook format with one variable per page. A large number of statistics describing the character of the variable's distribution are also available by statistic number. This subprogram takes full advantage of all the SPSS labeling options, and when a file has been fully labeled, the output from this program becomes a complete codebook documenting the file.

Subprogram CODEBOOK may operate on alphanumeric or numeric variables. However, statistics are computed only on numeric variables. CODEBOOK is most efficiently used with variables which are grouped into a relatively small number of categories (say, less than 20) for which the user desires complete and well-documented output. For variables with a large number of categories, and/or when the user is less interested in complete and labeled tables, subprogram MARGINALS provides a more efficient method for displaying one-way frequency distributions and related statistics. However, the complete labeling which is available in CODEBOOK is not available in subprogram MARGINALS. As with all SPSS subprograms, sampling, selecting, and weighting, as well as recoding and variable transformations, may be temporarily or permanently effected while using subprogram CODEBOOK.

### 11.2.1 THE CODEBOOK PROCEDURE CARD

Subprogram CODEBOOK is called and activated by a procedure card containing the control word CODEBOOK. The control word is followed by a list of the variables for which frequency tables and statistics are to be generated. The variables are entered onto the card by the same conventions used in subprogram CONDESCRIPTIVE, and a fuller explanation of these conventions may be found in the preceding descriptions of this program as well as in Secs. 4.7, 4.8, and 4.9 (describing the MISSING VALUES, VALUE LABELS, and PRINT FORMAT cards which all use the same conventions for printing variable lists). A summary of these conventions follows:

1. When codebook tables are to be computed from three or more *adjacent* variables, the variable names are entered onto the card by a notation of the following type:

   VARX TO VARY

   This notation will cause all variables in the file between and including VARX and VARY to be entered onto the calculation.

2. When two or more *nonadjacent* variables are to have codebook tables generated for them, the variable names are entered onto the card in the following manner:

   VARA,VARC,VARF,VARN

   These two conventions may be freely intermixed, producing a variable list of the following type:

   VARA TO VARF,VARN,VARO,VARP,VARQ TO VARZ

3. In addition, if the user wishes codebook tables generated for all of the variables in his file, he may utilize the keyword ALL.

The general format of the CODEBOOK is as follows:

```
1              16
CODEBOOK      ⎧ ALL          ⎫
              ⎨    or         ⎬
              ⎩ variable list ⎭
```

The following example CODEBOOK card would cause a codebook frequency table to be produced for each of the variables listed on the card.

```
1              16
CODEBOOK      AGE,RACE,SEX,VOTE,PARTY
```

### 11.2.2 OPTIONS AVAILABLE FOR SUBPROGRAM CODEBOOK

An OPTIONS card may follow the CODEBOOK card. As usual, the OPTIONS card contains the control word OPTIONS followed by a list of option numbers desired by the user.

*Option* 1. Instructs the system to include all cases in the computation of the tables and statistics regardless of whether their values were previously defined as missing. The default *missing-data option* instructs the system to delete cases which have values defined as missing from the computation of the statistics, so that the statistics computed for that variable will be based only on those cases which have values which have not been defined as missing.

*Option* 2. Instructs the system not to search or print any of the labeling information which is normally reported on all output from the CODEBOOK program. This option will effect a substantial increase in the efficiency or operating speed of the program. However, when the user wishes to suppress labeling while computing one-way frequency distributions, he should use subprogram MARGINALS which is a more efficient program for computing unlabeled one-way frequency distributions. The option does, however, remain available here.

*Option* 4.   Causes a histogram to be produced for each of the variables for which a codebook frequency table has been generated. Examples of these histograms are shown in sample output from this program on the following pages.

*Option* 5.   Causes histogram to be printed for each variable but suppresses the printing of the normal CODEBOOK frequency table.

The format of the OPTIONS card is, as always,

```
1                    16
OPTIONS              number list
```

As usual, the OPTIONS card may be deleted. If it is deleted, the following options will be in effect:

Option *a.*   Cases containing missing values will be excluded from the computation of the statistics.

Option *b.*   Full labeling will be printed wherever present.

Option *c.*   Histograms will *not* be presented.

### 11.2.3   STATISTICS AVAILABLE FOR SUBPROGRAM CODEBOOK

The user may select any of eleven statistics by number on the STATISTICS card which, as usual, directly follows the OPTIONS card. If the OPTIONS card is not prepared (i.e., if all of the default options are selected), the STATISTICS card directly follows the CODEBOOK card. Table 11.2 gives the statistics and their corresponding numbers. When a number is placed in the specification field, the corresponding statistic will be computed for all of the variables for which tables have been requested.

**TABLE 11.2   Correspondence between statistics and numbers in subprogram CODEBOOK**

| | | | |
|---|---|---|---|
| 1 | Mean | 7 | Kurtosis |
| 2 | Standard error | 8 | Skewness |
| 3 | Median | 9 | Range |
| 4 | Mode | 10 | Minimum |
| 5 | Standard deviation | 11 | Maximum |
| 6 | Variance | | |

If the user wishes all of the statistics computed for each of the variables, he may enter the keyword ALL in place of the number list. If the STATISTICS card is omitted, the system assumes (for this program) that no statistics are desired. A brief description of the available statistics can be found in Appendix D.

The format of the STATISTICS card is, as always,

```
1                    16
STATISTICS           ⎧ ALL        ⎫
                     ⎨ or         ⎬
                     ⎩ number list ⎭
```

### 11.2.4   PROGRAM LIMITATIONS FOR SUBPROGRAM CODEBOOK

The following limitations apply to the IBM 360 version of subprogram CODEBOOK.

*Limitation* 1.   No more than 250 variable names and/or keywords may be referenced on a CODEBOOK card. Names listed with the TO convention count as only three towards this total regardless of how many variables are implied.

*Limitation* 2. The maximum number of variables which can be processed on a single task is a function of the number of values or categories in the *largest variable* (i.e., the variable with the largest number of unique values) to be processed in that task. Clearly, the converse is also true: the largest number of values a variable may contain is a function of the number of variables to be processed. The user can determine if a planned run will fit in a single task by solving the following equation for either the maximum number of *variables* or the maximum number of *values*.[1]

$$MAXVALS = \frac{(SPACE/4) - (4 \times NVARS) - 15}{8 + (2 \times NVARS)}$$

where MAXVALS is the number of non-missing values in the *largest* variable to be processed (i.e., the variable taking the largest number of unique values), and where NVARS is the number of variables to be processed. Alternatively,

$$MAXVARS = \frac{(SPACE/4) - (8 \times NVALS) - 15}{4 + (2 \times NVALS)}$$

where MAXVARS is the maximum number of variables which can be processed for a value of NVALS; where NVALS is the number of values in the largest variable to be processed.

If the user violates limitation 1, an error message is printed and the run is terminated by the system before the data is processed. However, the system can never predetermine whether limitation 2 will be exceeded. If, as the data is being processed, the system encounters one or more variables which exceed the maximum number of permissible values (determined by the number of variables being run—see above formula), the offending variable or variables are deleted from the computations, and a message is printed listing the variable(s) which exceeded the maximum-value parameter. Frequency tables, desired statistics, and histograms, if requested, are produced for all other variables just as if no violation had occurred.

### 11.2.5   EXAMPLE DECK SETUPS FOR USING SUBPROGRAM CODEBOOK

Example 11.3 will be of particular interest to the reader, since it not only illustrates the use of subprogram CODEBOOK, but typifies the sort of run a user will often initially make to begin analysis of his data with SPSS. In this example, file-defining information and cases are input to the system from cards, a run of subprogram CODEBOOK is requested, and the file is saved as an SPSS system file for subsequent retrieval. We describe the composition of the control-card deck in detail below.

The FILE NAME identifies the file name as ORGSTUDY and associates an extended label with it. As the SUBFILE LIST card indicates, the file consists of three parts. The cases in the file are divided into subfiles labeled NEWYORK, NWJERSEY, and PENNSYLV, with 100, 115, and 135 cases, respectively, as shown on the # OF CASES card. The VARIABLE LIST card defines a variable list of 29 variables, and the VAR LABELS card associates extended labels with each variable name. The VALUE LABELS card details the values which each variable can assume and indicates the meaning of each value. Some of these values indicate that the case is to be considered missing. For example, the MISSING VALUES card shows that value zero for variable RACE is missing, and referring once again to the VALUE LABELS card, we see that this value indicates the condition NA (Not Applicable). The INPUT FORMAT card specifies that the cases are read as numeric values, since an F-type format specification is used, and that each case will occupy one card. Since the INPUT MEDIUM card specifies CARD input, cards containing the punched data for each of the 350 cases follow the READ INPUT DATA card in the deck. A listing of these cards appears in Appendix I. The PRINT FORMATS card specifies that if the values of any of the variables are to be written on an output report, the format to be used is numeric with no digits after the decimal point. Looking once again at the INPUT

---

[1]The default or normal value of the parameter SPACE is 80,000. The user may alter this parameter through the use of a JCL EXEC card (see Appendix F.1).

**EXAMPLE 11.3** The control cards required to define and save file ORGSTUDY and to produce a run of subprogram CODEBOOK

```
1                16
RUN NAME         CODEBOOK RUN FROM CARD INPUT, SAVE AN SPSS SYSTEM FILE
FILE NAME        ORGSTUDY,STUDY OF ORGANIZATIONAL MEMBERSHIP AND ACTIVITY
SUBFILE LIST     NEWYORK,NWJERSEY,PENNSYLV
# OF CASES       100,115,135
VARIABLE LIST    COMMID,RESPID,RESDYTH,MARITAL,FRATMEM,SERVMEM,VETMEM,
                 POLMEM,UNIONMEM,SPORTMEM,YOUTHMEM,SCHOLMEM,HOBMEM,SCHFRMEM,
                 NATMEM,FARMEM,LITMEM,PROFMEM,RELMEM,OTHMEM,NMEM,NACT,RELIG,AGE,
                 INCOME,EDRESPON,SEX,RACE,OCLEVRES
VAR LABELS       COMMID,US COMMUNITY ID NUMBER/
                 RESPID,RESPONDENT ID NUMBER/
                 RESDYTH,RESIDENCE FIRST 15 YEARS/
                 MARITAL,MARITAL STATUS/
                 FRATMEM,MEMB IN FRATERNAL ORGS/
                 SERVMEM,MEMB IN SERVICE CLUBS/
                 VETMEM,MEMB IN VETERANS GRPS/
                 POLMEM,MEMB IN POLITICAL ORGS/
                 UNIONMEM,MEMB IN LABOR UNION/
                 SPORTMEM,MEMB IN SPORTS CLUBS/
                 YOUTHMEM,MEMB IN YOUTH GROUPS/
                 SCHOLMEM,MEMB IN SCHOOL SERVICE GRPS/
                 HOBMEM,MEMB IN HOBBY-GARDEN CLUBS/
                 SCHFRMEM,MEMB SCHOOL FRAT-SORORITY/
                 NATMEM,MEMB NATIONAL ORGS/
                 FARMEM,MEMB FARM ORGS/
                 LITMEM,MEMB LIT-ART GRPS/
                 PROFMEM,MEMB PROF-ACADEMIC ORGS/
                 RELMEM,MEMB IN RELIGIOUS ORGS/
                 OTHMEM,OTHER MEMBERSHIPS/
                 NMEM,TOTAL NUMBER OF MEMBERSHIPS/
                 NACT,TOTAL NUMBER ACTIVE MEMBERSHIPS/
                 RELIG,RELIGIOUS AFFILIATION/
                 AGE,AGE LAST BIRTHDAY/
                 INCOME,FAMILY INCOME/
                 EDRESPON,LAST YEAR SCHOOL COMPLETED/
                 SEX,RESPONDENTS SEX/
                 RACE,RESPONDENTS RACE/
                 OCLEVRES,OCCUP LEVEL OF RESPONDENT
VALUE LABELS     RESDYTH (1)MOSTLY FARM(2)MSTLY SMALL TOWN (3)MSTLY SMALL CITY
                      (4)MSTLY BIG CITY,SUBERB(9)NA,DK(0)INAPPLICABLE/
                 MARITAL (1)MARRIED(2)WIDOWED(3)DIVORCED(4)SEPARATED
                      (5)NEVER MARRIED(8)DK(9)NA(0)REFUSED/
                 FRATMEM TO OTHMEM (1)YES(0)NO(8)NA/
                 NMEM,NACT (0)NONE(1)ONE(2)TWO(3)THREE(4)FOUR(5)FIVE(6)SIX
                      (7)SEVEN(8)8-12(9)13-16/
                 RELIG (1)PROTESTANT(2)CATHOLIC(3)JEWISH(4)SHINTO,TAO(5)NONE
                      (6)ORTHODOX(7)BUDDHIST,CONF(8)HINDU,MUSLIM(9)OTHER-NONPROT
                      (0)NA/
                 INCOME (01)LESS THAN 1000(02)1000-1999(03)2000-2999(04)3000-3999
                      (05)4000-4999(06)5000-5999(07)6000-6999(11)7000-7999
                      (21)8000-8999(31)9000-9999(41)10000-14999(51)15000-19999
                      (61)20000-24999(71)25000 AND OVER(88)REFUSED(98)NA(99)DK/
                 EDRESPON (1)NONE(2)1-8 YEARS (3)9-11 YEARS(4)12 YEARS
                      (5)COLLEGE INCOMPLETE(6)COLLEGE GRAD(7)COLLEGE PLUS
                      (9)DK(0)NA/
                 SEX (1)MALE(2)FEMALE/
                 RACE (1)WHITE(2)NEGRO(3)ORIENTAL(4)INDIAN AMERICAN
                      (5)LATIN AMERICAN(8)OTHER(0)NA/
                 OCLEVRES (1)UNSKILLED(2)AMBIG SKILL (3)INDEPENDENTS(4)SKILLED
                      (5)CLRC,SALE,LOTEC(6)PROF,MANG(0)OTHER
MISSING VALUES   RESDYTH(0,7,9)/MARITAL(0,8,9)/FRATMEM TO OTHMEM(8)/
                 RELIG(9)/AGE(98,99)/INCOME(88,98,99)/EDRESPON(0,9)/
                 RACE(0)/OCLEVRES(0)
INPUT FORMAT     FIXED (F3.0,F2.0,1X,21F1.0,2F2.0,1X,4F1.0)
INPUT MEDIUM     CARD
PRINT FORMATS    COMMID TO OCLEVRES (0)
PROCESS SBFILES     ALL
CODEBOOK         RESDYTH TO RELIG,SEX TO OCLEVRES
READ INPUT DATA
 11 1 420000000000000000000176 3 2215
 11 2 110000000000000000000124 6 3210
  .
  .
  DATA CARDS FOR FILE ORGSTUDY (SEE APPENDIX I)
  .
  .
13211 010001100100000000020236 7 3114
13212 050000000010000000001023151 5115
SAVE FILE
FINISH
```

FORMAT card we see that this requirement is consistent with the way the variables are read in, since each variable is read as an integer.

The CODEBOOK card indicates that a codebook-format tabulation is to be performed for each variable in the variable list from variable RESDYTH to variable RELIG, inclusive, and for variable SEX to variable OCLEVRES, inclusive. Thus 24 tabulations are requested. Since no STATISTICS or OPTIONS cards follow the CODEBOOK card, the following conditions are in force: full labeling will appear on the output reports, no histograms are written, and no statistics are calculated. Each of the 24 tables is compiled from all 350 cases, since the PRO-CESS SBFILES card contains the keyword ALL, indicating that all three subfiles are to be processed as a group.

```
CODEBOOK RUN FROM CARD INPUT, SAVE AN SPSS SYSTEM FILE                07/25/69        PAGE    4

FILE    ORGSTUDY (CREATION DATE = 07/25/69)    STUDY OF ORGANIZATIONAL MEMBERSHIP AND ACTIVITY
SUBFILE    NEWYORK    NWJERSEY    PENNSYLV

VARIABLE    MAPITAL    MARITAL STATUS
```

| VALUE LABEL | VALUE | ABSOLUTE FREQUENCY | RELATIVE FREQUENCY (PERCENT) | ADJUSTED FREQUENCY (PERCENT) | CUMULATIVE ADJ FREQ (PERCENT) |
|---|---|---|---|---|---|
| MARRIED | 1. | 276 | 78.9 | 78.9 | 78.9 |
| WIDOWED | 2. | 29 | 8.3 | 8.3 | 87.1 |
| DIVORCED | 3. | 11 | 3.1 | 3.1 | 90.3 |
| SEPARATED | 4. | 11 | 3.1 | 3.1 | 93.4 |
| NEVER MARRIED | 5. | 23 | 6.6 | 6.6 | 100.0 |
| REFUSED | 0. | 0 | 0.0 | MISSING | 100.0 |
| DK | 8. | 0 | 0.0 | MISSING | 100.0 |
| NA | 9. | 0 | 0.0 | MISSING | 100.0 |
| TOTAL | | 350 | 100.0 | 100.0 | 100.0 |

```
VALID    OBSERVATIONS -      350
MISSING OBSERVATIONS -        0
```

**FIG. 11.3**  Sample page of output from subprogram CODEBOOK.

A typical page of output from the run is reproduced in Fig. 11.3. At the top of the output appears the run label as given by the RUN NAME card, the date, and page number. Next appears the file name and label and the names of the subfiles from which the data in the table are compiled. Next the variable name, in this case MARITAL, and the variable label are printed. The body of the table contains, for each value of the variable MARITAL which was encountered, the value label, the value itself, the number of times the value occurred and its percentage of the whole, the percentage adjusted for the occurrence of missing values, and cumulative adjusted percentage frequency. Notice in this case that no missing values, that is, 0, 8, or 9 were encountered, so that the adjusted percent frequency is equal to the relative percent frequency. This checks with the tally of valid observations which is 350. The other pages of output are similar in format.

The above run is typical of the situation where the user has measured a number of variables of nominal character, and where, on the initial run, the user wishes to both document and save his data for subsequent analysis. The SAVE FILE card causes this information to be written on an output device as an SPSS system file. The precise device to be used is specified the user with an FT04 JCL card in the set of JCL cards which are prepared for the run. As a by-product of this process, a codebook tabulation is produced which the user will probably refer to repeatedly as his analysis proceeds.

Notice that certain variables have not been tabulated in codebook format. For example, it would be quite meaningless to request a codebook tabulation of variable RESPID, the respondent identification number. Such a listing would have included 350 valid values, each of frequency 1, and no missing data! The point is that the user should exercise some discretion in the tables he requests from subprogram CODEBOOK. Generally, continuous variables or variables with a large number of valid values are not suitable for tabulation with this subprogram.

Example 11.4 illustrates the use of subprogram CODEBOOK in a run utilizing an SPSS system file. The system file named ORGSTUDY has been saved on a previous run such as that of Example 11.3. In this case the tabulation is compiled from the cases of a single subfile NEWYORK. The CODEBOOK card names a single variable NMEM. The OPTIONS card requests a histogram as well as a codebook format tabulation, and the STATISTICS card causes

**EXAMPLE 11.4**

```
1                16
RUN NAME         CODEBOOK RUN FROM AN SPSS SYSTEM FILE
GET FILE         ORGSTUDY
PROCESS SBFILES(NEWYORK)
CODEBOOK         NMEM
OPTIONS          4
STATISTICS       1,4
FINISH
```

the mean and modal value of the variable NMEM to be printed. The output from this run is shown in Fig. 11.4. The reader may find it instructive to relate this output to the file-defining information which was input in the previous example run.

CODEBOOK RUN FROM AN SPSS SYSTEM FILE                                          07/25/69        PAGE    2

FILE    ORGSTUDY (CREATION DATE = 07/25/69)    STUDY OF ORGANIZATIONAL MEMBERSHIP AND ACTIVITY
SUBFILE    NEWYORK

VARIABLE    NMEM        TOTAL NUMBER OF MEMBERSHIPS

| VALUE LABEL | VALUE | ABSOLUTE FREQUENCY | RELATIVE FREQUENCY (PERCENT) | ADJUSTED FREQUENCY (PERCENT) | CUMULATIVE ADJ FREQ (PERCENT) |
|---|---|---|---|---|---|
| NONE | 0. | 59 | 59.0 | 59.0 | 59.0 |
| ONE | 1. | 29 | 29.0 | 29.0 | 88.0 |
| TWO | 2. | 9 | 9.0 | 9.0 | 97.0 |
| THREE | 3. | 1 | 1.0 | 1.0 | 98.0 |
| FOUR | 4. | 1 | 1.0 | 1.0 | 99.0 |
| SEVEN | 7. | 1 | 1.0 | 1.0 | 100.0 |
| TOTAL | | 100 | 100.0 | 100.0 | 100.0 |

**FIG. 11.4**    Output from subprogram CODEBOOK.

```
CODEBOOK RUN FROM AN SPSS SYSTEM FILE                              07/25/69        PAGE   3

FILE   ORGSTUDY (CREATION DATE = 07/25/69)     STUDY OF ORGANIZATIONAL MEMBERSHIP AND ACTIVITY
SUBFILE   NEWYORK

VARIABLE   NMEM       TOTAL NUMBER OF MEMBERSHIPS

    CODE
          I
     0.   *************************************************** (     59)   59.0 PCT
          I     NONE
          I
          I
     1.   *************************** (     29)   29.0 PCT
          I     ONE
          I
          I
     2.   ********** (      9)    9.0 PCT
          I     TWO
          I
          I
     3.   ** (      1)    1.0 PCT
          I     THREE
          I
          I
     4.   ** (      1)    1.0 PCT
          I     FOUR
          I
          I
     7.   ** (      1)    1.0 PCT
          I     SEVEN
          I
          I.........I.........I.........I.........I.........I.........I.........I.........I.........I.........I
          0        10        20        30        40        50        60        70        80        90       100
          FREQUENCY

STATISTICS..

MEAN          0.610              MODE         0.0

VALID   OBSERVATIONS −       100
MISSING OBSERVATIONS −         0
```

**FIG. 11.4**    *(Continued)*

# 11.3    SUBPROGRAM MARGINALS: ONE-WAY FREQUENCY DISTRIBUTIONS AND RELATED STATISTICS

Subprogram MARGINALS computes and presents tables containing (1) simple raw frequencies, (2) relative frequencies, and (3) cumulative relative frequencies for classificatory or grouped variables. The same statistics available in subprogram CODEBOOK describing the character of frequency distributions are also available in MARGINALS by statistics number. While this program does not have the full labeling capabilities of CODEBOOK and does not enable the user to produce histograms, it maintains some features unavailable in CODEBOOK: (1) the printed output is more convenient to read for variables containing a large number of categories, and (2) it has an option which enables the user to suppress the printing of frequency tables, producing only the statistics which the user desires. As usual, sampling, selecting, and weighting, as well as recoding and variable transformations, may be temporarily or permanently effected while using subprogram MARGINALS.

### 11.3.1    THE MARGINALS PROCEDURE CARD

Subprogram MARGINALS is called and activated by a procedure card containing the control word MARGINALS. The control word is followed by a list of the variables for which marginal frequency tables and statistics are to be generated. The variables are entered onto the card according to the same conventions used in subprograms CONDESCRIPTIVE and CODEBOOK, and a fuller explanation of these conventions may be found in the preceding descriptions of these two procedure cards (see Secs. 11.1.1 and 11.2.1). Adjacent variables may be entered onto the card with the usual TO convention, and nonadjacent variables are listed in any order and separated by one or more common delimiters. If the user wishes to have frequency tables produced for all the variables in his file, the variable list can be replaced by the keyword ALL. The general format of the MARGINALS card is as follows:

1                 16
MARGINALS         ⎧ variable list ⎫
                  ⎨      or       ⎬
                  ⎩ ALL           ⎭

The following example card would cause one-way frequency distributions to be produced (along with the desired statistics for each variable named).

```
1              16
MARGINALS      AGE,SEX,PARTY,VAR010 TO VAR020
```

### 11.3.2   OPTIONS AVAILABLE FOR SUBPROGRAM MARGINALS

An OPTIONS card follows the MARGINALS card. As usual, the OPTIONS card contains the control word OPTIONS, followed by a list of the option numbers desired by the user. The missing-data options available in MARGINALS differ slightly from those in CODEBOOK. The format of the OPTIONS card is

```
1              16
OPTIONS        number list
```

*Option* 1.  Causes the missing values to be included in the tables and statistics. The *default option for missing data* instructs the system to delete cases which have values defined as missing from the relative frequencies, as well as from that of statistics. However, the number of missing cases is reported.

*Option* 2.  Suppresses the extended-variable label printing.

*Option* 3.  Suppresses the printing of cumulative frequencies.

*Option* 5.  Suppresses the printing of the frequency table, yielding only the statistics. The user must remember that the statistics will be computed according to the missing-value option selected above, even though the table will not be printed.

*Option* 6.  Causes the missing values to be included in the table, but deletes them from the computation of statistics.

If the OPTIONS card is deleted, missing data will be excluded from both the tables and the computations of the statistics, and options 2 to 6 will *not* be in effect. The number of missing cases for each missing variable will, however, be reported.

### 11.3.3   STATISTICS AVAILABLE FOR SUBPROGRAM MARGINALS

The user may select any of the following 11 statistics by number on the STATISTICS card which, as usual, directly follows the OPTIONS card. When the OPTIONS card is not prepared, the statistics card directly follows the MARGINALS card. Table 11.3 gives the statistics and their corresponding numbers. When a number is placed in the specification field, that statistic will be computed on all the variables for which marginals have been requested.

**TABLE 11.3   Correspondence between statistics and numbers for subprogram MARGINALS**

| | | | |
|---|---|---|---|
| 1 | Mean | 7 | Kurtosis |
| 2 | Standard error | 8 | Skewness |
| 3 | Median | 9 | Range |
| 4 | Mode | 10 | Minimum |
| 5 | Standard deviation | 11 | Maximum |
| 6 | Variance | | |

If the user wishes all of the statistics computed for each of the variables, he may enter the keyword ALL in place of the number list. If the STATISTICS card is omitted, the system assumes that no statistics are desired. (A brief description of the statistics can be found in Appendix D.) As usual, the format of the STATISTICS card is:

```
1              16
STATISTICS     ⎧ ALL        ⎫
               ⎨ or         ⎬
               ⎩ number list ⎭
```

### 11.3.4    PROGRAM LIMITATIONS FOR SUBPROGRAM MARGINALS

The following program limitations apply to the IBM 360 version of subprogram MARGINALS.

*Limitation* 1.   No more than 250 variable names may be referenced on a MARGINALS card. Names listed with the TO convention count as only three names, regardless of how many variables have been implied between the two names.

*Limitation* 2.   The maximum number of variables which can be processed on a single task is a function of the number of values or categories in the largest variable (i.e., the variable with the largest number of unique values) to be processed in that task. Clearly, the converse is also true; the largest number of values a variable may contain is a function of the number of variables to be processed. The user can determine if a planned run will fit in a single task by solving the following equations for either the maximum number of variables or the maximum number of values:[1]

$$MAXVALS = \frac{(SPACE/4) - (2 \times NVARS)}{(2 \times NVARS) + 3}$$

where MAXVALS is the number of values in the largest variable to be processed (i.e., the variable taking the largest number of values) and NVARS is the number of variables to be processed. Alternatively,

$$MAXVARS = \frac{(SPACE/4) - (3 \times NVALS)}{(2 \times NVALS) + 2}$$

where MAXVARS is the maximum number of variables which can be processed for a value of NVALS and NVALS is the number of values in the largest variable to be processed.

If the user violates limitation 1, an error message is printed and the run is terminated by the system before the data is processed. However, the system can never predetermine whether limitation 2 will be exceeded. If, as the data is being processed, the system encounters one or more variables which exceed the maximum number of permissible values (determined by the number of variables being processed—see the above formula), the offending variable or variables are deleted from the computations, and a message is printed listing the variable(s) which exceeded the maximum-value parameter. Frequency tables and desired statistics are produced for all other variables just as if no violation had occurred.

### 11.3.5    EXAMPLE DECK SETUP USING SUBPROGRAM MARGINALS

Example 11.5 illustrates the use of subprogram MARGINALS in a run using an SPSS system file; it also shows how multiple uses of a subprogram can be made in a single run. The system file named ORGSTUDY is retrieved with the use of a GET FILE card. This system file has been saved in a previous run.

**EXAMPLE 11.5**

```
1               16
RUN NAME        MARGINALS RUN FROM A SYSTEM FILE
GET FILE        ORGSTUDY
PROCESS SBFILES(NEWYORK,NWJERSEY)
COMMENT           NOTE THAT TWO SUBFILES ARE PROCESSED AS A GROUP
MARGINALS       AGE,INCOME
STATISTICS      1,2,3,4,5,6,9,10,11
PROCESS SBFILES(PENNSYLV)
COMMENT           NOTE ONLY ONE SUBFILE IS PROCESSED IN THE FOLLOWING
MARGINALS       INCOME
FINISH
```

ORGSTUDY contains three subfiles, labeled NEWYORK, NWJERSEY, and PENNSYLV. The PROCESS SUBFILE cards specify that in the first MARGINALS computation, the cases

---

[1]The default or normal value of the parameter SPACE is 80,000. The user may alter this parameter through the use of a JCL EXEC card (see Appendix A.1).

for subfiles NEWYORK AND NWJERSEY are to be processed as a group. In the second MARGINALS computation, only the cases of subfile PENNSYLV are to be included. For a complete listing of the file-defining information and cases for file ORGSTUDY, the reader is referred to Appendix I.

The first MARGINALS control card requests frequencies and statistics for the two variables AGE and INCOME. Both of these variables assume a large number of values. As mentioned previously, the MARGINALS subprogram is more appropriate than subprogram CODEBOOK for variables with a large number of distinct values. Notice that all available statistics except kurtosis and skewness are computed in this first task.

The second MARGINALS control card specifies that a computation and listing be performed for the variable INCOME. No statistics are computed, since the STATISTICS card is absent following the second MARGINALS card. The OPTIONS card has also been deleted and the default options will therefore be in force. Notice that it requires three pages of output to display the frequencies and statistics for variable AGE.

Note that COMMENT cards have been inserted in the control-card deck for improved legibility. These optional cards have no effect upon the results of the run.

The results of the run are reproduced in Fig. 11.5.

```
MARGINALS RUN FROM A SYSTEM FILE                                        07/25/69      PAGE   2

FILE    ORGSTUDY (CREATION DATE = 07/25/69)    STUDY OF ORGANIZATIONAL MEMBERSHIP AND ACTIVITY
SUBFILE    NEWYORK    NWJERSEY

VARIABLE    AGE        AGE LAST BIRTHDAY


CODE                             18.           20.           21.           22.           23.

ABSOLUTE FREQUENCY                2             3             1             2             2
RELATIVE FREQUENCY (PERCENT)     0.9           1.4           0.5           0.9           0.9
CUMULATIVE FREQUENCY (PERCENT)   0.9           2.3           2.8           3.7           4.7


CODE                             24.           25.           26.           27.           28.

ABSOLUTE FREQUENCY                11            7             5             3             4
RELATIVE FREQUENCY (PERCENT)     5.1           3.3           2.3           1.4           1.9
CUMULATIVE FREQUENCY (PERCENT)   9.8           13.0          15.3          16.7          18.6


CODE                             29.           30.           31.           32.           33.

ABSOLUTE FREQUENCY                4             6             3             1             4
RELATIVE FREQUENCY (PERCENT)     1.9           2.8           1.4           0.5           1.9
CUMULATIVE FREQUENCY (PERCENT)   20.5          23.3          24.7          25.1          27.0


CODE                             34.           35.           36.           37.           38.

ABSOLUTE FREQUENCY                3             5             2             3             4
RELATIVE FREQUENCY (PERCENT)     1.4           2.3           0.9           1.4           1.9
CUMULATIVE FREQUENCY (PERCENT)   28.4          30.7          31.6          33.0          34.9


CODE                             39.           40.           41.           42.           43.

ABSOLUTE FREQUENCY                3             4             8             6             3
RELATIVE FREQUENCY (PERCENT)     1.4           1.9           3.7           2.8           1.4
CUMULATIVE FREQUENCY (PERCENT)   36.3          38.1          41.9          44.7          46.0


CODE                             44.           45.           46.           47.           48.

ABSOLUTE FREQUENCY                3             2             6             3             7
RELATIVE FREQUENCY (PERCENT)     1.4           0.9           2.8           1.4           3.3
CUMULATIVE FREQUENCY (PERCENT)   47.4          48.4          51.2          52.6          55.8
```

**FIG. 11.5**  Output from subprogram MARGINALS.

MARGINALS RUN FROM A SYSTEM FILE                                                          07/25/69          PAGE    3

| CODE | 49. | 50. | 51. | 52. | 53. |
|---|---|---|---|---|---|
| ABSOLUTE FREQUENCY | 3 | 5 | 2 | 4 | 5 |
| RELATIVE FREQUENCY (PERCENT) | 1.4 | 2.3 | 0.9 | 1.9 | 2.3 |
| CUMULATIVE FREQUENCY (PERCENT) | 57.2 | 59.5 | 60.5 | 62.3 | 64.7 |

| CODE | 54. | 55. | 56. | 57. | 58. |
|---|---|---|---|---|---|
| ABSOLUTE FREQUENCY | 6 | 2 | 4 | 5 | 5 |
| RELATIVE FREQUENCY (PERCENT) | 2.8 | 0.9 | 1.9 | 2.3 | 2.3 |
| CUMULATIVE FREQUENCY (PERCENT) | 67.4 | 68.4 | 70.2 | 72.6 | 74.9 |

| CODE | 59. | 60. | 61. | 62. | 63. |
|---|---|---|---|---|---|
| ABSOLUTE FREQUENCY | 5 | 4 | 1 | 3 | 2 |
| RELATIVE FREQUENCY (PERCENT) | 2.3 | 1.9 | 0.5 | 1.4 | 0.9 |
| CUMULATIVE FREQUENCY (PERCENT) | 77.2 | 79.1 | 79.5 | 80.9 | 81.9 |

| CODE | 64. | 65. | 66. | 67. | 68. |
|---|---|---|---|---|---|
| ABSOLUTE FREQUENCY | 3 | 4 | 2 | 3 | 2 |
| RELATIVE FREQUENCY (PERCENT) | 1.4 | 1.9 | 0.9 | 1.4 | 0.9 |
| CUMULATIVE FREQUENCY (PERCENT) | 83.3 | 85.1 | 86.0 | 87.4 | 88.4 |

| CODE | 69. | 70. | 72. | 73. | 74. |
|---|---|---|---|---|---|
| ABSOLUTE FREQUENCY | 2 | 1 | 3 | 3 | 3 |
| RELATIVE FREQUENCY (PERCENT) | 0.9 | 0.5 | 1.4 | 1.4 | 1.4 |
| CUMULATIVE FREQUENCY (PERCENT) | 89.3 | 89.8 | 91.2 | 92.6 | 94.0 |

| CODE | 75. | 76. | 77. | 78. | 79. |
|---|---|---|---|---|---|
| ABSOLUTE FREQUENCY | 2 | 3 | 1 | 1 | 2 |
| RELATIVE FREQUENCY (PERCENT) | 0.9 | 1.4 | 0.5 | 0.5 | 0.9 |
| CUMULATIVE FREQUENCY (PERCENT) | 94.9 | 96.3 | 96.7 | 97.2 | 98.1 |

| CODE | 81. | 83. | 84. | 87. |
|---|---|---|---|---|
| ABSOLUTE FREQUENCY | 1 | 1 | 1 | 1 |
| RELATIVE FREQUENCY (PERCENT) | 0.5 | 0.5 | 0.5 | 0.5 |
| CUMULATIVE FREQUENCY (PERCENT) | 98.6 | 99.1 | 99.5 | 100.0 |

MARGINALS RUN FROM A SYSTEM FILE                                                          07/25/69          PAGE    4

FILE    ORGSTUDY (CREATION DATE = 07/25/69)    STUDY OF ORGANIZATIONAL MEMBERSHIP AND ACTIVITY
SUBFILE    NEWYORK    NWJERSEY

DESIRED STATISTICS..

| MEAN | 46.605 | STD ERROR | 1.140 | MEDIAN | 46.083 |
|---|---|---|---|---|---|
| MODE | 24.000 | STD DEV | 16.712 | VARIANCE | 279.279 |
| RANGE | 69.000 | MINIMUM | 18.000 | MAXIMUM | 87.000 |

VALID    OBSERVATIONS –        215
MISSING OBSERVATIONS –          0   OR    0.0 PERCENT OF TOTAL

**FIG. 11.5**    (*Continued*)

```
MARGINALS RUN FROM A SYSTEM FILE                                      07/25/69     PAGE  5

FILE   ORGSTUDY (CREATION DATE = 07/25/69)   STUDY OF ORGANIZATIONAL MEMBERSHIP AND ACTIVITY
SUBFILE   NEWYORK    NWJERSEY

VARIABLE   INCOME    FAMILY INCOME


CODE                              1.          2.          3.          4.          5.

ABSOLUTE FREQUENCY                18          16          23          25          13
RELATIVE FREQUENCY (PERCENT)      8.7         7.7        11.1        12.1         6.3
CUMULATIVE FREQUENCY (PERCENT)    8.7        16.4        27.5        39.6        45.9


CODE                              6.          7.         11.         21.         31.

ABSOLUTE FREQUENCY                18          17          22          15           5
RELATIVE FREQUENCY (PERCENT)      8.7         8.2        10.6         7.2         2.4
CUMULATIVE FREQUENCY (PERCENT)   54.6        62.8        73.4        80.7        83.1


CODE                             41.         51.         61.         71.

ABSOLUTE FREQUENCY                19          11           2           3
RELATIVE FREQUENCY (PERCENT)      9.2         5.3         1.0         1.4
CUMULATIVE FREQUENCY (PERCENT)   92.3        97.6        98.6       100.0



MISSING VALUES..

CODE                             88.         99.

ABSOLUTE FREQUENCY                5           3



DESIRED STATISTICS..

MEAN        14.000          STD ERROR      1.177          MEDIAN        5.972

MODE         4.000          STD DEV       16.941          VARIANCE    286.990

RANGE       70.000          MINIMUM        1.000          MAXIMUM      71.000

VALID   OBSERVATIONS -    207
MISSING OBSERVATIONS -      8   OR   3.7 PERCENT OF TOTAL



MARGINALS RUN FROM A SYSTEM FILE                                      07/25/69     PAGE  6

FILE   ORGSTUDY (CREATION DATE = 07/25/69)   STUDY OF ORGANIZATIONAL MEMBERSHIP AND ACTIVITY
SUBFILE   PENNSYLV

VARIABLE   INCOME    FAMILY INCOME


CODE                              1.          2.          3.          4.          5.

ABSOLUTE FREQUENCY                 2           8           9           7           5
RELATIVE FREQUENCY (PERCENT)      1.5         6.0         6.8         5.3         3.8
CUMULATIVE FREQUENCY (PERCENT)    1.5         7.5        14.3        19.5        23.3


CODE                              6.          7.         11.         21.         31.

ABSOLUTE FREQUENCY                14          17           8          12          11
RELATIVE FREQUENCY (PERCENT)     10.5        12.8         6.0         9.0         8.3
CUMULATIVE FREQUENCY (PERCENT)   33.8        46.6        52.6        61.7        69.9


CODE                             41.         51.         61.         71.

ABSOLUTE FREQUENCY                27           8           2           3
RELATIVE FREQUENCY (PERCENT)     20.3         6.0         1.5         2.3
CUMULATIVE FREQUENCY (PERCENT)   90.2        96.2        97.7       100.0



MISSING VALUES..

CODE                             99.

ABSOLUTE FREQUENCY                2


VALID   OBSERVATIONS -    133
MISSING OBSERVATIONS -      2   OR   1.5 PERCENT OF TOTAL
```

**FIG. 11.5**   (*Continued*)

# 12
# TABLE DISPLAYS OF RELATIONSHIPS BETWEEN TWO OR MORE VARIABLES: CROSSTABULATION AND DESCRIPTION OF SUBPOPULATIONS

After the researcher has examined the distribution of each of his variables, he normally begins to investigate sets of relationships among two or more of these variables. Based on the characteristics of the variables and the purposes of his analysis, one or more procedures for examining relationships will be selected. SPSS contains three programs which permit the user to examine relationships in a table-type format. There are two subprograms for computing and displaying two-way to *n*-way crosstabulation tables—CROSSTABS and FASTABS. The third subprogram, BREAKDOWN, computes the means and standard deviations of a dependent variable (which normally must be interval in scale) for specified subgroups in the sample or population.

The two subprograms CROSSTABS and FASTABS serve the same basic functions. They both permit the user to compute bivariate joint frequency distributions with varying levels of control variables. They both have complete variable- and value-labeling capabilities. Both programs permit the user to process missing data by a number of different options, and the two programs contain a rather complete complement of significance tests and measures of association which may be selected by the user. As usual, all of the SPSS recoding, variable-transformations, and data-selection features may be utilized when using either one of these programs.

The two programs differ insofar as FASTABS is restricted to operating on variables which are integer numbers, while CROSSTABS can operate on any type of variable—alphanumeric or numeric. FASTABS also requires a slightly greater amount of control-card preparation in that the user must specify the upper and lower limits of the variables to be entered into the crosstabulation tables. CROSSTABS, on the other hand, only requires the user to know and submit the names of the variables to be crosstabulated. The sole advantage of subprogram FASTABS is its processing speed, which is *significantly faster* than the more general CROSS-TABS subprogram. This discrepancy in processing speed should not be taken lightly, for FASTABS can result in enormous savings in machine time, particularly with large files. Furthermore, the recoding and variable transformation capabilities of SPSS will usually enable the user to make variables compatible with subprogram FASTABS with a minimal amount of effort.

The subgroup means and standard deviations produced by subprogram BREAKDOWN are analogous in many respects to crosstabulation where each mean and standard deviation summarizes a complete row or column of a contingency table. The output from this program presents the mean, standard deviation, and variance of the dependent variable for the entire population. These same statistics are then computed for each subgroup or category of each independent variable included in the table along with the number of cases falling into that group. The means, standard deviations, and variances are presented as a logical breakdown or tree—first for groups, then for subgroups within groups, next for sub-subgroups within subgroups, etc. Up to five independent variables may be entered into a single table.

The detailed specifications for CROSSTABS and FASTABS are presented in Secs. 12.2 and 12.3, respectively. Subprogram BREAKDOWN is described in Sec. 12.4. Because of the prominence of crosstabulation in social research—reflected by the fact that SPSS contains two programs for crosstabulation—an introduction to crosstabulation is presented before these programs are described in detail.

## 12.1     AN INTRODUCTION TO CROSSTABULATION

A crosstabulation is basically a joint frequency distribution of cases according to two or more classificatory variables. The display of the distribution of cases by their position on two or more variables is the chief component of contingency-table analysis and indeed the most commonly used analysis method in the social sciences.[1] These joint frequency distributions can be statistically analyzed by certain tests of significance (e.g., the chi-square statistic) and can be summarized by a number of measures of association between pairs of variables within the joint frequency tables, such as the contingency coefficient, phi, tau, gamma, etc. (See Appendix D for a definition of these statistics.)

The nature of crosstabulation tables can perhaps be best illustrated by a typical example of such an analysis and a hypothesis concerning its results. The most basic form of crosstabulation is the 2 × 2 table. Consider a study which hypothesizes that the frequency of blue-eyed persons among individuals with blonde hair is considerably greater than the incidence of blue-eyed persons among individuals with brunette hair. If a survey collecting this information were taken, the above hypothesis could be tested by the following 2 × 2 table:

|  | Blonde | Brunette |
|---|---|---|
| Blue |  |  |
| Nonblue |  |  |

Let us further assume that the study examined 100 blonde individuals and 200 brunettes, and that the tabulation of the data indicated the following frequency distribution:

[1]For an excellent introduction to the logic of contingency table analysis, see Morris Rosenberg, "The Logic of Survey Analysis," Basic Books, New York, 1968.

|  | Blonde | Brunette |  |
|---|---|---|---|
| Blue | 75 | 40 | 115 |
| Nonblue | 25 | 160 | 185 |
|  | 100 | 200 |  |

A quick perusal of this table indicates that there are dramatic differences in the proportions of blondes and brunettes with blue eyes. Because, however, there are different total numbers of blondes and brunettes, the exact difference is most clearly revealed when the proportions are examined:

|  | Blonde | Brunette |  |
|---|---|---|---|
| Blue | (75) 75% | (40) 20% | 115 |
| Nonblue | (25) 25% | (160) 80% | 185 |
|  | 100% 100 | 100% 200 |  |

Obviously, there is a strong relationship between the color of hair and the color of eyes. But the results of contingency tables are often less dramatic, and the question usually emerges as to whether the differences in percentage are statistically significant. Without attempting here to raise a question best answered in basic statistics books, there are a number of ways in which the percentage may be examined (provided the sample is more or less random) which can determine whether discrepancies in percentages are due solely to sampling error or reflect statistically significant relationships. (A number of tests of significance and association, available in FAS-TABS and CROSSTABS, are described briefly in Appendix D.)

There are two logical extensions of this basic table: the addition of other variables as controls and the addition of categories within each of the variables. In order to demonstrate these logical extensions, let us shift to a less obvious and more interesting hypothesis. Consider a study which is concerned with the very basic determinates of individual income and first hypothesizes that there is a strong relationship between level of education and level of income, and next hypothesizes that this basic relationship is affected by racial prejudice. One might, in this case, draw a random sample of adult Americans, collecting measurements on race, education, and income. The initial table testing the hypothesis of a strong positive relation between income and education might appear as follows, depending on the amount of detail used in classifying the data which has been gathered:

|  | Education | | |
|---|---|---|---|
| Income | Grade school or less | 1–4 years high school | 1 or more years college |
| Under $3000 | 40% | 25% | 5% |
| $3000–$6000 | 35% | 30% | 15% |
| $6000–$10,000 | 20% | 35% | 40% |
| Over $10,000 | 5% | 10% | 40% |
|  | 100% | 100% | 100% |

It is evident from this table that there is a strong relationship between education and income. As the level of education increases, the proportion of individuals in the lower-income categories decreases while the proportion in the higher-income categories increases. The second hypothesis that race affects this relationship and specifically that nonwhites will have lower incomes at all levels of education requires a three-dimensional table. Because printing surfaces are two-dimensional, three-dimensional tables are usually presented in the following format:

| Income | Whites | | |
| | Education | | |
| | Grade school or less | 1—4 years high school | 1 or more years college |
|---|---|---|---|
| Under $3000 | 35% | 15% | 2% |
| $3000–$6000 | 35% | 35% | 13% |
| $6000–$10,000 | 25% | 40% | 40% |
| Over $10,000 | 5% | 10% | 45% |
| | 100% | 100% | 100% |

| Income | Nonwhites | | |
| | Education | | |
| | Grade school or less | 1—4 years high school | 1 or more years college |
|---|---|---|---|
| Under $3000 | 50% | 35% | 10% |
| $3000–$6000 | 45% | 45% | 25% |
| $6000–$10,000 | 5% | 15% | 50% |
| Over $10,000 | 0% | 5% | 15% |
| | 100% | 100% | 100% |

It is clear from these tables, which are actually subtables in a three-dimensional table, that the second as well as the first hypothesis is confirmed.

Again, we have ignored the problem of tests of significance and measures of association. The statistics available for the two SPSS crosstabulation subprograms are briefly defined in Appendix D. The user should, however, consult a statistics book before using these measures.[1] Sections 12.2 and 12.3 are devoted to the write-ups of the two SPSS subprograms which compute two-way to $n$-way crosstabulation tables.

## 12.2    SUBPROGRAM CROSSTABS: TWO-WAY TO n-WAY CROSSTABULATION TABLES AND RELATED STATISTICS

Subprogram CROSSTABS enables the user to compute two-way to $n$-way joint frequency distributions of the type described in the previous section for either alphanumeric or numeric variables. Any type of variable may be entered into a crosstabulation table so long as it has no more than 250 individual or unique values. Unlike most crosstabulation programs, subprogram CROSSTABS does not require that the user specify the number of categories in the variables being entered into the tables. This program also enables the user to take advantage of the full variable- and value-labeling features of the SPSS system, and all labels are automatically reported when present unless suppressed by the user.

Each of the two-way tables and subtables may be percentaged by column, by row, by the percent of the total table, or any combination of the three. Alternatively, all percentages can be suppressed so only the raw frequency distributions are presented. Column and row totals and percentages are also reported in the tables. In addition to the table-presentation options, a rather complete complement of significance tests and measures of association are available. Alphanumeric and numeric variables can both be input into the CROSSTABS program; however, the user should be careful when interpreting those statistics that make ordinal assumptions

---

[1]Two widely used statistics books explaining most of the statistics available in CROSSTABS and FASTABS are Hubert Blalock, "Social Statistics," McGraw-Hill, New York, 1960, and Sidney Siegel, "Nonparametric Statistics for the Behavioral Sciences," McGraw-Hill, New York, 1956.

about the data when alphanumeric variables are present. Of course, like all subprograms in the SPSS system, missing data can be handled according to a number of options; and recoding and variable transformations, either permanent or temporary, as well as the sampling, selecting, and weighting of cases, can be accomplished for any set of crosstabulations.

### 12.2.1  THE CROSSTABS PROCEDURE CARD

The user specifies the desired tables by means of the CROSSTABS procedure card. The CROSS-TABS card may reference any variable name which has been previously defined, either on a variable-list card, in an existing file, or by means of a variable transformation. The variable names on the CROSSTABS card are linked by the keyword BY. The card has the following general format:

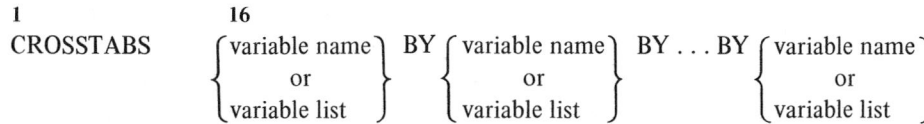

As usual, the keyword BY must be separated from the variable names by one or more common delimiters, and the variable names must be spelled correctly. The CROSSTABS card may be continued from one physical card to the next as long as columns 1 to 15 of all succeeding cards are left blank. All conventions applying to names and keywords must be followed. (Be careful not to split variable names between cards.) The following example illustrates how two- to five-way tables can be produced by means of the CROSSTABS card.

```
1               16
CROSSTABS       AGE BY SEX
CROSSTABS       AGE BY SEX BY RACE
CROSSTABS       AGE BY SEX BY RACE BY INCOME
CROSSTABS       AGE BY SEX BY RACE BY INCOME BY EDUCATN
```

The first CROSSTABS card indicates a simple two-way frequency table: the variable AGE by the variable SEX. The second will yield a number of tables for AGE by SEX, one for each value of the variable RACE. The third card specifies a table of AGE by SEX for all possible combinations of the values of the variables RACE and INCOME. If, for example, there were three categories of INCOME (high, medium, and low) and two of RACE (white and nonwhite) six subtables would be produced. The tables would be put out in the order of the value of the last variable named changing most slowly; that is, there would be two subtables of AGE by SEX, one for whites and one for nonwhites, for each category of INCOME. It is very important to understand the sequential order of the variables surrounding the BY designation: the first variable mentioned always becomes the row variable and the second is always the column variable; and if three or more variables are involved in one set of tables, the third variable becomes the lowest-order control variable, and so forth, moving to the right. The values of the last variable mentioned change most slowly. The following examples illustrate how different tables can be requested by changing the order of the variables.

```
1               16
CROSSTABS       RACE BY INCOME
CROSSTABS       INCOME BY RACE
```

The first card will produce a table where RACE is the row variable, while the second will specify INCOME as the row variable:

The user should be particularly careful in sequencing his variables and selecting whether he desires his percentages to be based on column or row tables.

Multiple tables can be specified on a single CROSSTABS card by several conventions. First, a number of individual tables can be specified by placing a slash [/] between the table requests, as in the following example, which will cause one table to be computed for RACE BY INCOME, another for URB BY EDUCATN, and a third for SEX BY OCCUPATN.

```
1                16
CROSSTABS        RACE BY INCOME/URB BY EDUCATN/SEX BY OCCUPATN
```

The order in which tables are requested is unimportant except that the tables will be printed in that order.

Multiple tables can also be requested by placing more than one variable name to the right or left of any BY. These variable lists may consist of lists of nonadjacent variables set off by one or more common delimiter(s), or when groups of adjacent variables are to be crosstabulated, variable lists utilizing the normal TO convention may be entered. As usual, these two conventions may be intermixed, producing lists of variables for crosstabulations of the following sort:

VARA,VARD,VARF TO VARJ BY VARN, VARP TO VARQ,VARZ

These multiple lists will produce one table for each variable named or implied on the left side of the BY for every variable named or implied to the right of the BY. The first variable named to the left of the BY becomes the row variable and will be crosstabulated with each variable named or implied to the right of the BY beginning with the leftmost variable directly following the keyword BY and ending with the last variable named. When tables for all of the column variables have been generated for the first row variable, the process is repeated for the next row variable. This procedure is repeated, moving from left to right, for all variables named or implied to the left of the keyword BY. The user should note that while the values of the last variable change most slowly, the identity of the last variable changes most rapidly. The following examples demonstrate in greater detail how multiple table requests may be constructed.

```
1                16
CROSSTABS        RACE,SEX,INCOME BY EDUCATN,OCCUPATN
CROSSTABS        RACE BY SEX TO INCOME
CROSSTABS        RACE TO OCCUPATN BY EDUCATN
CROSSTABS        RACE TO OCCUPATN BY INCOME TO EDUCATN
CROSSTABS        RACE TO OCCUPATN BY INCOME TO EDUCATN BY CITY
```

In the first example, RACE will become the first row variable and will be crosstabulated first with EDUCATN and then with OCCUPATN. SEX will then become the row variable to be crosstabulated with EDUCATN and OCCUPATN. This will be repeated for INCOME, which is the last row variable. In the second example, RACE is the only row variable, and one table will be produced for each variable (in the file) from SEX to and including INCOME. If there were five variables between and inclusive of these variables, five tables would be produced with RACE by SEX being the first table and RACE by INCOME being the last. In the third example, RACE will again become the first row variable, while EDUCATN will always be the column variable, and RACE will be replaced in turn by all variables falling between it and OCCUPATN in the variable list. In the fourth example, RACE will become the first row variable, and one table will be produced for each variable between and inclusive of INCOME and EDUCATN, which will all be column variables. A similar set of tables will be produced for each row variable between RACE and OCCUPATN. In the last and most complex example, there will be one table for each value of CITY for every combination specified (i.e., each combination of RACE TO OCCUPATN BY INCOME TO EDUCATN will have one subtable printed for each value of CITY). In effect, CITY becomes the control variable for the entire set of tables that were generated in the fourth example.

In the above examples each set of table requests was placed on a separate CROSSTABS card. This was done solely for the sake of clarity, for many such lists can be entered onto a single CROSSTABS card and its continuations as long as each list is separated from the next by the special delimiter, the slash [/]. All the usual rules concerning continuing SPSS control cards from one physical card to the next apply (see Sec. 3.1, and particularly Sec. 3.1.3).

### 12.2.2   PRINTED OUTPUT FROM SUBPROGRAM CROSSTABS

The printed output from subprogram CROSSTABS is designed to give a complete representation of joint frequency distributions in a readily understandable table form.[1] The sample output shown in Fig. 12.1 demonstrates a simple two-way table crosstabulating number of organizational memberships by level of education. The example also illustrates all statistics which subprogram CROSSTABS enables the user to generate for any given table. The table was requested with raw frequencies and column percentages (as indicated in the section on the OPTIONS card, the table may be percentaged by any combination of column percentages, row percentages, and percentage of the entire table). The numbers on the left margin and the upper margin of the table are the value codes themselves. The labels to the left of and above the value codes are the value labels corresponding to the first and second variables, respectively. They are optional and will only be printed when they have already been input into the file. The upper number in each cell is the cell count or absolute frequency; the lower number is the column percentage. With allowance made for rounding, the sum of each column's percentages should approximate 100 percent. The upper numbers in the row totals and column totals are equal to the sum of the raw cell frequencies for the respective rows and columns. The lower number in each of these cases is the percentage which that row or column is of all rows or columns. The total number of cases on which the table is based is given in the lower right corner of the table. When there are missing cases, the number is indicated below the statistics list.

Figure 12.2 indicates how three- to $n$-way tables are printed. This table displays the crosstabulation of education by number of memberships, controlled by sex.

[1]We are grateful to the designers of the DATATEXT crosstabulation program, since the output format of that program greatly influenced the design of our own.

```
CROSSTABS RUN                                                    07/25/69      PAGE   38

FILE    ORGSTUDY (CREATION DATE = 07/25/69)     STUDY OF ORGANIZATIONAL MEMBERSHIP AND ACTIVITY
SUBFILE   PENNSYLV

* * * * * * * * * * * * * * * *  C R O S S T A B U L A T I O N   O F  * * * * * * * * * * * * * * * * * *
    EDRESPON  LAST YEAR SCHOOL COMPLETED              BY  NMEM      TOTAL NUMBER OF MEMBERSHIPS
* * * * * * * * * * * * * * * * * * * * * * * * * * * * * * * * * * * * * * * * * * * * *  PAGE  1 OF  1

                    NMEM
             COUNT  I
             COL PCT INONE    ONE     TWO      THREE   FOUR    FIVE     SEVEN    ROW
                    I                                                           TOTAL
                    I    0. I   1. I    2. I    3. I    4. I    5. I    7. I
EDRESPON     --------I-------I-------I-------I-------I-------I-------I-------I
             1.  I     2  I    0  I    0  I    0  I    0  I    0  I    0  I     2
NONE         I     3.7  I  0.0  I  0.0  I  0.0  I  0.0  I  0.0  I  0.0  I   1.5
             -I-------I-------I-------I-------I-------I-------I-------I
             2.  I    16  I   10  I    3  I    2  I    0  I    0  I    0  I    31
1-8 YEARS    I    29.6  I 27.0  I 10.3  I 33.3  I  0.0  I  0.0  I  0.0  I  23.0
             -I-------I-------I-------I-------I-------I-------I-------I
             3.  I    13  I    3  I    6  I    1  I    0  I    0  I    0  I    23
9-11 YEARS   I    24.1  I  8.1  I 20.7  I 16.7  I  0.0  I  0.0  I  0.0  I  17.0
             -I-------I-------I-------I-------I-------I-------I-------I
             4.  I    13  I   16  I    6  I    0  I    0  I    0  I    0  I    35
12 YEARS     I    24.1  I 43.2  I 20.7  I  0.0  I  0.0  I  0.0  I  0.0  I  25.9
             -I-------I-------I-------I-------I-------I-------I-------I
             5.  I     8  I    8  I    7  I    1  I    1  I    1  I    1  I    27
COLLEGE INCOMPLE I  14.8  I 21.6  I 24.1  I 16.7  I 20.0  I 33.3  I100.0  I  20.0
             -I-------I-------I-------I-------I-------I-------I-------I
             6.  I     2  I    0  I    5  I    1  I    3  I    0  I    0  I    11
COLLEGE GRAD I     3.7  I  0.0  I 17.2  I 16.7  I 60.0  I  0.0  I  0.0  I   8.1
             -I-------I-------I-------I-------I-------I-------I-------I
             7.  I     0  I    0  I    2  I    1  I    1  I    2  I    0  I     6
COLLEGE PLUS I     0.0  I  0.0  I  6.9  I 16.7  I 20.0  I 66.7  I  0.0  I   4.4
             -I-------I-------I-------I-------I-------I-------I-------I
             COLUMN     54      37      29       6       5       3       1      135
             TOTAL    40.0    27.4    21.5     4.4     3.7     2.2     0.7    100.0

CHI SQUARE =     86.77995 WITH   36 DEGREES OF FREEDOM
CRAMER'S V =     0.32732
CONTINGENCY COEFFICIENT =      0.62553
KENDALL'S TAU B =     0.33896
KENDALL'S TAU C =     0.29946
GAMMA =     0.43711
SOMER'S D =     0.35907
```

**FIG. 12.1**   A two-way crosstabulation produced by subprogram CROSSTABS.

```
CROSSTABS RUN                                                    07/25/69      PAGE  39

FILE    ORGSTUDY (CREATION DATE = 07/25/69)   STUDY OF ORGANIZATIONAL MEMBERSHIP AND ACTIVITY
SUBFILE   PENNSYLV

* * * * * * * * * * * * * * * *  C R O S S T A B U L A T I O N   O F  * * * * * * * * * * * * * * * * * * * * * *
     EDRESPON  LAST YEAR SCHOOL COMPLETED                    BY  NMEM     TOTAL NUMBER OF MEMBERSHIPS
CONTROLLING FOR..
     SEX       RESPONDENTS SEX                                   VALUE =        1.  MALE
* * * * * * * * * * * * * * * * * * * * * * * * * * * * * * * * * * * * * * * * * * * * * *  PAGE  1 OF  1
```

|  |  | NMEM |  |  |  |  |  |  |  |
|---|---|---|---|---|---|---|---|---|---|---|
| COUNT | I | NONE | ONE | TWO | THREE | FOUR | FIVE | SEVEN | ROW |
| COL PCT | I | | | | | | | | TOTAL |
| | I | 0. I | 1. I | 2. I | 3. I | 4. I | 5. I | 7. I | |
| EDRESPON |  |  |  |  |  |  |  |  |  |
| 1. NONE | I | 2 I 8.3 | 0 I 0.0 | 0 I 0.0 | 0 I 0.0 | 0 I 0.0 | 0 I 0.0 | 0 I 0.0 | 2 3.0 |
| 2. 1-8 YEARS | I | 6 I 25.0 | 7 I 35.0 | 3 I 21.4 | 1 I 33.3 | 0 I 0.0 | 0 I 0.0 | 0 I 0.0 | 17 25.8 |
| 3. 9-11 YEARS | I | 4 I 16.7 | 1 I 5.0 | 3 I 21.4 | 1 I 33.3 | 0 I 0.0 | 0 I 0.0 | 0 I 0.0 | 9 13.6 |
| 4. 12 YEARS | I | 5 I 20.8 | 8 I 40.0 | 2 I 14.3 | 0 I 0.0 | 0 I 0.0 | 0 I 0.0 | 0 I 0.0 | 15 22.7 |
| 5. COLLEGE INCOMPLE | I | 5 I 20.8 | 4 I 20.0 | 3 I 21.4 | 0 I 0.0 | 1 I 33.3 | 0 I 0.0 | 1 I 100.0 | 14 21.2 |
| 6. COLLEGE GRAD | I | 2 I 8.3 | 0 I 0.0 | 3 I 21.4 | 0 I 0.0 | 1 I 33.3 | 0 I 0.0 | 0 I 0.0 | 6 9.1 |
| 7. COLLEGE PLUS | I | 0 I 0.0 | 0 I 0.0 | 0 I 0.0 | 1 I 33.3 | 1 I 33.3 | 1 I 100.0 | 0 I 0.0 | 3 4.5 |
| COLUMN TOTAL | | 24 36.4 | 20 30.3 | 14 21.2 | 3 4.5 | 3 4.5 | 1 1.5 | 1 1.5 | 66 100.0 |

```
CHI SQUARE =     58.19641 WITH  36 DEGREES OF FREEDOM
CRAMER'S V =    0.38335
CONTINGENCY COEFFICIENT =    0.68453
KENDALL'S TAU B =    0.22786
KENDALL'S TAU C =    0.20355
GAMMA =    0.29096
SOMER'S D =    0.24020
```

```
CROSSTABS RUN                                                    07/25/69      PAGE  40

FILE    ORGSTUDY (CREATION DATE = 07/25/69)   STUDY OF ORGANIZATIONAL MEMBERSHIP AND ACTIVITY
SUBFILE   PENNSYLV

* * * * * * * * * * * * * * * *  C R O S S T A B U L A T I O N   O F  * * * * * * * * * * * * * * * * * * * * * *
     EDRESPON  LAST YEAR SCHOOL COMPLETED                    BY  NMEM     TOTAL NUMBER OF MEMBERSHIPS
CONTROLLING FOR..
     SEX       RESPONDENTS SEX                                   VALUE =        2.  FEMALE
* * * * * * * * * * * * * * * * * * * * * * * * * * * * * * * * * * * * * * * * * * * * * *  PAGE  1 OF  1
```

|  |  | NMEM |  |  |  |  |  |  |
|---|---|---|---|---|---|---|---|---|
| COUNT | I | NONE | ONE | TWO | THREE | FOUR | FIVE | ROW |
| COL PCT | I | | | | | | | TOTAL |
| | I | 0. I | 1. I | 2. I | 3. I | 4. I | 5. I | |
| EDRESPON |  |  |  |  |  |  |  |  |
| 2. 1-8 YEARS | I | 10 I 33.3 | 3 I 17.6 | 0 I 0.0 | 1 I 33.3 | 0 I 0.0 | 0 I 0.0 | 14 20.3 |
| 3. 9-11 YEARS | I | 9 I 30.0 | 2 I 11.8 | 3 I 20.0 | 0 I 0.0 | 0 I 0.0 | 0 I 0.0 | 14 20.3 |
| 4. 12 YEARS | I | 8 I 26.7 | 8 I 47.1 | 4 I 26.7 | 0 I 0.0 | 0 I 0.0 | 0 I 0.0 | 20 29.0 |
| 5. COLLEGE INCOMPLE | I | 3 I 10.0 | 4 I 23.5 | 4 I 26.7 | 1 I 33.3 | 0 I 0.0 | 1 I 50.0 | 13 18.8 |
| 6. COLLEGE GRAD | I | 0 I 0.0 | 0 I 0.0 | 2 I 13.3 | 1 I 33.3 | 2 I 100.0 | 0 I 0.0 | 5 7.2 |
| 7. COLLEGE PLUS | I | 0 I 0.0 | 0 I 0.0 | 2 I 13.3 | 0 I 0.0 | 0 I 0.0 | 1 I 50.0 | 3 4.3 |
| COLUMN TOTAL | | 30 43.5 | 17 24.6 | 15 21.7 | 3 4.3 | 2 2.9 | 2 2.9 | 69 100.0 |

```
CHI SQUARE =     63.31844 WITH  25 DEGREES OF FREEDOM
CRAMER'S V =    0.42841
CONTINGENCY COEFFICIENT =    0.69176
KENDALL'S TAU B =    0.46988
KENDALL'S TAU C =    0.41941
GAMMA =    0.60730
SOMER'S D =    0.49970
```

**FIG. 12.2**   A three-way crosstabulation produced by subprogram CROSSTABS.

When using alphanumeric variables, the user should note that the printing sequence places all numeric characters first in descending order (highest to lowest), then the letters of the alphabet, again in descending order (Z to A), followed by any special characters ('–', '&', etc.). This will affect the way in which tables are printed and also the interpretation of statistics which depend on ordinal order. For example, if the user had two variables, each coded 1,2,3,A,B,C, the row variable would be printed down the page with 3 as the first value, 2 and 1 as the second and third, and then the alphabetics C,B, and A. The column variable would be printed 3, 2, 1, C, B, and A from the left to the right.

There are occasional instances in which the user desires to print very large tables which are too large to fit onto a single page of printed output. When this is the case, the table will be segmented and printed on successive pages until it has been entirely printed. A table of this type is printed starting at the northwest corner and moving across the row toward the northeast corner. When the width of the table has been printed, the next segment is started from the western side, and so forth, until the whole table is printed. This process might look as follows:

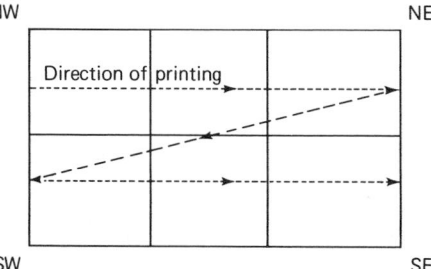

An example of a segmented table is shown in Fig. 12.3.

### 12.2.2.1  A note on value labels for CROSSTABS

Value labels are automatically printed on all crosstabulation tables (wherever present) unless the user explicitly suppresses them through the use of option 2. However, because of space requirements, only the first 16 characters of these 20 character labels are printed. Furthermore, when a variable appears in a table as the column variable, its value labels are broken into two lines for printing purposes. The first eight characters appear on the first line and the second eight on a following line. If the user is concerned about the format of the labels, he should

```
CROSSTABS RUN FROM A SYSTEM FILE                                      07/25/69      PAGE   42

FILE    ORGSTUDY (CREATION DATE = 07/25/69)    STUDY OF ORGANIZATIONAL MEMBERSHIP AND ACTIVITY
SUBFILE    PENNSYLV

* * * * * * * * * * * * * *    C R O S S T A B U L A T I O N   O F   * * * * * * * * * * * * * * * * *
   RACE      RESPONDENTS RACE                     BY  INCOME    FAMILY INCOME
* * * * * * * * * * * * * * * * * * * * * * * * * * * * * * * * * * * * * * * * *   PAGE  1 OF  2

                  INCOME
           COUNT  I
           ROW PCT ILESS THA 1000-199 2000-299 3000-399 4000-499 5000-599 6000-699 7000-799 8000-899 9000-999   ROW
           COL PCT IN 1000    9        9        9        9        9        9        9        9        9        TOTAL
           TOT PCT I    1.I     2.I      3.I      4.I      5.I      6.I      7.I     11.I     21.I     31.I
          -------I--------I--------I--------I--------I--------I--------I--------I--------I--------I--------I
RACE
              1.  I     1  I     6  I     7  I     6  I     2  I    10  I    15  I     7  I    11  I    10  I    115
WHITE            I   0.9  I   5.2  I   6.1  I   5.2  I   1.7  I   8.7  I  13.0  I   6.1  I   9.6  I   8.7  I   86.5
                 I  50.0  I  75.0  I  77.8  I  85.7  I  40.0  I  71.4  I  88.2  I  87.5  I  91.7  I  90.9  I
                 I   0.8  I   4.5  I   5.3  I   4.5  I   1.5  I   7.5  I  11.3  I   5.3  I   8.3  I   7.5  I
              -I--------I--------I--------I--------I--------I--------I--------I--------I--------I--------I
              2.  I     1  I     2  I     1  I     0  I     3  I     3  I     2  I     0  I     0  I     1  I     13
NEGRO            I   7.7  I  15.4  I   7.7  I   0.0  I  23.1  I  23.1  I  15.4  I   0.0  I   0.0  I   7.7  I    9.8
                 I  50.0  I  25.0  I  11.1  I   0.0  I  60.0  I  21.4  I  11.8  I   0.0  I   0.0  I   9.1  I
                 I   0.8  I   1.5  I   0.8  I   0.0  I   2.3  I   2.3  I   1.5  I   0.0  I   0.0  I   0.8  I
              -I--------I--------I--------I--------I--------I--------I--------I--------I--------I--------I
              3.  I     0  I     0  I     0  I     0  I     0  I     0  I     0  I     0  I     1  I     0  I      1
ORIENTAL         I   0.0  I   0.0  I   0.0  I   0.0  I   0.0  I   0.0  I   0.0  I   0.0  I 100.0  I   0.0  I    0.8
                 I   0.0  I   0.0  I   0.0  I   0.0  I   0.0  I   0.0  I   0.0  I   0.0  I   8.3  I   0.0  I
                 I   0.0  I   0.0  I   0.0  I   0.0  I   0.0  I   0.0  I   0.0  I   0.0  I   0.8  I   0.0  I
              -I--------I--------I--------I--------I--------I--------I--------I--------I--------I--------I
              5.  I     0  I     0  I     1  I     1  I     0  I     1  I     0  I     1  I     0  I     0  I      4
LATIN AMERICAN   I   0.0  I   0.0  I  25.0  I  25.0  I   0.0  I  25.0  I   0.0  I  25.0  I   0.0  I   0.0  I    3.0
                 I   0.0  I   0.0  I  11.1  I  14.3  I   0.0  I   7.1  I   0.0  I  12.5  I   0.0  I   0.0  I
                 I   0.0  I   0.0  I   0.8  I   0.8  I   0.0  I   0.8  I   0.0  I   0.8  I   0.0  I   0.0  I
              -I--------I--------I--------I--------I--------I--------I--------I--------I--------I--------I
           COLUMN      2        8        9        7        5       14       17        8       12       11        133
           TOTAL     1.5      6.0      6.8      5.3      3.8     10.5     12.8      6.0      9.0      8.3      100.0
(CONTINUED)
```

**FIG. 12.3**  An example of a segmented crosstabulation table.

```
CROSSTABS RUN FROM A SYSTEM FILE                                      07/25/69        PAGE  43

FILE   ORGSTUDY (CREATION DATE = 07/25/69)    STUDY OF ORGANIZATIONAL MEMBERSHIP AND ACTIVITY
SUBFILE   PENNSYLV

* * * * * * * * * * * * * * *   C R O S S T A B U L A T I O N   O F   * * * * * * * * * * * * * * * *
      RACE     RESPONDENTS RACE                              BY  INCOME    FAMILY INCOME
* * * * * * * * * * * * * * * * * * * * * * * * * * * * * * * * * * * * * * * * * * * *  PAGE  2 OF  2


                   INCOME
              COUNT I
              ROW PCT I10000-14 15000-19 20000-24 25000 AN   ROW
              COL PCT I 999       999      999     D OVER    TOTAL
              TOT PCT I     41.I     51.I     61.I     71.I
RACE          --------I--------I--------I--------I--------I
                1.  I     27  I     8  I     2  I     3  I    115
WHITE           I   23.5  I   7.0  I   1.7  I   2.6  I   86.5
                I  100.0  I 100.0  I 100.0  I 100.0  I
                I   20.3  I   6.0  I   1.5  I   2.3  I
              -I--------I--------I--------I--------I
                2.  I      0  I     0  I     0  I     0  I     13
NEGRO           I    0.0  I   0.0  I   0.0  I   0.0  I    9.8
                I    0.0  I   0.0  I   0.0  I   0.0  I
                I    0.0  I   0.0  I   0.0  I   0.0  I
              -I--------I--------I--------I--------I
                3.  I      0  I     0  I     0  I     0  I      1
ORIENTAL        I    0.0  I   0.0  I   0.0  I   0.0  I    0.8
                I    0.0  I   0.0  I   0.0  I   0.0  I
                I    0.0  I   0.0  I   0.0  I   0.0  I
              -I--------I--------I--------I--------I
                5.  I      0  I     0  I     0  I     0  I      4
LATIN AMERICAN  I    0.0  I   0.0  I   0.0  I   0.0  I    3.0
                I    0.0  I   0.0  I   0.0  I   0.0  I
                I    0.0  I   0.0  I   0.0  I   0.0  I
              -I--------I--------I--------I--------I
         COLUMN       27        8        2        3       133
         TOTAL      20.3      6.0      1.5      2.3     100.0
```

**FIG. 12.3**  *(Continued)*

remember to (1) restrict the length of his value labels to 16 characters and (2) space his labels so that the break between the eighth and ninth characters will not produce undesired effects.

### 12.2.3   OPTIONS AVAILABLE FOR SUBPROGRAM CROSSTABS: THE OPTIONS CARD

The OPTIONS card provides the user with three types of options for subprogram CROSSTABS: First, it enables him to control the handling of missing data and allows him to either include or exclude missing values for his tables; second, it allows him to have label printing suppressed; and third, it allows him to control the percentaging of tables. These options are selected by number on the OPTIONS card which has the following format:

| 1 | 16 |
|---|---|
| OPTIONS | number list |

The following is a list of the options available and their corresponding option numbers:

*Option* 1.   Causes values declared as missing to be included in the tables. If not used, the default option assumes that values defined as missing on the MISSING VALUES card are to be excluded from the table. The number of missing cases for any given table will, however, be reported.

*Option* 2.   Causes the search for and printing of labels to be suppressed. Both variable labels and value labels are suppressed by this option. When option 2 is not used, the default option searches for and prints labels whenever present. Some increase in speed is achieved by suppressing labels.

Options 3 to 5 deal with the table percentages to be printed. When the options are not used, each table is percentaged by row, by column, and by the cell percent of the total.

*Option* 3.   Causes row percentages to be deleted.

*Option* 4.   Causes column percentages to be deleted.

*Option* 5.   Causes total percentages to be deleted.

If, for example, the user desires a run in which missing values are to be included in the analysis and wishes to have his tables percentaged by column only, the following OPTIONS card would be required:

```
1              16
OPTIONS        1,3,5
```

The OPTIONS card directly follows the CROSSTABS card and controls the options on all tables requested for that task. If the OPTIONS card is deleted, the default options will all be in force; i.e., missing values will be excluded from the tables, labels will be printed where present, and all tables will be percentaged by column, by row, and by total.

### 12.2.4 STATISTICS AVAILABLE FOR SUBPROGRAM CROSSTABS: THE STATISTICS CARD

As with all SPSS subprograms, optional support statistics desired by the user are selected by means of the STATISTICS card which directly follows the OPTIONS card. Table 12.1 indicates the statistics available and their corresponding statistic numbers. Computing formulas and basic assumptions, as well as some description of these statistics, can be found in Appendix D. If the keyword ALL is placed in the specification field instead of the number list, all statistics will be reported; if the card is deleted, no statistics will be reported.

**TABLE 12.1**  **Correspondence between statistics and numbers for subprogram CROSSTABS**

| | |
|---|---|
| 1. Chi square[†] | 6. Kendall's tau B |
| 2. Phi for 2 X 2 | 7. Kendall's tau C |
|    Cramer's V for | 8. Gamma |
|    larger tables | 9. Somer's D (symmetric) |
| 3. Contingency coefficient | |

[†]For 2 X 2 tables, Fisher's exact text is applied when there are fewer than 21 cases. Yates' corrected chi square is applied for all other 2 X 2 tables.

The format of the STATISTICS card is:

```
1              16
STATISTICS     ⎧ ALL        ⎫
               ⎨ or         ⎬
               ⎩ number list ⎭
```

The STATISTICS card directly follows the OPTIONS card or the CROSSTABS card if the OPTIONS card is deleted.

### 12.2.5 PROGRAM LIMITATIONS FOR SUBPROGRAM CROSSTABS

The following limitations are presently set for subprogram CROSSTABS; these parameters will, however, be significantly increased in the near future.

*Limitation* 1.   200 is the maximum number of variable names which can be referenced on the CROSSTABS card. Each reference of a variable name counts as '1' and all variables implied by a TO statement count as '1' towards the total of 200.

*Limitation* 2.   250 is the maximum number of individual values which a given variable may take.

*Limitation* 3.   The following formula sets the limit MAXCELLS on the maximum number of table cells which may be generated on any given run:[1]

$$MAXCELLS = \frac{(SPACE/4)}{D + 2}$$

where D is the number of dimensions of the table having the largest dimensions among those to be generated on the specific run. Therefore, if all the tables on a run were two-dimensional and space were 80,000, there would be 5,000 available cells on that run.

*Limitation* 4.   A maximum of 20 individual table-request lists may be processed from any given CROSSTABS card and its continuations. A table request list is defined by all tables requested between slashes, unless of course, it is the first or last list.

[1]For a discussion of the parameter SPACE, see Appendix F.2. The default value of SPACE is 80,000.

*Limitation* 5.    The maximum number of dimensions available for any crosstabulation is 10. This means that control variables can be stacked eight deep, but no more than eight control variables may be involved in any set of subtables.

### 12.2.6    EXAMPLE DECK SETUPS FOR SUBPROGRAM CROSSTABS

Example 12.1 illustrates the calculation of a number of two-way crosstabulations using an SPSS system file. In this case the system file used is named ORGSTUDY. See Appendix I for a listing of the file-defining cards and data cases for this file. This file has three subfiles named NEW-YORK, NWJERSEY, and PENNSYLV. The PROCESS SBFILES card calls for the crosstabulation to be performed on subfiles NEWYORK and PENNSYLV as a group.

**EXAMPLE 12.1**

```
1                16
RUN NAME         CROSSTABS RUN FROM A SYSTEM FILE
GET FILE         ORGSTUDY
PROCESS SBFILES(NEWYORK,PENNSYLV)
CROSSTABS        FRATMEM TO YOUTHMEM BY NATMEM,FARMEM,RELMEM
STATISTICS       1,8
OPTIONS          3
FINISH
```

A total of 21 tables are requested (see the VARIABLE LIST card for file ORGSTUDY in Appendix I). The STATISTICS card causes chi-square and Gamma to be computed for each table; the OPTIONS card causes the suppression of row percentages. The first and the last table output from the run are reproduced in Fig. 12.4.

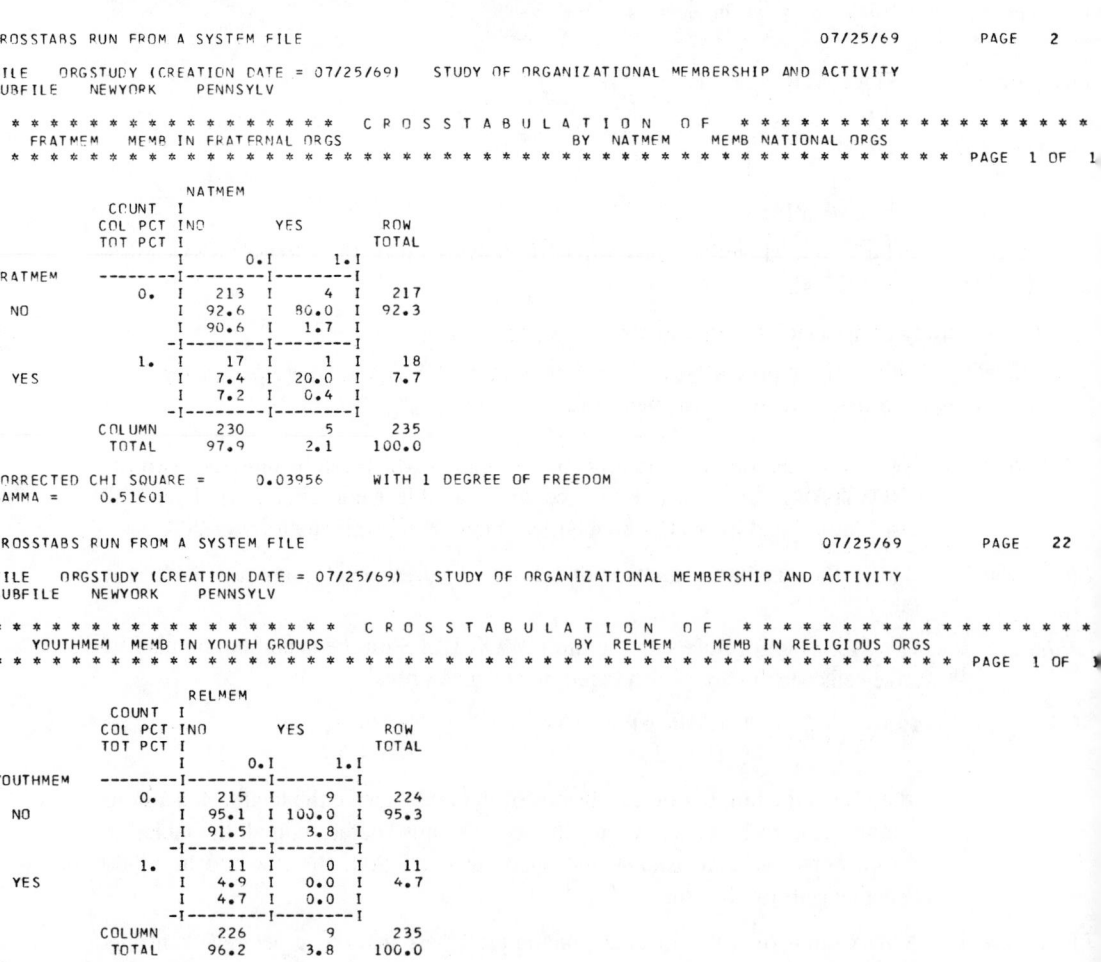

**FIG. 12.4**    Two-way crosstabulation tables produced by subprogram CROSSTABS.

Example 12.2 illustrates the use of subprogram CROSSTABS for production of multiple tables on a single run. The first table is a two-way crosstabulation of variable RACE by EDRESPON. This table is reproduced in Fig. 12.5. The second table is a three-way crosstabulation of variables RACE by EDRESPON by RESDYTH. Actually four tables are produced—a two-way crosstabulation of RACE by EDRESPON for each value of variable RESDYTH—since RESDYTH assumes four valid values. The first and last of these tables are reproduced in Fig. 12.6.

**EXAMPLE 12.2**

```
1                  16
RUN NAME           CROSSTABS RUN FROM A SYSTEM FILE
GET FILE           ORGSTUDY
PROCESS SBFILES        ALL
CROSSTABS          RACE BY EDRESPON/RACE BY EDRESPON BY RESDYTH
STATISTICS         ALL
FINISH
```

Each table is calculated using all three of the subfiles of file ORGSTUDY, since the PROCESS SBFILES card contains the keyword ALL. This card was inserted by way of illustration; it could have been removed from the control-card deck without affecting the results of the run since the default subfile processing mode is to run all subfiles as a combined file.

```
CROSSTABS RUN FROM A SYSTEM FILE                                    07/25/69      PAGE   2

FILE   ORGSTUDY (CREATION DATE = 07/25/69)    STUDY OF ORGANIZATIONAL MEMBERSHIP AND ACTIVITY
SUBFILE   NEWYORK    NWJERSEY   PENNSYLV

* * * * * * * * * * * * * * * *  C R O S S T A B U L A T I O N   O F  * * * * * * * * * * * * * * * * * *
    RACE        RESPONDENTS RACE                      BY  EDRESPON  LAST YEAR SCHOOL COMPLETED
* * * * * * * * * * * * * * * * * * * * * * * * * * * * * * * * * * * * * * * * * * * * * *  PAGE  1 OF  1

                    EDRESPON
             COUNT  I
             ROW PCT INONE    1-8 YEAR 9-11 YEA 12 YEARS COLLEGE  COLLEGE  COLLEGE      ROW
             COL PCT I        S        RS                INCOMPLE GRAD     PLUS         TOTAL
             TOT PCT I   1. I    2. I     3. I     4. I     5. I    6. I     7. I
RACE         --------I--------I--------I--------I--------I--------I--------I--------I
        1.   I    7  I   69  I    52 I     76 I     45 I    20  I     9  I    278
WHITE        I   2.5  I  24.8 I   18.7 I   27.3 I   16.2 I   7.2  I    3.2 I   79.4
             I 100.0  I  71.1 I   77.6 I   79.2 I   93.8 I  83.3  I   81.8 I
             I   2.0  I  19.7 I   14.9 I   21.7 I   12.9 I   5.7  I    2.6 I
             -I--------I--------I--------I--------I--------I--------I--------I
        2.   I    0  I   27  I    13 I     15 I      2 I     3  I     1  I     61
NEGRO        I   0.0  I  44.3 I   21.3 I   24.6 I    3.3 I   4.9  I    1.6 I   17.4
             I   0.0  I  27.8 I   19.4 I   15.6 I    4.2 I  12.5  I    9.1 I
             I   0.0  I   7.7 I    3.7 I    4.3 I    0.6 I   0.9  I    0.3 I
             -I--------I--------I--------I--------I--------I--------I--------I
        3.   I    0  I    0  I     0 I      2 I      0 I     1  I     1  I      4
ORIENTAL     I   0.0  I   0.0 I    0.0 I   50.0 I    0.0 I  25.0  I   25.0 I    1.1
             I   0.0  I   0.0 I    0.0 I    2.1 I    0.0 I   4.2  I    9.1 I
             I   0.0  I   0.0 I    0.0 I    0.6 I    0.0 I   0.3  I    0.3 I
             -I--------I--------I--------I--------I--------I--------I--------I
        5.   I    0  I    1  I     2 I      3 I      1 I     0  I     0  I      7
LATIN AMERICAN I 0.0  I  14.3 I   28.6 I   42.9 I   14.3 I   0.0  I    0.0 I    2.0
             I   0.0  I   1.0 I    3.0 I    3.1 I    2.1 I   0.0  I    0.0 I
             I   0.0  I   0.3 I    0.6 I    0.9 I    0.3 I   0.0  I    0.0 I
             -I--------I--------I--------I--------I--------I--------I--------I
         COLUMN     7       97       67       96       48      24       11       350
         TOTAL     2.0     27.7     19.1     27.4     13.7     6.9      3.1     100.0

CHI SQUARE =    29.20448 WITH  18 DEGREES OF FREEDOM
CRAMER'S V =     0.16677
CONTINGENCY COEFFICIENT =     0.27752
KENDALL'S TAU B =    -0.10035
KENDALL'S TAU C =    -0.06901
GAMMA =    -0.19677
SOMER'S D =    -0.06581
```

**FIG. 12.5** A two-way crosstabulation produced by subprogram CROSSTABS.

```
CROSSTABS RUN FROM A SYSTEM FILE                                          07/25/69      PAGE    68

FILE    ORGSTUDY (CREATION DATE = 07/25/69)    STUDY OF ORGANIZATIONAL MEMBERSHIP AND ACTIVITY
SUBFILE   NEWYORK   NWJERSEY   PENNSYLV

* * * * * * * * * * * * * * * *   C R O S S T A B U L A T I O N   O F   * * * * * * * * * * * * * * * * * *
    RACE      RESPONDENTS RACE                           BY  EDRESPON  LAST YEAR SCHOOL COMPLETED
CONTROLLING FOR..
    RESDYTH   RESIDENCE FIRST 15 YEARS                        VALUE =        1.  MOSTLY FARM
* * * * * * * * * * * * * * * * * * * * * * * * * * * * * * * * * * * * * * * * * * * * * *   PAGE  1 OF  1
```

|   | EDRESPON<br>COUNT<br>ROW PCT I NONE<br>COL PCT I<br>TOT PCT I 1. I | 1-8 YEAR<br>S<br>2. I | 9-11 YEA<br>RS<br>3. I | 12 YEARS<br>4. I | COLLEGE<br>INCOMPLE<br>5. I | COLLEGE<br>GRAD<br>6. I | ROW<br>TOTAL |
|---|---|---|---|---|---|---|---|
| RACE | --------I--------I | --------I | --------I | --------I | --------I | --------I |  |
| WHITE 1. | I     2 I    34 I<br>I   2.5 I  43.0 I<br>I 100.0 I  65.4 I<br>I   1.9 I  33.0 I | 15 I<br>19.0 I<br>75.0 I<br>14.6 I | 16 I<br>20.3 I<br>94.1 I<br>15.5 I | 11 I<br>13.9 I<br>100.0 I<br>10.7 I | 1 I<br>1.3 I<br>100.0 I<br>1.0 I | 79<br>76.7 |
| NEGRO 2. | I     0 I    18 I<br>I   0.0 I  78.3 I<br>I   0.0 I  34.6 I<br>I   0.0 I  17.5 I | 5 I<br>21.7 I<br>25.0 I<br>4.9 I | 0 I<br>0.0 I<br>0.0 I<br>0.0 I | 0 I<br>0.0 I<br>0.0 I<br>0.0 I | 0 I<br>0.0 I<br>0.0 I<br>0.0 I | 23<br>22.3 |
| ORIENTAL 3. | I     0 I     0 I<br>I   0.0 I   0.0 I<br>I   0.0 I   0.0 I<br>I   0.0 I   0.0 I | 0 I<br>0.0 I<br>0.0 I<br>0.0 I | 1 I<br>100.0 I<br>5.9 I<br>1.0 I | 0 I<br>0.0 I<br>0.0 I<br>0.0 I | 0 I<br>0.0 I<br>0.0 I<br>0.0 I | 1<br>1.0 |
| COLUMN<br>TOTAL | 2<br>1.9 | 52<br>50.5 | 20<br>19.4 | 17<br>16.5 | 11<br>10.7 | 1<br>1.0 | 103<br>100.0 |

```
CHI SQUARE =    18.09859 WITH  10 DEGREES OF FREEDOM
CRAMER'S V =     0.29641
CONTINGENCY COEFFICIENT =      0.38659
KENDALL'S TAU B =   -0.24384
KENDALL'S TAU C =   -0.17985
GAMMA =   -0.52303
SOMER'S D =    -0.17941
```

```
CROSSTABS RUN FROM A SYSTEM FILE                                          07/25/69      PAGE    71

FILE    ORGSTUDY (CREATION DATE = 07/25/69)    STUDY OF ORGANIZATIONAL MEMBERSHIP AND ACTIVITY
SUBFILE   NEWYORK   NWJERSEY   PENNSYLV

* * * * * * * * * * * * * * * *   C R O S S T A B U L A T I O N   O F   * * * * * * * * * * * * * * * * * *
    RACE      RESPONDENTS RACE                           BY  EDRESPON  LAST YEAR SCHOOL COMPLETED
CONTROLLING FOR..
    RESDYTH   RESIDENCE FIRST 15 YEARS                        VALUE =        4.  MSTLY BIG CITY,SUBER
* * * * * * * * * * * * * * * * * * * * * * * * * * * * * * * * * * * * * * * * * * * * * *   PAGE  1 OF  1
```

|   | EDRESPON<br>COUNT I<br>ROW PCT I 1-8 YEAR<br>COL PCT I S<br>TOT PCT I 2. I | 9-11 YEA<br>RS<br>3. I | 12 YEARS<br>4. I | COLLEGE<br>INCOMPLE<br>5. I | COLLEGE<br>GRAD<br>6. I | COLLEGE<br>PLUS<br>7. I | ROW<br>TOTAL |
|---|---|---|---|---|---|---|---|
| RACE | --------I--------I | --------I | --------I | --------I | --------I | --------I |  |
| WHITE 1. | I    11 I<br>I  17.2 I<br>I 100.0 I<br>I  13.9 I | 11 I<br>17.2 I<br>78.6 I<br>13.9 I | 15 I<br>23.4 I<br>62.5 I<br>19.0 I | 13 I<br>20.3 I<br>92.9 I<br>16.5 I | 11 I<br>17.2 I<br>91.7 I<br>13.9 I | 3 I<br>4.7 I<br>75.0 I<br>3.8 I | 64<br>81.0 |
| NEGRO 2. | I     0 I<br>I   0.0 I<br>I   0.0 I<br>I   0.0 I | 1 I<br>11.1 I<br>7.1 I<br>1.3 I | 6 I<br>66.7 I<br>25.0 I<br>7.6 I | 1 I<br>11.1 I<br>7.1 I<br>1.3 I | 1 I<br>11.1 I<br>8.3 I<br>1.3 I | 0 I<br>0.0 I<br>0.0 I<br>0.0 I | 9<br>11.4 |
| ORIENTAL 3. | I     0 I<br>I   0.0 I<br>I   0.0 I<br>I   0.0 I | 0 I<br>0.0 I<br>0.0 I<br>0.0 I | 1 I<br>50.0 I<br>4.2 I<br>1.3 I | 0 I<br>0.0 I<br>0.0 I<br>0.0 I | 0 I<br>0.0 I<br>0.0 I<br>0.0 I | 1 I<br>50.0 I<br>25.0 I<br>1.3 I | 2<br>2.5 |
| LATIN AMERICAN 5. | I     0 I<br>I   0.0 I<br>I   0.0 I<br>I   0.0 I | 2 I<br>50.0 I<br>14.3 I<br>2.5 I | 2 I<br>50.0 I<br>8.3 I<br>2.5 I | 0 I<br>0.0 I<br>0.0 I<br>0.0 I | 0 I<br>0.0 I<br>0.0 I<br>0.0 I | 0 I<br>0.0 I<br>0.0 I<br>0.0 I | 4<br>5.1 |
| COLUMN<br>TOTAL | 11<br>13.9 | 14<br>17.7 | 24<br>30.4 | 14<br>17.7 | 12<br>15.2 | 4<br>5.1 | 79<br>100.0 |

```
CHI SQUARE =    22.55096 WITH  15 DEGREES OF FREEDOM
CRAMER'S V =     0.30847
CONTINGENCY COEFFICIENT =      0.47124
KENDALL'S TAU B =   -0.01440
KENDALL'S TAU C =   -0.00983
GAMMA =   -0.02857
SOMER'S D =    -0.00921
```

**FIG. 12.6**   A three-way crosstabulation produced by subprogram CROSSTABS.

## 12.3 SUBPROGRAM FASTABS: TWO-WAY TO n-WAY CROSSTABULATION TABLES AND RELATED STATISTICS FOR INTEGER VARIABLES

Subprogram FASTABS has the same basic function as subprogram CROSSTABS, and the printed output from the two programs is identical. FASTABS differs from CROSSTABS, however, in several respects: (1) it is *significantly faster*, (2) it can handle a larger number of tables, (3) it requires a slightly greater amount of card preparation, and (4) it can only process variables which are numerically coded and integer in form. FASTABS also requires that the user know the lowest and highest valid (i.e., nonmissing) values taken by each of the variables for which he desires crosstabulation tables. In short, FASTABS should be chosen over CROSS-TABS whenever the user is able to input his data in integer form (remember recodes and variable transformations can be used for this purpose) and feels that the saving in machine time outweighs the cost of a slightly greater amount of card preparation.

### 12.3.1 THE FASTABS PROCEDURE CARD

The FASTABS card has two portions or segments. The first portion of the card defines the variables (and their limiting values) to be used in building the tables. The second portion of the card actually defines the tables to be generated.

The control word FASTABS is followed by the keyword VARIABLES and the special delimiter =. The = sign is followed by one or more variable names for which a single set of lowest and highest values are to be defined. This variable name or list of variable names is followed by a left parenthesis [ ( ], the lowest valid value associated with the preceding variable or variables, one or more common delimiters, the highest valid value, and then a right parenthesis [ ) ]. The right, or closing, parenthesis is followed by a slash [/], and the next variable or list of variables and the associated lowest and highest values follow in exactly the same format. This process is repeated until all of the variables to be used in generating the tables and their associated lowest and highest values have been defined. Any variable which has been previously defined (on a variable list, in a file, or by means of a transformation) may appear on these lists, and the variables may appear in any order specified by the user. (The order in which they appear, however, will affect the way in which the actual tables are requested, so the user should read on before deciding on the order.)

Where three or more *adjacent* variables have the same delimiting values, the variable names may be entered on the card by a notation of the following type:

VARX TO VARY (lowest value, highest value)/

where both VARX and VARY are variables which have been previously defined, where VARX precedes VARY on the variable list, and where all variables falling between VARX and VARY are to take the same delimiting values. As usual, the keyword TO must be separated from VARX and VARY by one or more common delimiters. This notation enables the user to simultaneously define the delimiting values for large numbers of adjacent variables.

When two or more *nonadjacent* variables are to take the same delimiting values, the variable names are entered onto the FASTABS card in the following manner:

VARA,VARC,VARF,VARJ (lowest value, highest value)/

where the variables VARA,VARC,VARF, and VARJ have been previously defined and are to take the same delimiting values. These two notations may be freely mixed to produce a list of variable names of the following type:

VARA TO VARE, VARK,VARP,VARR,VART TO VARZ (lowest value, highest value)/

The delimiting values, which are set off by parentheses, are followed by a slash [/] and then by a similar variable list and its associated delimiting values, until all variables to be used in the task have been listed. No more than 100 variable names may be named or implied (by the TO convention) on these lists. The general format of the first portion of the FASTABS card, which defines the variables to be used and their associated delimiting values, is then as follows:

```
1                      16
FASTABS                VARIABLES=    ⎧ variable name ⎫    (lowest value, highest value)/
                                     ⎨      or       ⎬
                                     ⎩ variable list ⎭

                                     ⎧ variable name ⎫    (lowest value, highest value)/ . . .
                                     ⎨      or       ⎬
                                     ⎩ variable list ⎭
```

In the second segment of the specification field of the FASTABS card the user specifies the desired crosstabulation tables from the variables defined in the first portion of the card. The last variable list and its associated delimiting values is followed by one or more common delimiters and the keyword TABLES which is in turn followed by the special delimiter =. The = sign is then followed by the variables to be crosstabulated. The variable names are linked with the keyword BY which specifies the crosstabulations. The following examples illustrate how two- to five-way tables can be requested by means of the FASTABS card.

```
1          16
FASTABS    VARIABLES=AGE(0,8)/SEX(1,2)/TABLES=AGE BY SEX
FASTABS    VARIABLES=AGE(0,8)/SEX,RACE(1,2)/TABLES=AGE BY SEX BY RACE
FASTABS    VARIABLES=AGE(0,8)/SEX,RACE(1,2)/INCOME(1,3)/TABLES=
           AGE BY SEX BY RACE BY INCOME
FASTABS    VARIABLES=AGE(0,8)/INCOME(1,3)/EDUCATN(0,5)/SEX,RACE(1,2/
           TABLES=AGE BY SEX BY RACE BY INCOME BY EDUCATN
```

The first FASTABS card requests a simple two-way frequency table; the variable AGE by the variable SEX. The second will yield a number of tables for AGE by SEX, one for each value of the variable RACE. The third card specifies a table of AGE by SEX for all possible combinations of the values of the variables RACE and INCOME. If, for example, there were three categories of INCOME (high, medium, and low) and two of RACE (white and nonwhite), six subtables would be produced. The tables would be put out in the order of the value of the last variable named changing most slowly; that is, there would be two subtables of AGE by SEX, one for whites and one for nonwhites, for each category of INCOME. It is very important to understand the sequential order of the variables surrounding the BY designation: The first variable mentioned always becomes the row variable, and the second is always the column variable; if three or more variables are involved in one set of tables, the third variable becomes the lowest-order control variable, and so forth, moving to the right. Thus, the last variable mentioned rotates most slowly. The following examples illustrate how different tables can be requested by changing the order of the variables. Note that the order in which the variables are defined in the VARIABLES portion of the FASTABS card is independent (in this case) of the order used to request the tables. The first card will produce a table where RACE is the row variable, while the second will specify INCOME as the row variable.

```
1               16
FASTABS         VARIABLES=RACE(0,1)/INCOME(1,3)/TABLES=RACE BY INCOME
FASTABS         VARIABLES=RACE(0,1)/INCOME(1,3)/TABLES=INCOME BY RACE
```

The user should be particularly careful in sequencing his variables and selecting whether he desires his percentages to be based on column or row tables.

Multiple tables can be specified on a single FASTABS card by several conventions. First, a number of individual tables can be specified by placing a slash [/] between the table requests, as in the following example, which will cause one table to be computed for RACE BY INCOME, another for URB BY EDUCATN, and a third for SEX BY OCCUPATN.

```
1               16
FASTABS         VARIABLES=RACE,SEX(0,1)/URB,INCOME,OCCUPATN(1,3)/
                EDUCATN(0,5)/TABLES=RACE BY INCOME/URB BY EDUCATN/
                SEX BY OCCUPATN
```

The order in which tables are requested is unimportant except that the tables will be printed in that order.

Multiple tables can also be requested by placing more than one variable name to the right or left of any BY. In the case of FASTABS, however, this capability is somewhat more limited than in subprogram CROSSTABS. Any *two or more* variables which have been defined adjacently on the VARIABLES portion of the FASTABS card may be entered on the right or left side of a BY using the usual TO convention. Remember, however, that the definition of adjacent on the TABLES portion of the FASTABS card refers to the order in which the variables were defined on the VARIABLES portion of the card and not to their location in the file. Furthermore, unlike the CROSSTABS card, lists of nonadjacent variables separated by common delimiters such as VARX,VARA,VARZ BY VARD,VARF *may not be entered* and will cause program termination and an error message.

Multiple lists entered by means of the TO convention will produce one table for each variable named or implied on the left side of a BY for every variable named or implied to the right of the BY. The first variable of the inclusive list on the left of the BY becomes the first row variable, and a table will be produced for the variable named or all of the variables implied by the TO to the right of the BY. Beginning with the variable which begins the inclusive list (to the left of the BY), one table is produced for each variable included in the list to the right of the BY, and these column variables are processed sequentially. When the last table has been produced for the first row variable, the process is repeated for the next row variable implied by the inclusive list.

The following is the general format of the FASTABS card:

```
1               16
FASTABS         VARIABLES= ⎰ variable name ⎱ (low value, high value)/ ⎰ variable name ⎱
                           ⎰      or        ⎰                        ⎰      or        ⎰
                           ⎱ variable list  ⎰                        ⎱ variable list  ⎰
```

(low variable, high variable) . . . / TABLES= ⎰ variable name ⎱ BY
                                              ⎰      or        ⎰
                                              ⎱ variable list  ⎰

⎰ variable name ⎱ BY . . . / ⎰ variable name ⎱ BY ⎰ variable name ⎱ . . .
⎰      or        ⎰           ⎰      or        ⎰    ⎰      or        ⎰
⎱ variable list  ⎰           ⎱ variable list  ⎰    ⎱ variable list† ⎰

†Variable lists on the TABLES portion of the FASTABS card are limited to those of the VARA TO VARD variety.

The next four examples demonstrate the use of these multiple lists. These examples should also make the user sensitive to the importance of the order in which the variables are defined on the VARIABLES portion of the card, if he wishes to employ multiple lists.

```
1                16
FASTABS          VARIABLES=RACE(0,1)/SEX(1,2)/INCOME(0,9)/ITEM1 TO ITEM6
                 ITEM9,ITEM13(1,5)/TABLES=RACE BY ITEM1 TO ITEM13

FASTABS          VARIABLES=RACE(0,1)/SEX(1,2)/INCOME(0,9)/ITEM1 TO ITEM6
                 ITEM9,ITEM13(1,5)/TABLES=RACE TO INCOME BY ITEM13

FASTABS          VARIABLES=RACE(0,1)/SEX(1,2)/INCOME(0,9)/ITEM1 TO ITEM6
                 ITEM9,ITEM13(1,5)/TABLES=RACE TO INCOME BY ITEM1 TO
                 ITEM13

FASTABS          VARIABLES=RACE(0,1)/SEX(1,2)/INCOME(0,9)/ITEM1 TO ITEM6
                 ITEM9,ITEM13(1,5)/TABLES=RACE TO SEX BY ITEM1 TO ITEM13
                 BY INCOME
```

In the first example, RACE will become the row variable, and one table will be produced for each of the eight variables defined between and including ITEM1 and ITEM13. RACE by ITEM1 will be the first table generated, and RACE by ITEM13 will be the last table produced. In the second example, three row variables have been defined, but only one column variable has been entered. This would cause three tables to be generated in which ITEM13 will always be the column variable. The tables would be produced in the following order: RACE BY ITEM13, SEX BY ITEM13, INCOME BY ITEM13. In the third example, RACE will again become the first row variable, and one table will be produced with RACE as the row variable for each variable between and inclusive of ITEM1 and ITEM13, which will all be column variables. An identical set of tables will be generated for SEX and INCOME (as the row variables) in that order. In the last and most complex example, there will be one table for each value of the variable INCOME for every combination of variables specified (i.e., each combination of RACE TO INCOME BY ITEM1 TO ITEM13 will have one subtable for every value of the variable INCOME). In effect, INCOME becomes an additional control variable for the entire set of tables that were generated in the third example.

In the above examples each set of table requests was placed on a separate FASTABS card. This was done solely for the sake of clarity, and up to 20 such lists can be entered onto a single FASTABS card and its continuations as long as each list is separated from the next by the special delimiter, the slash [/]. All of the usual rules concerning continuing SPSS control cards from one physical card to the next apply.

### 12.3.2 PRINTED OUTPUT FROM SUBPROGRAM FASTABS

The printed output for subprogram FASTABS is identical to that of subprogram CROSSTABS. The user is referred to Sec. 12.1.2. All points made in the discussion in that section apply to FASTABS as well as to CROSSTABS.

### 12.3.3 OPTIONS AVAILABLE FOR SUBPROGRAM FASTABS: THE OPTIONS CARD

The options available in subprogram FASTABS enable the user to control the processing of missing data, suppress the labeling of tables, and select among various table-percentaging options. The options available for subprogram FASTABS are identical to those available in CROSSTABS. The numbers used to activate the various options and the format of the OPTIONS cards for these two programs are also identical. Therefore, the user is referred to Sec. 12.2.3 for direction in preparing the OPTIONS card for FASTABS. There is, however, one addition for subprogram FASTABS: Option 6 is available in FASTABS, but not in CROSSTABS. Option 6 causes the deletion of value labels, but has the variable labels retained and printed on the output.

### 12.3.4 STATISTICS AVAILABLE FOR SUBPROGRAM FASTABS: THE STATISTICS CARD

The statistics available for subprogram FASTABS include all those available for subprogram CROSSTABS and some additional statistics appropriate for numerical data. A complete list of the statistics available and their corresponding statistics numbers are provided in Table 12.2.

**TABLE 12.2**   **Correspondence between statistics and numbers for subprogram FASTABS**

| | |
|---|---|
| 1. Chi square[†] | 6. Kendall's tau B |
| 2. Phi for 2 X 2 | 7. Kendall's tau C |
|    Cramer's V for | 8. Gamma |
|    larger tables | 9. Somer's D symmetric |
| 3. Contingency coefficient |    and asymmetric |
| 4. Lamda symmetric and | 10. Eta |
|    asymmetric | |
| 5. Uncertainty coefficient | |
|    symmetric and asymmetric | |

[†]For 2 X 2 tables, Fisher's exact test is applied when there are fewer than 21 cases. Yates' corrected chi square is applied for all other 2 X 2 tables.

A mathematical discussion of the above measures of association can be found in Appendix D.2. To cause the program to calculate the statistics, the user prepares a STATISTICS card with appropriate number of numbers in the specification field. The STATISTICS card directly follows the OPTIONS card, or the FASTABS card if the OPTIONS card is deleted.

The format of the STATISTICS card is

$$\overset{1}{\text{STATISTICS}} \qquad \overset{16}{\left\{ \begin{matrix} \text{ALL} \\ \text{or} \\ \text{number list} \end{matrix} \right\}}$$

### 12.3.5   PROGRAM LIMITATIONS FOR SUBPROGRAM FASTABS

The following limitations apply to the IBM 360 version of subprogram FASTABS:

*Limitation* 1.   100 is the maximum number of variable names which may be referenced on a FASTABS card. This applies only to the VARIABLES portion of the card.

*Limitation* 2.   No variable which has more than 250 individual or unique values may be entered into the FASTABS subprogram. Recoding (temporary or permanent) may, of course, be used to avoid overflowing this limitation.

*Limitation* 3.   A maximum of 20 individual lists may be entered onto the TABLES portion of the FASTABS card. By individual lists we mean complete table requests separated by slashes.

*Limitation* 4.   The maximum number of table cells which may be generated on a given task is determined by the following formula:

$$\text{MAXCELLS} = (\text{SPACE}/4) - (10 \times \text{NVARS})$$

where NVARS is the number of variables named and/or implied on the VARIABLES portion of the FASTABS card. If NVARS=100 and SPACE=80,000 (which is its default value, see Appendix F.2), then the maximum number of cells which could be produced on that task would be 19,000.

*Limitation* 5.   The maximum number of dimensions available for any FASTABS is eight. This means that control variables can be stacked six deep, but no more than six control variables may be involved in any set of subtables.

The user should note that the program allocates one cell for every value between the lowest and the highest; so if, for example, a variable is coded to take the values 1, 2, 3, 4, or 9, recoding 9 to an adjacent value (i.e., 0 or 5) will save core and enable the user to generate many more tables.

### 12.3.6    EXAMPLE DECK SETUP AND OUTPUT FOR SUBPROGRAM FASTABS

Example 12.3 illustrates the use of subprogram FASTABS to produce 2 two-way crosstabulations from an SPSS system file. The file named ORGSTUDY is retrieved by use of the GET FILE card. (For a listing of the file-defining control cards and cases of this file, see Appendix I.) For purposes of the crosstabulation, a variable named INCOME already contained in the file is used to calculate a new variable NEWINC. Then NEWINC is crosstabulated with variable RELIG and with variable RESDYTH. The possible values of INCOME and the resulting values of NEWINC are shown below.

| Values of variable INCOME | Resulting value of NEWINC |
|---|---|
| 1, 2, 3, 4, 5 | 1 |
| 6, 7, 11, 21, 31, 41 | 2 |
| 51, 61, 71, 88, 98, 99 | 3 |

A VALUE LABELS card is inserted to create labels for the three valid resulting values of variable NEWINC, and a MISSING VALUE card to define zero as a missing value.

**EXAMPLE 12.3**

```
1                16
RUN NAME         FASTABS RUN FROM A SYSTEM FILE
GET FILE         ORGSTUDY
COMMENT          VARIABLE INCOME IS TRICHOTOMIZED FOR THIS RUN, AND A NEW
                 VARIABLE 'NEWINC' IS CREATED
IF               (INCOME LE 5) NEWINC=1
IF               ((INCOME GE 6) AND (INCOME LE 41)) NEWINC=2
IF               (INCOME GE 51) NEWINC=3
FASTABS          VARIABLES=NEWINC(1,3)/RELIG(0,9)/RESDYTH(0,9)/
                 TABLES=NEWINC BY RELIG,RESDYTH
STATISTICS       1,6,7
FINISH
```

The user should note that it would have been necessary to include an FT03 JCL card (see Appendix F) in the deck accompanying the control cards for the above runs since retrieval of an SPSS system file with the use of the GET FILE card is desired.

The FASTABS card provides for values 0, 1, 2, and 3 for variable NEWINC, values 0, 1, 2, ..., 9 for variable RELIG, and values 0, 1, 2, ..., for variable RESDYTH. These are the only variables for which values must be specified since only these variables are referenced on the TABLES= portion of the card.

All statistics available from subprogram FASTABS are computed for both tables, and full labeling and cell percentages by row, column, and total are presented since all default options are in force.

The output from this run is reproduced in Fig. 12.7. It is worth noting that a SAVE FILE card could have been inserted in the deck directly preceding the FINISH card; in this case a new updated system file would have been written containing the variable NEWINC. Also, the user would have had to prepare an FT04 JCL card (see Appendix F).

## 12.4    SUBPROGRAM BREAKDOWN: DESCRIPTION OF SUBPOPULATIONS

Subprogram BREAKDOWN provides a simple technique for examining the means, standard deviations, and variances of a criterion or dependent variable among various subgroups in a sample or total population. In many respects, this operation is analogous to crosstabulation where each mean and standard deviation summarizes the distribution of a complete row or column of a contingency table. Given a dependent variable (which may be either continuous or discrete) for which a mean is a reasonable measure of central tendency, BREAKDOWN will enable the user to obtain means, standard deviations, and variances of the variable for complex classifications involving from one to five independent variables. In its simplest form, for example, the mean level of income may be determined for each of a number of categories of education. This example can be extended so that the mean level of income is computed for

```
FASTABS RUN FROM A SYSTEM FILE                                    07/25/69        PAGE   2

FILE   ORGSTUDY (CREATION DATE = 07/25/69)    STUDY OF ORGANIZATIONAL MEMBERSHIP AND ACTIVITY
SUBFILE   NEWYORK    NWJERSEY   PENNSYLV

* * * * * * * * * * * * * * * *   C R O S S T A B U L A T I O N   O F   * * * * * * * * * * * * * * * * *
    NEWINC                                     BY  RELIG    RELIGIOUS AFFILIATION
* * * * * * * * * * * * * * * * * * * * * * * * * * * * * * * * * * * * * * * * * * * * * * *  PAGE  1 OF  1

               RELIG
        COUNT  I
        ROW PCT IPROTESTA CATHOLIC  JEWISH    NONE    ORTHODOX BUDDHIST    ROW
        COL PCT INT                                            .CONF      TOTAL
        TOT PCT I    1 I     2 I     3 I     5 I     6 I     7 I
NEWINC  --------I--------I--------I--------I--------I--------I--------I
      1 I     96 I    22 I     2 I     6 I     0 I     0 I     126
LOW INCOME I 76.2 I  17.5 I   1.6 I   4.8 I   0.0 I   0.0 I    37.3
        I   41.6 I  27.2 I  33.3 I  33.3 I   0.0 I   0.0 I
        I   28.4 I   6.5 I   0.6 I   1.8 I   0.0 I   0.0 I
        -I--------I--------I--------I--------I--------I--------I
      2 I    115 I    53 I     2 I    11 I     1 I     1 I     183
MEDIUM INCOME I 62.8 I 29.0 I  1.1 I   6.0 I   0.5 I   0.5 I    54.1
        I   49.8 I  65.4 I  33.3 I  61.1 I 100.0 I 100.0 I
        I   34.0 I  15.7 I   0.6 I   3.3 I   0.3 I   0.3 I
        -I--------I--------I--------I--------I--------I--------I
      3 I     20 I     6 I     2 I     1 I     0 I     0 I      29
HIGH INCOME I 69.0 I  20.7 I   6.9 I   3.4 I   0.0 I   0.0 I     8.6
        I    8.7 I   7.4 I  33.3 I   5.6 I   0.0 I   0.0 I
        I    5.9 I   1.8 I   0.6 I   0.3 I   0.0 I   0.0 I
        -I--------I--------I--------I--------I--------I--------I
      COLUMN    231       81        6       18        1        1      338
      TOTAL    68.3     24.0      1.8      5.3      0.3      0.3    100.0

RAW CHI SQUARE =   13.12073 WITH    10 DEGREES OF FREEDOM.  SIGNIFICANCE = 0.2170
CRAMER'S V = 0.13932
CONTINGENCY COEFFICIENT = 0.19331
LAMDA (ASYMMETRIC) = 0.0     WITH NEWINC    DEPENDENT.       = 0.0    WITH RELIG    DEPENDENT.
LAMDA (SYMMETRIC) = 0.0
UNCERTAINTY COEFFICIENT (ASYMMETRIC) = 0.01991 WITH NEWINC  DEPENDENT.     = 0.02097 WITH RELIG    DEPENDENT.
UNCERTAINTY COEFFICIENT (SYMMETRIC) = 0.02043
KENDALL'S TAU B = 0.10207.    SIGNIFICANCE =  0.0026
KENDALL'S TAU C = 0.07878.    SIGNIFICANCE =  0.0153
GAMMA =  0.19936
SOMER'S D (ASYMMETRIC) = 0.11119 WITH NEWINC   DEPENDENT.       = 0.09369 WITH RELIG    DEPENDENT.
SOMER'S D (SYMMETRIC) = 0.10170

NUMBER OF MISSING OBSERVATIONS =    12


FASTABS RUN FROM A SYSTEM FILE                                    07/25/69        PAGE   3

FILE   ORGSTUDY (CREATION DATE = 07/25/69)    STUDY OF ORGANIZATIONAL MEMBERSHIP AND ACTIVITY
SUBFILE   NEWYORK    NWJERSEY   PENNSYLV

* * * * * * * * * * * * * * * *   C R O S S T A B U L A T I O N   O F   * * * * * * * * * * * * * * * * *
    NEWINC                                     BY  RESDYTH    RESIDENCE FIRST 15 YEARS
* * * * * * * * * * * * * * * * * * * * * * * * * * * * * * * * * * * * * * * * * * * * * * *  PAGE  1 OF  1

               RESDYTH
        COUNT  I
        ROW PCT IMOSTLY F MSTLY SM MSTLY SM MSTLY BI   ROW
        COL PCT IARM     ALL TOWN ALL CITY G CITY,S  TOTAL
        TOT PCT I    1 I     2 I     3 I     4 I
NEWINC  --------I--------I--------I--------I--------I
      1 I     58 I    26 I     9 I    17 I     110
LOW INCOME I 52.7 I  23.6 I   8.2 I  15.5 I    36.7
        I   58.0 I  29.2 I  28.1 I  21.5 I
        I   19.3 I   8.7 I   3.0 I   5.7 I
        -I--------I--------I--------I--------I
      2 I     39 I    56 I    18 I    51 I     164
MEDIUM INCOME I 23.8 I 34.1 I  11.0 I  31.1 I    54.7
        I   39.0 I  62.9 I  56.3 I  64.6 I
        I   13.0 I  18.7 I   6.0 I  17.0 I
        -I--------I--------I--------I--------I
      3 I      3 I     7 I     5 I    11 I      26
HIGH INCOME I 11.5 I  26.9 I  19.2 I  42.3 I     8.7
        I    3.0 I   7.9 I  15.6 I  13.9 I
        I    1.0 I   2.3 I   1.7 I   3.7 I
        -I--------I--------I--------I--------I
      COLUMN   100       89       32       79      300
      TOTAL   33.3     29.7     10.7     26.3    100.0

RAW CHI SQUARE =   34.44661 WITH     6 DEGREES OF FREEDOM.  SIGNIFICANCE = 0.0000
CRAMER'S V = 0.23961
CONTINGENCY COEFFICIENT = 0.32093
LAMDA (ASYMMETRIC) = 0.13971 WITH NEWINC   DEPENDENT.       = 0.12500 WITH RESDYTH  DEPENDENT.
LAMDA (SYMMETRIC) = 0.13095
UNCERTAINTY COEFFICIENT (ASYMMETRIC) = 0.06316 WITH NEWINC  DEPENDENT.     = 0.04365 WITH RESDYTH DEPENDENT.
UNCERTAINTY COEFFICIENT (SYMMETRIC) = 0.05162
KENDALL'S TAU B = 0.28074.    SIGNIFICANCE =  0.0000
KENDALL'S TAU C = 0.26723.    SIGNIFICANCE =  0.0000
GAMMA =  0.42943
SOMER'S D (ASYMMETRIC) = 0.24733 WITH NEWINC   DEPENDENT.       = 0.31859 WITH RESDYTH  DEPENDENT.
SOMER'S D (SYMMETRIC) = 0.27851

NUMBER OF MISSING OBSERVATIONS =    50
```

**FIG. 12.7**  Output from subprogram FASTABS.

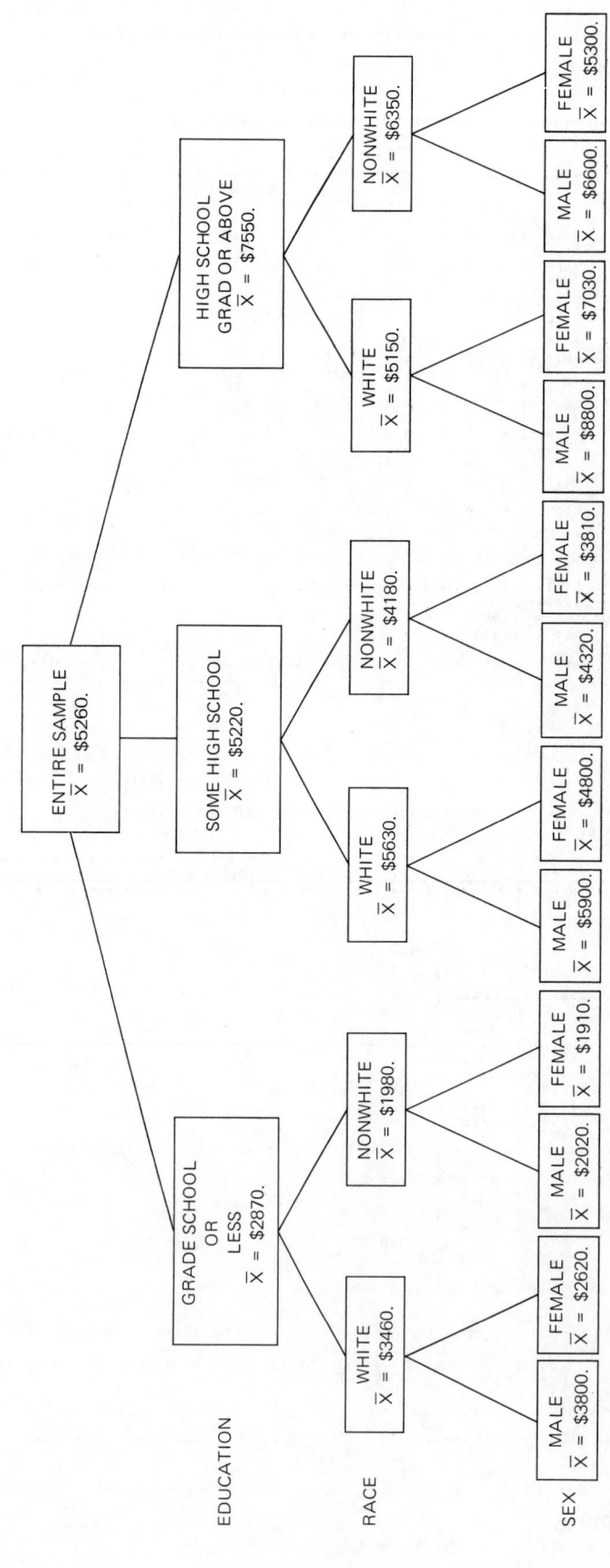

**FIG. 12.8**  Subsample structure for procedure BREAKDOWN. $\overline{X}$ refers to the mean of the variable INCOME within each subsample.

whites and nonwhites within each level of education and further elaborated so that means are produced comparing males and females within each racial group within each educational group. Up to five independent variables may be entered. The independent variables may be nominal, ordinal, or interval so long as they are classified into a limited number of discrete groups. The dependent variable may be either continuous or discrete, but clearly must be a variable for which a mean represents a meaningful measure of central tendency.

The output of subprogram BREAKDOWN presents the mean, standard deviation, and variance of the dependent variable for the entire population. These same statistics are then presented for each subgroup or class of each independent variable to be included in the table along with the number of cases falling into that subgroup. The procedure can be best understood when the above example is presented in terms of a tree, as in Fig. 12.8. This type of tree closely parallels the output format of BREAKDOWN. For clarity, however, only the means are presented below. The user must also remember that all of the means refer to mean level of income (i.e., the dependent variable) within all the different subgroups.

The research utility of this procedure is substantial. The first two rows of Fig. 12.8, for example, represent an analysis which is conceptually identical to that previously demonstrated on page 118 in the introduction to crosstabulation. The hypothetical findings also closely parallel those presented in that example and indicate that racial prejudice seems to affect levels of income at all levels of education. The findings also suggest that it is not just discrepancies in educational levels which account for the differences in income levels between the white and nonwhite segments of our society.

While the results of these analyses are parallel, there are clearly some differences in the type of information that one obtains from them. First, the mean breakdown analysis is considerably more succinct; that is, one gets the same information out of fewer numbers. In the same light and for the same reasons, one loses some information as well. For example, an examination of the means does not allow the researcher to compare the proportion of whites and nonwhites with high-school educations who earn less than $3,000 a year. On the other hand, had the income measure been collected as a continuous variable (say to the nearest thousand dollars) BREAKDOWN would have enabled the researcher to attach an actual dollar average to the income of each of the groups. In this instance, dividing the sample into a smaller number of discrete groups (a requirement of crosstabulation analysis) would have caused a loss of a valuable empirical hold on the data.

As usual, the choice of statistical methods depends upon both the nature of the data and the type of questions being asked.

As with all SPSS subprograms, all of the data modification and data selection procedures may be used with subprogram BREAKDOWN. There are also several options for processing missing data.

**12.4.1   THE BREAKDOWN PROCEDURE CARD**

The procedure card contains the control word BREAKDOWN followed by (in or after column 16) the list of variables for which breakdown tables are desired. The specification field begins with a variable name or list of variable names which are to be the dependent variables. One complete table will be presented for each variable named on this portion of the card. The dependent variable name or list is followed by the keyword BY which in turn is followed by a variable name or variable list of independent variables. This list may then also be followed by an additional BY and yet another list of variable names. This process may be repeated so that tables involving as many as five variables may be specified.

The BREAKDOWN procedure card may be best understood by a series of examples. The following BREAKDOWN card specifies a single two-dimensional table to obtain the mean level of INCOME for each value of the variable EDUCATN. The standard deviation and variance would of course also be computed.

```
1                16
BREAKDOWN        INCCME BY EDUCATN
```

Adding additional variables to a table is simply accomplished by inserting a variable linked with the keyword BY. The following BREAKDOWN card, for example, would produce a table identical in content to the example presented in Fig. 12.8.

```
1                   16
BREAKDOWN           INCOME BY EDUCATN BY RACE BY SEX
```

Note that the first variable always becomes the dependent or criterion variable and that the independent variables are entered into the table in the order in which they appear on the card proceeding from left to right.

Multiple tables can be specified in two ways. First a slash [/] may be placed after the first table requested, and a second table is then defined in a matter identical to the first such as:

```
1                   16
BREAKDOWN           INCOME BY EDUCATN BY RACE BY SEX/NMEM BY SES BY LRES BY RACE
```

Multiple tables can also be requested by placing more than one variable name to the right or left of any BY. These variable lists may consist of lists of nonadjacent variables set off by one or more common delimiter(s) of the type

VARX,VARY BY VARA,VARC,VARF

When groups of adjacent variables are to be entered, variable lists utilizing the usual TO convention may be entered. For example,

VARA TO VARD BY VARN TO VARZ

As usual, these two conventions may be intermixed, producing lists of variables of the following sort:

VARA,VARD,VARF TO VARJ BY VARN, VARP TO VARQ,VARZ

These multiple lists will produce one table for each variable named or implied on the left side of the BY for every combination of variables named or implied to the right of the BY. The following sample BREAKDOWN cards illustrate the use of these lists:

```
1                   16
BREAKDOWN           INCOME,EDUCATN,SAVINGS BY RACE BY SEX

BREAKDOWN           INCOME TO VAR073 BY RACE TO AGE

BREAKDOWN           VARL TO VARN,VARQ  BY VARA,VARB BY VARX TO VARZ
```

In the first card, three tables are specified: INCOME by RACE by SEX, EDUCATN by RACE by SEX, and SAVINGS by RACE by SEX. In the second card, there are two multiple-variable lists. If there were two variables implied between INCOME and VAR073 (i.e., a total of four variables) and three variables between RACE and AGE (a total of five), then a total of 20 tables would be produced. The tables would be produced in the following order: the first table would be INCOME by RACE, the second table would be INCOME by the variable directly following RACE in the RACE TO AGE list. One table would be produced for each variable in that list with INCOME as the dependent variable, and the last table would be INCOME by AGE. Following this, a new series of tables would be produced for the dependent variable directly following the variable INCOME in the INCOME TO VAR073 list. This process would be repeated so that the last table produced would be VAR073 by AGE.

These examples illustrate the rules of order, which are more clearly brought out in the third and last BREAKDOWN card; namely, the variables to the right of the last BY changes most quickly. Within lists separated with a BY, variables rotate from left to right. For the third BREAKDOWN card above, the first table produced would be VARL by VARA by VARX; the second table VARL by VARA by VARY; and the third VARL by VARA by VARZ. Having then produced all combinations for VARL and VARA, a second sequence of tables would be produced for all combinations of VARL and VARB. With this completed, the entire procedure would be repeated using VARM as the dependent variable. Finally, the entire process would be repeated for dependent variable VARN.

Up to five BY's may occur in a given list. Each list is delineated by a /, and a new list commences following the slash. The last list need not be followed by a slash. A maximum of 30 such lists may appear on a given BREAKDOWN card and its continuations. The general format of the BREAKDOWN card is then as follows:

```
1                    16
BREAKDOWN        ⎧ dependent variable ⎫    BY    ⎧ 1st independent variable ⎫    BY
                 ⎨        or          ⎬          ⎨          or              ⎬
                 ⎩   variable list    ⎭          ⎩      variable list       ⎭

                 ⎧ 2nd independent variable ⎫  BY . . . BY  ⎧ nth independent variable ⎫   / . . .
                 ⎨          or              ⎬               ⎨          or              ⎬
                 ⎩      variable list       ⎭               ⎩      variable list       ⎭
```

### 12.4.2  OPTIONS AVAILABLE FOR SUBPROGRAM BREAKDOWN: THE OPTIONS CARD

The BREAKDOWN procedure card is followed by an OPTIONS card which informs the BREAKDOWN program of the processing options desired by the user (see Sec. 5.2). The OPTIONS card contains the control word OPTIONS followed by a number list indicating the desired processing options.

There are three ways of handling missing data in subprogram BREAKDOWN.

*Default missing data option–table-wide deletion.*    The default or normal means of handling missing data with subprogram BREAKDOWN is *table-wide deletion.* Under table-wide deletion, a case is omitted from the computations for a given table when the value of any variable in that table is missing. This means that any case contained in a table will have a complete set of nonmissing values for all variables in that table. *This method of processing missing data will be employed unless option 1 or 3 is selected.*

*Option* 1.  *Inclusion of missing data.* This option causes missing-value indicators to be ignored and enters all data into the computation of the BREAKDOWN tables. This option is equivalent to deleting all missing value indicators for the variables being entered.

*Option* 2.  *Exclusion of missing data for dependent variables only.* This option causes missing data to be excluded only when data is missing for the dependent or criterion variable. In all other instances, the case is included, and the means, standard deviations, variances, and numbers of cases in each missing-data category are reported, as well as for valid values of the independent variables. This option can be very useful for examining biases of nonrespondent cases. If there are systematic biases in the types of respondents, nations, etc., which correlate with absent data, this technique will help determine what these biases are and their order of importance.

*Option* 3.  *Suppression of labels.* Selection of option 3 will cause the program to suppress the search for labels. When selected, no labels will be printed. Selection of this option will cause a small increase in processing speed.

As usual, the OPTIONS card may be deleted if all of the default options are selected. When this is done, the following options will be in force:

*Option a.*    Missing data will be excluded on a table-wide basis (see definition above).

*Option b.*    Labels will be printed wherever present.

### 12.4.3  STATISTICS FOR SUBPROGRAM BREAKDOWN

Subprogram BREAKDOWN, unlike any other program in the SPSS package, has *no* additional statistics. The mean, standard deviation, variance, and number of cases of each subgroup in the population are always printed, but no other statistics are available. For this reason, *there is no STATISTICS card for subprogram BREAKDOWN.*

### 12.4.4 PROGRAM LIMITATIONS FOR SUBPROGRAM BREAKDOWN

The following limitations are presently in effect for subprogram BREAKDOWN:

*Limitation* 1.   No more than 200 variables may be referenced on a given BREAKDOWN procedure card and its continuations. Each occurrence of a variable name counts as one towards this 200, even though the variable name has previously appeared on the card.

*Limitation* 2.   250 is the maximum number of tables which can be requested on a given procedure card and its continuations.

*Limitation* 3.   The maximum number of dimensions available for any given BREAKDOWN table is six—the dependent variable plus five independent or control variables. In practice this means that the keyword BY may be used a maximum of five times in constructing individual tables or lists of tables.

*Limitation* 4.   No more than 30 complete lists of tables may be specified on any given BREAKDOWN card and its continuations. A complete list is defined by all the tables requested between slashes [/], unless of course, it is the first or last list.

*Limitation* 5.   The maximum number of cells available is defined by the formula

$$\text{MAXCELLS} = \frac{(\text{SPACE}/4)}{(\text{MD} + 4)} - 1$$

where a cell is defined as a unique combination of the values of the independent or control variables. MAXCELLS is then the sum of these unique combinations. SPACE is in *bytes*. SPACE is set at 80,000 unless it has been altered by use of the PARM field on the EXEC card (see Appendix F. MD is the maximum number of uses of the keyword BY in any list appearing on the BREAKDOWN card or its continuations. If the list or individual tables with the largest number of dimensions uses five control or independent variables, MD would be equal to 5.

### 12.4.5 EXAMPLE DECK SETUP FOR SUBPROGRAM BREAKDOWN

Example 12.4 illustrates the use of subprogram BREAKDOWN to produce subsample tabulations when processing with a system file. It also points up some of the practical difficulties of using this procedure.

#### EXAMPLE 12.4

```
1                16
RUN NAME         BREAKDOWN RUN USING A SYSTEM FILE
GET FILE         ORGSTUDY
PROCESS SBFILES(NEWYORK)
BREAKDOWN        NMEM BY SEX BY RACE/INCOME BY FRATMEM BY SERVMEM BY VETMEM
FINISH
```

The data for the subsample tabulations are contained in a previously saved system file named ORGSTUDY. See Appendix I for a listing of file-defining control cards and data cases for this file. Only one of the three subfiles in this file, NEWYORK, is selected for the tabulation.

The first tabulation is reproduced in Fig. 12.9. The dependent or control variable is NMEM, the total number of memberships in organizations held by each respondent. From the table, we see that for the entire sample (NEWYORK), there were 100 valid cases; among these, the mean number of memberships is 0.610 per respondent, the standard deviation of the number of memberships is 1.014, and the variance is 1.028. Reading downward in the table, we find that in the two subsamples of 44 males and 56 females, the mean number of memberships is 0.773 and 0.482, respectively. The second column of tabulations shows the results when each of these two subsamples is further subdivided by race (white or Negro). We find, for example, that among the 16 male Negroes in the sample, the mean number of memberships is 1.000, and so forth.

```
BREAKDOWN RUN USING A SYSTEM FILE                                07/25/69        PAGE   76

FILE   ORGSTUDY (CREATION DATE = 07/25/69)    STUDY OF ORGANIZATIONAL MEMBERSHIP AND ACTIVITY
SUBFILE   NEWYORK

- - - - - - - - - -   D E S C R I P T I O N   O F   S U B P O P U L A T I O N S - - - - - - - - - -
CRITERION VARIABLE    NMEM        TOTAL NUMBER OF MEMBERSHIPS
     BROKEN DOWN BY   SEX         RESPONDENTS SEX
               BY     RACE        RESPONDENTS RACE
- - - - - - - - - - - - - - - - - - - - - - - - - - - - - - - - - - - - - - - - - - - - - -

FOR ENTIRE POPULATION
MEAN          0.610
STD DEV       1.014
VARIANCE      1.028
N           (  100)


VARIABLE    SEX              VARIABLE    RACE

CODE          1.            CODE          1.
MALE                        WHITE
MEAN          0.773         MEAN          0.643
STD DEV       1.309         STD DEV       1.026
VARIANCE      1.715         VARIANCE      1.053
N           (  44)          N           (  28)

                            CODE          2.
                            NEGRO
                            MEAN          1.000
                            STD DEV       1.713
                            VARIANCE      2.933
                            N           (  16)

CODE          2.            CODE          1.
FEMALE                      WHITE
MEAN          0.482         MEAN          0.486
STD DEV       0.687         STD DEV       0.702
VARIANCE      0.472         VARIANCE      0.492
N           (  56)          N           (  35)

                            CODE          2.
                            NEGRO
                            MEAN          0.476
                            STD DEV       0.680
                            VARIANCE      0.462
                            N           (  21)

   TOTAL CASES =      100
```

**FIG. 12.9**   Printout of subsample characteristics by subprogram BREAKDOWN.

The second tabulation, reproduced in Fig. 12.10, is actually a poor use of the BREAK-DOWN program. However, it points up some pitfalls in using this procedure. In this case, the sample has been broken down according to the values of three variables, FRATMEM, SERV-MEM, and VETMEM. For each subsample, statistics of the dependent variable INCOME have been calculated.

Each of the three variables FRATMEM, SERVMEM, and VETMEM can take the value 1 or 0, depending upon whether or not the respondent is a member of a fraternal organization, service organization, or veteran's group, respectively. Therefore there is a total of eight possible categories. Some of these are not listed, however, because there were no respondents in certain categories. For example, there were apparently no persons among the 94 valid cases who were not members of a fraternal organization, were members of a service organization, and also were members of a veteran's group. There were eight persons, however, who were members of fraternal organizations and not members of either service organizations or veteran's groups. The printout yields the interesting information that the eight persons who were members of fraternal organizations had an average of $17,000 annual income, as opposed to an average of $7,670 for the sample as a whole.

Asterisks appear for the standard deviation and variance of the dependent variable within subsamples with only one member, since these numbers are undefined. This illustrates what can happen when a small sample is broken down too finely. The number of cases in each subsample will tend to be too small for statistically meaningful conclusions.

Since no OPTIONS card follows the BREAKDOWN card in the deck, the default option of table-wide deletion is in force. In the context of the second table, this means that there were six cases which contained a missing-data value for either the variable INCOME, FRATMEM, SERVMEM, or VETMEM.

```
BREAKDOWN RUN USING A SYSTEM FILE                                      07/25/69      PAGE   77

FILE    ORGSTUDY (CREATION DATE = 07/25/69)    STUDY OF ORGANIZATIONAL MEMBERSHIP AND ACTIVITY
SUBFILE    NEWYORK

- - - - - - - - - -  D E S C R I P T I O N   O F   S U B P O P U L A T I O N S  - - - - - - - - - -
CRITERION VARIABLE    INCOME     FAMILY INCOME
     BROKEN DOWN BY    FRATMEM    MEMB IN FRATERNAL ORGS
                BY    SERVMEM    MEMB IN SERVICE CLUBS
                BY    VETMEM     MEMB IN VETERANS GRPS
- - - - - - - - - - - - - - - - - - - - - - - - - - - - - - - - - - - - - - - - - - - - - - - - -

FOR ENTIRE POPULATION
MEAN          7.670
STD DEV      11.404
VARIANCE    130.051
N         (    94)


VARIABLE    FRATMEM        VARIABLE    SERVMEM        VARIABLE    VETMEM

CODE          0.           CODE          0.           CODE          0.
NO                         NO                         NO
MEAN          6.802        MEAN          6.835        MEAN          6.928
STD DEV      10.267        STD DEV      10.323        STD DEV      10.430
VARIANCE    105.408        VARIANCE    106.568        VARIANCE    108.775
N         (    86)         N         (    85)         N         (    83)

                                                      CODE          1.
                                                      YES
                                                      MEAN          3.000
                                                      STD DEV       1.414
                                                      VARIANCE      2.000
                                                      N         (     2)

                          CODE          1.            CODE          0.
                          YES                         NO
                          MEAN          4.000         MEAN          4.000
                          STD DEV  **********          STD DEV  **********
                          VARIANCE **********          VARIANCE **********
                          N         (     1)          N         (     1)

CODE          1.          CODE          0.            CODE          0.
YES                       NO                          NO
MEAN         17.000       MEAN         17.000         MEAN         17.000
STD DEV      18.416       STD DEV      18.416         STD DEV      18.416
VARIANCE    339.143       VARIANCE    339.143         VARIANCE    339.143
N         (     8)        N         (     8)          N         (     8)

     TOTAL CASES =      100
   MISSING CASES =        6 OR    6.0 PCT.
```

**FIG. 12.10**    Printout of subsample characteristics by subprogram BREAKDOWN.

# 13
# BIVARIATE CORRELATION ANALYSIS: PEARSON AND RANK-ORDER CORRELATION

The SPSS system furnishes two programs for performing correlation analysis: PEARSON CORR and NONPAR CORR. PEARSON CORR computes standard product-moment or zero-order correlations, while NONPAR CORR computes Spearman and/or Kendall rank-order correlations for ordinal data. Both programs provide the user with significance tests and have the capability of producing matrices (on an output medium of the user's choice) for input into other programs. Each of the programs also contains several options for handling missing data. As usual, all of the data-selection and data-modification procedures available in SPSS may be employed while using these correlation programs.

## 13.1    INTRODUCTION TO CORRELATION ANALYSIS

Correlation analysis provides the researcher with a single summary statistic describing the strength of association between two variables. Like bivariate crosstabulation tables, correlation coefficients enable the researcher to determine the degree of covariation between two variables. In crosstabulation the degree of association is determined by examining the joint frequency distribution of the two variables in tabular form. In correlation analysis the strength of association is indicated by a single summary statistic—the coefficient. The types of correlation analysis included in this chapter do, in actuality, test only a special case in the overall realm of correlation: the case of linear correlation among variables which are at least ordinal in scale. Measures of association for nominal variables, like the *contingency coefficient,* are available in the crosstabulation subprograms CROSSTABS and FASTABS. Procedures for nonlinear correlation analysis (because of their much more limited use in the social sciences) are not presently included in the SPSS system.

Linear correlation analysis has become quite widely used in social science research for a number of different types of problems. First, correlation analysis is used to describe the strength of association between an independent and a dependent variable. Second, correlation analysis is often used in examining sets of independent or dependent variables in order to determine if they are related in a way which would allow them to be combined into a composite scale or index. Finally, correlation analysis is often employed as a first step to more complicated multivariate procedures which build on correlation coefficients such as partial correlation, multiple regression, causal modeling, factor analysis, etc. It is for this reason that we enable the user to output a correlation matrix for direct input into other SPSS programs or into other statistical packages.

The choice of the correlation procedure to be used is usually based on the type of data being employed. In general, Pearson product-moment correlations are used with *interval scales.* By this we mean that the variables are measured in common established units, and the units are real numerical quantities (i.e., where 10 units of variable X are to 5 units of variable X as 25 units is to 20 units). Rankings and ordinal categories do not usually have these qualities. The Spearman and Kendall rank-order correlation coefficients are generally used with these ordinal variables. By *ordinal* we mean that the values are numeric and can be arranged in increasing or decreasing order, but the numeric values assigned to cases do not correspond to a cardinal metric. For example, the beauty contestant who ranked first in a contest is not necessarily 5 times as beautiful as the fifth-ranked contestant. We do know, however, that she is ranked first, and there are four contestants ranked more beautiful than the fifth-ranked contestant, as well as a number below her depending upon the number of contestants.

Further, Spearman rank-order coefficients are generally preferred over Kendall's tau when the number of ordinal categories that a variable takes is large and the number of ties relatively small. Kendall's tau, on the other hand, is usually preferred when the number of categories are few and/or the number of ties large. This usually means that Spearman rank-order coefficients are preferred when the ordinal scale is more or less continuous, and Kendall's tau is selected when the data is grouped into a more limited number of categories.

However, in actuality there is no firm agreement among practicing researchers on the selection of correlation coefficients—particularly on the advisability of the use of Pearson correlations with ordinal data. This discussion should in no instance be used as an authoritative guide in the selection of correlation procedures.

As indicated above, the three correlation procedures described in this chapter measure only linear relationships. All three coefficients vary from $-1.0$ to $+1.0$. A coefficient of 0 always indicates that no *linear* relationship exists; a $+1.0$ coefficient implies a "perfect" positive relationship (i.e., an increase in one variable is always associated with a concommitant increase in the other variable); and a coefficient of $-1.0$ indicates a "perfect" negative relationship (i.e., one in which an increase in one variable is always associated with a decrease in the other variable).

While the computational procedure for the three types of correlations differ, they all have a common and rather direct relation to the underlying geometrical representation of a relationship—the scatter diagram. And perhaps the best intuitive way to understand and interpret all types of correlations is to visualize the relationship as a scatter diagram. Figure 13.1 displays the characteristics of a strong positive linear relationship. In this diagram let us assume, for example, that the vertical axis represents the proportion of a nation's population which is literate, while the horizontal axis represents a per capita measure of newspaper circulation. A given nation's level of literacy and per capita circulation can be jointly recorded on this scatter diagram by placing a dot at the intersection of its values on the two variables. Once this procedure has been accomplished for all the nations under investigation, the relationship can be

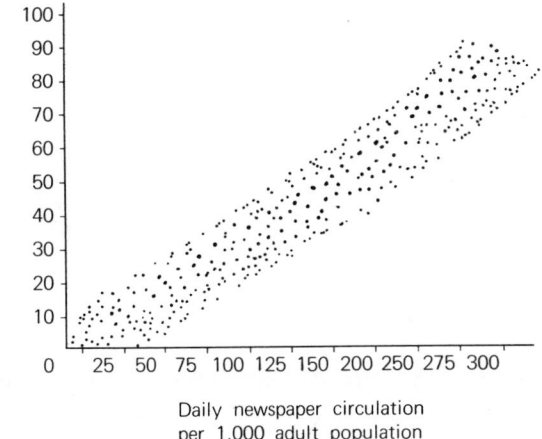

Daily newspaper circulation
per 1,000 adult population

**FIG. 13.1**    A scattergram illustrating a strong positive linear relationship.

examined. Given that we are not interested in the regression, but only in the correlation, the interpretation of this scatter diagram is quite straightforward. First, it is clear that the two variables are strongly related; as the level of literacy of a nation increases, so does its newspaper circulation. The clear pattern and tight scatter make this a very clear relationship. While one would normally use a Pearson correlation to measure this type of relationship, the pattern would remain pretty much the same if the actual values were replaced by rankings of the type used to compute Spearman and Kendall coefficients.

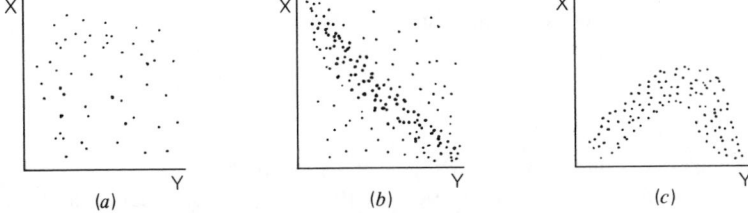

**FIG. 13.2**    Scattergrams illustrating different types of relationships.

Figure 13.2 demonstrates three different types of relationships. In scatter diagram (*a*) there is little or no relationship, linear or otherwise. The dots are randomly distributed, and the correlation coefficient for these two variables would approach zero no matter what type of linear coefficient was computed. Scatter diagram (*b*) reveals a weak negative relationship in which an increase in either one of the variables is mildly associated with a decrease in the other. In this case the correlation coefficient would be negative and small in quantity. The relationship revealed by scatter diagram (*c*) is of the most troublesome sort when using correlational procedures which test only the linear hypothesis, for the two variables in this diagram are quite strongly related. However, their relationship is nonlinear, and in this case all three correlation procedures available would yield a coefficient approaching zero for these two variables, when in reality they are quite strongly related. This last diagram should serve as a warning to the user to take caution in interpreting correlation coefficients.

## 13.2   SUBPROGRAM PEARSON CORR: PEARSON PRODUCT-MOMENT CORRELATION COEFFICIENTS

Subprogram PEARSON CORR computes zero-order product-moment correlation coefficients which are often termed Pearson correlations after their originator. This most common and widely applied correlation coefficient measures the amount of spread about the linear least-squares equation. More precisely, this correlation coefficient *is the ratio of the covariation to the square root of the product of the variation in X and the variation in Y.*[†] It is defined by the

---

[†]Hubert Blalock, "Social Statistics," p. 287, McGraw-Hill, New York, 1960.

following formula:

$$r = \frac{\sum_{i=1}^{N}(X_i - \bar{X})(Y_i - \bar{Y})}{\left\{ [\sum_{i=1}^{N}(X_i - \bar{X})^2][\sum_{i=1}^{N}(Y_i - \bar{Y})^2] \right\}^{\frac{1}{2}}}$$

where $X_i$ = ith observation of variable X

$Y_i$ = ith observation of variable Y

N = number of observations

$\bar{X} = \sum_{i=1}^{N} X_i/N$ = mean of variable X

$\bar{Y} = \sum_{i=1}^{N} Y_i/N$ = mean of variable Y

This formula can be restated by dividing the numerator and denominator by N − 1 to show that the correlation coefficient can also be defined as the covariance in X and Y divided by the product of their standard deviations. The covariance in X and Y is defined as

$$\frac{\sum_{i=1}^{N}(X_i - \bar{X})(Y_i - \bar{Y})}{N - 1}$$

The actual formula used by SPSS for computing Pearson correlation coefficients is

$$r = \frac{\sum_{i=1}^{N} X_i Y_i - (\sum_{i=1}^{N} X_i)(\sum_{i=1}^{N} Y_i)/N}{\left\{ \left[ \sum_{i=1}^{N} X_i^2 - (\sum_{i=1}^{N} X_i)^2/N \right] \left[ \sum_{i=1}^{N} Y_i^2 - (\sum_{i=1}^{N} Y_i)^2/N \right] \right\}^{\frac{1}{2}}}$$

Significance tests are reported for each coefficient and are derived from the use of Student's *t* with N − 2 degrees of freedom for the computed quantity:

$$r \left[ \frac{N - 2}{1 - r^2} \right]^{\frac{1}{2}}$$

The user has an option of selecting a one- or two-tailed test of significance.

Output from this program always includes the coefficient, the test of significance, and the number of cases [N] upon which the correlation coefficient was computed. The user may optionally have a matrix of correlations written or punched on cards, tape, or disk for input into other SPSS subprograms, into his own program, or into other statistical packages. A matrix of correlations may be produced or specific sets of coefficients can be requested. Multiple matrices and/or multiple lists of specific correlations may be produced on a given pass. In other words, the user has complete control over the variables to be entered into the correlations within the size limits of the program. Cases containing missing values may be excluded from the computations pairwise or listwise. In *pairwise deletion* a case is deleted from the computation of a given coefficient when either one of the variables involved in that coefficient is missing; that case will, however, be included in the computation of all coefficients for which there is complete information for that case. When the *listwise-deletion* option is selected, the case is deleted from the computation of all coefficients within that list or matrix, if that case has a missing value for any one of the variables in the list. This means that within a given list or matrix, all correlation coefficients are computed for an identical population.

The means and standard deviations, as well as the cross-product deviations and covariances, can be printed if the user requests them. All of the options and statistics, as well as the procedure for requesting correlations, are described in detail in the following sections.

### 13.2.1 THE PEARSON CORR PROCEDURE CARD

The user specifies the desired correlation coefficients by means of the PEARSON CORR procedure card. The control words PEARSON CORR are followed (beginning in column 16, as usual) by the variable names and/or variable lists for which correlation coefficients are desired. The PEARSON CORR card may reference any variable which has been previously defined, including those defined by variable transformations. The variables are entered onto the card in the usual manner. Nonadjacent variable names must be separated from each other by one or more common delimiters. Three or more *adjacent* variables may be entered with the usual TO convention (as in VARX TO VARZ), where both VARX and VARZ are variables which have been previously defined and where VARX precedes VARZ on the cases in the file. As is usually the case, these two conventions may be used together to produce variable lists of the following type:

VARA,VARC,VARL TO VARN,VARZ

All other rules and conventions concerning the use of variable names and the construction of SPSS control cards also apply (see Chap. 3 and particularly Secs. 3.1.2.1 and 3.1.3).

The keyword WITH specifies that a correlation coefficient is to be computed for each variable named preceding this keyword paired with each variable named following the keyword. For example,

```
1              16
PEARSON CORR   AGE,INCOME,SEX WITH SCALE1,SCALE2
```

would inform the system that six correlation coefficients are to be computed and printed: AGE with SCALE1, AGE with SCALE2, INCOME with SCALE1, INCOME with SCALE2, SEX with SCALE1, and SEX with SCALE2. The correlation coefficients, the number of cases upon which they are based, and their level of statistical significance are then printed in serial order, six coefficients across the page. The left-most variable in the correlation list is paired with the left-most variable on the right side of the keyword WITH. Then, each successive variable to the right of the keyword WITH is paired with this first variable in the list. This process is then repeated for each successive variable in the list which lies to the left side of the keyword WITH. All coefficients requested are computed and printed so that a control card of the type

```
1              16
PEARSON CORR   A TO D WITH A TO D
```

would produce the following 16 coefficients, their N's, and their levels of statistical significance: A with A, A with B, A with C, A with D, B with A, B with B, B with C, B with D, C with A, C with B, C with C, C with D, D with A, D with B, D with C, and D with D, in exactly that order.

When a *correlation matrix* is to be punched on cards or written on tape or disk for future use, the keyword WITH *must not be used in the specification field*. When this matrix form is utilized (i.e., whenever the keyword WITH is not used to separate the variables being correlated), the system computes all possible nonredundant correlations from the variables on the list. By *nonredundant*, we mean all unique coefficients. Because the correlation of a variable with itself is always unity, and the correlation of Y with X is identical to the correlation of X with Y, these redundant correlations are not printed. However, if the user requests that a correlation matrix be punched or written for future use, the complete square matrix is assembled and written or punched on the device specified by the user in his JCL cards, even though the complete matrix is not printed. See Sec. 12.1.3 for a more complete explanation of punched matrices.

The following example PEARSON CORR card demonstrates the matrix-form convention for the same variable list used in the example above. This time, however, a correlation matrix is to be computed.

```
1              16
PEARSON CORR   AGE,INCOME,SEX,SCALE1,SCALE2
```

This card would cause the 10 nonredundant coefficients to be computed and reported on the printed output. If the user also wished to have a matrix written or punched, a full 5 X 5 matrix would be assembled and produced on the device requested by him. Hence, the following two PEARSON CORR cards yield basically the same information:

```
1              16
PEARSON CORR   AGE,INCOME,SEX,IQ WITH AGE,INCOME,SEX,IQ

PEARSON CORR   AGE,INCOME,SEX,IQ
```

However, a punched or written matrix cannot be produced with the first card because of the WITH, and the redundant coefficients will be computed, printed, and counted in the first card, but will not appear in the second. When the user is dealing with relatively large matrices, he will achieve considerable savings in machine time and will be able to process a much larger matrix if the matrix form is utilized. We therefore suggest that it be used with large matrices even when a punched or written matrix is not requested.

Multiple matrices, multiple lists, and multiple combinations of matrices and lists can be requested on a single PEARSON CORR card (and on its continuation cards) as long as each list or matrix to be computed is separated from the next by a single slash [/]. The general format of the PEARSON CORR procedure card is then as follows:

```
1                16
PEARSON CORR ⎰variable name⎱ ⎡WITH ⎰variable name⎱⎤  /...
             ⎱    or       ⎰ ⎢     ⎱    or        ⎰⎢
             ⎰variable list ⎱ ⎣     ⎰variable list  ⎰⎦
```

Note that there must be *no* slash preceding the first list and there need be no slash following the last list.

The following example PEARSON CORR procedure card illustrates a run in which the user is requesting four separate correlation lists. The second and fourth lists are of the matrix form. If the user had requested that matrices be punched, all four lists would have been computed and printed in the manner described above. Punched matrices would, however, have been produced only for lists 2 and 4.

```
1                16
PEARSON CORR   ITEM1 TO ITEM9 WITH SCALE1,SCALE3,SCALE7 TO SCALE9/AGE
               TO INCOME/VAR003 TO VAR008 WITH VAR112,VAR124/IQ,EDUC,TESTA,
               TESTB,APTITUD
```

### 13.2.2   OPTIONS AVAILABLE FOR SUBPROGRAM PEARSON CORR

The PEARSON CORR procedure card is followed by an OPTIONS card which instructs the PEARSON CORR subprogram as to the processing options desired by the user (see Sec. 5.2). The OPTIONS card contains the control word OPTIONS followed by a number list indicating the desired options. *The first three options deal with the handling of missing data.* There are three ways of handling missing data in subprogram PEARSON CORR:

*Default missing-data option—pairwise deletion.*   The default or normal means of handling missing data with subprogram PEARSON CORR is pairwise deletion. With pairwise deletion, a case is omitted from the computation of a given coefficient if the value of either of the two variables being considered is missing. A case is therefore included in the computation of all coefficients for which it has complete data. Pairwise deletion has the advantage of utilizing as much of the data as possible in the computation of each coefficient. It has the disadvantage, however, of (under some circumstances) producing coefficients which are based on a different number of cases and perhaps on even quite different subpopulations of the file. *This default option is in force unless the user selects option 1 or 2.*

*Option* 1.   *Inclusion of missing data.*   This option causes the subprogram to include all cases in the calculation of the correlation coefficients regardless of any missing data values which may be defined.

*Option* 2.   *Listwise deletion of missing data.*   Causes cases containing missing data to be deleted listwise. Listwise deletion has a case omitted from the calculation of *all* coefficients specified in a single list if a case contains a missing value for any variable entered into that list. In general, listwise deletion has the effect of reducing the number of cases upon which the coefficients are computed. How large this reduction will be depends of course upon the overall amount of missing data and its distribution among the cases. If the missing data is highly concentrated by case, the net effect will not be much different than pairwise deletion. If, on the other hand, missing data is randomly spread among a large proportion of the cases, a major reduction in the workable N will result when this option is selected. The workable N is further affected by the distribution of missing values among the variables; the variable with the largest amount of missing data will establish the maximum number of cases on which all coefficients within a given list will be computed. Option 2, on the other hand, is particularly important when the researcher wishes to do further multivariate analysis on the correlations and wishes to ensure that all the coefficients are derived from the same cases. Note that if more than one list of correlations is specified, this option will result in a different number and configuration of valid cases for each list.

*Option 3.*    *One- and two-tailed tests of statistical significance.*    *Causes a two-tailed test of statistical significance to be applied to each coefficient requested* rather than the normal one-tailed test. A two-tailed test is normally used when the researcher does not have an explicit hypothesis concerning expected direction of the coefficient (i.e., whether it will be positive or negative). The one-tailed test is normally used when there are rather explicit expectations about the direction of the coefficient. *Note that the one-tailed test is the default option and is universally applied unless option 3 is selected.*

*Option 4.*    *Punching or writing matrices for future access.*    This option causes a matrix of coefficients to be punched or written (on the medium of the user's choice) for all lists which are specified in matrix form. The keyword WITH must never be used in a list for which the user desires a punched or written matrix. In runs in which the user has multiple correlation lists and desires that one or more of these lists be output as punched or written matrices, only those lists which do *not* contain the keyword WITH will be output on a medium other than the printer.

When more than one matrix is requested, the matrices are written, in the order requested, one behind each other, until all the desired matrices have been written or punched. All matrices are written or punched on the standard SPSS BCD output device presently termed FT09F001. Instructions for completing the requisite JCL card so that the user may have matrices punched on cards or written on tape or disk are to be found in Appendix F (Job Control Language For SPSS). This JCL card must be filled out if the user requests written or punched matrices.

All matrices are output in card image (irrespective of the output device used) with a format of 8F10.7. Each row of the matrix starts on a new card, and the row continues onto as many cards as required. When a row has been completed, a new card is started for the next row in the matrix. This procedure is repeated until the entire matrix has been output. The diagonal elements of the matrix are always output as 1.0, and all redundant coefficients are also output so that the matrix is complete and square. Note that this is not true of the accompanying printed matrix which contains only the nonredundant coefficients.

The output format of 8F10.7 means that eight coefficients will be output per card-image record. Each coefficient will have seven significant digits to the right of the decimal point, and the seventh or last digit will always be in a position or column of an even multiple of 10 (e.g., in terms of card images, the last digit of the first coefficient will be punched in column 10, and the last digit of the eighth coefficient will be in column 80). When one of these matrices is to be input into one of the SPSS subprograms which accept correlation matrices (such as PARTIAL CORR, REGRESSION, or FACTOR), it should be read in under an equivalent format (e.g., 8F10.0). This is also true when the user wishes to read any of these matrices into one of his own programs or into another statistical package.

As usual, the OPTIONS card may be deleted if all of the default options are selected. When this is done, the following options will be executed on the data:

Option *a.*    Missing data will be excluded pairwise (see definition above).

Option *b.*    A one-tailed test of statistical significance will be computed for all coefficients requested.

Option *c.*    Correlation matrices will *not* be output on devices other than the printer, but correlation lists of the matrix form (i.e., lists without the keyword WITH) will be accepted and printed in the normal fashion on the printer along with all other specified lists.

### 13.2.3    STATISTICS AVAILABLE FOR SUBPROGRAM PEARSON CORR

The correlation coefficients, the number of nonmissing cases upon which they were computed, and their level of statistical significance are always reported. A number of other supporting statistics are also available and, as usual, are requested by statistic number on the STATISTICS card. The STATISTICS card directly follows the OPTIONS card. If all of the default options are selected and the OPTIONS card is omitted, the STATISTICS card directly follows the PEARSON CORR procedure card. The STATISTICS card may also be omitted, in which case only the coefficients, the N on which they were computed, and their significance level will be reported. If any of the following statistics are desired, the control word STATISTICS is followed (beginning in column 16) with one or more of the following numbers or the keyword ALL which will cause all of the following statistics to appear on the printed output. The statistics in no way affect the written or punched matrices.

*Statistic* 1.    Causes the means and standard deviations of each variable referenced on the PEARSON CORR card to be computed and printed. These means and standard deviations are based on all cases containing valid or nonmissing values for that variable unless option 1 is selected, in which case all values are entered into the computation of the means and standard deviations. Neither the default option nor option 2 has any effect on the computation of these statistics.

*Statistic* 2.    Causes the cross-product deviations and the covariance to be printed for each pair of variables for which a correlation coefficient was requested. These statistics (unlike the means and standard deviations) are based on the same cases as the correlation coefficients.

### 13.2.4    PROGRAM LIMITATIONS FOR SUBPROGRAM PEARSON CORR

*Limitation* 1.    A maximum of 40 individual specification lists may appear on a given PEAR-SON CORR card and its continuations. Note that each specification list must be separated from the next by the special delimiter /, but there should be *no* / before the first list, and there need be no / after the last list.

*Limitation* 2.    A maximum of 500 variable names may be referenced on a given PEARSON CORR card and its continuations. This limitation of 500 names applies to the sum of all variables named in all lists, and therefore variables which appear in more than one list must be counted as one name each time they appear.

*Limitation* 3.    No more than 250 individual elements may appear on a PEARSON CORR card or its continuations. Each occurrence of a variable name, keyword, and special delimiter counts as "one" towards this total.

*Limitation* 4.    The maximum number of coefficients which may be computed on a single pass varies depending upon which missing-data option is selected. If the *default missing-data option* (i.e., the pairwise deletion) is selected, a maximum of (SPACE/24) coefficients may be computed.[1] Note that an 82 × 82 matrix involves 3,321 nonredundant pairs and is therefore the maximum-size matrix which can be handled by the program when the pairwise-deletion option is selected. This maximum applies to the sum of all coefficients requested by all lists on a given PEARSON CORR card and its continuations. When either missing-data options 1 or 2 are selected, the maximum number of coefficients which can be computed is 7,750. This permits a maximum matrix size of 125 × 125 variables. Again this maximum applies to the sum of all coefficients requested by all lists on a given PEARSON CORR card.

[1] For a discussion of the parameter SPACE, see Appendix F.2. The default value of SPACE is 80,000.

In determining whether a given problem will fit on a single pass, the user should be aware of the following issues. The number of nonredundant coefficients generated by a matrix is determined by the formula $(NVAR^2 - NVAR)/2$ where NVAR is the number of variables entered into the matrix. When using the matrix-form list (i.e., a list without the keyword WITH), the number of coefficients used can always be determined by the solution of this formula. For lists utilizing the keyword WITH, the number of coefficients requested is the simple product of the number of variables to the right of the WITH times the number of variables to the left of the WITH. In this case the actual number of variables employed by the use of the TO convention must be counted, as must all redundant coefficients requested. Thus, whenever matrices are contemplated, the use of the matrix form will result in a considerable savings in terms of both machine time and the number of coefficients which must be stored.

### 13.2.5  SAMPLE DECK SETUP AND OUTPUT FOR SUBPROGRAM PEARSON CORR

Example 13.1 illustrates the use of subprogram PEARSON CORR in a run using an SPSS system file. The system file named COMSTUDY has been saved in a previous run and is retrieved with the use of the GET FILE card.

**EXAMPLE 13.1**

```
1                    16
RUN NAME             RUN PEARSON CORRELATIONS WITH SYSTEM FILE AND PUNCH CORRELATIONS
GET FILE             COMSTUDY
PEARSON CORR         MEDSCH TO PTTERTRY WITH POP60/TIME WITH NEWSWEEK
OPTIONS              2
PEARSON CORR         MEDSCH TO PTTERTRY
OPTIONS              2,4
FINISH
```

The user should be aware that in order to retrieve this file, it would be necessary for him to include an FT03 JCL card in the deck of JCL cards which accompany this run. The variable list in file COMSTUDY was defined by the use of the following VARIABLE LIST card:

```
1                    16
VARIABLE LIST        COMCO01,CARDNO1,MEDSCH,MEDFINC,PTGOHS,PTAGRI,PTMANU,PTTERTRY,
                     POP60,POPLAT,PTCHGN,SPISOL,WHTCOLAR,LIFE,TIME,NEWSWEEK,READDIG,
                     HRSWORK,GOVSELCT,CONELECT,PARTISAN,PARTROLE
```

A complete listing of the file-defining control cards and cases for this file may be found in Appendix I.

The first list on the first PEARSON CORR card (MEDSCH TO PTTERTRY WITH POP60) causes the following variables to be correlated:

MEDSCH with POP60
MEDFINC with POP60
PTGOHS with POP60
PTAGRI with POP60
PTMANU with POP60
PTTERTRY with POP60

The second list causes the correlation TIME with NEWSWEEK to be produced. Output from this first PEARSON CORR procedure is reproduced in Fig. 13.3. The OPTIONS card causes listwise deletion of missing data.

```
RUN PEARSON CORRELATIONS WITH SYSTEM FILE AND PUNCH CORRELATIONS                    07/25/69        PAGE    2

FILE   COMSTUDY (CREATION DATE = 07/25/69)    STUDY OF AMERICAN SMALL COMMUNITIES

- - - - - - - - - - - - - P E A R S O N   C O R R E L A T I O N   C O E F F I C I E N T S - - - - - - - - - - - -

VARIABLE            VARIABLE            VARIABLE            VARIABLE            VARIABLE            VARIABLE
PAIR                PAIR                PAIR                PAIR                PAIR                PAIR
--------            --------            --------            --------            --------            --------


MEDSCH    -0.0119   MEDFINC    0.2361   PTGOHS     0.2403   PTAGRI    -0.2828   PTMANU     0.0942   PTTERTRY   0.0611
WITH      N( 64)    WITH      N( 64)    WITH      N( 64)    WITH      N( 64)    WITH      N( 64)    WITH      N( 64)
POP60     SIG .463   POP60     SIG .030  POP60     SIG .028  POP60     SIG .012  POP60     SIG .229  POP60     SIG .316

RUN PEARSON CORRELATIONS WITH SYSTEM FILE AND PUNCH CORRELATIONS                    07/25/69        PAGE    3

FILE   COMSTUDY (CREATION DATE = 07/25/69)    STUDY OF AMERICAN SMALL COMMUNITIES

- - - - - - - - - - - - - P E A R S O N   C O R R E L A T I O N   C O E F F I C I E N T S - - - - - - - - - - - -

VARIABLE            VARIABLE            VARIABLE            VARIABLE            VARIABLE            VARIABLE
PAIR                PAIR                PAIR                PAIR                PAIR                PAIR
--------            --------            --------            --------            --------            --------


TIME       0.4135
WITH      N( 64)
NEWSWEEK  SIG .001
```

**FIG. 13.3**    Output from subprogram PEARSON CORR.

The second PEARSON CORR control card in Example 3.1 specifies a number of correlations to be computed from the same file. This time, the variable list is in matrix form: MEDSCH TO PTTERTRY. The following table shows the correlations calculated and printed:

| Variable | Variable | | | | |
| | MEDSCH | MEDFINC | PTGOHS | PTAGRI | PTMANU | PTTERTRY |
|---|---|---|---|---|---|---|
| MEDSCH | | X | X | X | X | X |
| MEDFINC | | | X | X | X | X |
| PTGOHS | | | | X | X | X |
| PTAGRI | | | | | X | X |
| PTMANU | | | | | | X |
| PTTERTRY | | | | | | |

The output from this run is reproduced in Fig. 13.4. The second OPTIONS card specified listwise deletion for this calculation, and in addition, causes a square matrix of correlation coefficients to be punched on cards. (The user would have to prepare an FT09 JCL card to specify the output device for this punched matrix.) Output of the matrix is appropriate in this case since the keyword WITH did not appear on the PEARSON CORR card. The reader is referred to Sec. 13.2.2 where it is explained that listwise deletion is the most appropriate statistical procedure where a correlation matrix is to be input to another program; for example, the SPSS subprograms PARTIAL CORR or REGRESSION. A listing of the punched matrix is shown in Fig. 13.5.

```
RUN PEARSON CORRELATIONS WITH SYSTEM FILE AND PUNCH CORRELATIONS                    07/25/69        PAGE    5

FILE   COMSTUDY (CREATION DATE = 07/25/69)    STUDY OF AMERICAN SMALL COMMUNITIES

- - - - - - - - - - - - - P E A R S O N   C O R R E L A T I O N   C O E F F I C I E N T S - - - - - - - - - - - -

VARIABLE            VARIABLE            VARIABLE            VARIABLE            VARIABLE            VARIABLE
PAIR                PAIR                PAIR                PAIR                PAIR                PAIR
--------            --------            --------            --------            --------            --------


MEDSCH     0.7162   MEDSCH     0.5383   MEDSCH    -0.1945   MEDSCH     0.0809   MEDSCH     0.6015   MEDFINC    0.5267
WITH      N( 64)    WITH      N( 64)    WITH      N( 64)    WITH      N( 64)    WITH      N( 64)    WITH      N( 64)
MEDFINC   SIG .001  PTGOHS    SIG .001  PTAGRI    SIG .062  PTMANU    SIG .263  PTTERTRY  SIG .001  PTGOHS    SIG .001


MEDFINC   -0.1569   MEDFINC    0.3957   MEDFINC    0.3599   PTGOHS    -0.3149   PTGOHS     0.2353   PTGOHS     0.3789
WITH      N( 64)    WITH      N( 64)    WITH      N( 64)    WITH      N( 64)    WITH      N( 64)    WITH      N( 64)
PTAGRI    SIG .108  PTMANU    SIG .001  PTTERTRY  SIG .002  PTAGRI    SIG .006  PTMANU    SIG .031  PTTERTRY  SIG .001


PTAGRI    -0.2148   PTAGRI    -0.3379   PTMANU    -0.3303
WITH      N( 64)    WITH      N( 64)    WITH      N( 64)
PTMANU    SIG .044  PTTERTRY  SIG .003  PTTERTRY  SIG .004
```

**FIG. 13.4**    Output from subprogram PEARSON CORR.

```
1.0000000  0.7161650  0.5382863-0.1944827  0.0808510  0.6015470
0.7161650  1.0000000  0.5266900-0.1568862  0.3956798  0.3599354
0.5382863  0.5266900  1.0000000-0.3149385  0.2352718  0.3788608
-0.1944827-0.1568862-0.3149385  1.0000000-0.2147607-0.3378556
0.0808510  0.3956798  0.2352718-0.2147607  1.0000000-0.3303398
0.6015470  0.3599354  0.3788608-0.3378556-0.3303398  1.0000000
```

**FIG. 13.5**    The punched matrix produced by the PEARSON CORR run shown in Example 13.1.

## 13.3    SUBPROGRAM NONPAR CORR: SPEARMAN AND/OR KENDALL RANK-ORDER CORRELATION COEFFICIENTS

Subprogram NONPAR CORR computes Spearman and/or Kendall rank-order correlation co-efficients. The control word NONPAR is based on the fact that these two correlation coefficients are nonparametric. That is, neither depends upon a normal distribution or on the metric quality of interval scales. Both of these procedures do require that the variables be at least ordinal in scale and numeric in type.

Both Spearman's $r_s$ and Kendall's tau require the use of rankings rather than the absolute values of variables in the computation of the coefficients; hence, the first task of the NONPAR CORR subprogram is to read the variables in and to replace their initial values with ordinal rankings. The processing of missing data often requires the rankings to be continuously adjusted as each variable for which coefficients are desired is paired with each other variable. For these reasons, NONPAR CORR is the only subprogram in the SPSS system which requires that all the data be *core resident* (i.e., in the computer's memory) during the entire computational procedure. The requirement of core residency places severe limitations on the quantity of data which can be processed. This is, for example, the only SPSS subprogram which cannot theoretically process an infinite number of cases. It is also the only program in which there is a direct trade-off between the number of coefficients which can be produced and the number of cases which can be processed. The nature of the computations also makes this subprogram relatively slower than PEARSON CORR, for example.

Output from this program may include either or both the Spearman $r_s$ and Kendall tau coefficients. A test of statistical significance and the number of cases upon which the coefficient was computed accompanies each coefficient, just as in PEARSON CORR. Also like PEARSON CORR, a matrix of coefficients may be output on a medium of the user's choice for future use. Similarly, a matrix of correlations may be produced, or specific sets of coefficients can be requested. Multiple matrices and/or multiple lists of specific correlations may be produced on a given pass. Also like PEARSON CORR, missing data may be excluded pairwise, listwise, or it may be included in the computation of the coefficients. Because of the many similarities between NONPAR CORR and PEARSON CORR, the reader will often be referred to the description of PEARSON CORR rather than having identical detailed descriptions repeated here.

The chief differences between Spearman's $r_s$ and Kendall's tau seem to be that the Kendall coefficients are somewhat more meaningful when the data contain a large number of tied ranks. Spearman's $r_s$ on the other hand, seems to yield a closer approximation to product-moment correlation coefficients when the data is more or less continuous (i.e., not characterized by a large number of ties at each rank). As a rule of thumb, one might use tau more readily when a fairly large number of cases were classified into a relatively small number of categories and $r_s$ when the ratio of cases to categories is smaller. Each of the procedures, however, has a correction for ties, and there is no fixed rule about selecting one over the other. In actuality, the basic concepts underlying these two coefficients are quite similar as are usually the resulting coefficients when the two are computed on the same data. Both coefficients vary from +1.0 to −1.0, but in general, the absolute value of tau tends to be slightly smaller than that of r.

Spearman's $r_s$ is defined as the sum of the squared differences in the paired ranks for two variables over all cases, divided by a quantity which can perhaps best be described as what the sum of the squared differences in ranks would have been had the two sets of rankings been totally independent. This quotient is then subtracted from 1 to produce the standardized coefficient. Spearman $r_s$ is then formally defined as

$$r_s = 1 - \frac{6 \sum\limits_{i=1}^{N} |d_i^2|}{N^3 - N}$$

For computational purposes and particularly to correct for the occurrence of tied ranks, Spearman's $r_s$ can be redefined as

$$r_s = \frac{T_x + T_y - \sum\limits_{i=1}^{N} d_i^2}{2(T_x T_y)^{\frac{1}{2}}}$$

where D is the difference between the ranks of the two variables for each case, and where $T_x$ or $T_y$ is to be defined by the quantity

$$\frac{N(N^2 - 1) - \Sigma R(R^2 - 1)}{12}$$

where R is the number of ties at a given rank for X or Y, respectively. The significance on any $r_s$ coefficient can be determined by comparing the quantity

$$r_s \left( \frac{N - 2}{1 - r_s^2} \right)^{\frac{1}{2}}$$

with the Student's t distribution with $N - 2$ degrees of freedom.

Kendall's tau is quite similar to $r_s$ in that both are techniques for producing standardized coefficients based on the amount of agreement between two sets of ordinal rankings. While we arrive at $r_s$ by manipulating (in order to standardize) the square of the differences in the two sets of rankings, Kendall's tau begins by computing a statistic called S. Given that the rankings of one variable are placed in their natural order (i.e., arranged by their ranks in order from 1 to N), S is computed by comparing the number of pairs of rankings of a second variable which are also arranged in their correct or natural order when they are sorted according to the natural order of the rankings of the first variable. S is then computed by beginning with the observation ranked 1 on the first variable and counting the number of ranks on the second variable which are greater than the rank of that case on the second variable. Once this has been done, the number of ranks below this observation which are smaller than its rank on the second variable are subtracted from the first quantity. When this procedure is repeated for all ranks, the sum of these remainders is equal to the statistic S. The computed or actual S is then divided by the maximum possible S which could have been obtained with that number of rankings had the two sets of rankings been in total agreement. This number can be expressed as $\frac{1}{2}N(N - 1)$ where N is the number of observations or cases. The general formula for tau is then

$$\tau = \frac{S}{\frac{1}{2}N(N - 1)}$$

When the correction for tied ranks is introduced, the formula becomes

$$\tau = \frac{S}{\sqrt{\frac{1}{2}N(N - 1) - T_x} \sqrt{\frac{1}{2}N(N - 1) - T_y}}$$

where $T_x = \frac{1}{2}\Sigma(t - 1)$, where t is the number of tied observations in each group of ties on the X variable, and where $T_y$ is the same quantity for the Y variable. The significance of tau is determined by comparing tau to a normal distribution with a standard deviation equal to

$$\left( \frac{4N + 10}{9N(N - 1)} \right)^{\frac{1}{2}}$$

### 13.3.1 THE NONPAR CORR PROCEDURE CARD

Subprogram NONPAR CORR computing Spearman and/or Kendall rank-order correlation coefficients is called and activated by a procedure card containing the control words NONPAR CORR. The control words are followed by one or more lists of variables for which coefficients are desired. The format of this card is identical to the format of the PEARSON CORR procedure card, and the user is referred to Sec. 13.1.1 for a detailed discussion of the format.

Briefly, variable names may be entered as lists of individual variables and/or utilizing the TO convention. As with the PEARSON CORR card, the keyword WITH may be omitted to obtain all possible correlation coefficients from a given variable list. The two forms of variable lists may be mixed in multiple specification lists which are separated from one another by slashes. As with PEARSON CORR, a matrix of coefficients may be output (punched on cards or written on tape or disk) when the WITH is not present in the list.

### 13.3.2 OPTIONS AVAILABLE FOR SUBPROGRAM NONPAR CORR

As with all SPSS programs, the desired options are selected by number on an OPTIONS card which directly follows the NONPAR CORR procedure card. Options 1 to 4 for this subprogram are identical to those listed in subprogram PEARSON CORR, and they are therefore not listed here. The following problems concerning several of these options when used with subprogram NONPAR CORR are noted here. The use of option 1 or 2 for processing missing data will significantly decrease the processing time over the default missing-data option which deletes missing values pairwise. It should be noted that the difficulties and magnitude are in this case quite significant.

The maximum-size correlation matrix which can presently be punched or written on a BCD output file is now set at 30. This is significantly smaller than the matrix which can be produced by PEARSON CORR.

Options 5 and 6 control the selection of Spearman or Kendall correlations. Specifically, use of neither option results in getting only Spearman correlations. Option 5 yields only Kendall correlations, and option 6 yields both Kendall and Spearman. If options 4 and 6 are used together, all Kendall correlation matrices will precede all Spearman correlation matrices on the BCD output device.

### 13.3.3 STATISTICS AVAILABLE FOR SUBPROGRAM NONPAR CORR

Correlation coefficients, level of statistical significance and the number of cases upon which each correlation was calculated are always printed. No further statistics are available so that subprogram NONPAR CORR *is one of the subprograms not utilizing a* STATISTICS *card.*

### 13.3.4 PROGRAM LIMITATIONS FOR SUBPROGRAM NONPAR CORR

The following limitations are currently in effect for this subprogram:

*Limitation* 1. A maximum of 100 variables may be referenced on any given NONPAR CORR procedure card and its continuations. Each name implied by the utilization of the TO convention must be counted.

*Limitation* 2. A maximum of 25 specification lists may appear. All specification lists except the last are followed by a slash. This means that no more than 24 slashes may appear.

*Limitation* 3. Unlike any other subprogram in the SPSS system, there is a finite number of cases which can be processed on any given pass. Sampling and selecting may, of course, be used to manipulate this maximum. The maximum number of cases is determined by the expression

$$\frac{(SPACE/2)}{2 \times NVAR + 1}$$

where NVAR is the number of variables used.[1] If option 2 is used, NVAR is the total number of variables. Otherwise, it is the number of unique variables (i.e., a variable appearing in more than one list is counted more than once only if option 2 is in effect). If the default missing value option is selected, the denominator of the expression is modified to $2 \times (NVAR + 2) + 1$.

### 13.3.5 SAMPLE DECK SETUP AND OUTPUT FOR SUBPROGRAM NONPAR CORR

Example 13.2 illustrates the use of subprogram NONPAR CORR in a run using an SPSS system file. The system file has been saved in a previous run and is retrieved with the use of the GET FILE card. A listing of the file-defining control cards and cases for file ORGSTUDY may be found in Appendix I. In this case two of the three subfiles are processed together as a group. The NONPAR CORR control card specifies a total of 10 correlations to be calculated, since it contains five variable names in matrix form. The keyword WITH is omitted and the correlations to be calculated are as shown in the table.

**EXAMPLE 13.2**

```
1              16
RUN NAME       RUN SPEARMAN CORRELATIONS WITH SYSTEM FILE INPUT
GET FILE       ORGSTUDY
PROCESS SBFILES (NWJERSEY,PENNSYLV)
NONPAR CORR    RESDYTH,INCOME,NACT,EDRESPON,OCLEVRES
OPTIONS        1
FINISH
```

**Table of correlations produced by the example run 13.2**

| Variable | RESDYTH | INCOME | Variable<br>NACT | EDRESPON | OCLEVRES |
|---|---|---|---|---|---|
| RESDYTH |  | X | X | X | X |
| INCOME |  |  | X | X | X |
| NACT |  |  |  | X | X |
| EDRESPON |  |  |  |  | X |
| OCLEVRES |  |  |  |  |  |

The OPTIONS card provides for the inclusion of missing variable values in the correlation calculations. A one-tailed test of statistical significance is made since the default of option 3 is in force. A matrix of correlation coefficients is not punched since the default of option 4 is in force, but it could have been punched because the matrix form of the variable list was used on the NONPAR CORR card.

```
RUN SPEARMAN CORRELATIONS WITH SYSTEM FILE INPUT                          07/25/69      PAGE   2

FILE    ORGSTUDY (CREATION DATE = 07/25/69)    STUDY OF ORGANIZATIONAL MEMBERSHIP AND ACTIVITY
SUBFILE   NWJERSEY   PENNSYLV

- - - - - - - - - - - - - - S P E A R M A N   C O R R E L A T I O N   C O E F F I C I E N T S - - - - - - - - - - - - -

VARIABLE        VARIABLE        VARIABLE        VARIABLE        VARIABLE        VARIABLE
PAIR            PAIR            PAIR            PAIR            PAIR            PAIR
--------        --------        --------        --------        --------        --------

RESDYTH 0.0936  RESDYTH 0.0202  RESDYTH 0.2022  RESDYTH 0.0119  INCOME  0.1807  INCOME  0.4311
WITH    N( 250) WITH    N( 250) WITH    N( 250) WITH    N( 250) WITH    N( 250) WITH    N( 250)
INCOME  SIG .070 NACT   SIG .375 EDRESPON SIG .001 OCLEVRES SIG .426 NACT  SIG .002 EDRESPON SIG .001

INCOME  0.2647  NACT    0.2126  NACT    0.1100  EDRESPON 0.2455
WITH    N( 250) WITH    N( 250) WITH    N( 250) WITH    N( 250)
OCLEVRES SIG .001 EDRESPON SIG .001 OCLEVRES SIG .041 OCLEVRES SIG .001
```

**FIG. 13.6**  Output from subprogram NONPAR CORR.

The output from this run is reproduced in Fig. 13.6. For each variable pair, the correlation coefficient, number of cases used to calculate the correlation, and significance level of the correlation coefficient are listed.

[1] For a discussion of the parameter SPACE, see Appendix F.2. The default value of SPACE is 80,000.

# 14
# PARTIAL CORRELATION: SUBPROGRAM PARTIAL CORR

Subprogram PARTIAL CORR provides the user with the capability of computing large numbers of partial-correlation coefficients of any order or combination of orders. The program has been designed so that the user may conveniently define multiple levels of control variables and multiple lists of independent and dependent variables on a single PARTIAL CORR procedure card. Up to 25 distinct sets of partials may be specified and each set may itself specify a large number of coefficients.

Input to the program may be either raw data (from a BCD or an SPSS system file) or one or more matrices of simple correlations. These correlation matrices may be ones which have been generated by the user's own programs or by one of the SPSS subprograms. (See Sec. 16.3 for procedures required for matrix input into this program.) Output from subprogram PARTIAL CORR consists of the desired partial-correlation coefficients, the degrees of freedom, and a one- or two-tailed test of statistical significance. All simple correlations (zero-order partials) used in computing the partials may be printed if the user desires. The means and standard deviations of all variables entered onto the PARTIAL CORR procedure card may also be requested by means of the STATISTICS card. Punched matrices of simple correlation coefficients may also be output on a medium of the user's choice for future access.

Missing data may be excluded from the computation of the coefficients in either a pairwise or listwise fashion. As usual, pairwise deletion causes a case to be excluded from the computation of a given simple correlation (all partials are based on the simple correlations) if either of the two variables involved in the computation of that coefficient has a value that has been defined as missing. Listwise deletion causes a case to be deleted if any variable in the entire partial list has a value which has been tagged as missing. Alternatively, missing data may, of course, be included in the computation of the partials, or the user may estimate missing data by recoding missing values to means, medians, etc.

As usual, all of the data-modification and data-selection procedures of SPSS may be employed while using subprogram **PARTIAL CORR**. This is not true, however, when the user is inputting matrices rather than raw data. Section 14.3 describes all the special conventions for matrix input.

Before proceeding to the detailed description of this program and the control cards required to use it, a brief introduction to partial correlation will be presented for users wishing to review partial correlation. Others may wish to proceed directly to Sec. 14.2.

## 14.1   INTRODUCTION TO PARTIAL-CORRELATION ANALYSIS

Partial correlation provides the researcher with a single measure of association describing the relationship between two variables while adjusting for the effects of one or more additional variables. Conceptually then, at least, partial correlation is analogous to crosstabulation with control variables. In crosstabulation the control is accomplished by examining the joint frequency distribution of two variables among two or more categories of one or more control variables (e.g., education's relationship to income, controlling for the effects of age). With crosstabulation the control is literal; i.e., one simultaneously locates each observation according to the values it takes on three or more variables. This is indeed one of the major problems with crosstabulation analysis, for each additional category of each variable in the relationship exerts a tremendous drain on the average cell frequencies. It takes a very large sample to execute even relatively simple controls.

In partial correlation, on the other hand, the control is statistical rather than literal and is based on the simplifying assumptions of linear relationships among the variables. In essence, partial correlation enables the researcher to remove the effect of the control variable from the relationship between the independent and dependent variables without physically manipulating the raw data. In partial correlation the effect of the control variable(s) is assumed to be linear throughout the range of the control variable, and it is this linear assumption that makes partial correlation possible.

Once one knows the linear relationship among the independent, dependent, and control variables, the partial correlation coefficient can be calculated by constructing (statistically, that is) new independent and dependent variables with the effect of the control variable(s) removed. This is done by making a prediction (based on the simple correlation coefficients) of both the independent and dependent variables from the knowledge of the effect that the control variable has on them. The new or adjusted independent variable is constructed by taking the difference between the actual value of the original independent variable (for each observation) and its value as predicted by the control variable. This new variable is, by definition, uncorrelated with each and/or all control variables which have been entered. The same procedure is then repeated for the dependent variable.

The linear effect of the control variable(s) has now been removed from both the independent and dependent variables, and the simple correlation between these adjusted variables is the partial correlation. However, since correlation coefficients are a complete description of the bivariate linear relationships among all the variables involved, this procedure can be statistically achieved from the correlation matrix alone, without reference to the individual observations. Therefore, when one computes the partial-correlation coefficient from the correlation matrix, the result is the same as if one had calculated the residuals for each observation [based on the effects of the control variables(s)] and had then computed a new simple correlation between the two sets of residuals. That is what we mean by adjusting the value based on the prediction from the simple correlation.

PARTIAL CORRELATION: SUBPROGRAM PARTIAL CORR

The basic formula for the computation of partial-correlation coefficients is

$$r_{ij.k} = \frac{r_{ij} - (r_{ik})(r_{jk})}{\sqrt{1 - r_{ik}^2}\ \sqrt{1 - r_{jk}^2}}$$

where k is the control variable, and i and j are the independent and dependent variables (the order is immaterial, since the correlation of i on j is the same as that of j on i). The extension of this formula to more than one control variable (that is, n + 1) is made by replacing the simple correlation coefficients (or zero-order partials) on the right-hand side of the equation with the nth-order partial coefficients. In this way the above formula can be used to recursively define and compute each higher-order partial from the previous one. It can be shown mathematically that the order in which one adds control variables has no effect on the ultimate partial. This is a result of the fact that the above formula is simply a computational shortcut of the residual-prediction procedure where the order in which the control variables are entered is clearly immaterial.

Partial correlation can be used in a wide variety of ways to aid the researcher in understanding and clarifying relationships between three or more variables. When properly employed, partial correlation becomes an excellent technique for uncovering spurious relationships, locating intervening variables, and can even be used to help the researcher make certain types of causal inferences.[1] In this brief introduction to partial correlation, we will attempt only to illustrate a few of the many types of conceptual problems for which partial-correlation analysis can be used. We will not, however, attempt to go beyond the simple statistical discussion presented above, and we strongly urge the user to consult one of the many available detailed statistical discussions of partial correlation.[2]

Partial correlation can be a very helpful tool for enabling the researcher to locate spurious relationships. A *spurious correlation* is defined as a relationship between two variables (A and B for example) in which A's correlation with B is solely the result of the fact that A varies along with some other variable (C for example) which is indeed the true predictor of B. In this case, when the effects of C are controlled, held constant, etc., B no longer varies with A. As an illustration, let us take a hypothetical study of the determinants of crime rates in a sample of American communities. Let us further assume that the initial investigation has revealed a moderately strong positive correlation between the racial makeup of communities (measured as the proportion of nonwhites living there) and a composite crime-rate index. The researcher suspects, however, that the relationship is spurious and due solely to the fact that two other variables, (1) poverty (measured as the proportion of families with incomes less than $3,000) and (2) size of community, covary strongly with both racial makeup and crime rates, and therefore the relationship between racial composition and crime rates is purely a function of the former's relationship to both poverty levels and community size. The question is then, does racial composition have any effect on crime rates when the effects of poverty and community size are removed? Let us examine some hypothetical data in order to indicate how partial correlation can address itself to this type of problem. Assume the following correlations existed between the four variables:

|  | Percent nonwhite | Percent below $3,000 | City size | Crime index |
|---|---|---|---|---|
| Percent nonwhite | 1.00 | .51 | .41 | .36 |
| Percent below $3,000 |  | 1.00 | .29 | .60 |
| City size |  |  | 1.00 | .49 |
| Crime index |  |  |  | 1.00 |

[1] Hubert M. Blalock, "Causal Inference in Non-experimental Research," The University of North Carolina Press, Chapel Hill, N.C., 1964, and Herbert A. Simon, "Models of Man," Wiley, New York, 1957.

[2] M. G. Kendall and A. Stuart, "The Advanced Theory of Statistics," vol. 2, chap. 27, Griffin, London, 1961.

First, it is clear from the simple correlations that the relationships between poverty and crime rate, and between city size and crime rate, are even stronger than that between racial composition and crime rate. Second, the correlations between racial makeup and the other two independent variables are quite strong. These are the researcher's first indications that the relationship between racial composition and crime rate may be a spurious one. The computation of three partial-correlation coefficients (two first-order partials and one second-order partial) will produce some relatively precise answers to these questions. If the correlation between racial composition and crime rate disappears (i.e., becomes zero) when we control for the effects of poverty and city size, we will have considerable evidence that the relationship is indeed a spurious one.

To begin, we will compute the first-order partial between racial composition and crime rate, controlling for the effects of poverty. This partial is .09 indicating that the initial correlation of .36 has been drastically reduced by simply controlling for the effects of poverty. Next we compute the second first-order partial, controlling for the effects of city size. This partial is .25. While the reduction is not as dramatic, it is still quite substantial. Finally we compute the second-order partial indicating the relationship between racial composition and crime rate while simultaneously controlling for the effects of poverty and city size; this partial is −.02 or essentially zero. These relationships have now been clarified considerably; the relationship between racial composition and crime rate is spurious; the effects of both poverty and city size are acting to create the spurious relationship; but poverty is the variable having the greatest contaminating effect and is the major cause of the spurious relationship. Restated, these finding suggest that when one controls for the effects of city size and particularly for levels of poverty, crime rates are similar irrespective of the racial composition of the city.

With a relatively small sample of cities, this type of multivariate analysis would have been extremely difficult, if possible at all, with crosstabulation. Partial correlation, on the other hand, provides a relatively easy and quite precise technique for this type of problem.

Another important feature of partial correlation lies in its ability to aid the researcher in a search for intervening linking variables. While there is no statistical difference between the computation of partials employed to locate spurious relationships and those used to determine intervening variables, the conceptual issues are different enough to merit separate treatment. The search for intervening variables is highly related to the issue of causality insofar as the researcher wishes to make statements of the sort: A leads to B which in turn leads to C. While partial correlation can be of great assistance in such problems, the researcher's theory (i.e., his ability to place a time-series ordering to his variables) becomes much more important in these types of situations.

Take, for example, a hypothetical study concerned with the transfer of wealth from parent to offspring. Given a strong correlation between parental wealth and that of their grown children, as well as high correlations between parental wealth and child's educational attainment and between offspring's educational attainment and his own wealth, an important issue might be the determination of the mechanisms which link parental wealth to that of their children. Given a matrix of correlations such as the following, one might hypothesize (A) that there is a direct transfer of wealth from parents to their offspring and that while the correlation of parents' wealth and child's education is supportive of this relationship, it is not critical; or (B) that the major proportion of the correlation between the wealth of parents and offspring is due to the impact that parents' wealth has on the educational attainment of their children which is in turn the major predictor of the wealth of offspring.

| | Parental wealth | Offspring's education | Offspring's wealth |
|---|---|---|---|
| Parental wealth | 1.00 | .52 | .45 |
| Offspring's education | | 1.00 | .65 |
| Offspring's wealth | | | 1.00 |

The simple correlations indicate that approximately 20 percent of the variance in the wealth of all offspring sampled was determined by the wealth of their parents. The degree to which this represents direct transfers of wealth as opposed to the indirect effects via parental wealth's impact on the educational attainment of their offspring can be determined by computing a partial correlation between parental wealth and that of their offspring. The size of that partial will indicate the proportion of the initial relationship which is due to direct transfers as opposed to educational attainment. This partial is .17, indicating that less than 3 percent out of the original 20 percent of the explained variance between wealth of parents and their children is due to direct transfers of wealth while the remaining 17 percent seems to be the result of the impact that parental wealth has on educational attainment.

The last example usage of partial correlation deals again with a slightly different problem: locating relationships where none appear to exist. Here too the statistical method is identical, but the conceptual issues are a bit different. One sometimes encounters situations where theory or intuitive judgment leads one to believe that there should be a relationship between two variables, but the data simply do not indicate any relationship. When this is the case, there is the possibility that some other variable or variables are acting to hide or suppress the relationship. These suppressor relationships often take the form of "A shows no relationship to B because A is negatively related to C which in turn is positively related to B." Hence A is positively related to B when one controls for the effects of C.

Take the following hypothetical example of a marketing study attempting to determine what types of families purchase second automobiles. The initial investigation of the data surprisingly found that there was almost no correlation ($r = .081$) between a measure of family need for a second car and whether or not a family owned a second automobile. However upon closer scrutiny, the researchers became suspicious of the possibility of a confounding or masking variable. They noticed that family income was strongly related to the purchase of a second car ($r = .55$) and that family income was, on the other hand, somewhat negatively related to need for a second automobile ($r = -.32$). A partial coefficient was then computed between need and purchase, removing the effects of family income from both of these variables in order to determine if income had acted to hide a potentially important relationship.

When this partial was computed, it became clear that family income was indeed masking a rather strong relationship ($r_{12.3} = .33$) between need and purchase. From this partial the researchers were able to state that at any given level of family income, need for a second automobile explained about 11 percent of the variance in the purchases.

This introduction to partial correlation hopefully indicates how versatile and useful a research tool partial correlation can be. In the first instance it served to help locate a spurious correlation, in the second it enabled us to determine the importance of a particular intervening variable, and in the third its ability to help uncover a relationship where none appeared to exist was demonstrated. The types of analyses which can be accomplished with partial correlation are numerous, and this very brief introduction is not meant to be in any way a substitute for the excellent literature which exists on the subject.

## 14.2    THE PARTIAL CORR PROCEDURE CARD

Subprogram PARTIAL CORR is called and activated by a procedure card with the control words PARTIAL CORR followed by a specification field (beginning in or after column 16) containing three types of information which must be entered in order to specify the desired partial correlations. First, one or more pairs of independent and dependent variables for which one or more partials are desired must be entered (these *do not* include the control variables) and they are referred to as the *correlation list*. Second, one or more control variables which are to be used as controls for the variables in the correlation list must be entered, and this portion of the specification field is referred to as the *control list*. Third and finally, the user must enter the *order values* indicating the order of partials desired from the correlation and control lists. The general format of the PARTIAL CORR card is then as follows:

```
1               16
PARTIAL CORR    correlation list BY control list (order values) / correlation
                list BY control list (order values) / . . .
```

Because of the complexity of this card, we will break its explanation down into the individual portions of the card.

### 14.2.1     THE CORRELATION LIST

The *correlation list* specifies pairs of variables to be correlated while partialling or controlling for the variable(s) which appear in the control list. It is termed correlation list because the first task in computing partials is to compute zero-order or simple correlations. Relationships are specified and variables entered onto the correlation list in a manner identical to that used in specifying the simple correlations in the PEARSON CORR and NONPAR CORR subprograms. In fact, the function of the correlation list on the PARTIAL CORR card is identical to that of the entire specification field on the PEARSON CORR and NONPAR CORR cards (i.e., specifying the pairs of correlation coefficients desired). In this instance, however, it is just the beginning, for the control variables must also be specified (as must the instructions for their specific application).

Variables are entered onto the correlation list in one of two manners depending upon whether the user desires partials to be computed for all possible combinations of the variables entered or for only specified combinations of these variables. As in PEARSON CORR specific combinations of variables are specified by the use of the keyword WITH. This keyword causes at least one partial (depending, of course, on the control list and the order values) to be computed for each variable appearing to the left of the keyword WITH paired with each variable entered to the right of the WITH. The following correlation list would cause one partial to be produced for each control variable and/or combinations of control variables (specified on the control list and order values) for INCOME with EDUCATN, INCOME with RACE, OCCU-PATN with EDUCATN, OCCUPATN with RACE.

INCOME, OCCUPTN WITH EDUCATN, RACE

In all instances the leftmost variable on the left side of the WITH is paired *first* with the leftmost variable to the right of the WITH. Then the former is paired with each successive variable to the right of the WITH moving from left to right. When all the variables to the right of the keyword have been paired against the leftmost variable to the left of the WITH, the procedure is repeated for the next variable, again moving from left to right. In short, the variables to the right of the WITH rotate before those to its left. This procedure is repeated until all the specified variables have been paired. If a variable appears on both sides of the WITH, the redundant coefficient *will be* computed.

If the user desires one or more partials for all possible combinations (of nonredundant) variables entered onto the correlation list, he enters the variables without the keyword WITH. The deletion of the keyword WITH from the correlation list causes the leftmost variable on the list to be paired with each variable to its right. Then the same procedure is repeated for the variable immediately to its left, and the process is repeated until all nonredundant pairs of correlations have been specified.

As usual the correlation list may reference any variable which has been previously defined, including any defined by temporary or permanent variable transformations. Nonadjacent variables must be separated from each other by one or more common delimiters. Three or more *adjacent* variables may be entered with the usual TO convention (such as VARX TO VARZ) where VARX precedes VARZ on the cases in the file. This will cause all variables between VARX and VARZ to be entered into the correlation list.

Examples of the alternative forms of the correlation list for the PARTIAL CORR card are

VARA,VARC TO VARM WITH VARQ, VARR, VARX TO VARZ
VARA,VARC TO VARM,VARQ,VARR,VARX TO VARZ

### 14.2.2     THE CONTROL LIST

The last variable in the correlation list is followed by the keyword BY, and the list of control variables follows this keyword. The *control list* is simply the list of variables to be used as controls for each pair of variables specified by the correlation list. However, the control list itself does not carry the information on how these control variables will be applied to the variable pairs for this is done by the order values. Variables are entered into the control list in the normal list fashion. Any variable which has been previously defined may be entered, and three or more adjacent variables may be simultaneously entered by means of the TO convention. The detailed format of the PARTIAL CORR card is then

```
1                 16
PARTIAL CORR  ⎰ variable list WITH variable list ⎱  BY variable list (order values)
              ⎨             or                    ⎬
              ⎩ matrix type variable list         ⎭
```

### 14.2.3   THE ORDER VALUE(S)

The last variable in the control list is followed by a set of from one to five separate values enclosed in parentheses. These values, termed the *order values*, specify the exact partials which are to be computed from the correlation and control lists. Each of the individual numbers in this set of parentheses indicates a desired order of partials. This means that one partial will be produced for every unique combination of control variables (which add to that number) for each pair of correlations specified on the correlation list. This is perhaps most clearly explained by a series of examples. The following PARTIAL CORR card would cause two first-order partials to be computed: EDUCATN with INCOME, controlling first for FATHRED and then for FATHRINC.

```
1          16
PARTIAL CORR    EDUCATN WITH INCOME BY FATHRED,FATHERINC(1)
```

With one slight modification this same card would cause one second-order partial to be computed rather than two first-order partials (e.g., EDUCATN with INCOME, controlling simultaneously for FATHRED and FATHERIN).

```
1          16
PARTIAL CORR    EDUCATN WITH INCOME BY FATHRED,FATHERIN (2)
```

One list could have been used to specify both sets of partials by simply placing both a 1 and a 2 in the parentheses containing the order values:

```
1          16
PARTIAL CORR    EDUCATN WITH INCOME BY FATHRED,FATHERIN (1,2)
```

There is a maximum of *five* order values which may appear at the end of any control list. Each of these values must also be separated from each other by one or more common delimiters. The interaction between the order values and the control list may be further clarified by the following. First, any order value may be specified from 1 to the number of variables on the control list. One complete set of partials will be produced by each order value inserted. When the value 1 is specified, a single first-order partial will be produced for each control variable with each pair of variables specified by the correlation list. When a value equal to the number of control values is specified, a single partial (of Nth order where N is the number of control variables) will be produced for each pair of variables specified by the correlation list using *all* the control variables simultaneously as the control. When a value somewhere between 1 and the number of variables on the control list is inserted, a partial will be computed for every possible unique combination of control variables for each pair of variables in the correlation list. The following PARTIAL CORR card would, for example, produce a total of 25 partial coefficients for the single variable INCOME with EDUCATN. These 25 coefficients would be from three complete sets (5 first-order partials, 10 second-order partials, and 10 third-order partials). The table below the card indicates the exact partials that would be produced by the following card. This table contains every possible unique combination of first-, second-, and third-order partials which can be obtained from the control list containing five control variables.

<sup>1</sup>
**PARTIAL CORR** <sup>16</sup> INCOME WITH EDUCATN BY VAR001 TO VAR005 (1,2,3)

| First-order partials | Second-order partials | Third-order partials |
|---|---|---|
| INCOME WITH EDUCATN | INCOME WITH EDUCATN | INCOME WITH EDUCATN |
| BY | BY | BY |
| VAR001 | VAR001 and VAR002 | VAR001, VAR002 and VAR003 |
| VAR002 | VAR001 and VAR003 | VAR001, VAR002 and VAR004 |
| VAR003 | VAR001 and VAR004 | VAR001, VAR002 and VAR005 |
| VAR004 | VAR001 and VAR005 | VAR001, VAR003 and VAR004 |
| VAR005 | VAR002 and VAR003 | VAR001, VAR003 and VAR005 |
| | VAR002 and VAR004 | VAR001, VAR004 and VAR005 |
| | VAR002 and VAR005 | VAR002, VAR003 and VAR004 |
| | VAR003 and VAR004 | VAR002, VAR003 and VAR005 |
| | VAR003 and VAR005 | VAR002, VAR004 and VAR005 |
| | VAR004 and VAR005 | VAR003, VAR004 and VAR005 |

The order values are followed by a slash [/], and a second complete partial list may then be entered. A maximum of 25 such lists may appear on any given PARTIAL CORR card and its continuations. (The user should, however, consult the program limitations in Sec. 16.4 before constructing his run, for there are a number of other program limitations which can be exceeded even though the above limitation is not.)

## 14.3 SPECIAL CONVENTIONS FOR MATRIX INPUT FOR SUBPROGRAM PARTIAL CORR

Subprogram PARTIAL CORR, like the subprogram REGRESSION and FACTOR, permits the user to enter his data in the usual form as cases or observations (which may be in BCD form or reside in an SPSS system file) or, alternatively, to input data in the form of a matrix of simple correlation coefficients. This feature enables the user to skip the first and most costly step in generating partials, the computation of the matrix of simple correlations. Once the simple correlations have been computed, the user may make any number of runs computing various partials for a small fraction of the cost which would have been involved in computing them from a large file of raw observations.

However, the concept of entering a matrix of coefficients is quite different from that of entering a file of cases, and for this reason there are a number of special conventions which must be followed when the matrix input feature is utilized. Some of these conventions deal with the format of the correlation matrices themselves, and others deal with the control cards and procedures required to enter them.

### 14.3.1 REQUIREMENTS ON THE FORM AND FORMAT FOR CORRELATION MATRICES

All correlations entered must be in the form of a standard SPSS matrix of 8F10.7. They must be BCD card-image records, but they may physically reside on any medium—card, tape, disk, etc. Each new row of the matrix must begin on a new physical record. The format of 8F10.7 also means that the last significant digit of the coefficient will be in columns which are even multiples of 10 (that is, columns 10, 20, 30, 40, . . . 80). The maximum precision which may be entered is seven digits to the right of the decimal point. However, the user is not required to enter his coefficients with this much accuracy, because the decimal point appearing in the field will override the .7 specification of the format list as long as the coefficients are right justified to the columns which are an even multiple of 10. Coefficients taking a positive value need not be preceded by a sign, but all negative coefficients must be directly preceded by a minus sign [−]. A complete square matrix must always be entered.

### 14.3.2 CONVENTIONS AND CONTROL CARDS REQUIRED TO ENTER MATRICES

Each complete partial-correlation list requires its own matrix of simple coefficients between *all* variables named in both the correlation and control lists. This matrix may contain coefficients which are not actually required given the specific partials requested, but a complete matrix must nevertheless be entered. The order of the variables in each matrix is determined complete-ly by the order in which the variables have been entered onto the correlation and control lists. The matrix must be set up so that the first variable entered into the correlation list is paired with each other variable in the correlation list (including the correlation with itself) moving from left to right and then with each variable in the control list again in left-to-right order. This then constitutes the first row of the matrix. The second row is formed by obtaining a complete set of correlations for the variable found immediately to the right of the first variable. This variable is paired with the first variable, then with itself, and then with each other variable named on the correlation list and control list moving from left to right. In other words, each variable named will produce an entire row of coefficients in the matrix. Half of these coeffi-cients will be redundant in that the matrix will contain the correlation of B with A as well as A with B. The matrix must also contain a complete set of diagonals even though these will always be unity, that is, A with A, B with B, etc. Matrices produced by all SPSS subprograms are always written or punched in this form; however, the user still must be sure that the correlation matrix has been generated with the variables in the right order.

The following illustrates the matrix required by a sample PARTIAL CORR card:

```
1               16
PARTIAL CORR    A,B,C WITH D,E BY X,Y,Z(1,2)
```

**Example matrix required by above partial list**

```
AA   AB   AC   AD   AE   AX   AY   AZ
BA   BB   BC   BD   BE   BX   BY   BZ
CA   CB   CC   CD   CE   CX   CY   CZ
DA   DB   DC   DD   DE   DX   DY   DZ
EA   EB   EC   ED   EE   EX   EY   EZ
XA   XB   XC   XD   XE   XX   XY   XZ
YA   YB   YC   YD   YE   YX   YY   YZ
ZA   ZB   ZC   ZD   ZE   ZX   ZY   ZZ
```

The following PEARSON CORR card would be used to generate the above matrix on a medium specified by the user:

```
1               16
PEARSON CORR    A,B,C,D,E,X,Y,Z
```

One matrix is required for each complete partials list. Because there is a maximum of 25 lists, there is also a maximum of 25 matrices which may be entered for any single task.

In addition, the following cards are required when entering a matrix or series of matrices:

1. A VARIABLE LIST card constructed in the usual manner (see Sec. 4.2) containing the name of each variable which is to appear on *any* of the lists on the PARTIAL CORR card. Variables are defined only once and even though a variable may appear on more than one correlation or control list, it is defined only a single time on the VARIABLE LIST. The order in which the variables are named on the VARIABLE LIST is unimportant *unless* the user wishes to employ the TO convention to enter adjacent variables onto correlation or control lists. When the TO convention is used, the order of the variables in the matrix is assumed to be the same as the order in which they appear on the VARIABLE LIST.

2. An INPUT MEDIUM card containing one of the following keywords—CARD, TAPE, DISK, OTHER—specifying the location of the matrix must also be prepared. When matri-ces are located on a medium other than CARD, the JCL cards for a BCD input file (FT08) must also be completed (see Appendix F).

3. A # OF CASES card must also be prepared containing the user's best estimate of the number of cases upon which the correlations in the matrix or matrices are based. This card is used only for purposes of computing the tests of significance and *should not* be con-fused with specifying the number of rows in the matrix. The program automatically computes the number of rows on the matrix from knowledge of the number of variables in the correlation and control lists. If the user is entering more than one matrix, and the matrices were computed on a different number of cases, he must either ignore the tests of

significance on partials computed from some of the matrices or enter them on separate runs. The one exception to this is computing partials on identical matrices produced from subfiles (see 6 below).

4.  An OPTIONS card must follow the PARTIAL CORR card and its continuations. This card must contain option 4 which informs the system that a matrix rather than raw data is to be read. The only other option which may be used when matrices rather than raw data are being input is option 3 which causes a two- rather than a one-tailed test of significance to be applied to the partials.

5.  A READ MATRIX card follows the OPTIONS card, or the STATISTICS card if it is used, and informs the system that one or more matrices of coefficients will follow. The READ MATRIX card has the same location and serves the same function as the READ INPUT DATA card. The matrix or matrices directly follow this card if they are on cards. When there is more than one matrix, the matrices are placed one behind each other in the order in which the PARTIAL CORR card requests them. (This is true no matter where the matrices physically reside.) There must be nothing separating the matrices.

6.  If the user has produced a set of identical matrices from a file with a subfile structure, he may use the subfile-processing features to obtain identical sets of partial correlations from his matrices. This requires that he insert a SUBFILE LIST which is prepared in the usual manner (see Sec. 4.3). It also requires that he supply a number of cases for each subfile on the # OF CASES card. And a PROCESS SBFILES card must be placed directly before the PARTIAL CORR card.

Other data-definition cards (e.g., labels and formats) are not applicable to matrices and may not therefore be entered. The same is true for all of the data-modification and data-selection control cards which clearly have no meaning when matrices are being input. For similar reasons correlation matrices may not be retained as SPSS system files. A RUN NAME card may be optionally used, and as usual, a FINISH card is required. An example deck setup for computing partial correlations from matrix input appears in Sec. 16.7.

## 14.4   OPTIONS AVAILABLE FOR SUBPROGRAM PARTIAL CORR

The PARTIAL CORR procedure card is followed by an OPTIONS card which instructs the PARTIAL CORR subprogram as to the processing options desired by the user (see Sec. 5.2). The OPTIONS card contains the control word OPTIONS followed by a number list indicating the options desired. The format of the OPTIONS card is then

```
1                16
OPTIONS          number list
```

The first three options determine how missing data will be processed.[1] All these options refer to the manner in which the matrix of simple correlations will be computed, since all partial coefficients are computed from the initial matrix of simple correlations.

*The default missing-data option—listwise deletion.*    The default or normal means of handling missing data with subprogram PARTIAL CORR is listwise deletion. Listwise deletion causes a case to be omitted from the calculation of *all* coefficients specified in a partial list when that case contains a missing value on any variable entered onto either the correlation or control list. In general, listwise deletion has the effect of reducing the number of cases upon which the coefficients are computed. How large this reduction will be depends, of course, upon the overall amount of missing data, the number of variables in the list, and the distribution of the missing data among the cases and the variables. If the missing data is highly concentrated by case, the

---

[1]The missing-data options are, of course, irrelevant when the input is a correlation matrix. However, the discussions of the effects that these different procedures have on the interpretation of partial coefficients should be carefully considered before the user prepares his matrix of correlations for input into subprogram PARTIAL CORR.

net effect will not be great. If, on the other hand, missing data is evenly spread among a large proportion of the cases, a major reduction in the workable N will result when this option is selected. The workable N is further affected by the distribution of missing values among the variables; the variable with the largest amount of missing data will establish the maximum possible number of cases on which all coefficients in a given list will be computed. Further, the greater the number of variables involved in a list the smaller will tend to be the effective N, unless, of course, the missing data is highly concentrated in only a few variables. On the other hand, listwise deletion is the only way to ensure that the partial correlations are computed from the same population. Since the missing-data option affects the computation of the pairs of simple correlations on which all partials are then based, it is possible to compute partials which are based on correlations which were computed for very different segments of the population if the pairwise-deletion method is used rather than the listwise procedure. The user, however, must make his own decision based on his methodological assumptions and knowledge of his own data. *This default option is in force unless the user selects option 1 or 2.*

*Option 1.*   *Inclusion of missing data.*    Selection of this option causes missing-value indicators to be totally ignored and enters all data into the computation of the simple correlations upon which the partials will be based. This option is equivalent to deleting all references to missing values for the variables being entered.

*Option 2.*   *Pairwise deletion of missing data.*    Under pairwise deletion, a case is omitted from the computation of a given simple coefficient if the value of either of the two variables being considered is missing. A case is therefore included in the computation of all simple coefficients for which it has complete data. Pairwise deletion has the advantage of utilizing as much of the data as possible in the computation of each of the simple coefficients for which partials are to be calculated. It has the distinct disadvantage, however, of (under some circumstances) producing partial coefficients from simple correlations which are themselves based on a very different number of cases and perhaps even on quite different subpopulations. Here again only the researcher with knowledge of *his* goals, *his* assumptions, and *his* data can make the decision of whether to use pairwise deletion or listwise deletion of missing data.

*Option 3.*   *One- and two-tailed tests of statistical significance.*    Each partial-correlation coefficient computed is accompanied by a test of its statistical significance. The test of significance used is the quantity

$$t = r \left( \frac{df}{1 - r^2} \right)^{\frac{1}{2}}$$

This quantity is then compared with Student's t. The resulting level of statistical significance will be one of two values depending upon whether a one- or two-tailed test is being applied. *The selection of option 3 causes a two-tailed test* to be applied to each partial coefficient requested rather than the normal (or default) one-tailed test. A two-tailed test is normally used only when the researcher does *not* have an explicit hypothesis concerning the expected direction of the coefficient (i.e., whether it will be positive or negative). DF, the degrees of freedom for a coefficient calculated under pairwise deletion of missing observations, are derived from the minimum number of cases used in the calculation of any simple correlation coefficient in the list. Under listwise deletion all correlation coefficients will have been computed on the same number of cases, determined, of course, by the relationship with the largest amount of missing data. In both instances the number of variables involved in any partial coefficient is subtracted from the number of nonmissing cases to give the degrees of freedom. *Note that the one-tailed test is the default option and is always applied unless option 3 is selected.*

*Option* 4.  *Matrix input.*   Informs subprogram PARTIAL CORR that a correlation matrix rather than raw data is to be read. This option must always be used when a matrix is to be read and, of course, may never be used when processing from raw data. All the other conventions for matrix input discussed in Sec. 16.4 must also be followed.

*Option* 5.  *Punching or writing matrices for future access.*   This option causes a complete matrix of simple coefficients among all variables in a given partials list (including both correlation and control lists) to be written or punched on a medium of the user's choice. We should stress that unlike matrices produced from PEARSON CORR, these matrices contain all combinations of variables before and after the keyword WITH, if used, and the variables after the keyword BY. In all other respects, these matrices are in the standard SPSS form: their format is 8F10.7, and each new row begins on a new card-image record. A set of JCL cards for the BCD output file (FT09) must be filled out when matrices are to be output (see JCL, Appexdix F). More complete descriptions of the form and format of SPSS matrices may be found in Sec. 13.1.2. When this option is selected and more than one partial list is specified, one matrix will be output for each partial list appearing on the PARTIAL CORR card.

As usual, the OPTIONS card may be deleted if all the default options are selected. When this is done, the following options will be executed on the data:

*Option a.*   Missing data will be excluded from the computations listwise (see definition above).

*Option b.*   A one-tailed test of statistical significance will be computed for all partials requested.

*Option c.*   Raw data (from either BCD or SPSS system file) must be input. Input of correlation coefficients must be specified under option 4.

*Option d.*   Output correlation matrices will *not* be written or punched.

## 14.5   STATISTICS AVAILABLE FOR SUBPROGRAM PARTIAL CORR

The partial-correlation coefficients, their degrees of freedom, and their level of statistical significance are always reported. The means and standard deviations of the variables, as well as all of the zero-order or simple correlations used in computing the partials, may be optionally requested in the usual manner via the STATISTICS card. As usual, the STATISTICS card directly follows the OPTIONS card. If all the default options are selected and the OPTIONS card is therefore not entered, the STATISTICS card directly follows the PARTIAL CORR procedure card. The STATISTICS card may, of course, also be deleted, in which case only the coefficients, the degrees of freedom, and levels of statistical significance will be reported.

The STATISTICS card has its usual format of the control word STATISTICS followed by a number list or the keyword ALL. In this case, however, there are only two statistics available.

*Statistic* 1.   Instructs the system to print out the simple or zero-order correlations used in computing the partial correlations. Each is printed with the degrees of freedom and significance. In the case of pairwise deletion, the number of degrees of freedom is based on the number of cases used to calculate the specific correlation coefficient. In listwise deletion, the degrees of freedom will be the same for all correlations computed from a given list. The correlations printed include all possible combinations of variables appearing in the list on the PARTIAL CORR card.

*Statistic* 2.   Causes the means and standard deviations of the variables listed on the PARTIAL CORR card to be printed along with the number of valid cases observed for each of the variables. In the case of listwise deletion, the mean and standard deviation for a variable will be based on those cases in which none of the variables in the list has a missing value. In pairwise deletion these statistics are based on all nonmissing cases for each variable. These statistics are clearly not available when data is being entered in the form of correlation matrices.

## 14.6    PROGRAM LIMITATIONS FOR SUBPROGRAM PARTIAL CORR

*Limitation 1.*    No more than 25 complete lists may appear on the PARTIAL CORR card. A list consists of a correlation list, a control list, and the order values.

*Limitation 2.*    No more than 400 variables may be mentioned implicitly or explicitly on the card. Each occurrence of a variable counts once, so that a given variable which is used on a number of lists must be counted each time.

*Limitation 3.*    No more than five orders of partial correlations (excluding the zero-order correlations produced with statistic 2) may be requested of a single list. Partial coefficients of greater than the fifth order may be requested, but no more than five orders may be computed.

*Limitation 4.*    The core storage available is (SPACE/8) units.[1] Using listwise or no missing cases, each variable requires three units, and each N X N matrix (where N is the number of variables mentioned in a list) requires N X N units. Using pairwise missing cases, the following quantities are required:
  (a)    If the mean and standard deviation are requested (statistic 1), three units for each variable mentioned.
  (b)    Three times N X N for each N X N matrix.

Briefly, the core storage limitation means that the maximum number of variables in a single list (when there is only one list on the PARTIAL CORR card) is 98 if missing cases are not excluded at all or are excluded listwise and is 57 if missing cases are excluded pairwise.

## 14.7    EXAMPLE DECK SETUPS FOR SUBPROGRAM PARTIAL CORR

Example 14.1 illustrates the use of subprogram PARTIAL CORR in a run using an SPSS system file. The system file used is named COMSTUDY; file-defining control cards and cases for this file are listed in Appendix I. The partial correlation between a single pair of variables, MEDFINC and SPISOL, is calculated. The partial correlation will be calculated with the effect of variable MEDSCH removed, with the effect of variable PTTERTRY removed, and with the effects of MEDSCH and PTTERTRY both removed. The OPTIONS card specifies pairwise deletion of missing data, and a two-tailed test of significance is to be applied. The STATISTICS card causes the means and standard deviations and number of valid cases for each variable to be printed. The output from this run is listed in Fig. 14.1.

**EXAMPLE 14.1**

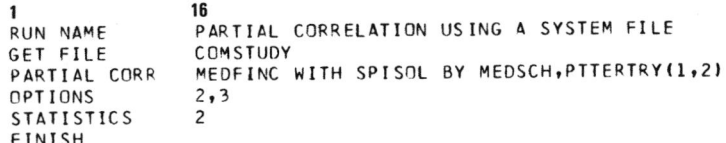

```
1               16
RUN NAME        PARTIAL CORRELATION USING A SYSTEM FILE
GET FILE        COMSTUDY
PARTIAL CORR    MEDFINC WITH SPISOL BY MEDSCH,PTTERTRY(1,2)
OPTIONS         2,3
STATISTICS      2
FINISH
```

[1] For a discussion of the parameter SPACE, see Appendix F.2. The default value of SPACE is 80,000.

```
PARTIAL CORRELATION USING A SYSTEM FILE                              07/25/69        PAGE   2

FILE   COMSTUDY (CREATION DATE = 07/25/69)    STUDY OF AMERICAN SMALL COMMUNITIES


VARIABLE          MEAN        STANDARD DEV    CASES

MEDFINC       5355.3125       1685.3795        64
SPISOL           6.8125          3.1667        64
MEDSCH          10.2344          2.0992        64
PTTERTRY        41.3187         12.4078        64



PARTIAL CORRELATION USING A SYSTEM FILE                              07/25/69        PAGE   3

FILE   COMSTUDY (CREATION DATE = 07/25/69)    STUDY OF AMERICAN SMALL COMMUNITIES
- - - - - - - - - - - - P A R T I A L   C O R R E L A T I O N   C O E F F I C I E N T S - - - - - - - - - - - - - - -

CONTROLLING FOR..   MEDSCH


VARIABLE          VARIABLE        VARIABLE        VARIABLE        VARIABLE        VARIABLE
PAIR              PAIR            PAIR            PAIR            PAIR            PAIR
--------          --------        --------        --------        --------        --------


MEDFINC   -0.6730
WITH   DF =   61
SPISOL    SIG .001



PARTIAL CORRELATION USING A SYSTEM FILE                              07/25/69        PAGE   4

FILE   COMSTUDY (CREATION DATE = 07/25/69)    STUDY OF AMERICAN SMALL COMMUNITIES
- - - - - - - - - - - - P A R T I A L   C O R R E L A T I O N   C O E F F I C I E N T S - - - - - - - - - - - - - -

CONTROLLING FOR..   PTTERTRY


VARIABLE          VARIABLE        VARIABLE        VARIABLE        VARIABLE        VARIABLE
PAIR              PAIR            PAIR            PAIR            PAIR            PAIR
--------          --------        --------        --------        --------        --------


MEDFINC   -0.6216
WITH   DF =   61
SPISOL    SIG .001



PARTIAL CORRELATION USING A SYSTEM FILE                              07/25/69        PAGE   5

FILE   COMSTUDY (CREATION DATE = 07/25/69)    STUDY OF AMERICAN SMALL COMMUNITIES
- - - - - - - - - - - - P A R T I A L   C O R R E L A T I O N   C O E F F I C I E N T S - - - - - - - - - - - - - -

CONTROLLING FOR..   MEDSCH    PTTERTRY


VARIABLE          VARIABLE        VARIABLE        VARIABLE        VARIABLE        VARIABLE
PAIR              PAIR            PAIR            PAIR            PAIR            PAIR
--------          --------        --------        --------        --------        --------


MEDFINC   -0.6680
WITH   DF =   60
SPISOL    SIG .001
```

**FIG. 14.1**   Output from subprogram PARTIAL CORR.

Example 14.2 illustrates the use of subprogram PARTIAL CORR when using matrices of correlation coefficients as inputs. It also illustrates the ability of SPSS to execute more than one task in a single run. In this case subprogram PARTIAL CORR is used twice. The first use causes a number of partial conditions to be calculated using a 5 x 5 matrix supplied by the user in the run deck immediately following the first READ MATRIX card. The partial correlations are all between variable BA and variable PSGPA with the effect of the following sets of variables removed:

SEX
GREV
GREQ
SEX and GREV
SEX and GREQ
GREV and GREQ
SEX and GREV and GREQ.

**EXAMPLE 14.2**

```
1                    16
RUN NAME             PARTIAL CORRELATIONS USING MATRIX INPUT
VARIABLE LIST        BA,PSGPA,SEX,GREV,GREQ,MARITAL,AGE
INPUT MEDIUM         CARD
# OF CASES           300
PARTIAL CORR         BA WITH PSGPA BY SEX,GREV,GREQ (1,2,3)
OPTIONS              3,4
READ MATRIX
        1.000        .120        .053        .072        .015
         .120       1.000       -.058        .281        .175
         .063       -.058       1.000       -.053       -.035
         .072        .281       -.053       1.000        .351
         .015        .172       -.356        .351       1.000
PARTIAL CORR         BA WITH PSGPA BY MARITAL,AGE (1,2)
OPTIONS              3,4
READ MATRIX
        1.000        .120       -.274       -.143
         .120       1.000        .101        .001
        -.274        .018       1.000        .511
        -.143        .001        .511       1.000
FINISH
```

The first OPTIONS card specifies a two-tailed test of significance and matrix input.

The second PARTIAL CORR card calls for partial correlations between variables BA and PSGPA to be calculated with the effect of the following sets of variables removed:

MARITAL
AGE
MARITAL and AGE

The output from this run is shown in Fig. 14.2.

```
PARTIAL CORRELATIONS USING MATRIX INPUT                           07/25/69        PAGE    2

FILE   NONAME   (CREATION DATE = 07/25/69)

- - - - - - - - - - - - P A R T I A L   C O R R E L A T I O N   C O E F F I C I E N T S - - - - - - - - - - - - -

CONTROLLING FOR..    SEX


VARIABLE              VARIABLE              VARIABLE              VARIABLE              VARIABLE              VARIABLE
PAIR                  PAIR                  PAIR                  PAIR                  PAIR                  PAIR
--------              --------              --------              --------              --------              --------


BA        0.1241
WITH    DF =  297
PSGPA     SIG .032
```

```
PARTIAL CORRELATIONS USING MATRIX INPUT                           07/25/69        PAGE    3

FILE   NONAME   (CREATION DATE = 07/25/69)

- - - - - - - - - - - - P A R T I A L   C O R R E L A T I O N   C O E F F I C I E N T S - - - - - - - - - - - - -

CONTROLLING FOR..    GREV


VARIABLE              VARIABLE              VARIABLE              VARIABLE              VARIABLE              VARIABLE
PAIR                  PAIR                  PAIR                  PAIR                  PAIR                  PAIR
--------              --------              --------              --------              --------              --------


BA        0.1042
WITH    DF =  297
PSGPA     SIG .072
```

```
PARTIAL CORRELATIONS USING MATRIX INPUT                           07/25/69        PAGE    4

FILE   NONAME   (CREATION DATE = 07/25/69)

- - - - - - - - - - - - P A R T I A L   C O R R E L A T I O N   C O E F F I C I E N T S - - - - - - - - - - - - -

CONTROLLING FOR..    GREQ


VARIABLE              VARIABLE              VARIABLE              VARIABLE              VARIABLE              VARIABLE
PAIR                  PAIR                  PAIR                  PAIR                  PAIR                  PAIR
--------              --------              --------              --------              --------              --------


BA        0.1192
WITH    DF =  297
PSGPA     SIG .039
```

```
PARTIAL CORRELATIONS USING MATRIX INPUT                           07/25/69        PAGE    5

FILE   NONAME   (CREATION DATE = 07/25/69)

- - - - - - - - - - - - P A R T I A L   C O R R E L A T I O N   C O E F F I C I E N T S - - - - - - - - - - - - -

CONTROLLING FOR..    SEX        GREV


VARIABLE              VARIABLE              VARIABLE              VARIABLE              VARIABLE              VARIABLE
PAIR                  PAIR                  PAIR                  PAIR                  PAIR                  PAIR
--------              --------              --------              --------              --------              --------


BA        0.1076
WITH    DF =  296
PSGPA     SIG .064
```

```
PARTIAL CORRELATIONS USING MATRIX INPUT                           07/25/69        PAGE    6

FILE   NONAME   (CREATION DATE = 07/25/69)

- - - - - - - - - - - - P A R T I A L   C O R R E L A T I O N   C O E F F I C I E N T S - - - - - - - - - - - - -

CONTROLLING FOR..    SEX        GREQ


VARIABLE              VARIABLE              VARIABLE              VARIABLE              VARIABLE              VARIABLE
PAIR                  PAIR                  PAIR                  PAIR                  PAIR                  PAIR
--------              --------              --------              --------              --------              --------


BA        0.1193
WITH    DF =  296
PSGPA     SIG .040
```

**FIG. 14.2**   Output from subprogram PARTIAL CORR.

PARTIAL CORRELATIONS USING MATRIX INPUT                          07/25/69        PAGE    7

FILE   NONAME  (CREATION DATE = 07/25/69)

- - - - - - - - - - - - - P A R T I A L   C O R R E L A T I O N   C O E F F I C I E N T S - - - - - - - - - - - - - -

CONTROLLING FOR..    GREV     GREQ

| VARIABLE<br>PAIR<br>-------- | VARIABLE<br>PAIR<br>-------- | VARIABLE<br>PAIR<br>-------- | VARIABLE<br>PAIR<br>-------- | VARIABLE<br>PAIR<br>-------- | VARIABLE<br>PAIR<br>-------- |
|---|---|---|---|---|---|

BA        0.1055
WITH    DF =  296
PSGPA     SIG .069

PARTIAL CORRELATIONS USING MATRIX INPUT                          07/25/69        PAGE    8

FILE   NONAME  (CREATION DATE = 07/25/69)

- - - - - - - - - - - - - P A R T I A L   C O R R E L A T I O N   C O E F F I C I E N T S - - - - - - - - - - - - - -

CONTROLLING FOR..    SEX      GREV     GREQ

| VARIABLE<br>PAIR<br>-------- | VARIABLE<br>PAIR<br>-------- | VARIABLE<br>PAIR<br>-------- | VARIABLE<br>PAIR<br>-------- | VARIABLE<br>PAIR<br>-------- | VARIABLE<br>PAIR<br>-------- |
|---|---|---|---|---|---|

BA        0.1069
WITH    DF =  295
PSGPA     SIG .066

PARTIAL CORRELATIONS USING MATRIX INPUT                          07/25/69        PAGE   10

FILE   NONAME  (CREATION DATE = 07/25/69)

- - - - - - - - - - - - - P A R T I A L   C O R R E L A T I O N   C O E F F I C I E N T S - - - - - - - - - - - - - -

CONTROLLING FOR..    MARITAL

| VARIABLE<br>PAIR<br>-------- | VARIABLE<br>PAIR<br>-------- | VARIABLE<br>PAIR<br>-------- | VARIABLE<br>PAIR<br>-------- | VARIABLE<br>PAIR<br>-------- | VARIABLE<br>PAIR<br>-------- |
|---|---|---|---|---|---|

BA        0.1299
WITH    DF =  297
PSGPA     SIG .025

PARTIAL CORRELATIONS USING MATRIX INPUT                          07/25/69        PAGE   11

FILE   NONAME  (CREATION DATE = 07/25/69)

- - - - - - - - - - - - - P A R T I A L   C O R R E L A T I O N   C O E F F I C I E N T S - - - - - - - - - - - - - -

CONTROLLING FOR..    AGE

| VARIABLE<br>PAIR<br>-------- | VARIABLE<br>PAIR<br>-------- | VARIABLE<br>PAIR<br>-------- | VARIABLE<br>PAIR<br>-------- | VARIABLE<br>PAIR<br>-------- | VARIABLE<br>PAIR<br>-------- |
|---|---|---|---|---|---|

BA        0.1214
WITH    DF =  297
PSGPA     SIG .036

PARTIAL CORRELATIONS USING MATRIX INPUT                          07/25/69        PAGE   12

FILE   NONAME  (CREATION DATE = 07/25/69)

- - - - - - - - - - - - - P A R T I A L   C O R R E L A T I O N   C O E F F I C I E N T S - - - - - - - - - - - - - -

CONTROLLING FOR..    MARITAL    AGE

| VARIABLE<br>PAIR<br>-------- | VARIABLE<br>PAIR<br>-------- | VARIABLE<br>PAIR<br>-------- | VARIABLE<br>PAIR<br>-------- | VARIABLE<br>PAIR<br>-------- | VARIABLE<br>PAIR<br>-------- |
|---|---|---|---|---|---|

BA        0.1299
WITH    DF =  296
PSGPA     SIG .025

FIG. 14.2    (*Continued*)

# 15
# MULTIPLE-REGRESSION ANALYSIS: SUBPROGRAM REGRESSION†

The SPSS multiple-regression program is designed to allow the researcher access to a wide variety of multiple-regression techniques without making the use of the program overly difficult or complicated. In particular, the SPSS multiple-regression program combines standard multiple regression and stepwise regression in a manner which provides considerable control over the inclusion of independent variables in the regression equation. Output of normalized regression coefficients in addition to the standard regression coefficients allows the program to be used for the calculation of the path coefficients used in path analysis. The variable transformation features of the SPSS package also allow the regression program to be used for harmonic and polynomial regression.

Input to the regression program may consist of either raw data or a correlation matrix. If the input consists of raw data, then any of the SPSS variable-transformation features may be used, and several options are available for the handling of missing data. The alternative possibility of using a correlation matrix for input, with or without means and standard deviations, allows the researcher to perform extended analysis without calculating the correlation matrix more than once. This provides considerable savings of time when large files are involved. It also permits regression analysis based on correlations obtained from other sources, such as the SPSS

†The computational method used in this multiple-regression subprogram was designed and programmed by William C. Mitchell. This chapter describing the program was also written by him.

subprograms PEARSON CORR and NONPAR CORR. Computational techniques developed for this program permit the handling of a large number of independent and dependent variables in a fast and accurate manner.

Section 15.1.1 presents a general description of multiple-regression analysis while Sec. 15.1.2 contains an introductory mathematical discussion of multiple regression. Section 15.1.3 describes stepwise multiple regression as implemented in this program. Users familiar with these subjects may wish to proceed directly to Sec. 15.2 for a detailed description of the use of the SPSS multiple-regression program.

## 15.1 INTRODUCTION TO MULTIPLE-REGRESSION ANALYSIS

Multiple regression is an extension of the use of the bivariate correlation coefficient to multivariate analysis. The correlation coefficient, or normalized simple regression coefficient, allows the researcher to measure the linear relationship between one independent variable and a dependent variable. Multiple regression allows one to study the linear relationship between a set of independent variables and a number of dependent variables while taking into account the interrelationships among the independent variables. If the simple correlation coefficient is viewed as the continuous analog of a two-way crosstabulation, then multiple regression is the continuous analogue of an n-way crosstabulation.

The basic concept of multiple regression is to produce a linear combination of independent variables which will correlate as highly as possible with the dependent variable. This linear combination can then be used to "predict" values of the dependent variable. The difference between the value of the dependent variable and the value predicted by the linear combination of the independent variables is known as the residual. The regression equation is then written as follows:

$$D = b_1 I_1 + b_2 I_2 + \cdots + b_n I_n + c + r$$

where D is the dependent variable, the I's are the independent variables, the b's are the regression coefficients (unnormalized), c is a constant, and r is the residual.

Many of the properties of multiple regression may be understood by considering the residual. The residual has mean zero, and its standard deviation is the smallest possible for any linear combination of the given independent variables. In other words, if the b's in the regression equation are replaced by any other values, then the standard deviation of the residual will be larger. In this sense, the regression equation provides an optimum prediction of the dependent variable. A consequence of this optimization, which will be explained in the next section, is that the residual and any independent variable have zero correlation.

### 15.1.1 AN EXAMPLE

A good method of understanding the role and power of multiple regression is to consider an example. Consider the following case, based on ficticious data, of a university administrator who wants a basis for admitting students who will have the best opportunity of obtaining a degree and the least probability of flunking out. Three pieces of information are available for each prospective student:

1. College Board test scores
2. Quality of high school attended
3. Family income of student's parents

The researcher wants to know how he can use this information to predict the freshman grade-point averages of prospective students.

As a first phase of analysis, the researcher calculates simple correlation coefficients between each of the three independent variables and the dependent variable. He finds that freshman GPA correlates .70 with College Board scores, .01 with quality of high-school education, and .12 with family income. Since the researcher had expected that the quality of the high school would have a significant effect, but that family income would have no effect, he wonders if the interrelationships among the independent variables are influencing his results. To pursue this he constructs the following tables for students from two extremes—prep schools and ghetto schools:

| High school | | Prep school | | Ghetto school | |
|---|---|---|---|---|---|
| College Board | | High | Low | High | Low |
| Freshman GPA | High | 60% (450) | 30% ( 75) | 75% (300) | 33% (200) |
| | Low | 40% (300) | 70% (175) | 25% (100) | 67% (400) |
| | | 100% (750) | 100% (250) | 100% (400) | 100% (600) |

The researcher studies this table and observes that among students with high College Board scores, 75 percent of the ghetto students have high freshman GPA's while only 60 percent of those from prep schools have high freshman GPA's. The researcher is thus further confounded by the fact that, after controlling for College Board scores, students from ghetto schools do better than their counterparts from prep schools. The slight positive correlation between freshman GPA and quality of high school results from the fact that prep-school students tend to do better on the College Board tests. The researcher suspects that this is because ghetto students are required to have more ability to do as well with inferior preparation. In a common environment, this added ability has a chance to come forward, resulting in unexpected achievement.

This analysis is sufficient for the two extreme cases of private prep schools and ghetto schools, but what does it tell the administrator to do when confronted with students with identical College Board scores from a suburban high school and a consolidated school in a small college town? To construct tables for every type of school would be impractical. A more difficult question is what the administrator should do when a ghetto student has a College Board score 10 points lower than a prep-school student. Does the quality of high school attended represent more or less than a 10-point difference on College Board scores? To answer questions like these the researcher needs a single continuous prediction equation based on all available information. Multiple regression provides this.

To do this, the researcher calculates correlation coefficients among all the variables and enters the following into the SPSS multiple-regression program:

| | Mean | St dev | Correlations | | | |
|---|---|---|---|---|---|---|
| | | | GPA | Board | QHS | FI |
| Freshman GPA | 2 | 1 | 1.000 | .700 | .013 | .120 |
| College Board | 500 | 100 | .700 | 1.000 | .400 | .250 |
| Quality high school | 50 | 20 | .013 | .400 | 1.000 | .500 |
| Family income | 8 | 5 | .120 | .250 | .500 | 1.000 |

In this table the College Board scores range from 0 to 800, quality of high school (QHS) is rated on a 0 to 100 scale, family income (FI) is in thousands, and the GPA varies from 0.0 to 4.0. The resulting prediction equation obtained from multiple regression is

Predicted GPA = .0082 X College Board score
− .018 X Quality of high school
+ .02 X Family income
− 1.36

This prediction equation explains 58 percent of the variance in freshman GPA.

To show how this formula works, a student with a College Board score of 550 from a high school rated at 43 and with a family income of $8,000 would have a predicted GPA of 2.536. That is,

Predicted GPA = .0082 X 550 − .018 X 43 + .02 X 8 − 1.36
= 4.510 − .774 + .16 − 1.36
= 2.536

If the student's actual GPA were 2.7, then the residual, or error, would be .164.

This regression equation can be used two ways. As a prediction equation it can be used as above to provide an estimated value of the dependent variable GPA from known values of the independent variables. The second use is to provide understanding of the relation of each independent variable to the dependent variable. This is achieved primarily by examination of the signs of the regression coefficients. A positive coefficient means that, other things being equal, the larger the value of the independent variable, the larger the value of the dependent variable. In the above example, College Board score and family income have positive coefficients, while quality of high school has a negative coefficient. The researcher expected that College Board score would have a positive coefficient while family income would have little effect. He explains the negative coefficient of quality of high school as a result of holding the College Board score constant. To do equally well on the College Board tests, the student with inferior preparation must have more potential ability. The effect of such a negative coefficient is to give "bonus" points to students with inferior preparation, only in this case such points are based on quantitative experience rather than on subjective judgments.

Apart from consideration of the sign of the coefficient, the next important factor in understanding the relationships expressed by the regression equation is to consider the size of the coefficients. Since the independent variables are measured on different scales, the researcher wonders which variable is the most important predictor of freshman GPA and if any variables can be left out of the equation without losing much predictive ability. The coefficient of the College Board score is the smallest, even though it had the largest correlation with the dependent variable and was expected to be the most important. This avenue may be explored by looking at the normalized regression equation. In this equation, all variables are expressed in standard units. The standardized variables are denoted by the symbol Z. We obtain

$$\text{Predicted } Z_{\text{GPA}} = .82 \times Z_{\text{College Board score}}$$
$$- .36 \times Z_{\text{Quality of high school}}$$
$$+ .10 \times Z_{\text{Family income}}$$

These coefficients reflect the strength of the relationship between the independent and dependent variables as well as the direction of the relationship. It is now apparent that the College Board score is the most important part of the prediction equation, and family income is the least important. If there is only one independent variable, then the normalized regression coefficient is the correlation coefficient. For example, suppose that we had used only the College Board scores in the regression equation. We would have obtained

$$\text{Predicted GPA} = .007 \times \text{College Board score} - 1.5$$

In standardized form, the computed regression equation becomes

$$Z_{\text{GPA}} = .70 \times Z_{\text{College Board score}}$$

The simple regression coefficient of GPA on College Board score is .007. The normalized simple regression coefficient .70 is also the the correlation coefficient. It should be noted that there is no regression constant in the normalized regression equation. This reflects the fact that when all the independent variables take on their mean value, the predicted value is the mean value of the dependent variable.

Since the coefficient of family income was insignificant, it is logical to remove it from the equation. Such small coefficients might be the result of statistical sampling error or other external factors. It is not sufficient merely to remove this term from the equation since it is correlated with the other independent variables. To get an optimum prediction equation with just two variables, a new regression equation must be calculated. The resulting equation is

$$\text{Predicted GPA} = .0083 \times \text{College Board score}$$
$$- .016 \times \text{Quality of high school}$$
$$- 1.34$$

The change in the equation is quite small, and this equation accounts for 57 percent of the variance in GPA compared with 58 percent for the three-term prediction equation.

Returning to the normalized regression equation, the researcher notices that the correlation coefficient between family income and freshman GPA (.12) is larger than the regression coefficient of family income (.10). This leads the researcher to hypothesize that the positive correlation between family income and freshman GPA is a result of the fact that students with higher family income generally get better schooling and thus better College Board scores and higher freshman GPA's. This hypothesis is supported by the fact that family income and quality of high school correlate .50 and quality of high school and College Board scores correlate .40. However, family income and College Board scores correlate only .25. This suggests that quality of high school is an important link in the relationship between family income and College Board scores. That is, if a student from a high-income family doesn't go to a good high school, he will probably not do as well on his College Boards or freshman GPA as would be predicted from family income alone.

Findings of this type come under the heading of *causal modeling*. This method of analysis attempts to explain empirical findings in a manner that reflects the total process which the researcher believes underlies the situation under study rather than just the bivariate relationships. For instance, family income does *not* cause higher College Board scores even though there is a positive bivariate relationship between the two variables. The causal process is through the intervening variable quality of high school. The technique of ascertaining causal links is calculation of path coefficients. These coefficients are the standardized regression coefficients when the independent variables are limited to those which have a prior effect on the dependent variable. Thus, it would not be realistic to expect a student's freshman GPA to have a causal effect on his College Board scores or on the quality of the high school he attended. There will be a correlation, but the causal interpretation is in the other direction. The causal model with path coefficients is shown in the accompanying figure. Paths with small coefficients have been eliminated.

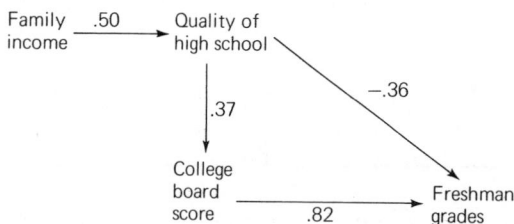

The researcher observes that College Board score is by far the best predictor of freshman GPA. However, this prediction is based on a linear model which assumes that if A does twice as well as B on the College Board test (in standard score), then A will do twice as well as B as a college freshman (once again, in terms of standard scores). The researcher wonders if this is a valid assumption. To answer this question he decides to do polynomial regression. He does this by using the variable-transformation features of SPSS to create a variable equal to the square of the students standardized College Board score. This new variable will be zero for the mean College Board score of 500 and will become larger for values which differ from the mean in either direction. College Board scores of 400 or 600 will give this variable values of 1, scores 300 or 700 will result in values of 4, and scores of 200 or 800 will give a Z-square value of 9. Multiple regression with these two forms of College Board score will give the following regression equation:

$$Z_{GPA} = .70 \times Z_{College\ Board} - .15 \times Z^2_{College\ Board} + .15$$

where $Z^2_{College\ Board}$ is the square of a standard variable and is not itself a standard variable. This is why there is a regression constant in the above equation.

This polynomial regression equation suggests to the researcher that students with extreme scores will not do as well as the simple linear model predicts. For students with very high College Board scores this could mean that other factors such as motivation and interest are necessary to predict college GPA, while for students with low College Board scores, it indicates a threshold effect. Students below this threshold simply have no chance of success in college.

Other variations of multiple regression such as harmonic or asymtopic regression can be performed in a similar fashion. The only requirement is that the researcher have a sufficiently thorough knowledge of the variation he wants to use to perform the necessary variable transformations. Only the ingenuity of the researcher limits such applications.

### 15.1.2   MATHEMATICAL DESCRIPTION OF MULTIPLE REGRESSION

The preceding example demonstrated how a social scientist might use multiple regression. The following is a heuristic mathematical analysis of the method. It is intended only to give the reader a feeling for the mathematics underlying multiple regression; a more advanced and rigorous description may be obtained by consulting a statistics text or a mathematics book which describes least-squares fitting techniques.[1]

In the preceding section multiple regression was introduced as a means of constructing a linear combination of independent variables $X_1, X_2, \ldots, X_n$ which best predicts the dependent variable $X_0$. Although many users will prefer to give a causal interpretation to the individual regression coefficients, the idea of prediction leads most easily to an understanding of multiple regression. For the sake of convenience, let us assume that all the variables are standardized, that is, they have mean 0 and standard deviation 1. Designate the correlation coefficient between $X_i$ and $X_j$ by $r_{ij}$. Since the variables $X_i$ are standardized, the correlation coefficient $r_{ij}$ is the expected value of the product of $X_i$ and $X_j$. That is, $r_{ij} = E(X_i \times X_j)$.

We desire a prediction equation of the form

$$X_0 = b_1 X_1 + b_2 X_2 + \cdots + b_n X_n + R$$

where the coefficients $b_i$ are chosen to make the residual R as small as possible.

To show how the $b_i$ can be chosen to minimize R, let us consider in detail the case of simple regression with one independent variable. This example will also demonstrate the role of the correlation coefficient in prediction. The simple regression equation for standardized variables is

$$X_0 = b_1 X_1 + R$$

The objective is to choose $b_1$ so that when $R^2$ is averaged over all observations, the expected value will be as small as possible. We want to minimize

$$\sum_{i=1}^{m} \frac{R_i^2}{m} = E(R^2) = E[(X_0 - b_1 X_1)^2]$$
$$= E(X_0^2 - 2b_1 X_1 + b_1^2 X_1^2)$$
$$= E(X_0^2) - 2b_1 E(X_0 X_1) + b_1^2 E(X_1^2)$$
$$= 1 - 2b_1 r_{01} + b_1^2$$

It can be shown that this minimum is obtained when $b_1 = r_{01}$. This confirms the earlier statement that the standardized simple regression coefficient is equivalent to the correlation coefficient. Another fact of interest is that the correlation between the independent variable $X_1$ and the residual R is zero. This may be proven mathematically, but at the current intuitive level, we can justify the statement as follows. If there were a nonzero correlation between the independent variable and the residual, then the prediction could be improved because we would be able to predict the residual from knowledge of the independent variable. Thus a better prediction would be possible with a different $b_1$. Only when the independent variable and the residual are uncorrelated do we have the optimum prediction equation.

This relationship also holds in the multiple-regression case. Only when each of the independent variables is uncorrelated with the residual do we have the optimum prediction equation. This condition may be written mathematically as follows:

$$r_{0i} = b_1 r_{1i} + b_2 r_{2i} + \cdots + b_n r_{ni} \qquad (i = 1, 2, \ldots, n)$$

[1]Whitaker and Robinson, "Calculus of Observations", Dover, New York, 1967.

We thus have n linear equations in n unknowns. The solution of this system of equations will yield the optimum prediction coefficients. This solution will exist unless one of the independent variables is a linear combination of the other independent variables. However, in this case, the offending independent variable may be removed from the prediction equation without effecting the residual R.

Thus far we have discussed multiple regression in terms of standardized variables. For general variables we need to add a constant term to the regression equation, as follows:

$$X_0 = C + B_1 X_1 + B_2 X_2 + \cdots + B_n X_n + R$$

In this case we have $B_i = b_i S_0 / S_i$ where $S_k$ is the standard deviation of the k-th variable and $S_0$ is the standard deviation of the dependent variable.

### 15.1.3 STEPWISE MULTIPLE REGRESSION

Stepwise regression is a powerful variation of multiple regression which provides a means of choosing independent variables which will provide the best prediction possible with the fewest independent variables. In the earlier case, an application of stepwise regression would have led to the retention of College Board score and quality of high school as predictors of freshman GPA, but family income would have been left out of the equation.

To illustrate the ideas underlying stepwise regression, consider the following problem. Suppose we have 20 possible independent variables, and we want a prediction equation using the best five of these. One way of choosing the best five-term equation is to construct all possible prediction equations using different combinations of independent variables. There are over 15,000 such combinations. Since the exhaustive search method is not feasible, a more convenient method is required. Stepwise regression is a quick and efficient method which provides a near-optimum solution to the problem. The method recursively constructs a prediction equation one independent variable at a time. The first step is to choose the single variable which is the best predictor. The second independent variable to be added to the regression equation is that which provides the best prediction in conjunction with the first variable. You then proceed in this recursive fashion adding variables step-by-step until you have the desired number of independent variables or until no other variable will make a significant contribution to the prediction equation. At each step the optimum variable is selected, given the other variables in the equation. This procedure does not always yield the true optimum, but it usually does fairly well.

Stepwise regression is based upon a common method of solving the system of linear equations in multiple regression, that is, Gauss elimination with row and column interchanges. It happens that this computational method provides the information necessary to select the next variable to be brought into the equation. There are two pieces of information which are used in this selection process. The first is the normalized regression-coefficient value b that the prospective independent variable would have if it were brought into the equation on the next step. The significance of b is measured by the F statistic. If F is too small, there is little reason to add that independent variable to the prediction equation.

The second piece of information used in the selection process is the pivot element which would be involved in bringing that variable into the equation. This value is known as the *tolerance.* If the tolerance is small, then that variable is nearly a linear combination of variables already in the equation. If it is really a linear combination of independent variables already in the equation, then the tolerance will be zero. A large tolerance indicates that a new "dimension" is being added to the prediction equation. The tolerance is never larger than 1. The amount of additional variance explained by adding the new variable is the product of the normalized regression coefficient b squared and the tolerance. Thus, even if the prospective b is large, a small tolerance value will negate the value of that variable being added to the equation. Consequently, stepwise regression never brings a variable into the equation if the tolerance is below a specified minimum. This also helps to ensure the computational accuracy of the program.

#### 15.1.4  COMPUTATIONAL METHODS

The basic computational method of this multiple regression program is Gauss elimination with some row and column interchanges. This method also underlies stepwise regression. However, the regular stepwise-regression technique has been refined computationally to ensure accuracy and to save computer time. The mathematics involved have not been changed. The program could easily be refined to include iterative refinement on the regression coefficients, but double-precision arithmetic has been used in all sensitive calculations. In addition, the tolerance level ensures some computational accuracy if stepwise regression is used. It is believed that the accuracy of this program is sufficient for social science problems. Researchers with more stringent needs should be familiar with the remedies available.

Considerable savings in computer time result from a new method of handling variables which are not in the regression equation. Variables which are not in the inclusion list of a REGRESSION list are entirely excluded from the calculations involved in that REGRESSION problem (see Sec. 15.5). The researcher should not hesitate to add variables to the VARIABLES list unless he feels that the time required to calculate additional correlations is too great. In addition, there are savings nearly as great for variables which are in the inclusion list, but are not yet in the regression equation. Only those calculations necessary to determine the statistics printed for variables not in the equation are done until the variable is actually brought into the regression equation. When not all variables in the inclusion list are brought into the equation, this results in considerable savings. If all the variables in the inclusion list are brought into the regression equation, this method allows no savings. In many cases, however, a significant reduction in computer time may be realized using the above technique.

## 15.2  THE REGRESSION PROCEDURE CARD

The SPSS control cards for linear stepwise regression are quite straightforward and easy to use. More complicated applications, such as polynomial regression, are handled through the use of the variable-transformation features of SPSS described in Chap. 8.

The multiple-regression subprogram is called and activated by a procedure card containing the control word REGRESSION in columns 1 to 15. Each regression calculation consists of two steps. First, a square correlation matrix must be assembled or computed. This is accomplished through the use of a VARIABLES list. Second, one or more regression calculations are made using the assembled matrix. This is accomplished through the use of one or more REGRESSION lists. Finally, the whole procedure may be repeated, so that another VARIABLES list may be used followed by one or more REGRESSION lists. The format of the REGRESSION procedure card is, therefore

```
1                 16
REGRESSION        VARIABLES=variables list/REGRESSION=regression list/ . . . /
                  REGRESSION=regression list/VARIABLES=variables list/
                  REGRESSION=regression list/ . . . /REGRESSION=regression
                  list/ . . . etc.
```

#### 15.2.1  THE VARIABLES LIST

Prior to the use of a REGRESSION procedure card, a variable list must have been defined. This variable list may be the list of variables for cases to be read from cards or tape. In this case the user would insert a VARIABLE LIST card in the control-card deck. Alternatively, the user may have retrieved a system file with the use of a GET FILE card. In this case the variable list is the one associated with the system file. In addition, the user may have computed some new variables with the use of a series of COMPUTE or IF cards or their starred [*] counterparts, in which case, new variable names would have been added to the current variable list.

Suppose that the variable list which is currently defined when the REGRESSION card is encountered is the following:

VARA,VARB,VARC, . . . , VARZ

The VARIABLES list consists of the keyword VARIABLES, followed by [=], a special delimiter, and a list of variable names separated by blanks or commas. Each of the variable must be one of the variables named in the current variables list. The TO convention may be used. Thus for the above example, acceptable VARIABLES lists are

VARIABLES = VARA,VARB,VARC
VARIABLES = VARA,VARZ,VARD
VARIABLES = VARD TO VARL,VARA,VARZ

The purpose of the VARIABLES list is to cause the regression subprogram to assemble a matrix of correlations to be used in the regression calculations. The matrix is square and of the same dimension as the number of variables referenced in the VARIABLES list.

### 15.2.2   THE REGRESSION LIST

The multiple-regression calculations desired are specified by a REGRESSION list. This list is of the form

REGRESSION = dependent variable, {parameters} WITH inclusion list

The {parameters} are an optional input to the regression program which will be described later in this section. The parameter specification can, and in most cases will, be left blank. The inclusion list is a set of inclusion names separated from each other by blanks or a comma. An *inclusion list* is a variable name or list of names from the VARIABLES list which may be followed by an inclusion level enclosed in a pair of parentheses. Examples of inclusion names are

VARA(3)

or

VARA,VARB(4)

or

VARA,VARL TO VARZ(2).

The inclusion level is a number from 0 to 99 which controls the selection of independent variables for the regression equation. The use of the inclusion level will be described later in this section. Because there is no default value for the inclusion level, each prospective independent variable in the regression list must be assigned an inclusion level. This may be done in two ways. If a variable name in the regression list is followed by a number in parentheses, then that is its inclusion level; if not, then it is assigned the value of the next inclusion level to follow in the regression list. It follows that in order for each variable in the list to have an inclusion level, the final variable name in the regression list must be followed by an inclusion level enclosed in parentheses.

The TO convention may be used in the regression list under the following conditions. First, the order of the variables is taken as they appear in the variables list of the REGRESSION card, not as they appeared in the file. Second, all the variables denoted by a TO convention must have the same inclusion level. Consider the following example:

```
1               16
VARIABLE LIST   A B C D E F G H I
REGRESSION      VARIABLES = A, D TO G, I/
                REGRESSION = A WITH D (3) E TO F (1) /
                REGRESSION E WITH D (1) F TO I, A (3)
```

This REGRESSION card specifies the following two multiple-regression calculations:

|  | Problem 1 | | Problem 2 | |
|---|---|---|---|---|
| Dependent variable | A | | E | |
| | → | ← | → | ← |
| Independent variables | D | 3 | D | 1 |
| and inclusion level | E | 1 | F | 2 |
| | F | 1 | I | 2 |
| | I | 1 | H | 2 |

Notice the difference between the use of the TO convention in the variable list and the regression list. The variables specified by D TO F in the regression list are D, E, and F since the TO convention is based on the original order of variables in the file specification. The use of the TO convention in the regression list does not refer back to the original file specification, but only to the variables list of the REGRESSION card. Thus E TO I in the regression list means E, F, and I. The F TO H list specifies F, I, and H. H is excluded from the first regression list and I is included in the first because I precedes H in the variables list of the REGRESSION card. The fact that H precedes I in the original file specification has no effect at this point.

Regardless of whether regular multiple regression or stepwise regression is desired, the SPSS regression calculations are performed in steps. Each step involves adding one or more independent variables to the regression equation. If the user knows exactly what variables he wishes included in the regression equation, he may bring them all into the equation on the first step and limit his calculations to that one step. If the user has one set of variables which he is sure he wants in the equation and a secondary set of less interesting variables, then he may bring the first set into the equation on the first step, and the second set of variables can be added on the second step. Or he may combine regular multiple regression with stepwise regression by forcing the first set of variables into the equation on the first step and allowing additional independent variables to be selected from the second set of variables by the stepwise option. These later variables will be added one variable per step until all variables have been added or no other variable in the inclusion list makes a significant contribution to the regression equation. Alternatively, the user may specify that only the three best variables of the second set be added to the regression equation. Or he may specify that the variables of the first set be added in a stepwise fashion, and when these have been brought into the regression equation, then the variables of the second set will be brought into the equation in either one step or in stepwise fashion.

The user may tailor the multiple-regression calculations to his own needs in the above fashion through the use of inclusion levels. Variables with higher inclusion levels are brought into the regression equation (provided they satisfy the other requirements) before variables with lower inclusion levels. The *inclusion level* is an integer from 0 to 99 which is enclosed in parentheses in the inclusion list of the REGRESSION procedure card. There are two modes of inclusion, multiple and stepwise. Variables with odd inclusion levels are in stepwise mode and enter the regression equation in accordance with the procedures of stepwise regression. If several variables have the same odd inclusion level, they are entered one at a time as long as the variable makes a significant contribution to the regression equation. Variables with even inclusion levels are in multiple mode and are brought into the equation regardless of how significant a contribution they might make. If several variables have the same even inclusion level, then they are all entered on the same step. As soon as all variables at a given level have been considered, variables at the next lower inclusion level are considered.

A variable with inclusion level zero will never be brought into the regression equation, but it is included in certain parts of the output as if it were being considered for inclusion. See the description of the output in Sec. 15.4 for further details.

The parameters in the regression list are the final element of the user's control of the regression calculations. These optional parameters permit the user to specify the maximum number of steps in the calculation, the minimal F level, and the tolerance level for the inclusion of variables in stepwise mode. Since each of these parameters has a default value, the use of parameters is optional. If the researcher wishes to limit the number of steps, then he encloses the desired number of steps in a pair of parentheses, for example, (5). After this number of steps no more independent variables will be added to the equation regardless of inclusion level or significance. If the researcher desires to change the F-level, he does it as follows: ( n , F ) where n is the maximum number of steps and F is the desired F-level. If the user desires to change the F-level he must specify the number of steps whether he wants to limit the number of steps or not. He can choose a large number of steps if he wants to change only the F-level. The tolerance level may be specified as follows: ( n , F , T ). To specify a tolerance level, the user must also specify the number of steps and the F-level. The default values for the parameters are equivalent to (80, .01, .001). Examples of parameter specifications are

(5, .02)

or

(10, .025, .0003)

The first parameter set specifies a maximum of five steps and an F-level of .02; the second parameter set specifies a maximum of 10 steps, an F-level of .025, and a tolerance level of .0003.

A VARIABLES list may be followed by any number of REGRESSION lists. A REGRESSION list may be followed by a VARIABLES list, in which case the REGRESSION lists which follow the second (or succeeding) are based on the variables in the second VARIABLES list only. Only one VARIABLES list is "in effect" for any REGRESSION list, and the relevant VARIABLES list is the last one before the REGRESSION list. However, the same variables may appear in more than one VARIABLES list. The last REGRESSION list need not be followed by a slash [/] .

## 15.3   SPECIAL CONVENTIONS FOR MATRIX INPUT FOR SUBPROGRAM REGRESSION

Since multiple regression requires only means, standard deviations, and correlations, some researchers may want to do multiple regression directly from the correlation matrix. This can be done with the SPSS multiple-regression subprogram. This capability is particularly important if the researcher wants to use correlations generated by nonparametric techniques (e.g., Spearman correlations) or if the correlations are based on such a large number of cases that recalculating the correlations each time a different run is made is impractical. Matrix input allows the researcher to calculate the correlations once and then do multiple regression at his leisure. If some multiple-regression run suggests something unexpected, the researcher can investigate this without recalculating the correlation matrix.

The principal requirement for matrix input is that all variables which may be included in the regression calculations at some time be included in the correlation matrix. Variables can be left out of regression calculations by leaving them out of the inclusion list with no increase in computer time, but if the variable is not in the correlation matrix, it cannot be added without calculating more correlations. The multiple-regression program has an option (option 8) which permits the correlation matrix to be saved for later use (see Sec. 15.5). In addition, the PEARSON CORR and NONPAR CORR subprograms have an option which permits a correlation matrix to be saved for later use. The only restriction for using such a matrix for the multiple-regression program is that the WITH convention not be used in the PEARSON CORR or NONPAR CORR subprograms since a square matrix is required for input to the multiple regression program.

The REGRESSION card is the same for matrix input and raw-data input. However the order of the variables in the VARIABLES list must be the same as the order of the variables in the correlation matrix.

The format for the correlation matrix is ( 8F10.7 ). This is the only format which may be used. Each new row of the correlation matrix must start on a new card. A detailed discussion of the construction of a correlation matrix may be found in Sec. 14.3.2. Means and standard deviations are read in as an additional two rows of the matrix which come before the correlation matrix. The format for means and standard deviations is ( 8F10.0 ). There is an option on the OPTIONS card which permits input of a correlation matrix without means or standard deviations. In this case, means of 0 and standard deviations of 1 are assumed.

If there is more than one VARIABLES list in the REGRESSION card, then the second correlation matrix follows the first. Means and standard deviations once again go before the correlation matrix and after the previous correlation matrix. The same option as to inclusion of means and standard deviations must be used for all VARIABLES lists on the REGRESSION card.

When matrix input is used, the READ INPUT DATA card is replaced by a READ MATRIX card. This card is then directly followed by the cards containing the punched means and standard deviations (if present) and the correlation matrix. The INPUT MEDIUM card is retained and plays the same role as for raw-data input. There is no provision for saving files of correlation matrices in the SPSS system. The # OF CASES card is used and specifies the number of cases the correlations were based on, *not* the number of rows in the correlation matrix. This number is used for statistical computations in the multiple-regression subprogram.

## 15.4    PRINTED OUTPUT FROM SUBPROGRAM REGRESSION

The output from the multiple-regression subprogram can be divided into two parts: step-by-step results and a summary table, as shown in Fig. 15.1. The first type of output is printed for each regression equation calculated. This provides the user with output every time variables are added to the regression equation. The summary table is provided only after the final step and gives a brief description of the situation at each step. All output is labeled, but this section gives a more detailed description of the output.

The dependent variable is printed at the top of each page of multiple-regression output. The output at each step consists of the following. First appears a list of the variables entered during the current step. This will be one variable in stepwise mode and one or more in multiple mode. Below this is the statistical summary of the total prediction equation. This includes multiple r, r-square, and the standard error. The r-square can be interpreted as the proportion of the variance in the dependent variable accounted for by the regression equation. The standard error is the standard deviation of the residual. Since the mean of the residual is zero the standard error can thus be considered the typical size of a residual. Because the residual is the difference between prediction and actual value, the standard error is thus the typical error in prediction. The remainder of this summary includes an analysis of the regression. The first line is for the regression equation, the second for the residuals. In each case the sum of squares and mean sum of squares is presented. The F is the ratio of the two mean squares and measures the significance of the regression equation representing more than mere chance. For the proper interpretation of the F-level, the researcher should consult a table giving the probability of obtaining a given F by mere chance. The proper degrees of freedom are included in the output.[1]

The remainder of the step-by-step output is divided into two halves which appear side by side. The left half is for the variables in the regression equation, and the right half is for variables in the inclusion list, but not yet in the regression equation. The right half contains information on prospective independent variables.

For variables in the regression equation, four values are presented for each independent variable. The B and the BETA values are the regular and normalized regression coefficients, respectively. The normalized regression coefficient BETA is also the path coefficient. The third value is the standard error of B. This measures the significance of the regression coefficient. The range of the regular regression coefficient should be interpreted as B $\pm$ S, where S is the standard error. If S is much smaller in magnitude than B, then the sign of the regression coefficient may be interpreted with confidence. If S is nearly as large as B, then the coefficient should be used with care since there is a significant chance, at least 15 percent, that the true

---

[1] For a more complete statistical discussion of multiple regression consult J. Johnston, "Econometric Methods", McGraw-Hill, New York, 1963.

```
STEPWISE MULTIPLE REGRESSION RUN FROM A SYSTEM FILE                          06/24/69        PAGE    2

FILE    STOCKP   (CREATION DATA = 06/24/69)    DATA FOR PREDICTION OF INVESTORS INDEX

* * * * * * * * * * * * * * * * * * * * * *  M U L T I P L E   R E G R E S S I O N  * * * * * * * * * * * * * * * * * * * * * * * *

DEPENDENT VARIABLE..    INVINDEX   INVESTORS INDEX 1949=100

VARIABLE(S) ENTERED ON STEP NUMBER  1..    GNP      GROSS NATIONAL PRODUCT
```

| | | ANALYSIS OF VARIANCE | DF | SUM OF SQUARES | MEAN SQUARE | F |
|---|---|---|---|---|---|---|
| MULTIPLE R | 0.93729 | | | | | |
| R SQUARE | 0.87852 | REGRESSION | 1. | 339937.40614 | 339937.40614 | 216.946 |
| STANDARD ERROR | 39.58437 | RESIDUAL | 30. | 47004.68172 | 1566.92272 | |

```
--------------- VARIABLES IN THE EQUATION ------------------        ------------- VARIABLES NOT IN THE EQUATION -------------
```

| VARIABLE | B | BETA | STD ERROR B | F | VARIABLE | BETA IN | PARTIAL | TOLERANCE | F |
|---|---|---|---|---|---|---|---|---|---|
| GNP | 0.01357 | 0.93729 | 0.00092 | 216.946 | CORPPROF | -0.75329 | -0.47045 | 0.04738 | 8.243 |
| (CONSTANT) | -85.48109 | | | | CORPDIV | 0.50029 | 0.72182 | 0.25289 | 31.545 |

```
* * * * * * * * * * * * * * * * * * * * * * * * * * * * * * * * * * * * * * * * * * * * * * * * * * * * * * * * * * * * * * *

VARIABLE(S) ENTERED ON STEP NUMBER  2..    CORPPROF   CORPORATE PROFITS BEFORE TAXES
```

| | | ANALYSIS OF VARIANCE | DF | SUM OF SQUARES | MEAN SQUARE | F |
|---|---|---|---|---|---|---|
| MULTIPLE R | 0.95153 | | | | | |
| R SQUARE | 0.90540 | REGRESSION | 2. | 350341.48912 | 175170.74456 | 138.783 |
| STANDARD ERROR | 35.52736 | RESIDUAL | 29. | 36603.59874 | 1262.19306 | |

```
--------------- VARIABLES IN THE EQUATION ------------------        ------------- VARIABLES NOT IN THE EQUATION -------------
```

| VARIABLE | B | BETA | STD ERROR B | F | VARIABLE | BETA IN | PARTIAL | TOLERANCE | F |
|---|---|---|---|---|---|---|---|---|---|
| GNP | 0.02421 | 1.67252 | 0.00380 | 40.635 | CORPDIV | 0.45524 | 0.73122 | 0.24406 | 32.174 |
| CORPPROF | -0.20923 | -0.75329 | 0.07288 | 8.243 | | | | | |
| (CONSTANT) | -75.40775 | | | | | | | | |

```
MULTIPLE REGRESSION RUN ILLUSTRATING USE OF INCLUSION LEVELS                 06/24/69        PAGE    3

FILE    STOCKP   (CREATION DATA = 06/24/69)    DATA FOR PREDICTION OF INVESTORS INDEX

* * * * * * * * * * * * * * * * * * * * * *  M U L T I P L E   R E G R E S S I O N  * * * * * * * * * * * * * * * * * * * * * * * *

DEPENDENT VARIABLE..    INVINDEX   INVESTORS INDEX 1949=100

VARIABLE(S) ENTERED ON STEP NUMBER  3..    CORPDIV   CORPORATE DIVIDENDS PAID
```

| | | ANALYSIS OF VARIANCE | DF | SUM OF SQUARES | MEAN SQUARE | F |
|---|---|---|---|---|---|---|
| MULTIPLE R | 0.97774 | | | | | |
| R SQUARE | 0.95598 | REGRESSION | 3. | 369912.82879 | 123304.27626 | 202.705 |
| STANDARD ERROR | 24.66364 | RESIDUAL | 28. | 17032.25906 | 608.29497 | |

```
--------------- VARIABLES IN THE EQUATION ------------------        ------------- VARIABLES NOT IN THE EQUATION -------------
```

| VARIABLE | B | BETA | STD ERROR B | F | VARIABLE | BETA IN | PARTIAL | TOLERANCE | F |
|---|---|---|---|---|---|---|---|---|---|
| GNP | 0.01574 | 1.08714 | 0.00303 | 26.967 | | | | | |
| CORPPROF | -0.15462 | -0.55669 | 0.05150 | 9.014 | | | | | |
| CORPDIV | 0.42586 | 0.45524 | 0.07508 | 32.174 | | | | | |
| (CONSTANT) | -111.70268 | | | | | | | | |

```
MAXIMUM STEP REACHED


STEPWISE MULTIPLE REGRESSION RUN FROM A SYSTEM FILE                          07/25/69        PAGE   11

FILE    STOCKP   (CREATION DATE = 07/25/69)    DATA FOR PREDICTION OF INVESTORS INDEX

* * * * * * * * * * * * * * * * * * * * * *  M U L T I P L E   R E G R E S S I O N  * * * * * * * * * * * * * * * * * * * * * * * *

DEPENDENT VARIABLE..    INVINDEX   INVESTORS INDEX 1949=100

                                               SUMMARY TABLE
```

| VARIABLE | | MULTIPLE R | R SQUARE | RSQ CHANGE | SIMPLE R | B | BETA |
|---|---|---|---|---|---|---|---|
| GNP | GROSS NATIONAL PRODUCT | 0.93729 | 0.87852 | 0.87852 | 0.93729 | 0.01574 | 1.08714 |
| CORPPROF | CORPORATE PROFITS BEFORE TAXES | 0.95153 | 0.90540 | 0.02689 | 0.87912 | -0.15462 | -0.55669 |
| CORPDIV | CORPORATE DIVIDENDS PAID | 0.97774 | 0.95598 | 0.05058 | 0.93667 | 0.42586 | 0.45524 |
| (CONSTANT) | | | | | | -111.70268 | |

**FIG. 15.1**  Output from subprogram REGRESSION.

regression coefficient is of the opposite sign as the calculated value due to random errors in the data. The fourth value of the left side of the output measures the relative size of B and S. F is calculated as (B/S)**2. One should consult a statistical table for the exact significance of the F statistic, but the usual cutoff values are 1, 2, and 4. Values larger than these represent statistically significant coefficients.

The constant of the regression coefficient appears below the final independent variable. It has little meaning unless one wants to use the regression equation for prediction purposes.

For variables not in the regression equation, but in the inclusion list, a different four values are presented in the right-hand side of the output. The first is the BETA coefficient which each variable would have if it alone were brought into the regression equation on the next step; the second is the partial correlation between the prospective independent variable and the dependent variable when the independent variables in the regression equation are controlled for. The third value is the tolerance, which is explained in Sec. 15.3. The final value is the F statistic for the significance of the potential independent variable. The F also measures the significance of the partial correlation. If that variable is entered on the next step, the F value will remain the same.

The summary table presents information for each independent variable at the conclusion of the final step. Presented here are the multiple r, the r-square, and the change in r-square from the value of the previous step. When several variables are entered during the same step in multiple mode, each variable will appear to have been entered on a separate step. The only piece of information which appears in the summary table, but not in the other output, is the simple r, which is the correlation between the independent variable and the dependent variable. This is presented so that the researcher may see what effect the other independent variables have on the relationship between the two variables. The researcher should take particular note if the two are of opposite sign.

The B and BETA values presented in the summary table are taken from the final step and bear no relation to the B and BETA of other steps.

## 15.5   OPTIONS AVAILABLE FOR SUBPROGRAM REGRESSION

There are eight options available with subprogram REGRESSION. The first two options determine the way missing values are handled during the calculation of the correlation matrix. The default condition (that is, the case in which neither of the first two options are exercised) is that a missing value for one variable causes that case to be ignored for all variables. This is listwise deletion of cases. Under these conditions, all means, standard deviations, and correlations are based on the same universe of data. There are sound statistical reasons for using this procedure. For a detailed discussion of listwise deletion, see Sec. 14.4.

Options are selected for this subprogram by the insertion of an OPTIONS card in the control-card deck immediately following the REGRESSION card (see Sec. 5.2). The OPTIONS card contains the control word OPTIONS followed by a number list indicating the options desired. The format of the OPTIONS card is then

| 1 | 16 |
|---|---|
| OPTIONS | number list |

*Option* 1.   *Inclusion of missing data.*   This option causes the subprogram to include all cases in the calculation of the correlation coefficients regardless of any missing data values which may be defined.

*Option* 2.   *Pairwise deletion of cases.*   This option causes pairwise deletion of cases which contain missing data values. A missing value for a particular variable causes that case to be eliminated from the calculations involving that variable only. This option should be used when a researcher has many variables each with a few missing values, and listwise deletion would reduce his number of cases farther than desired. The number of cases used in subprogram REGRESSION for computation purposes under this option is the minimum number of cases any correlation is based on. The researcher should have a good familiarity with his data and the statistics involved before using this option. For further discussion of options 1 and 2, the reader may refer to Sec. 14.4, making the obvious modifications.

*Option* 3.   *Suppression of variable labels.*   Selection of this option causes suppression of the variable labels on the printed output. This results in a slight increase in processing speed.

*Option 4. and 5.*   *Matrix input.*   Option 4 specifies that a matrix of correlation coefficients will be input by the user. The use of this option has been discussed in Sec. 15.5. Option 5 specifies that means and standard deviations are going to be read in with the correlation matrix as described in Sec. 15.4. Option 5 cannot be used without the use of option 4. However, when option 4 is used without option 5, means and standard deviations are not included in the user-supplied data. In this case standardized variables with mean 0 and standard deviation 1 will be assumed in all calculations. This will result in the b and beta values being identical, and the regression coefficient will be zero.

*Option 6.*   *Suppression of step-by-step output.*   In this case only a summary table at the conclusion of the final step will appear.

*Option 7.*   *Suppression of the summary table.*

*Option 8.*   *Matrix output.*   This option causes the correlation matrix (or matrices) used in the calculations to be printed on an output unit of the user's choice. In this case, a set of JCL cards for the BCD output file FT09 must be inserted in the deck (see the JCL, Appendix F). The format of the resulting matrices is compatible with the format required of matrices to be input to subprogram REGRESSION. See Sec. 15.3 for details.

## 15.6   STATISTICS AVAILABLE FOR SUBPROGRAM REGRESSION

The optional statistics which one may obtain from subprogram REGRESSION are selected by the use of a STATISTICS card. If present, this card directly follows the OPTIONS card in the control-card deck, or if there is no OPTIONS card, this card directly follows the REGRESSION card. The STATISTICS card has its usual format, that is, the control word STATISTICS appears beginning in column 1 and beginning in column 16 appear the numbers 1 and/or 2 or the keyword ALL. In the last case statistics 1 and 2 are both selected. If no STATISTICS card appears in the deck directly following the REGRESSION card, neither statistic is selected.

*Statistic 1.*   *Printout of the correlation matrix (matrices).*   More than one matrix may appear if there is more than one REGRESSION list.

*Statistic 2.*   *Means, standard deviations, and number of valid cases.*   If this statistic is selected, these numbers are printed for each variable. Here *number of valid cases* means the number of cases which did not have missing values. If option 1 is selected, missing data values are counted as valid.

## 15.7   PROGRAM LIMITATIONS OF SUBPROGRAM REGRESSION

*Limitation 1.*   There is a maximum of 10 VARIABLES lists per REGRESSION card. This is equivalent to a limit of 10 correlation matrices per run.

*Limitation 2.*   There is a maximum of 50 REGRESSION lists per REGRESSION card regardless of how many VARIABLES lists are on the card.

*Limitation 3.*   There is a limit of 200 variable names in the combined VARIABLES lists on any REGRESSION card. Each occurrence of a variable name in a list counts as one in this total.

*Limitation 4.*   A maximum of 400 variable names may be used in the combined REGRESSION lists on any REGRESSION card. Each occurrence of a variable name as either a dependent or independent variable counts as one in this total.

*Limitation* 5.    The core storage required is SPACE, defined by the following formula:

$$SPACE = 8 \times (NVARS + MATRIX)$$

where NVARS is the number of variable names in the combined VARIABLES lists. If pairwise deletion of missing values (option 2) is specified, then

$$MATRIX = \Sigma_i \; 3 \times N_i^2$$

where $N_i$ is the number of variable names in a given VARIABLES list, and the sum is over all lists. If listwise deletion of missing values (default of option 2) is specified then

$$MATRIX = \Sigma_i \; N_i^2 + \max_i \left\{ \max_j (M_{ij}) \times N_i \right\}$$

where $M_{ij}$ is the number of variables in REGRESSION list j of VARIABLES list i. Consider the following example:

| i | $N_i$ | $N_i^2$ | M | $N_i \times M$ |
|---|-------|---------|---|----------------|
| 1 | 5     | 25      | 8 | 40             |
| 2 | 20    | 400     | 7 | 140            |
| 3 | 10    | 100     | 5 | 50             |
| 4 | 30    | 900     | 6 | 180            |
| 5 | 5     | 25      | 3 | 15             |
|   | 70    | 1450    |   |                |

If pairwise deletion is specified, MATRIX will be $3 \times 1450 = 4350$. Since NVARS is 70, SPACE will be $8 \times 70 + 4350 = 4910$. If pairwise deletion is not specified, then space will be $8 \times 70 + 1450 + 180 = 2190$, since 180 is the largest $N_i \times M$ value.

## 15.8    EXAMPLE DECK SETUPS AND OUTPUT FOR SUBPROGRAM REGRESSION

Example 15.1 illustrates the most straightforward and elementary use of subprogram REGRESSION. In this example, the user wishes to enter his data from cards and wishes to perform a normal multiple-regression run (not stepwise). Five variables are involved, INVINDEX, GNP, CORPPROF, CORPDIV, and YEAR. The purpose of the regression run is to calculate a regression equation to predict INVINDEX (Investor's Index) as a function of GNP (Gross National Product), CORPPROF (Corporate Profits), and CORPDIV (Corporate Dividends). The variable YEAR is not used in the calculations. The cases are each punched on a single card in the format specified by the INPUT FORMAT card, and follow the READ INPUT DATA card in the deck.

The VARIABLES list portion of the REGRESSION card in this case specifies that all the variables found in each case except YEAR are to be used to calculate the correlation matrix. The REGRESSION list specifies that a regression equation is to be calculated with INVINDEX as the dependent variable and GNP, CORPPROF and CORPDIV as independent or explanatory variables. The output from this example run is shown in Fig. 15.2.

Example 15.2 is a variation of Example 15.1. In this case, data is read in from cards as before, and the same cards containing the cases follow the READ INPUT DATA card in the deck. The same variables are used for the regression calculation. This time, however, the calculation is performed in a stepwise fashion. The REGRESSION list specifies that first a regression equation will be fitted with GNP as a single independent variable, next the variable CORPPROF is introduced into the calculations, and finally the variable CORPDIV. The output from this run is shown in Fig. 15.3. At the conclusion of the run an SPSS system file is saved for use in subsequent runs.

**EXAMPLE 15.1**     Deck setup for subprogram REGRESSION

```
1                16
RUN NAME         MULTIPLE REGRESSION RUN USING CARD INPUT AND RAW DATA
VARIABLE LIST    INVINDEX,GNP,CORPPROF,CORPDIV,YEAR
VAR LABELS       INVINDEX,INVESTORS INDEX 1949=100/
                 GNP,GROSS NATIONAL PRODUCT/
                 CORPPROF,CORPORATE PROFITS BEFORE TAXES/
                 CORPDIV,CORPORATE DIVIDENDS PAID
INPUT FORMAT     FIXED (F6.1,4F6.0)
PRINT FORMATS    INVINDEX(1), GNP TO CORPDIV(0)
# OF CASES       32
REGRESSION       VARIABLES=INVINDEX,GNP,CORPPROF,CORPDIV/
                 REGRESSION=INVINDEX WITH GNP TO CORPDIV(2)
READ INPUT DATA
   76.4   7678    269    216   1935
   99.5   8022    351    251   1936
  105.9   8820    403    250   1937
   86.7   8871    362    290   1938
   83.7   9536    541    304   1939
   70.7  10911    619    317   1940
   61.7  12486    801    273   1941
   58.7  14816    917    243   1942
   76.3  15357    882    233   1943
   76.6  15927    858    211   1944
   91.0  15552    852    195   1945
  105.8  15251    966    230   1946
   96.8  15446   1008    286   1947
  102.8  15735    908    240   1948
  100.0  16343    851    278   1949
  120.3  17471   1065    361   1950
  153.8  18547   1034    300   1951
  158.2  20027   1C81    296   1952
  146.5  20794   1089    287   1953
  165.6  20186    953    282   1954
  212.7  21920   1206    321   1955
  245.9  23811   1313    340   1956
  236.0  24117   1202    364   1957
  218.8  24397   1242    371   1958
  242.6  25242   1378    388   1959
  256.9  25849   1295    397   1960
  326.1  26515   1314    436   1961
  314.4  28287   1422    470   1962
  336.0  29740   1525    511   1963
  394.0  31650   1718    583   1964
  433.1  33814   1836    629   1965
  4C8.5  35822   1762    655   1966
FINISH
```

**EXAMPLE 15.2**

```
1                16
RUN NAME         MULTIPLE REGRESSION RUN ILLUSTRATING USE OF INCLUSION LEVELS
FILE NAME        STOCKP,DATA FOR PREDICTION OF INVESTORS INDEX
VARIABLE LIST    INVINDEX,GNP,CORPPROF,CORPDIV,YEAR
VAR LABELS       INVINDEX,INVESTORS INDEX 1949=100/
                 GNP,GROSS NATIONAL PRODUCT/
                 CORPPROF,CORPORATE PROFITS BEFORE TAXES/
                 CORPDIV,CORPORATE DIVIDENDS PAID
INPUT FORMAT     FIXED (F6.1,4F6.0)
PRINT FORMATS    INVINDEX(1), GNP TO CORPDIV(0)
# OF CASES       32
REGRESSION       VARIABLES=INVINDEX,GNP,CORPPROF,CORPDIV/
                 REGRESSION=INVINDEX WITH GNP(5)CORPPROF(3)CORPDIV(1)
READ INPUT DATA
   76.4   7678    269    216   1935
   99.5   8022    351    251   1936
    .
    .
    .
  SAME DATA CARDS AS FOR EXAMPLE 15.1
    .
    .
    .
  433.1  33814   1836    629   1965
  4C8.5  35822   1762    655   1966
SAVE FILE
FINISH
```

```
MULTIPLE REGRESSION RUN USING CARD INPUT AND RAW DATA                          06/24/69        PAGE    2

FILE   NONAME   (CREATION DATA = 06/24/69)

* * * * * * * * * * * * * * * * * * * *  M U L T I P L E   R E G R E S S I O N  * * * * * * * * * * * * * * * * * * * * * *

DEPENDENT VARIABLE..    INVINDEX    INVESTORS INDEX 1949=100

VARIABLE(S) ENTERED ON STEP NUMBER  1..      CORPDIV    CORPORATE DIVIDENDS PAID
                                             GNP        GROSS NATIONAL PRODUCT
                                             CORPPROF   CORPORATE PROFITS BEFORE TAXES


MULTIPLE R          0.97774               ANALYSIS OF VARIANCE    DF      SUM OF SQUARES       MEAN SQUARE            F
R SQUARE            0.95598               REGRESSION              3.      369912.82879        123304.27626      202.705
STANDARD ERROR     24.66364               RESIDUAL               28.       17032.25906           608.29497


-------------- VARIABLES IN THE EQUATION -----------------        ------------- VARIABLES NOT IN THE EQUATION -------------

VARIABLE        B          BETA       STD ERROR B       F          VARIABLE      BETA IN      PARTIAL     TOLERANCE        F

CORPDIV       0.42586     0.45524      0.07508       32.174
GNP           0.01574     1.08714      0.00303       26.967
CORPPROF     -0.15462    -0.55669      0.05150        9.014
(CONSTANT)  -111.70268


ALL VARIABLES ARE IN THE EQUATION


MULTIPLE REGRESSION RUN USING CARD INPUT AND RAW DATA                          07/25/69        PAGE    3

FILE   STOCKP   (CREATION DATE = 07/25/69)    DATA FOR PREDICTION OF INVESTORS INDEX

* * * * * * * * * * * * * * * * * * * *  M U L T I P L E   R E G R E S S I O N  * * * * * * * * * * * * * * * * * * * * * *

DEPENDENT VARIABLE..    INVINDEX    INVESTORS INDEX 1949=100

                                              SUMMARY TABLE

VARIABLE                               MULTIPLE R   R SQUARE   RSQ CHANGE   SIMPLE R            B              BETA

CORPDIV   CORPORATE DIVIDENDS PAID        0.93667    0.87735    0.87735     0.93667         0.42586          0.45524
GNP       GROSS NATIONAL PRODUCT          0.97047    0.94181    0.06446     0.93729         0.01574          1.08714
CORPPROF  CORPORATE PROFITS BEFORE TAXES  0.97774    0.95598    0.01417     0.87912        -0.15462         -0.55669
(CONSTANT)                                                                               -111.70268
```

**FIG. 15.2**   Output from subprogram REGRESSION.

```
MULTIPLE REGRESSION RUN ILLUSTRATING USE OF INCLUSION LEVELS                   06/24/69        PAGE    2

FILE   STOCKP   (CREATION DATA = 06/24/69)    DATA FOR PREDICTION OF INVESTORS INDEX

* * * * * * * * * * * * * * * * * * * *  M U L T I P L E   R E G R E S S I O N  * * * * * * * * * * * * * * * * * * * * * *

DEPENDENT VARIABLE..    INVINDEX    INVESTORS INDEX 1949=100

VARIABLE(S) ENTERED ON STEP NUMBER  1..      GNP        GROSS NATIONAL PRODUCT


MULTIPLE R          0.93729               ANALYSIS OF VARIANCE    DF      SUM OF SQUARES       MEAN SQUARE            F
R SQUARE            0.87852               REGRESSION              1.      339937.40614        339937.40614      216.946
STANDARD ERROR     39.58437               RESIDUAL               30.       47004.68172          1566.92272


-------------- VARIABLES IN THE EQUATION -----------------        ------------- VARIABLES NOT IN THE EQUATION -------------

VARIABLE        B          BETA       STD ERROR B       F          VARIABLE      BETA IN      PARTIAL     TOLERANCE        F

GNP           0.01357     0.93729      0.00092      216.946        CORPPROF    -0.75329     -0.47045     0.04738       8.243
(CONSTANT)  -85.48109                                              CORPDIV      0.50029      0.72182     0.25289      31.545


* * * * * * * * * * * * * * * * * * * * * * * * * * * * * * * * * * * * * * * * * * * * * * * * * * * * * * * * * * * * * *


VARIABLE(S) ENTERED ON STEP NUMBER  2..      CORPPROF   CORPORATE PROFITS BEFORE TAXES


MULTIPLE R          0.95153               ANALYSIS OF VARIANCE    DF      SUM OF SQUARES       MEAN SQUARE            F
R SQUARE            0.90540               REGRESSION              2.      350341.48912        175170.74456      138.783
STANDARD ERROR     35.52736               RESIDUAL               29.       36603.59874          1262.19306


-------------- VARIABLES IN THE EQUATION -----------------        ------------- VARIABLES NOT IN THE EQUATION -------------

VARIABLE        B          BETA       STD ERROR B       F          VARIABLE      BETA IN      PARTIAL     TOLERANCE        F

GNP           0.02421     1.67252      0.00380       40.635        CORPDIV      0.45524      0.73122     0.24406      32.174
CORPPROF     -0.20923    -0.75329      0.07288        8.243
(CONSTANT)  -75.40775
```

**FIG. 15.3**   Output from subprogram REGRESSION: stepwise calculation.

```
STEPWISE MULTIPLE REGRESSION RUN FROM A SYSTEM FILE                          06/24/69        PAGE    3

FILE    STOCKP   (CREATION DATA = 06/24/69)    DATA FOR PREDICTION OF INVESTORS INDEX

* * * * * * * * * * * * * * * * * * *  M U L T I P L E   R E G R E S S I O N  * * * * * * * * * * * * * * * * * * * * * *

DEPENDENT VARIABLE..    INVINDEX   INVESTORS INDEX 1949=100

VARIABLE(S) ENTERED ON STEP NUMBER  3..    CORPDIV    CORPORATE DIVIDENDS PAID


MULTIPLE R          0.97774                   ANALYSIS OF VARIANCE     DF      SUM OF SQUARES        MEAN SQUARE           F
R SQUARE            0.95598                   REGRESSION               3.       369912.82879        123304.27626       202.705
STANDARD ERROR     24.66364                   RESIDUAL                28.        17032.25906           608.29497


---------------- VARIABLES IN THE EQUATION -----------------        ------------- VARIABLES NOT IN THE EQUATION -------------

VARIABLE         B          BETA        STD ERROR B      F           VARIABLE      BETA IN      PARTIAL     TOLERANCE        F

GNP           0.01574     1.08714        0.00303       26.967
CORPPROF     -0.15462    -0.55669        0.05150        9.014
CORPDIV       0.42586     0.45524        0.07508       32.174
(CONSTANT)  -111.70268


MAXIMUM STEP REACHED


MULTIPLE REGRESSION RUN ILLUSTRATING USE OF INCLUSION LEVELS                  07/25/69        PAGE    7

FILE    STOCKP   (CREATION DATE = 07/25/69)    DATA FOR PREDICTION OF INVESTORS INDEX

* * * * * * * * * * * * * * * * * * *  M U L T I P L E   R E G R E S S I O N  * * * * * * * * * * * * * * * * * * * * * *

DEPENDENT VARIABLE..    INVINDEX   INVESTORS INDEX 1949=100

                                               SUMMARY TABLE

VARIABLE                                MULTIPLE R  R SQUARE  RSQ CHANGE  SIMPLE R           B              BETA

GNP         GROSS NATIONAL PRODUCT        0.93729    0.87852    0.87852    0.93729         0.01574        1.08714
CORPPROF    CORPORATE PROFITS BEFORE TAXES 0.95153   0.90540    0.02689    0.87912        -0.15462       -0.55669
CORPDIV     CORPORATE DIVIDENDS PAID      0.97774    0.95598    0.05058    0.93667         0.42586        0.45524
(CONSTANT)                                                                              -111.70268
```

**FIG. 15.3**   *(Continued)*

As a final variation of Example 15.1, we present Example 15.3. This run produces the output shown in Fig. 15.1. In this case, however, the run is accomplished with use of an SPSS system file. Such a file would have been saved in a previous run in a manner similar to that shown in Example 15.2.

**EXAMPLE 15.3**

```
1                       16
RUN NAME                STEPWISE MULTIPLE REGRESSION RUN FROM A SYSTEM FILE
GET FILE                STOCKP
REGRESSION              VARIABLES=INVINDEX,GNP,CORPPROF,CORPDIV/
                        REGRESSION=INVINDEX WITH GNP(6),CORPPROF(4),CORPDIV(2)
FINISH
```

**EXAMPLE 15.4**

```
1                       16
RUN NAME                MULTIPLE REGRESSION WITH MEANS, STD.DEVS., AND MATRIX INPUT
VARIABLE LIST           FRESHGPA, COLBOARD, HIGHSCH, FAMINC, COLBRDSQ
# OF CASES              69
INPUT MEDIUM            CARD
REGRESSION              VARIABLES = FRESHGPA, COLBOARD TO FAMINC/
                        REGRESSION = FRESHGPA WITH COLBOARD, HIGHSCH (2) FAMINC (1)/
                        REGRESSION = COLBOARD (2) WITH HIGHSCH (4), FAMINC (2)/
                        REGRESSION = HIGHSCH (1,.02) WITH FAMINC (1)/
                        VARIABLES = FRESHGPA, COLBRDSQ, COLBOARD/
                        REGRESSION = FRESHGPA WITH COLBRDSQ TO COLBOARD (4)
OPTIONS                 4,5
STATISTICS              2
READ MATRIX
             2.         500.         50.          8.
             1.         100.         20.          5.
       1.0000000   0.7000000   0.0130000   0.1200000
       0.7000000   1.0000000   0.4000000   0.2500000
       0.0130000   0.4000000   1.0000000   0.5000000
       0.1200000   0.2500000   0.5000000   1.0000000
             0.          0.          0.
             1.          1.          1.
       1.0000000   0.7000000  -0.1500000
       0.7000000   1.0000000   0.0000000
      -0.1500000   0.0000000   1.0000000
FINISH
```

Our final run (Example 15.4) is based upon the example discussed in detail in Sec. 15.1.1. Four separate regression equations are formed, using two matrices of correlation coefficients with means and standard deviations supplied by the user. The first card immediately following the READ MATRIX card is the means of the variables FRESHGPA, COLBOARD, HIGHSCH, and FAMINC. The second card contains the standard deviations of the same variables. A 4 × 4 matrix of correlation coefficients for the same variables follows on the succeeding four cards. Three separate multiple-regression runs are made using this data. The next two cards contain means and standard deviations for variables FRESHGPA, COLBOARD, and COLBRDSQ. There follows a 3 × 3 matrix of correlation coefficients for the same variables. This data is used to calculate a single regression equation. The STATISTICS card indicates that means and standard deviations will be printed, but not correlations. The output from this run is listed in Fig. 15.4.

```
MULTIPLE REGRESSION WITH MEANS, STD.DEVS., AND MATRIX INPUT                    07/25/69        PAGE    2

FILE   NONAME    (CREATION DATE = 07/25/69)


VARIABLE          MEAN        STANDARD DEV     CASES

FRESHGPA        2.0000         1.0000           69
COLBOARD      500.0000       100.0000           69
HIGHSCH        50.0000        20.0000           69
FAMINC          8.0000         5.0000           69
FRESHGPA        0.0            1.0000           69
COLBRDSQ        0.0            1.0000           69
COLBOARD        0.0            1.0000           69



MULTIPLE REGRESSION WITH MEANS, STD.DEVS., AND MATRIX INPUT                    06/24/69        PAGE    3

FILE   NONAME    (CREATION DATA = 06/24/69)

* * * * * * * * * * * * * * * * * * * * *  M U L T I P L E   R E G R E S S I O N  * * * * * * * * * * * * * * * * * * * * * * * * *

DEPENDENT VARIABLE..     FRESHGPA

VARIABLE(S) ENTERED ON STEP NUMBER  1..     COLBOARD
                                            HIGHSCH


MULTIPLE R        0.75820              ANALYSIS OF VARIANCE    DF      SUM OF SQUARES      MEAN SQUARE           F
R SQUARE          0.57487              REGRESSION              2.        39.09101          19.54551         44.623
STANDARD ERROR    0.66183              RESIDUAL               66.        28.90899           0.43801


--------------- VARIABLES IN THE EQUATION ------------------     ------------- VARIABLES NOT IN THE EQUATION ------------

VARIABLE         B         BETA      STD ERROR B      F          VARIABLE      BETA IN     PARTIAL     TOLERANCE         F

COLBOARD      0.00827     0.82714     0.00088      89.220        FAMINC       0.09657     0.12801      0.74702       1.083
HIGHSCH      -0.01589    -0.31786     0.00438      13.175
(CONSTANT)   -1.34107


* * * * * * * * * * * * * * * * * * * * * * * * * * * * * * * * * * * * * * * * * * * * * * * * * * * * * * * * * * * * * * * *

VARIABLE(S) ENTERED ON STEP NUMBER  2..     FAMINC


MULTIPLE R        0.76278              ANALYSIS OF VARIANCE    DF      SUM OF SQUARES      MEAN SQUARE           F
R SQUARE          0.58183              REGRESSION              3.        39.56478          13.18826         30.147
STANDARD ERROR    0.66141              RESIDUAL               65.        28.43522           0.43746


--------------- VARIABLES IN THE EQUATION ------------------     ------------- VARIABLES NOT IN THE EQUATION ------------

VARIABLE         B         BETA      STD ERROR B      F          VARIABLE      BETA IN     PARTIAL     TOLERANCE         F

COLBOARD      0.00821     0.82139     0.00088      87.745
HIGHSCH      -0.01819    -0.36384     0.00490      13.773
FAMINC        0.01931     0.09657     0.01856       1.083
(CONSTANT)   -1.35188


ALL VARIABLES ARE IN THE EQUATION
```

**FIG. 15.4**   Output from subprogram REGRESSION generated by example run 15.4.

```
MULTIPLE REGRESSION WITH MEANS, STD.DEVS., AND MATRIX INPUT                    07/25/69      PAGE    4

FILE   NONAME   (CREATION DATE = 07/25/69)

* * * * * * * * * * * * * * * * * * * M U L T I P L E   R E G R E S S I O N * * * * * * * * * * * * * * * * * * * * * * * *

DEPENDENT VARIABLE..    FRESHGPA

                                                    SUMMARY TABLE

VARIABLE                               MULTIPLE R  R SQUARE  RSQ CHANGE  SIMPLE R              B              BETA

COLBOARD                                 0.70000    0.49000    0.49000    0.70000          0.00821          0.82139
HIGHSCH                                  0.75820    0.57487    0.08487    0.01300         -0.01819         -0.36384
FAMINC                                   0.76278    0.58183    0.00697    0.12000          0.01931          0.09657
(CONSTANT)                                                                               -1.35188
```

```
MULTIPLE REGRESSION WITH MEANS, STD.DEVS., AND MATRIX INPUT                    06/24/69      PAGE    5

FILE   NONAME   (CREATION DATA = 06/24/69)

* * * * * * * * * * * * * * * * * * * M U L T I P L E   R E G R E S S I O N * * * * * * * * * * * * * * * * * * * * * * * *

DEPENDENT VARIABLE..    COLBOARD

VARIABLE(S) ENTERED ON STEP NUMBER  1..    HIGHSCH


MULTIPLE R        0.40000              ANALYSIS OF VARIANCE   DF     SUM OF SQUARES        MEAN SQUARE           F
R SQUARE          0.16000              REGRESSION             1.      108800.00000        108800.00000       12.762
STANDARD ERROR   92.33295              RESIDUAL              67.      571200.00000          8525.37313

----------------- VARIABLES IN THE EQUATION ------------------        ------------- VARIABLES NOT IN THE EQUATION -------------

VARIABLE         B         BETA    STD ERROR B      F          VARIABLE       BETA IN    PARTIAL    TOLERANCE       F

HIGHSCH       2.00000    0.40000     0.55985     12.762        FAMINC          0.06667    0.06299     0.75000      0.263
(CONSTANT)  400.00000


* * * * * * * * * * * * * * * * * * * * * * * * * * * * * * * * * * * * * * * * * * * * * * * * * * * * * * * * * * * * * *

VARIABLE(S) ENTERED ON STEP NUMBER  2..    FAMINC


MULTIPLE R        0.40415              ANALYSIS OF VARIANCE   DF     SUM OF SQUARES        MEAN SQUARE           F
R SQUARE          0.16333              REGRESSION             2.      111066.66667        55533.33333        6.442
STANDARD ERROR   92.84504              RESIDUAL              66.      568933.33333          8620.20202

----------------- VARIABLES IN THE EQUATION ------------------        ------------- VARIABLES NOT IN THE EQUATION -------------

VARIABLE         B         BETA    STD ERROR B      F          VARIABLE       BETA IN    PARTIAL    TOLERANCE       F

HIGHSCH       1.83333    0.36667     0.65005      7.954
FAMINC        1.33333    0.06667     2.60018      0.263
(CONSTANT)  397.66667


ALL VARIABLES ARE IN THE EQUATION
```

```
MULTIPLE REGRESSION WITH MEANS, STD.DEVS., AND MATRIX INPUT                    07/25/69      PAGE    6

FILE   NONAME   (CREATION DATE = 07/25/69)

* * * * * * * * * * * * * * * * * * * M U L T I P L E   R E G R E S S I O N * * * * * * * * * * * * * * * * * * * * * * * *

DEPENDENT VARIABLE..    COLBOARD

                                                    SUMMARY TABLE

VARIABLE                               MULTIPLE R  R SQUARE  RSQ CHANGE  SIMPLE R              B              BETA

HIGHSCH                                  0.40000    0.16000    0.16000    0.40000          1.83333          0.36667
FAMINC                                   0.40415    0.16333    0.00333    0.25000          1.33333          0.06667
(CONSTANT)                                                                              397.66667
```

**FIG. 15.4**   *(Continued)*

MULTIPLE REGRESSION WITH MEANS, STD.DEVS., AND MATRIX INPUT                    06/24/69        PAGE    7

FILE    NONAME    (CREATION DATA = 06/24/69)

* * * * * * * * * * * * * * * * * * * * *  M U L T I P L E    R E G R E S S I O N  * * * * * * * * * * * * * * * * * * * * * * *

DEPENDENT VARIABLE..    HIGHSCH

VARIABLE(S) ENTERED ON STEP NUMBER  1..    FAMINC

| | | | | | | | | |
|---|---|---|---|---|---|---|---|---|
| MULTIPLE R | 0.50000 | | ANALYSIS OF VARIANCE | DF | SUM OF SQUARES | MEAN SQUARE | | F |
| R SQUARE | 0.25000 | | REGRESSION | 1. | 6800.00000 | 6800.00000 | | 22.333 |
| STANDARD ERROR | 17.44929 | | RESIDUAL | 67. | 20400.00000 | 304.47761 | | |

---------------- VARIABLES IN THE EQUATION ------------------          ------------- VARIABLES NOT IN THE EQUATION -------------

| VARIABLE | B | BETA | STD ERROR B | F | | VARIABLE | BETA IN | PARTIAL | TOLERANCE | F |
|---|---|---|---|---|---|---|---|---|---|---|
| FAMINC | 2.00000 | 0.50000 | 0.42321 | 22.333 | | | | | | |
| (CONSTANT) | 34.00000 | | | | | | | | | |

ALL VARIABLES ARE IN THE EQUATION


MULTIPLE REGRESSION WITH MEANS, STD.DEVS., AND MATRIX INPUT                    07/25/69        PAGE    8

FILE    NONAME    (CREATION DATE = 07/25/69)

* * * * * * * * * * * * * * * * * * * * *  M U L T I P L E    R E G R E S S I O N  * * * * * * * * * * * * * * * * * * * * * * *

DEPENDENT VARIABLE..    HIGHSCH

                                            SUMMARY TABLE

| VARIABLE | MULTIPLE R | R SQUARE | RSQ CHANGE | SIMPLE R | B | BETA |
|---|---|---|---|---|---|---|
| FAMINC | 0.50000 | 0.25000 | 0.25000 | 0.50000 | 2.00000 | 0.50000 |
| (CONSTANT) | | | | | 34.00000 | |


MULTIPLE REGRESSION WITH MEANS, STD.DEVS., AND MATRIX INPUT                    06/24/69        PAGE    9

FILE    NONAME    (CREATION DATA = 06/24/69)

* * * * * * * * * * * * * * * * * * * * *  M U L T I P L E    R E G R E S S I O N  * * * * * * * * * * * * * * * * * * * * * * *

DEPENDENT VARIABLE..    FRESHGPA

VARIABLE(S) ENTERED ON STEP NUMBER  1..    COLBOARD
                                           COLBRDSQ

| | | | | | | | | |
|---|---|---|---|---|---|---|---|---|
| MULTIPLE R | 0.71589 | | ANALYSIS OF VARIANCE | DF | SUM OF SQUARES | MEAN SQUARE | | F |
| R SQUARE | 0.51250 | | REGRESSION | 2. | 34.85000 | 17.42500 | | 34.692 |
| STANDARD ERROR | 0.70871 | | RESIDUAL | 66. | 33.15000 | 0.50227 | | |

---------------- VARIABLES IN THE EQUATION ------------------          ------------- VARIABLES NOT IN THE EQUATION -------------

| VARIABLE | B | BETA | STD ERROR B | F | | VARIABLE | BETA IN | PARTIAL | TOLERANCE | F |
|---|---|---|---|---|---|---|---|---|---|---|
| COLBOARD | -0.15000 | -0.15000 | 0.08594 | 3.046 | | | | | | |
| COLBRDSQ | 0.70000 | 0.70000 | 0.08594 | 66.338 | | | | | | |
| (CONSTANT) | 0.0 | | | | | | | | | |

ALL VARIABLES ARE IN THE EQUATION


MULTIPLE REGRESSION WITH MEANS, STD.DEVS., AND MATRIX INPUT                    07/25/69        PAGE    10

FILE    NONAME    (CREATION DATE = 07/25/69)

* * * * * * * * * * * * * * * * * * * * *  M U L T I P L E    R E G R E S S I O N  * * * * * * * * * * * * * * * * * * * * * * *

DEPENDENT VARIABLE..    FRESHGPA

                                            SUMMARY TABLE

| VARIABLE | MULTIPLE R | R SQUARE | RSQ CHANGE | SIMPLE R | B | BETA |
|---|---|---|---|---|---|---|
| COLBOARD | 0.15000 | 0.02250 | 0.02250 | -0.15000 | -0.15000 | -0.15000 |
| COLBRDSQ | 0.71589 | 0.51250 | 0.49000 | 0.70000 | 0.70000 | 0.70000 |
| (CONSTANT) | | | | | 0.0 | |

**FIG. 15.4**    (*Continued*)

# 16
# SCALOGRAM ANALYSIS: SUBPROGRAM GUTTMAN SCALE

Subprogram GUTTMAN SCALE[1] provides the user with the capability of producing up to 50 separate Guttman scales on a single task. The scales are evaluated by a simplified variant of the Goodenough technique.[2] Each item included in a scale may have up to three cutting points, and an individual scale is computed for each possible combination of cutting points specified. While the user selects the cutting points, the subprogram itself accomplishes the dichotomization. Scales with multiple cutting points count only as one scale in terms of the 50-scale limitation, even though a unique scale is produced for each combination of cutting points.

The order of the items may be automatically determined by the subprogram according to the percentage of the respondents who "fail" or "reject" each of the items. Alternatively, the user may fix the order of the items himself. In addition to the basic table giving the frequencies,

[1]The Guttman Scale program is based in part upon routines developed by Ronald E. Anderson. See R. E. Anderson, A Computer Program for Guttman Scaling with the Goodenough Technique, *Behavioral Science*, Vol. 11, No. 3, p. 235, May, 1966. Anderson's original program, developed at the Institute of Sociological Research, University of Washington, was later modified to handle multiple cutting points by Anderson and Lynne Ofshe in affiliation with the Stanford Computation Center.

[2]See W. H. Goodenough, A Technique for Scale Analysis, *Educ. Psychol. Measmt.*, pp. 179-190; 1944, and A. L. Edwards, On Guttman Scale Analysis, *Educ. Psychol. Measmt.*, Vol. 8, pp. 313-318, 1948.

errors, and scale types, the user may request a number of statistics which will aid him in evaluating the scales. Included in the available statistics are: (1) the coefficient of reproducibility, (2) the minimum marginal reproducibility, (3) the percent improvement, and (4) the coefficient of scalability. Inter-item correlations and part-whole correlations may also be requested. Missing data may be included or excluded from the scales.

As usual, all the data-selection and data-modification procedures may be employed (for either temporary or permanent modifications) while using subprogram GUTTMAN SCALE. Before proceeding to the detailed description of the program or the features described above, a brief introduction to Guttman scaling will be presented for users who are not completely familiar with the Guttman scaling technique.

## 16.1   AN INTRODUCTION TO GUTTMAN SCALE ANALYSIS[1]

In the course of data analysis, the social science researcher may construct many types of indexes. The term *index* has come to mean any measure which combines the values of several variables or items into a composite measure. In general, indexes are used to predict or gauge some underlying continuum which can be only partially measured by any single item or variable which is included in the index. The Dow Jones Index, which evaluates the overall performance of the New York Stock Exchange, averaging the losses and gains of a selected number of individual issues, is an excellent example of a multiple-item index.

Social scientists, particularly those engaged in psychological and attitudinal research, have developed a large number of techniques for combining individual items into scales and indexes. Some of these techniques are quite simple. For example, Likert indexes are computed by simply summing the responses to a number of items each taking a value from 5 (agree strongly) to 1 (disagree strongly) assumed to be measuring part of the same underlying continuum. Other techniques which attempt to assess and utilize the interrelationships and/or operating characteristics of the component items (such as factor indexes and Guttman scales) are considerably more complicated.[2]

One of these techniques, scalogram analysis, commonly termed *Guttman scaling* after its originator, has become widely used in many types of social science research, particularly in the area of attitude measurement in survey research. Because of its wide application, the SPSS system includes subprogram GUTTMAN SCALE which enables the user to perform basic scalogram analysis on any set of variables in his file.

Guttman scale analysis is a means of analyzing the underlying operating characteristics of three or more items in order to determine if their interrelationships meet several special properties which define a Guttman scale. Guttman scales must first be unidimensional; that is, the component items must all measure movement toward or away from the same single underlying object. The substance of the object is unimportant; it may be racial prejudice, sense of political efficacy, or even the technological development of societies. Similarly, the unit of analysis may be individuals, nations, etc.

Second, Guttman scales must be cumulative, and it is this property which differentiates Guttman scales from almost all other types of scales and indexes. Operationally, a cumulative scale implies that the component items can be ordered by degree of difficulty and that respondents who reply positively to a difficult item will always respond positively to less difficult items and vice versa. Perhaps the best method for explaining the basic concepts behind Guttman scales is to introduce a hypothetical example and to trace the items in this example through the scaling procedure.

[1]This brief discussion is in no way complete and should not be used as a substitute for a detailed explanation of the logic or method behind scalogram analysis. A large and excellent literature exists on scalogram analysis. See, for just a few examples, Allen L. Edwards, "Techniques of Attitude and Scale Construction", Chaps. 7 and 9, Appleton-Century-Crofts, New York, 1957; Warren S. Torgerson, "Theory and Methods of Scaling", Wiley, New York, 1958, and Bert F. Green, Jr., Attitude Measurement, in G. Lindzey (ed.), "Handbook of Social Psychology", Addison-Wesley, Cambridge, Mass., 1956.

[2]The variable transformation capabilities of SPSS were specifically designed so that the user could employ a number of these techniques as well as his own index constructions by utilizing the arithmetic and logical expressions available on the COMPUTE and IF cards (see Secs. 3.1.2.1 and 3.1.3).

One of the early and classical applications of Guttman scaling was in the creation of social distance or prejudice scales.[1] The *social-distance* scale is an excellent example of the Guttman scale, because the underlying concepts of these types of scales are directly related to the operational definitions and procedures used in building the scales.

Let us assume that a researcher wished to determine if the following five items from a sample survey would form a Guttman scale of racial prejudice. Let us further assume that respondents were asked to tell the interviewer whether he or she agreed or disagreed with each of the five statements, and that agreement with any statement was coded as a 1 and disagreement as a 0.

A.   In general, I would have no objections to my son or daughter dating a Negro as long as (he or she) were a good person.
B.   At a party with my friends, I would not hesitate at all to ask a Negro to dance if I were attracted to (him or her) as a person.
C.   I would have no objections to inviting a Negro to dine in my house.
D.   In general, I would not object to having a Negro family live next door.
E.   In general, I would not object to sitting next to a Negro on a bus.

First, it is clear that each of these items attempts to measure distance from a single object, individuals of the Negro race. Second, it is also clear that the items have been designed to reflect different positions on the continuum of racial prejudice, so that the mildly prejudiced person would be more likely to respond "yes" to item E than to item A.

Specifically, each item in a Guttman scale must be ordinal to the degree of having the capacity of being divided at some point into two portions—pass or fail or yes or no. These items clearly meet these criteria, and because they have been precoded into yes and no responses, there is no need to select cutting points. In general, however, respondents or observations which have values equal to or greater than the selected cutting points are considered to have "passed" an item, while those having values less than the cutting point are considered to have "failed" the item. From this point on in the discussion, passing or accepting an item will be indicated by a score of 1, while failing or rejecting an item will be indicated by a score of 0.

Once all of the constituent items have been assigned a pass-fail cutting point, they must display the capacity of being ordered from most difficult to least difficult. This ordering is usually, but not necessarily, obtained by sorting the items in descending order according to the proportion of respondents who fail or reject the items. Alternatively, the researcher may himself decide on the order of the items. However, major differences from the order suggested by the proportion of respondents passing and failing the items will decrease the probability that the scale will meet the Guttman criteria. In this case, let us assume that item A contains the highest proportion of respondents replying negatively, item E contains the lowest, and items B, C, and D fall between A and E and can be placed in that order by the proportion of respondents who replied "no" to these items.

The logic behind the above procedures becomes clear when the test of unidimensionality and cumulativeness devised by Guttman is applied to the items. The degree to which a group of items is both unidimensional and cumulative is determined by the extent to which "passes" (scores of 1) on any item are associated with scores of 1 on all items which have been ranked as less difficult. The inverse is also true; that is, a scale is unidimensional and cumulative insofar as scores of 0 (rejection) on any item are associated with scores of 0 on all items which have been judged to be more difficult.

This fits nicely with the concept behind the items in our social distance or racial-prejudice scale. One would expect, for example, that it would be perfectly plausible for a respondent to reply that he did not mind sitting next to a Negro on a bus, but at the same time respond that he would not be willing to invite a Negro to dine in his home. However, the same logic would suggest that one would *not* expect respondents who did not object to inviting a Negro to dine in their homes to object to sitting next to Negroes on a bus. By intuitive standards, inviting

[1]Emory S. Bogardus, Racial Distance Changes in the United States During the Past Thirty Years, *Sociology and Social Research*, Vol. XLIII, pp. 127-134, November, 1958.

a Negro to dine in one's own home means the acceptance of a greater amount of social intimacy with members of the Negro race than does simply sitting next to a Negro on a bus. On the other hand, sitting next to Negroes on a bus gives us only partial information about the likelihood of a respondent agreeing with the statement concerning inviting Negroes to dine in one's home. If the respondent rejected even the notion of sitting next to Negroes, we would not expect him to invite a Negro to dine in his home. However, he may be only somewhat prejudiced, believing that Negroes can sit anywhere they wish on a bus, but still feel that he does not want the more intimate contact implied in having a Negro dine in his home.

Extending the logic of this particular scale as well as the general logic of Guttman scale analysis, one would expect the responses to items to form the following pattern:

| Scale type | Items | | | | |
|---|---|---|---|---|---|
| | A | B | C | D | E |
| 5 | 1 | 1 | 1 | 1 | 1 |
| 4 | 0 | 1 | 1 | 1 | 1 |
| 3 | 0 | 0 | 1 | 1 | 1 |
| 2 | 0 | 0 | 0 | 1 | 1 |
| 1 | 0 | 0 | 0 | 0 | 1 |
| 0 | 0 | 0 | 0 | 0 | 0 |

If the five items under analysis formed a perfect Guttman scale, all the responses would conform to the ideal pattern above. That is, all respondents who passed only one item would pass item E and no others. Respondents passing two items would always pass items D and E and not items A, B, or C. The passing of a more difficult item would never be associated with rejecting a less difficult one.

But data rarely, if ever, perfectly fit the expectations of the researcher.[1] And the test of scalability of the items in the Guttman procedure is the degree to which the data indeed fit the model. Each deviation from the expected pattern is counted as an error. The errors are then accumulated, and a number of standardized coefficients are produced from them to enable the researcher to determine if the items do indeed form a Guttman scale, i.e., a scale which is both unidimensional and cumulative.

The following section indicates the exact procedure used to evaluate Guttman scales and presents some sample output from subprogram GUTTMAN SCALE so that the user may tie this discussion directly to the use of the subprogram.

### 16.1.1 EVALUATING GUTTMAN SCALES

An examination of the following sample output (Fig. 16.1) should enable the user to better understand the GUTTMAN SCALE subprogram as well as the general evaluation of Guttman scales. First, examine the respondents who are of scale type 2; that is, all the respondents who passed two of the three items in the scale. Had these items formed a perfect Guttman scale, all 57 of these respondents would have passed items NHELP and NMEM but none of them would have passed INCOMER. As it stands, however, 23 of the 57 respondents with a scale score of two failed NHELP, the least difficult item. Note also that 11 of the 57 respondents failed item NMEM when they should have passed it. Furthermore, and most devastating to this Guttman scale, 34 of these 57 respondents passed the most difficult item INCOMER when they should have failed it. As an aid to interpreting those responses which are to be considered errors, the subprogram prints the term ERR above those responses which (based on their scale score)

[1]Many factors may cause deviations from the expected pattern. The attitudes of many citizens, for example, may be poorly organized and their prejudices inconsistant as measured from one item to another. It is also conceivable for the perfectly rational nonprejudiced respondent to be more concerned with the value of his property than with equality for Negro citizens. While he personally has no objection to a Negro living in his neighborhood, his perceived concern for his property value may cause him to pass an item which the researcher feels is difficult, while rejecting one which the researcher has designed to be considerably less difficult. One could obviously go on at great length speculating as to why respondents deviate from the expected Guttman pattern.

```
DEMONSTRATE THE SPSS PACKAGE

FILE    DEMO      DEMONSTRATION FILE FROM VERBA'S U.S. STUDY
SUBFILE CITY1     CITY2
```

```
* * * * * * * * *   G U T T M A N   S C A L E   ( S C A L E 0 1  )  U S I N G
INCOMER    RECODED ANNUAL FAMILY INCOME            DIVISION POINT =     5.00
NMEM       TOTAL # ORGANIZATIONAL MEMBERSHIPS      DIVISION POINT =     1.00
NHELP      # OF RECEIPTS OF WELFARE SERVICES       DIVISION POINT =     8.00
* * * * * * * * * *     RESP = 1 FOR VALUES EQUAL TO DIVISION POINT AND ABOVE  * *
```

Scale type                    Responses below here are errors

```
ITEM.. INCOMER    NMEM       NHELP

RESP.. 0    1 I  0  1 I  0    1 I TOTAL
--I--I-ERR-----I-ERR----I-ERR-----I
S    I       I       I          I
C  3 I 0   13I  0  13I  0    13I   13
A    I------ERRI       I          I
L    I       I       I          I
E  2 I 23  34I 11  46I 23   34I   57
0    I      I------ERRI          I
1    I      I       I          I
   1 I 83   8I 74  17I 25   66I   91
     I       I       I------ERRI
     I       I       I          I
   0 I 47   0I 47   0I 47    0I   47
     I---------I---------I---------I
SUMS   153  55 132  76  95  113    208
PCTS    74  26  63  37  46   54
ERRORS   0  42  11  17  48    0    118
```

Failed—should have passed
Passed—should have failed

```
     220 CASES WERE PROCESSED
      12 (OR  5.5 PTC) WERE MISSING
```

Respondents with a score of 2
Who failed item 'NHELP'

Respondents with a score of 2
Who passed item 'NHELP'

Total respondents with
a score of 2

Total nonmissing cases

Total errors

Respondents passing item
% passing item
Respondents failing item
% failing item

```
STATISTICS..

COEFFICIENT OF REPRODUCIBILITY = 0.8109
MINIMUM MARGINAL REPRODUCIBILITY = 0.6378
PERCENT IMPROVEMENT = 0.1731
COEFFICIENT OF SCALABILITY = 0.4779


CORRELATION COEFFICIENTS..

            INCOMER    NMEM       NHELP

INCOMER      1.0000   0.6852    -0.2847
NMEM         0.6852   1.0000    -0.2174
NHELP       -0.2847  -0.2174     1.0000
SCALE-ITEM  -0.1166  -0.2384    -0.6491
```

**FIG. 16.1**   Output from subprogram GUTTMAN SCALE.

passed an item when they should have failed it or failed an item which should have passed.

The percent of the respondents passing and failing each item are printed at the bottom of the table along the row marked PCTS. This should give the user some notion as to the efficacy of the dividing points he has chosen. Note particularly the percentage pass and fail of NHELP compared to that of NMEM. The division point selected for NHELP has made it almost as difficult to pass as NMEM and INCOMER, the division point selected has therefore caused the accumulation of many more errors than might have occurred had a lower cutting point for NHELP been chosen.

An item-by-item accumulation of errors is printed across the bottom of the table alongside the heading ERRORS. The left value under each of the items gives the number of respondents who failed the item when they should have passed it, and the right value indicates the number of respondents who passed the item when they should have failed it. The left value (under the heading ERRORS) of the most difficult item in any scale will always be zero, as will be right-most value of the least difficult item, for this is the only way that respondents can enter the maximum and minimum scale types. Again, the large number of errors among those who should have passed the least difficult item but failed it, and the large number of errors among those who passed the most difficult item, but should have failed it, point to the weakness of these items as a Guttman scale. It is unclear whether a change in the cutting points and/or in the order of the items would improve this scale. The interitem correlations suggest it would not. The correlations indicate that item NHELP has little business in this scale; the correlations between this item and the other two variables are not only quite small, but negative.

The program also enables the user to select among four statistics which can aid him in evaluating the scalability of the items. First, the *coefficient of reproducibility* is a measure of the extent to which a respondent's scale score is a predictor of his response pattern. Mathematically, it is 1 minus the result of dividing the total number of errors by the total number of responses,[1] and it varies from 0 to 1. A general guideline to the interpretation of this measure is that a coefficient of reproducibility higher than .9 is considered to indicate a valid scale. Note that in the above example, the coefficient of reproducibility is only .8109. Since it is possible to dichotomize variables at the user's discretion, it is obvious that judicious manipulating of the cutting points can result in a very high coefficient of reproducibility. A second measure, the *minimum marginal reproducibility,* constitutes the minimum coefficient of reproducibility that could have occurred for the scale given the cutting points used and the proportion of respondents passing and failing each of the items. It is calculated by summing the maximum marginals for each item and dividing this sum by the total number of responses. The difference between the coefficient of reproducibility and the minimum marginal reproducibility indicates the extent to which the former is due to response patterns rather than the inherent cumulative interrlation of the variables used. This difference is called *the percent improvement* and is actually the difference in two percents rather than a ratio itself. Note that in this case it is quite small. The final measure is obtained by dividing the percent improvement by the difference between 1 and the minimum marginal reproducibility. The denominator represents the largest value that the percent improvement may attain, and the resulting ratio is called the *coefficient of scalability.* The coefficient of scalability also varies from 0 to 1, and should be well above .6 if the scale is truly unidimensional and cumulative. In this case the coefficient is below .5.

As an aid to the user in determining whether a particular item or group of items did or did not constitute a scale, the SPSS system can provide a set of correlation coefficients. First, each item is correlated with every other item to yield the inter-item correlation matrix. The correlation coefficients are Yules Q. Second, a set of part-whole correlations is printed. The part-whole correlations consist of each item being correlated with the sum of all other items. The coefficients are Bi-serial. These measures enable the user to easily spot items that are not positively related to the other items in the scale.

### 16.1.2 BUILDING GUTTMAN SCALES

Once the data has been processed through subprogram GUTTMAN SCALE and the user has obtained one or more sets of items which meet the Guttman criteria, the next step will be to actually construct the scale or scales. Each respondent may be assigned a scale score based on the number of items passed. The COMPUTE and IF cards described in Secs. 8.2, 8.2.1, and 8.2.2, are used to specify the values to be assigned to the new scale variable. The new scale or scales can be permanently added to the variables in an existing SPSS system file by saving a new file at the conclusion of the run (see Secs. 7.2 and 7.2.1). Alternatively, the user may wish to have the cases containing the new scales (as well as some or all the existing variables) punched on cards or written in BCD form on tape, disk, etc. This can be accomplished by using the WRITE CASES procedure card described in Sec. 10.5.

Unfortunately, there is not total agreement among researchers as to the best procedure to be used in assigning scale scores to those cases or respondents who do not conform to one of the *perfect scale types*[2] We feel that if a group of items passes the rather stringent require-

---

[1]The total number of responses is the total number of (nonmissing) respondents times the number of items.

[2]A perfect scale type is one of the types of patterns predicted or expected by the scale and one which contributes no errors in the evaluation of the scale. In a four-item Guttman scale, where the items have been ordered by their degree of difficulty, the following five patterns are all of the perfect scale types: 0000, 0001, 0011, 0111, 1111. All other patterns of pass and fail contribute one or more errors to the scale.

ments of the Guttman evaluating procedure, assigning each case a scale score based on the number of items passed (whether or not they are perfect scale types) is a sound procedure. After all, if a group of items meets the test of unidimensionality and cumulativeness, the number of items passed will be an excellent predictor of the pattern of the responses, for this is precisely the operational procedure employed in accumulating the errors and generating the coefficients. For these reasons, subprogram GUTTMAN SCALE makes no special provisions for identifying nonscale types.

However, we should note that some researchers feel that special procedures should be followed in assigning scores to nonscale types. One of these procedures, the *modified latent distance* technique, involves a rather complicated method for computing the joint probability of a respondent falling between points on the scale or continuum being constructed.[1] Another technique, the *minimum error criterion*, which is computationally much simpler, is often employed in assigning scale scores to nonscale types and assigns respondents' scale scores which minimize the number of errors they add to the overall scale.[2]

If the user wishes to utilize one of these techniques, he may dichotomize the items at their cutting points (using the RECODE procedure) and pass the data through subprograms CROSSTABS or FASTABS to obtain all the information required to determine the scale score for each nonscale-type response pattern. The user may then construct COMPUTE and IF statements to assign scores to the nonscale types as well as to the scale types. If there is a large number of items involved in the scale, these statements will, however, get quite complicated. The authors are quite aware that this is a terribly cumbersome procedure. However, to have included this capability in the GUTTMAN SCALE subprogram itself would have meant imposing severe limitations on the number of scales which could be evaluated on a single pass, the number of cases which could have been processed, as well as causing a significant decrease in the processing speed on the subprogram. We frankly do not feel that the capability of identifying nonscale types justifies its cost in terms of the sacrifices it would require of other capabilities presently contained in subprogram GUTTMAN SCALE.

Scale scores for the new variable (i.e., the Guttman scale being generated) may be assigned by a sequence of COMPUTE and IF cards of the following type:

```
1                   16
COMPUTE             GUTSCAL1 = 0
IF                  (ITEMA GE 2) GUTSCAL1 = 1
IF                  (ITEMB GE 3) GUTSCAL1 = GUTSCAL1 + 1
IF                  (ITEMC GE 5) GUTSCAL1 = GUTSCAL1 + 1
IF                  (ITEMD GE 2) GUTSCAL1 = GUTSCAL1 + 1
```

In the above sequence of cards, the new scale variable GUTSCAL1 is first set equal to zero. The four IF cards specify the conditions under which 1 will be added to the scale score of each respondent. The GE-constant portion of the logical expression informs the system to execute the indicated operations on variable GUTSCAL1 (i.e., those operations specified to the right of the =) when, and only when, the case contains a value for the item greater than or equal to the constant. The constant is, of course, the division point. The operations always add 1 to the previous scale score. If the case contains a value less than the cutting point, no operations will be executed, and the scale score will remain as it was at the conclusion of the previous statement. That is to say, the COMPUTE and IF statements are cumulative. The results of the sequence of cards will always be a single value, in this case, between 0 and 4. For cases in which the respondent failed all four of the items, the scale score will be zero. It was initially set to zero and would be unaltered by the IF cards, because its values on all four of the items are below the specified cutting point. If a case contains two values greater than the specified constant, its scale score would be 2. If it had four such values, its score would be 4, etc. The order of the IF statements if unimportant as long as each pass (i.e., a value greater than or equal to the cutting point) adds 1 to the overall score. Had all the items in the scale been

---

[1] Improved Model for a Latent Distance Scale, paper 3, *The Use of Mathematical Models in the Measurement of Attitudes, H.M.-455, Part II,* prepared under the direction of Paul F. Lazarsfeld, Columbia University, U. S. Air Force Project "Rand", The Rand Corporation, Santa Monica, California, 1951.

[2] Andrew F. Henry, A Method of Classifying Non-Scale Response Patterns in a Guttman Scale, *P.O.Q.,* vol. 16, no. 1, pp. 94-106, 1952.

precoded with 0 and 1 values, the same results would be achieved by simply summing the items by means of a COMPUTE card of the following type:

```
1              16
COMPUTE        GUTSCAL1 = ITEMA + ITEMB + ITEMB + ITEMC + ITEMD
```

If the user desires to have cases with missing values on component items to also be considered missing on the new scale, he must define the missing values for the scale. As with all variables generated by variable transformations, cases to be designated as missing can be assigned a special value by means of an IF statement. If we desired, for example, to exclude any case which contained a missing value on one or more items composing the above scale, we could do so by means of the following IF statement and an accompanying MISSING VALUES card which actually defines the missing value for the new variable. This statement assumes that the value 9 was used as the missing value for all variables being used to build the scale.

```
1              16
IF             (ITEMA EQ 9 OR ITEMB EQ 9 OR ITEMC EQ 9 OR ITEMD EQ 9)
               GUTSCAL1 = 9
MISSING VALUES GUTSCAL1(9)
```

These two cards would directly follow the cards used to construct the scale.

## 16.2    THE GUTTMAN SCALE PROCEDURE CARD

The user calls and activates subprogram GUTTMAN SCALE by a procedure card containing the control words GUTTMAN SCALE followed by the name to be given to the first scale to be produced on that task. The scale name serves only to identify the scale and its associated table on the printed output. The name is not entered into the variable list, nor do the scale scores become part of the file. Any name of the user's choice may be selected as long as it does not exceed eight characters in length and the first character is an alphabetic letter. All other rules and conventions concerning the use of names on SPSS control cards must also be followed (see Secs. 3.1.2.1 and 3.1.3). The scale name is followed by the special delimiter, the equal sign [=]. The equal sign is in turn followed by a list of individual variable names and their associated division points to be included in the scale. Any variable which has been previously defined on a variable list, from an existing system file, or a variable created by means of a transformation, may be included on the list. A maximum of 12 variables may be entered onto a single scale. Each variable named on this list is directly followed by from one to three division points enclosed in parentheses. When there is a single division point, the variable name is followed by a left parenthesis, the value to become the division point, and then a right parenthesis. When there is to be more than one division point (two or three), the left parenthesis is followed by the value to become the first division point, one or more common delimiters, the value to become the second division point, etc. Multiple cutting points must be separated from each other by one or more common delimiters.

When all the variables to be included in a scale and their associated cutting points have been entered, the user may place a slash [/] following the closing parenthesis of the division point(s) of the last variable. The slash may be followed by a second scale name, and the procedure of entering the variables and their cutting points is repeated. Up to 50 individual scales may be defined on the GUTTMAN SCALE card and its continuations. As usual, no variable name or individual value can be split between physical cards, and columns 1 to 15 of all cards after the first must be left blank. The general format of the GUTTMAN SCALE card is then as follows:

```
1              16
GUTTMAN SCALE  scale name=variable name (division point) variable name
               (division point) variable name (division point) . . . /
               scale name=variable name (division point) variable name
               (division point) . . .
```

If the user is allowing the subprogram to automatically order the variables by the percentage of respondents failing the item, the order he uses to input the variable names is unimportant. If, however, he selects option 3 (which forces his ordering on the items), the variable names must be entered on the GUTTMAN SCALE card in the order he desires. The left-most variable named will be considered the most difficult item, the right-most, the least difficult. All variables in between will be taken from left to right and are assumed to be in decreasing order of difficulty.

As explained previously, the division or cutting point is the value which will be used to determine whether a respondent has passed or failed the item. Respondents with values greater than or equal to the cutting point will be assumed to have passed the item, while those with values less than the cutting point will be assumed to have failed it. Integers or decimal numbers may be used as cutting points. Each item may have a maximum of three division points associated with it. When one or more items have multiple cutting points, one scale will be produced for each possible combination of cutting points, so that a three-item scale with three specified cutting points per item will produce 27 scales, each with its own table, statistics, etc. These 27 scales will, however, only count as one scale towards the maximum of 50 scales which can be produced from a single GUTTMAN SCALE card. When one or more items in a scale have multiple cutting points, the left-most cutting points of all variables are used to compute the first scale. The second cutting point of the left-most variable is then used, and a second scale is produced. The cutting points associated with the left-most variable are rotated first, and those applying to the last or right-most variable are rotated last. The number of scales which will be produced is the product of the number of cutting points for the first variable times the number of cutting points in the second times . . . the number of cutting points in the last variable. As the user can readily see, a great number of scales can be produced with just the addition of a few cutting points. Be judicious, or you will be buried in output.

The following example GUTTMAN SCALE card will cause two independent Guttman scales, named PREJSCAL and GUTSCAL2, to be generated. The second scale, GUTSCAL2, will actually produce four scales, because ITEM3 and ITEM4 each have two associated division points.

```
1                    16
GUTTMAN SCALE   PREJSCAL = DATE(2)DINE(3)NEIGHBOR(1)SITBUS(4)/GUTSCAL2=
                ITEM1(3)ITEM2(4.3)ITEM3(1,2)ITEM4(0.5,1)
```

## 16.3   OPTIONS AVAILABLE FOR SUBPROGRAM GUTTMAN SCALE

The following options are available for subprogram GUTTMAN SCALE. As usual, the options are selected by number on an OPTIONS card which directly follows the procedure card.

*Option* 1.   Causes missing data to be entered into all scales and computations. The default option for missing values causes a case to be deleted from an entire scale if the value of any variable or item in that scale is missing. The user should be aware in building scales with a large number of items that this deletion procedure can drastically reduce the number of cases which will be included in the scale.

*Option* 2.   Causes the printing of variable labels to be suppressed. Normally, the variable labels for all component items appear in the header describing each scale.

*Option* 3.   Causes the automatic ordering of variables from most to least difficult to be suppressed. When the option is used, the order of difficulty of the items in the scale will be taken from the GUTTMAN SCALE procedure card. The left-most variable will be considered the most difficult, and the variables will be entered from left to right; the last variable entered will be considered the least difficult item in the scale. Normally (i.e., when option 3 is not employed), the items are ordered in the degree of difficulty according to the proportion of respondents failing or rejecting the item. The variable or item having the greatest proportion of respondents failing it is considered the most difficult. The item with the next highest proportion of rejections is second, and so on. If the OPTIONS card is deleted, missing data will be excluded, variable labels will be printed, and items will be ordered by the proportion of respondents failing each of the items.

## 16.4  STATISTICS AVAILABLE FOR SUBPROGRAM GUTTMAN SCALE

The following statistics are available for subprogram GUTTMAN SCALE. They are, as usual, requested by means of the STATISTICS card. Each statistic and its corresponding statistic number is listed below. If the user desires all of the statistics, he may replace the number list with the keyword ALL. A brief discussion of these statistics can be found in Sec. 16.2. As usual, the STATISTICS card is placed directly behind the OPTIONS card. If the OPTIONS card is deleted, the STATISTICS card directly follows the GUTTMAN SCALE procedure card.

*Correspondence between Statistics and Statistics Numbers*

1 = *Inter-item and Part-Whole Correlation Coefficients*
   Selection of this statistic will cause a matrix of Yules Q correlation coefficients to be printed for all items included in the scale. In addition, the correlation between each item with the sum of all other items in the scale (i.e., part-whole correlations of the Bi-serial type) will also be printed.
2 = *Coefficient of Reproducibility*
3 = *Minimum Marginal Reproducibility*
4 = *Percent Improvement Achieved by Guttman Scale*
5 = *Coefficient of Scalability*

## 16.5  LIMITATIONS OF SUBPROGRAM GUTTMAN SCALE

The following limitations are presently in effect for subprogram GUTTMAN SCALE:

*Limitation* 1.  No more than 50 scales can be constructive exclusive of additional scales accounted for by use of multiple cutting points.

*Limitation* 2.  No more than 12 items (variables) may be used in any single scale.

*Limitation* 3.  No more than 3 cutting points may be present for any single item in any scale.

*Limitation* 4.  No more than 100 unique items (variables) may be mentioned in all the scales.

*Limitation* 5.  No more than (SPACE/4) cells may be required for computations.[1]

Cell usage may be calculated as follows, where N is the number of variables or items. Each scale requires $2 \times N \times (N + 1)$ cells for each possible combination of cutting points. Additionally, $(N \times N - N)/2$ cells are required for each possible combination of cutting points if correlations are to be printed. For example, 20 scales of 12 items each with 1 cutting point per item with correlations will require

$$2 \times 12 \times (12 + 1) + (12 \times 12 - 12)/2$$

or

$312 + 66$ or 378 cells for each scale or 7560 cells total.

## 16.6  SAMPLE DECK SETUP AND OUTPUT FOR SUBPROGRAM GUTTMAN SCALE

Example 16.1 illustrates the use of subprogram GUTTMAN SCALE in a run utilizing an SPSS system file. The system file used is named ORGSTUDY and is retrieved with the use of the GET FILE card. The purpose of the run is to create three scale items RECMEM, OCCMEM, and ALTMEM, and to test if they pass the tests required to form a Guttman scale. In the file ORGSTUDY, there are a number of variables which are coded 1 if the respondent is a member of a certain type of organization, and 0 otherwise.

[1]For a discussion of the parameter SPACE, see Appendix F.2. The default value of SPACE is 80,000.

**EXAMPLE 16.1**

```
1               16
RUN NAME        GUTTMAN SCALE CONSTRUCTION
GET FILE        ORGSTUDY
COMPUTE         ALTMEM=FRATMEM+VETMEM+SCHOLMEM+NATMEM+RELMEM
IF              (ALTMEM GT 1) ALTMEM=1
COMPUTE         OCCMEM=SERVMEM+UNIONMEM+PROFMEM+FARMEM
IF              (OCCMEM GT 1) OCCMEM=1
COMPUTE         RECMEM=SPORTMEM+HOBMEM+LITMEM+SCHFRMEM
IF              (RECMEM GT 1) RECMEM=1
VAR LABELS      ALTMEM,MEMBER OF SERVICE-ORIENTED GROUP/
                OCCMEM,MEMBER OF OCCUPATIONAL GROUP/
                RECMEM,MEMBER OF RECREATIONAL GROUP
GUTTMAN SCALE   MEMBSCAL=ALTMEM(1)OCCMEM(1)RECMEM(1)
STATISTICS      ALL
FINISH
```

For purposes of building this Guttman scale, the ORGSTUDY variables are grouped as follows:

*Service-oriented organization member* (*Variable* ALTMEM)

| | |
|---|---|
| FRATMEM | member of fraternal organizations |
| VETMEM | member of veterans groups |
| SCHOLMEM | member in school service groups |
| NATMEM | member of national organizations |
| RELMEM | member in religious organizations |

*Occupational organization member* (*Variable* OCCMEM)

| | |
|---|---|
| SERVMEM | member of service clubs |
| UNIONMEM | member in labor union |
| PROFMEM | member in professional-academic organizations |
| FARMEM | member of farmers' organizations |

*Recreational organization member* (*Variable* RECMEM)

| | |
|---|---|
| SPORTMEM | member in sport clubs |
| HOBMEM | member in hobby-garden clubs |
| LITMEM | member of literary-art groups |
| SCHFRMEM | member of school fraternity or sorority |

A listing of the file-defining cards and cases for file ORGSTUDY can be found in Appendix I. We notice that if variable FRATMEM and SERVMEM have the value 1 and the other variables have the value 0, this indicates that the respondent is a member of a fraternal organization and a service club, but of no other type of organization listed in the table. We wish to create a new variable, ALTMEM, which equals 1 if the respondent was a member of a fraternal organization, a veterans group, a school service group, a national organization, or a religious organization, and 0 otherwise. This is accomplished by use of the two SPSS control cards:

```
1               16
COMPUTE         ALTMEM = FRATMEM+VETMEM+SCHOLMEM+NATMEM+RELMEM
IF              (ALTMEM GT 1) ALTMEM = 1
```

The variables OCCMEM and RECMEM are created in a similar fashion to indicate whether the respondent was a member of the second and third groups of organizations, respectively. The VAR LABELS card defines labels for the new variables.

To test whether the three new variables pass the requirements for a Guttman scale, the GUTTMAN SCALE control card is used. This card names the scale being constructed as MEMBSCAL and indicates that the scale items in decreasing order of difficulty are the new variables ALTMEM, OCCMEM, and RECMEM. The pass-reject level for each scale item is specified as 1, according to the way these scale items have been constructed.

```
GUTTMAN SCALE CONSTRUCTION                                        07/25/69      PAGE   81

 FILE   ORGSTUDY (CREATION DATE = 07/25/69)    STUDY OF ORGANIZATIONAL MEMBERSHIP AND ACTIVITY
 SUBFILE   NWJERSEY   PENNSYLV

 * * * * * * *   G U T T M A N   S C A L E   ( M E M B S C A L )   U S I N G   * * * * * * * *
 ALTMEM    MEMBER OF SERVICE-ORIENTED GROUP           DIVISION POINT =     1.00
 OCCMEM    MEMBER OF OCCUPATIONAL GROUP               DIVISION POINT =     1.00
 RECMEM    MEMBER OF RECREATIONAL GROUP               DIVISION POINT =     1.00
 * * * * * * * *   RESP = 1 FOR VALUES EQUAL TO DIVISION POINT AND ABOVE   * * * * * * * * * *


ITEM.. RECMEM     ALTMEM     OCCMEM

RESP..   0    1 I   0    1 I   0    1 I  TOTAL
  ---I-ERR-----I-ERR-----I-ERR-----I
     I        I        I        I
   3 I   0   11I   0   11I   0   11I     11
     I------ERRI        I        I
     I        I        I        I
   2 I   27  16I   7   36I   9   34I     43
     I        I------ERRI        I
     I        I        I        I
   1 I   81  10I  52   39I  49   42I     91
     I        I        I------ERRI
     I        I        I        I
   0 I  105   0I 105    0I 105    0I    105
     I---------I---------I---------I
SUMS    213  37  164   86  163   87    250
PCTS     85   15   66   34   65   35
ERRORS    0   26    7   39   58    0    130


    250 CASES WERE PROCESSED
      0 (OR  0.0 PCT) WERE MISSING


STATISTICS..

COEFFICIENT OF REPRODUCIBILITY = 0.8267
MINIMUM MARGINAL REPRODUCIBILITY = 0.7200
PERCENT IMPROVEMENT = 0.1067
COEFFICIENT OF SCALABILITY = 0.3810


CORRELATION COEFFICIENTS..

           ALTMEM     OCCMEM     RECMEM

ALTMEM     1.0000     0.1427     0.1724
OCCMEM     0.1427     1.0000     0.1212
RECMEM     0.1724     0.1212     1.0000
SCALE-ITEM 0.2058     0.1731     0.1942
```

**FIG. 16.2**   Output from subprogram GUTTMAN SCALE.

The output listing from the **GUTTMAN SCALE** subprogram for this example is shown in Fig. 16.2. All statistics available for this subprogram have been printed, since the keyword ALL appears on the **STATISTICS** card.

The user will note that if the user had included a **SAVE FILE** card in the control-card deck immediately preceding the **FINISH** card, a new SPSS system file would have been saved including the values of the new variables for each case, and labeling information for these new variables would have been retained. (In this event, the user would also insert an FT04 JCL card in the set of JCL cards accompanying the deck listed).

# 17
# FACTOR ANALYSIS†

Subprogram FACTOR performs a variety of factor-analytic techniques. Input may be raw data (from either a BCD or SPSS system file), a correlation matrix, or a factor matrix. Five different factoring methods are available: (1) principal factoring without iteration, (2) principal factoring with iterations, (3) Rao's canonical factoring, (4) alpha factoring, and (5) image factoring. Four alternative rotational methods may be applied to the various factoring solutions, three being orthogonal and one oblique. The three orthogonal solutions are varimax, quartimax, and equimax. In the oblique rotation, the user can control the degree of correlations between factors. Graphical plotting for visual display of the relationship between pairs of rotated factors is also available and may be used in conjunction with any of the orthogonal rotation procedures.

The user has total control over the criteria for extracting and rotating factors. He may directly specify the number of factors to be extracted and rotated, specify his own minimum eigenvalue criterion, or rely on default options. If he wishes he may also control the iterative procedures by specifying the maximum number of permissible iterations. Furthermore, diagonal values of the correlation matrix may be altered at will.

The STATISTICS card permits the user to control the precise configuration of his output so that only the information he desires will be printed. Factor-score matrices are optionally

†This chapter has been prepared by Jae-On Kim with the assistance of Norman H. Nie.

available for each of the rotational methods and may be used in conjunction with the SPSS data-modification cards to produce factor scores for each case in the file.

As usual, several options are provided for the processing of missing data, and all the file management procedures in SPSS may be used in conjunction with this subprogram.

## 17.1   INTRODUCTION TO FACTOR ANALYSIS

The purpose of this introduction is to provide the user with a working understanding of the basic concepts of factor analysis without burdening him with statistical details. The emphasis is more on providing the user with a general orientation to the topic than on presenting calculating algorithms. It will be assumed in the following discussion, however, that the user has some grasp of the meaning of correlation and regression coefficients. Verbal descriptions of a complex statistical method without recourse to exact mathematical representations are bound to be misleading if taken verbatim. The user is therefore advised to consult at least one standard treatment of the subject in conjunction with this chapter.[1]

The single most distinctive characteristic of factor analysis is its data-reduction capability. Given an array of correlation coefficients for a set of variables, factor-analytic techniques enable us to see whether some underlying pattern of relationships exists such that the data may be "rearranged" or "reduced" to a smaller set of *factors* or *components* that may be taken as *source variables* accounting for the observed interrelations in the data.

Possible uses of this capability are many and varied. Nevertheless, the most common applications of the method may be classified into one of the following categories: (1) exploratory uses—the exploration and detection of patterning of variables with a view to the discovery of new concepts and a possible reduction of data; (2) confirmatory uses—the testing of hypotheses about the structuring of variables in terms of the expected number of significant factors and factor loadings; and (3) uses as a measuring device—the construction of indices to be used as new variables in later analysis. The exploratory uses of factor analysis are the most common but should not be taken as the sole rationale for factor analysis. As more factor-analytic studies are made, the confirmatory uses of factor analysis, or hypothesis testing, will take on greater importance. It should be noted also that although all the factor-analytic applications are ultimately based on the data-summarizing capability of the method, the specific applications to various research problems are bounded only by the user's imagination.[2]

### TYPES OF FACTOR ANALYSIS

The term *factor analysis* is not a unitary concept, and it subsumes a fairly large variety of procedures, the most general classification of which may be organized around the major alternatives available at each of the three customary steps of factor analysis. The three ordinary steps are (1) the preparation of the correlation matrix, (2) the extraction of the initial factors—the exploration of possible data reduction, and (3) the rotation to a terminal solution—the search for simple and interpretable factors. Major options at each stage may be summed up by three dichotomies: R-type versus Q-type factor analysis in step 1, defined versus inferred factors in step 2, and orthogonal versus oblique in step 3. Each will be taken up in greater detail later.

### Preparation of Correlation Matrix

The first step in factor analysis involves the calculation of appropriate measures of association for a set of *relevant variables*. The user has to define the relevant universe of his analysis. The nature and scope of the variables included in the analysis have crucial implications for the

---

[1]Those who have some mathematical training might wish to read Harman (1967) as an introduction. Unfortunately, however, three of the five factoring methods used in this program are not covered in his book. A minimum number of references to the relevant literature—most of which are highly technical—will be found at the end of this chapter. Since the technique is still being improved, especially with the advent of computers, the user is also advised to consult recent issues of *Psychometrika*. Those who have limited mathematical training might prefer a less technical but conceptually lucid treatment by Rozeboom (1966) or a nontechnical introduction by Rummel (1967).

[2]See Rummel (1967) for references to the social science application.

factor results and for the possible interpretation of them. Also closely related is the selection of appropriate measures of association; most factor analyses require product-moment correlation coefficients. Granted that some type of correlation matrix is used as the basic input to the factor analysis, the user has some alternatives; he may calculate correlations between variables (or attributes), or he may calculate "association" between individuals or objects. Suppose we have data on 10 individuals in terms of eight social characteristics. We could calculate the correlation between each pair of social characteristics (R-type) or between each pair of individuals (Q-type). If factor analysis is applied to a correlation matrix of *units* (objects, individuals, communities, or the like), it is called *Q-factor analysis*, while the more common variety based on correlations between *variables* is known as *R-factor analysis*. [1]

### Extraction of Initial Factors

The second step in factor analysis is to explore the data-reduction possibilities by constructing a set of new variables on the basis of the interrelations exhibited in the data. In doing so, the analyst may define the new variables as exact mathematical transformations of the original data, or he may make inferential assumptions about the structuring of variables and about their source of variation. The former approach, which uses defined factors, is called *principal-component* analysis, while the latter, which uses inferred factors, is generically called *classical-* or *common-factor analysis*. Whether factors are exactly defined or are inferred, initial factors are usually extracted in such a way that one factor is independent from the other; that is, factors are *orthogonal*. Furthermore, effort is made not so much on locating meaningful dimensions as on detecting possible reductions of data.

### 1. Defined Factors

Principal-component analysis is a relatively straightforward method of transforming a given set of variables into a new set of composite variables or principal components that are orthogonal (uncorrelated) to each other. No particular assumption about the underlying structure of the variables is required. One simply asks what would be the best linear combination of variables— best in the sense that the particular combination of variables would account for more of the variance in the data as a whole than any other linear combination of variables. The first principal component, therefore, may be viewed as the single best summary of linear relationships exhibited in the data. The second component is defined as the second best linear combination of variables, under the condition that the second component is orthogonal to the first. To be orthogonal to the first component, the second one must account for the proportion of the variance not accounted for by the first one. Thus the second component may be defined as the linear combination of variables that accounts for the most residual variance after the effect of the first component is removed from the data. Subsequent components are defined similarly until all the variance in the data is exhausted. Unless at least one variable is perfectly determined by the rest of the variables in the data, the principal-component solution requires as many components as there are variables.

The principal-component model may be compactly expressed as follows:

$$z_j = a_{j1}F_1 + a_{j2}F_2 + \cdots + a_{jn}F_n$$

where each of the n observed variables is described linearly in terms of n new uncorrelated components $F_1, F_2, \ldots, F_n$, each of which is, in turn defined as a linear combination of the n original variables. [2]

---

[1] The factor-analysis program in SPSS routinely handles R-type analysis. For Q factoring, the data have to be transposed first before the calculation of suitable measures of association. For a discussion of Q methodology, see Stephenson (1953); for a discussion of Q technique for dichotomous raw data, see Holley and Guilford (1965).

[2] Rozeboom succinctly comments on the aspect of circular reasoning: "If the data variables are to be analyzed as linear combinations of factors which are themselves, in turn, defined as composites of the data variables, aren't we just going in circles? Well, yes—in a way we are, but sometimes the view from one point on a circle is more interesting than from another. Complete analysis of a set of variables into defined factors

Since each component is defined as the *best* linear summary of variance left in the data after the previous components are taken care of, the first m components—usually much smaller than the number of variables in the set—may explain most of the variance in the data. For factor-analytic purposes, the analyst normally retains the first few components for further rotation. (More discussion will be found in Sec. 17.2, which deals with specific methods of extracting factors.)

## 2. Inferred Factors

*Classical-factor analysis,* on the other hand, is basically based on the faith that the observed correlations are mainly the results of some underlying regularity in the data. More specifically, it is assumed that the observed variable is influenced by various determinants, some of which are shared by other variables in the set while others are not shared by any other variable. The part of a variable that is influenced by the shared determinants is usually called *common,* and the part that is influenced by idiosyncratic determinants is usually called *unique.* Under this assumption, the unique part of a variable does not contribute to relationships among variables. It also follows from the preceding assumption that the observed correlations must be the result of the correlated variables sharing some of the common determinants. The implicit faith on our part is that those assumed common determinants will not only account for all the observed relations in the data, but will also be smaller in number than the variables. The basic model may compactly be expressed as follows:

$$z_j = a_{j1} F_1 + a_{j2} F_2 + \cdots + a_{jm} F_m + d_j U_j \qquad (j = 1, 2, \ldots, n)$$

where  $z_j$ = variable j in standardized form
  $F_i$ = hypothetical factors
  $U_j$ = unique factor for variable j
  $a_{ji}$ = standardized multiple-regression coefficient of
    variable j on factor i (factor loading)
  $d_j$ = standardized regression coefficient of variable
    j on unique factor j

The following are assumed to hold among the hypothesized variables:

$$COR(F_i, U_j) = 0 \qquad (i = 1, 2, \ldots, n, \quad j = 1, 2, \ldots, n)$$
$$COR(U_j, U_k) = 0 \qquad (j \neq k)$$

That is, the unique factor $U_j$ is assumed to be orthogonal to all the common factors and unique factors associated with other variables. This means that the unique portion of a variable is not related to any other variable or to that part of itself which is due to the common factor.

Therefore, if there is any correlation between the two variables j and k, it is assumed to be due to the common factors. Further, if the common factors are assumed to be orthogonal to each other, i.e., unrelated, the following fundamental factor theorem emerges:

$$r_{jk} = r_{jF_1} r_{kF_1} + r_{jF_2} r_{kF_2} + \cdots + r_{jF_m} r_{kF_m}$$
$$= a_{j1} a_{k1} + a_{j2} a_{k2} + \cdots + a_{jm} a_{km}$$
$$= \sum_{i=1}^{m} a_{ji} a_{ki}$$

That is, the correlation between variables j and k is the sum of the cross-products of the correlations of j and k with the respective common factors. If there is only a single common

---

is merely a linear transformation of the set, and a person's scores on such factors jointly contain exactly as much information about him, no more and no less, as do his scores on the original variables. But some ways to say the same thing are more illuminating than other ways . . . , and transformation of a set of data variables into a set of factors may very well reveal important relationships which are difficult to discern among the variables in their original form. In particular, extraction of factors economically exhibits the degree of linear dependence among the data variables." (Rozeboom, 1966:213)

factor, the above expression will reduce to

$$r_{jk} = r_{jF_1} r_{kF_1}$$

This means that the correlation between j and k is due solely to the factor $F_1$, or if one were to control the hypothetical factor $F_1$, the partial correlation between j and k would be zero.

Factor analysis can be thought of as a technique by which a minimum number of hypothetical variables are specified in such a way that after controlling for these hypothetical variables, all the remaining (partial) correlations between the variables would become zero.

The basic factor postulate assumes the existence of residual variance, which is not accounted for by common factors and does not contribute to the intercorrelations of the variables. However, the exact amount of the *unique* variance or its complement, communality, is not known; it has to be estimated from the given data. The determination of communalities remains one of the most difficult and ambiguous tasks in factor analysis. One of the main characteristics that differentiates one method of factoring from another is the procedure used for estimating the communalities.

Whether a solution employs defined factors or inferred factors depends on whether the existence of unique variance is assumed. More practically, one differs from the other depending on whether the correlation matrix is altered before doing the factor analysis. All inferential factor techniques replace the main diagonals of the correlation matrix with communality estimates before factoring.

If true communalities are inserted in the diagonal of the correlation matrix, the rank of the correlation matrix should be reduced if the factor-analytic assumptions are to be valid. Ideally, therefore, the question of the number of factors required to account for a given correlation matrix can be solved by examining the rank of the matrix. However, random errors of measurement and indeterminacy in selecting communalities confound the situation. (More specific topics will be taken up in Sec. 17.2.)

### Rotation of Factors into Terminal Factors

We now turn to the final step in factor analysis. Regardless of whether factors are defined or inferred, the exact configuration of the factor structure is not unique; one factor solution can be transformed into another without violating the basic assumptions or the mathematical properties of a given solution. In other words, there are many statistically equivalent ways to define the underlying dimensions of the same set of data. This indeterminacy in a factor solution is in a way unfortunate because there is no unique and generally accepted best solution. On the other hand, not all the statistical factor solutions are equally meaningful in theoretical terms. Some are more parsimonious and simpler than other; some are more informative than others; and each tells us something slightly different about the structure of the data. Therefore, one is left to choose the best rotational method to arrive at the terminal solution that satisfies the theoretical and practical needs of the research problem.

The major option available to the analyst at this point is whether to choose an orthogonal rotational method or an oblique rotational method.[1] The basic impetus for employing any rotational method is the same: somehow to achieve simpler and theoretically more meaningful factor patterns. Orthogonal factors are mathematically simpler to handle, while the oblique factors are empirically more realistic. There is no compelling reason to favor one method over another, and the choice should be made on the basis of the particular needs of a given research problem. (See Sec. 17.3 for further discussion.)

### SUMMARY

It should be noted here that the three steps are not invariably followed in every factor analysis and that the three dichotomies by no means exhaust the possible alternatives. For a quick review and as a *general* guide, the classification of the types of factor analysis is presented in Table 17.1.

[1]Orthogonal factors are uncorrelated, while oblique factors may be correlated.

**TABLE 17.1** Types of factor analysis

| Steps in factor analysis | Major options | | Key references to literature | |
|---|---|---|---|---|
| 1. Preparation of correlation matrix | (a) | Correlation between variables | (a) | R factoring |
| | (b) | Correlation between units | (b) | Q factoring |
| 2. Extraction of initial factors | (a) | Defined factors | (a) | *Principal-component* solution |
| | (b) | Inferred factors | (b) | *Classical* or *common*-factor solution |
| 3. Rotation to terminal factors | (a) | Uncorrelated factors | (a) | Orthogonal factors or rotation |
| | (b) | Correlated factors | (b) | Oblique factors or rotation |

Any combination of the three dichotomies may occur. For instance, a factor analysis may have been based on an R-type matrix, extracted by principal-component solution, then rotated to oblique factors. No wonder there are so many kinds of factor analysis if we consider all the subdivisions that exist within each of the general categories mentioned above.[1]

### 17.1.1 MEANING OF ESSENTIAL TABLES AND STATISTICS IN FACTOR-ANALYSIS OUTPUT

A complete factor analysis solution will provide at least the following six matrices:

1. Correlation matrix for input variables
2. Initial factor loadings
3. Weights to estimate variables from factors (factor-*pattern* matrix)
4. Weights to estimate factors from variables (factor-*estimate* matrix)
5. Correlation between factors and variables (factor-*structure* matrix)
6. Correlation matrix for terminal factors

The user should be familiar with each of the six matrices because understanding one is essential for understanding the proper meaning of the others. In the following, we shall assume that the user is familiar with correlation matrices, and therefore, we will not discuss 1. The matrices from 3 to 6 pertain to the terminal solution. These four constitute the main sources of information for interpreting and constructing new indices. Therefore, we shall describe them first. Initial factor matrix 2 will be discussed briefly at the end of this section and will be covered in detail in Sec. 17.2.

*Rotated factor-pattern matrix* To *factor analyze,* at the most general level, means to express a variable as a linear combination of independent variables, either defined or inferred. The factor-pattern matrix contains the regression weights of the common factors and therefore tells us the composition of a variable in terms of hypothetical factors.

*Factor-estimate matrix* A complete solution should also provide a means of estimating factor scores from the observed variables. This matrix consists of the regression weights to be used in estimating factors from the observed variables.

*Rotated factor-structure matrix* Every factor solution also gives us the correlation coefficient between each variable and each factor. *In an orthogonal solution, the pattern matrix and the structure matrix are identical.* Therefore, the two matrices are presented in a single table simply labeled *factor matrix* or *factor loadings.*

*Correlation matrix among factors* In an orthogonal solution, factors are imposed to be orthogonal. Therefore the correlation between factors is arbitrarily determined to be zero. However, in a general (or oblique) solution, the correlations among factors have the same importance as information as pattern and structure matrices have. This matrix will show the

---

[1]For further differentiation of factor analysis on the basis of the nature of data, see Cattell (1965).

interrelations of the underlying dimensions and may be used as an input for further factor analysis (higher-order factoring).

Table 17.2 presents the expected essential outputs for orthogonal and oblique solutions in tabular form.

**TABLE 17.2    Basic matrices of factor analysis**

|  | Orthogonal solution | Oblique solution |
|---|---|---|
| Basic data | The same correlation matrix | |
| Initial factors | The same orthogonal-factor matrix | |
| Terminal factors | Factor matrix | (a) Pattern matrix<br>(b) Structure matrix |
| Correlation between factors | No matrix output | Factor-correlation matrix |
| Factor-estimate matrix | Factor-estimate matrix | Factor-estimate matrix |

We shall first discuss the terminal solution of orthogonal factors and then turn to oblique factors.

*Rotated orthogonal-factor matrix*    Table 17.3 presents the terminal solution of orthogonally rotated factors. Since it is an orthogonal-factor matrix, it stands for both a *pattern* and a *structure* matrix. That is, the coefficients in the table represent both regression weights and correlation coefficients.

**TABLE 17.3    Varimax rotated factor matrix**

|  | FACTOR 1 | FACTOR 2 | FACTOR 3 |
|---|---|---|---|
| VAR001 | 0.88920 | 0.07829 | 0.03230 |
| VAR002 | 0.78523 | 0.14023 | 0.05768 |
| VAR003 | 0.10210 | 0.67352 | 0.06342 |
| VAR004 | 0.07237 | 0.85632 | 0.09643 |
| VAR005 | 0.08390 | 0.09470 | 0.76480 |
| VAR006 | 0.12345 | 0.00320 | 0.69532 |
| VAR007 | 0.32460 | 0.34210 | 0.04274 |

The loadings or numbers in a given row represent regression coefficients of factors to describe a given variable. The three columns in Table 17.3, therefore, stand for three factors or hypothetical constructs as yet unnamed, and the numbers in each row represent regression weights. More specifically, we should recall the basic factor postulate:

$$z_j = a_{j1}F_1 + a_{j2}F_2 + \cdots + a_{jm}F_m + d_jU_j$$

where $z_j$ stands for a variable, $F_i$ for common factors, $U_j$ for a unique factor, and $a_{ji}$ and $d_j$ for regression weights. (All the variables are assumed to be normalized.) Each row of Table 17.3 is simply an abbreviated presentation of this postulate. The unique factor and its loading are not reported in the matrix simply because the information is, in a sense, redundant and can be obtained from other information contained in the table. For instance, the first row may be used in the following regression formula:

$$z_1 = 0.88920F_1 + 0.07829F_2 + 0.03230F_3 + d_1U_1$$

It is obvious that the most important determinant of VAR001 is FACTOR 1, and the influence of the other common factors is negligible. Likewise, the only significant common factor for VAR003 is FACTOR 2. By reading every row in the same manner, we can describe the linear composition of each variable in terms of three hypothetical factors. Note, however, that each variable except the last one loads significantly only on one factor. The factorial complexity of these variables is therefore 1. The last variable, on the other hand, loads moderately on both FACTOR 1 and FACTOR 2, indicating a factorial complexity of 2. If a variable loads on more than one factor, or its complexity is greater than 1, the "meaning" of that variable is no longer simple: It measures more than one theoretical dimension.

In a regression equation, the independent variables (in this particular case, the hypothetical factors) are said to *control* or *account for* a certain proportion of the variance in the dependent variable (in this case, VAR001 to VAR007). The importance of a given factor for a given variable can be exactly expressed in terms of the variance in the variable that can be accounted for by the factor. For instance, the variance of VAR001 accounted for by the variation in FACTOR 1 is

$$a_{11}^2 = (0.88920)^2 = 0.79067$$

That is, 79 percent of the total variance of VAR001 is accounted for by FACTOR 1.

Likewise, the variance of a variable accounted for by a factor is given by the square of the respective factor loadings. (However, this is true only in an orthogonal solution. Oblique solution will be discussed later.)

Similarly, the proportion of the variance in VAR001 accounted for by all three common factors is

$$h_1^2 = a_{11}^2 + a_{12}^2 + a_{13}^2$$
$$= (0.88920)^2 + (0.07829)^2 + (0.03230)^2$$
$$= 0.79783$$

Compare this value with the variance accounted for by FACTOR 1 alone—0.79067. The contribution of FACTOR 2 and FACTOR 3 to the variance of VAR001 is only

$$0.79783 - 0.79067 = 0.00716$$

The total variance of a variable accounted for by the combination of all common factors, designated $h_j^2$, is usually referred to as the *communality* of the variable. This value indicates the amount of the variance of a variable that is shared by at least one other variable in the set. The complement of communality represents the proportion of the unique variance of a variable and is given by

$$1 - h_j^2$$

This proportion is not accounted for by the common factors or by any variable in the set. (The omitted regression coefficient for the unique factor $d_i$ is given by $\sqrt{1 - h_j^2}$.)

As mentioned earlier, the coefficients in Table 17.3 also represent correlation coefficients between factors (presented in the columns) and variables (presented in the rows). For example, the correlation between FACTOR 1 and VAR001 is 0.88920 and that between FACTOR 2 and VAR007 is 0.34210.

Finally, the user may compare any pair of rows in Table 17.3 and, recalling the fundamental factor theorem, find out the sources of common variation (or correlation). For instance, the correlation between VAR001 and VAR002 is given by

$$r_{12} = r_{1f_1} r_{2F_1} + r_{1F_2} r_{2F_2} + r_{1F_3} r_{2F_3}$$
$$= a_{11} a_{21} + a_{12} a_{22} + a_{13} a_{23}$$
$$= (0.88920)(0.78523) + (0.07829)(0.14023) + (0.03230)(0.05768)$$
$$= (0.69882 + 0.01097 + 0.00186)$$
$$= 0.71105$$

In factor-analytic solutions, the estimated correlation given above should be very close to the observed correlation.

Note that the correlation between VAR001 and VAR002 is mainly due to FACTOR 1. Were it not for FACTOR 1, $r_{12}$ would be close to zero. Note, for instance, that the correlation between VAR002 and VAR007 is due mainly to FACTOR 1 and FACTOR 2. The correlation between VAR001 and VAR003 should be relatively small because these two variables do not load highly on the same common factor.

*Rotated oblique-factor matrices*    In an oblique solution, there will be two separate matrices, an example of which is presented in Table 17.4.

**TABLE 17.4    Oblique factor matrices**

|  | Pattern matrix | | Structure matrix | |
|---|---|---|---|---|
|  | FACTOR 1 | FACTOR 2 | FACTOR 1 | FACTOR 2 |
| VAR001 | .99978 | −.11012 | .97652 | .08240 |
| VAR002 | .88724 | −.08012 | .87234 | .08902 |
| VAR003 | .76098 | .34380 | .82600 | .43000 |
| VAR004 | −.08202 | .99870 | .11721 | .99668 |
| VAR005 | .05368 | .96723 | .24231 | .97823 |

The pattern matrix delineates more clearly the grouping or clustering of variables than the structure matrix. The square of a pattern coefficient represents the *direct* contribution of a given factor to the variance of a variable. However, a factor may also contribute to a given variable indirectly through other correlated factors. Therefore, the total variance of a variable accounted for *by a factor* is not given by the sum of direct contributions. By the same token, the total variance of a variable accounted for by *all the common factors*—the communality of a variable—is no longer given by the sum of square of pattern coefficients. The communality of a variable consists in direct as well as joint contributions. All these complications are due to the correlations between the factors.

The structure matrix, on the other hand, consists of correlation coefficients. For instance, the correlation between VAR001 and FACTOR 1 is 0.97652. The total variance of VAR001 accounted for by FACTOR 1 is, therefore, $(.97652)^2$. Note that this value is no longer identical to the total direct contribution given by $(.99978)^2$, and that its indirect contribution must be negative.

Parenthetically, it may be noted that the oblique-pattern matrix is simpler than the corresponding orthogonal matrix, while the structure matrix is more complex than the orthogonal matrix. The loadings in the structure matrix are partly due to the correlations between the factors.

*Initial-factor matrix and importance of factors*    The initial-factor matrix contains orthogonal factors and thus stands for both a pattern and a structure matrix. Therefore, all the descriptions of rotated orthogonal matrix are pertinent here. We may recall, however, that this matrix is produced primarily as a means of data reduction. Regardless of whether factors are inferred or defined, they are ordered in descending importance.

On the basis of this matrix, one would normally decide how many factors to retain and evaluate how complete a given factor analysis is. Therefore, it is important to examine the proportion of variance accounted for by each factor and jointly by the first m significant factors that will be used in further rotation.

An example of initial factors is given in Table 17.5. The solution is based on principal component with unities in the main diagonal of the correlation coefficients.

**TABLE 17.5    Initial factor matrix**
**(Factor matrix using principal factor, no iterations)**

|             | FACTOR 1 | FACTOR 2 |
|-------------|----------|----------|
| VAR01       | 0.74407  | −0.21249 |
| VAR02       | 0.79059  | −0.35333 |
| VAR03       | 0.75725  | −0.19206 |
| VAR04       | −0.44525 | 0.09777  |
| VAR05       | 0.29515  | −0.68438 |
| VAR06       | 0.73981  | 0.58467  |
| VAR07       | 0.66588  | 0.59194  |
|             |          |          |
| EIGENVALUE[†] | 3.02819 | 1.37704 |
| PCT OF VAR[†] | 43.3     | 19.7     |
| CUM PCT[†]    | 43.3     | 62.9     |

[†]In actual computer output, these statistics
are printed on a separate page.

We can examine the importance of a given factor in terms of the amount of total variance in the data it accounts for. By recalling that the variance of variable j accounted for by factor i is the square of the respective factor loadings, $a_{ji}^2$, one may calculate the *total* amount of variance accounted for by a factor by adding the square of the loadings in each column:

$$\text{Variance accounted for by FACTOR } 1 = \sum_{j=1}^{n} a_{j1}^2 \qquad (j = 1, 2, \ldots, n)$$

$$= (0.74407)^2 + (0.79059)^2 + \cdots + (0.66588)^2$$

$$= 3.02819$$

$$= \text{respective eigenvalue}^{†}$$

Since all the variables are normalized, the variance of each variable is 1; thus, the total variance in the data equals the number of variables in the set. It is therefore easy to calculate the *proportion of total variance* accounted for by a given factor, say FACTOR 1:

$$\text{Proportion of total variance accounted for by FACTOR } 1 = \frac{\sum_{j=1}^{n} a_{j1}^2}{n}$$

$$= \frac{3.02819}{7} = 3.02819 = .433$$

One may also want to know the proportion of *common variance* (the variance accounted for by all the common factors) accounted for by each factor. For this, one has to add up the communality ($h_j^2$) of each variable and then calculate:

$$\text{Proportion of common variance accounted for by Factor } 1 = \frac{\sum_{j}^{n} a_{j1}^2}{\sum_{j}^{n} h_j^2}$$

$$= \frac{3.02819}{3.02819 + 1.37704}$$

$$= .687$$

The statistics, the proportion of total variance and the proportion of common variance accounted for by a given factor, are calculated by the program, if appropriate. However, the importance of a factor as indicated by "variance accounted for" is of no particular interest in a terminal solution (rotated one), because the importance of a factor in a terminal solution often

[†]If the initial matrix contains *inferred* factors, the sum of eigenvalues equals the sum of communalities, and some of the eigenvalues will be negative. Therefore, eigenvalues may not be interpreted as amounts of explained variance.

reflects only the number of variables for a given factor included in the data relative to the total number of variables.[1]

*Other tables and statistics*     Other statistics will be discussed briefly in Sec. 17.8, and the factor-estimate matrix will be discussed fully in Sec. 17.4.

## 17.2    METHODS OF FACTORING AVAILABLE IN SUBPROGRAM FACTOR

There are five different methods of factoring available in this program. These five initial factor solutions can be rotated in turn to the terminal solution by any one of the three orthogonal rotation methods or by the oblique rotation. The five methods are:

PA1—principal factoring without iteration
PA2—principal factoring with iteration
RAO—Rao's canonical factoring
ALPHA—alpha factoring
IMAGE—image factoring

The mnemonics to the left are the SPSS keywords that are used on the FACTOR procedure card whenever reference is made to the factoring methods.

The immediate result of initial factoring is the extraction of an unrotated factor matrix. There are several features common to all these extracting methods:

1.    All factors are imposed to be orthogonal.
2.    Factors are arranged in the order of their importance; the first factor is the most important component, and the second factor is the second most important, and so on.
3.    The first factor tends to be a general factor; that is, it has significant loading on every variable. Subsequent factors tend to be bipolar, that is, some factor loadings are positive while others are negative.

One variant of PA1, known as the *principal-component solution,* employs defined factors, while all the other factoring methods use some inferential assumptions. In image factoring, some properties of the *image-covariance* structure are used as estimates of the underlying factor structure; but after this matrix is obtained, the subsequent factors are exactly defined. In this sense, image factors are both inferred and defined.

### 17.2.1    PRINCIPAL FACTORING WITHOUT ITERATION: PA1†

The PA1 factoring method (principal factoring without iteration) is actually two separate methods that differ drastically from each other. In practice, the difference is the result of a simple decision by the user whether or not to replace the main diagonal of the correlation matrix with estimates of communality.

1. In the first method, when the main diagonal of the correlation matrix is not altered, the program will extract principal components, which are defined as exact mathematical transformations of original variables. This method does not require any assumptions about the general structure of the variables.

---

[1]In an oblique solution, the *direct* or *independent* contribution of a factor can be calculated in the same manner. The calculation of the total contribution of a factor (or total variance accounted for by a given factor) involves joint contributions with other correlated factors. As mentioned, the contribution of a factor in a terminal solution is not of very much interest. Therefore, the relevant statistical formula is not presented here.

†There are three terms in the literature referring to the same style of factoring: *principal components, principal axes, principal factors.* They differ only in the scaling of the composite variables (factors or components): a principal axis is usually standardized to have a mean of zero and a variance equal to the total variance it accounts for; a principal component is the same as a principal axis except that its mean is not standardized to zero; a principal factor is normalized to have a zero mean and a unit variance. However, much confusion exists in actual usage. Following Harman (1967), for convenience here, the solution of factoring with unities in the diagonals of the correlation matrix will be called the *principal-component solution,* and the solution with communalities in the diagonals of the correlation matrix will be called the *principal-factor solution.*

A variable can be decomposed into n components and can be predicted exactly from these components. However, our main interest does not lie in a mathematical transformation itself. We are primarily interested in finding whether some small number of components account for most of the variance in the data. It is quite possible that the first few components account for most of the variance and that the remaining components account for only small amounts of variance that are often due to idiosyncratic variations in the individual variables.

In the principal-component matrix, the eigenvalues associated with each component represent the amount of total variance accounted for by the factor. Therefore, the importance of a component may be evaluated by examining the proportion of the total variance accounted for as follows:

$$\text{Proportion of total variance accounted for by component } i = \frac{\lambda_i}{n}$$

where $\lambda_i$ represents the eigenvalue of ith component and n represents the number of variables in the set. These statistics will be automatically calculated by the program and printed.

The number of significant components to be retained for the final rotated solution will ordinarily be determined by the specification of the minimum eigenvalue criterion. The program retains and prints only components with eigenvalues greater than or equal to 1.0. This criterion ensures that only components accounting for at least the amount of average variance of a variable will be treated as significant.

There is, however, no absolute criterion, and the user may control the number of components to be retained through specification of the MINEIGEN and/or NFACTORS parameters, which will be described in Section 17.5.4.

2. In the second method, the principal-component solution can be modified by replacing the main diagonal of the correlation matrix with some estimates of communality. Factors extracted from such a reduced correlation matrix are often called *principal factors* to differentiate them from principal components, which are extracted from a correlation matrix with unities in the main diagonal.[1] The most commonly used estimates are (1) the squared multiple correlation between a variable and the rest of the variables in the set and (2) the absolute value of the highest element in each column of the correlation matrix.

The factors or components so extracted are no longer exact transformations of the original variables. By replacing the main diagonals of the correlation matrix, we are making an inferential leap. We assume that only some portions of the variables are involved in the patterning of variables and that if we remove common sources of variance, the remaining correlations between variables will all become zeros.

In this model, we are assuming the existence of a unique factor or a unique variance of a variable not involved with any other variables. By replacing the diagonal elements in the correlation matrix, we are taking out the presumed unique variance of each variable and only analyzing the remaining portions of the variables.

A diagonal element has to be less than unity and greater than zero. Whatever value we may put in as the communality estimate, we intend to decompose only that proportion of the variable into "factors."

There is, however, no agreed upon method of calculating communalities, although the theoretical lower bounds of communalities and their absolute upper bounds are known. Since *communality* is defined as the proportion of a variable sharing something in common with other variables in the set, the communality of a variable cannot be smaller than the squared multiple correlation between a variable and all others in the set. That portion of a variable that can be predicted by other variables must be related to them. Other than that, any value between this lower bound and 1.0 can be used as the communality estimate.

## 17.2.2  PRINCIPAL FACTORING WITH ITERATION: PA2

The second method of factoring in subprogram FACTOR is a modification of PA1. It differs from PA1 in two important respects. First, PA2 automatically replaces the main diagonal elements of the correlation matrix with communality estimates. Initial estimates of the communalities are given by the squared multiple correlation between a given variable and the rest of

[1] See footnote † on p. 218

the variables in the matrix. (In cases where the determinant of the matrix is smaller than $10^{-8}$ or the matrix is singular, the absolute value of the biggest element in each column is used instead of the squared multiple correlation.)[1] In this method, therefore, the user automatically gets so-called *inferred factors.*

The second difference from PA1 is that PA2 employs an iteration procedure for improving the estimates of communality. First, the program determines the number of factors to be extracted from the original or unreduced correlation matrix. The program then replaces the main diagonal elements of the correlation matrix with initial estimates of communalities, the $R^2$ estimates. Next it extracts the same number of factors from this reduced matrix, and the variances accounted for by these factors become new communality estimates. The diagonal elements are then replaced with these new communalities. This process continues until the differences in the two successive communality estimates are negligible.

It may be noted that PA2 can handle most of the intial factoring needs of the user. At present this is the most universally accepted *factoring* method. Those who have limited experience with factor analysis might do well to stay with this method.

### 17.2.3 THE REMAINING METHODS OF FACTORING

The remaining three factoring methods available in subprogram FACTOR—RAO, ALPHA, and IMAGE—are relatively new and the merits of them are still the subject of some debate. They are provided mainly for those users who have some grasp of factor-analytic procedures and who wish to explore more subtle patterning of their data. For these reasons, the following discussions are quite brief and a few technical terms are used without explanation.

#### 17.2.3.1 Rao's canonical factoring: RAO

The guiding principle of canonical factoring is to find a factor solution in which the correlation between the set of hypothesized factors and the set of data variables is maximized. It follows the classical-factor model (in contrast to the principal-component model) in the sense that the hypothesized factors are assumed to be determined by the linear combination of the *common* variance portion of the observed variables. Estimation of communality or unique variance becomes the central problem.

In addition, Rao's canonical factoring assumes that the given correlation matrix is based upon a *sample* of cases and asks what the most likely population parameters would be. Since some sampling errors are assumed to exist, it is also expected that the hypothesized factor structure would not exactly fit the data.

By recalling that in the classical-factor solution one is seeking a minimum number of factors to account for the observed correlation matrix, it is therefore relevant to ask at least how many factors are required so that the fit between the data and the hypothesized factors does not deviate *significantly* (on a specified level) from chance expectation. The existence of such a significance test for the number of factors is a distinctive feature of Rao's canonical factoring.

#### 17.2.3.2 Alpha factoring: ALPHA

The special features of alpha factoring can be grasped when it is compared to Rao's canonical factoring. Like canonical factoring, alpha factoring follows the basic factor postulate in which the variables are assumed to consist of two parts: one that is determined by common factors and one that is unique to each variable.

In alpha factoring, however, *variables* included in the factor analysis are considered a sample from the universe of *variables* (or characteristics of individuals, communities, and the like) in contrast to canonical factoring where the units such as individuals or communities are taken as samples, and the variables are taken to be the entire universe of attributes. In this method, one seeks to define factors that have maximum generalizability (the measure of which is known as *Kuder-Richardson's reliability coefficient* or *Cronbach's alpha*). One seeks to make inferences about the universe of variables from a *sample* of variables; it is simply assumed that

---

[1] If the determinant is negative, run will be terminated.

the variables are observed over a given *population* of individuals. This involves a *psychometric* inference, not a statistical inference in the usual sense.

In actual calculation, one starts with the communality estimates given by the squared multiple correlation and readjusts the correlation matrix following the assumption that the observed n variables are only a sample from the universe of variables. Another contrast with Rao's canonical factoring is that in alpha factoring the variables are rescaled according to the communality while in Rao's solution the variables are rescaled according to the unique variance estimate. The iteration process continues until the communalities converge. [Since the iteration process is not only more complex than that of PA2, but also involves matrices not yet discussed, no description is given here. Interested readers are referred to Kaiser and Caffrey (1965).] The number of factors to be retained will be determined by the number of factors with positive generalizability. If the associated eigenvalue of a factor is less than 1.0, it is hard to assign any meaning to it. Thus only those factors that indicate some generalizability to other variables in the universe are retained.

### 17.2.3.3 Image factoring: IMAGE

As in other classical-factoring methods, the image-factoring method implicitly assumes that a variable can be decomposed into two parts: one part due to common factors and the other a unique part unassociated with other variables. The exact proportions of these two parts are, of course, unknown and must be estimated on the basis of the correlation matrix. Image theory developed by Guttman provides us with such an approximation.

It has been demonstrated by image theory that the true communality of a variable will be equal to the square of the multiple correlation between that variable and all others in the set provided the total universe of the variables is included in the set. In other words, the best estimate of the common part of a variable is given by the image of variable j, denoted by $P_j$:

$$P_j = \sum^n W_{jk} Z_k \qquad k = 1, 2, \ldots, n - 1$$

where $W_{jk}$ are the standardized regression coefficients for predicting variable j from the rest of the variables in the set, as denoted by k. Then the anti-image ($e_j$) of a variable, which is the best estimate of the unique portion of a variable, is simply given by

$$e_j = z_j - P_j$$

Whether the images approximate the true communalities, therefore, depends on how well the set of variables represents a given universe of relevant variables. Actual extraction of factors is performed from an image covariance matrix, which contains the squares of the images in the main diagonal and the adjusted correlation coefficients as the off-diagonal elements. This readjustment of the correlation matrix assures that the resultant matrix is *Gramian*. Description of the nature of this matrix is beyond the scope of this chapter, but it may be noted that if the factor-analytic assumptions about the structure of the variables are correct, the resultant *anti-image covariance* matrix will reveal certain properties, namely, the entire matrix should be approximately zero. Image factoring can therefore routinely tell us the validity of the factor-analytic inferences about the data (Kaiser, 1963).

The number of factors are determined by the eigenvalue of the image covariance matrix, and factors with eigenvalues greater than 1.0 will be retained. The number of factors so determined is usually n/2, that is, one-half of the number of variables in the set. This number is usually greater than the user can possibly interpret or is willing to retain.

The inclusion of several trivial factors in the *orthogonal* rotation does not affect the terminal solution very much. Therefore, it is possible to discard some of the trivial and uninterpretable factors even after rotation (Kaiser, 1963).

## 17.3 METHODS OF ROTATION AVAILABLE IN SUBPROGRAM FACTOR

The unrotated factors extracted through various factoring methods may or may not give us a meaningful patterning of variables. As indicated in the previous section, all the initial solutions used in this program extract orthogonal factors in the order of their importance. The first

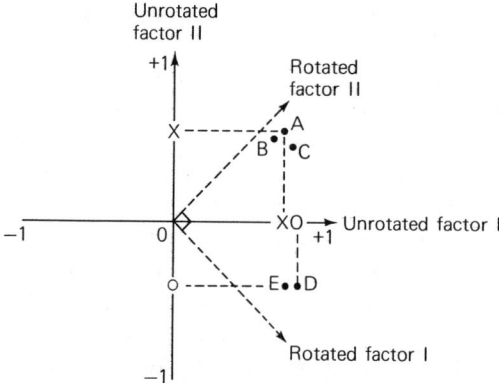

**FIG. 17.1**    Orthogonal factor rotation.

factor so extracted tends to be a general factor; that is, it tends to load significantly on every variable. However, the second factor tends to be bipolar; that is, approximately half of the variables have positive loadings and the other half negative loadings. The remaining factors also tend to be bipolar, and it is often hard to interpret such factors. Furthermore, every variable tends to be decomposed into positive as well as negative factors, and the complexity of each variable is usually greater than 1.

For an illustration, examine Fig. 17.1, in which five variables (A, B, C, D, and E) are depicted in a two-dimensional factor space.

On the unrotated first factor, all the variables load very high. On the unrotated second factor, variables A, B, and C are moderately high in the positive direction, while variables E and D are moderately high in the negative direction. A's loadings on the unrotated factors are indicated by the crossmarks on each axis; the distances of these marks from the origin represent the loadings. Likewise, the loadings of D are indicated by circles. Note that D's loading on the unrotated second factor is negative. The unrotated factor loadings for these variables are presented in Table 17.6.

**TABLE 17.6    Comparison between two factor loadings**

|  | Unrotated factors | | Rotated factors | |
|---|---|---|---|---|
| VARA | .75 | .63 | .14 | .95 |
| VARB | .69 | .57 | .14 | .90 |
| VARC | .80 | .49 | .18 | .92 |
| VARD | .85 | −.42 | .94 | .09 |
| VARE | .76 | −.42 | .92 | .07 |

From inspection of Fig. 17.1, it is obvious that there are two clusters of variables: variables A, B, and C go together, as do variables D and E. However, such patterning of variables is not so obvious from the unrotated factor loadings. By rotating the original axis to the dotted lines in Fig. 17.1, however we get completely different factor loadings. Note that variable D loads high on rotated factor I, but almost zero on rotated factor II. On the other hand, variable A loads very high on rotated factor II, but almost zero on rotated factor I. The clustering or patterning of these variables into two groups is more obvious after the rotation than before, even though the relative position or configuration of the variables remains unchanged.

In the unrotated solution, every variable is decomposed into two significant common factors, while in the rotated solution, each variable is decomposed into a single significant common factor. Therefore, the rotated factor loadings are conceptually simpler than the unrotated ones. In fact, if there were more than two factors, the meaning of the unrotated factors could be even harder to comprehend because some variable might load on many factors. Another important reason for rotation is that the loadings in the unrotated solution depend heavily on the relative number of variables; if you delete one variable, which presumably stands for a certain theoretical dimension, the relative loadings on the unrotated factors may change drastically. The rotated factors are more stable in this respect than the unrotated ones.

The same general principles apply to oblique rotations as apply to orthogonal rotations. The oblique rotation method is more flexible because the factor axes need not be orthogonal

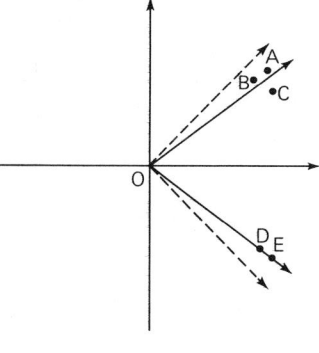

---→ Orthogonal rotated factors
——→ Oblique rotated factors      **FIG. 17.2**    Oblique rotation factor.

(uncorrelated) and is more realistic because the theoretically important underlying dimensions are not assumed to be unrelated to each other. In Fig. 17.2, the two rotational methods are compared. Note that the oblique factor axes represent the clustering of variables more accurately insofar as each axis is closer to the respective group of variables. Furthermore, the oblique solution provides us with information about the amount of *actual* correlation between the factors. In this particular example, the two groups are in fact fairly orthogonal to each other.

The ultimate goal of any rotation is to get some theoretically meaningful factors and, if possible, the simplest factor structure. To achieve such a simple structure, Thurstone tried to establish some rules of thumb, which have been neatly summarized by Harman (1967:98):

1. Each row of the factor matrix should have at least one zero.
2. If there are m common factors, each column of the factor matrix should have at least m zeros.
3. For every pair of columns of the factor matrix there should be several variables whose entries vanish in one column, but not in the other.
4. For every pair of columns of factor matrix, a large proportion of the variables should have vanishing entries in both columns when there are four or more factors.
5. For every pair of columns of the factor matrix there should be only a small number of variables with nonvanishing entries on both columns.

The above criterion can be paraphrased in geometric terms. Going back to Fig. 17.1, the above criterion ensures that (1) many points will lie near the final factor axes; (2) a large number of points will lie near the origin (this will be the case only when there are many factors); and (3) only a small number of points will remain removed from both axes (Harman, 1967:99).

In practice, all objective or analytical methods of rotation boil down to this: Given the fixed number of factors and the fixed amount of variance accounted for by these factors (or the fixed amount of total communality), how do we go about simplifying the rows of the factor matrix and/or simplifying the columns of the factor matrix? By simplifying the rows, we mean making as many values as possible in each row close to zero, and by simplifying the columns, we mean making as many values as possible in each column close to zero. Both simplifications ultimately lead to the same simple structure. With these general remarks in mind, let us compare the specific rotational methods.

### 17.3.1   ORTHOGONAL ROTATION: QUARTIMAX

The guiding principle of quartimax rotation is to make the complexity of a variable a minimum, that is, to rotate the initial factors in such a way that a variable loads high on one factor, but almost zero on all others. (Recall the example of rotation in Fig. 17.1.) Such a criterion means in analytic terms the minimization of the cross-product of factor loadings for variable j:

$$\sum_{p<q=1}^{m} \sum_{j=1}^{n} (a_{jp}a_{jq})^2 \to \text{minimum}$$

where $p < q$, and each refers to common factors. If one of the cross-product terms (factor loading) is zero, the cross-product will be zero.

Let us note that the communalities do not change under orthogonal rotation. This also implies that the amount of variance accounted for by any orthogonal solution will remain the same. Therefore, the square of the total communality will also remain constant.

$$\sum_{p=1}^{m} \sum_{j=1}^{n} a_{jp}^4 + 2 \sum_{p>q=1}^{m} \sum_{j=1}^{n} a_{jp}^2 a_{jq}^2 = (\text{total common variance})^2$$

$$= \text{constant}^\dagger$$

If one wants to minimize the cross-product term in the above equation, one has to maximize the first term, i.e., the sum of the factor loadings to its fourth power; hence the name QUARTIMAX.

$$\sum_{}^{m} \sum_{}^{n} a_{jp}^4 \rightarrow \text{maximum}$$

The maximum possible simplification is reached if every variable loads only on one factor. The rotational method QUARTIMAX seeks to attain such simplicity under the restraints imposed by the data.

Since the method emphasizes simplification of the rows of the factor matrix, the first rotated factor tends to be a general factor, (that is, many variables tend to load high on it), while subsequent factors tend to be subclusters of variables.

### 17.3.2 ORTHOGONAL ROTATION: VARIMAX

In contrast to QUARTIMAX, which centers on simplifying the *rows* of a factor matrix, the VARIMAX criterion centers on simplifying the *columns* of a factor matrix. Note that in QUARTIMAX many variables can load high or near high on the same factor (because the main focus is on simplifying the rows), but VARIMAX defines a simple factor as one with only 1's and 0's in the column.

Such a simplification is equivalent to maximizing the variance of the squared loadings in each column. Hence the name VARIMAX. This method of rotation is the most widely used and is in a way a modification of quartimax. Compare this computational formula with the preceding one.

$$n \sum_{p=1}^{m} \sum_{j=1}^{n} \left(\frac{a_{jp}}{h_j}\right)^4 - \sum_{p=1}^{m} \left(\sum_{j=1}^{n} \frac{a_{jp}^2}{h_j^2}\right)^2 \rightarrow \text{maximum}$$

### 17.3.3 ORTHOGONAL ROTATION: EQUIMAX

EQUIMAX follows the general line of reasoning of the QUARTIMAX and VARIMAX criteria. It can be thought of as a compromise solution of the preceding two. Instead of concentrating either on simplification of the rows or on simplification of the columns, it tries to accomplish some of each. Hence the name EQUIMAX.

### 17.3.4 OBLIQUE ROTATION: OBLIQUE

Oblique rotation involves a similar type of simplifying principle. Here, however, the requirement of orthogonality among the factor axes is relaxed. In principle, the initial factor axes are allowed to rotate freely to best summarize any clustering of variables. Such rotation, however, can be adequately achieved only with some visual or graphical aid and the discerning eye of the researcher.

Most objective methods of oblique rotation have been traditionally achieved *indirectly* by defining the so-called *reference axes* and simplifying them. The idea is to minimize the cross-

$^\dagger \sum_{j=1}^{n} h_j^2 = \sum_{j=1}^{n} \sum_{p=1}^{m} a_{jp}^2 = \text{proportion of total variance accounted for by m common factors} = \text{constant}$

$$\left(\sum_{p=1}^{m} \sum_{j=1}^{n} a_{jp}^2\right)^2 = \sum_{p=1}^{m} \sum_{j=1}^{n} a_{jp}^4 + 2 \sum_{p<q=1}^{m} \sum_{j=1}^{m} a_{jp}^2 a_{jq}^2 = \text{constant}$$

products of the factor loadings on reference axes in order to simplify the primary factor loadings. Hence, the generic name of the rotational methods based on this idea is indirect "oblimin". Since we believe that the introduction of reference axes unnecessarily complicates the presentation and that the theoretical payoff is negligible, we opted for the direct "oblimin" criterion in which the simplification of the pattern matrix is achieved by simplifying the expression:

$$\sum_{p<q=1}^{m} \left( \sum_{j=1}^{n} a_{jp}^2 a_{jq}^2 - \frac{\delta}{n} \sum_{j=1}^{n} a_{jp}^2 \sum_{j=1}^{n} a_{jq}^2 \right)$$

where a's are factor pattern loadings and $\delta$ is an arbitrary value by means of which the analyst can control the obliqueness of his solution.

In this method, the factors are allowed to be correlated if such correlations exist in the data. However, none of the objective, or machine-determined, methods designed so far produce the best, undisputable, terminal solution. Some methods tend to make the resulting factors more correlated than others. In the rotational method OBLIQUE, the default value of $\delta$ (controlled by DELTA) is set at zero, which is known to produce a fairly oblique solution. This value can be altered by the user to make the terminal solution more oblique or less oblique.

| Some suggested values of $\delta$ | |
| --- | --- |
| Any positive value | Extremely oblique (correlated) solution |
| 0 | Default value—fairly oblique (correlated) solution |
| −.5 to −5 | Less oblique (correlated) solution |
| Less than −5 | Nearly orthogonal (uncorrelated) solution |

The user must make the final decision on which value of DELTA best fits his data. Comparison of the results of direct "oblimin" rotations with other more traditional methods of rotation is given in Harman (1967:334-341).

### 17.3.5 GRAPHICAL PRESENTATION OF ROTATED ORTHOGONAL FACTORS

Subprogram FACTOR provides the user with a graphical presentation of the rotated factors that have been determined by any of the three orthogonal rotations. If the user desires to output these plots, he may do so by inserting the appropriate number on his STATISTICS card (see Sec. 17.8). Since only two-dimensional space can be effectively plotted, the program will take every possible pair of factors one by one. If, for instance, there are three rotated factors (FACTOR 1, FACTOR 2, and FACTOR 3), the program will give three different plots: one graph with FACTOR 1 and FACTOR 2, another with FACTOR 1 and FACTOR 3, and the third with FACTOR 2 and FACTOR 3.

In reading the graphs, the user should pay attention to the following three aspects: (1) the relative distance of a variable from the two axes, (2) the direction of a variable in relation to the axes (it may indicate either a positive or a negative loading), and finally (3) the clustering of variables and their relative position to each other. In this way, the user can acquire some information on the degree of *actual* correlation between the factors.

In the accompanying example (Fig. 17.3), we see that variables 4, 5, 7, 8, 9, and 13 are all close to the origin and therefore have small loadings on both factors. The cluster of variables 1, 2, 3, 6, and 10 load high on FACTOR 1, but low on FACTOR 2. Similarly, variables 11, 12, and 14 load high on FACTOR 2, but low on FACTOR 1. Note, however, that both variables 6 and 12, unlike the others, have some loading on both factors. As a whole, the graph separates the clustering of 11, 12, and 14 from the clustering of 1, 2, 3, 6, and 10. The clustering of these two groups also seems to indicate some degree of correlation between them. If one were to draw a line through the middle of each clustering from the origin, the two lines will be less than 90 degrees apart.

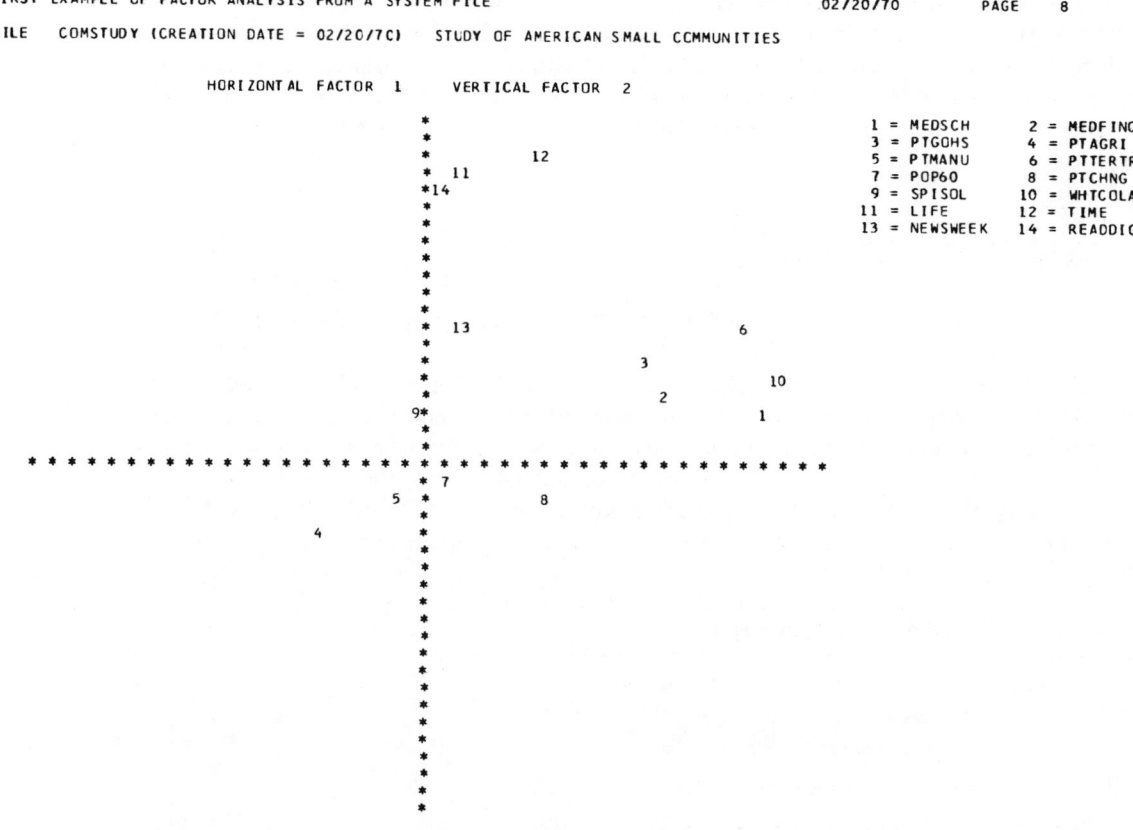

FIRST EXAMPLE OF FACTOR ANALYSIS FROM A SYSTEM FILE          02/20/70     PAGE   8

FILE   COMSTUDY (CREATION DATE = 02/20/7C)    STUDY OF AMERICAN SMALL COMMUNITIES

**FIG. 17.3**    An example of graphic presentation.

## 17.4    BUILDING COMPOSITE INDICES WITH A FACTOR-SCORE COEFFICIENT (OR FACTOR ESTIMATE) MATRIX

After the proper terminal solution is obtained, the user may wish to build composite scales that represent the theoretical dimensions associated with the respective factors. By means of a factor-score matrix and the SPSS data-modification cards (COMPUTE's and IF's), the user may assign factor scores to each case in his file.

Subprogram FACTOR uses the least-squares regression method to estimate factors. The program defines the best set of coefficients for the variables in such a way that the correlation between the composite variable and the hypothetical factor is maximum. Except in the principal-component solution (where the diagonals of the correlation matrix are not altered), the correlation between such a composite variable and the respective factor will not be perfect.[1]

The coefficients displayed in Table 17.7 represent regression weights of each standardized variable (z score) to construct a composite factor index.[2] For example, the best estimate of FACTOR 1 will be given by

$$f_1 = .83200z_1 + .22120z_2 + .10000z_3 + .21267z_4 + .00389z_5$$

---

[1]The actual formula used in calculating the score coefficient matrix is

$$\overline{F} = S'R^{-1}$$

where $\overline{F}$ represents the factor-score coefficient matrix, S the rotated factor structure matrix, and R the correlation matrix [see Harman (1967:352)].

[2]It has been customary to build factor scales employing only those variables that have substantial loadings on a given factor. It seems, however, that the complete-estimation method (as shown in SPSS) has some advantages over such shorthand methods. In the shorter method, the influence of variables not included in the scale construction is not controlled; they will affect the scale through their intercorrelations with the variables used in the scale. In the complete-estimation method, on the other hand, some variables are simply used as *supression* variables to give the best estimate of the given factor. Ultimately the user must decide for himself which of these methods is to be used.

**TABLE 17.7    Factor-score coefficient matrix**

|         | FACTOR 1 | FACTOR 2 |
|---------|----------|----------|
| VAR001  | .83200   | −.23168  |
| VAR002  | .22120   | .00193   |
| VAR003  | .10000   | .52354   |
| VAR004  | −.21267  | .62138   |
| VAR005  | .00389   | .82124   |

where $f_1$ stands for a factor scale (of FACTOR 1) and $z_n$ represents the standardized variables of VAR001 to VAR005, respectively. Construction of a factor scale or index requires information about the mean and standard deviation of each variable (in addition to the factor-score matrix), because one has to convert the variables into z scores. For instance, $z_1$ in the preceding equation is given by

$$z_1 = (VAR001 - \text{mean of VAR001}) / \text{standard deviation of VAR001}$$

hence the type of statement used for constructing a factor scale would look something like the following:

```
1                 16
COMPUTE           SCALE1 = (.83200 (VAR001 − X₁) / SD₁)
                  + (.22120 (VAR002 − X̄₁) / SD₂) + (.1000 (VAR003 X̄₃)/SD₃) +
                  (−.21267 (VAR004 − X̄₄) / SD₄) + (.00389 (VAR005 − X̄₅) / SD₅)
```

where the actual means and standard deviations would be substituted for $\bar{X}_i$ and $SD_i$.

## 17.5    THE FACTOR PROCEDURE CARD

The user activates the factor analysis subprogram by specifying the control word FACTOR in the control field. This control word is followed by the keyword VARIABLES= as the first parameter in the specification field.[1] The keyword is in turn followed by a list of variables to be included in the factor analysis.

The first portion of the FACTOR procedure card has the following general format

```
1                 16
FACTOR            VARIABLES=variable list/
```

### 17.5.1    THE VARIABLES= LIST

The variable list following the keyword VARIABLES= names all the variables to be included in the factor analysis, no matter which solution is specified.

Variables may be entered onto the FACTOR card according to the usual conventions. Lists of nonadjacent variable names may be entered in any order the user desires as long as they are separated by one or more common delimiters. Three or more adjacent variables may be declared by means of the usual TO convention. However, when TO is used, the user relinquishes control of the order in which the variables will appear in his output. The two types of lists may be intermixed, producing a variable list of the following type:

VARIABLES = VARA, VARD, VARF TO VARN, VARX/

The last variable in the list must be followed by a / (slash).

No more than 69 variables can normally be included in a given variable list. However, this may be increased to an absolute maximum of 80 by increasing the SPACE parameter on the JCL card (see Appendix F.2).

All other rules of syntax applying to variable names must be followed, and of course, no variable may be included in the list that has not been previously defined via a VARIABLE LIST card or by means of a variable transformation.

---

[1]The special delimiter = (equal sign) used to separate the variable list from the keyword variables may have on one or both sides of it one or more common delimiters (blanks or commas) if the user wishes. This is also true wherever it is employed in the FACTOR procedure card.

### 17.5.1.1    The variable list for the input of matrices

Subprogram FACTOR, like PARTIAL CORR and REGRESSION, enables the user to enter correlation matrices. In addition, subprogram FACTOR provides for the input of factor matrices with communalities vector. When the user is entering either type of matrix, the variable list refers to the order of the variables as they appear in the matrix. These names are then associated with the appropriate elements (rows and columns) of the matrix. Additional information concerning the conventions of entering matrices is contained in Sec. 17.6.

### 17.5.2    SELECTION OF FACTORING METHODS: BY THE TYPE= KEYWORD

The user selects the desired method for the initial factor solution by inserting the keyword TYPE= directly after his variable list. This keyword is then followed by another keyword specifying the type of factoring method to be employed. The available keywords are listed below, along with a brief identifying description of the solution.

| Keywords | Meanings |
|----------|----------|
| PA1 | Principal factor without iteration |
| PA2 | Principal factor with iteration |
| RAO | Rao's canonical factoring |
| ALPHA | Alpha factoring |
| IMAGE | Image factoring |

The keyword TYPE may be omitted, in which case the PA2 solution is assumed and will be executed. Note that the keyword specifying the type of solution must be followed by a /. The general format of the FACTOR procedure card up to this point is as follows:

```
1                 16
FACTOR            VARIABLES = variable list/
                  TYPE =  ⎧ PA1   ⎫
                          ⎪ PA2   ⎪
                          ⎨ RAO   ⎬   /
                          ⎪ ALPHA ⎪
                          ⎩ IMAGE ⎭
```

### 17.5.3    ALTERING THE DIAGONAL OF THE CORRELATION MATRIX
### BY MEANS OF THE DIAGONAL VALUE LIST

If the user specifies TYPE = PA1 (principal-factor solution without iteration), he may wish to alter the main diagonals of the correlation matrix. This is accomplished by inserting the keyword DIAGONAL=. This keyword is followed by a list of communality estimates for each of the variables in the matrix. These new diagonal elements will replace the usual 1.0 in the matrix. They, therefore, must be entered according to the order of the variables specified in the VARIABLES list portion of the FACTOR procedure card.

When the user wishes to change the diagonal, he will usually use one of the following: (1) the highest absolute values of the correlation coefficients in each column; (2) the squared multiple correlation of each variable with the rest of the variables; (3) any value that falls between 1.0 and the squared multiple correlation. This means that the values will always be positive and will never exceed 1.0.

The values are inserted to the right of the keyword DIAGONAL= and must be separated by one or more common delimiters as is always the case in lists of values on SPSS control cards.

A special convention exists for instances where the user wishes the same value to be applied to a number of adjacent diagonals. This repeat convention is activated by entering an integer equal to the number of times the value is to be repeated and then entering the value to be repeated following as asterisk. The form of this repeat convention is then *"n\*value"* where *n* is the number of times the value is to be repeated, and value is the desired diagonal element. The two conventions for entering the diagonal values can be intermixed to produce a diagonal list of the following type:

```
                  16
                  DIAGONAL = value, value,  n*value, . . . , value/
```

Of course, the DIAGONAL= keyword and the associated value list are totally optional. If the DIAGONAL= keyword is not entered, 1.0 will *always* be assumed to be the value of the diagonal elements of the correlation matrix. (This will be the case even if the original correlation matrix is changed to contain values other than 1.0.)

In factoring methods other than PA1, however, these diagonals are automatically replaced by the values required by each factoring method. Therefore, the DIAGONAL= keyword *should* be used *only* with PA1.

When DIAGONAL= is used, the general format of the FACTOR procedure card is

```
1                16
FACTOR           VARIABLES= variable list/
                 TYPE = PA1/ DIAGONAL = value list/
```

### 17.5.4  CONTROLLING THE FACTORING PROCESS: THE NFACTORS, MINEIGEN, ITERATE, AND STOPFACT PARAMETERS

The user controls the factoring procedure by entering a series of keywords that provide the FACTOR program with instructions for extracting the factors. There are four keywords: NFACTORS, MINEIGEN, ITERATE, and STOPFACT. However, not all the keywords are applicable to all the factoring methods. NFACTORS and MINEIGEN, which are alternative methods for determining the number of factors to be extracted, may always be used with PA1 and PA2, but only users well acquainted with the theory of factor analysis should attempt to use them with the other techniques. ITERATE and STOPFACT, which control the iterative processes in PA2, RAO, and ALPHA, have no meaning for IMAGE and PA1 and therefore may not be used with them.

All the keywords and their associated parameters are optional since the program provides standard default values for them. In most cases the parameters have been set to values that have become more or less standard conventions in the various factoring methods. In other instances, such as ITERATE, they have been set to values that will protect the user from inadvertently consuming large quantities of machine time. In general, it is probably a good idea to change these default parameters only when the user has a specific reason for doing so.

When more than one of these keywords are employed, they may be entered in any internal order the user desires. However, each parameter must be terminated with a slash [/].

#### 17.5.4.1  Controlling the number of factors with the NFACTORS parameter

Whenever the user knows the number of factors that he wishes extracted, he may specify this number by entering the keyword NFACTORS= and following this with the value equal to the number of factors desired. NFACTORS will normally only be used with factoring methods PA1 and PA2. With other factoring methods, he may use NFACTORS only after examining the rotated factors to delete some of the trivial factors.

Whenever the user desires the complete principal-component solution, NFACTORS must be set equal to the number of variables. Note that the NFACTORS parameter must be followed by a /. NFACTORS is required if input is a factor matrix with communalities vector.

Some example usages of NFACTORS are

```
16
NFACTORS = 3/
NFACTORS = 12/
```

#### 17.5.4.2  Controlling the number of factors with the MINEIGEN parameter

The number of factors extracted is normally determined by the specification of the minimum eigenvalue. According to accepted conventions, the SPSS FACTOR ANALYSIS program automatically deletes all factors with an associated eigenvalue of less than 1.0. If the user wishes to alter this criterion, he may either raise or lower the acceptable eigenvalue by entering the keyword MINEIGEN= and follow it with the desired eigenvalue.

However, if the NFACTORS parameter is used, it will take precedence over the MINE-IGEN parameter. Normally the user will use the MINEIGEN parameter *only* if he has some special reason for increasing or decreasing the number of factors to be extracted. Otherwise, the default eigenvalue of 1.0 should suffice.

The user should be very wary of using MINEIGEN with factoring procedures other than PA1 and PA2. As usual, the argument must be terminated with a slash [/].

Some example usages of MINEIGEN are

```
16
MINEIGEN = 1.5 /
MINEIGEN = .8 /
```

### 17.5.4.3  Controlling the number of iterations with the ITERATE parameter

Factoring methods PA2, RAO, and ALPHA employ an iterative convergence method to reach the final communalities. Such iterative procedures are costly in terms of machine time, and large matrices can require literally hundred of iterations to achieve a more or less accurate convergence. On the other hand, social scientists are rarely concerned about accuracy beyond the second or third digit. For these reasons we have set the maximum number of iterations at 25.

If the user desires more accuracy, he may increase the number of permissible iterations by means of the ITERATE= keyword and its associated value. When the user does not specify the maximum number of iterations, the program will accept the solution of the twenty-fifth iteration whether or not acceptable convergence has been reached. The number of iterations performed is reported in the output with a message indicating whether an adequate conversion has or has not been reached.

Example usages of the ITERATE= parameter to increase or decrease a number of permissible iterations follow:

```
16
ITERATE = 99 /
ITERATE = 1 /
```

The keyword ITERATE= must be followed by an integer value equal to the maximum permissible number of iterations. Like all parameters on the FACTOR procedure cards, the argument must be concluded with a /.

### 17.5.4.4  Controlling the number of iterations with the STOPFACT parameter

Satisfactory convergence in the iterative process is indicated by the convergence criterion specified by the STOPFACT= parameter. If the user does not specify the STOPFACT value, the iteration stops if two successive sets of communality estimates are different from each other by not more than 0.001.

If the user wishes to lower or raise this value and thus increase or decrease the number of iterations, he may do so by entering the keyword STOPFACT= and following it with the desired value. No more than seven significant digits to the right of decimal points may be specified, and 1.0 is the maximum value that may be entered.

If the value specified by ITERATE or the default 25 iterations is reached before the STOPFACT criterion has been satisfied, iteration will cease. Remember that the STOPFACT argument must terminate with a /.

Example usages of STOPFACT are

```
16
STOPFACT = .0001/
STOPFACT = .05/
```

The default values for each of the four parameters are listed in Table 17.8.

**TABLE 17.8     Values for the four parameters that control the factoring process**

| Parameter | Default values |
|---|---|
| NFACTORS | Minimum eigenvalue |
| MINEIGEN | 1.0 |
| ITERATE | 25 |
| STOPFACT | 0.001 |

The user should remember that some of these parameters are subordinate to others. The number of factors, for example, will be determined by the minimum eigenvalue unless explicitly specified by NFACTORS. MINEIGEN, on the other hand, will always be overridden by the NFACTORS parameter. Normally the number of iterations is determined by the default STOP-FACT criterion, which is .001 unless it has been changed by the user. However, if the specified level of convergence has not been reached by the time that the maximum permissible iteration cycle has been performed, iteration will stop. This is true whether the user has altered the ITERATE value or not.

### 17.5.5  SELECTING THE METHOD OF ROTATION WITH THE ROTATE PARAMETER

The user may select among four methods of rotation by means of the ROTATE parameter—three of the methods of rotation by means of the ROTATE parameter—three of the methods are orthogonal and one is oblique. The three orthogonal methods are varimax, quartimax, and equimax. The oblique method can be further modified by specification of DELTA. Each of these methods has been described in some detail in Sec. 17.3, and the user should read that section before attempting to select the rotation procedure. Like the factoring method, only one type of rotation may be selected for a given factor solution. The number of factors rotated will always be equal to the number of factors extracted during the initial factoring process.

The user selects the rotational method by entering the keyword ROTATE= and following this with VARIMAX, QUARTIMAX, EQUIMAX, or OBLIQUE. If the ROTATE parameter is not entered, VARIMAX rotation will be executed.[1]

The general structure of this portion of the FACTOR procedure card is

$$
\begin{array}{l}
\mathbf{16} \\
\text{ROTATE} = \left\{ \begin{array}{l} \text{VARIMAX} \\ \text{or} \\ \text{QUARTIMAX} \\ \text{or} \\ \text{EQUIMAX} \\ \text{or} \\ \text{OBLIQUE} \end{array} \right\} \ /
\end{array}
$$

The following are valid examples:

```
16
ROTATE = VARIMAX/
ROTATE = EQUIMAX/
ROTATE = OBLIQUE/
```

#### 17.5.5.1  Controlling oblique rotation with the DELTA parameter

The user may control oblique rotation by specifying the DELTA parameter. The default value is set at zero. If the user wishes less oblique rotation, he may do so by decreasing the value. The general format of the DELTA parameter is

**16**
DELTA = value/

A valid example of DELTA used in conjunction with ROTATE is

```
16
ROTATE = OBLIQUE/DELTA = -.5/
```

### 17.5.6  SUMMARY OF THE FORMAT OF THE FACTOR PROCEDURE CARD

With the exception of the VARIABLES= keyword and its associated variable list, which must be the first set of parameters on a FACTOR card, the order of all other parameters are optional, and the user may enter them in any order he desires.

However, because of the sequential logic of the factor-analysis procedure and the large number of controlling parameters, we suggest that the user follow the sequence we have used in

---

[1] Although some of these keywords are larger than the usual eight characters, the program identifies the rotational procedure by the first eight characters and then simply ignores the remaining characters up to the /.

preparing his FACTOR card. The system will, however, accept any order as long as all necessary information has been entered and the VARIABLE= list appears first.

Because so many parameters are optional, it is difficult to specify the general format of the card. We shall instead list a series of concrete examples that display most of the usual configurations of the FACTOR procedure card.

### EXAMPLE 17.1

```
1              16
FACTOR         VARIABLES=A, B, C, D, E, F, G/
```

This first example illustrates the most simple version of the factor card where all the default options are selected. PA2 with iterations will be the factoring method; the number of factors extracted will be determined by the number of factors with an eigenvalue greater than or equal to 1.0; the diagonals of the correlation matrix will be initially replaced by squared multiple correlations; the iteration will be stopped if the convergence reaches the .001 criterion; the maximum number of iterations will be 25; and finally, the varimax rotation will be used.[1]

### EXAMPLE 17.2

```
1              16
FACTOR         VARIABLES = A, B, C, D TO H/
               TYPE = RAO/ ITERATE = 99/
```

Example 17.2 will produce a factor analysis with the following specifications: Rao's canonical factoring will be executed; the number of factors will be determined by the default option (only factors with eigenvalues greater than or equal to 1.0 will be retained); the maximum iteration allowed will be 99; the convergence criterion will be the default .001; and the terminal solution will be based upon the varimax rotation.[1]

### EXAMPLE 17.3

```
1              16
FACTOR         VARIABLES = A, B, C, D, E, F, G/
               TYPE = PA1/NFACTORS = 7/
```

Example 17.3 displays a FACTOR procedure card in which (1) PA1 is selected, and (2) the number of factors to be extracted is the same as the number of variables. This example will give the user a complete principal-component solution. As it stands, it will rotate the seven components according to the varimax criterion. (However, the user may not be interested in rotating a complete principal-component solution and can indicate this on the STATISTICS card.)

### EXAMPLE 17.4

```
1              16
FACTOR         VARIABLES = A, B, C, D, E, F/
               TYPE = PA1/ DIAGONAL = .95, .96, .93, .78, .88, .77/
               ROTATE = OBLIQUE
```

Example 17.4 shows the user how to change the diagonal elements of the correlation matrix. Specification of DIAGONAL values is not permitted for factoring methods other than PA1. The rotational method will be oblique, with default value of DELTA = 0.

### EXAMPLE 17.5

```
1              16
FACTOR         VARIABLES = A, B, C, D, E, F, G, H, K/
               TYPE = IMAGE/ ROTATE = EQUIMAX/
```

[1]The user *must always* prepare a STATISTICS card when using subprogram FACTOR.

For image factoring, the user has to specify the VARIABLES parameter and the TYPE parameter and that will be all that is normally needed. The user may, however, choose any one of the rotational methods.

Table 17.9 summarizes all the keywords and their associated arguments that may be used on the FACTOR procedure card.

**TABLE 17.9    Summary table of keywords and keyword parameters for subprogram factor**

| Keyword | Argument(s) | Function performed |
|---|---|---|
| VARIABLES= | variable list | Lists the variables to be included in the factor analysis. |
| TYPE= | PA1, PA2, ALPHA, RAO, IMAGE | Selects the initial factoring method. PA2 is the default option if the TYPE parameter is deleted. |
| DIAGONAL= | Value list of the type: value$_i$, value$_j$, . . . , value n or n*value or value$_i$, n*value, value$_j$ | Permits the user to alter the diagonal elements. To be used only with PA1. |
| NFACTORS= | value | Specifies the number of factors to be extracted for the initial solution. Is superordinate to MINEIGEN. |
| MINEIGEN= | value | Permits the user to alter the minimum eigenvalue for factors to be extracted. The default value is 1.0. |
| ITERATE= | value | Specfies the maximum number of iterations permitted. The default value is set to 25. |
| STOPFACT= | value | Permits the user to alter the test criterion for stopping the iterative process. Default is .001. If this value is reached, iteration will stop no matter how many iterations were permissible under the ITERATE parameter. |
| ROTATE= | VARIMAX, QUARTIMAX, EQUIMAX, or OBLIQUE | Selects the desired rotational method. Only one may be used, and if the ROTATE parameter is deleted, VARIMAX will be the rotational method. |
| DELTA= | value | Permits the user to select the desired degree of obliqueness of his rotation. This parameter must be used only in conjunction with ROTATE=OBLIQUE. If not used, the program assumes DELTA = 0. |

## 17.6    SPECIAL CONVENTION FOR MATRIX INPUT AND OUTPUT FOR SUBPROGRAM FACTOR

Subprogram FACTOR allows the user to enter his data in the usual form as cases or observations (which may be in BCD form or reside in SPSS system file) or, alternately, to input a simple correlation matrix or factor matrix directly to the program. This feature enables the user to skip the first and costly step—the computation of the matrix of simple correlations. Once the simple correlations have been computed, the user may try different methods of factoring and rotation without performing the costly and redundant step of reading the raw data.

However, the process of entering a matrix of coefficients is quite different from entering a file of cases. For this reason, a number of special conventions must be followed, and the meaning of a number of the control cards is altered.

### 17.6.1  CONTROL CARDS REQUIRED TO ENTER MATRICES

Whenever either a correlation matrix or a factor matrix is being entered rather than actual data cases, the user must inform the system via the OPTIONS card. Option 3 is used when a matrix of simple correlations is being input, and option 4 is used when a factor matrix is being input. In addition, the user must prepare the following SPSS control cards:

1.   A VARIABLE LIST card is prepared in the usual manner. The list must include all the variables in the matrix. This list serves to name the variables so that they may be appropriately labeled at various points in the output.

2.   An INPUT MEDIUM card containing one of the following keywords—CARD, TAPE, DISK, OTHER—specifying the location of the matrix must also be prepared. When matrices are located on a medium other than CARD, the JCL cards for a BCD input file (FT08) must also be prepared (see Appendix F).

3.   A # OF CASES card must also be prepared containing the user's best estimate of the number of cases upon which the matrix was computed. This card is used only for purposes of computing tests of significance and has nothing to do with the number of variables in the matrix or the number of cards to be read.

4.   A READ MATRIX card must follow the OPTIONS card or the STATISTICS card and must precede the actual matrix if it is input on cards. The READ MATRIX card serves the same purpose as the READ INPUT DATA card.

5.   Some data-definition cards (e.g., formats) and data-modification cards are not applicable to matrices and therefore may not be entered. For similar reasons, matrices may not be retained as SPSS system files.

#### 17.6.1.1  Input of correlation matrix

Subprogram FACTOR accepts correlation matrices in the standard SPSS matrix format. These matrices may be output from subprograms PEARSON CORR, NONPAR CORR, PARTIAL CORR, or REGRESSION, or from subprogram FACTOR itself. Alternatively, the user may input correlation matrices produced by hand or by a non-SPSS program. However, in the latter instance, the matrix must be prepared in the standard SPSS format, which assumes that variables are punched 8F10.7, and each row of the matrix must begin on a new physical card.

Further details on the format of a standard SPSS matrices are given in Sec. 14.3.1. The user must also remember to input an OPTIONS card and activate option 3 whenever the matrix of simple correlations is being input. Finally, if the matrix resides on a medium other than cards, the user must remember to prepare an FT08 JCL card (see Appendix F.4).

#### 17.6.1.2  Input of the factor matrix

When the user wants to input some results of orthogonal factoring and wishes to rotate and/or plot the result, he may do so by inputting the factor matrix and the corresponding communalities vector.[1] This factor matrix may be based on any of the factoring procedures, but the user should remember that not all rotational methods are applicable to all factoring procedures.

Factor matrices to be entered into subprogram FACTOR must be in a standard format. When the matrix and associated communalities have been output from SPSS subprogram FACTOR itself, the user need not worry about this format problem. However, if the matrix is prepared by hand or is being generated by another factor-analysis program, the user must make sure that it is compatible.

The matrices are in card image irrespective of the medium on which they reside. All the factor loadings for the first variable are entered in serial order in a format of 8F10.7. If there are more than eight factors, the ninth to sixteenth loadings are entered on a second card, the

---

[1] Oblique matrices may not be entered.

seventeenth to twenty-fourth on the third, and so on until the last loading for the first variable has been entered. The first loading for each variable begins on a new card. There will, therefore, be one or more cards for each variable in the factor matrix, and the number of cards will depend on the number of factors extracted. The communality estimates follow the factor matrix and are also entered in a format of 8F10.7. The format of these matrices is then

$$
\begin{array}{ccccc}
L_{1,1} & L_{1,2} & L_{1,3} & \cdots & L_{1,m} \\
L_{2,1} & L_{2,2} & L_{2,3} & \cdots & L_{2,m} \\
\multicolumn{5}{c}{\dotfill} \\
L_{n,1} & L_{n,2} & L_{n,3} & \cdots & L_{n,m} \\
C_1 & C_2 & C_3 & \cdots & C_n
\end{array}
$$

where $L_{i,j}$ stands for factor loading for variable $i$ on factor $j$, and $C_i$ stands for communality for variable $i$.

### 17.6.2    OUTPUT OF CORRELATION AND FACTOR MATRICES

The user may wish to output a simple correlation or a factor matrix or both on any run employing subprogram FACTOR. The output of such matrices may be exceedingly useful since they can save a large amount of computer time when different types of factoring and rotational methods are desired for the same body of the data.

The matrices are output in the standard SPSS format as described in the previous section. Option 5 on the OPTIONS card causes the matrix of simple correlations to be produced, and option 6 similarly activates the production of the initial orthogonal-factor matrix and corresponding communalities. If both options are desired, the correlation matrix will be written or punched before the factor matrix. The communalities of the factor matrix are the last series of elements in the factor matrix.

These matrices may be written or punched on any device of the user's choice. An FT09 card specifying their form and location must be prepared (see Appendix F.7).

## 17.7    OPTIONS AVAILABLE IN SUBPROGRAM FACTOR

The FACTOR procedure card is followed by an OPTIONS card, which instructs the program on the processing options desired by the user (see Sec. 5.2, the OPTIONS card). The OPTIONS card contains the control word OPTIONS followed by a number list indicating the options desired.

The first three options determine how missing data will be processed.[1] All these options refer to the manner in which the matrix of simple correlations is to be computed, since this is always the first step in all the factoring procedures.

*The default missing data option—listwise deletion.*    The default or normal means of handling missing data with subprogram FACTOR is listwise deletion. Listwise deletion causes a case to be omitted from the calculation of all coefficients when that case contains a missing value on any variable entered on the variables list. In general, listwise deletion has the effect of reducing the number of cases upon which the factor analysis will be performed. On the other hand, listwise deletion is the only way to insure that the factor analysis is computed on the same set of cases. Since the missing data option affects the computation of the correlations on which the factor analysis is based, it is possible (if pairwise rather than listwise deletion is used) to produce a very artificial factor analysis from correlations that were computed for very different segments of the population. The user himself, however, must make his own decision based on his methodological assumptions and knowledge of his own data. *Listwise deletion, the default missing data option, will be in force unless the user selects* option 1 or 2.

[1]The missing data options are, of course, irrelevant when the input is either a correlation or factor matrix. However, the discussions of the effects of these different procedures on the interpretation of factor solution should be carefully considered before the user produces the matrix of correlations.

*Option* 1.   *Inclusion of missing data.*    Selection of this option causes missing value indicators to be totally ignored and enters all data into the computation of the simple correlation upon which factor analysis will be based. This option is equivalent to deleting all references to missing values of the variables being entered.

*Option* 2.   *Pairwise deletion of missing data.*    Under pairwise deletion, a case is omitted from the computation of a given simple coefficient if the value of either of the variables being considered is missing. A case is therefore included in the computation of all simple correlation coefficients for which it has complete data. Pairwise deletion has the advantage of utilizing as much data as possible in the computation of each of the simple coefficients. It has the disadvantage, however, of (under some circumstances) producing highly artificial correlations that are based on a very different number of cases and perhaps even on quite different subpopulations.

*Options 3 to 6 deal with input and output of matrices.*

*Option* 3.   *Input of the correlation.*    Subprogram FACTOR can operate on a matrix of simple correlations generated on previous runs of any SPSS subprogram that produces a correlation matrix as output (e.g., PEARSON CORR, NONPAR CORR, PARTIAL CORR, REGRESSION). Matrices produced by other programs may be entered as long as they conform to the SPSS matrix format. We highly recommend production of such matrices if the user contemplates extensive experimentation with different factoring and rotational methods. With a large file, input of the correlation matrix can save the user *enormous* amounts of machine time. Option 3 informs subprogram FACTOR that a correlation matrix rather than raw data is to be read. All the other conventions for matrix input discussed in Sec. 17.6 must also be followed.

*Option* 4.   *Input of the factor matrix and communalities.*    When the user has decided on the desired factoring method, but wishes to experiment with different rotational solutions, he may enter a factor matrix and the vector of communalities. Option 5 explains how to produce written or punched factor matrices with SPSS subprogram FACTOR. The user may, of course, also input factor results produced by other programs such as BMD; however, these matrices and their associated communalities must be in the format expected by subprogram FACTOR. Section 17.6 presents detailed instructions for preparing and entering these matrices.

*Option* 5.   *Output of the simple correlation matrix.*    This option causes the correlation matrix used in subprogram FACTOR to be written on an output medium of the user's choice. A complete matrix of all variables entered into the factor analysis will be produced. The matrix will be in the standard SPSS format of 8F10.7, and each row of the matrix will begin a new physical card. As is always the case when matrices are being output, an FT09 JCL card must be prepared (see Appendix F.7).

*Option* 6.   *Output of the factor matrix and communalities.*    The selection of option 6 will cause the factor matrix and the associated communalities to be written on a medium of the user's choice. This matrix may then be reentered into the FACTOR subprogram for different rotational solutions, calculation of factor-score coefficients, or plotting factor results. The format of the factor matrix and associated communalities will be identical to that described in the requirements for entering this type of information (see Sec. 17.6). The user must remember to prepare an FT09 JCL card as he always must when producing a matrix output (see Appendix F.7).

As usual, the OPTIONS card may be deleted if all the default options are selected. When this is done, the following options will be executed on the data:

1. Matrix input will not be accepted.
2. Missing data will be excluded by the listwise convention.
3. Matrix output will not be produced.

## 17.8    STATISTICS AVAILABLE FOR SUBPROGRAM FACTOR

The role of the STATISTICS card in subprogram FACTOR is fundamentally different from its role in all other SPSS procedures. Because there are no standard or core computations, all information to be output must be specified on the STATISTICS card. If no STATISTICS card is entered, no output will be produced. In this way, the user has complete control over what is to be printed on his output as well as what is to be calculated.

As usual, statistics are selected by statistics number and any combination of statistics may be requested. If all the available statistics are desired, the user may enter the keyword ALL in lieu of a number list. The general format of the STATISTICS card is then

**1**                        **16**

STATISTICS        $\left\{ \begin{array}{c} \text{number list} \\ \text{or} \\ \text{ALL} \end{array} \right\}$

The following are the statistics available:

*Statistic 1.*   *Means and standard deviations.*   Causes the means and standard deviations of the variables listed on the VARIABLES= list of the FACTOR procedure card to be printed along with the number of valid cases observed for each of the variables.

*Statistic 2.*   *Correlation matrix.*   This option instructs the system to print out a simple or zero-order correlation matrix for all variables entered into the factor analysis.

*Statistic 3.*   *Inverse and determinant of correlation matrix.*   Causes the inverse of the correlation matrix and its determinant to be printed. These intermediary statistics are required for factor solution, but are not usually interpreted. They are made available for those special situations where the researcher might wish to have access to an inverted matrix for his own computations.

*Statistic 4.*   *Communalities, eigenvalues, and proportion of total and common variance.*   Instructs the program to print out the following statistics: (1) the eigenvalues associated with the initial unrotated and rotated factors; (2) the proportion of total variance accounted for by the initial factors; (3) if applicable, the proportion of the common variance accounted for by the rotated factors; and (4) the initial communality estimates (if applicable) and the final communalities.

*Statistic 5.*   *Initial factor matrix.*   Causes the initial unrotated factor matrix to be printed. This matrix contains only the number of significant factors or the number requested with the NFACTORS parameter. If the user wishes to see the entire matrix, NFACTORS should be set equal to the number of variables. This matrix usually contains a large amount of valuable information about the structure of the variables. Thus, we recommend the user obtain it even if he is primarily interested in the rotated solution.

*Statistic 6.*   *Rotated factor matrix and transformation matrix.*   Causes the selected rotated matrix, VARIMAX, QUARTIMAX, EQUIMAX, or OBLIQUE, to be printed. The accompanying transformation matrix used in converting the initial matrix to the terminal rotated matrix will be printed. Statistic 6 will almost always be requested.

*Statistic 7.*   *Factor-score coefficient matrix.*   Instructs the program to print the factor-score coefficient matrix, which is commonly used to construct composite variables based on the rotated factor solution. See Sec. 17.4, which describes how this matrix can be used in conjunction with SPSS data-modification cards to construct factor scores. Calculation of this statistic requires additional computer time because the correlation matrix must be inverted again. When input is a factor matrix, this option is not available.

*Statistic 8.*  *Plot of rotated factors.*  In orthogonal solution, selection of this statistic causes the program to plot the relative position of each variable in all possible pairs of factor axes. For example, if there are three factors, A, B, and C, there will be three diagrams in which factors A and B, A and C, and B and C constitute the vertical and horizontal axes (see Sec. 17.3.5).

Table 17.10 gives a summary of the correspondence between statistics and statistics numbers.

**TABLE 17.10    Table of statistics**

| Statistics | Description |
|---|---|
| 1 | Means and standard deviations |
| 2 | Correlation matrix |
| 3 | Inverse and determinant of correlation matrix |
| 4 | Communalities, eigenvalues, and proportion of total and common variance |
| 5 | Initial-factor matrix |
| 6 | Rotated factor matrix and transformation matrix |
| 7 | Factor-estimate matrix |
| 8 | Plot of rotated factors |

## 17.9    PROGRAM LIMITATIONS FOR SUBPROGRAM FACTOR

The following limitations exist for subprogram FACTOR:

*Limitation 1.*    One and only one factor analysis may be specified on a given FACTOR procedure card and its continuations. This means that only one variable list can be entered and that only one method of factoring and one method of rotation may be specified.

*Limitation 2.*    No more than 66 variables may be entered into the factor analysis when the default value of 80,000 is used as the SPACE parameter. Under no circumstances can the number of variables exceed 80, regardless of how much core is available at the user's installation.

The amount of SPACE required for the execution of subprogram FACTOR is determined by the following formula:

$$SPACE = 2(9m^2 + m)$$

where m stands for the total number of variables entered after the VARIABLES= parameter.

## 17.10    EXAMPLE DECK SETUPS FOR SUBPROGRAM FACTOR

Example 17.6 illustrates the uses of subprogram FACTOR in a run from an SPSS system file named COMSTUDY. (The data-definition cards, control cards, and cases are listed in Appendix I.)

Factor analysis has been executed for 14 variables in this file which contains selected population and communications data for a sample of 64 small American communities.

## EXAMPLE 17.6

```
                16
RUN NAME        FIRST EXAMPLE OF FACTOR ANALYSIS FROM A SYSTEM FILE
GET FILE        COMSTUDY
FACTOR          VARIABLES = MEDSCH TO POP60, PTCHNG TO READDIG/
                TYPE=PA2/ ITERATE = 99/
STATISTICS      2, 4, 5, 6, 7, 8
FINISH
```

The FACTOR card specifies factoring procedure PA2 (principal factoring with iterations). A maximum of 99 iterations is permitted, and the number of factors will be determined by the default eigenvalue, i.e., only factors with eigenvalue greater than or equal to 1.0 will be extracted. The method of rotation will be VARIMAX, which is the default rotational method when none is specified.

No OPTIONS card has been prepared, and therefore, all the default options will be in force. Missing data will be excluded by the listwise convention, and no matrices will be written or punched.

The statistics requested on the STATISTICS card will cause the following information to be printed:

1. The correlation matrix
2. Communalities, eigenvalues, and proportion of total and common variance
3. Unrotated principal factor matrix
4. Varimax rotated factor matrix
5. Matrix of factor-score coefficients
6. Plot of rotated factors

Figures 17.4 to 17.9 contain the output from this run. However, only the first page of the plotted factors is presented.

```
FIRST EXAMPLE OF FACTOR ANALYSIS FROM A SYSTEM FILE                02/20/70      PAGE   3

FILE   COMSTUDY (CREATION DATE = 02/20/70)   STUDY OF AMERICAN SMALL COMMUNITIES

CORRELATION COEFFICIENTS..
```

|          | MEDSCH   | MEDFINC  | PTGOHS   | PTAGRI   | PTMANU   | PTTERTRY | POP60    | PTCHNG   | SPISOL   | WHTCOLAR |
|----------|----------|----------|----------|----------|----------|----------|----------|----------|----------|----------|
| MEDSCH   | 1.00000  | 0.71617  | 0.53829  | -0.19448 | 0.08085  | 0.60155  | -0.01193 | 0.21827  | -0.05821 | 0.74307  |
| MEDFINC  | 0.71617  | 1.00000  | 0.52669  | -0.15689 | 0.39568  | 0.35994  | 0.23615  | 0.03174  | -0.51058 | 0.62609  |
| PTGOHS   | 0.53829  | 0.52669  | 1.00000  | -0.31494 | 0.23527  | 0.37886  | 0.24026  | 0.23116  | 0.09121  | -0.36135 |
| PTAGRI   | -0.19448 | -0.15689 | -0.31494 | 1.00000  | -0.21476 | -0.33786 | -0.28284 | -0.13735 | -0.33069 | 0.00934  |
| PTMANU   | 0.08085  | 0.39568  | 0.23527  | -0.21476 | 1.00000  | -0.33034 | 0.09422  | -0.12863 | 0.16935  | 0.71837  |
| PTTERTRY | 0.60155  | 0.35994  | 0.37886  | -0.33786 | -0.33034 | 1.00000  | 0.06109  | 0.16074  | -0.45053 | 0.16889  |
| POP60    | -0.01193 | 0.23615  | 0.24026  | -0.28284 | 0.09422  | 0.06109  | 1.00000  | -0.01544 | 0.02260  | 0.21626  |
| PTCHNG   | 0.21827  | 0.03174  | 0.23116  | -0.13735 | -0.12863 | 0.16074  | -0.01544 | 1.00000  | 1.00000  | -0.11522 |
| SPISOL   | -0.05821 | -0.51058 | -0.23206 | 0.09121  | -0.33069 | 0.16935  | -0.45053 | 0.02260  | 1.00000  | 1.00000  |
| WHTCOLAR | 0.74307  | 0.62609  | 0.61897  | -0.36135 | 0.00934  | 0.71837  | 0.16889  | 0.21626  | -0.11522 | 1.00000  |
| LIFE     | 0.22723  | 0.33037  | 0.31230  | -0.17550 | 0.01367  | 0.31888  | 0.09032  | 0.00014  | -0.03873 | 0.30218  |
| TIME     | 0.36968  | 0.36036  | 0.40195  | -0.27962 | -0.07349 | 0.49613  | 0.09060  | 0.00439  | 0.02665  | 0.50310  |
| NEWSWEEK | 0.03787  | -0.03460 | 0.17128  | -0.08798 | -0.16779 | 0.25293  | -0.08440 | -0.06258 | 0.17443  | 0.09416  |
| READDIG  | 0.12198  | -0.00716 | 0.19664  | -0.17913 | -0.17982 | 0.34106  | -0.13705 | -0.10052 | 0.20752  | 0.10858  |

|          | LIFE     | TIME     | NEWSWEEK | READDIG  |
|----------|----------|----------|----------|----------|
| MEDSCH   | 0.22723  | 0.36968  | 0.03787  | 0.12198  |
| MEDFINC  | 0.33037  | 0.36036  | -0.03460 | -0.00716 |
| PTGOHS   | 0.31230  | 0.40195  | 0.17128  | 0.19664  |
| PTAGRI   | -0.17550 | -0.27962 | -0.08798 | -0.17913 |
| PTMANU   | 0.01367  | -0.07349 | -0.16779 | -0.17982 |
| PTTERTRY | 0.31888  | 0.49613  | 0.25293  | 0.34106  |
| POP60    | 0.09032  | 0.09060  | -0.08440 | -0.13705 |
| PTCHNG   | 0.00014  | 0.00439  | -0.06258 | -0.10052 |
| SPISOL   | -0.03873 | 0.02665  | 0.17443  | 0.20752  |
| WHTCOLAR | 0.30218  | 0.50310  | 0.09416  | 0.10858  |
| LIFE     | 1.00000  | 0.81186  | 0.14379  | 0.64125  |
| TIME     | 0.81186  | 1.00000  | 0.41354  | 0.58991  |
| NEWSWEEK | 0.14379  | 0.41354  | 1.00000  | 0.36860  |
| READDIG  | 0.64125  | 0.58991  | 0.36860  | 1.00000  |

**FIG. 17.4**  Printout of correlation matrix by subprogram FACTOR.

| VARIABLE | EST COMMUNALITY | | FACTCR | EIGENVALUE | PCT OF VAR | CUM PCT |
|----------|-----------------|---|--------|------------|------------|---------|
| MEDSCH   | 0.77798 | | 1  | 4.44502 | 31.8 | 31.8  |
| MEDFINC  | 0.84166 | | 2  | 2.45029 | 17.5 | 49.3  |
| PTGOHS   | 0.55287 | | 3  | 1.58099 | 11.3 | 60.5  |
| PTAGRI   | 0.41984 | | 4  | 1.13526 | 8.1  | 68.7  |
| PTMANU   | 0.58936 | | 5  | 0.93891 | 6.7  | 75.4  |
| PTTERTRY | 0.74506 | | 6  | 0.89132 | 6.4  | 81.7  |
| POP60    | 0.36138 | | 7  | 0.78887 | 5.6  | 87.4  |
| PTCHNG   | 0.22295 | | 8  | 0.47702 | 3.4  | 90.8  |
| SPISOL   | 0.59173 | | 9  | 0.43167 | 3.1  | 93.9  |
| WHTCOLAR | 0.78638 | | 10 | 0.31201 | 2.2  | 96.1  |
| LIFE     | 0.80718 | | 11 | 0.20697 | 1.5  | 97.6  |
| TIME     | 0.82276 | | 12 | 0.15863 | 1.1  | 98.7  |
| NEWSWEEK | 0.42618 | | 13 | 0.10053 | 0.7  | 99.4  |
| READDIG  | 0.63451 | | 14 | 0.08246 | 0.6  | 100.0 |

**FIG. 17.5**　Estimated communalities (squared multiple correlation), eigenvalues, and proportion of variance, calculated from the unaltered correlation matrix.

FACTOR MATRIX USING PRINCIPAL FACTOR WITH ITERATIONS

|          | FACTOR 1 | FACTOR 2 | FACTCR 3 | FACTOR 4 |
|----------|----------|----------|----------|----------|
| MEDSCH   | -0.75380 | 0.19234  | 0.39434  | -0.24910 |
| MEDFINC  | -0.72105 | 0.54392  | -0.07052 | -0.30248 |
| PTGOHS   | -0.66335 | 0.20449  | -0.01332 | 0.03380  |
| PTAGRI   | 0.38883  | -0.06675 | 0.06901  | -0.25453 |
| PTMANU   | -0.06410 | 0.48931  | -0.29405 | -0.25403 |
| PTTERTRY | -0.73018 | -0.26090 | 0.40367  | 0.23366  |
| POP60    | -0.20840 | 0.40680  | -0.31590 | 0.58099  |
| PTCHNG   | -0.15315 | 0.05537  | 0.25658  | 0.10430  |
| SPISOL   | 0.15381  | -0.61194 | 0.34397  | -0.06937 |
| WHTCOLAR | -0.83816 | 0.15740  | 0.31587  | 0.09654  |
| LIFE     | -0.60975 | -0.33791 | -0.47111 | -0.10859 |
| TIME     | -0.76393 | -0.40977 | -0.33008 | -0.01292 |
| NEWSWEEK | -0.22697 | -0.37280 | -0.05043 | 0.04312  |
| READDIG  | -0.41339 | -0.61748 | -0.29288 | -0.07789 |

| VARIABLE | COMMUNALITY | | FACTCR | EIGENVALUE | PCT OF VAR | CUM PCT |
|----------|-------------|---|--------|------------|------------|---------|
| MEDSCH   | 0.82277 | | 1 | 2.04634 | 37.7 | 37.7  |
| MEDFINC  | 0.91223 | | 2 | 1.43414 | 26.4 | 64.1  |
| PTGOHS   | 0.48317 | | 3 | 1.10353 | 20.3 | 84.4  |
| PTAGRI   | 0.22520 | | 4 | 0.84915 | 15.6 | 100.0 |
| PTMANU   | 0.39452 | |   |         |      |       |
| PTTERTRY | 0.81878 | |   |         |      |       |
| POP60    | 0.64627 | |   |         |      |       |
| PTCHNG   | 0.10323 | |   |         |      |       |
| SPISOL   | 0.52125 | |   |         |      |       |
| WHTCOLAR | 0.83639 | |   |         |      |       |
| LIFE     | 0.71971 | |   |         |      |       |
| TIME     | 0.86063 | |   |         |      |       |
| NEWSWEEK | 0.19490 | |   |         |      |       |
| READDIG  | 0.64402 | |   |         |      |       |

**FIG. 17.6**　Printout of unrotated factor matrix (initial solution), final communalities, and percent of common variance accounted for by unrotated factors.

VARIMAX ROTATED FACTOR MATRIX

|          | FACTOR  1 | FACTOR  2 | FACTOR  3 | FACTOR  4 |
|----------|-----------|-----------|-----------|-----------|
| MEDSCH   | 0.84587   | 0.14575   | 0.25471   | -0.14543  |
| MEDFINC  | 0.59223   | 0.15180   | C.72839   | 0.08886   |
| PTGOHS   | 0.53111   | 0.26136   | 0.28220   | C.23054   |
| PTAGRI   | -0.26934  | -0.19044  | -0.03567  | -0.33929  |
| PTMANU   | -0.05313  | -0.08750  | 0.61625   | 0.06546   |
| PTTERTRY | 0.76335   | 0.35350   | -0.31555  | 0.10746   |
| POP60    | 0.04923   | -0.03754  | 0.17168   | 0.78292   |
| PTCHNG   | 0.28992   | -0.08864  | -0.09762  | 0.04234   |
| SPISOL   | -0.01446  | 0.12347   | -0.57696  | -0.41583  |
| WHTCOLAR | 0.86305   | 0.21674   | 0.10753   | 0.18163   |
| LIFE     | 0.09918   | 0.81821   | 0.17987   | 0.08978   |
| TIME     | C.29359   | C.86941   | 0.05232   | 0.12578   |
| NEWSWEEK | 0.07221   | 0.38474   | -0.20287  | -0.02255  |
| READDIG  | 0.01229   | 0.78332   | -0.15467  | -0.07973  |

TRANSFCRMATION MATRIX

|          |   | FACTOR  1 | FACTOR  2 | FACTOR  3 | FACTOR  4 |
|----------|---|-----------|-----------|-----------|-----------|
| FACTOR   | 1 | -0.75514  | -0.58143  | -0.23086  | -0.19596  |
| FACTOR   | 2 | 0.18413   | -0.62222  | 0.68674   | 0.32760   |
| FACTOR   | 3 | 0.62861   | -0.51130  | -0.45653  | -0.36742  |
| FACTOR   | 4 | 0.02673   | -0.11551  | -0.51640  | 0.84810   |

**FIG. 17.7**   Rotated orthogonal factor matrix (terminal solution) and transformation matrix used to rotate the initial factor matrix to the terminal solution.

FACTOR SCORE COEFFICIENTS

|          | FACTOR  1 | FACTOR  2 | FACTOR  3 | FACTOR  4 |
|----------|-----------|-----------|-----------|-----------|
| MEDSCH   | C.34627   | -0.07878  | 0.13738   | -0.34526  |
| MEDFINC  | 0.13172   | 0.01351   | 0.46410   | -0.21440  |
| PTGOHS   | 0.13250   | 0.03047   | 0.08541   | 0.10721   |
| PTAGRI   | -0.04962  | -0.02234  | C.11258   | -0.34917  |
| PTMANU   | -0.10564  | 0.02478   | 0.45928   | -0.12904  |
| PTTERTRY | C.32594   | -0.02698  | -0.36585  | 0.14531   |
| POP60    | -0.06781  | -0.05454  | -0.14982  | 0.85358   |
| PTCHNG   | 0.16938   | -0.12026  | -0.14436  | 0.06095   |
| SPISCL   | 0.09270   | 0.03044   | -0.29164  | -0.28977  |
| WHTCOLAR | 0.33201   | -0.07936  | -0.08928  | 0.08227   |
| LIFE     | -0.16689  | 0.40176   | 0.17478   | -0.01118  |
| TIME     | -0.07024  | 0.37086   | 0.03900   | 0.05542   |
| NEWSWEEK | -0.01663  | C.15846   | -0.12374  | 0.01726   |
| READDIG  | -0.13522  | 0.37983   | -0.01813  | -0.08246  |

**FIG. 17.8**   Factor estimate matrix.

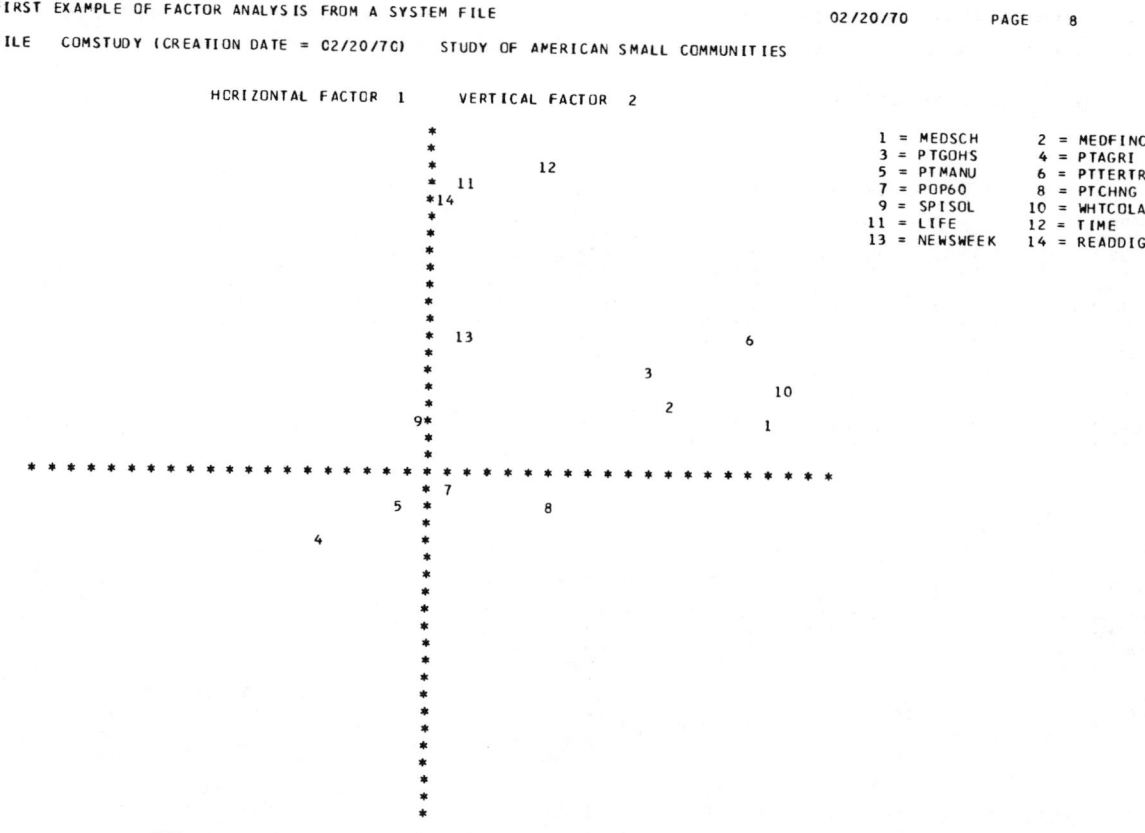

**FIG. 17.9**    An example printout of plotted factors.

Example 17.7 demonstrates the deck setup for running from a correlation matrix. The **VARIABLE LIST** card specifies seven variables whose order must agree with their position in the matrix. The #OF CASES card is used only for computation of statistics and has nothing to do with the number of cases to be read by the program.

The **FACTOR** procedure card indicates that all the variables in the matrix are to be entered in the factor analysis. The initial factoring method is PA1 (principal factoring without iterations). Three factors are specified by the NFACTORS parameter, and the rotational method will be EQUIMAX.

Option 3 on the **OPTIONS** card indicates that a correlation matrix will be read. A READ MATRIX card and the actual matrix follow the STATISTICS card. The STATISTICS card requests only the correlation matrix and the two factor matrices. Figures 17.10 to 17.13 contain the output produced from this run.

**EXAMPLE 17.7**

```
1                       16
RUN NAME                FACTOR ANALYSIS FROM A CORRELATION MATRIX
VARIABLE LIST           MEDSCH, MEDFINC, PTGOHS, PTAGRI, PTMANU, TIME, LIFE
INPUT MEDIUM            CARD
# OF CASES              64
FACTOR                  VARIABLES= MEDSCH TO LIFE/ TYPE = PA1/
                        NFACTORS= 3/ROTATE = EQUIMAX/
OPTIONS                 3
STATISTICS              2,4,5,6
READ MATRIX
    1.00000     0.71622     0.53826    -0.19451     0.08083     0.36970     0.22723
    0.71622     1.00000     0.52672    -0.15688     0.39568     0.36035     0.33037
    0.53826     0.52672     1.00000    -0.31495     0.23527     0.40196     0.31230
   -0.19451    -0.15688    -0.31495     1.00000    -0.21477    -0.27963    -0.17551
    0.08083     0.39568     0.23527    -0.21477     1.00000    -0.07349     0.01366
    0.36970     0.36035     0.40196    -0.27963    -0.07349     1.00000     0.81186
    0.22723     0.33037     0.31230    -0.17551     0.01366     0.81186     1.00000
FINISH
```

CORRELATION COEFFICIENTS..

|        | MEDSCH | MEDFINC | PTGOHS | PTAGRI | PTMANU | TIME | LIFE |
|--------|--------|---------|--------|--------|--------|------|------|
| MEDSCH | 1.00000 | 0.71622 | 0.53826 | -0.19451 | 0.08083 | 0.36970 | 0.22723 |
| MEDFINC | 0.71622 | 1.00000 | 0.52672 | -0.15688 | 0.39568 | 0.36035 | 0.33037 |
| PTGOHS | 0.53826 | 0.52672 | 1.00000 | -0.31495 | 0.23527 | 0.40196 | 0.31230 |
| PTAGRI | -0.19451 | -0.15688 | -0.31495 | 1.00000 | -0.21477 | -0.27963 | -0.17551 |
| PTMANU | 0.08083 | 0.39568 | 0.23527 | -0.21477 | 1.00000 | -0.07349 | 0.01366 |
| TIME | 0.36970 | 0.36035 | 0.40196 | -0.27963 | -0.07349 | 1.00000 | 0.81186 |
| LIFE | 0.22723 | 0.33037 | 0.31230 | -0.17551 | 0.01366 | 0.81186 | 1.00000 |

**FIG. 17.10**   Printout of correlation matrix from a correlation input matrix.

| VARIABLE | EST COMMUNALITY | | FACTOR | EIGENVALUE | PCT OF VAR | CUM PCT |
|----------|-----------------|--|--------|------------|------------|---------|
| MEDSCH | 0.62178 | | 1 | 3.02819 | 43.3 | 43.3 |
| MEDFINC | 0.66891 | | 2 | 1.37704 | 19.7 | 62.9 |
| PTGOHS | 0.40777 | | 3 | 0.98192 | 14.0 | 77.0 |
| PTAGRI | 0.19106 | | 4 | 0.77973 | 11.1 | 88.1 |
| PTMANU | 0.34735 | | 5 | 0.48151 | 6.9 | 95.0 |
| TIME | 0.72842 | | 6 | 0.19663 | 2.8 | 97.8 |
| LIFE | 0.68448 | | 7 | 0.15497 | 2.2 | 100.0 |

**FIG. 17.11**   Estimated communalities (squared multiple correlation), eigenvalues, and percent of variance accounted for by initial factors. (Note: Estimated communalities are irrelevant for the solution.)

FACTOR MATRIX USING PRINCIPAL FACTOR, NO ITERATIONS

|        | FACTOR 1 | FACTOR 2 | FACTOR 3 |
|--------|----------|----------|----------|
| MEDSCH | 0.74407 | -0.21249 | 0.44301 |
| MEDFINC | 0.79059 | -0.35333 | 0.29365 |
| PTGOHS | 0.75725 | -0.19206 | 0.02865 |
| PTAGRI | -0.44525 | 0.09777 | 0.72920 |
| PTMANU | 0.29515 | -0.68438 | -0.37811 |
| TIME | 0.73981 | 0.58467 | -0.08767 |
| LIFE | 0.66588 | 0.59194 | -0.12736 |

| VARIABLE | COMMUNALITY |
|----------|-------------|
| MEDSCH | 0.79504 |
| MEDFINC | 0.83610 |
| PTGOHS | 0.61114 |
| PTAGRI | 0.73955 |
| PTMANU | 0.69845 |
| TIME | 0.89684 |
| LIFE | 0.81002 |

**FIG. 17.12**   Unrotated factor matrix and associated communalities. (Since factors are exactly defined, eigenvalues and variances given in Fig. 17.11 are relevant for this matrix.

FACTOR ANALYSIS FROM A CORRELATION MATRIX                          02/20/70      PAGE   5

FILE   NONAME   (CREATION DATE = 02/20/70)


EQUIMAX ROTATED FACTOR MATRIX


|        | FACTOR  1 | FACTOR  2 | FACTOR  3 |
|--------|-----------|-----------|-----------|
| MEDSCH | 0.87199   | 0.18583   | -0.01160  |
| MEDFINC| 0.88410   | 0.13300   | 0.19179   |
| PTGOHS | 0.64957   | 0.29204   | 0.32235   |
| PTAGRI | 0.02692   | -0.33202  | -0.79283  |
| PTMANU | 0.29694   | -0.28502  | 0.72735   |
| TIME   | 0.25062   | 0.91185   | 0.05066   |
| LIFE   | 0.17207   | 0.88171   | 0.05471   |


TRANSFORMATION MATRIX


|          | FACTOR  1 | FACTOR  2 | FACTOR  3 |
|----------|-----------|-----------|-----------|
| FACTOR 1 | 0.73177   | 0.59139   | 0.33878   |
| FACTOR 2 | -0.41640  | 0.78145   | -0.46470  |
| FACTOR 3 | 0.53956   | -0.19899  | -0.81809  |

**FIG. 17.13**    An example of equimax rotated factor matrix and associated transformation matrix.


## REFERENCES

Cattell, Raymond F.: Factor Analysis: An Introduction to Essentials. (I) The Purpose and Underlying Models, (II) The Role of Factor Analysis in Research, *Biometrics*, vol. 21, pp. 190-215, 405-435, 1965.

Guttman, Louis: Some Necessary Conditions for Common-Factor Analysis, *Psychometrika*, vol. 19, pp. 149-161, 1954.

Harman, Harry H.: "Modern Factor Analysis," The University of Chicago Press, Chicago, 1967.

Harris, Chester W. (ed.): "Problems in Measuring Change," The University of Wisconsin Press, Madison, 1963.

————: Some Rao-Guttman Relationships, *Psychometrica*, vol. 27, pp. 247-263, 1962.

Holley, J.W. and J.P. Guilford: A Note on the G Index of Agreement, *Educational and Psychological Measurement*, vol. 24, pp. 749-753, 1964.

Kaiser, Henry F.: Image Analysis, in Chester W. Harris (ed.) "Problems in Measuring Change," The University of Wisconsin Press, Madison, 1963.

———— and John Caffry: Alpha Factor Analysis, *Psychometrika*, vol. 30, pp. 1-14, 1965.

Rao, C. Radhakrishna: Estimation and Tests of Significance in Factor Analysis, *Psychometrika*, vol. 20, pp. 93-111, 1955.

Rozeboom, William W.: "Foundations of the Theory of Prediction," Dorsey Press, Homewood, Ill., 1966.

Rummel, R.J.: Understanding Factor Analysis, *Conflict Resolution*, vol. 11, pp. 444-480, 1967.

Stephenson, W.: "*The Study of Behavior*," The University of Chicago Press, Chicago, 1953.

# A
# SPSS ERROR MESSAGES

When the SPSS system encounters a syntax error on a control card, it will print out an error number which will correpond to one of the error messages listed below. The researcher can use this list to debug his control cards.

SPSS error messages are numeric and must be looked up in the accompanying list. They are normally printed out after the control card following the card in error. No further processing is performed on the card causing the error.

The list is organized according to the card being processed when the error was encountered.

## GENERAL ERRORS
1. A control card has been read which has an unrecognized control field.
5. A control card has too many symbols.

## VARIABLE LIST or ADD VARIABLES
10. Too many variables have been declared.
11. Invalid use of the VARxxx TO VARyyy convention.
12. There are no variable names on the VARIABLE LIST card.
13. A variable has been declared twice.
14. The deck placement of the VARIABLE LIST or ADD VARIABLES card is incorrect.

## GET FILE

20. No file name appears on the GET FILE card.
21. The system-file tape that is mounted has a name other than that which is on the GET FILE card.
22. The system-file tape has an invalid format.

## INPUT MEDIUM

30. The specified medium is not recognizable; it must be CARD, TAPE, DISK, or OTHER.

## INPUT FORMAT

35. Either FIXED or FREEFIELD must be specified.
36. The parentheses on the INPUT FORMAT card do not balance.
37. The parentheses on the INPUT FORMAT list are nested too deeply.
38. A format specification has a missing or invalid width.

## PROCESS SBFILES

40. A subfile is declared to be in more than a single group.
41. The format of the PROCESS SBFILES card is incorrect.
42. A subfile name appearing on the PROCESS SBFILES card has not been declared on a SUBFILE LIST card.

## PRINT FORMAT

45. The variable list on the PRINT FORMAT card is invalid.
46. The format of the PRINT FORMAT card is incorrect.
47. An invalid format specification appears on the PRINT FORMAT card.

## VALUE LABEL or VAR LABEL

49. A variable name appears on more than one VALUE LABEL card.
50. The format of the VALUE LABEL card is incorrect.
51. A variable list on the VALUE LABEL or VAR LABEL card is invalid.
52. The VALUE LABEL card has an invalid use of the TO convention.
53. The deck placement of the VALUE LABEL card is incorrect.
54. The deck placement of the VAR LABEL card is incorrect.

## MISSING VALUE

55. The format of the MISSING VALUE card is incorrect.
56. A variable list on the MISSING VALUE card is invalid.
57. Too many missing values have been declared for a variable.

## SUBFILE LIST or ADD SUBFILES

60. A subfile name has been declared twice.
61. The deck placement of the SUBFILE LIST or ADD SUBFILES card is incorrect.

## DELETE SUBFILE

65. A subfile name on the DELETE SUBFILE card has never been declared.
66. The DELETE SUBFILE card has an invalid use of the TO convention.
67. The deck placement of the DELETE SUBFILE card is incorrect.

## DELETE VARS or KEEP VARIABLES

70. The variable list on the DELETE VARIABLE or KEEP VARIABLE card is invalid.

## SAMPLE or *SAMPLE

75. The percentage for sampling is missing.
76. The deck placement of the SAMPLE OR *SAMPLE card is incorrect.

## #OF CASES

80.  There was no SUBFILE LIST card appearing before the #OF CASES card.
81.  The number of arguments on the #OF CASES card does not agree with the number of subfiles declared on the SUBFILE LIST card.
82.  The number of cases specified for some subfile is invalid.
83.  The #OF CASES card contains an improper use of the ESTIMATED convention.

## KEYPUNCH

90.  The argument on the KEYPUNCH card is neither 026 nor 029.

## NUMBERED

95.  The NUMBERED card specifies neither YES nor NO.

## WEIGHT or *WEIGHT

100.  The variable name on the weight card is undefined.
101.  The deck placement of the WEIGHT or *WEIGHT card is incorrect.

## OPTIONS or STATISTICS

111.  The deck placement of the OPTIONS card is incorrect.
112.  The deck placement of the STATISTICS card is incorrect.

## DOCUMENT

120.  There are too many DOCUMENT cards on a single run.
121.  The deck placement of the DOCUMENT card is incorrect.

## WRITE CASES

150.  The format on the WRITE CASES card has no left parenthesis.
151.  The format on the WRITE CASES card has no right parenthesis.
152.  The format on the WRITE CASES card contains an invalid character.
153.  A format specification on the WRITE CASES card is incomplete.
154.  The variable list on the WRITE CASES card is invalid.
155.  The variable list on the WRITE CASES card is not of the same length as the format list.
156.  The WRITE CASES card specifies too many variables.
157.  The WRITE CASES format contains a Hollerith field of invalid length.
158.  The WRITE CASES format contains a literal string on which the apostrophes do not balance.
159.  The WRITE CASES format is too long.

## RECODE OR *RECODE

201.  The format of the RECODE card is incorrect.
202.  A variable list on the RECODE card is invalid.
203.  A value list on the RECODE card is invalid.
204.  There are too many recodes for a single run.
205.  The keyword HIGHEST or LOWEST has been used incorrectly.
206.  The deck placement of the RECODE card is incorrect.

## IF, *IF, COMPUTE, *COMPUTE, SELECT IF, OR *SELECT IF

221.  The parentheses on an IF card do not balance.
222.  An undefined variable name has been encountered in an expression.
223.  Too many transformations have been encountered for a single run.
224.  The assignment operator = has been used incorrectly.
225.  Too many variables have been declared.
226.  Too many IF, COMPUTE, etc., cards have been encountered.
227.  The IF, COMPUTE, etc., cards involve too many operations.
228.  The deck placement of the COMPUTE or IF card is incorrect.

IF, *IF, COMPUTE, *COMPUTE, SELECT IF, OR *SELECT IF    (*Continued*)

229.    The deck placement of the *COMPUTE or *IF card is incorrect.
241.    An operator is missing from an expression.
242.    An operand is missing from an expression.

FASTABS

300.    The FASTABS card is missing either the TABLES or the VARIABLES keyword.
305.    A pair of values in the VARIABLES list is missing a right parenthesis.
310.    An improper value pair appears in the VARIABLES list.
315.    A table has been requested which has too many or too few dimensions.
320.    A variable name in the TABLES list did not appear in the VARIABLES list.
325.    There is an improper use of the TO convention in the TABLES list.
330.    An invalid delimiter has been encountered.
335.    The format of the FASTABS card is incorrect.
340.    An undeclared variable has appeared in the VARIABLES list.
345.    The FASTABS card requests too many individual cells.
346.    The FASTABS run has produced too many rows or columns.
350.    The FASTABS card requests too many tables.
355.    Too many variables are declared in the VARIABLES list.
356.    There are too many table lists on the FASTABS card.

CODE BOOK

400.    The variable list on the CODEBOOK card is invalid.

REGRESSION

450.    The REGRESSION specification list is incomplete.
455.    The REGRESSION card has too many VARIABLES lists.
460.    The REGRESSION card has an invalid VARIABLES list.
465.    Too many variable names appear in the VARIABLES lists on the REGRESSION card.
470.    The REGRESSION card has too many REGRESSION lists.
475.    A variable in a REGRESSION list on the REGRESSION card did not appear in the preceding VARIABLES list.
480.    A REGRESSION list on the REGRESSION card is invalid.
485.    Too many variable names appear in the REGRESSION lists on the REGRESSION card.
487.    There are too many variables in a REGRESSION = list.
490.    The REGRESSION problem exceeds the core limitations.
495.    A READ MATRIX card was expected, but was not found while performing REGRESSION.

MARGINALS

500.    The variable list on the MARGINALS card is invalid.

PARTIAL CORR

550.    The format of the PARTIAL CORR card is invalid.
553.    The PARTIAL CORR card references an undefined variable or has an invalid use of the TO convention.
556.    Too many variables are referenced on the PARTIAL CORR card.
559.    There are too many correlation lists on the PARTIAL CORR card.
562.    Too many orders of partial correlations are requested.
565.    An order of partial correlations is invalid.
568.    The PARTIAL CORR problem requires too much core storage.
571.    A correlation list on the PARTIAL CORR card has more than one occurrence of the keyword WITH.
574.    A correlation list has fewer than two dependent variables.

## CROSSTABS

600.   The variable list on the CROSSTABS card is invalid.
605.   The format of the CROSSTABS card is incorrect.
610.   The CROSSTABS run has produced too many individual cells.
615.   The CROSSTABS card lists too many variables.
620.   A table on the CROSSTABS card has too many dimensions.
625.   The CROSSTABS run has produced too many rows or columns.
630.   A table on the CROSSTABS card has too few dimensions.
635.   There are too many table primaries on the CROSSTABS card.

## BREAKDOWN

650.   The variable list on the BREAKDOWN card is invalid.
655.   The format of the BREAKDOWN card is incorrect.
660.   The BREAKDOWN run has produced too many individual cells.
665.   The BREAKDOWN card lists too many variables.
670.   A table on the BREAKDOWN card has too many dimensions.
675.   The BREAKDOWN card requests too many tables.
680.   A table on the BREAKDOWN card has too few dimensions.
685.   There are too many table primaries on the BREAKDOWN card.

## READ INPUT DATA or READ MATRIX

700.   The READ INPUT DATA card is missing.
701.   The READ MATRIX card is missing.
705.   There was no # OF CASES card read prior to encountering the READ INPUT DATA card.
710.   Due to permanent file modifications, there are no cases left.
740.   An invalid field was encountered while performing freefield input.
745.   On freefield input, an alpha string had no closing quote.

## CONDESCRIPTIVE

801.   The variable list on a CONDESCRIPTIVE card is invalid.

## FACTOR

820.   The VARIABLES = list on the FACTOR card is invalid.
822.   The FACTOR card format is invalid.
824.   The FACTOR card has no VARIABLES = list.
826.   The FACTOR problem exceeds the core limitations.
828.   The FACTOR card contains an invalid argument type.
830.   The argument for TYPE = is invalid on the FACTOR card.
832.   The DIAGONAL = list on the FACTOR card has an invalid use of the * convention.
834.   An element in the DIAGONAL = list on the FACTOR card is less than zero or greater than unity.
836.   The length of the DIAGONAL = list is incorrect.
838.   The argument for ROTATE = is invalid on the FACTOR card.

## PEARSON CORR

850.   The PEARSON CORR card contains an invalid variable list.
855.   The PEARSON CORR card contains too many correlation lists.
860.   The PEARSON CORR card contains too many variable names.
865.   There is more than one use of the keyword WITH in a correlation list on the PEARSON CORR card.
870.   A correlation list on the PEARSON CORR card is invalid.
875.   The PEARSON CORR card requests too many correlations.

## NONPAR CORR

900. The NONPAR CORR card contains too many correlation lists.
905. The NONPAR CORR card contains an invalid variable list.
910. The NONPAR CORR card contains too many variable names.
915. There is more than one use of the keyword WITH in a correlation list on the NONPAR CORR card.
920. A correlation list on the NONPAR CORR card is invalid.
925. Too many cases were encountered while processing nonparametric correlations.

## GUTTMAN SCALE

950. A GUTTMAN SCALE item is an undefined variable.
955. The format of the GUTTMAN SCALE card is invalid.
960. The GUTTMAN SCALE card specifies too many scales.
965. A scale on the GUTTMAN SCALE card is composed of too few or too many items.
970. The division point specification for an item on the GUTTMAN SCALE card is invalid.
975. The GUTTMAN SCALE problem exceeds the core limitations.
980. The GUTTMAN SCALE card specifies too many variable names.

## SYSTEM ERRORS (These messages should never appear.)

1001. The transformations routine compiled an invalid string.
1003. The sort routine in CROSSTABS blew up.
1006. File IOSCR1 has a subfile error found in reading data.
1010. CODEBOOK or MARGINALS has encountered difficulty computing the median.
1015. BREAKDOWN has produced duplicate cells.
1019. The partial correlation program requested a nonexistent control variable.

1770. An attempt to shift from reading to writing on a file.
1771. A record which is to be written is too long for the buffer.
1772. An attempt to shift from writing to reading without rewinding the file.
1773. An attempt to read past the end of the data set.
1774. An attempt to note a record that has been read.
1775. An attempt to point to a record that has been written.
1776. A data set cannot be opened.

# B

# SUMMARY OF SPSS CONTROL CARDS: FUNCTIONS, STATUS, FORMATS, AND POSITION IN CARD DECK

The following table lists all SPSS control cards (except the statistical procedure cards) in alphabetical order, along with their appendix section numbers. The format, function, status, and reference section in the book of each of the cards is then given. In this appendix, the cards are ordered according to their function so that they may be more conveniently used in preparing SPSS runs.

| SPSS control fields | Appendix section | SPSS control fields | Appendix section |
|---|---|---|---|
| ADD SUBFILES | B.9 | Procedures cards | B.19 |
| ADD VARIABLES | B.6 | PROCESS SBFILES | B.18 |
| COMMENT | B.37 | READ INPUT DATA | B.30 |
| COMPUTE | B.23 | READ MATRIX | B.31 |
| DELETE VARS | B.8 | RECODE | B.22 |
| DELETE SUBFILE | B.10 | RUN NAME | B.1 |
| DOCUMENT | B.38 | SAMPLE | B.26 |
| DUMP | B.36 | SAVE FILE | B.32 |
| FILE NAME | B.3 | SELECT IF | B.27 |
| FINISH | B.33 | Starred [*] data-modification | |
| GET FILE | B.2 | and data-selection cards | B.29 |
| IF | B.24 | STATISTICS | B.21 |
| INPUT FORMAT | B.13 | SUBFILE LIST | B.5 |
| INPUT MEDIUM | B.11 | TMISS | B.25 |
| KEEP VARIABLES | B.7 | VALUE LABELS | B.15 |
| KEYPUNCH | B.34 | VARIABLE LIST | B.4 |
| MISSING VALUES | B.14 | VAR LABELS | B.17 |
| NUMBERED | B.39 | WEIGHT | B.28 |
| OPTIONS | B.20 | WRITE CASES | B.40 |
| PRINT BACK | B.35 | #OF CASES | B.12 |
| PRINT FORMATS | B.16 | | |

The next table gives the precedence order or ranking of all SPSS control cards so that the user can quickly check to ensure that the sequence of his control statements is correct. These precedence numbers range from 0 (highest precedence) to 24 (lowest precedence), and no card with a lower precedence may be placed before a card with a higher precedence. The order of cards with the same precedence is of no consequence. Remember, though, the lower the precedence number the higher the precedence, so that the numbers will increase moving from the first to last control cards in the user's deck. These numbers can also be found in brackets under the heading of STATUS for each card covered in this appendix.

The COMMENT is not given a precedence number, for it may appear anywhere in the user's deck except between the READ INPUT DATA or READ MATRIX cards and the data cases or matrices.

| Precedence | Control card | Precedence | Control card |
|---|---|---|---|
| 0 | NUMBERED | 13 | *SAMPLE |
| 1 | KEYPUNCH / PRINT BACK | 14 | TMISS / *COMPUTE / *IF / *SELECT IF / *RECODE |
| 2 | RUN NAME | | |
| 3 | GET FILE | 15 | *WEIGHT |
| 4 | FILE NAME | 16 | MISSING VALUES / PRINT FORMATS |
| 5 | ADD VARIABLES / VARIABLE LIST | 17 | DUMP |
| 6 | ADD SUBFILES / DELETE SUBFILES / SUBFILE LIST | 18 | PROCESS SUBFILES |
| 7 | INPUT MEDIUM / INPUT FORMAT | 19 | procedure card / WRITE CASES |
| 8 | # OF CASES | 20 | OPTIONS / STATISTICS |
| 9 | SAMPLE | 21 | READ INPUT DATA / READ MATRIX |
| 10 | TMISS / COMPUTE / IF / SELECT IF / RECODE | 22 | DELETE VARS / KEEP VARIABLES |
| | | 23 | SAVE FILE |
| 11 | WEIGHT | 24 | FINISH |
| 12 | VAR LABELS / VALUE LABELS / DOCUMENT | | |

## B.1   THE RUN NAME CARD

1
RUN NAME

16
run label of up to 64 characters

FUNCTION:  Provides a header label at the top of each page of printed output generated by the run.

STATUS:  Optional. [2]

Reference Sec. 6.1

## B.2   THE GET FILE CARD

1
GET FILE

16
file name

FUNCTION:   Retrieves for processing any SPSS system file which has been previously retained.

STATUS:   Required whenever the user wishes to access an existing file. Not used on runs from cards or BCD tape. [3]

Reference Sec. 7.3.1

## B.3   THE FILE NAME CARD

1
FILE NAME

16
file name [optional file label up to 64 characters]

FUNCTION:   Provides the file being input with a file name of up to eight characters in length. May also provide the file with an optional file label. Can also be used to rename an existing file which is being updated.

STATUS:   Required whenever a file is to be retained as an SPSS system file. Otherwise optional. [4]

Reference Secs. 4.1 and 7.3.2.1

## B.4   THE VARIABLE LIST CARD

1
VARIABLE LIST

16
variable list

FUNCTION:   Provides each variable to be entered into the file with a name of up to eight characters in length. All subsequent processing of data is accomplished by reference to these variable names. A variable name is either
(*a*) a name of the user's choice up to eight characters using alphabetic letters, or

(*b*) the special convention VARXXX TO VAR-YYY

STATUS:   Required on file-generating runs or whenever processing directly from cards or BCD tape. [5]

Reference Secs. 4.2 and 4.6.4

## B.5    THE SUBFILE LIST CARD

1
SUBFILE LIST

16
subfile name list in order of input

FUNCTION:    Provides each subfile with a subfile name of up to eight characters in length, the first four of which must be unique. All subsequent processing of subfiles is accomplished by reference to these names.

STATUS:    Required whenever the file contains a subfile structure. Otherwise *it is not prepared.* It is, of course, used only when inputting data directly from cards or BCD tape. [6]

Reference Sec. 4.3

## B.6    THE ADD VARIABLES CARD

1
ADD VARIABLES

16
list of new variable names

FUNCTION:    Names the variables being added to an existing SPSS system file. Variable name conventions are the same as for the VARIABLE LIST card.

STATUS:    Required whenever new variables are being added to an existing SPSS system file. [6]

Reference Sec. 10.2

## B.7    THE KEEP VARIABLES CARD

1
KEEP VARIABLES

16
variable list

FUNCTION:    Lists those variables which are to be saved on a new or updated SPSS system file at the end of the run. The variable list may utilize the TO convention. All variables not named on the KEEP VARIABLES card are deleted at the end of the current run.

STATUS:    May be used whenever an SPSS system file is being saved. [22]

Reference Sec. 10.1

## B.8   THE DELETE VARS CARD

1                                      16
DELETE VARS                            variable list

FUNCTION:   Lists those variables which are not to be saved on a new SPSS system file at the end of the run. All variables not named on the DELETE VARS card will be saved when a SAVE FILE card is encountered.

STATUS:   May be used whenever an SPSS system file is being saved. [22]

Reference Sec. 10.1

## B.9   THE ADD SUBFiLES CARD

1                                      16
ADD SUBFILES                           list of subfile names

FUNCTION:   Provides a name for each subfile which is to be added to an existing SPSS system file.

STATUS:   Must be used whenever observations are being added to an existing file. Whenever it is used, INPUT MEDIUM and # OF CASES cards must also be present. [6]

Reference Sec. 10.4

## B.10   THE DELETE SUBFILE CARD

1                                      16
DELETE SUBFILE                         list of subfile names

FUNCTION:   Lists those subfiles which are to be deleted from an SPSS system file named on the GET FILE card. The subfiles named on the DELETE SUB-FILE card may not be processed during the run and will not be saved on the new system file if a SAVE FILE card is encountered.

STATUS:   May be used whenever a GET FILE card is present. [6]

Reference Sec. 10.3

### B.11    THE INPUT MEDIUM CARD

1                                    16
INPUT MEDIUM                    { CARD
                                  DISK
                                  TAPE
                                  or
                                  OTHER }

FUNCTION:   Informs system as to whether user will enter data from cards or from other input media, such as magnetic tape, disk, or data cell.

STATUS:   Required on all runs using cards, disk, or BCD tape. [7]

Reference Sec. 4.5

### B.12    THE # OF CASES CARD

1                                    16
# OF CASES                      { number of cases
                                  ESTIMATED number of cases
                                  or
                                  number of cases in each subfile }

FUNCTION:   Provides the system with the number of cases in the user's file or the number of cases in each of the file's subfiles. When a file has a subfile structure, the number of cases in each of the subfiles must be entered in the same order as they appear on the SUBFILE LIST card. These numbers must be separated by one or more common delimiters. The keyword ESTIMATED may be used only in the absence of a subfile structure when the input medium is other than CARD.

STATUS:   Required on all file-generating runs and on all runs involving BCD tape or cards. [8]

Reference Sec. 4.4

### B.13    THE INPUT FORMAT CARD

1                                    16
INPUT FORMAT                    { FIXED
                                  or
                                  FREEFIELD }      [format list if fixed]

FUNCTION: Provides the SPSS system with information concerning (1) the organization of data cases (i.e.,
whether they are in fixed or free-field format),
(2) type of variable (i.e., numeric or alphanumeric), and (3) card and column location of the
variable (when data are in fixed form). When
data are in free-field format, no format list is
required.

STATUS: Required on all file-generating runs from cards
or BCD tape in which the user's data are not
being entered directly from an SPSS system file.
[7]

Reference Sec. 4.6

## B.14 THE MISSING VALUES CARD

1
MISSING VALUES
$\left\{\begin{array}{l}\text{variable list}\\\text{or}\\\text{variable name}\end{array}\right\}$ (missing value list) / ...

FUNCTION: Informs the system as to the missing values for
any or all of the variables in the user's file. May
also be used to define missing values for recoded
or transformed variables.

STATUS: Optional. May be used whenever the user wishes
to declare or change one or more missing values
for any variable in his file. [16]

Reference Sec. 4.7

## B.15 THE VALUE LABELS CARD

1
VALUE LABELS
$\left\{\begin{array}{l}\text{variable name}\\\text{or}\\\text{variable list}\end{array}\right\}$ (value1) label1 (value2) label 2 ...
(valueN) labelN/

$\left\{\begin{array}{l}\text{variable name}\\\text{or}\\\text{variable list}\end{array}\right\}$ (value1) label1 (value2) label 2 ...
(valueN) labelN/

FUNCTION: Associates a label of up to 40 characters with
each value of any or all of the variables in a file.

STATUS: Optional. May be prepared whenever the user
wishes to declare or alter a label for any value in
his file. [12]

Reference Sec. 4.8

### B.16    THE PRINT FORMATS CARD

1                             16
PRINT FORMATS    $\left\{\begin{array}{c}\text{variable name}\\ \text{or}\\ \text{variable list}\end{array}\right\}$ (value)/ $\left\{\begin{array}{c}\text{variable name}\\ \text{or}\\ \text{variable list}\end{array}\right\}$ (value)

FUNCTION:    (a) Enables the user to control the number of digits to the right of the decimal point when reporting the values of numeric variables on output from SPSS statistical subprograms.

(b) Informs the system that a variable is alphanumeric.

STATUS:    Required for alphanumeric variables. Optional for numeric variables. When it is not used with numeric variables, two digits to the right of the decimal point are printed. [16]

Reference Sec. 4.9

### B.17    THE VAR LABELS CARD

1                             16
VAR LABELS      variable name1, variable label / variable name2, variable label / ...

FUNCTION:    Enables the user to associate an extended-variable label of up to 40 characters in length with any or all of the variables in his file.

STATUS:    Optional. May be prepared whenever the user wishes to provide extended labels for his variables. [12]

Reference Sec. 4.10

### B.18    THE PROCESS SBFILES CARD

1                             16
PROCESS SBFILES    $\left\{\begin{array}{l}\text{EACH}\\ \text{or}\\ \text{ALL}\\ \text{or}\\ \text{(subfile list 1)(subfile list 2) ...}\end{array}\right\}$

FUNCTION:    Instructs the system as to how the user wishes the subfiles to be processed as single subfiles. The keyword EACH specifies that each subfile is to be treated independently; ALL indicates that the subfile structure is to be ignored and that the file is to be treated as a unit; and combinations of subfiles are formed by placing two or more subfiles within the same set of ( ).

STATUS:    Required on all runs with files having subfile structures. Not prepared, of course, for files not having a subfile structure. [18]

Reference Sec. 5.5

## B.19   THE PROCEDURE CARDS

FUNCTION:   Individual procedure cards enable the user to call upon the desired subprograms and to enter specified variables into the calculation. Each subprogram has its own procedure card with a unique control field and its own conventions for entering variables onto the card. See the appropriate subprogram write-ups, beginning with Chap. 11, for a complete explanation.

STATUS:   Every run does, of course, require at least one procedure card. [19]

Reference Sec. 5.1

## B.20   THE OPTIONS CARD

1
OPTIONS

16
options number list

FUNCTION:   Provides the subprogram activated by the procedure card with information concerning the desired options, such as how to process missing data. Options are specified by number in the individual subprogram write-ups.

STATUS:   Required with the exception of a few subprograms which enable the user to declare a default option by omitting the card. See the individual subprogram write-ups. [20]

Reference Sec. 5.2

## B.21   THE STATISTICS CARD

1
STATISTICS

16
$\left\{ \begin{array}{l} \text{statistics number list} \\ \text{or} \\ \text{ALL} \end{array} \right\}$

FUNCTION:   Provides the subprogram activated on the procedure card with instructions concerning the desired statistics to be computed for the output. Each subprogram has its own list of available statistics and a corresponding number list for their selection and activation.

STATUS:   Required except for a few subprograms where its omission causes no statistics to be printed. [20]

Reference Sec. 5.3

### B.22   THE RECODE CARD

1                                    16
RECODE          $\left\{\begin{array}{c}\text{variable list} \\ \text{or} \\ \text{variable name}\end{array}\right\}$ (value list = new value) $\left\{\begin{array}{c}\text{(value list = new value)} \\ \text{or} \\ \text{(CONVERT)}\end{array}\right\}$ / . . .

> FUNCTION:   Recodes the values of a variable.
>
> STATUS:     Optional. [10]

Reference Sec. 8.1

### B.23   THE COMPUTE CARD

1                                    16
COMPUTE                              computed variable = arithmetic expression

> FUNCTION:   Performs unconditional variable transformations which involve one or more arithmetic operations.
>
> STATUS:     Optional. [10]

Reference Sec. 8.2.1

### B.24   THE IF CARD

1                                    16
IF                                   (logical expression) computed variable = arithmetic expression

> FUNCTION:   Permits the user to generate variable transformations contingent upon prespecified conditions.
>
> STATUS:     Optional. [10]

Reference Sec. 8.2.2

### B.25   THE TMISS CARD

1                                    16
TMISS                                any number

> FUNCTION:   Changes the initialization value which is automatically provided for transformed variables from zero to any other number which the user may desire.
>
> STATUS:     Optional. [10]

Reference Sec. 8.2.4.1

### B.26   THE SAMPLE CARD

1                                    16
SAMPLE                               factor (where factor is any positive decimal number less than 1.0 and represents the percentage of his file which the user wishes to analyze)

FUNCTION:    Draws a random sample of the cases in the user's file.

STATUS:    Optional. [9]

Reference Sec. 9.1

## B.27    THE SELECT IF CARD

| 1 | 16 |
|---|---|
| SELECT IF | (logical expression) |

FUNCTION:    Selects for processing only those cases which meet the criteria specified in the logical expression.

STATUS:    Optional. [10]

Reference Sec. 9.2

## B.28    THE WEIGHT CARD

| 1 | 16 |
|---|---|
| WEIGHT | variable name |

FUNCTION:    When used in conjunction with a variable transformation, causes the weighting of selected cases within the file.

STATUS:    Optional. [11]

Reference Sec. 9.3

## B.29    THE TEMPORARY (STARRED) DATA-MODIFICATION AND DATA-SELECTION CARDS

The following permanent data-modification and data-selection cards may also appear in a temporary form: RECODE, COMPUTE, IF, SAMPLE, SELECT IF, and WEIGHT. In each case, the only difference in format between the permanent and temporary cards is that the control field of all temporary cards contains an asterisk [*] in column 1, directly followed by the control word(s). For example, the general format of the temporary RECODE card is

| 1 | 16 |
|---|---|
| *RECODE | $\left\{ \begin{array}{c} \text{variable list} \\ \text{or} \\ \text{variable name} \end{array} \right\}$ (value list = new value) $\left\{ \begin{array}{c} \text{(value list = new value)} \\ \text{or} \\ \text{CONVERT} \end{array} \right\}$ |

FUNCTION:    Executes temporary data modifications or selections which are only in effect for the set of task-definition cards immediately following.

STATUS:    Optional. [14]

Reference Sec. 8.2.3

### B.30    THE READ INPUT DATA CARD

1                                          16
READ INPUT DATA

FUNCTION:    Instructs the system to begin reading the input data.

STATUS:    Required when processing from cards or BCD tape; not used when processing from an SPSS system file. [21]

Reference Sec. 5.4

### B.31    THE READ MATRIX CARD

1                                          16
READ MATRIX

FUNCTION:    Instructs the system to begin reading correlation matrices or other calculated data.

STATUS:    Required when subprograms such as REGRESSION will be reading calculated data rather than raw data. Must be used in conjunction with an INPUT MEDIUM card. [21]

Reference Sec. 15.4

### B.32    THE SAVE FILE CARD

1                                          16
SAVE FILE                                  file name

FUNCTION:    Retains data input in the form of an SPSS system file.

STATUS:    Required whenever the user wishes to retain a file which has been generated on a run or to permanently retain any modifications which have been made on an existing file during the run. [23]

Reference Sec. 7.2.1

### B.33    THE FINISH CARD

1                                          16
FINISH

FUNCTION:    Terminates the processing for the run and switches control back to the installation's monitoring system.

STATUS:    Required. [24]

Reference Sec. 6.2

## B.34    THE KEYPUNCH CARD

| 1 | 16 |
|---|----|
| KEYPUNCH | 026 |

FUNCTION:    Informs the system that control cards have been punched with an IBM 026 keypunch, rather than an 029.

STATUS:    Optional. [1]

Reference Sec. 6.3.1

## B.35    THE PRINT BACK CARD

| 1 | 16 |
|---|----|
| PRINT BACK | NO |

FUNCTION:    Suppresses the printing back of control cards.

STATUS:    Optional. [1]

Reference Sec. 6.4

## B.36    THE DUMP CARD

| 1 | 16 |
|---|----|
| DUMP | keyword |

FUNCTION:    Lists an SPSS file's data-defining information on the output.

STATUS:    Optional. [17]

Reference Sec. 6.3.5

## B.37    THE COMMENT CARD

| 1 | 16 |
|---|----|
| COMMENT | any text |

FUNCTION:    Serves to insert a comment of the user's choice in the control-card deck. This card does not affect the functioning of the programs in any way.

STATUS:    Optional. [Anywhere]

Reference Sec. 6.3.3

### B.38 THE DOCUMENT CARD

1                                 16
DOCUMENT                          any text

FUNCTION: Retains the text appearing on the card as part of a system file. This documenting information may be retrieved by the use of the DUMP card.

STATUS: Optional. [12]

Reference Sec. 6.3.4

### B.39 THE NUMBERED CARD

1                                 16
$\begin{Bmatrix} YES \\ or \\ NO \end{Bmatrix}$

FUNCTION: Causes columns 73 to 80 of all SPSS control cards and their continuations to be ignored so that the user may use these columns for sequence numbers or other identifying information.

STATUS: Optional. [0]

### B.40 THE WRITE CASES CARD

1                                 16
WRITE CASES                       format list, variable list

FUNCTION: Enables the user to write out any or all of the variables in his file in BCD format. The selection of cases and the format of the cases can be controlled by the user.

STATUS: Required whenever the user wishes to execute this function. It is not otherwise used. [19]

Reference Sec. 10.4

# C
# SPSS SYNTAX [†]

CONVENTIONS..
" – USED TO DELIMIT LITERAL ELEMENTS
| – USED FOR LOGICAL OR
& – USED FOR LOGICAL AND
¬ – USED FOR LOGICAL NOT
|| – USED FOR CONCATENATION

\* \* \* \* \* \* \* \*    B A S I C    E L E M E N T S    \* \* \* \* \* \* \* \* \*

⟨DIGIT⟩                = ⟨"0"⟩ | ⟨"1"⟩ | ⟨"2"⟩ | ⟨"3"⟩ | ⟨"4"⟩ |
                         ⟨"5"⟩ | ⟨"6"⟩ | ⟨"7"⟩ | ⟨"8"⟩ | ⟨"9"⟩

⟨SPECIAL CHARACTER⟩     = ⟨" "⟩ | ⟨","⟩ | ⟨""""⟩ | ⟨"*"⟩ | ⟨"–"⟩ |
                         ⟨"+"⟩ | ⟨"/"⟩ | ⟨"("⟩ | ⟨")"⟩ | ⟨"="⟩

⟨LETTER⟩                = ¬⟨DIGIT⟩ & ¬⟨SPECIAL CHARACTER⟩ &
                         ¬⟨"."⟩

[†]For simplicity, certain liberties have been taken with formal Bacus-normal notation in this appendix.

| | | |
|---|---|---|
| \<CHARACTER\> | = | \<DIGIT\> \| \<SPECIAL CHARACTER\> \| \<LETTER\> \| \<"."\> |

\<INTEGER\>  = \<DIGIT\> \| \<DIGIT\>\|\|\<INTEGER\>

\<VALUE\>  = \<NUMERIC VALUE\> \| \<ALPHA VALUE\>
\<NUMERIC VALUE\>  = \<POSITIVE VALUE\> \| \<"−"\>\<POSITIVE VALUE\>
\<POSITIVE VALUE\>  = \<INTEGER\> \| \<"."\>\|\|\<INTEGER\> \|
\<INTEGER\>\|\|\<"."\> \|
\<INTEGER\>\|\|\<"."\>\|\|\<INTEGER\>

\<ALPHA VALUE\>  = \<""\>\|\|\<ALPHA STRING\>\|\|\<""\>
\<ALPHA STRING\>  = \<STRING CHARACTER\> \|
\<STRING CHARACTER\>\|\|\<ALPHA STRING\>

\<STRING CHARACTER\>  = \<CHARACTER\> & ¬\<""\>

\<NAME\>  = \<LETTER\> \| \<NAME\>\|\|\<LETTER\> \|
\<NAME\>\|\|\<DIGIT\> \| \<NAME\>\|\|\<"."\>

\<LABEL\>  = \<CHARACTER\> \| \<CHARACTER\>\|\|\<LABEL\>

\<ARITH EXPR\>  = \<ARITH PRIMARY\> \|
\<"("\>\<ARITH EXPR\>\<")"\> \|
\<ARITH EXPR\>\<BINARY OP\>\<ARITH EXPR\> \|
\<UNARY OP\>\<"("\>\<ARITH EXPR\>\<")"\>

\<ARITH PRIMARY\>  = \<VARIABLE NAME\> \| \<VALUE\>
\<UNARY OP\>  = \<"SQRT"\> \| \<"EXP"\> \| \<"LN"\> \|
\<"SIN"\> \| \<"COS"\> \| \<"ATAN"\> \|
\<"RND"\> \| \<"LG10"\>

\<BINARY OP\>  = \<"+"\> \| \<"−"\> \| \<"*"\> \| \<"/"\> \| \<"**"\>

\<LOGICAL EXPR\>  = \<RELATION\> \| \<"("\>\<LOGICAL EXPR\>\<")"\> \|
\<"NOT"\>\<LOGICAL EXPR\> \|
\<LOGICAL EXPR\>\<LOGICAL OP\>\<LOGICAL EXPR\>

\<RELATION\>  = \<ARITH EXPR\>\<RELATIONAL OP\>\<ARITH EXPR\>
\<RELATIONAL OP\>  = \<"GT"\> \| \<"GE"\> \| \<"EQ"\> \| \<"NE"\> \|
\<"LE"\> \| \<"LT"\>
\<LOGICAL OP\>  = \<"AND"\> \| \<"OR"\>

\<VARIABLE NAME\>  = \<NAME\>

\<FILE NAME\>  = \<NAME\>

\<SUBFILE NAME\>  = \<NAME\>

\<VARIABLE LIST\>  = \<VARIABLE PRIMARY\> \|
\<VARIABLE PRIMARY\>\<VARIABLE LIST\>

\<VARIABLE PRIMARY\>  = \<VARIABLE NAME\> \|
\<VARIABLE NAME\>\<"TO"\>\<VARIABLE NAME\>

\<SUBFILE LIST\>  = \<SUBFILE NAME\> \|
\<SUBFILE NAME\>\<SUBFILE LIST\>

\<VARIABLE LABEL\>  = \<LABEL\>

\<VALUE LABEL\>  = \<LABEL\>

```
<FILE LABEL>              = <LABEL>

<RUN LABEL>               = <LABEL>

<FORTRAN FORMAT>          = <"(">< FORMAT LIST><")">
<FORMAT LIST>             = <CONVERSION LIST> |
                            <CONVERSION LIST><"/"><FORMAT LIST>
<CONVERSION LIST>         = <"/"> | <CONVERSION GROUP>
<CONVERSION GROUP>        = <FORMAT ELEMENT> |
                            <FORMAT ELEMENT><","><CONVERSION GROUP>
<FORMAT ELEMENT>          = <LITERAL ELEMENT> |
                            <CONVERSION ELEMENT> |
                            <INTEGER>||<CONVERSION ELEMENT>
<CONVERSION ELEMENT>      = <"X"> |
                            <"F">||<INTEGER>||<".">||<INTEGER> |
                            <"A">||<INTEGER>
<LITERAL ELEMENT>         = <INTEGER>||<"H">||<ALPHA STRING> |
                            <ALPHA VALUE>
```

```
* * * * * * * * * *   C O N S T R U C T S   * * * * * * * * * * *
```

```
NUMBERED..
DATA FIELD               = <NUMBERING OPTION>
<NUMBERING OPTION>       = <"YES"> | <"NO">

KEYPUNCH..
DATA FIELD               = <KEYPUNCH MODEL NO.>
<KEYPUNCH MODEL NO.>     = <"026"> | <"029">

PRINT BACK..
DATA FIELD               = <PRINT OPTION>
<PRINT OPTION>           = <"YES"> | <"NO">

RUN NAME..
DATA FIELD               = <RUN LABEL>

GET FILE..
DATA FIELD               = <FILE NAME>

FILE NAME..
DATA FIELD               = <FILE NAME><FILE LABEL>

VARIABLE LIST..
DATA FIELD               = <DECLARATIONS>
<DECLARATIONS>           = <DECL PRIMARY> |
                            <DECL PRIMARY><DECLARATIONS>
<DECL PRIMARY>           = <VARIABLE NAME> | <DECL PAIR>
<DECL PAIR>              = <SPECIAL NAME><"TO"><SPECIAL NAME>
<SPECIAL NAME>           = <"VAR">||<DIGIT>||<DIGIT>||<DIGIT>

DELETE VARIABLE..
DATA FIELD               = <VARIABLE LIST>
```

```
        SUBFILE LIST..
        DATA FIELD                          = <SUBFILE LIST>

        DELETE SUBFILE..
        DATA FIELD                          = <SUBFILE LIST>

        MISSING VALUE..
        DATA FIELD                          = <MISSING LIST>
        <MISSING LIST>                      = <MISSING PRIMARY> |
                                              <MISSING PRIMARY><"/"><MISSING LIST>
        <MISSING PRIMARY>                   = <VARIABLE LIST><VALUE PART>
        <VALUE PART>                        = <"("><VALUE LIST><")"> |
                                              <"("><")">
        <VALUE LIST>                        = <VALUE> | <VALUE><VALUE LIST>

        VAR LABEL..
        DATA FIELD                          = <LABEL LIST>
        <LABEL LIST>                        = <LABEL PRIMARY> |
                                              <LABEL PRIMARY><"/"><LABEL LIST>
        <LABEL PRIMARY>                     = <VARIABLE NAME><VARIABLE LABEL>

        VALUE LABEL..
        DATA FIELD                          = <LABEL LIST>
        <LABEL LIST>                        = <LABEL PRIMARY> |
                                              <LABEL PRIMARY><"/"><LABEL LIST>
        <LABEL PRIMARY>                     = <VARIABLE LIST><LABEL SECONDARY>
        <LABEL SECONDARY>                   = <LABEL ASSIGNMENT> |
                                              <LABEL ASSIGNMENT><LABEL SECONDARY>
        <LABEL ASSIGNMENT>                  = <"("><VALUE><")"><VALUE LABEL>

        INPUT MEDIUM..
        DATA FIELD                          = <MEDIUM>
        <MEDIUM>                            = <"CARD"> | <"TAPE"> | <"DISK"> |
                                              <"OTHER">

        # OF CASES..
        DATA FIELD                          = <CASES LIST>
        <CASES LIST>                        = <PRECISE LIST> | <ESTIMATED LIST>
        <PRECISE LIST>                      = <INTEGER> | <INTEGER><PRECISE LIST>
        <ESTIMATED LIST>                    = <"ESTIMATED"><INTEGER>

        INPUT FORMAT..
        DATA FIELD                          = <FORMAT DECLARATION>
        <FORMAT DECLARATION>                = <"FREEFIELD"> | <"FIXED"><FORTRAN FORMAT>

        PRINT FORMAT..
        DATA FIELD                          = <PRINT LIST>
        <PRINT LIST>                        = <PRINT PRIMARY> |
                                              <PRINT PRIMARY><"/"><PRINT LIST>
        <PRINT PRIMARY>                     = <VARIABLE LIST><"("><FORMAT SPECS><")">
        <FORMAT SPECS>                      = <DIGIT> | <"A">

        PROCESS..
        DATA FIELD                          = <"EACH"> | <"ALL"> | <PROCESS LIST>
```

```
<PROCESS LIST>                    = <GROUP LIST> |
                                    <GROUP LIST><PROCESS LIST>
<GROUP LIST>                      = <"("><SUBFILE LIST><")">

READ INPUT DATA..
DATA FIELD                        = <EMPTY>

COMMENT..
DATA FIELD                        = <LABEL>

RECODE..
DATA FIELD                        = <RECODE LIST>
<RECODE LIST>                     = <RECODE PRIMARY> |
                                    <RECODE PRIMARY><"/"><RECODE LIST>
<RECODE PRIMARY>                  = <RECODE VARIABLES><CONVERSION SPECS>
<RECODE VARIABLES>                = <"ALL"> | <VARIABLE LIST>
<CONVERSION SPECS>                = <ALPHA SPECS> | <VALUE SPECS> |
                                    <VALUE SPECS><ALPHA SPECS>
<ALPHA SPECS>                     = <"("><"CONVERT"><")">
<VALUE SPECS>                     = <SET PART> | <SET PART><VALUE SPECS>
<SET PART>                        = <"("><INPUT LIST><"="><VALUE><")">
<INPUT LIST>                      = <VALUE PRIMARY> |
                                    <VALUE PRIMARY><INPUT LIST>
<VALUE PRIMARY>                   = <VALUE> | <VALUE PAIR>
<VALUE PAIR>                      = <VALUE><"THRU"><VALUE> |
                                    <"LOWEST"><"THRU"><VALUE> |
                                    <VALUE><"THRU"><"HIGHEST">

SELECT IF..
DATA FIELD                        = <"("><LOGICAL EXPR><")">

IF..
DATA FIELD                        = <"("><LOGICAL EXPR><")">
                                    <VARIABLE NAME><"="><ARITH EXPR>

COMPUTE..
DATA FIELD                        = <VARIABLE NAME><"="><ARITH EXPR>

SAMPLE..
DATA FIELD                        = <VALUE>

WEIGHT..
DATA FIELD                        = <VARIABLE NAME>

DUMP..
DATA FIELD                        = <DUMP LIST>
<DUMP LIST>                       = <DUMP ITEM> | <DUMP ITEM><DUMP LIST>
<DUMP ITEM>                       = <"VARLIST"> | <"SUBDIRECTORY"> |
                                    <"LABELS"> | <"TRANSFORMS"> |
                                    <"SORTVARS">| <"DOCUMENTS"> |
                                    <"RECODES"> | <"VARINFO">

SAVE FILE..
DATA FIELD                        = <EMPTY>
```

```
OPTIONS..
DATA FIELD                      = <OPTION LIST>
<OPTION LIST>                   = <INTEGER> | <INTEGER><OPTION LIST>


STATISTICS..
DATA FIELD                      = <STATISTIC OPTION>
<STATISTIC OPTION>              = <"ALL"> | <STATISTIC LIST>
<STATISTIC LIST>                = <INTEGER> | <INTEGER><STATISTIC LIST>

FASTABS..
DATA FIELD                      = <"VARIABLES"><"="><VARIABLE PART>
                                  <"TABLES"><"="><TABLE PART>
<VARIABLE PART>                 = <VARIABLE PRIMARY> |
                                  <VARIABLE PRIMARY><"/"><VARIABLE PART>
<VARIABLE PRIMARY>              = <VARIABLE LIST><"("><VALUE><VALUE><")">
<TABLE PART>                    = <TABLE DECLARATION> |
                                  <TABLE DECLARATION><"/"><TABLE PART>
<TABLE  DECLARATION>            = <TABLE PRIMARY><"BY"><TABLE PRIMARY> |
                                  <TABLE PRIMARY><"BY"><TABLE DECLARATION>
<TABLE PRIMARY>                 = <VARIABLE NAME>  |
                                  <VARIABLE NAME><"TO"><VARIABLE NAME>


CROSSTABS..
DATA FIELD                      = <CROSSTABS LIST>
<CROSSTABS LIST>                = <CROSSTABS TABLE> |
                                  <CROSSTABS TABLE><"/"><CROSSTABS LIST>
<CROSSTABS TABLE>               = <VARIABLE LIST><"BY"><VARIABLE LIST> |
                                  <VARIABLE LIST><"BY"><CROSSTABS TABLE>


MARGINALS..
DATA FIELD                      = <MARGINALS VARIABLES>
<MARGINALS VARIABLES>           = <"ALL"> | <VARIABLE LIST>

CODEBOOK..
DATA FIELD                      = <CODEBOOK VARIABLES>
<CODEBOOK VARIABLES>            = <"ALL"> | <VARIABLE LIST>

CONDESCRIPTIVE..
DATA FIELD                      = <CONDESCRP VARIABLES>
<CONDESCRP VARIABLES>           = <"ALL"> | <VARIABLE LIST>

PEARSON CORR..
DATA FIELD                      = <CORR LIST>
<CORR LIST>                     = <CORR PRIMARY> |
                                  <CORR PRIMARY><"/"><CORR LIST>
<CORR PRIMARY>                  = <VARIABLE LIST><"WITH"><VARIABLE LIST> |
                                  <VARIABLE LIST>


NONPAR CORR..
DATA FIELD                      = <CORR LIST>
<CORR LIST>                     = <CORR PRIMARY> |
                                  <CORR PRIMARY><"/"><CORR LIST>
<CORR PRIMARY>                  = <VARIABLE LIST><"WITH"><VARIABLE LIST> |
                                  <VARIABLE LIST>
```

```
BREAKDOWN..
DATA FIELD                    = <BREAKDOWN LIST>
<BREAKDOWN LIST>              = <BREAKDOWN TABLE> |
                                <BREAKDOWN TABLE><"/"><BREAKDOWN LIST>
<BREAKDOWN TABLE>             = <VARIABLE LIST><"BY"><VARIABLE LIST> |
                                <VARIABLE LIST><"BY"><BREAKDOWN TABLE>

WRITE CASES
DATA FIELD                    = <FORTRAN FORMAT><VARIABLE LIST>

GUTTMAN SCALE..
DATA FIELD                    = <SCALE LIST>
<SCALE LIST>                  = <SCALE SPEC> |
                                <SCALE SPEC><"/"><SCALE LIST>
<SCALE SPEC>                  = <SCALE NAME><"="><ITEM LIST>
<SCALE NAME>                  = <NAME>
<ITEM LIST>                   = <SCALE ITEM> | <SCALE ITEM><SCALE LIST>
<SCALE ITEM>                  = <VARIABLE NAME>
                                <"("><DIVISION PT LIST><")">
<DIVISION PT LIST>            = <NUMERIC VALUE> |
                                <NUMERIC VALUE><DIVISION PT LIST>

REGRESSION..
DATA FIELD                    = <MATRIX LIST>
<MATRIX LIST>                 = <MATRIX SPEC> |
                                <MATRIX SPEC><"/"><MATRIX LIST>
<MATRIX SPEC>                 = <VARIABLE PART><REGRESSION PART>
<VARIABLE PART>               = <"VARIABLES ="><VARIABLE LIST>
<REGRESSION PART>             = <REGRESSION LIST> |
                                <REGRESSION LIST><"/"><REGRESSION PART>
<REGRESSION LIST>             = <"REGRESSION ="><VARIABLE NAME>
                                <"("><LEVELS><")"><"WITH"><INDP LIST>
<LEVELS>                      = <NUMERIC VALUE> |
                                <NUMERIC VALUE><LEVELS>
<INDP LIST>                   = <INDP VARIABLES> |
                                <INDP VARIABLES><INDP LIST>
<INDP VARIABLES>             = <VARIABLE LIST><"("><INTEGER><")">

PARTIAL CORR
DATA FIELD                    = <MATRIX LIST>
<MATRIX LIST>                 = <MATRIX SPEC> |
                                <MATRIX SPEC><"/"><MATRIX LIST>
<MATRIX SPEC>                 = <CORR LIST><"BY"><VARIABLE LIST>
                                <"("><ORDER LIST><")">
<CORR LIST>                   = <VARIABLE LIST><"WITH"><VARIABLE LIST> |
                                <VARIABLE LIST>
<ORDER LIST>                  = <INTEGER> | <INTEGER><ORDER LIST>
```

# D
# REFERENCE FOR STATISTICAL FORMULAS

## D.1 STATISTICS EMPLOYED IN SUBPROGRAMS CONDESCRIPTIVE, CODEBOOK, AND MARGINALS

### D.1.1 THE ARITHMETIC MEAN

The arithmetic mean is defined as the sum of the scores of a variable divided by the total number of valid cases for that variable. The formula for the arithmetic mean $\bar{X}$ is

$$\bar{X} = \frac{\sum_{i=1}^{N} X_i}{N}$$

where $X_i$ equals the score of each case, and where N represents the total number of valid cases. When the data is given in grouped form, which is a common practice when a large number of cases is involved, it is conventionally assumed for the purpose of computing the mean that the values within each category are concentrated at the midpoint of their respective interval rather than evenly distributed throughout it. The formula for computing the mean when grouped data is involved then becomes

$$\bar{X} = \frac{\sum_{i=1}^{k} f_i m_i}{N}$$

where $f_i$ equals the number of cases in the ith category, $m_i$ equals the midpoint of the ith category, and k equals the number of categories involved. In this case

$$N = \Sigma_{i=1}^{k} f_i \ .$$

### D.1.2   STANDARD ERROR

Standard error is defined as the standard deviation of a sampling distribution (see D.1.5).

### D.1.3   THE MEDIAN

The median of a given group of cases is defined as that score which is larger than the value of half the scores and smaller than the value of the other half of the scores. In order to compute the median, the cases are arranged in order according to the numerical values of the scores. When an odd number of cases is involved, the median will be the value of the score of the middle case; however, when an even number of cases is involved, the median will be determined by computing the mean of the scores of the two middle cases. For an odd number of cases the median is the value of the $(N + 1)/2$ case (where N equals the total number of cases); for an even number of cases, the median is equal to the value of the mean of the values of the $N/2$ and the $(N/2) + 1$ cases. When the scores for these two middle cases are the same, the median is simply equal to their common value.

In computing the median from grouped data, the values within each category are assumed to be distributed evenly throughout it. The first step in the computation is to determine the interval which contains the median. Suppose that the data has been grouped as shown in the accompanying table.

| Interval number | Range of scores $X_i$ falling in this interval | Frequency of scores falling in this interval | Cumulative frequency |
|---|---|---|---|
| 1 | $L_1 \leqslant X_i < L_2$ | $f_1$ | $F_1 = f_1$ |
| 2 | $L_2 \leqslant X_i < L_3$ | $f_2$ | $F_2 = f_1 + f_2$ |
| 3 | $L_3 \leqslant X_i < L_4$ | $f_3$ | $F_3 = f_1 + f_2 + f_3$ |
| $\vdots$ | $\vdots$ | $\vdots$ | $\vdots$ |
| k | $L_k \leqslant X_i < L_{k+1}$ | $f_k$ | $F_k = \Sigma_{i=1}^{k} f_i = N$ |

We now determine which interval will contain that case whose score X is such that half the cases had a score smaller than X and half greater than X. This will be the interval i where $F_{i-1} < N/2 \leqslant F_i$, and $F_o = 0$. The formula for the median is then

$$L_i + \frac{(N/2) - F_{i-1}}{f_i} (L_{i+1} - L_i)$$

### D.1.4   MODE

The mode is a measure of distribution which consists of the most frequently appearing score or scores.

### D.1.5   STANDARD DEVIATION

Standard deviation is the square root of the arithmetic mean of the squared deviations from the mean. In other words, the deviations of the scores from the mean are determined, each deviation is squared and the arithmetic mean of these numbers is calculated, then the square root of that mean is taken. The formula for the standard deviations is

$$s = \left[ \frac{\Sigma_{i=1}^{N} (X_i - \overline{X})^2}{N} \right]^{\frac{1}{2}}$$

where $\overline{X}$ equals the mean of the original scores. Several other formulas can be used when computing from ungrouped data. Two of these are

$$s = \left[ \frac{\Sigma_{i=1}^{N} X_i^2 - \frac{(\Sigma_{i=1}^{N} X_i)^2}{N}}{N} \right]^{\frac{1}{2}} \qquad \text{or} \qquad s = \frac{1}{N} \left[ N\Sigma_{i=1}^{N} X_i^2 - (\Sigma_{i=1}^{N} X_i)^2 \right]^{\frac{1}{2}}$$

When computing from grouped data, it is assumed that each case within a given interval i is located at the midpoint $d_i$ of that interval. If $x_i$ is set equal to $d_i - \overline{X}$, $x_i$ represents the deviation of the midpoint from the mean. The general formula then becomes

$$s = \left[ \frac{\Sigma_{i=1}^{N} f_i x_i^2}{N} \right]^{\frac{1}{2}}$$

### D.1.6 VARIANCE

Variance is equal to the square of standard deviation. Its formula therefore becomes

$$\text{Variance} = s^2 = \frac{\Sigma_{i=1}^{N}(X_i - \overline{X})^2}{N}$$

and its computing formulas are found by simply removing the square-root sign from any of the computing formulas for standard deviation.

### D.1.7 KURTOSIS

Kurtosis is the measure of the general peakedness of distribution for a given set of scores. Its formula is

$$\text{Kurtosis} = \frac{\Sigma_{i=1}^{N}\left(\frac{X_i - \overline{X}}{s}\right)^4}{N} - 3$$

The positive values indicate leptokurtosis (more peaked in the middle than the normal distribution), and negative values indicate platykurtosis.

### D.1.8 SKEWNESS

A distribution is considered to be skewed when there is a considerably larger number of extreme cases on one side of the distribution curve than on the other. Its formula is

$$\text{Skewness} = \frac{\Sigma_{i=1}^{N}\left(\frac{X_i - \overline{X}}{s}\right)^3}{N}$$

When the result is a positive number, the distribution is skewed to the right (extremely high scores are farther away from the mean than extremely low scores); when the result is negative, the distribution is skewed to the left.

### D.1.9 RANGE

Range is a measure of dispersal which is equal to the difference between the highest and lowest scores. When the data is grouped, it is computed as the difference between the midpoints of the highest and lowest intervals.

### D.1.10 MINIMUM

The minimum is the lowest score given for the data.

### D.1.11 MAXIMUM

The maximum is the highest score given for the data.

## D.2    STATISTICS AVAILABLE FOR SUBPROGRAMS CROSSTABS AND FASTABS

### D.2.1    CHI-SQUARE

The Chi-square statistic given in the tables of the CROSSTABS and FASTABS subprograms is based upon Pearson's Chi-square test of association. It tests the independence (or lack of statistical association) between two variables. It does *not* measure the degree of association; it only indicates the likelihood of having a distribution as different from statistical independence by chance alone as the observed distribution. Its formula is

$$\chi^2 = \sum_i \frac{(f_o^i - f_e^i)^2}{f_e^i}$$

with $(r - 1)(c - 1)$ degrees of freedom, where $f_o^i$ equals the observed frequency in each cell, $f_e^i$ equals the expected frequency, c equals the number of columns in the table, and r equals the number of rows in the table. The expected frequence $f_e^i$ is calculated as

$$f_e^i = \left(\frac{c_i r_i}{N}\right)$$

where $c_i$ is the frequency in a respective column marginal, $r_i$ is the frequency in a respective row marginal, and N stands for total number of valid cases.

The probability figure given in the table indicates on what level the difference between the observed distribution and the expected distribution can be thought as significant. It shows the probability of having as much difference between the sample distribution and the expected distribution if in fact the population distribution were independent.

For example, if the probability associated with given value of $X^2$ is .05, one can reject the null hypothesis that the two variables are independent at the significance level of .05 or greater.

Chi-square gives the most accurate result when applied to tables with a large value of N, as chi-square distribution tables are based on large sampling. Therefore, when the expected frequencies in some cells of the table run as low as 5, it is a good idea to make some correction for continuity, as the possibilities of different values for chi-square are rather limited when the cell frequencies are small integers. The correction, which will tend to make the value for chi-square somewhat smaller, consists of bringing all observed frequencies closer to the values of the expected frequencies by either adding or subtracting 0.5 in each cell before computing chi-square. Another way of getting around the problem of small frequencies is combining two or more categories. If most cell values are fairly large and only a few are as small as 5, it is not really necessary to make any adjustment at all before computing chi-square.

### D.2.2    FISHER'S EXACT TEST

Fisher's exact test is used with 2 X 2 contingency tables to yield exact, rather than approximate, probabilities. It is most useful for small samples. Its formula is

$$P_i = \frac{R_1! R_2! C_1! C_2!}{N! a! b! c! d!}$$

where $R_1$ equals the frequency total for row 1, $R_2$ equals the total for row 2, $C_1$ equals the total for column 1, $C_2$ equals the total for column 2; a, b, c, and d are all the frequencies of cells a, b, c, and d, respectively (assuming that the cells are lettered as in the accompanying diagram).

| a | b | $R_1$ |
|---|---|---|
| c | d | $R_2$ |

$C_1$  $C_2$

If one finds the probability of the observed distribution, as well as every other possible distribution giving as much or more evidence of association, then one can test the hypothesis that the given distribution is purely a product of chance by taking the calculated sum of $P_i$ values (or probability) as the significance level. Fisher's exact test is essentially one tailed.

The value of the exact significance level (or probability) is calculated by computing $P_i$ for the given table and also for each possible table with a variation on the distribution that is more extreme than that of the given table and then adding up all the values of $P_i$.

### D.2.3   PHI

Phi makes a correction for the fact that the value of chi-square is directly proportional to that of N by adjusting the $x^2$ value. Its formula is

$$\text{Phi } (\phi) = \frac{\chi^2}{N}$$

and for a $2 \times 2$ table, its values range from 0, when there is no relationship between the two variables, to 1, when the relationship between the two variables is perfect.

### D.2.4   CRAMER'S V

When phi is calculated for a table which is not $2 \times 2$, it has no upper limit. Therefore, Cramer's V is used to adjust phi for either the number of rows or the number of columns in the table, depending on which of the two is smaller. Its formula is

$$V = \left( \frac{\phi^2}{\text{Min } (r - 1),(c - 1)} \right)^{\frac{1}{2}}$$

and its values will range from 0 to 1, regardless of the size of the table being tested. When the table being tested is actually $2 \times 2$, the value of Cramer's V will be equal to that of phi.

### D.2.5   CONTINGENCY COEFFICIENT

Pearson's contingency coefficient adjusts chi-square for chi-square plus N. Its formula is

$$C = \frac{\chi^2}{\chi^2 + N}$$

and its values range from 0 to .707 for a $2 \times 2$ table; but the upper limit changes size as the table size increases. For this reason it should only be used to compare tables having the same dimensions.

### D.2.6   LAMBDA ASYMMETRIC

Lambda asymmetric is used only for asymmetrical tables whose columns define an independent variable and whose rows define a dependent variable. Its formula is

$$\text{Lambda} = \lambda_b = \frac{\sum_k \max.f_{jk} - \max.f_{.k}}{N - \max.f_{.k}}$$

where $\sum_k \max.f_{jk}$ represents the sum of the maximum values of the cell frequencies in each column and $\max.f_{.k}$ represents the maximum value of the row totals.

### D.2.7   LAMBDA SYMMETRIC

Unlike lambda asymmetric, lambda symmetric makes no assumption that one of the two variables in a table is dependent on the other one.

$$\text{Lambda} = \frac{\sum_k \max.f_{.k} + \sum_j \max.f_{jk} - \max.f_{.k} - \max.f_{j.}}{2N - \max.f_{.k} - \max.f_{j.}}$$

where $\sum_k \max.f_{jk}$ and $\max.f_{.k}$ are as defined for lambda asymmetric, $\max.f_{j.}$ is the maximum column total, and $\sum_j \max.f_{jk}$ is the sum of the maximum values of the cell frequencies in each row.

### D.2.8   KENDALL'S TAU B AND TAU C

Kendall's tau b and tau c both depend upon rank order, but tau c is intended for tables with an unequal number of rows and columns. The value of tau b can vary from $-1$ to $+1$, depending on how much agreement exists between the ranks of the rows.

In calculating tau b and tau c, count all possible number of pairs, $(\frac{1}{2})N(N-1)$, then partition these into the following three groups:

$P$ = all pairs in which the order on one variable is the same as the order
     on the other—concordant pairs

$Q$ = all pairs in which the order on one variable is the opposite of the order
     on the other—discordant pairs

$T$ = all pairs in which at least one variable shows a tie

Then

$$\text{Tau } b = \frac{P - Q}{1/2N(N - 1)}$$

Tau b can be computed with adjustment for ties by the use of the formula

$$\text{Tau } b = \frac{P}{1/2N(N-1) - T_1} - \frac{Q}{1/2N(N-1) - T_2}$$

where $T_1$ equals the number of ties in the first variable, and $T_2$ equals the number of ties in the second variable. Tau c has the formula

$$\text{Tau } c = \frac{2m(P - Q)}{N^2(m - 1)}$$

where m represents either the number of rows or the number of columns in the table, whichever is smaller.

### D.2.9   GAMMA

Gamma is another ordinal symmetric measure. Its formula is

$$\text{Gamma} = \frac{P - Q}{P + Q}$$

where P and Q have the same meaning as they do for Kendall's tau.

### D.2.10   SOMER'S D

Somer's D is similar to gamma but considers ties as valid information and is applied to both symmetric and asymmetric cases. Its formula is

$$\text{Asymmetric} = \frac{2(P - Q)}{N^2 - \Sigma j C j^2} = \frac{P - Q}{1/2(N^2 - \Sigma j C_j^2)}$$

where P and Q have the same meaning as for Kendall's tau b, and jCj represents the count of each column. As for lambda asymmetric, this measure assumes that the column variable is independent, and the row variable is dependent.

Likewise, asymmetric d with the column as dependent variable may be expressed as

$$\text{Asymmetric } d = \frac{2(P - Q)}{N^2 - \Sigma j R j^2}$$

where jRj represents the counts in each row.

Symmetric d utilizes the same strategy as symmetric lambda and can be expressed as follows:

$$\text{Symmetric } d = \frac{2(P - Q)}{1/2[(N^2 - \Sigma j C j^2) + (N^2 - \Sigma j R j^2)]}$$

### D.2.11   UNCERTAINTY COEFFICIENT

Uncertainty coefficient is based upon information theory and indicates the degree to which the knowledge of the independent variable reduces the amount of information uncertainty in the dependent variable.

The asymmetric coefficient when X is the independent variable and Y the dependent variable is

$$\text{Uncertainty coefficient} = \frac{U(Y) - U(Y|X)}{U(Y)}$$

where $U(Y)$ represents the average uncertainty in the marginal distribution of Y and is calculated by

$$U(Y) - -\sum_{j} p(Y_j) \log p(Y_j)$$

where $p(Y_j)$ stands for the probability of a particular category in Y or proportion of $Y_j$.

$U(Y|X)$ stands for a conditional uncertainty of Y given X and is calculated by

$$U(Y|X) = -\sum_{k}\sum_{j} p(Y_j, X_k) \log p(Y_j|X_k)$$

Likewise, an asymmetric measure where X is the dependent variable can be defined as

$$\frac{U(X) - U(X|Y)}{U(X)}$$

and a symmetric coefficient as

$$\frac{U(Y) + U(X) - U(Y,X)}{U(Y) + U(X)}$$

where $U(Y,X)$ stands for the joint uncertainty

$$U(Y,X) = -\sum_{j}\sum_{k} P(Y_j, X_k) \log p(Y_j X_k)$$

All uncertainty coefficients vary from 0 to 1.

# E
# GLOSSARY OF TECHNICAL TERMS

There follows an alphabetical listing of terms used frequently in the text and their meanings. Many SPSS terms are included as are terms relating to the use of computers and coding of data using punched cards.

| | |
|---|---|
| A-format element | A specification used on the INPUT FORMAT and WRITE CASES control card for alphanumeric variables, i.e., variables having alphanumeric values. |
| Alphabetic | Symbol or value composed entirely of alphabetic characters, e.g., control words DOCUMENT, OPTIONS and values MALE, FEMALE. |
| Alphanumeric | Mnemonic (nonnumeric) values composed from the letters A, B to Z, and digit symbols 0, 1 to 9, for example, LOG10, EDUC, or NMEM. Type of a variable, data, or coding scheme. |
| Argument | Values of variables upon which a specific function is to be performed, for example, SQRT(VARA) causes the square-root function to be performed upon the values of the variable VARA. VARA is the argument for the function. |

| | |
|---|---|
| Arithmetic expression | A mathematical formula consisting of variable names, operators, functions, and constants which may be evaluated for each case in a file, using values of variables in each case. |
| Array | Presentation of data in row and column (two-dimensional) format. |
| Assembly language | A lower-level code for the computer which was used to write certain SPSS subprograms. |
| BCD | Binary coded decimal. A coding scheme for the representation of characters in a computer. |
| Binary representation | Internal computer representation of data. |
| Bit | A 0 or 1. A series of bits constitutes binary representation. |
| Blocking factor | The number of individual cases (or card images) to be written or read at one time from a peripheral device such as tape or disk. |
| BPI | Bits per inch. A measure of the density or amount of information recorded on a magnetic tape. |
| Byte | Eight bits of information. The basic storage unit of the IBM/360 computer. |
| Card | See punched card. |
| Card image | An 80-column record on a tape or disk file. |
| Cardinal values | Numeric or counting values, as opposed to nominal values. |
| Case | The unit of measurement within the SPSS system. Each case consists of the simultaneous determination of values for all variables in the file. |
| CASWGT | An SPSS-created variable which contains the weight factor for each case of a permanently weighted file. It is used by the statistical subprograms and by the WRITE CASES output routine. |
| Character | Graphic symbol (letter, digit, or special symbol) occupying one column or position. See character set. |
| Character set | The permissable set of graphics or symbols recognizable by a computer. |
| Coding | Coding scheme for data. Reduction of information obtained from a study to a set of numeric or alphanumeric (mnemonic or non-numeric) values suitable for input into an analysis procedure. |
| Column | Card column. A single position on a card, capable of representing a single character. |
| Column width | The number of characters in a field. |
| COMMENT | A control card for user comments which is printed back on the output along with the other control cards. It has no other affect on job processing. |
| Common delimiter | A blank or comma. A symbol required to separate names, values, etc., which are in free-field format on data or control cards. |
| COMPUTE | Control card for variable transformations. It allows a new set of variable values to be created from an arithmetic function of one or more existing variables. The set of values may be assigned to an old or new variable. See also computed variable. |

| | |
|---|---|
| Computed variable | A variable created using the variable-transformation facilities of SPSS and whose set of values are computed from one or more existing variables, for example, NEWVAR = OLDVAR−0.5*− CTRLVAR. |
| Contiguous | Without intervening blanks, in immediately adjacent positions, e. g., contiguous characters of a keyword: STATISTICS. |
| Continuous | Continuous variable. A variable which could logically assume a continuum of values, e.g., income. |
| Control card | SPSS control card. A user-supplied card which specifies a task or information for the SPSS system. See control field and specification field. |
| Control field | The first 16 columns of a control card. See control word. |
| Control word | The information in the first 16 columns of a control card which identifies the control card. |
| Core storage | A high-speed recording device used within the computer for manipulation of data. |
| Crosstabulation | A table display of the frequencies of data cases among values of two or more variables; e.g., sex according to age group. |
| Data | Values, on a control card or in the data file, to be passed to the system. Input, control cards, and data file containing the set of data values for analysis to be processed by the SPSS system. |
| Data analysis | The process of categorizing or summarizing data for the purpose of drawing inferences, usually with use of statistical techniques. |
| Data cell | A data-storage device allowing for large quantities of information, but only moderately fast access. |
| Data definition | Control cards. Required or optional control cards which define the user's data file. These cards include the FILE NAME, VARIABLE LIST, and SUBFILE LIST control cards. |
| Data modification | Control cards. A group of control cards which permit the user to permanently or temporarily alter the values of variables in a file. The group includes the COMPUTE, IF, and RECODE control cards and their starred [*] counterparts. |
| Data selection | Control cards. A group of control cards which allow the sampling or weighting of cases in a file. The WEIGHT, SAMPLE, and SELECT IF control cards and their starred [*] counterparts are included in this group. |
| Debug | Error elimination. Checking of input and output from a job or procedure for completeness and accuracy. |
| Deck | A set of punched cards submitted to a computer for processing. |
| Define | To identify or describe an item to the SPSS or operating system by the use of appropriate control cards. |
| Delimiter | Symbols which set apart items of information on a control card. The common delimiters are the blank and the comma. The special delimiters are the left and right parenthesis [( and )] and the slash [/] and are used according to certain rules in specific contexts. |
| Dependent variable | The variable which one wishes to explain as a function of other variables (the independent variables). |

| | |
|---|---|
| Descriptive statistics | Numbers which summarize a body of data. |
| Device | Input device, output device. Input medium, output medium. The mechanism attached to the computer by which information is entered or output. |
| Direct access | A mode of operation of the operating system which allows non-sequential access of data stored on a memory device of the computer. |
| Discrete | Discrete variable. A variable which can logically assume only a finite number of values, e.g., political affiliation. |
| Disk | Disk file, disk pack. A data-storage device used on a computer for quick access to information. |
| Distribution | The variability of values of data. |
| DOCUMENT | A control card for user comments and descriptive information. It is saved as part of a system file and can be printed back out on subsequent runs using the DUMP card. |
| DUMP | A control card which, for the system file being processed, will cause all data-defining and data-modification information to be printed out. |
| Embedded blank | A space or blank character appearing in the middle of a field. |
| Error message | A message which may be printed out during an SPSS processing run. The error messages are numbered, and the user should consult the error-message list (Appendix A) to determine the source of difficulty. |
| Extended label | A specification which may be associated by a user with a file, variable, or variable value which is printed on the output. Labels are specified by control cards and may extend from one control card to the next. |
| F-format element | A specification used on the INPUT FORMAT and WRITE CASES control cards for numeric variables, i.e., variables having only numerical values for each case. |
| Field | One or more adjacent positions in a control card or data record which specifies a single value or item. |
| File | Grouping of data cases for analysis. Data is entered into the SPSS system as a file. The file may be substructured (see subfile), and may be saved along with its defining control cards (see system file). |
| File-generating run | An SPSS job run where an input data file and data-defining cards are saved as a system file (SAVE FILE card) at the end of the job. |
| File modification | The process of addition or deletion of specific variables, cases, or subfiles from an SPSS system file. |
| Fixed column | Located in a fixed column or position and of fixed-column width; fixed-column format. Data-organization method using a fixed-field format, i.e., values are located in fixed columns on a record. |
| Format | Of data: data-organization method, fixed or free field. Of variable: numeric or alphanumeric. |
| Format list | The specifications for fixed-column data on input (INPUT FORMAT card) or output (WRITE CASES card) from SPSS. The for- |

mat list gives the variable type (numeric or alphanumeric) and column locations for each variable.

FORTRAN IV — A common version of the FORTRAN language in which most of the SPSS system was written. Some version of FORTRAN (FORmula TRANslator) is acceptable to most modern computer systems.

Free field — Field delimited by some specified character. Data-organization method where values are separated by a delimiting character, e.g., a blank or comma. SPSS control-card specifications are mostly free field.

Frequency distribution — A mathematical or empirical curve or histogram which summarizes the frequency with which a variable assumes its various values.

FTxx cards — JCL cards required by the operating system for reading and writing of SPSS tape and disk files. To save and retrieve a system file, FT04 and FT05 cards are used; to read and write card-image files, the FT08 and FT09 cards.

Function — SPSS supplied "built-in" mathematical function for use in constructing a mathematical expression with a variable-transformation card. These functions include log functions, trigonometric functions, square root, etc.

Graphic — Graphic symbol. The visual representation of a character of the character set.

H-format element — Specification of a Hollerith constant.

Hexidecimal — A system of number representation used by computers based on 16 symbols.

HIGHEST — A keyword (RECODE CARD) which may be used as a substitute for the maximum value when recoding continuous variables.

Hollerith constant — A string of characters or field which may form part of the format list for output of cases using the WRITE CASES control card.

IBM 360 — A series of computing machines manufactured by International Business Machines Corporation. The series is composed of several related machines having the same internal logic, but providing for several levels of "computing power." The SPSS system has been implemented for this system, for models having certain minimum specifications.

Identification field — Field reserved for or containing identification information. The field on the data record reserved by the user for case identification.

Identification number — For a file, a number assigned by the user for the identification and sequencing of case, and for a card file, for the card within each case. This number is generally sequentially assigned and appears in the first or last columns of the card or record.

IF — Control card for variable transformations which specifies a conditional assignment of a computed value to a variable. The assignment may be temporary (*IF card), and a defined value is ensured for all cases of a new variable by the TMISS variable.

Independent variable(s) — The explanatory variable(s) in a statistical analysis. In multiple linear regression, the variables used to make up the linear form.

| | |
|---|---|
| JCL | Job Control Language. A language designed for use with the IBM 360 series computers to allow the user to control the flow of his program steps and the use of input and output devices. Certain JCL cards must be prepared by the user to allow the use of the SPSS system. |
| K | 1,000 |
| Keypunching | Manual punching of punched cards, as in the preparation of control cards. |
| Keyword | A preset sequence of alphabetic characters which have a reserved meaning in the SPSS system, e.g., TO or THRU. |
| Kurtosis | A measure of the concentration of variable values about the mean (average) value. |
| Label | See extended label. |
| Language | The set of terms and rules of syntax which make up the code used for communicating with the SPSS or operating systems. |
| Left justified | Positioning of information to the left in a field. |
| Listwise deletion | An option in certain of the statistical subprograms for the processing of cases with missing values. For a given list of variables, if a case contains a missing value for one or more of the variables listed, it is omitted for the entire set of variables. |
| Logical expression | The expression or formula on an IF control card which is evaluated to determine if a computed value will be assigned to a variable. The formula yields the value true or false. |
| Logical operators | The keywords AND, OR, and NOT which are used to form a logical expression. |
| LOWEST | A keyword (RECODE card) which may be used as a substitute for the minimum value when recoding (continuous) variables. |
| Machine readable | Prepared in a form suitable for input to a computer. |
| MARGINALS | The simple frequency distribution of the cases in a data file among the values of a discrete variable. |
| Mathematical operators | Graphic symbols used to form mathematical expressions for variable-transformation cards. The symbols and meanings are: + addition, − subtraction, * multiplication, / division, and = equals (assignment). |
| Medium | The device to be used to read an SPSS file. This is specified on the INPUT MEDIUM card by the use of a mnemonic. |
| Missing values | Values which may be assigned to a variable to indicate why the data is incomplete. Up to three different codes may be used to specify, for example; not applicable, not obtained, invalid response (MISSING VALUES card). |
| Mnemonics | A sequence of characters which uniquely identify a name or value, e.g., a file name STUDY/69, a variable value for SEX, MALE. |
| Mixed number | A whole number and a fraction; e.g., 10.5. |
| Name | A tag or mnemonic of up to eight characters used to refer to a file or variable. |

| | |
|---|---|
| Nominal | Nominal variable. A variable whose values have no numeric significance, e.g., the variable sex. |
| Nonparametric | Nonparametric statistics. Distribution-free statistics, statistics which do not require the variables to have some special distribution, e.g., normality. |
| Normalized score | A continuous variable which has been transformed so that it has a mean of 0 and a standard deviation of 1. |
| Numeric | Arithmetic value, either integer (I format) or decimal (F format). Type of variable, data, or coding scheme using the digits 0, 1 to 9, plus optionally the $+$, $-$, ., and E symbols. |
| Operator | A special symbol or keyword which causes the values of variables to be combined to produce new values. See mathematical operators, logical operators, and relational operators. |
| Operating system | See system. |
| OPTIONS | Control card which allows the user to specify the processing options to apply for a given statistical subprogram. The set of default options (defined for each subprogram) which apply if no OPTIONS card appears, can be selectively overridden. |
| Ordinal | Ordinal variable. A variable whose values denote an ordering, rather than relative magnitude. |
| OS/360 | The operating system of the IBM 360. |
| Pairwise deletion | An option in certain of the statistical subprograms for the processing of cases with missing values. If a case contains a missing value for one of the two variables involved in computing a statistic, the case is omitted from the computation of that statistic but may be included in the computation of others. |
| Parameter | Information (values, numbers, etc.) which is supplied by the user to select options allowed by a subprogram. |
| Percentage base | The percentage of cases to be used from a file or designated set of subfiles when sampling occurs (as with control card SAMPLE). |
| Physical card | A punched card as opposed to a card image. |
| PRINT FORMATS | A control card used to (a) identify all alphanumeric coded variables (mandatory), and (b) for numeric variables, to specify the number of digits following the decimal point on output. The default is two digits, the maximum is five. |
| Procedure | An SPSS subprogram for a specific statistical or data manipulation. |
| Procedure cards | Control cards which cause an SPSS procedure to be executed. |
| Processing | Run. The process carried out by the computer to perform a calculation or data manipulation. |
| Processing mode | The method of processing a file with a subfile structure, e.g., one or more subfiles processed separately, subfile structure to be ignored, etc. (PROCESS SBFILES). |
| Program | The set of instructions which causes the computer to operate. The SPSS system is a large program. |
| Punching | The process of recording information on cards with the use of a keypunch. |

| | |
|---|---|
| Raw data | Data prior to input to the SPSS system, that is, which has not been processed or affected in any way by the system. |
| RECODE | Control card for the selective recoding of existing variables. Any value or group of values may be replaced by a single new value. The recoding may be temporary (*RECODE). |
| Recode | To convert data from one set of values to another according to some rule, e.g., variable transformation using IF, COMPUTE, RECODE. |
| Relational operator | The keywords LE, LT, EQ, NE, GT, GE which express a relation between two values which could be true or false. |
| RND | An SPSS arithmetic function to round a decimal value to the nearest integer. It can be used in constructing a mathematical or logical expression on a variable-transformation card. |
| Rounding error | In the processing of a weighted file, the reported number of cases falling into some category may differ from one statistical procedure to another, due to the technicalities of the procedures used. Such inaccuracies are inevitable in many statistical techniques. |
| Run | Processing run or computer run. Processing of an SPSS job by computer. |
| Run cards | A set of control cards which give additional control and descriptive information for a processing run. Most (but not all) are optional. |
| Run termination | The end of processing of an SPSS job, normal or error, and return of control to the operating system. |
| SAMPLE | A random sample of data from a file may be made using the SAMPLE control card. A sample of any size (fraction of cases in the file) sufficient to give significant results may be specified. The sampling may be temporary (*SAMPLE). |
| Scratch file | External storage media (tape or direct access) used by SPSS or the operating system to hold information temporarily during a processing run. |
| SEQNUM | An SPSS created variable which contains, for each file or subfile, a unique SPSS-assigned case-sequence number. For a substructured file, the variables SUBFIL and SEQNUM together give a unique case-identification code. |
| Setup | Deck setup. The required order of control cards and data in the input deck. |
| Special characters | Single character symbols with reserved meanings. For example, delimiters on control cards, or arithmetic operators. See character set. |
| Special delimiters | See delimiter. |
| Specification field | Columns 17 to 80 of control cards. |
| Starred [*] cards | See temporary cards. |
| Statistically significant | A statistic is said to be statistically significant (with a specified confidence level) when certain tests, which are based on assumptions about the nature of the statistic, are met. Many SPSS subprograms compute measures of statistical significance. |

| | |
|---|---|
| STATISTICS | The control card used to specify the statistics to be reported by a given subprogram. There are no default statistics associated with the card. |
| Statistics | Numbers which are derived from and summarize a body of data. |
| String | String of free-field values. Names or values in an ordered list. |
| SUBFIL | An SPSS-created variable containing, for each case of a file with a subfile structure, the subfile name (alphanumeric value). |
| Subfile | A grouping of related cases in a substructured file. The subfile is created from BCD input cases as specified by the appropriate control cards. Data analysis may be done at the file or subfile level (processing mode). |
| Subfile list | The specification for subfile processing of the subfiles which together compose the overall file. For subfile-processing mode, the specification of individual subfiles to be processed. |
| Subprogram | SPSS statistical subprogram. A subroutine or part of the SPSS system to perform a specific calculation or manipulation. |
| Syntax | The rules for the construction of meaningful SPSS control cards or JCL cards. |
| System | SPSS system: The set of programs which execute the functions discussed in the text. Operating system: The programs of the computer, which provide the environment within which the SPSS system operates. |
| System file | Input data file plus data-defining information saved at the end of a run (SAVE FILE). A system file can be input into a run (GET FILE card), modified, and a new system file saved. Cases and data-defining information can be retrieved from the file (see WRITE CASES and DUMP). |
| Tape | A high-volume storage medium used on computers. This will typically be used for storage of SPSS system files, provided access is not required too frequently. |
| Task | Statistical calculations to be performed upon a file. |
| Task definition | Specification, by means of control cards, of the procedures to be executed, the options to be exercised, and the files to be manipulated during a given processing run. |
| Temporary [*] cards | A class of control cards which cause temporary transformations to be performed upon a file which affect only the task they immediately precede. The control field begins with an asterisk or star (*RECODE or *COMPUTE or *IF). |
| TMISS | A control card which permits the user to specify a default value for a variable created using the IF card. |
| Transformation | The use of the value of one or more variables to compute the values of a new variable. Transformations may be performed by use of the COMPUTE, RECODE, and IF control cards and their starred [*] counterparts. |
| 12-punch | One of the nonnumeric hole positions on a punched card. Such a punch is invalid for numeric data. |

| | |
|---|---|
| Unified file | A file for which processing is performed upon all cases, that is, a subfile structure is ignored. |
| Value | A number or alphanumeric character assumed by a variable for a particular case. |
| Value labels | A description of up to 20 characters in length for particular values of a variable which may be specified by the user with a VALUE LABELS control card. These descriptions may be saved in a system file to be printed automatically on the output. |
| Variable | A determination of values for a set of cases. Each variable is given a variable name or mnemonic. |
| Variable length | Values or names. Names, labels, and values may consist of varying numbers of characters. |
| VARIABLE LIST | A control card which specifies the variable list for a file. |
| Variable list | The sequential set of variables whose values constitute the cases in a file. Each variable has a mnemonic, and this sequence of mnemonics constitutes the variable list. |
| Variable order | The sequential order of variables as specified on a VARIABLE LIST control card and retained in the data file. |
| Variable type | The values of a variable may be stored, retrieved, and manipulated in the SPSS system in two modes—alphanumeric or floating point. The mode of a variable is its type. |
| WEIGHT | A control card which specifies the weighting of cases in a file for sampling purposes. |
| Weighted file | A file for which the values of the variable CASWGT have been altered so that some cases will be counted more heavily than others. |
| WRITE CASES | A control card which permits the output of a selected set of variables from a data file. |
| X-format element | An element of the specification field of the INPUT FORMAT or WRITE CASES control cards used to skip columns. |
| Z score | A value obtained by subtracting from a variable value its mean and dividing the result by the standard deviation of the variable. |

# F
# OS 360 JOB CONTROL LANGUAGE (JCL) FOR THE SPSS SYSTEM AT THE STANFORD INSTALLATION

JCL or job control language for OS 360 is the means by which the user controls the interaction between his data, the program he is using, and the computer's operating system. The IBM 360 operating system and the job control language which enables the user to instruct it is among the most flexible and versatile available. Unfortunately, versatility and flexibility in this case also mean greater complexity, and the operating system of the 360 requires the user to supply the computer with additional information (about his data files) beyond that which he has already supplied on his SPSS control cards.

The major function of JCL, for users of the SPSS system is to provide the operating system with information on the exact location, type, and form of the user's data files—both input and output. And it is precisely because the SPSS system provides the user with so many options for the input and output of data that he must also suffer through the additional pains of preparing JCL cards for his files. When the user is, for example, entering his data from a BCD tape or disk file, rather than from cards, the JCL requirement varies slightly. Or if the user wishes to save his file at the conclusion of a run, in the form of an SPSS system file, this too requires the addition of several JCL cards. Then, when the user reenters his data into the system as an SPSS system file, some modifications in the JCL cards must be made again.

The JCL cards required for all the input and output options have been prepared for the user and are presented in this appendix. The user may simply copy the required cards and fill in several blank fields which contain information specific to his data files. The instructions for filling in these blanks are presented in detail along with the cards, and the user should have little trouble with JCL if he reads this appendix carefully.

This appendix presents instructions for the preparation of JCL for the SPSS system at the Stanford Computation Center (campus facility). The Stanford installation runs under an MFT monitor with a modified HASP spooling program. While users at other installations will find this appendix useful in preparing JCL for SPSS on their machine, they should consult with the appropriate personnel at their installation before attempting to operate the SPSS system. The basic concepts and deck setups will be the same from one installation to another. However, differences in monitors, spooling procedures, the handling of labeled tapes, as well as discrepancies in the versions of OS being used, will often cause some particulars on the JCL cards to vary from one installation to another.

## F.1    BASIC JCL CARDS ALWAYS REQUIRED WHEN OPERATING THE SPSS SYSTEM

The following 10 JCL cards constitute the basic group of cards which are always required when operating the SPSS system. They are also identical to those cards required when the user is entering his data from cards and *is not* attempting to save an SPSS system file, output cases in BCD form, or produce punched or written correlation matrices. If the user is entering his data from cards and none of the aforementioned features are being employed, the *basic* JCL cards may be used with no additions or modifications. If the user is employing any of the above features or is entering his data from a BCD file residing on tape or disk, or is inputting an SPSS system file from any device, additional JCL must be prepared and inserted into the basic JCL deck. Appendix A.2 may be used to determine which JCL cards are to be prepared when the user is employing the various input/output capabilities of SPSS. Each of the subsequent sections of the appendix presents detailed instructions for the preparation of the various JCL cards required to use all the options for input and output of data files. The first nine JCL cards are placed directly in front of the RUN NAME card; all SPSS control cards follow in the sequence indicated throughout the text. JCL card 10, the /* card, must always follow the FINISH card.

### F.1.1    BASIC SPSS JCL CARDS

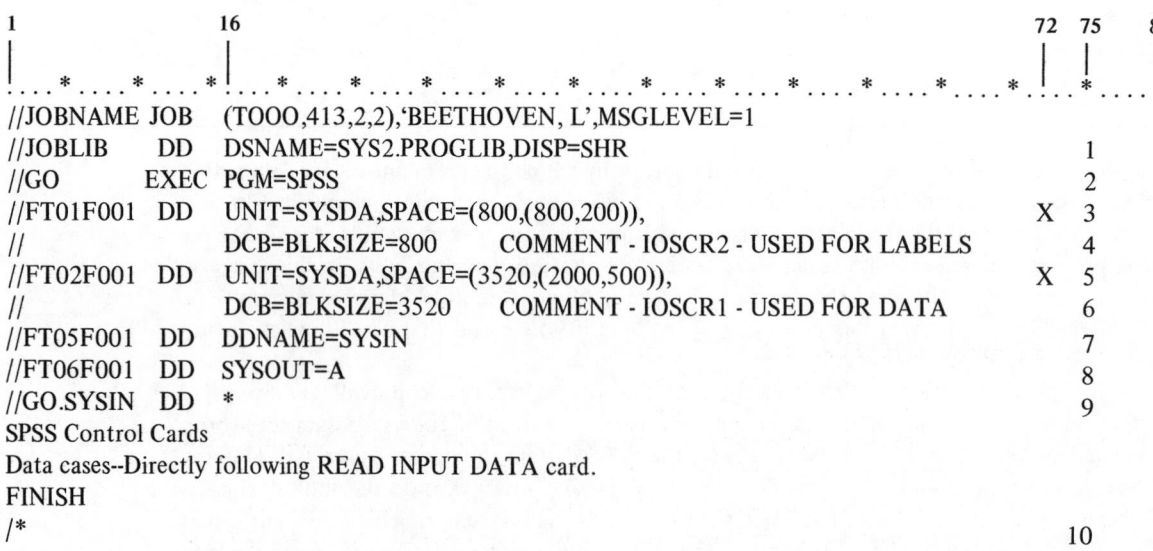

```
1                        16                                              72  75    80
|                         |                                              |    |     |
|  . . . * . . . . * . . . . * . . . * . . . . * . . . * . . . . * . . . * . . . . * . . . * . . . * . . . . * . . . . * . . .|   . * . . . . *
//JOBNAME  JOB     (TOOO,413,2,2),'BEETHOVEN, L',MSGLEVEL=1
//JOBLIB   DD      DSNAME=SYS2.PROGLIB,DISP=SHR                          1
//GO       EXEC    PGM=SPSS                                              2
//FT01F001 DD      UNIT=SYSDA,SPACE=(800,(800,200)),                 X   3
//                 DCB=BLKSIZE=800       COMMENT - IOSCR2 - USED FOR LABELS   4
//FT02F001 DD      UNIT=SYSDA,SPACE=(3520,(2000,500)),              X   5
//                 DCB=BLKSIZE=3520      COMMENT - IOSCR1 - USED FOR DATA     6
//FT05F001 DD      DDNAME=SYSIN                                         7
//FT06F001 DD      SYSOUT=A                                             8
//GO.SYSIN DD      *                                                    9
SPSS Control Cards
Data cases--Directly following READ INPUT DATA card.
FINISH
/*                                                                      10
```

### F.1.1.1

The user may follow his data with one or more additional sets of task-definition cards. He in turn follows these with a FINISH card. The /* card, JCL card 10, always follows the FINISH card irrespective of the number of tasks to be performed.

**F.1.1.2**

The very first card in the deck, the *job card* (which is unnumbered), is not a JCL card specific to SPSS, but is required on *all* jobs being entered at the Stanford installation. This card carries all the accounting information, the user's bin number, and tape mounting instructions. It is highly specific to the individual installation.

**F.1.2    EXAMPLE RUN AND DECK SETUP WITH BASIC JCL**

## F.2    ALTERING THE SPACE PARAMETER FOR THE ALLOCATION OF CORE

SPSS has been set up so that the amount of space or core available for the execution of the statistical subprograms may be altered by the user at the time of processing. The largest segment of the SPSS program itself requires approximately 135,000 bytes. The program then automatically allocates an additional 80,000 bytes of core (for the tables, sums, matrices, etc., required by the statistical subprogram being utilized) unless this parameter is altered by the user at the time of the run. Normally this means that SPSS will require a partition or region of approximately 215,000 bytes.[1]

[1]The exact amount of core required by SPSS will vary from one installation to another because of differences in the way in which buffers are allocated, etc.

If the user is operating SPSS at an installation running under MVT and is paying core-residency charges, or is running SPSS at an installation which has less than 215,000 bytes available for user programs, or the user has a very large task and is operating on a machine large enough to increase the core allocation of SPSS, the normal or default space allocation of 80,000 bytes may be altered. This is accomplished by adding a space parameter to JCL card 2 which normally appears as follows:

```
1                 16
//GO    EXEC      PGM=SPSS
```

When the SPACE parameter is to be altered JCL card 2 is modified in the following manner:

```
1                 16
//GO    EXEC      PGM=SPSS,PARM=xxxxx
```

where

1. The keyword SPSS (or the name of the SPSS program at the user's installation) is followed by a comma and the keyword PARM=. (Note There may be no additional blanks.)
2. The keyword PARM= is directly followed by an integer number which must be (a) greater than 3,000, (b) divisible by 8, and (c) must be no larger than the maximum number of bytes available for user programs at the user's installation.[1]

Altering the SPACE parameter affects only those parameters in SPSS subprograms which directly employ the value of SPACE in computing the program limitations. The number of cells available for a FASTABS procedure, the number of correlation coefficients which can be simultaneously computed by PEARSON CORR, the number of cases and coefficients which can be computed with NONPAR CORR are a few of the limitations which will be modified when the SPACE parameter is changed.

The upper limit on the total number of cells which may be generated during a FASTABS run serves as a good example for demonstrating the effect of changing the SPACE parameter on JCL card 2. The maximum number of available cells is computed by the following formula:

$$MAXCELLS = (SPACE/4) - ( 10 \text{ X NVARS})$$

where SPACE is either 80,000 or the number following the keyword PARM= on JCL card 2, and NVARS is the number of variables named and/or implied on the VARIABLES portion of the FASTABS procedure card.

If NVARS were 100 and the default SPACE option was in effect, then the maximum number of available cells (i.e., the sum of the rows times the columns in each table) would be 19,000. If SPACE were doubled (i.e., 160,000) and the number of variables remained at 100 the total number of available cells would become

$$(160,000/4) - 1000 = 39,000$$

Similarly, if the SPACE parameter where set at 40,000 and NVARS remained 100, the total number of available cells would become 9,000.

The following example JCL cards demonstrate the appearance of this card when the SPACE parameter is altered. The user should note that the number must be evenly divisible by 8 and no embedded commas may appear in this number.

```
1                 16
//GO    EXEC      PGM=SPSS,PARM=160000

//GO    EXEC      PGM=SPSS,PARM=40000

//GO    EXEC      PGM=SPSS,PARM=61320
```

[1]The user should consult with the appropriate computer-center personnel to determine the maximum permissible value for SPACE at his installation.

# F.3  DETERMINING THE REQUIRED JCL

Table F.1. should enable the user to determine which JCL cards he will need to prepare. It also gives the section numbers of Appendix F which contain the detailed instructions for preparing each of the JCL cards. The table is organized under four major headings corresponding to the major input and output options of SPSS. If the user is entering data in BCD form from a medium other than CARD, the information under section heading BCD INPUT FILES FT08 will be relevant. If the user is making a run on which he plans to save an SPSS system file, the information under SPSS OUTPUT SYSTEM FILES FT04 will be relevant. The table is supplemented by some common configurations of JCL that are required when utilizing various combinations of input/output options.

**TABLE F.1    Key to required JCL**

| JCL for input files | Applicable section(s) of Appendix F |
|---|---|
| BCD input files: FT08 | F.4 |
|     Cards | No additional JCL cards required |
|     9-track tape | F.4.1 |
|     7-track tape | F.4.2 |
|     BCD disk files | F.4.3 |
| | |
| SPSS input system files: FT03 | F.6 |
|     9-track tape | F.6.1 |
|     7-track tape | F.6.2 |
|     Disk files | F.6.3 |
| **JCL for output files** | |
| Output system files FT04 | F.5 |
|     9-track tape | F.5.1 |
|     7-track tape | F.5.2 |
|     Disk files | F.5.3 |
| | |
| BCD output files: FT09 (For WRITE CASES | |
|     or outputting correlation matrices) | F.7 |
|     Cards | F.7.1 |
|     9-track tape | F.7.2 |
|     7-track tape | F.7.3 |
|     BCD disk files | F.7.4 |

The following are some common configurations of input and output options which may be desired, and the JCL which would be necessary for such runs.

1.  Data being entered on cards and a system file being saved at the conclusion of the run on 9-track tape.

    When the BCD input medium is cards, no additional JCL is required to define that file.

    Saving a system file always requires the preparation of an FT04 set of JCL cards. Section F.5.1 defines the cards required when the system file is being saved on 9-track tape.

2.  Data being entered on 7-track BCD tape and a system file being saved on disk.

    JCL cards for FT08 (BCD input files) must be prepared. FT08 for 7-track tape is defined in Sec. F.4.2.

    JCL specifications for output system files FT04 on disk required by this run can be found in Sec. F.5.3.

3.  Data is being entered from an SPSS system file residing on 9-track tape for a statistical processing run only. No permanent transformations are to be retained and no other output device utilized.

This run would require the basic group of JCL, as always, plus JCL cards for an input system file FT03 residing on 9 track tape. Section F.6.1 contains instructions for preparing these cards.

4. On this complicated run, data is being entered from an SPSS system file residing on disk. Variables are being added with the ADD VARIABLES feature; the cases containing the variables to be added reside on 9-track tape. Furthermore, the user wishes to output a new BCD file containing some variables from the system file and some from the variables he is adding. A new system file containing all the variables in the old system file plus all of the new variables will also be retained on 7-track tape at the conclusion of the run.

This run would require the basic JCL group plus:

(*a*)  JCL for an input system file FT03 residing on disk, defined in Sec. F.6.3.

(*b*)  JCL for a BCD input file FT08 residing on 9-track tape, defined in Sec. F.4.1.

(*c*)  JCL for a BCD output file on 9-track tape, defined in Sec. F.7.2.

(*d*)  JCL for an output system file FT04 to reside on a 7-track tape. This JCL is defined in Sec. F.5.2.

## F.4   JCL REQUIRED FOR BCD INPUT FILES: FT08

The user may input BCD files consisting of data cases or correlation matrices from cards, 7-track tape, 9-track tape, or disk. When the user has indicated on his INPUT MEDIUM card that data is to be entered from a BCD medium other than CARD (i.e., TAPE, DISK), JCL cards for a BCD input file FT08 must be prepared and inserted into the basic JCL cards. If the user is entering BCD data directly from cards, an FT08 card and its continuations *need not* be prepared. Similarly, an FT08 card need not be prepared if the user is entering his data from an SPSS system file unless he is utilizing the ADD VARIABLES or ADD SUBFILES features, and the new variables or subfiles are being entered from a medium other than CARD. In short, any run which requires an INPUT MEDIUM card and on which the INPUT MEDIUM card specifies a medium other than CARD will require the preparation of an FT08 card and its continuations. JCL cards for 9-track tapes are defined first, then 7-track tapes, and finally disks.

### F.4.1   JCL CARDS FT08 (BCD INPUT FILES) ON 9-TRACK TAPES

The following two JCL cards numbered 8.1 and 8.2 must be prepared whenever the user is entering a BCD file from 9-track tape. The cards are inserted in the basic JCL deck directly behind JCL card 8.

A.  JCL card 8.1 (BCD input files) for 9-track tapes.
    JCL card 8.1 is set up to bypass the label-processing procedure. Since it is the general practice at the Stanford installation to use unlabeled tapes, the modifications required to process standard OS labeled tapes will not be described. Users at other installations employing labeled tapes or the (,NL) label convention should consult with the appropriate personnel at their installation for instructions on modifying JCL card 8.1.

B.  JCL card 8.2 (BCD input files) for 9-track tapes.
    i.   xx following the keyword LRECL= is to be replaced by the physical length of the user's records. In most instances the user's data will be in card image, and xx will be 80 (the column length of an IBM card). If the user has data records which are not card image, xx will be replaced by the actual length of the records.
    ii.  yyy following the keyword BLKSIZE= is to be replaced by the block length used in

writing the tape. This information must be known before a tape can be read and processed.

  iii.  zzzz following the keyword VOLUME=SER= is to be replaced by the reel number of the tape.

### F.4.2  JCL CARDS FT08 (BCD INPUT FILES) ON 7-TRACK TAPES

The following three JCL cards numbered 8.1 to 8.3 must be prepared whenever a BCD input file residing on 7-track tape is entered into the system. These three JCL cards are inserted into the basic JCL deck following JCL card 8. The overlap in numbering between the JCL cards for 7- and 9-track BCD input tapes should not cause any problems, for they can never be used together on the same run (i.e., there can never be two BCD input files).

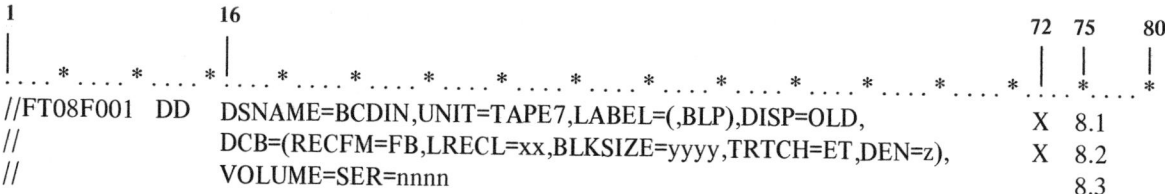

```
1                16                                                      72  75    80
|                |                                                       |   |     |
|....*....*....*.|..*....*....*....*....*....*....*....*....*....*....*...|...*....*
//FT08F001  DD   DSNAME=BCDIN,UNIT=TAPE7,LABEL=(,BLP),DISP=OLD,          X   8.1
//               DCB=(RECFM=FB,LRECL=xx,BLKSIZE=yyyy,TRTCH=ET,DEN=z),    X   8.2
//               VOLUME=SER=nnnn                                             8.3
```

A.  JCL card 8.1 (BCD input files) for 7-track tapes.

    JCL card 8.1 is set up to bypass the label-processing procedure. Since it is a general practice at the Stanford installation to use unlabeled tapes, the modifications required to process standard OS labeled tapes will not be described. Users at other installations employing labeled tapes or the (,NL) label convention should consult with the appropriate personnel at their installation for instructions on modifying JCL card 8.1.

B.  JCL card 8.2 (BCD input files) for 7-track tapes.

    i.  The xx following the keyword LRECL= is to be replaced by the physical length of the user's records. In most instances, the user's data will be in card image, and xx will be 80 (the column length of an IBM card). If the user has data records which are not card image, xx will be replaced by the actual length of the records.

    ii.  The yyyy following the keyword BLKSIZE= is to be replaced by the block length used in writing the tape. This information must be known before a tape can be read and processed.

    iii.  The z following the keyword DEN= must be replaced by the density under which the tape was written and is to be read. The density of a tape is the number of bytes recorded per tape inch. There are three common densities used on 7-track tapes— 200 BPI, 556 BPI, and 800 BPI. The z is replaced by a 0, if the BPI or density is 200, a 1 if it is 556, or 2 if it is 800.

Note:  The translating technique used for BCD tapes is almost universally ET. See TRTCH=ET on card 8.2. If for some reason the user has acquired a tape using another translation technique, he should consult his computation-center personnel for instructions on modifying this keyword for card 8.2.

C.  JCL card 8.3 (BCD input file) for 7-track tapes.

    The nnnn following the keywords VOLUME=SER= is to be replaced by the reel number of the tape.

### F.4.3  JCL CARDS FT08 (BCD INPUT FILES) FOR BCD DISK FILES

When the user has a BCD data file residing on one of the direct-access disk volumes that he wishes to enter into the SPSS system, JCL cards 8.1 and 8.2 for disk files must be prepared and inserted into the JCL deck directly behind JCL card 8. Again, the overlap in numbering should not cause confusion because there may be only one BCD input file used on a given run. The format of these two cards is slightly different than that defining the BCD tape files.

```
1                16                                                          72  75    80
|                |                                                           |   |     |
|....*....*....*!....*....*....*....*....*....*....*....*....*....*....*...*!...*....*
//FT08F001  DD    DSNAME=bbbbbbbb,UNIT=SYSDA,DISP=OLD,                       X   8.1
//                VOLUME=SER=zzzzzz                                              8.2
```

A.  JCL card 8.1 for BCD input disk files.

The parameter bbbbbbbb following the keyword DSNAME= is replaced by the name under which the data set was retained. This name must be spelled and spaced exactly as the name under which it was retained. Since the names may be variable in length, the user should take care to ensure that the X (indicating continuation) remains in column 72 of card 8.1.

B.  JCL card 8.2 for BCD input disk files.

The zzzzzz following the keywords VOLUME=SER= is replaced by the volume name of disk pack on which the data set resides. This is the volume upon which the data set was placed when it was generated.

### F.4.4  EXAMPLE DECK SETUP WITH DATA BEING ENTERED FROM BCD FILE ON DISK

A deck setup similar to the following would be used whenever the user is entering BCD data from a file residing on tape, disk, etc. The only differences would be in JCL cards 8.1 and 8.2. In this case the BCD input file is on disk. If the user were to desire to save a system file at the conclusion of the run or use the WRITE CASES or matrix output capability, additional JCL for these output files would, of course, have to be prepared.

```
1               16                                                          72 75   80
|               |                                                          |  |     |
|...|....*....*....|....*....*....*....*....*....*....*....*....*....|....*.....*
//JOBNAME JOB    (TOOO,413,2,2),'BEETHOVEN, L',MSGLEVEL=1
//JOBLIB    DD   DSNAME=SYS2.PROGLIB,DISP=SHR                                1
//GO        EXEC PGM=SPSS                                                    2
//FT01F001  DD   UNIT=SYSDA,SPACE=(800,(800,200)),                        X  3
//               DCB=BLKSIZE=800       COMMENT - IOSCR2 - USED FOR LABELS    4
//FT02F001  DD   UNIT=SYSDA,SPACE=(3520,(2000,500)),                      X  5
//               DCB=BLKSIZE=3520      COMMENT - IOSCR1 - USED FOR DATA      6
//FT05F001  DD   DDNAME=SYSIN                                               7
//FT06F001  DD   SYSOUT=A                                                   8
//FT08F001  DD   DSNAME=TOOO.DISKFILE,UNIT=SYSDA,DISP=OLD,                X  8.1
//               VOLUME=SER=SYS09                                           8.2
//GO.SYSIN  DD   *                                                          9
RUN NAME         EXAMPLE RUN FROM BCD FILE ON DISK
FILE NAME        STUDYA THIS IS THE OPTIONAL EXTENDED LABEL FOR FILE STUDYA
VARIABLE LIST    ID,AGE,INCOME,SEX,RACE,VAR006 TO VAR010
INPUT MEDIUM     DISK
# OF CASES       1540
INPUT FORMAT     FIXED (F4.0,2X,3F1.0,A1,F2.0)
MISSING VALUES   AGE TO RACE (0,8,9)/VAR005 TO VAR010 (0)
VAR LABELS       AGE RESPONDENTS AGE IN DECADES/INCOME YEARLY FAMILY INCOME IN
                 $1000
VALUE LABELS     AGE (1) UNDER 20 YEARS (2) BETWEEN 20 AND 29 (3) BETWEEN 30
                 AND 39 (4) BETWEEN 40 AND 49 (5) OVER 50 YEARS/SEX (1) MALE
                 (2) FEMALE/RACE (1) WHITE (2) NON-WHITE/AGE TO RACE (8) DK
                 (9) NA (O) OMITTED
PRINT FORMATS    AGE TO RACE (O)/VAR006 TO VAR010 (1)/AGE TO INCOME, RACE (0)/
                 SEX (A)
CROSSTABS        AGE BY RACE BY VAR001/RACE BY VAR001 TO VAR010
OPTIONS          3,5
STATISTICS       ALL
FINISH
/*                                                                          10
```

## F.5   JCL REQUIRED FOR THE OUTPUT SYSTEM FILE: FT04

Whenever the user wishes to create an SPSS system file, an FT04 card (and its continuations) must be prepared. In some instances the user will be generating a system file directly from a BCD input file; in other cases a new or updated file may be generated after data modification, data selection, or file maintenance. In all of these cases JCL for the "new" system file must be prepared. In short, the FT04 JCL card and its continuations must be prepared whenever a SAVE FILE card is used.

SPSS system files may be generated on 7- or 9- track tape, or on disk files. System files *may not*, however, be punched on cards.

### F.5.1   JCL CARDS FT04 (OUTPUT SYSTEM FILES) ON 9-TRACK TAPES

The following two JCL cards numbered 6.4 and 6.5 must be prepared whenever the user is saving an SPSS system file on 9-track tape. These two cards are normally inserted in the basic JCL deck directly following JCL card 6 unless the input data is being entered from an SPSS system file. If this is the case and the input system file resides on 9-track tape or on disk, JCL cards 6.4 and 6.5 for the output system file follow card 6.2. If the input system file is being entered from 7-track tape, they will follow card 6.3 (see Appendix F.6).

```
//FT04F001  DD   DSNAME=SYSOUT,UNIT=TAPE9,LABEL=(,BLP),DISP=(NEW,KEEP),    X  6.4
//               DCB=BLKSIZE=4000,VOLUME=SER=zzzz                              6.5
```

A.  JCL card 6.4 (output system files) for 9-track tapes.

JCL card 6.4 for 9-track tapes is set up to bypass the label-processing capability of the operating system. Since it is the general practice at the Stanford installation to use unlabeled tapes, the modifications of card 6.4 required to process standard OS labeled tapes will not be described. Users at other installations employing labeled tapes or the (,NL) label convention should consult with the appropriate personnel at their installation for instructions on modifying JCL card 6.4.

B.  JCL card 6.5 (output system files) for 9-track tapes.

    i.  Any **BLKSIZE** greater than 2012 is valid; however, a value of 4000 is economical.

    ii.  JCL card 6.5 for 9-track tape (output system files) requires only one modification. The zzzz field following the keyword VOLUME=SER= is to be replaced by the reel number of the tape.

### F.5.2   JCL CARDS FT04 (OUTPUT SYSTEM FILES) ON 7-TRACK TAPES

The following three JCL cards numbered 6.4 to 6.6 must be prepared whenever the user is saving an SPSS system file on 7-track tape. These three cards are normally inserted in the basic JCL deck directly following JCL card 6 unless the input data is being entered from an SPSS system file. If this is the case, and the input system file resides on 9-track tape or on disk, JCL cards 6.4 to 6.5 for the output system file follow card 6.2. If the input system file is being entered from 7-track tape, they will follow card 6.3 (see Appendix F.6).

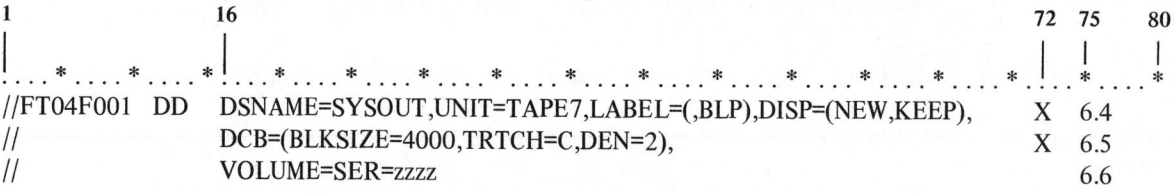

```
//FT04F001  DD   DSNAME=SYSOUT,UNIT=TAPE7,LABEL=(,BLP),DISP=(NEW,KEEP),    X  6.4
//               DCB=(BLKSIZE=4000,TRTCH=C,DEN=2),                         X  6.5
//               VOLUME=SER=zzzz                                             6.6
```

A.  JCL card 6.4 for 7-track tapes.

JCL card 6.4 for 7-track tapes is set up to bypass the label-processing capability of the operating system. Since it is the general practice at the Stanford installation to use unlabeled tapes, the modifications of card 6.4 required to process standard OS labeled tapes will not be described. Users at other installations employing labeled tapes or the (,NL) label convention should consult with the appropriate personnel at their installation for instructions on modifying JCL card 6.4.

B.  JCL card 6.5 for 7-track tapes will normally require no modifications. If for some reason 800 **BPI** 7-track tape drives are unavailable at the user's installation, another density can be specified (see DEN=2). The user should, however, use the highest density available.

C.  JCL card 6.6 for 7-track tapes requires only one modification.

The zzzz field following the keyword VOLUME=SER= is to be replaced by the reel number of the tape.

### F.5.3   JCL CARDS FT04 (OUTPUT SYSTEM FILES) FOR DISK

The following three JCL cards numbered 6.4 to 6.6 must be prepared whenever the user is saving an SPSS system file on a direct-access disk file. When the data is being input from a BCD file (residing on any medium), JCL cards 6.4 to 6.6 are inserted in the basic JCL deck following JCL card 6. If the data is being input from an SPSS system file and the input system file resides on 9-track tape or on disk, JCL cards 6.4 to 6.6 for the output system file follow card 6.2. If the input system file is being entered from 7-track tape, they will follow card 6.3 (see Appendix F.6). The format of these three cards is as follows:

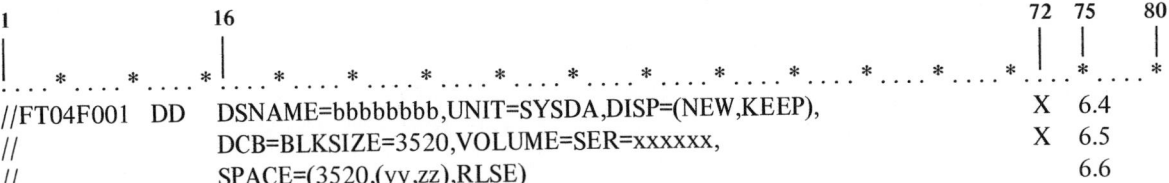

A.  JCL card 6.4 for output system files on disk.

   The parameter bbbbbbb following the keyword DSNAME is replaced by the name under which the data set was retained. This name must be spelled and spaced exactly as the name under which it was retained. Since the names may be variable in length, the user should take care to ensure that the X (indicating continuation) remains in column 72 of card 6.4.

B.  JCL card 6.5 for outputting files on disk.

   The xxxxxx following the keywords VOLUME=SER= should be replaced by the volume name of the disk on which the user wishes to retain the file. Users should check with their computation-center personnel to obtain the appropriate disk designations.

C.  JCL card 6.6 for outputting system files on disk.

   i.  The sole function of this card is to reserve and create adequate space for the system file being generated on disk. Space here is designated in blocks of 3520 bytes. The yy field is to be replaced by the number of blocks which will be required for the system file being saved on disk. The user may determine the number of blocks required by the following formulas:

$$\frac{NVARS \times NCASES}{750}$$

   where NVARS is the number of variables in the user's file and where NCASES is the total number of cases in all subfiles. The quantity resulting from the solution of this formula should be added to the quantity obtained by the solution of the following formula:

$$\frac{(NVARS \times 7) + (NSUBFLS \times 3) + (NVARLABS \times 13) + (NVALLABS \times 6)}{800}$$

   where NVARS is the number of variables in the user's file, NSUBFLS is the number of subfiles (if any), NVARLABS is the number of variable labels (if any), and NVALLABS is the number of value labels (if any).

   ii. The zz should be replaced by a number equaling 25 percent of the sum of the quantities of the above two formulas. This will ensure that the user is requesting sufficient space to retain his output system file. The RLSE keyword on this card instructs the operating system to release all unused space, so that the user will not be charged for space that he is not utilizing. In short, estimate safely high.

#### F5.4   EXAMPLE DECK SETUP WHEN SAVING A SYSTEM FILE ON DISK

The following example run and deck setup is typical of that used when data is being entered on cards and an SPSS system file is being saved on disk. If, however, the user were entering his data on a BCD medium other than cards, an FT08 card (and its continuations) would be required. If the user desired to utilize the WRITE CASES or matrix-output capability, additional JCL for these files would, of course, have to be prepared.

```
1                16                                                              72  75    '80
|                |                                                               |   |     |
 . . . . *  .  .  . *  . . | . . * . . . . * . . . . * . . . . * . . . . * . . . . * . | . . * . . *
//JOBNAME JOB    (TOOO,413,2,2),'BEETHOVEN, L',MSGLEVEL=1
//JOBLIB    DD    DSNAME=SYS2.PROGLIB,DISP=SHR                                       1
//GO        EXEC  PGM=SPSS                                                           2
//FT01F001  DD    UNIT=SYSDA,SPACE=(800,(800,200)),                              X   3
//                DCB=BLKSIZE=800       COMMENT - IOSCR2 - USED FOR LABELS           4
//FT02F001  DD    UNIT=SYSDA,SPACE=(3520,(2000,500)),                           X   5
//                DCB=BLKSIZE=3520      COMMENT - IOSCR1 - USED FOR DATA              6
//FT04F001  DD    DSNAME=TOOO.SYSFIL,UNIT=SYSDA,DISP=(NEW,KEEP),                X   6.4
//                DCB=BLKSIZE=3520,VOLUME=SER=SYS12,                            X   6.5
//                SPACE=(3520,(10,6),RLSE)                                          6.6
//FT05F001  DD    DDNAME=SYSIN                                                      7
//FT06F001  DD    SYSOUT=A                                                          8
//GO.SYSIN  DD    *                                                                 9
RUN NAME          EXAMPLE RUN SAVING A SYSTEM FILE ON DISK
FILE NAME         STUDYA
VARIABLE LIST     AGE,SEX,RACE,INCOME,EDUCATN
INPUT MEDIUM      CARD
# OF CASES        10
INPUT FORMAT      FIXED (10F1.0)
MISSING VALUES    AGE TO RACE (0,8,9)/INCOME(7)/EDUCATN(0)
VAR LABELS        AGE,AGE OF THE RESPONDENT/SEX,SEX OF THE RESPONDENT/INCOME,
                  FAMILY INCOME IN DOLLARS/EDUCATN,EDUCATN OF HEAD OF HOUSEHOLD
VALUE LABELS      SEX (1) MALE (2) FEMALE (3) NOT ASCERTAINED/RACE (1) WHITE
                  (2) NEGRO (3) ORIENTAL (4) OTHER (9) NOT ASCERTAINED/EDUCATN
                  (1) NONE (2) PRIMARY OR LESS (3) SOME SECONDARY (4) SECONDARY
                  GRADUATE (5) SOME COLLEGE (6) COLLEGE GRADUATE (7) GRAD SCHOOL
                  (8) OTHER (9) DONT KNOW (0) NOT ASCERTAINED
PRINT FORMATS     AGE TO EDUCATN (0)
CROSSTABS         RACE BY INCOME BY EDUCATN/INCOME BY RACE BY SEX
OPTIONS           1,3
STATISTICS        1,4,6
READ INPUT DATA
1234567891
9876543210
1357924681
2468135791
1472583261
9876543210
0123546789
2495643210
8976543271
2546475896
MARGINALS         AGE TO EDUCATN
OPTIONS           1,3
STATISTICS        ALL
→ SAVE FILE
FINISH
/*                                                                                  10
```

## F.6   JCL REQUIRED FOR INPUT SYSTEM FILES: FT03

Once the user has saved an SPSS system file, he will enter his data from this file on successive runs. Whenever entering data from an SPSS system file, an FT03 card (and its continuations) must be prepared. In short, an FT03 card will be required on any run which contains a GET FILE control card. In some instances, when adding data to an existing system file (e.g., adding variables or adding subfiles), the user will be required to define a BCD input file (FT08) as well as the system file. Normally, however, the FT03 cards which define the input system file will be the only input file with which the user need concern himself.

### F.6.1   JCL CARDS FT03 (INPUT SYSTEM FILE) ON 9-TRACK TAPE

The following two JCL cards numbered 6.1 and 6.2 must be prepared whenever the user is entering an SPSS system file on 9-track tape. These two JCL cards are inserted in the JCL deck directly following JCL card 6.

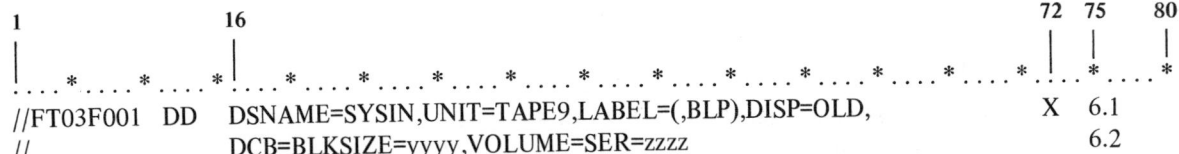

A.   JCL card 6.1 (input system file) for 9-track tapes.

JCL card 6.1 for 9-track tapes is set up to bypass the label-processing capability of the operating system. Since it is the general practice at the Stanford installation to use unlabeled tapes, the modifications of card 6.1 required to process standard OS labeled tapes will not be described. Users at other installations employing labeled tapes or the (,NL) label convention should consult with the appropriate personnel at their installation for instructions on modifying JCL card 6.1.

B.   JCL card 6.2 (input system file) for 9-track tapes.
  i.   The user must replace yyyy following BLKSIZE with the BLKSIZE used when the system file was saved. Normally this will be 4000.
  ii.   JCL card 6.2 for 9-track tape (input system files) requires only one modification. The zzzz field following the keywords VOLUME=SER= is to be replaced by the reel number of the tape.

### F.6.2   JCL CARDS FT03 (INPUT SYSTEM FILES) ON 7-TRACK TAPES[1]

The following three JCL cards numbered 6.1 to 6.3 must be prepared whenever the user is entering an SPSS system file which resides on 7-track tape. These three cards are inserted in the basic JCL deck directly following JCL card 6.

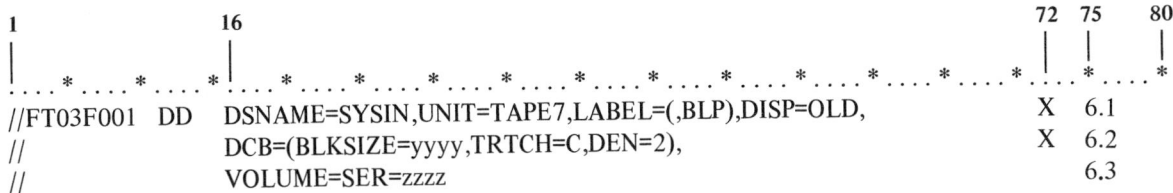

A.   JCL card 6.1 (input system files) for 7-track tapes.

As usual, the label-processing capability of OS has not been utilized. Users desiring labeled tapes should consult with their computation-center personnel.

B.   JCL card 6.2 (input system files) for 7-track tapes.
  i.   If 800 BPI 7-track tape drives are unavailable at the user's installation, the DEN=2 parameter can be altered. The user should, however, use the highest density available

---

[1]The use of 7-track tape for SPSS system files is dependent on the presence of the *data-conversion* special feature. 7-track tape drives not supporting this feature may not be used.

(see Sec. F.4.2.B which describes this problem in conjunction with generating SPSS system files).

    ii.    The user must replace yyyy following BLKSIZE with the BLKSIZE used when the system file was saved. Normally this will be 4000.

  C.    JCL card 6.3 (input system files) for 7-track tapes.
        Card 6.3 requires only one modification. The zzzz field following the keyword VOLUME=SER= is to be replaced by the reel number of the tape.

### F.6.3    JCL CARDS FT03 (INPUT SYSTEM FILES) FOR DISK

The following two JCL cards numbered 6.1 and 6.2 must be prepared whenever the user is entering an SPSS system file which resides on a direct-access disk file. These two cards are inserted in the basic JCL deck directly behind JCL card 6. The formats of these two cards are as follows:

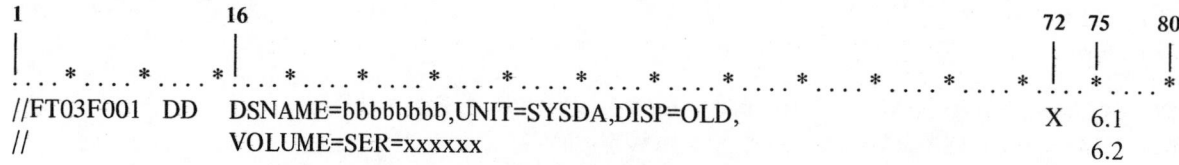

```
//FT03F001  DD    DSNAME=bbbbbbbb,UNIT=SYSDA,DISP=OLD,              X   6.1
//                VOLUME=SER=xxxxxx                                     6.2
```

  A.    JCL card 6.1 (input system files) for disk.
        The bbbbbbb field on this card must appear exactly as it was on JCL card 6.4 on the output system file, FT04 (see Sec. F.4.3.A).

  B.    JCL card 6.2 (input system file) for disk.
        This card should be prepared exactly as was JCL card 6.5 which was used to create the file. The xxxxxx following the keywords VOLUME=SER= should contain the volume name of the disk on which the file was saved.

### F.6.4    EXAMPLE DECK SETUP WITH DATA BEING ENTERED FROM AN SPSS SYSTEM FILE ON 9-TRACK TAPE

The following type of deck setup would be used whenever the user is entering his data from an SPSS system file residing on 9-track tape. If the user's system file resides on 7-track tape or on a disk, cards 6.1 and 6.2 (and 6.3 if 7-track tape) would be inserted as described above. The user would, of course, have to prepare additional JCL cards if any of the other input-output features of SPSS are being utilized. If, for example, an updated system file were to be created from the existing one, FT04 cards would have to be prepared.

```
1               16                                      72 75   80
|               |                                       |  |    |
|...*....*....*!...*....*....*....*....*....*....*....*....*!...*!...*
//JOBNAME JOB   (TOOO,413,2,2),'BEETHOVEN, L',MSGLEVEL=1
//JOBLIB    DD  DSNAME=SYS2.PROGLIB,DISP=SHR                        1
//GO       EXEC PGM=SPSS                                            2
//FT01F001 DD   UNIT=SYSDA,SPACE=(800,(800,200)),              X    3
//              DCB=BLKSIZE=800     COMMENT - IOSCR2 - USED FOR LABELS  4
//FT02F001 DD   UNIT=SYSDA,SPACE=(3520,(2000,500)),           X    5
//              DCB=BLKSIZE=3520    COMMENT - IOSCR1 - USED FOR DATA   6
//FT03F001 DD   DSNAME=SYSIN,UNIT=TAPE9,LABEL=(,BLP),DISP=OLD,  X    6.1
//              DCB=BLKSIZE=4000,VOLUME=SER=1088                    6.2
//FT05F001 DD   DDNAME=SYSIN                                       7
//FT06F001 DD   SYSOUT=A                                           8
//GO.SYSIN DD   *                                                  9
RUN NAME        PROCESSING FROM AN SPSS SYSTEM FILE ON 9 TRACK TAPE
GET FILE        STUDYB
PROCESS SBFILESEACH
MARGINALS       ALL
OPTIONS         1,3
STATISTICS      ALL
NONPAR CORR     AGE TO INCOME
OPTIONS         1
STATISTICS      2,3,5
FINISH
/*                                                                 10
```

## F.7   JCL REQUIRED FOR BCD OUTPUT FILES: FT09

Whenever the user is employing the WRITE CASES procedure, or whenever he is having correlation matrices written or punched from subprograms PEARSON CORR or NONPAR CORR, an FT09 card and its continuations must be prepared. The WRITE CASES procedure and the matrix-output capability permit the user to punch output on cards or to write it in BCD form on 9-track tape, 7-track tape, or disk. When the user is outputting such a BCD file on 9-track tape, two JCL cards numbered 8.4 and 8.5 are required. When the BCD output is being punched on cards, only one card, numbered 8.4, is required. BCD output files on 7-track tapes or disks require three cards numbered 8.4 to 8.6.

If the input data is being entered from cards or from an SPSS system file, the JCL cards defining the BCD output file directly follow JCL card 8. If data is being input from a BCD file residing on 7- or 9-track tape or on disk, the JCL cards for FT09 follow those for FT08.

### F.7.1   JCL CARDS FT09 FOR PUNCHED OUTPUT

The following JCL card numbered 8.4 must be prepared whenever the user is having cases or correlation matrices punched on cards. The format of this card is as follows:

```
1               16                                      72 75   80
|               |                                       |  |    |
|...*....*....*!...*....*....*....*....*....*....*....*....*!...*!...*
//FT09F001  DD   SYSOUT=B,DCB=(RECFM=F,LRECL=80,BLKSIZE=80)        8.4
```

Users should check with the appropriate personnel at their computation center for possible modifications of this card. When data is being input from cards or from an SPSS system file, the card is inserted in the basic JCL deck directly following card 8. If the data is being input from a BCD file residing on 7- or 9-track tape or on disk, the JCL cards for FT09 follow those for FT08. If the data is being input from a BCD file residing on 7- or 9-track tape or on disk, JCL cards 8.4 and 8.6 follow those defining FT08.

### F.7.2    JCL CARDS FT09 (BCD OUTPUT FILES) FOR 9-TRACK TAPES

The following two cards are required whenever the user is attempting to output data cases or correlation matrices onto 9-track tapes. When data is being input from cards or from an SPSS system file, JCL cards 8.4 and 8.5 defining the BCD output file are inserted into the basic JCL deck directly behind card 8. If the data is being input from a BCD file residing on 7- or 9-track tape or on disk, JCL cards 8.4 and 8.5 follow those JCL cards defining the BCD input device (FT08). The format of cards 8.4 and 8.5 for BCD output files on 9-track tapes are as follows:

```
//FT09F001  DD    DSNAME=BCDOUT,UNIT=TAPE9,LABEL=(,BLP),DISP=(NEW,KEEP),     X  8.4
//                DCB=(RECFM=FB,LRECL=80,BLKSIZE=2000),VOLUME=SER=yyyy           8.5
```

A.    JCL card 8.4 (BCD output files) for 9-track tapes.

JCL card 8.4 for 9-track tapes is set up to bypass the label-processing capability of the operating system. Since it is the general practice at the Stanford installation to use unlabeled tapes, the modifications of card 8.4 required to process standard OS labeled tapes will not be described. Users at other installations employing labeled tapes or the (,NL) label convention should consult with their computation-center personnel for instructions on modifying JCL card 8.4.

B.    JCL card 8.5 (BCD output files) for 9-track tapes.

i.    JCL card 8.5 for 9-track tapes will usually require only one modification. The yyyy field following the keyword VOLUME=SER= is to be replaced by the reel number of the tape.

ii.   The value 80 following the keyword LRECL= indicates card-image records. Correlation matrices are always written (by the SPSS subprograms) as card-image records. BCD output files used in conjunction with the WRITE CASES procedure card may be written with a record length other than 80. If the format list on the WRITE CASES card specifies a record length other than 80, that value should replace the 80 following the keyword LRECL=. We suggest, however, that unless the user has some computer experience and understands the ramifications of maintaining BCD files which are not card image, that he keep his BCD files in card image (i.e., LRECL=80. 80).

iii.  The block size of 2000 used on JCL card 8.5 is a suggested block length which is convenient. The user may alter this number if he understands its ramifications.

### F.7.3    JCL CARDS FT09 (BCD OUTPUT FILES) FOR 7-TRACK TAPES

The following three cards are required whenever the user is outputting cases or correlation matrices in BCD form onto 7-track tapes. When data is being input from cards or from an SPSS system file, JCL cards 8.4 and 8.6 are inserted into the basic JCL deck directly behind card 8. If the data is being input from a BCD file residing on 7- or 9-track tape or disk, the JCL cards 8.4 and 8.6 directly follow those defining FT08. The formats of these three cards are as follows:

```
//FT09F001  DD    DSNAME=BCDOUT,UNIT=TAPE7,LABEL=(,BLP),DISP=(NEW,KEEP),        X  8.4
//                DCB=(RECFM=FB,LRECL=80,BLKSIZE=2000,TRTCH=ET,DEN=2),          X  8.5
//                VOLUME=SER=yyyy                                                  8.6
```

A.    JCL card 8.4 (BCD output files) for 7-track tapes.

As usual, JCL card 8.4 is set up to bypass label processing. Users at other installations employing labeled tapes or the (,NL) label convention should consult with their computation-center personnel for the modifications required on card 8.4.

B.   JCL card 8.5 (BCD output files) for 7-track tapes.
   i.   JCL card 8.5 will normally require no modification. However, if density 2 (i.e., 800 BPI) 7-track tape drives are not available at the user's installation, the 2 following the keyword DEN= may be altered. The highest recording density available should, however, always be selected.
   ii.   The value 80 following the keyword LRECL= indicates card-image records. Correlation matrices are always written (by the SPSS subprograms) as card-image records. BCD output files used in conjunction with the WRITE CASES procedure card may be written with a record length other than 80. If the format list on the WRITE CASES card specified a record length other than 80, that value should replace the 80 following the keyword LRECL=. We suggest, however, that unless the user has some computer experience and understands the ramifications of maintaining BCD files which are not card image, that he keep his BCD files in card image (i.e., LRECL=80).
   iii.   The block size of 2000 used on JCL card 8.5 is a suggested block length which is convenient. The user may alter this number if he understands its ramifications.

C.   JCL card 8.6 (BCD output files) for 7-track tape.
   The yyyy field following the keyword VOLUME=SER= is to be replaced by the reel number of the tape.

## F.7.4   JCL CARDS FT09 (BCD OUTPUT FILES) FOR DISK

The following three JCL cards are required whenever the user is outputting cases or correlation matrices in BCD form onto 2314 disk volumes. When the data is being input from cards or from an SPSS system file, JCL cards 8.4 and 8.6 are inserted in the basic JCL deck directly behind card 8. If the data is being input from a BCD file residing on 7- or 9-track tape, or disk, the JCL cards 8.4 and 8.6 directly follow those defining FT08. The formats of these three cards are as follows:

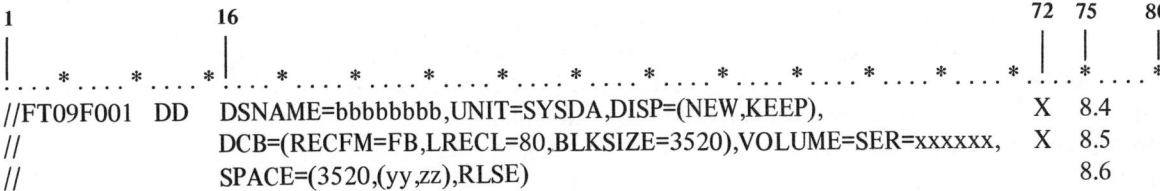

```
1                     16                                                    72  75    80
|                     |                                                     |   |     |
 . . . .*. . . .*. . . .*. . . .*. . . .*. . . .*. . . .*. . . .*. . . .*. . . .*. . . .*. . . .*. .*. . . .*
//FT09F001  DD    DSNAME=bbbbbbbb,UNIT=SYSDA,DISP=(NEW,KEEP),              X  8.4
//                DCB=(RECFM=FB,LRECL=80,BLKSIZE=3520),VOLUME=SER=xxxxxx,  X  8.5
//                SPACE=(3520,(yy,zz),RLSE)                                   8.6
```

A.   JCL card 8.4 (BCD output files) for disk.
   The bbbbbbb field following the keyword DSNAME= is to be replaced by a data-set name of up to eight characters in length, the first of which must be alphabetic. Like SPSS, some data-set names may not contain blanks or special characters. This data-set name is recorded on the disk's VTOC (volume table of contents) and is used whenever references to that data set is made after it has been written.

B.   JCL card 8.5 (BCD output files) for disk.
   i.   The only change normally required on this card is the replacement of the xxxxxx field following the keywords VOLUME=SER= with the volume name of the disk on which the user wishes to retain the BCD output file. The user should check with computation-center personnel before selecting a volume name.
   ii.   The value 80 following the keyword LRECL= indicates card-image records. Correlation matrices are always written (by the SPSS subprograms) as card-image records. BCD output files used in conjunction with the WRITE CASES procedure card may be written with a record length other than 80. If the format list on the WRITE CASES card specifies a record length other than 80, that value should replace the 80 following the keyword LRECL=. We suggest, however, that unless the user has some computer experience and understands the ramifications of maintaining BCD files which are not card image, that he keep his BCD files in card image (i.e., LRECL=80).

    iii.  The block length of 3520 following the keyword BLKSIZE= is a suggested value only. It happens also to be the maximum block length which permits writing two blocks on a 2314 track. The maximum block size which can be used on a 2314 is 7294. However, the block length must be an even multiple of the length of the record. 7280 is, therefore, the largest block length which can be used when the data is being written in card image.

  C.  JCL card 8.6 (BCD output files) for disk.

    i.  The yy field is to be replaced by the number of blocks required by the user's output file.

    ii.  When the user has determined the number of blocks required by his BCD output file, the zz field following the yy is replaced by a number equal to 25 percent of the number of tracks placed in yy. This zz is a secondary allocation and is the user's margin of error. The RLSE keyword on this card will cause all unused space to be released, so that the user will pay for only space being used.

### F.7.5    EXAMPLE DECK SETUP USING A PUNCHED BCD OUTPUT FILE

The following example demonstrates the JCL cards required on a run in which the data is being input from an SPSS system file on a 9-track tape and a selected group of variables from that file are being punched on cards with the WRITE CASES procedure card.

```
1                16                                                    72  75    80
|       *        |      *       *       *       *       *       *       *  |   *     |
 ....*....*....*|....*....*....*....*....*....*....*....*....*....*.|...*....*
//JOBNAME JOB    (TOOO,413,2,2),'BEETHOVEN, L',MSGLEVEL=1
//JOBLIB      DD   DSNAME=SYS2.PROGLIB,DISP=SHR                                1
//GO       EXEC PGM=SPSS                                                       2
//FT01F001  DD   UNIT=SYSDA,SPACE=(800,(800,200)),                       X     3
//               DCB=BLKSIZE=800       COMMENT - IOSCR2 - USED FOR LABELS      4
//FT02F001  DD   UNIT=SYSDA,SPACE=(3520,(2000,500)),                     X     5
//               DCB=BLKSIZE=3520      COMMENT - IOSCR1 - USED FOR DATA        6
//FT03F001  DD   DSNAME=SYSIN,UNIT=TAPE9,LABEL=(,BLP),DISP=OLD,          X     6.1
//               DCB=BLKSIZE=4000,VOLUME=SER=1088                              6.2
//FT05F001  DD   DDNAME=SYSIN                                                  7
//FT06F001  DD   SYSOUT=A                                                      8
//FT09F001  DD   SYSOUT=B,DCB=(RECFM=F,LRECL=80,BLKSIZE=80)                    8.4
//GO.SYSIN  DD   *                                                            9
RUN NAME         PUNCHING CARDS WITH THE WRITE CASES CARD
GET FILE         DEM01
WRITE CASES      (F3.0, 'A',1X,74F1.0) CASEID,VAR001 TO SEX
FINISH
/*                                                                          10
```

# G
# THE CDC 6000-SERIES VERSION OF SPSS†

In response to the need for a user-oriented system that could be utilized by any researcher, the Vogelback Computing Center at Northwestern University, in cooperation with the developers of the SPSS package for the IBM 360, initiated a project to translate SPSS for CDC 6000-series equipment. The SPSS project at Northwestern is under the direction of Mr. Larry Young, with assistance in programming and testing provided by Mrs. Lorraine Borman, and Messrs. Ron Witt and Donald Mazukelli. The programs have been written to be operational for the standard SCOPE 3 operating system. We shall refer to this system as SPSS 6000.

Compatibility with the SPSS 360 implementation was a prime conversion criterion, and every effort has been made to achieve this goal. The rationale for unity between systems was based on the belief that data files generated at one installation should be transportable and that the methods used to create the files should not have to be relearned. Too often a scholar who had learned to work with a system is forced to convert all his data bases to a new system upon moving to a new locale. Also, the increased use of common data sets and secondary analysis of social science data in the United States has stressed the importance of compatible statistical packages to analyze the data.

The sections below describe only those areas where hardware or software differences between the IBM 360- and CDC 6000-series computers required external changes to the SPSS

†This appendix was written by Lorraine Borman, Vogelback Computing Center, Northwestern University.

language conventions. In general, these changes are designed to produce the same output as the 360 version.

## G.1     DEFINING AN SPSS FILE: THE DATA-DEFINITION CARDS

### G.1.1     THE FILE NAME CARD

The FILE NAME card is used to (1) label output, (2) label an SPSS system file if created, and (3) provide a SCOPE file name for a SAVE FILE if the SAVE FILE card does not specify a file name (see Appendix G.3.1).

The SPSS file name may be up to eight characters in length, and the first character must be an alphabetic letter. The file name may be followed by an optional file label of up to 64 characters in length.

1               16

FILE NAME          STUDY1  THIS IS AN EXAMPLE OF A FILE NAME AND LABEL FOR STUDY1.

### G.1.2     THE NO. OF CASES CARD

The NO. OF CASES card informs the system of the number of cases in the user's file (see Sec. 4.4). The 360 SPSS card employs the symbol # which is not a legal character on the 6000-series computers; this has been replaced by NO.

1               16

NO. OF CASES     $\left\{ \begin{array}{l} \text{number of cases} \\ \text{or} \\ \text{ESTIMATED number of cases} \end{array} \right\}$

### G.1.3     THE INPUT MEDIUM CARD

The INPUT MEDIUM card serves to inform the SPSS system of the input device from which the user's data will be entered into the system. The control words INPUT MEDIUM are followed by either the keyword CARD or a file name if the input data is on magnetic tape or a disk file. If CARD is punched, input data is equated to the SCOPE INPUT file (job deck). If a file name is punched, it must be the name of an already existing SCOPE file; for example, a SCOPE file containing data cases may have been created by use of the REQUEST or ATTACH control cards (see Example G.5). If this card is not present in the SPSS job deck, the input medium is assumed to be the job deck.

1               16

INPUT MEDIUM     $\left\{ \begin{array}{l} \text{CARD} \\ \text{or} \\ \text{filename} \end{array} \right\}$

BCD data tapes created on a CDC 6000-series computer may be either unblocked or written as standard CDC 6000-series blocked tapes. Non-CDC 6000-series written data tapes are acceptable only in unblocked format, without header labels. If the ESTIMATED option is used on the NO. OF CASES card, an end-of-file mark must be present; if not, SPSS will read to the number of cases indicated on the NO. OF CASES card, and an end-of-file mark will not be necessary. If the user has a data tape written in blocked format on other than a CDC 6000-series computer, utility functions may be available to read the tape and rewrite it for input to SPSS. Users should check with the appropriate personnel concerning local procedures.

## G.2     SPECIAL-PURPOSE RUN CARDS

### G.2.1     THE KEYPUNCH CARD

The SPSS 6000 system assumes that control cards have been punched with an IBM 026 keypunch while the 360 system assumes 029 punched control cards. The KEYPUNCH card for SPSS 360 allows for conversion of 026 to 029 characters. This option is not implemented on the SPSS 6000; a message is printed informing the user of utility functions for 029 to 026 conversion available for this purpose and job processing is continued for as long as possible.

## G.3    GENERATING AND PROCESSING SPSS FILES: RETAINING FILES

### G.3.1    THE SAVE FILE CARD

The SAVE FILE card causes the SPSS file which is presently being processed to be saved in the form of a SCOPE system file at the conclusion of the run (see Sec. 7.2). The name of the SCOPE file is obtained from the first seven characters of "filename", if present. If "filename" is not punched, the first seven characters of the filename on the FILE NAME card is used. If the FILE NAME card is not present, and a name has not been specified on the SAVE FILE card, the file will not be saved. A diagnostic message will be issued.

```
1                16
SAVE FILE        filename
```

The file written by a SAVE FILE command uses standard CDC SCOPE file-creation procedures and is stored in a two-part binary format: the first part contains the information describing and defining the data; the second, the data. Thus, a SAVE FILE command writes a binary SCOPE 3 system file containing the SPSS created file. This file may be assigned to either magnetic tape or disk using SCOPE control cards (see Examples G.3 and G.4). If a new disk file is written, it may be made into a COMMON or permanent file using standard CDC file-disposition procedures.[1]

### G.3.2    THE GET FILE CARD

This command will access an SPSS created file from a SCOPE 3 system file. The GET FILE card causes the file to be positioned for processing and all the associated data-defining information passed to the system. The file name used must be the name of a SCOPE file which has been generated and retained by means of a SAVE FILE card in a previous run. The appropriate SCOPE control cards must be used to define the file, whether on tape or disk (see Example G.5).

```
1                16
GET FILE         STUDY1
```

## G.4    THE FILE-MODIFICATION CARDS

### G.4.1    THE WRITE CASES CARD

The WRITE CASES procedure enables the user to have any or all parts of his data punched on cards or written on tape or a disk file in BCD form (see Sec. 10.5). The user must specify the file name of the BCD output medium. For SPSS 6000, this file assignment is accomplished through the use of an additional SPSS control card, the BCD OUT MEDIUM card, one that is not required for SPSS 360 users.

```
1                16
WRITE CASES      (format) variable list
```

The WRITE CASES command for SPSS 6000 writes the BCD cases in exactly the format specified on the WRITE CASES card. This is not consistent with the 360 version. The format may contain any standard Fortran format conventions except I-type format.

### G.4.2    THE BCD OUT MEDIUM CARD

The BCD OUT MEDIUM card specifies the SCOPE file name to be used by the WRITE CASES command. This file may be either a magnetic tape or disk file, in which case, the file name must

---

[1]A COMMON file is a disk file which is saved after a job terminates and which can be later accessed. Permanent files have cataloging and editing capabilities and also may be password protected. Users should check with the appropriate personnel as to local procedures.

be equated to a SCOPE 3 system file using the appropriate SCOPE system control cards (see Example G.6).

The user may also elect to only print a listing of his data; in this case, he would specify OUTPUT as the file name. (OUTPUT is the standard SCOPE system output file.) To punch a BCD file, the file name PUNCH should be specified.

```
1                       16
BCD OUT MEDIUM   ⎧ filename ⎫
                 ⎪    or    ⎪
                 ⎨  OUTPUT  ⎬
                 ⎪    or    ⎪
                 ⎩  PUNCH   ⎭
```

The BCD OUT MEDIUM card must precede the WRITE CASES card. If absent, the default medium will be OUTPUT. This command remains in effect until another BCD OUT MEDIUM card is read or until job termination.

The filename specified must be seven characters or less in length and must have as its first character an alphabetic letter.

### G.4.3   THE OUTPUT MEDIUM CARD

The operating environment at Northwestern includes both central-site and remote-terminal batch processing. Because of various operational procedures, the need for writing output on a variety of output devices is required. One instance of this type of use is where an SPSS file has generated many different output listings, such as CODEBOOK, FASTABS, and REGRESSION. Since the printer at the remote-terminal site is slower than the central-site printer, the user may desire to divert his FASTABS output to the central-site printer, while printing the balance of the output at the terminal installation. Another type of use would be the need for multiple copies of output which, if printed at the time of job completion, might result in the printer being unavailable to other jobs for a long period of time. The use of the OUTPUT MEDIUM card would enable the user to write his output on a tape or disk file at job completion; he could then print this file at any later, more convenient date.

```
1                  16
OUTPUT MEDIUM   filename
```

The OUTPUT MEDIUM card remains in effect from its initial read time until either job termination or another OUTPUT MEDIUM card is read. If the card is not included in the SPSS job deck, the standard SCOPE OUTPUT file (line printer) is assumed.

The file name specified on the OUTPUT MEDIUM card must be equated to a SCOPE system file (see Example G.7). As with all file names which are passed to SCOPE, the name must be a maximum of seven characters and begin with an alphabetic letter.

One problem arising in social science data analysis is the need to differentiate between blanks and punched zeros. Since the CDC 6000-series computers read blanks as negative zeros, a nonvalid numeric value would result. SPSS 6000, therefore, handles blanks appearing in numeric variables as missing values and zeros are treated as valid numeric input. For most users, no additional declaration needs to be made to differentiate blank and zero information. Any other values may be user assigned through the use of the RECODE command. Blanks, of course, are valid values of alphabetic variables.

## G.5   NORTHWESTERN UNIVERSITY CDC 6400 ENVIRONMENT

The CDC 6400 installed at Northwestern consists of a 65k central memory, a 6603-II disk-storage unit, four 607 tape drives, two 854 disk packs, and a full complement of input/output units and remote terminals. Job processing is under the control of the SCOPE 3 operating system. SPSS has been written as an overlay system in the Fortran extended 2.0 language. SPSS users have complete access to standard CDC SCOPE software for job processing, file manipulation, file disposition, and file access. Any SPSS system file can be saved and later accessed from either a COMMON or permanent file by following the standard CDC control-card procedures for COMMON or permanent files.[1]

The examples that follow illustrate various SPSS programs as they apply to the Northwestern University installation. Although the basic concepts will be the same for all CDC 6000-series installations, local differences may necessitate changes in some of the SCOPE control cards.

Example G.1 shows the basic SCOPE system cards which are always required when operating the SPSS system. Input data is being entered on cards for a statistical-processing run only. The SPSS file created will not be saved at job termination.

**EXAMPLE G.1**

```
VJOB,CH . . . . . . . . . . ,CM77700,T50.
ATTACH(SPSS)
SPSS.
7-8-9 End of Record
RUN NAME            COMPLETE DECK SET UP FOR RUN FROM CARDS
VARIABLE LIST       AGE, SEX, RACE, INCOME, EDUCATN
INPUT MEDIUM        CARD
NO. OF CASES        10
INPUT FORMAT        FIXED (5X, 10F1.0)
MARGINALS           AGE TO EDUCATN
OPTIONS             1,4
STATISTICS          ALL
READ INPUT DATA
    2468579327
        .
        .
        .
FINISH
6-7-8-9 End of Information
```

The first SCOPE card in the deck is the job card containing the user's charge number, the core requirements for his job (CM77700), and a maximum time limit (T50). The form of this card will vary somewhat at different installations. The second card (ATTACH (SPSS)) attaches the SPSS overlay file to the job. The SPSS. card loads the SPSS object program from the file named SPSS and executes the job. The 7-8-9 End-of-Record card indicates the end of SCOPE system control information. SPSS control cards and data will then be read and processed. The 6-7-8-9 End-of-Information card indicates the end of the job and is required as the last card of any job deck. Depending upon local procedures at other CDC 6000-series installations, the ATTACH(SPSS) and SPSS. cards may vary slightly.

The remaining examples are sample configurations of input and output options using SPSS in the Northwestern University SCOPE 3 operating environment.

In Example G.2 data being entered on cards and a system file being saved at the conclusion of the run on magnetic tape.

At job termination, the SPSS system file generated would be assigned the name SAVET and be written on the user-supplied tape number 1234. The file name indicated on the SAVE FILE card must be equated to the name punched on the REQUEST card, in this case, SAVET. Since a tape density specification was not indicated on the REQUEST card, the SPSS file will automatically be written at 556 BPI.

In Example G.3 data is being entered on cards and an SPSS system file is to be saved on disk.

[1]On the 6400, storage requirements are one word per variable. The 6000-series computer word is 60 bits in length (10 characters).

**EXAMPLE G.2**

```
VJOB,CH. . . . . . . . . . ,CM. . . . . ,T50.
REQUEST(SAVET)     PLEASE HANG REEL NUMBER 1234
ATTACH(SPSS)
SPSS.
7-8-9 End of Record
RUN NAME           EXAMPLE RUN SAVING A SYSTEM FILE ON TAPE
FILE NAME          SAVETAPE
VARIABLE LIST      AGE, SEX, RACE, INCOME, EDUCATN
INPUT MEDIUM       CARD
          .
          .
          .
SAVE FILE          SAVET
FINISH
6-7-8-9 End of Information
```

**EXAMPLE G.3**

```
VJOB,CH. . . . . . . . . . ,CM. . . . . ,T. . .
ATTACH(SPSS)
SPSS.
COMMON(SAVET)
7-8-9 End of Record
RUN NAME           EXAMPLE RUN SAVING A SYSTEM FILE ON DISK
VARIABLE LIST      AGE, SEX, RACE, INCOME, EDUCATN
INPUT MEDIUM       CARDS
          .
          .
          .
SAVE FILE          SAVET
FINISH
6-7-8-9 End of Information
```

**EXAMPLE G.4**

```
VJOB,CH. . . . . . . . . . ,CM. . . . . ,T. . .
REQUEST(MYDATA)    PLEASE HANG REEL NO. 2345 CONTAINING MY DATA CASES
ATTACH(SPSS)
SPSS.
COMMON(SAVET)
7-8-9 End of Record
RUN NAME           SAMPLE RUN WITH TAPE INPUT AND SAVE FILE ON DISK
          .
          .
INPUT MEDIUM       MYDATA
          .
          .
          .
SAVE FILE          SAVET
FINISH
6-7-8-9 End of Information
```

The use of the COMMON(filename) card instructs the SCOPE 3 operating system to assign the file **SAVET** to a SCOPE COMMON system disk file. The file will be available for future processing as an SPSS system file.

In Example G.4 data is being entered on BCD tape and a SCOPE system file created by the use of the SAVE FILE command in SPSS will be saved on disk.

In Example G.5 data is being entered from an SPSS system file residing on tape for a statistical-processing run only. No permanent transformations are to be retained and no other output device utilized.

In Example G.6 data is being entered from an SPSS system file residing on a disk file (see Example G.3). Variables are being added with the ADD VARIABLES feature—the cases containing the variables to be added reside on magnetic tape. The user wishes to output a new BCD tape file containing some variables from the SPSS system file and some from the variables he is adding. A new system file containing all the variables in the old system file plus all the new variables will also be retained on tape at the conclusion of the run.[1]

**EXAMPLE G.5**

```
VJOB,CM. . . . . . . . . . ,CM. . . . . ,T. . .
REQUEST(SAVET)       PLEASE HANG REEL NUMBER 1234.
ATTACH(SPSS)
SPSS.
7-8-9 End of Record
RUN NAME             PROCESSING FROM AN SPSS SYSTEM FILE ON TAPE
GET FILE             SAVET
NONPAR CORR          AGE TO INCOME WITH AGE TO INCOME
      .
      .
      .
MARGINALS            ALL
      .
      .
      .
FINISH
6-7-8-9 End of Information
```

**EXAMPLE G.6**

```
VJOB,CH. . . . . . . . . . ,CM. . . . .T. . .
COMMON(SAVET)
REQUEST(ADDVAR)      PLEASE HANG REEL NO. 1357 WITH MY NEW CASES
REQUEST(NEWBCD)      PLEASE HANG REEL NO. 2468 FOR MY BCD OUTPUT
REQUEST(NEWFILE)     PLEASE HANG REEL NO. 9876 FOR MY NEW SPSS FILE
ATTACH(SPSS)
SPSS.
7-8-9 End of Record
RUN NAME             ADDING VARIABLES, WRITING CASES, AND UPDATING FILE
GET FILE             SAVET
ADD VARIABLES        X,Y,Z
INPUT MEDIUM         ADDVAR
INPUT FORMAT         FIXED (F.6.0, F1.0, F9.2)
MARGINALS            ALL
OPTIONS              ALL
READ INPUT DATA
BCD OUT MEDIUM NEWBCD
WRITE CASES          (F3.0, 1X, 75F10.2) CASEID, VAR1 to Z
SAVE FILE            NEWFILE
FINISH
6-7-8-9 End of Information
```

[1]When a user inputs one SPSS system file and outputs a new or updated system file, SCOPE cards for both input and output files must be prepared, in this case, COMMON(SAVET) and REQUEST(NEWFILE).

In Example G.7 data is being entered from an SPSS system file on tape. Output from FASTABS to be written on a disk file for future printing. The balance of the SPSS output to be normally printed at job termination.

**EXAMPLE G.7**

```
VJOB,CM. . . . . . . . . . ,CM. . . . . ,T. . .
REQUEST(NEWFILE)      HANG REEL NO. 9876
ATTACH(SPSS)
SPSS.
COMMON(FASTABS)
7-8-9 End of Record
RUN NAME              EXAMPLE OF THE USE OF THE OUTPUT MEDIUM CARD
GET FILE              NEWFILE
MARGINALS            ALL
        .
        .
        .

OUTPUT MEDIUM FASTABS
FASTABS              VARIABLES=AGE. . .
FASTABS              VARIABLES=. . . . . .
OUTPUT MEDIUM        OUTPUT
VARIABLES            A B C . . .
REGRESSION           VARIABLES = A, . . . .
                     REGRESSION = A . . .
FINISH
6-7-8-9 End of Information
```

# H
# A PROGRAMMER'S GUIDE TO SPSS

While the preceding parts of this text have dealt with guiding the reader in the use of SPSS, this appendix describes the actual computer program which performs tasks at the user's request. A knowledge of the contents of this appendix are in no way required for successful use of SPSS. The appendix is provided for two reasons. First, it is felt that some relatively sophisticated users may wish to have a better understanding of how the package actually works. For these users, this appendix provides technical documentation of the package. Second, the authors can foresee instances in which individuals will wish to modify the package or, more likely, will wish to write statistical procedures of their own within the framework of SPSS.

This appendix is divided into sections dealing with the following three general topics: (1) overall system flow and logic, (2) the logic of particular parts of SPSS, especially the statistical subprograms and the data-modification routines, and (3) guidelines for the incorporation of additional routines into SPSS. The first topic is treated at a relatively nontechnical level and should be of general interest. The remaining topics assume more than a cursory knowledge of computer fundamentals, and topic (3), in particular, assumes a knowledge of Fortran IV for the IBM system 360.

## H.1   SYSTEM FLOW AND LOGIC

The original logic for SPSS was set down, at least partly on paper, in late 1964 and early 1965.[†] To the extent that some of that original logic has transcended a switch from second- to third-generation hardware, to say nothing of various levels of software for each, the soundness of that logic speaks for itself. To the extent that entire concepts have been scrapped and replaced in the course of the intervening years, it is surprising that any logic at all remains. Nevertheless we feel confident in trying to describe the package as a logical entity.

We may start with an examination of the overall system flow chart shown in Fig. H.1. The flow chart on the left side of the diagram shows the logic of the control or supervisory portion of the program. The function of this portion of the program is to determine what the user wants done as opposed to actually doing it. Entering at the box labeled BEGIN, the control program first performs a small initialization procedure which, among other things, sets various switches to their default values and determines the correspondence between the data sets used in SPSS such as the printer and the numbers found on the DD cards of the JCL language. For example, during the initialization procedure, a switch is set indicating that the user wishes all his control cards to be printed as they are read and, in the version of the system in use at Stanford, assigns logical unit 6, as in FT06F001, as the line printer.

After finishing the initialization procedure, the control program enters a loop that continues until a FINISH card is encountered. Notice that such matters as error detection and subfile structure are ignored in this diagram. The loop begins with the reading of a control card. If this control card is not associated with a statistical procedure, the control program interprets the specification field and takes the action indicated. In the case of most control cards other than subprogram procedure cards, action consists of filing away the information on the card until subsequent processing of the data on the card is accomplished. For example, the INPUT FORMAT card is merely scanned and then stored away until it is time to read the input cases. Similarly, upon encountering a COMPUTE card, the program will simply code the specification field and store the coded information in such a way that it can be applied to each case as these cases become available. After taking an action appropriate to the control card which has been encountered, the control program returns to the top of the loop and reads another control card until a FINISH card is read, at which time execution is terminated. If, during repetition of this loop, a statistical-subprogram procedure card is encountered, the control program calls in the appropriate statistical subprogram which will then go about its business or issue an appropriate error message. Notice that completion of the loop contained in the control program depends upon the program's ability to recognize the procedure card which has been encountered. What happens if it encounters a card which it has never been programmed to recognize? It prints an error message and reads additional cards until it finds one that it can recognize. This action is similar to that resulting in the majority of SPSS error messages: if the program comes up against something unexpected, it accuses the user of committing a "fatal" error. Needless to say, no matter how many times SPSS encounters the same error, such as the occurrence of the letter I where the user meant to punch the number 1, it never learns to expect it and always flags it as an error.

The right side of Fig. H.1 represents the logic of a "typical procedure." This drawing is definitely not to scale since the typical procedure is composed of instructions to handle the procedure card, process the cases, and print the results on a relative ratio of about 25, 15, and 60 percent. Still the logic holds. The first action in each statistical subprogram is to interpret the control card applicable to the procedure. This consists largely of identifying the names of the variables which the user wishes to have considered. Next, a *call* or temporary relinquishment of control to a subprogram named STATOP will provide our typical procedure with the applicable statistics and options for this run.

Now we enter another loop. In this one, the statistical procedure calls another procedure named OBSERV. Normally, OBSERV will provide the statistical procedure with a value for every variable in the file for the next sequential case. Note that the statistical procedure must now operate on this single case and then get another. With the exception of the nonparametric-

[†]Dale Bent played the predominant role in the early *formal* definition of the internal logic of SPSS.

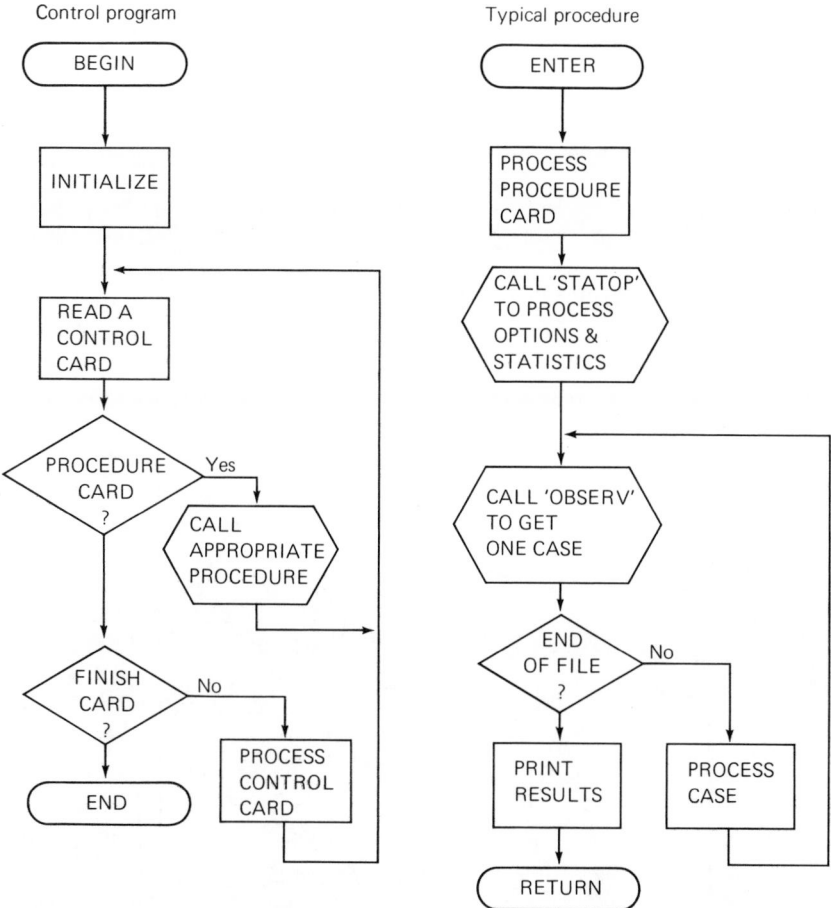

**FIG. H.1**   Overall system flowchart.

correlation routines, none of the statistical subprograms in SPSS have available more than a single case at any one time. This approach is necessitated, of course, by a desire to be able to process more or less indefinitely large files and is responsible for the lack of certain features in the system such as the availability of Z scores as a standard transformation or the reporting of residuals in connection with the regression program. The loop which processes the cases one at a time will sooner or later be interrupted by the occurrence of an end-of-file condition. As distinguished from the situation in which the program tries to read more cases than are physically in the user's file, this condition is sensed from the setting of a switch which is returned to the statistical program by OBSERV when all the cases have been processed.

Finally, after exiting from the case-processing loop, the statistical procedure is left with the task of formulating meaningful results from the data collected as the cases were processed and printing these results in an acceptable format. The kind of processing done here, for example, might be dividing the sum of the values of a variable by the number of cases to obtain the mean for that variable. After printing out the desired results, or rather the requested results, the statistical procedure returns control to the control program which will then read another control card, and so forth.

In the discussion above it should have become obvious that much of the actual work of processing the individual cases was left to a procedure called OBSERV. Let us now take a short look at how OBSERV works since it is called by each of the statistical procedures and governs in large part how the features of SPSS are implemented. The flow chart in Fig. H.2 shows a simplified version of the logic of OBSERV. In particular the logic necessary for subfile processing and for the addition of cases and variables has been ignored.

Upon entering the subprogram, a switch is examined to determine whether there have been any prior calls to OBSERV for the current task. If not, OBSERV goes through a short initialization routine which resets various switches and determines the degree of data modifica-

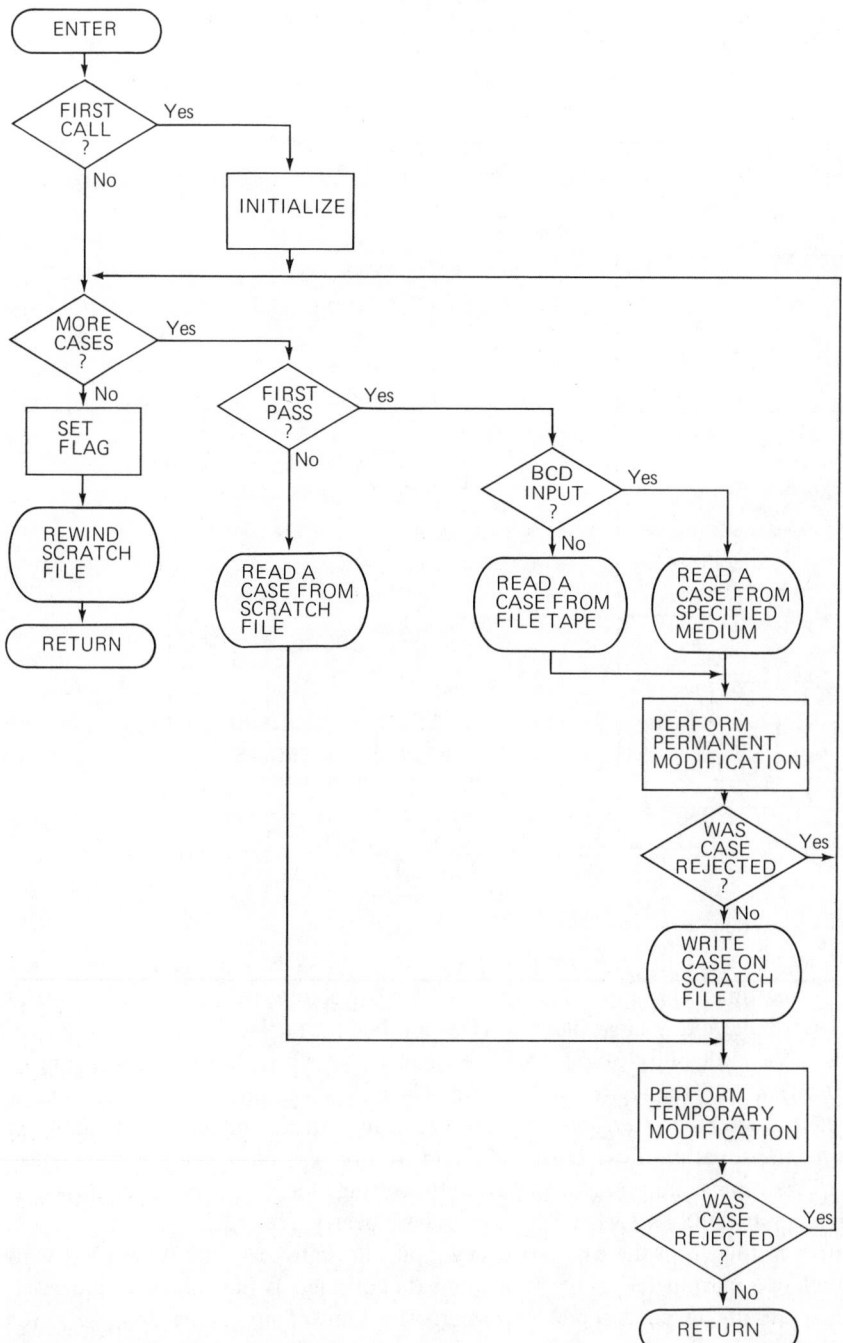

**FIG. H.2** Subprogram OBSERV.

tion necessary. Next a test is made to determine whether all the cases have been processed. If so, OBSERV returns control to the calling program with a switch setting to indicate that all the cases have been processed. This is the end-of-file indication discussed earlier. If there are more cases to be processed, OBSERV determines which logical unit the data is to be read from. If this is the first task in a job, the data will reside on either an SPSS system file or some BCD medium. The control program will have set two switches indicating (1) whether the data is on a system file and, if not, (2) whether the BCD data is on cards or some other medium. In either event, OBSERV reads the next case from the appropriate source and effects the required permanent data and file modifications. If the case was rejected by means of the sampling or selection mechanism, OBSERV will go back to the decision point concerning the availability of more cases. If the case is selected for processing, OBSERV will write the fully modified version of it on a scratch file which is normally on a disk. In every task after the first in a single job, the data is retrieved, complete with permanent modifications, from this scratch file. Regardless of the sequence number of the task within the job, the data is the same up to the point of temporary data and file modifications. Those file and data modifications specific to the current task are then carried out and either the fully prepared case is presented to the statistical subprogram or, in the case of temporary case rejection, OBSERV goes back to try to find another case.

If subfile processing is used, the logic of OBSERV differs on two main points. First, rather than determine whether there are more cases in the file to be processed, OBSERV must determine whether there are more cases in the current subfile group. If not, an end-of-group condition is returned to the calling statistical subprogram. Second, surrounding the *remaining-cases* logic is a test for *remaining-subfile groups*. Only when there are no remaining subfile groups to be processed is an end-of-file condition returned.

Central to the subject of program logic is the communication of various parameters between subprograms. The Fortran IV language is defined in such a way that each subprogram is a logical unit; whereas in other languages, such as ALGOL or PL/I, parameters known to the main program are accessible to all the subprograms, parameters are accessible to subprograms only when the Fortran programmer makes specific arrangements. In the SPSS system, while some information is passed in the form of *formal parameters,* most data is communicated via the central COMMON section. This central COMMON section is actually three named COMMON sections, but can be considered as a single section for practical purposes. A large portion of this COMMON section is allocated to various switches such as one which indicates that case selection is in force and another which indicates that at least one "fatal" error has been encountered.

Of more interest to the casual reader are the parameters related to the data itself. In particular there is a group of parameters which describe the characteristics of the individual variables. The name of each variable is entered into a "dictionary." Similarly, there is a vector for each variable which contains the appropriate missing-data indicators. Also associated with each variable are its print format and, most important, its value for the current case, and a switch which indicates whether this value should be considered missing. These last two items, the variable's value and its missing-data switch, are set by OBSERV as each case is read in and are in turn used by the statistical subprogram to build the various tables it requires in order to compute statistical measures. Similar to the entries for variables are dictionary entries and the numbers of cases for each subfile which the user has declared.

On a more technical plane, all the values which are manipulated by the system are in the form of so-called real numbers. Within the context of Fortran, *real* denotes floating point as opposed to fixed point, rather than noncomplex as it does in ordinary usage. Since no attempt is made to determine the possible outcome of data-modification procedures, the system is forced to assume that each variable can assume values varying from the lowest to the highest which can be represented in the floating-point format. As a consequence, whenever values are written in *internal* or binary format, they are written as 32-bit binary words. The importance of this fact is that, while a single-column variable requires only eight bits in its *external* form, i.e., in BCD, it requires 4 times this many bits to express it in internal form. Thus, for a great deal of social science data, files written in internal format will be considerably larger than the original BCD files. In those instances, of course, where only a small portion of the variables in the BCD file is entered into the SPSS system, a file written in internal format can be smaller than the BCD files from which they were created. This will frequently be the case when secondary analysis is performed. Within SPSS both the scratch file written by OBSERV to retain cases for later tasks within a single job and SPSS system files are written in internal format. While the physical reading and writing are handled by special-purpose assembly language routines, the effect is very similar to that achieved by the use of "unformatted" input/output in Fortran. It may, in fact, be of use to those using other systems or even their own programs, to know that the scratch file written by OBSERV, normally FT02F001, is a variable-length record blocked file in which each record contains a single case. In addition to those variables declared by the user, the weight of each case is written on this file. The case weight precedes the rest of the variables in each record. Since the maximum record which may evolve from this procedure contains four bytes for each of 500 user-defined variables plus four bytes each for the weight and the record-control information, the file is usually declared a logical record length of 2,008 and a (minimum) block length of 2,012. In fact if the user neglects to specify a block size in his job control language, the system will default to 2,012. The record format and record length are declared within the program and may not be overridden by declaring them on a job control card.

Although the actual method for effecting data and file modification is discussed later, the general logic relevant to OBSERV is considered here. The flow chart in Fig. H.3 provides a general outline of the logic for either permanent or temporary modifications. There are four basic steps in data modification: sampling, transformations (including IF, COMPUTE, SELECT IF, and RECODE), and weighting. It should be noted that the transformation and recoding information entered by the user has been translated into internal codes by the control program before OBSERV is called. OBSERV is unable to distinguish among the four external purposes of the internal codes grouped together as transformations, so they must be considered together as far as their execution is concerned.

The first step in the modification logic is to effect sampling if it has been requested. In order to decide whether to include a particular case in the sample, OBSERV generates a random

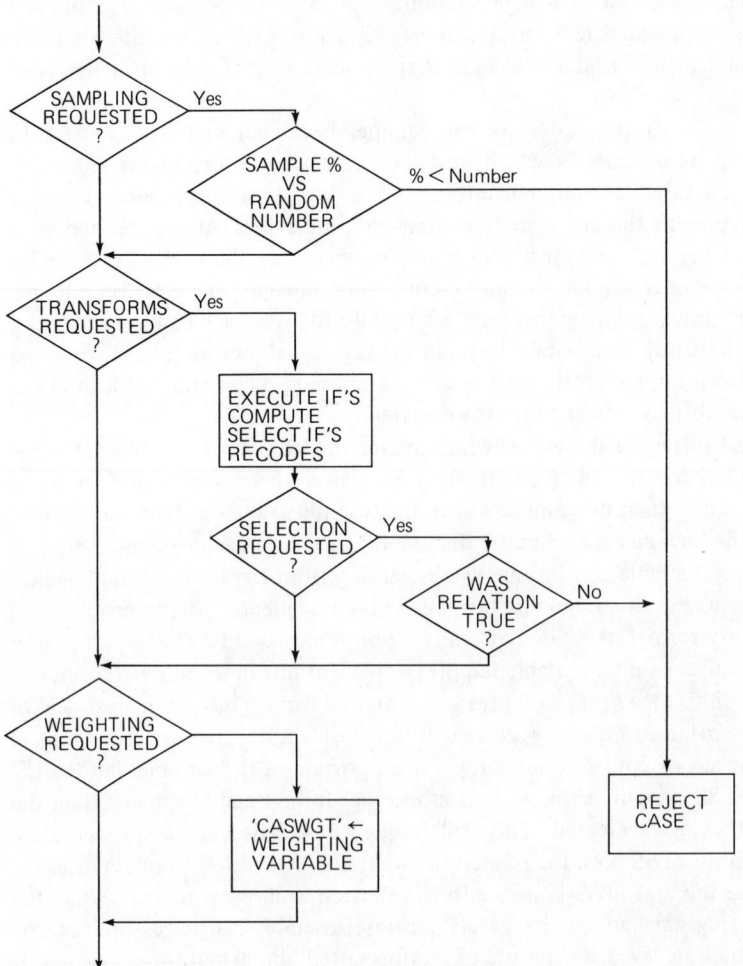

**FIG. H.3**   Data-modification logic.

number which varies continuously from zero to unity. This random number is then compared with the fraction of the cases which are to be included. If the random number is higher than this fraction, the case is rejected. A discussion of random numbers, or more properly pseudo-random-number generation, is outside the scope of this text. What is done in SPSS is generally described as the power-residue method in which the last-used random number is multiplied by a big hairy number. The result of this multiplication is a bigger, hairier number from which the middle bits or digits are extracted to give the new random number. Such a series of numbers is fixed and predictable and will eventually repeat itself. The random-number generator in SPSS was borrowed from the IBM Scientific Subroutine Package and will generate over a million numbers before repeating itself.

After sampling has been performed, transformations and recodes are executed if present. If any of the transformations was a SELECT IF, it will cause a switch to be set to indicate acceptance or rejection of the case. OBSERV tests the setting of this switch to determine whether to keep the current case. Finally, if the user has requested weighting, the value of the weighting variable is assigned to the system variable CASWGT where the statistical subprogram will use it to count the cases encountered.

Where do missing-data indicators fit into this discussion? Throughout the data- and file-modification procedure, all values of the variables are treated in the same manner. OBSERV does not address itself to the question of missing data until both permanent and temporary modifications are complete. It then examines the final value of each variable to determine whether to set the corresponding switch to indicate that the variable should be considered missing for the current case.

The above discussion has ignored some of the more technical points of SPSS. For instance, the discussion frequently alludes to a rather extensive control program. In fact, this control program is composed of several smaller subprograms each of which performs a specific task. For instance, there is one subprogram which has as its sole purpose the examining of the INPUT FORMAT card, another which concerns itself with the VAR LABELS, VALUE LABELS, and DOCUMENT cards and others which are concerned with the RECODE card or the transformation cards as a group. In addition, in an effort to conserve core storage, the control program isn't really the main program at all. In fact, there is a very small subprogram known as CALLER which calls the control program. The latter then processes control cards until a statistical-procedure card is encountered. It then returns control to CALLER with the number of the applicable statistical subprogram. CALLER then performs the actual call on the statistical subprogram. The savings in core storage are realized by overlaying the control program with the statistical subprogram.

## H.2   SPECIFIC SUBPROGRAM LOGIC

This section describes the logic of several specific subprograms in the SPSS system. These subprograms are divided into three major groups, the general-utility routines, the data-modification routines, and the statistical routines.

Most important among the subprograms in the utility category are those dealing with input and output. Within the SPSS system, there is a division of responsibility with respect to input and output. Specifically, all formatted I/O is left to Fortran while the unformatted I/O is handled by assembly language routines. That is, the two scratch data sets (FT01F001 and FT02F001) and the input and output SPSS system files (FT03F001 and FT04F001) are accessed in assembly language while the card reader and line printer (FT05F001 and FT06F001) and the BCD input and output data sets (FT08F001 and FT09F001) are handled by Fortran. Within the system, unformatted I/O is accomplished by calls to one of the two assembly-language I/O routines SPSSIOU and SPSSIOVB. The normal Fortran I/O commands READ, WRITE, and REWIND have as their equivalents READi, WRITEi, and RWINDi where i identifies the data set to be read from or written into. There are three additional I/O commands, CLOSEi, NOTEi, and POINTi. CLOSEi is roughly equivalent to the Fortran command END FILE in that it logically disconnects the data set or "closes" it. NOTEi causes a pointer to be returned which can be used to reference the last record written on the specified data set. POINTi causes the I/O routine to retrieve a specific record on the next READi command which references the same data set. The argument for POINTi is one which was returned by a NOTEi call. At present NOTE and POINT are used only with the scratch data set on which the labels reside.

The existence of two I/O routines is occasioned by the fact that there are two basically different access methods in use in SPSS. SPSSIOVB services the scratch data set on which the data is written for use by subsequent statistical routines and the input and output system files. The former is accessed by calls to READ1, WRITE1, and RWIND1 while the system files are accessed by calls to READF, WRITEF, and CLOSEF. CLOSEF closes whichever system file is currently open. Both of the system files, input and output, share the same DCB and buffers in an effort to conserve core storage. SPSSIOVB uses the basic sequential access method (BSAM), handles blocked variable-length records, and utilizes double buffering. Rewinds are accomplished by "pointing" to the initial record in the file or, if end-of-file has been reached since the file was last rewound, by a temporary close. The coding in SPSSIOVB is suitably generalized to permit addition of more files with a minimum of effort, however one should have a fairly thorough knowledge of OS/360 data management before attempting any major modification of these routines.

SPSSIOU exists solely to provide pseudodirect access for the labels. It uses BSAM and handles undefined length records with single buffering. Calls to WRITE2 cause records to be written. After a call to WRITE2, a call to NOTE2 returns the location of the last record written. Since the writing of a record must be physically complete before its location can be noted, calls to NOTE2 should be separated by as much processing as possible from preceding calls to WRITE2. After a call to RWIND2, the records can be retrieved sequentially by calls to READ2, and the order of retrieval can be altered by calls to POINT2. Calls to POINT2 actually start the reading of the requested record which is then passed to the processing program by the next call to READ2. As with calls to WRITE2 and NOTE2, calls to POINT2 and READ2 should take advantage of the processing overlap provided.

The use of single buffering in SPSSIOU was decided upon since it was recognized that (1) records are rarely retrieved sequentially, and (2) use of a work area in the calling program gives approximately the effect of double buffering when the file is written.

Both of the I/O routines have abnormal terminations which result in a user-completion code and a dump. The following completion codes may be encountered if a program error occurs:

1770    an attempt to shift from reading to writing on a file
1771    a record which is to be written is too long for the buffer
1772    an attempt to shift from writing to reading without rewinding the file
1773    an attempt to read past the end of the data set
1774    an attempt to note a record that has been read
1775    an attempt to point to a record that has been written
1776    unable to open a data set

In the dump that accompanies these completion codes, the registers contain their current information with the following exceptions:

1.    Register 0 contains what was in register 1 when the routine was called, i.e., the address of the calling program's argument list.
2.    Register 1 contains information used by the O/S abend routine.
3.    Register 14 contains what it did upon entering the I/O routine, i.e., the address of the next statement in the calling program.
4.    Register 15 contains what it did upon entering the I/O routine, i.e., the address of the entry point called. Examination of the contents of register 15 can usually help determine which data set caused the error. Similarly, an examination of the contents of register 14 can help determine which routine was calling the I/O routine.

What is physically contained in unformatted files? FT02F001, the scratch data set used for storage of the data file, contains one record for each case in the file. The first word in each record contains the weight for the case, and the additional words contain the values of the permanent variables in the order in which they were defined. Note that the system variables SEQNUM and SUBFIL are not contained on this file. These variables are generated by OBSERV each time the data is passed. FT01F001 contains label information. As variable labels are encountered, they are written on this data set, each one constituting a block. Calls to POINT2 are used to retain the locations of these labels. As value labels are encountered, they are also written on this data set. In this case, each is prefixed with the value to which it applies, and up to 800 bytes or 200 words of labels so coded are written as a single block. The starting block used for each set of labels encountered is retained through a call to POINT2. Associated with each variable in the file are three words of information used as pointers. The last of these three words is the pointer to the label for the variable. The other two words point to the first and second sets of value labels for the variable. The provision for two sets of labels for a variable allows for one set to be retrieved from a system file while the second can be entered with additional VAR LABEL cards. Both sets are considered by the statistical routines with the last value label which applies to a given value being the one which is used.

The system files contain three sections of information. First, they contain the variable dictionary and associated information such as the missing values, the output formats, the subfile dictionary, and associated numbers of cases. Second, they contain the information found on FT01F001, the label scratch data set. Each variable label is prefixed by the number of the variable to which it applies while the two possible sets of value labels are concatenated and prefixed with the number of the variable to which they apply. Finally, the data is recorded on the system files in exactly the same form as that in which it is found on FT02F001 Deletion of subfiles is accomplished when the file is initially read in by OBSERV while deletion of variables is accomplished when the file is saved.

The control program handles requests for getting a file by calling GTFILE. This subprogram transfers the initial portion of the input system file to core storage, transfers the labels to the label scratch data set, and positions the file so that the data portion can be read by OBSERV. A call to SVFILE reverses the flow and transfers the variable and subfile information from core storage to the new system file, transfers the labels from FT01F001 to the system file, and transfers the data from FT02F001 to the system file. Certain other information such as the file name and the creation date are also recorded on the system file. Any user interested in the precise format of an SPSS system file should examine the code of GTFILE and SVFILE.

The printer FT06F001 is accessed by the various subprograms as necessary. However, every time lines are printed, subprogram LINECT is called with the number of lines printed as the argument. LINECT then skips to the top of the page and prints the header as necessary. A variable in the main common section LINE always equals the number of lines remaining on a page so that various routines can check before printing information which should be contiguous whether there are sufficient lines remaining on the current page.

The card reader FT05F001 is accessed by OBSERV when data is to be read just as if it were any input device. The reading of control cards, however, is handled by a separate routine, CONCRD. A call to CONCRD causes a control card to be read. Columns 16 to 80 of the control card are transferred to an integer array STRING, and the current position in this array is initialized to 1. The latter pointer is contained in variable ISTR. Both STRING and ISTR are in the main common section. If the first 15 columns of the control card are other than blank, their contents are transferred to two double-word real variables, WORD1 and WORD2, and a switch QCHANG is set true. If these 15 columns are blank, WORD1 and WORD2 retain their prior contents.

In the case of the Fortran formats on the INPUT FORMAT and WRITE CASES cards, the individual processing programs, in this case INPFMT and WRCASE, scan columns 16 to 80. In all other cases, however, a set of free-field reading routines are utilized. Subprogram LABEL is used to retrieve consecutive columns until an appropriate delimiter is encountered. Subprogram STACK has two entries, SCAN and DECMAL, which are used to retrieve alphabetic and numeric arguments respectively. STACK returns all the words contained on a particular control card and all its extensions regardless of mode. Each word is returned as an element in a double-word real vector.

Two other routines helpful in the interpretation of control cards are STATOP and VAR-IND. STATOP looks for OPTIONS and STATISTICS cards and places their contents in the main common section in the form of settings in vectors of switches QOPTSR and QSTAT. It should be noted that another vector of switches, QOPT, is used solely for system options rather than those which apply to statistical procedures. VARIND is used in interpretation of parameter lists on statistical-procedure control cards. It examines successive double words in the vector returned by STACK to identify variable names and variable names separated by the keyword TO.

About the only thing that the two types of data-modification procedures have in common is that they both involve the translation of the user-prepared control cards into an intermediate set of symbols which direct the application of the modifications as the cases are read. The handling of the RECODE (and *RECODE) cards are discussed first since they are the easiest to understand. When a RECODE card is dissected by the subprogram RECODE, a series of interrelated lists are prepared. These lists are in a special common section known as CMREC. Taking as an example the following,

```
1                16
RECODE           AGE, SEX TO EDUC (5,8 THRU 10 = 0) (11 THRU HIGHEST = 5)
```

the numbers of the variables involved are entered into successive positions in the vector RECV. The single input value 5 is placed in a position in the vector RECIN1, and the associated output value 0 is placed in the corresponding position in the vector RECOT1. For each of the variable numbers in the vector RECV, a pointer is placed in the corresponding position of vector RECP1 so that RECP1 points to the first (and in this case the only) single-valued recode for each variable. For the two value-pair recodes a similar situation applies. A position in the vector RECIN2 receives the value 8, and corresponding positions in the vectors RECIN3 and RECOT2 receive the values 10 and 0 respectively. The next-higher positions in these three vectors receive the values 11, a very high number, and 5, respectively. A pointer is then placed in vector RECP2 for each applicable variable so that RECP2 points to the first value-pair recode for each variable. The first unused positions in vectors RECIN1 and RECIN2 are assigned a special number (which cannot be represented on a control card) to indicate that no more recodes exist for this set of variables. The special recode specification CONVERT is indicated by placing this same special value in a position in vector RECOT2.

The net result of all these pointers is that, for each variable to be recoded, there is an associated index of the vectors containing the single-valued recodes and another index of the vectors containing the value-pair recodes. Recoding actually takes place by first going through the list of applicable single values for each variable and then going through the list of value pairs until the input value fits into some category or the list is exhausted.

The IF, COMPUTE, SELECT IF and starred versions thereof are all translated by a pair of subroutines and evaluated by the subroutine EVAL. They are translated into a set of symbols occupying the following vectors in the main common section: INDTRA, ITRNSF, and ITR-NOP. For each assignment statement or complete logical expression, there is an entry in the vector INDTRA. This entry points to the first position in the vectors ITRNSF and ITRNOP which contain information pertaining to the arithmetic to be performed. Corresponding positions in these two vectors contain the four essential pieces of information for the performance of a single arithmetic operation. These four pieces of information are the actual operation (addition, subtraction, etc.), the two variables used in the operation and the variable which should receive the result of the operation. In the case of *unary* operators as opposed to *binary* operators, only a single variable or operand is coded. All the prepackaged functions are considered to be unary operators for these purposes. Four pieces of information are carried in these two vectors by "packing" the numbers of the three variables involved into ITRNSF. Specifically, the number of the first operand is multiplied by 491,401 (701 squared), and the number of the second operand is multiplied by 701, and then the three numbers are added together. The magic in the number 701 is that the transformation routines operate on the basis of 700 variables of which 197 are actually values or literals and temporary storage locations used for intermediate results. The operators are coded as numbers from 1 to 25 in the vector ITRNOP.

The transformation evaluation routine performs each of the operations until it reaches the first operation for the next assignment or complete logical expression. In the case of an IF statement, the next set of operations will be performed only if the result of evaluating the logical expression was true. A SELECT IF is composed of the logical expression coded by the user plus an assignment statement supplied by the system. This assignment statement sets a special variable's value to 1. It is executed only if the user-supplied logical expression is evaluated as true. OBSERV uses the value of the special variable to determine whether or not to select the case.

The process of building the vectors containing the information used by EVAL is performed by the subroutines FIXTRA and TRANS. The former performs a preliminary scan of the control card and calls TRANS which actually codes the necessary information into the three appropriate vectors. TRANS considers the precedence order of the operators and the user-supplied parentheses and constructs a reverse Polish string from which the ordered individual operations are built. A reverse Polish string is merely a convenient formula representation which depends on the order of appearance of the elements rather than a precedence of operators or the existence of parentheses to express the order of evaluation. The following pairs of formulas give an example of this notation:

| Conventional | Reverse Polish |
|---|---|
| A + B | A B + |
| A + B * C | B C * A + |
| A * (B + C) + D | B C + A * D + |
| A * B + C * D | A B * C D * + |

If one has a "push-down" stack, reverse Polish strings can be executed directly. As one encounters an operand, all operands already in the stack are pushed down one position and the new operand is placed on top. When an operator is encountered, it uses the top one or two operands in the stack depending upon whether it is a unary or binary operator. In the case of a unary operator, the result replaces the one and only operand in the top position of the stack. In the case of a binary operation, all operands in the stack are popped up one position and the result is placed in the top position. A variation of the stack concept is used to translate the reverse Polish string generated in TRANS into individual ordered operations.

The logic for creating the reverse Polish string from the expressions on the transformation control cards is shown in the accompanying flow chart (Fig. H.4). The arguments on the control card have been transferred to an integer vector called ITEMP prior to encountering this procedure in TRANS. The first decision point causes all operands, as opposed to parentheses and operators, to be placed in the string immediately. If the word being examined represents an operator, operators at the top of a temporary vector called ASTACK are pulled off and placed in the Polish string if their precedence is greater than or equal to the precedence of the current operator. Multiplication, for instance, has lower precedence than exponentiation, the same as division, and more than addition. While not shown in the flow chart, left parentheses always enter the temporary vector, and right parentheses cause all operators since the last left parenthesis to be pulled off. The paired parentheses are then ignored. As might be imagined, the pairing of parentheses is checked for prior to entering this routine. When all the contents of ITEMP have been processed, any operators still in the temporary vector ASTACK are released to the Polish string.

The logic of statistical procedures is demonstrated by examining two of them. FASTABS is a good example of those procedures which record occurrences of predefined conditions, e.g., the occurrence of values 3 and 5 for two specific variables, while CROSSTABS is an example of a program which records occurrences of conditions which are not expected until their first occurrence.

FASTABS is composed of three separate subroutines: FASTAB, FST2, and FST3. The functions of these three routines are to interpret the control card, read the observations, and

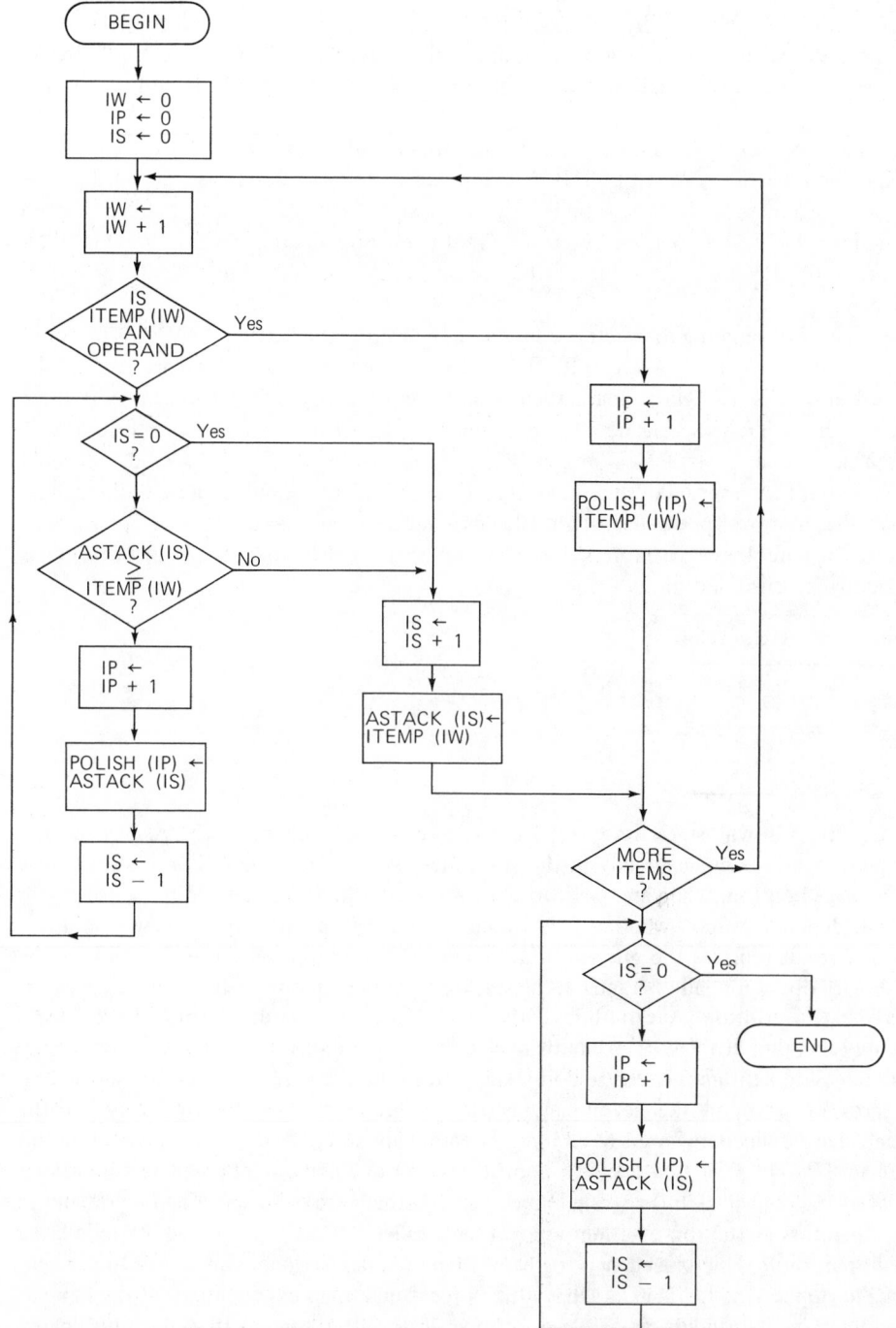

**FIG. H.4**    Creation of a Polish string.

produce the reports, respectively. The accompanying Table H.1 shows a hypothetical situation in which there are nine variables defined in the file. These are listed as the contents of the vector VARNAM. FASTAB is then called to interpret a procedure card calling for three tables involving a total of four variables. First, it constructs a vector KVAR which contains the position in the main variable dictionary (and in the observation vector, etc.) of the variables listed in the VARIABLES = list. Three associated lists which are not shown here receive the high and low values and the number of integral values between these limits for the variables in KVAR. In the example, each variable has a possible range of 0 to 9 for a total of 10 values. Next, FASTAB codes the TABLES = list. Each slash in this list delimits a *table primary*. In this example, there is only one such table primary. For later processing, FASTAB builds the vectors KLOVAR and KHIVAR which contain the first and last indices of variables in KVAR (not

VARNAM) which are to be used in the appropriate dimension of the tables for each primary. KHIVAR and KLOVAR are actually matrices, but can be thought of as containing a vector for each primary. In the case of the example, there are two entries in each, one for each of the two dimensions in the requested table primary. The variable in the first dimension will be varied from 1 to 1 and is always AGE. The variable in the second dimension varies from number 2 to 4 and changes from RACE to SEX to EDUC.

For the purposes of FASTABS, each table is imagined as an n-dimensional matrix, the indices of which are the indices of the n variables involved in the table, and the entries of which are the counts of the occurrences of the various combinations of values. All tables are constructed in a single vector. The relative position of a cell in the vector is calculated from the values of the variables comprising the individual table in which it resides plus the displacement of the first cell of its table within the vector as a whole. The displacement of this first cell is determined by summing the number of cells allocated to each previous table.

For each observation returned by OBSERV, FST2 calculates the variables involved in each table from the vectors prepared by FASTAB and then increments an appropriate cell for that table. FST3 takes the vector as filled by FST2 and extracts one table at a time from it.

**TABLE H.1    An example of the encoding of the FASTABS card**

| 1 | 16 |
|---|---|
| FASTABS | VARIABLES = AGE RACE SEX EDUC (0,9)/ |
|  | TABLES = AGE BY RACE TO EDUC |

| VARNAM | KVAR | KLOVAR | KHIVAR |
|---|---|---|---|
| 1. SEQNUM | 4 | 1 | 1 |
| 2. SUBFIL | 7 | 2 | 4 |
| 3. CASWGT | 6 |  |  |
| 4. AGE | 9 |  |  |
| 5. WEIGHT |  |  |  |
| 6. SEX |  |  |  |
| 7. RACE |  |  |  |
| 8. INCOME |  |  |  |
| 9. EDUC |  |  |  |

When calculating positions within the large vector, FASTABS uses the normal FORTRAN convention of varying the first dimension most rapidly. That is, successive cells represent successive values of the first variable. Incrementing the cell number by the number of values taken by the first variable is equivalent to incrementing the second variable's value by 1 while holding the first variable constant. Similarly, incrementing the cell number by the product of the possible values of the first and second variables results in locating a cell for which the value of the third variable has increased by 1 while the first and second variables have remained constant.

CROSSTABS is composed of five individual subroutines: CROSST, CRS1, CRS2, CRS3, and CRSORT. The respective functions of these subroutines are overall control, the examination of the control card, building of the tables from the observations encountered, printing of the tables, and sorting of the tables prior to printing. The control-card interpretation is similar to that in FASTABS with the exception that the vector corresponding to KVAR is constructed as variable names are encountered and contains duplicates. The building of the tables from observations is somewhat different from FASTABS since CROSSTABS does not know in advance what range of values a variable can take.

Figure H.5 demonstrates the logic by which CROSSTABS constructs the required tables. In this example, there are two tables each with two variables. The cell counts are kept in a single vector KCOUNT, as with FASTABS. Here, however, each cell must be identified by the values of the variables involved in matrix CVAL and the number of the table to which it belongs in vector KTABLE. In FASTABS, this information was implied by the location of the cell in the large vector. In CROSSTABS, the information must be provided explicitly. As CRS2 processes each observation, it must determine whether the combinations of values of the

| | KPREC | KTABLE | CVAL | | KCOUNT |
|------|-------|--------|------|------|--------|
| 1. | 4 | 1 | 2 | 1 | 5 |
| 2. | 6 | 2 | 1 | 2 | 9 |
| 3. | 2 | 2 | 1 | 1 | 8 |
| 4. | 7 | 1 | 1 | 2 | 7 |
| 5. | 1 | 1 | 1 | 1 | 10 |
| 6. | 5 | 2 | 2 | 2 | 8 |
| 7. | 3 | 1 | 2 | 2 | 3 |

|   | 1 | 2 |
|---|----|---|
| 1 | 10 | 7 |
| 2 | 5  | 3 |

|   | 1 | 2 |
|---|---|---|
| 1 | 8 | 9 |
| 2 |   | 8 |

**FIG. H.5**  Table construction by subprogram CROSSTABS.

variables involved in the tables have occurred before. If so, a cell in KCOUNT can be incremented. If not, a new entry must be created and initialized to a count of 1. To avoid having to search through all existing entries for the value combinations encountered, vector KPREC contains a path from each cell to the next higher one. In the example, cell 5 is the lowest in that it represents the variable values 1 and 1 for table 1. In vector KPREC there is a pointer from cell 5 to cell 1, the next higher cell. For each table, then, it is necessary to search through the cells in order until a match is found or until a cell is encountered which is higher than the one to be recorded. In this latter case, a new cell is inserted in the chain by pointing from the new cell to the higher one which was already encountered and pointing from the last lower cell to the new cell. Use of this ordering vector causes the program to have to search all existing entries only once regardless of the number of tables to be generated.

Prior to printing the tables, CRSORT is called to order the entries in ascending order according to the contents of KPREC. This reordering is not entirely necessary, but makes printing of the tables much easier and frees the storage used by KPREC for other uses.

## H.3  INCORPORATION OF A NEW SUBPROGRAM IN SPSS

There is little point in telling a programmer what he can and cannot do. However, there are some guidelines for the incorporation of a new subprogram in SPSS which may reduce the attendant difficulties somewhat.

First, in order to get a program called by the control program, one has to locate the table in CONTRL which contains the first eight characters of each recognized control card. If one of the entries of the form USER i is available, you can replace this entry with the first eight characters you intend to have on your program control card. The corresponding CALL statement in CALLER will have to be changed to call your program. If no such entry is available, you will have to make a new entry in the control-card list in CONTRL, enter a new statement number in the computed GO TO that is among the first executable statements after the initialization in CONTRL, set up an appropriate RETURN statement at the end of CONTRL, modify the computed GO TO in CALLER, and install a new CALL statement in CALLER.

After a new program has received control, it has three basic responsibilities: (1) cause CONCRD to read the control card following the control card for your program and its extensions, (2) do not stop calling OBSERV until the end of file is reached once you have called it at all, and (3) return control to CALLER when your program is finished. The first responsibility must be fulfilled prior to calling either STATOP or OBSERV and is probably best accomplished by calling STACK to interpret the control-card arguments since STACK always reads up to the next control card.

The accompanying program listing illustrates a simple program to calculate the mean and standard deviation of the variables listed on the procedure control card.

This sample program is divided into two separate subroutines. The first serves simply to read the control card while the second performs the actual processing on the basis of the information passed to it by the first. The major reason for using two subroutines concerns utilization of the block of storage obtained by the main program. It is convenient to use this block of storage (1) as a double-word vector which can contain the arguments found on the control card and (2) as three full-word vectors which can contain the information on each variable necessary for calculating the mean and standard deviation. Since Fortran takes a dim view of using a dummy parameter in an EQUIVALENCE statement, two separate routines are used.

The first task undertaken by the first subroutine is the determination of the size problem it can handle based on the size of the block of storage passed to it. Next, subroutines STACK and STATOP are called in succession to read the task control card and any associated OPTIONS and STATISTICS cards. The sample program considers the setting of only one switch, the one associated with option 1, but calling STATOP is a simple method of taking care of these two cards in a uniform manner.

Following the reading of the associated control cards, the sample program compares the items contained in the argument list which was returned by STACK with the contents of the variable-name vector VARNAM. If any items in the argument list cannot be found in VAR-NAM, an error is reported by calling subroutine ERROR. After processing the argument list, a check is made to ensure that not too many variables have been requested by considering the maximum size problem which can be handled given the core available.

By testing the logical value of QFATAL, the first subroutine is able to determine whether any errors have been detected so far on this run. If so, it is forbidden to call OBSERV, so the sample program elects to return control without calling the second subroutine. If there have not been any errors, the core which was passed from the calling program is allocated into three full-word vectors of length MXVAR. Notice that the block of core is being considered to be a double-word vector in the first subroutine, so it is actually passed as three double-word vectors of length MXVAR/2 each.

```
      SUBROUTINE MNSTD(SPACE,LSPACE)                             MNST0010
      INTEGER LSPACE                                             MNST0020
      REAL *8 SPACE(1)                                           MNST0030
C                                                                MNST0040
C     SAMPLE USER-PROVIDED SUBROUTINE FOR USE WITH SPSS.  IT IS IN MNST0050
C     TWO PARTS.                                                 MNST0060
C     THE FIRST PART READS THE CONTROL CARD,                     MNST0070
C     THE SECOND PART PROCESSES CASES AND PRINTS RESULTS.        MNST0080
C                                                                MNST0090
C     'SPACE' IS THE STORAGE ACQUIRED BY THE SO-CALLED 'MAIN' PROGRAM MNST0100
C     THRU A 'GETMAIN' SVC.  'LSPACE' IS THE LENGTH OF THIS AREA IN MNST0110
C     FULL-WORDS.  'SPACE' IS DOUBLE-WORD ALIGNED.               MNST0120
C                                                                MNST0130
C     'SPACE' IN THE CALL SEQUENCE WILL BE USED FIRST AS A       MNST0140
C     DOUBLE-WORD VECTOR.  IT IS THEN PASSED TO THE SECOND PART AS MNST0150
C     THREE FULL-WORD VECTORS.                                   MNST0160
C                                                                MNST0170
C     ................... MAIN SPSS COMMON SECTIONS .................MNST0180
      REAL *8 FILDAT,FILNAM,SFDIC(100),TDYDAT,VARNAM(506),WORD1,WORD2 MNST0190
     CREAL *4 B(200),FLABEL(16),FMTIN(200),OBS(700),RLABEL(16),  MNST0200
     1        SAMPCP,SAMPCT,TMISS,XMISS(506,3)                   MNST0210
     CINTEGER *4 DCMT1,DCMT2,IBLOCK,IDIC,IGP,IOBCD1,IOBCD2,IOCR,IOFILE, MNST0220
     1        IOFIL2,IOLP,IOSCR1,IOSCR2,IPAGE,ISF,ISTR,ITRNSF(1000), MNST0230
     2        LBLPNT(3,506),LINE,LINEMX,LITORG,NCARD,NCASES(100), MNST0240
     3        NCL,NCL1,NCL2,NDIC,NGP,NOOB,NPCL,NPTRN,NSF,NTR,NTRANS, MNST0250
     4        NVAR,NVNEW,NVOLD,NVTRN,NVTRNP,TRNORG,WGTVAR,WGTVRP  MNST0260
     OINTEGER *2 INDTRA(250),ITRNOP(1000),NMISS(506),SFGRP(100), MNST0270
     1        STRING(66),VFMT(506)                               MNST0280
     OLOGICAL *1 QCHANG,QFATAL,QMISS(506),QOPT(20),QOPTSR(20),QPASS2, MNST0290
     1        QSKEEP(100),QSTAT(24),QSTRNG(2,66),QSW(20),        MNST0300
     2        QVKEEP(506)                                        MNST0310
     OCOMMON /CMN1/ WORD1,WORD2,B,SAMPCP,SAMPCT,TMISS,DCMT1,DCMT2, MNST0320
     1        IBLOCK,IDIC,IGP,IOBCD1,IOBCD2,IOCR,IOFILE,IOFIL2,  MNST0330
     2        IOLP,IOSCR1,IOSCR2,IPAGE,ISF,ISTR,LINE,LINEMX,     MNST0340
     3        LITORG,NCARD,NCASES,NCL,NCL1,NCL2,NDIC,NGP,NOOB,   MNST0350
     4        NPCL,NPTRN,NSF,NTR,NTRANS,NVAR,NVNEW,NVOLD,NVTRN,  MNST0360
     5        NVTRNP,TRNORG,WGTVAR,WGTVRP,STRING,QCHANG,QFATAL,  MNST0370
     6        QMISS,QOPT,QOPTSR,QPASS2,QSKEEP,QSTAT,QSW,QVKEEP   MNST0380
     CCOMMON /CMN2/ FILDAT,FILNAM,SFDIC,TDYDAT,VARNAM,FLABEL,FMTIN, MNST0390
     1        RLABEL,INDTRA,ITRNOP,ITRNSF,LBLPNT,SFGRP,VFMT      MNST0400
      COMMON /CMN3/ OBS,NMISS,XMISS                              MNST0410
      EQUIVALENCE (STRING,QSTRNG)                                MNST0420
C     .........................................................MNST0430
```

```
C                                                                          MNST0440
C          ................. SPECIFIC TASK COMMON SECTION .................MNST0450
       COMMON /MSCMN/ MVAR,NMV                                             MNST0460
       INTEGER MVAR(500),NMV                                               MNST0470
C          ................................................................MNST0480
C                                                                          MNST0490
       INTEGER MXARG,NARG,IARG,MXVAR,IVAR,S2,S3                            MNST0500
C                                                                          MNST0510
C      CALCULATE PROGRAM LIMITATIONS.                                      MNST0520
       MXVAR = MINO(500,(LSPACE/6)*2)                                      MNST0530
       MXARG = MINO(500,LSPACE/2)                                          MNST0540
C                                                                          MNST0550
C      READ CONTROL CARD BY USING SUBROUTINE 'STACK'.                      MNST0560
C      ARGUMENTS TO 'STACK'..                                              MNST0570
C      1. REAL *8 VECTOR OF SYMBOLS FOUND.                                 MNST0580
C      2. INTEGER MAXIMUM NUMBER OF SYMBOLS TO RETURN.                     MNST0590
C      3. INTEGER NUMBER OF SYMBOLS ACTUALLY RETURNED.                     MNST0600
       CALL STACK(SPACE,MXARG,NARG)                                        MNST0610
C                                                                          MNST0620
C      PROCESS VECTOR.  DO NOT RECOGNIZE 'INCLUSIVE TO' CONVENTION.        MNST0630
C      INDICES OF REQUESTED VARIABLES GO IN VECTOR 'MVAR'.                 MNST0640
C      THE NUMBER OF VARIABLES IS ACCUMULATED IN 'NMV'.                    MNST0650
       NMV = 0                                                             MNST0660
       DO 120 IARG = 1,NARG                                                MNST0670
       DO 100 IVAR = 1,NVAR                                                MNST0680
  100 IF (VARNAM(IVAR) .EQ. SPACE(IARG)) GO TO 110                         MNST0690
C                                                                          MNST0700
C      ARGUMENT IS NOT A DECLARED VARIABLE - REPORT AN ERROR.              MNST0710
       CALL ERROR(2001)                                                    MNST0720
       GO TO 120                                                           MNST0730
  110 NMV = NMV+1                                                          MNST0740
       MVAR(NMV) = IVAR                                                    MNST0750
  120 CONTINUE                                                             MNST0760
C                                                                          MNST0770
C      CHECK FOR EXCESSIVE CORE REQUIREMENTS.                              MNST0780
       IF (NMV .GT. MXVAR) CALL ERROR(2002)                               MNST0790
C                                                                          MNST0800
C      GET OPTIONS AND STATISTICS CARDS READ AND INTERPRETED.             MNST0810
       CALL STATOP                                                         MNST0820
C                                                                          MNST0830
C      IF NO ERRORS HAVE OCCURRED, PASS CONTROL TO NEXT SUBROUTINE.        MNST0840
       IF (QFATAL) GO TO 900                                               MNST0850
       S2 = MXVAR/2+1                                                      MNST0860
       S3 = MXVAR/2+S2                                                     MNST0870
       CALL MST2(SPACE,SPACE(S2),SPACE(S3))                               MNST0880
  900 RETURN                                                               MNST0890
       END                                                                 MNST0900
       SUBROUTINE MST2(SUM,SUMSQ,NOBS)                                     MST20010
       REAL SUM(1),SUMSQ(1),NOBS(1)                                        MST20020
C                                                                          MST20030
C      MST2 PROCESSES CASES AND CALCULATES MEAN & STD DEVIATION.           MST20040
C      THE THREE VECTORS APPEARING AS ARGUMENTS ARE USED TO                MST20050
C      ACCUMULATE SUM, SUM OF SQUARES, AND SUM OF CASES.                   MST20060
C                                                                          MST20070
C          ................. MAIN SPSS COMMON SECTIONS .................MST20080
       REAL *8 FILDAT,FILNAM,SFDIC(100),TDYDAT,VARNAM(506),WORD1,WORD2     MST20090
      OREAL *4 B(200),FLABEL(16),FMTIN(200),OBS(700),RLABEL(16),          MST20100
      1         SAMPCP,SAMPCT,TMISS,XMISS(506,3)                          MST20110
      OINTEGER *4 DCMT1,DCMT2,IBLOCK,IDIC,IGP,IOBCD1,IOBCD2,IOCR,IOFILE,   MST20120
      1         IOFIL2,IOLP,IOSCR1,IOSCR2,IPAGE,ISF,ISTR,ITRNSF(1000),     MST20130
      2         LBLPNT(3,506),LINE,LINEMX,LITORG,NCARD,NCASES(100),        MST20140
      3         NCL,NCL1,NCL2,NDIC,NGP,NOOB,NPCL,NPTRN,NSF,NTR,NTRANS,     MST20150
      4         NVAR,NVNEW,NVOLD,NVTRN,NVTRNP,TRNORG,WGTVAR,WGTVRP         MST20160
      OINTEGER *2 INDTRA(250),ITRNOP(1000),NMISS(506),SFGRP(100),          MST20170
      1         STRING(66),VFMT(506)                                       MST20180
      OLOGICAL *1 QCHANG,QFATAL,QMISS(506),QOPT(20),QOPTSR(20),QPASS2,     MST20190
      1         QSKEEP(100),QSTAT(24),QSTRNG(2,66),QSW(20),               MST20200
      2         QVKEEP(506)                                                MST20210
      OCOMMON /CMN1/ WORD1,WORD2,B,SAMPCP,SAMPCT,TMISS,DCMT1,DCMT2,       MST20220
      1         IBLOCK,IDIC,IGP,IOBCD1,IOBCD2,IOCR,IOFILE,IOFIL2,          MST20230
      2         IOLP,IOSCR1,IOSCR2,IPAGE,ISF,ISTR,LINE,LINEMX,             MST20240
      3         LITORG,NCARD,NCASES,NCL,NCL1,NCL2,NDIC,NGP,NOOB,           MST20250
      4         NPCL,NPTRN,NSF,NTR,NTRANS,NVAR,NVNEW,NVOLD,NVTRN,          MST20260
      5         NVTRNP,TRNORG,WGTVAR,WGTVRP,STRING,QCHANG,QFATAL,          MST20270
      6         QMISS,QOPT,QOPTSR,QPASS2,QSKEEP,QSTAT,QSW,QVKEEP           MST20280
      OCOMMON /CMN2/ FILDAT,FILNAM,SFDIC,TDYDAT,VARNAM,FLABEL,FMTIN,      MST20290
      1         RLABEL,INDTRA,ITRNOP,ITRNSF,LBLPNT,SFGRP,VFMT             MST20300
       COMMON /CMN3/ OBS,NMISS,XMISS                                       MST20310
       EQUIVALENCE (STRING,QSTRNG)                                         MST20320
C          ................................................................MST20330
C                                                                          MST20340
```

```
C        ................... SPECIFIC TASK COMMON SECTION ................... MST20350
         COMMON /MSCMN/ MVAR,NMV                                             MST20360
         INTEGER MVAR(500),NMV                                              MST20370
C        ............................................................MST20380
C                                                                          MST20390
         REAL MEAN,STDDEV                                                  MST20400
         INTEGER IMV,MOOB,IOBS                                             MST20410
         LOGICAL *1 QFINF,QFING,QFIRST                                     MST20420
C                                                                          MST20430
C        INITIALIZE FOR ENTIRE TASK.                                       MST20440
         QFIRST = .TRUE.                                                   MST20450
C                                                                          MST20460
C        INITIALIZE FOR NEXT SUBFILE GROUP.                                MST20470
   100   DO 110 IMV = 1,NMV                                                MST20480
         SUM(IMV) = 0.                                                     MST20490
         SUMSQ(IMV) = 0.                                                   MST20500
   110   NOBS(IMV) = 0.                                                    MST20510
C                                                                          MST20520
C        PROCESS A CASE AT A TIME.  READ EACH CASE BY CALLING 'OBSERV'.    MST20530
C        ARGUMENTS TO 'OBSERV'..                                          MST20540
C        1. INTEGER CUMULATIVE UNWEIGHTED CASES PROCESSED                  MST20550
C        2. LOGICAL *1 END OF FILE INDICATOR.                             MST20560
C        3. LOGICAL *1 END OF SUBFILE GROUP INDICATOR.                    MST20570
C        4. LOGICAL *1 FIRST CALL INDICATOR.                              MST20580
   200   CALL OBSERV(MOOB,QFINF,QFING,QFIRST)                             MST20590
         IF (QFINF) RETURN                                                MST20600
         IF (QFING) GO TO 300                                             MST20610
C                                                                          MST20620
C        BUMP COUNTERS FOR EACH VARIABLE WHICH IS NOT 'MISSING' UNLESS    MST20630
C        OPTION 1 WAS SPECIFIED IN WHICH CASE NO CHECK IS MADE FOR        MST20640
C        MISSING VALUES.                                                  MST20650
         DO 210 IMV = 1,NMV                                               MST20660
         IF (QMISS(MVAR(IMV)) .AND. .NOT. QOPTSR(1)) GO TO 210            MST20670
         NOBS(IMV) = NOBS(IMV)+OBS(3)                                     MST20680
         SUM(IMV) = SUM(IMV)+OBS(MVAR(IMV))*OBS(3)                        MST20690
         SUMSQ(IMV) = SUMSQ(IMV)+OBS(MVAR(IMV))**2*OBS(3)                 MST20700
   210   CONTINUE                                                         MST20710
C                                                                          MST20720
C        END OF SUBFILE GROUP - PRINT FULL HEADER BY CALLING 'DPHEAD'.    MST20730
   300   CALL DPHEAD                                                      MST20740
         WRITE (IOLP,310)                                                 MST20750
   310   FORMAT (50HOVARIABLE          MEAN         STD DEV       CASES/)  MST20760
         CALL LINECT(3)                                                   MST20770
C                                                                          MST20780
C        CALCULATE AND PRINT MEAN & STANDARD DEVIATION FOR EACH VARIABLE  MST20790
         DO 410 IMV = 1,NMV                                               MST20800
         MEAN = SUM(IMV)/NOBS(IMV)                                        MST20810
         STDDEV = SQRT((SUMSQ(IMV)-SUM(IMV)**2/NOBS(IMV))/(NOBS(IMV)-1.)) MST20820
         IOBS = NOBS(IMV)+0.5                                             MST20830
         WRITE (IOLP,400) VARNAM(MVAR(IMV)),MEAN,STDDEV,IOBS             MST20840
   400   FORMAT (1X,A8,2(3X,F12.3),3X,I8)                                MST20850
   410   CALL LINECT(1)                                                  MST20860
C                                                                          MST20870
C        FINISHED PRINTING RESULTS, RE-INITIALIZE & GET ANOTHER           MST20880
C        SUBFILE GROUP IF ONE EXISTS.                                     MST20890
         GO TO 100                                                        MST20900
         END                                                             MST20910
```

The second subroutine uses the three vectors passed to it to hold the sum, sum of squares, and number of cases for each variable mentioned in the argument list on the control card. Note that, if option 1 is in effect, all values whether missing or not will be used in the computations so that all variables will have the same number of cases. By taking this fact into consideration, it would be possible to allocate the available core differently depending upon the setting of option switch 1. Many SPSS routines including REGRESSION and PARTIAL CORR do in fact allocate core based on the settings of option and statistics switches.

Following a straightforward initialization, the second subroutine enters a loop which is ended only when the end of a subfile group of observations has been reached. This same body of code is returned to successive times until all subfile groups have been processed as evidenced by the setting of the logical variable QFINF. In this loop, the sample program refers to the value and missing condition of each variable by using MVAR as the subscript of the vectors OBS and QMISS respectively. Successive variables which were found on the task card are reached by incrementing the subscript of MVAR itself. Thus MVAR provides the same indirect specification function fulfilled by KVAR in the FASTABS series.

Upon reaching the end of a subfile group, as indicated by the setting of the logical variable QFING, the sample program obtains a page ejection on the printer accompanied by the printing of the run name, the file name, and the names of the subfiles being processed by calling DPHEAD. It then prints the header for its own printout and calls LINECT to specify the number of lines printed. There follows a loop to print a line for each variable. Notice that LINECT is called after each line is printed so that a new header will be printed when the current page is filled. Finally the sample program goes back to try to read another subfile group.

In summary, the following points should be kept in mind when adding a new procedure to SPSS:

1.  Modify CONTRL and CALLER to pass control to your routine.
2.  Use the double-word aligned full-word vector which is passed to your program at your discretion.
3.  Cause CONCRD to read the control card following those concerned with your program.
4.  If you are going to use OBSERV to read the cases, do not return to the calling program until the end of file has been reached.
5.  Leave LINECT with a good estimate of the number of lines printed on the last page on which you printed output.

# I
# LISTING OF CASES AND DATA-DEFINITION CARDS FOR EXAMPLE FILES

## I.1  FILE COMSTUDY

### I.1.1  DATA-DEFINITION CARDS FOR FILE COMSTUDY

```
1               16
FILE NAME       COMSTUDY,STUDY OF AMERICAN SMALL COMMUNITIES
VARIABLE LIST   COMCO01,CARDN01,MEDSCH,MEDFINC,PTGOHS,PTAGRI,PTMANU,PTTERTRY,
                POP60,POPLAT,PTCHNG,SPISOL,WHTCOLAR,LIFE,TIME,NEWSWEEK,READDIG,
                HRSWORK,GOVSELCT,CONELECT,PARTISAN,PARTROLE
VAR LABELS      COMCO01,COMMUNITY CODE/
                CARDN01,CARD NUMBER/
                MEDSCH,MEDIAN SCHOOL YEARS FOR POPULATION OVER 25/
                MEDFINC,MEDIAN FAMILY INCOME/
                PTGOHS,PERCENT TOTAL UNITS GOOD HOUSING/
                PTAGRI,PERCENT LABOR IN AGRICULTURE-FOREST-FISHING/
                PTTERTRY,PERCENT LABOR IN TERTIARY INDUSTRY/
                POP60,TOTAL POPULATION IN 1960/
                POPLAT,TOTAL POPULATION LATEST ESTIMATE/
                PTCHNG,PERCENT POPULATION CHANGE 1960-66/
                SPISOL,DEGREE OF SPATIAL ISOLATION/
                WHTCOLAR,PERCENT CIVILIAN LABOR IN WHITE COLLAR OCCUPATIONS/
                LIFE,LIFE MAGAZINE SALES PER 1000 POPULATION/
                TIME,TIME MAGAZINE SALES PER 1000 POPULATION/
                NEWSWEEK,NEWSWEEK SALES PER 1000 POPULATION/
                READDIG,READERS DIGEST SALES PER 1000 POPULATION/
                HRSWORK,WORKING HOURS PER WEEK HEAD OF GOVERNMENT/
```

```
                      GOVSELCT,METHOD OF SELECTING HEAD OF GOVERNMENT/
                      CONELECT,ELECTION OF HEAD OF GOVERNMENT CONTESTED/
                      PARTISAN,ELECTION HEAD LEGALLY PARTISAN/
                      PARTROLE,ACTUAL ROLE OF PARTIES ELEC HEAD
VALUE LABELS          HRSWORK (1) LESS THAN 5 HRS (2) 6-10 HRS (3) 11-20 HRS
                      (4) 21-30 HRS (5) 31-40 HRS (6) OVER 40 HRS
                      (7) MISSING (8) INAPPLICABLE (9) NA/
                      GOVSELCT (1) DIRECT ELECTION (2) ELECT LOCAL BOARD
                      (3) APPOINTED BY HIGHER ATH (4) OTHER (8) NO LOCAL HEAD
                      (9) NA (0) MISSING/
                      CONELECT (1) ALWAYS CONTESTED (2) USUALLY CONTESTED
                      (3) OCCASIONALLY CONTEST (4) NEVER CONTESTED
                      (8) APPOINTED (9) NA (0) MISSING/
                      PARTISAN (1) NONPARTSN BY LAW (2) PARTISAN
                      (8) NO LOCAL GOVT HEAD (9) NA (0) MISSING/
                      PARTROLE (1) RUN WITH PART LABEL (2) NO LABEL BUT AFFIL
                      (3) TOTALLY NONPARTSN (8) NO GOVT HEAD (9) NA (0) MISSING
MISSING VALUES HRSWORK (7,8,9)/GOVSELCT TO PARTROLE (8,9,0)
PRINT FORMATS  COMC001,CARDN01,MEDFINC,POP60,POPLAT,SPISOL,LIFE TO PARTROLE(0),
               MEDSCH,PTGOHS TO PTTERTRY,PTCHNG,WHTCOLAR(1)
INPUT MEDIUM   CARD
INPUT FORMAT   FIXED (F3.0,F2.0,F4.1,F5.0,4F4.1,2F7.0,F5.1,F2.0,F4.1,4F3.0,
               5F1.0)
# OF CASES     64
```

### I.1.2    DATA CASES FROM FILE COMSTUDY

```
 22 1  86 5097 217 720  33 247  8350      0    0 4 170  0  0  0 005020
 41 1  86 2757 557 613 151 168   417      0    010 168  0  0  0 006080
 61 1  95 6100 819   5 426 355 19062  21200  112 0 339 39  7  5 8505060
 72 1  94 4917 775 262  61 471 11913  13400  125 5 408 34 10  8 7605010
 81 1 126 8191 946  17 213 574 40568  42800   55 0 622 68 34 12 005060
 82 1 114 6718 977  17 294 350 24723  30000  213 0 327102 25 2231205060
123 1  85 4417 568 102 150 451  4835   6000  241 8 259  0  0  0 6705060
131 1 121 7908 873  85 574 341  4785   5300  108 5 628 91 50 22 9905060
141 1 119 4444 966  16  66 569  3197  11000 2441 9 555 34 15  0 099999
142 1 101 3685 723   6  32 517  3157   3157    0 9 334 84 36 6377288800
152 1  94 5278   0  16 176 424 20117      0    0 1 352  0  0  0 006060
181 1  98 5963 778 341 325 334 11880      0    0 6 400  0  4  4 6805060
231 1 108 4655   0 358 223 262   538      0    010  13  0  0  0 006080
232 1 121 5815 701  12 278 526  2517   2517    010 498 91 21 2326305010
241 1 108 6632 601 310 341 349 17184      0    010 403  0  0  0 005016
261 1  99 6340 501 295 475 243  1217      0    0 2 280  0  0  0 005060
272 1 114 4513 623 165   7 517  1674      0    010 421  0 17 017905010
281 1 120 4786 698  36 181 533  3028   3028    010 440 32 12 1014501060
291 1  74 1678 790 338  56 327  3986      0    010 211  0  0  0 004080
292 1 108 4439 806   9  59 536  7819      0    010 541 27  7  7 9505010
301 1  89 4189 568  21 347 375 15193  15500   20 7 368 13  4  5 6045010
311 1  65 2894 647  75  79 441  6468   6468    0 9 322 25  8  0 2901010
321 1 119 4050 7C3  42 268 379  1715   1750  2010 376 79 31 1820705080
342 1  89 3980 409 142 419 295  1160      0    010 301  0  0 1320005010
352 1  94 6405 621 366  94 538  1196      0    010 363347 81 4659605010
391 1  88 3242   0  83 330 275   541      0    010 239  0  0  0 004080
412 1  86 6375 855 201 443 354 49658      0    0 3 298 30  7  4 7805015
421 1 137 7171 915   6 367 399 15173  24789  634 7 446  0  4  0 005060
442 1 119 5595 762   4  47 466 17731  16800  -53 8 487 46 27 1212601010
451 1 117 7216 952   4 408 373 18676  20300   87 7 469 19  6  0 005060
471 1 122 6279 765  31  45 550 10740  11800   99 8 463 46 22 2214105010
482 1  95 4092 844 115  67 560  1513      0    011 409  0 4328819401060
491 1  86 6291 906   2 585 260 29253  29300    2 6 281 64  6  4 5715060
502 1 102 5956 755  10 300 421 35789  33500  -64 3 428 53 18 32 8105016
513 1  93 5862 689   0 435 302  5862      0    0 7 262  0  0  0 005010
542 1 128 8517 948 348 126 526 11037      0    0 3 510  0  0  0 045010
552 1 121 7244 822   1 345 476 21261  21146   -5 4 578104 61  0 005010
581 1 118 8463 941   2 248 541 17499  17762   15 3 640121 40 3823505010
622 1  86 4827 659   5 469 311 37276  45429  219 6 319 36  8  7 9101510
632 1 102 4410 729  15 301 455  6159   6159    0 7 406 55 22 1725101510
651 1 122 5849 781  11  71 624 34451  38500 11811 530 56 43 2311405010
661 1 101 4703 524  90  41 622  1566      0    011 590  0 20 017504510
672 1  94 6879 968 230 540 229  9286      0    0 2 322  0 16 11 5605070
682 1 125 9384 995   5 382 468 16805  18500  101 3 658 75 32  0 005010
692 1 105 5155 756  25 385 415  3116   3116    0 8 357 42 33 1117705060
711 1 121 6000 881  14 385 644 24411  25500   45 7 525 36 17 1514201010
721 1  87 2942   0 463  74 379   239      0    011 368  0  0  0 005080
732 1 110 5945 680  35 210 498  3263   3594  101 9 420 53 33 2020205070
742 1 113 6005   0 151 179 465  3084      0    0 6 383  0  0  0 005060
743 1 115 5859 831  19 121 645 49142  63500  292 6 552 71 35 1917305060
751 1 122 7475 908 327 288 385 25952  32283  244 1 562  0  0  0 005016
781 1  90 4338 741   0 436 384  5958   5958    0 9 357 21  8 14 7045016
782 1  72 5339   0  91 212 394   661      0    0 9 205  0  0  0 005060
791 1 114 6828 928   5 423 372  7249   88C0  214 6 448 95 22 1113488800
```

```
802 1  90 4406 845    6 306 424   13674   12600   -79 8 373 62 14   813705C060
821 1 109 5313 780   11 385 368    3982    3982     C 7 410 35 14  2012105010
831 1  63 2326 316   73 352 258     700       0     0 9 258  0  0    0  C05010
861 1 104 4745 665   7C 3C1 395    4642    4642     C 5 426 27 11    0 8205010
881 1 125 5142 843   31  21 266    5864    8500   450 7 469 42 19  2211105010
891 1 121 5478 772   15 177 478   51230   56000   931C 502 34 13   810005010
893 1  89 3327 583  485 201 314    3335       0    C10 385  0  0    0  005080
912 1 113 5521 849   11 197 511    952C   10300    82 4 395  0  0    0  C05016
932 1   0    0  U    0   C   0    49845       0     C 3   0  0  0    0  005060
951 1 118 6390 788    9 277 515   37987   38600    16 6 489 65 30 15   005060
```

## I.2    FILE ORGSTUDY

### I.2.1    DATA-DEFINITION CARDS FOR FILE ORGSTUDY

```
1                  16
FILE NAME          ORGSTUDY,STUDY OF ORGANIZATIONAL MEMBERSHIP AND ACTIVITY
SUBFILE LIST       NEWYCRK,NWJERSEY,PENNSYLV
# OF CASES         100,115,135
VARIABLE LIST      COMMID,RESPID,RESDYTH,MARITAL,FRATMEM,SERVMEM,VETMEM,
                   POLMEM,UNIONMEM,SPORTMEM,YOUTHMEM,SCHOLMEM,HOBMEM,SCHFRMEM,
                   NATMEM,FARMEM,LITMEM,PROFMEM,RELMEM,OTHMEM,NMEM,NACT,RELIG,AGE,
                   INCOME,EDRESPON,SEX,RACE,OCLEVRES
VAR LABELS         COMMID,US COMMUNITY ID NUMBER/
                   RESPID,RESPONDENT ID NUMBER/
                   RESDYTH,RESIDENCE FIRST 15 YEARS/
                   MARITAL,MARITAL STATUS/
                   FRATMEM,MEMB IN FRATERNAL ORGS/
                   SERVMEM,MEMB IN SERVICE CLUBS/
                   VETMEM,MEMB IN VETERANS GRPS/
                   POLMEM,MEMB IN POLITICAL ORGS/
                   UNIONMEM,MEMB IN LABOR UNION/
                   SPORTMEM,MEMB IN SPORTS CLUBS/
                   YOUTHMEM,MEMB IN YOUTH GROUPS/
                   SCHOLMEM,MEMB IN SCHOOL SERVICE GRPS/
                   HOBMEM,MEMB IN HOBBY-GARDEN CLUBS/
                   SCHFRMEM,MEMB SCHOOL FRAT-SORORITY/
                   NATMEM,MEMB NATIONAL ORGS/
                   FARMEM,MEMB FARM ORGS/
                   LITMEM,MEMB LIT-ART GRPS/
                   PROFMEM,MEMB PROF-ACADEMIC ORGS/
                   RELMEM,MEMB IN RELIGIOUS ORGS/
                   OTHMEM,OTHER MEMBERSHIPS/
                   NMEM,TOTAL NUMBER OF MEMBERSHIPS/
                   NACT,TOTAL NUMBER ACTIVE MEMBERSHIPS/
                   RELIG,RELIGIOUS AFFILIATION/
                   AGE,AGE LAST BIRTHDAY/
                   INCCME,FAMILY INCOME/
                   EDRESPON,LAST YEAR SCHOOL COMPLETED/
                   SEX,RESPONDENTS SEX/
                   RACE,RESPONDENTS RACE/
                   OCLEVRES,OCCUP LEVEL OF RESPONDENT
VALUE LABELS       RESDYTH (1)MOSTLY FARM(2)MSTLY SMALL TOWN (3)MSTLY SMALL CITY
                           (4)MSTLY BIG CITY,SUBERB(9)NA,DK(0)INAPPLICABLE/
                   MARITAL (1)MARRIED(2)WIDOWED(3)DIVORCED(4)SEPARATED
                           (5)NEVER MARRIED(8)DK(9)NA(0)REFUSED/
                   FRATMEM TO OTHMEM (1)YES(0)NO(8)NA/
                   NMEM,NACT (0)NONE(1)ONE(2)TWO(3)THREE(4)FOUR(5)FIVE(6)SIX
                           (7)SEVEN(8)8-12(9)13-16/
                   RELIG (1)PROTESTANT(2)CATHOLIC(3)JEWISH(4)SHINTO,TAO(5)NONE
                           (6)ORTHODOX(7)BUDDHIST,CONF(8)HINDU,MUSLIM(9)OTHER-NONPROT
                           (0)NA/
                   INCOME (01)LESS THAN 1C00(02)1000-1999(03)2000-2999(04)3000-3999
                           (05)4000-4999(06)5000-5999(07)6000-6999(11)7000-7999
                           (21)8000-8999(31)9000-9999(41)10000-14999(51)15000-19999
                           (61)20000-24999(71)25000 AND OVER(88)REFUSED(98)NA(99)DK/
                   EDRESPON (1)NONE(2)1-8 YEARS (3)9-11 YEARS(4)12 YEARS
                           (5)COLLEGE INCOMPLETE(6)COLLEGE GRAD(7)COLLEGE PLUS
                           (9)DK(0)NA/
                   SEX (1)MALE(2)FEMALE/
                   RACE (1)WHITE(2)NEGRO(3)ORIENTAL(4)INDIAN AMERICAN
                           (5)LATIN AMERICAN(8)OTHER(0)NA/
                   OCLEVRES (1)UNSKILLED(2)AMBIG SKILL (3)INDEPENDENTS(4)SKILLED
                           (5)CLRC,SALE,LOTEC(6)PROF,MANG(0)OTHER
MISSING VALUES     RESDYTH(0,7,9)/MARITAL(0,8,9)/FRATMEM TO OTHMEM(8)/
                   RELIG(9)/AGE(98,99)/INCOME(88,98,99)/EDRESPON(0,9)/
                   RACE(0)/OCLEVRES(0)
INPUT FORMAT       FIXED (F3.0,F2.0,1X,21F1.0,2F2.0,1X,4F1.0)
INPUT MEDIUM       CARD
PRINT FORMATS      COMMID TO OCLEVRES (0)
```

## I.2.2   DATA CASES FOR FILE ORGSTUDY

```
11  1  42000000000000000000176 3 2215
11  2  11000000000000000000124 6 3210
11  3  11000000000000000000150 4 2114
11  4  11000000000000000000124 7 2112
11  5  11000000000000000014141   4212
11  6  01000000000000000000140 7 4115
11  7  11000000000000000013421   4215
11  8  31100000000000000001115441 5116
11  9  31000000000000000000145 2 2220
1110  05000000000000000000125 1 3122
1111  95000000000000000000129 2 3221
1112  01000000000000000000126 1 3221
1113  01000000000000000000126 2 3221
1114  92000000000000000110165 1 4121
1115  01000000000000000000137 3 2122
21  1  42000000000000001011179 6 3210
21  2  11000000000000000000015711   3210
21  3  22000000000000001012115488   4215
21  4  21100010010000000003116711   5112
21  5  21000000000000001001015488   3116
21  6  21000010000000000001014888   4114
21  7  12000000010000000011149 6 4215
21  8  12000000000000000000138 1 2221
21  9  14000000000000000000151 1 2222
2110  13000010000000000010154 4 2121
2111  12000010000000000010173 2 2121
2112  01000010000000000010129 4 4124
2113  13000000000000000000174 3 2122
2114  45000000000000000000144 1 4221
2115  45000000000000000000135 3 4221
22  1  01000010000000001021123 4 4122
22  2  15000000000000000000125 4 3222
22  3  21000010000000000001114441 2122
22  4  11000100000000000000164 2 2122
22  5  11000000000000000110161 5 2220
22  6  11100000010000000002113311 3220
22  7  12100000000000000010166 3 2220
22  8  11000010000000000010154 4 2124
22  9  14000000000000000110140 2 2221
2210  11100000000000000120165 4 2220
2211  21000000000000000110129 3 2220
2212  41000010000000000011152 4 3124
2213  21000000000000000000141 6 2220
2214  41000000000000000000121 4 4121
2215  11000000000000000000168 3 2220
2216  25000000000000000000124 4 4121
2217  21000000010000000011163 5 4221
2218  41000000000000000000013511   4222
2219  15000000000000000000149 7 3221
2220  21000000000000000000137 5 4124
2221  41100101110110010077713951 6120
2222  31000000010000000011173 3 6220
31  1  01000000000000000000246 7 1210
31  2  11000000000000000000126 7 4115
31  3  41000000000000000000013611   6113
31  4  21011011000000000004104388   6115
31  5  11010000000000000011160 4 5216
31  6  11000000000000001001114411 5115
31  7  01000000000000000000548 7 2210
31  8  21000000000000000000120 3 2210
31  9  22000000000000000000164 3 3212
3110  11000000000000000000128 7 3210
3111  21100010000000000002215911 2114
3112  31000010000000000011235 3 4114
3113  11000000000000000000175 3 5116
3114  21000000000000000000157 5 3113
3115  11000000000000001011174 2 2210
41  1  11000000000000000000156 4 2210
41  2  01000000010000000011127 6 3210
41  3  11000000000000000000156 3 2210
41  4  11000000000000000000167 3 2112
41  5  11000000000000000000122 5 4214
41  6  11000000000000000000153 3 2112
41  7  11000000000000000000170 3 2113
41  8  11001000000001000022141 4 4111
41  9  11000000000000000000146 1 2113
4110  11000000000000000000168 1 2210
4111  01000000000000000000159 6 2113
4112  11000000000000000000137 2 2210
4113  11000000000000000000172 2 2210
```

```
4114 110000000010000000001114099 3212
4115 110000000100000000011248 4 4210
4116 110000000000000000000152 1 2111
4117 210000001001000000021125551 5210
4118 210000000100000000010148°9 2210
4119 110000000000000000000550 1 1111
4120 410000000100010000021134511 5210
4121 110010000000000000010176 2 2113
4122 210000000000000000000130 1 3212
42  1 210000000000000000000127 6 4210
42  2 110000000000000000000138 4 3210
42  3 110000000000000000000153 1 2210
42  4 110001010000000000011133 7 3215
42  5 110000000000000000000172 1 2113
42  6 111001000000000000011164 4 2113
42  7 110000000000000000000141 5 5112
43  1 110000000000000000015241 3116
43  2 010000001100000002124211 4215
43  3 210000000000000000012421 4210
43  4 020000000000000000000169. 1 2210
43  5 111000000000000000011163 3 2122
43  6 110000000000000000000152 2 2210
43  7 210000000000000000000125 4 4111
51  1 410001000000000000000181 7 4116
51  2 320000000000000000000179 3 4212
51  3 410000000010000000010559 7 5113
51  4 410000000000000000000525 6 6215
51  5 450000000000000000000324 1 5110
51  6 420000000001000000121383 5 3210
51  7 410000000000010010010524 5 6215
61  1 110000100000000000010275 4 3112
61  2 030000010000000000121228 6 5115
61  3 110000100000000000001015621 4112
61  4 011100001000000000003224841 2114
61  5 020100100000000000021260 6 2211
61  6 211000000000000000010178 4 1210
61  7 410000000000010000011253 7 7230
61  8 410000100000000000102024621 2210
61  9 240000000000000000000142 4 2221
6110 011000000100000000022141 3 3220
6111 350000000000000000000126 2 3221
6112 050000000000000010122253 5 4116
6113 226000000000000000000266 2 2112
6114 250000000000000000000228 6 2112
6115 210000000000000000000265 6 1112
6116 210000000000000001011139 3 3222
6117 140000100000000000001113371 2121
6118 450000100000010000021253 5 4111
6119 210000000010000000011127 4 4210
6120 410000100000000000001014311 2112
6121 010011000100000000021125 7 3210
6122 210000000000000000000246 7 3210
6123 010000000000000000000218 2 3211
71  1 410000000100000000001113831 4210
71  2 410000100000000000011548 7 3112
71  3 011000000000000000001012841 4210
71  4 110000001100000000022230411 4210
71  5 410000110000000000002215131 3115
71  6 110000100000000000001014731 4115
71  7 211000100000000000002115071 4114
71  8 310100000000000001002213951 4215
72  1 310100000000000000001156011 2113
72  2 111000100000000000013057388 2116
72  3 110000000000000000000258 6 5114
72  4 121010000000000000114417441 5216
72  5 110010000000000000001027611 2113
72  6 110000000000000001010177 3 2210
72  7 110000000100000001022148411 3212
72  8 210000000000000000000162 1 2220
72  9 210000000000000000000014121 3210
7210 210000000000000000000014511 4221
7211 310000000000000000000158 2 1111
7212 110000000000000000000015511 2123
7213 210000000000000000000160 3 2121
7214 110000000000000000000243 4 2111
7215 120000000000000000000187 1 2210
7216 210000000000000000000015811 6216
7217 220000000000000000000018499 2210
7218 250010100000100000030269 1 2111
7219 111000000000000000001015711 3113
7220 210000000000000000000262 3 2111
7221 210000000000010000001016541 6135
```

```
7222 14000CC0000C000CC000142 2 2211
 81 1 410000000000000000111126 6 4210
 81 2 110000000000000000000172 5 2112
 81 '3 31000C11CC010C000033142 4 6122
 81 4 410000000C0000000000225 6 3154
 81 5 110000C0C00000000000257 5 3215
 81 6 41000000010000000011124051 4215
 81 7 21000CC0000000000C000220 7 3210
 81 8 210100000C100000002215461 5210
 81 9 220110000C000000C02216711 6116
8110 310100CC1100000003315071 7210
8111 23000000C00000000000124 4 4111
8112 210000000000000000J0033051 7215
8113 210100001100000C1004113541 6116
8114 12000C000C0000C00000558 5 4214
8115 31000C000C00000CC00013551 4210
8116 41000C0C000000000000014151 4215
8117 21080100110000000002215061 4210
8118 41000C01C000C00012112221 3113
8119 120000000C0000000000155 6 4215
8120 110000100000000C001115921 2112
8121 3110001000000000002125841 4112
8122 420000018100001100C4214621 7216
 82 1 140000000000000000111159 6 5111
 82 2 41000000000000000011022431 4210
 82 3 410000100100C00000021136 7 4215
 82 4 110000111100000000004214711 5210
 82 5 21000010000000000001122411 4114
 82 6 21000000000000000000013041 4112
 82 7 21000C1001C00000002024231 3112
 82 8 41000C00000C0000000022921 3250
 82 9 41000000J0000000000012321 5210
8210 45000000000000000000012441 5110
8211 2110000000000000000010149 6 4115
8212 4100C010000000000001023121 4154
8213 1100C00000000C00000142 4 4114
8214 41000000000000000000013011 4215
8215 110000000C100C00000001014611 3210
8216 250100010100001000041218 7 4215
8217 111010100000000000003013151 5114
8218 41000011001000000003222421 3114
8219 21000C00000000000000022C11 3210
8220 410000000000000000000013121 3212
8221 41000C01000000000012123341 5116
8222 310000100000000000001123041 4114
 83 1 41C0000CC1000000000001113821 4230
 83 2 21000100000000000000016241 6210
 83 3 21000000010000001002014151 7116
 83 4 41C110011000000010521324l 6116
 83 5 310000C010000001002115651 5116
 83 6 130000000000001C01115711 4213
 83 7 01000100000000000000013441 4115
 83 8 31000000000000000094721 4210
 83 9 110100010000000002116441 6115
8310 210000000000000000C026841 5115
8311 420100000C0000000C1037311 3210
8312 21001100000C00000012114841 4115
8313 230100000C001C110044345 7 6215
8314 41100000000000000012197441 5116
8315 01000000000000000000223 7 5215
8316 11000000010000000C011142 6 2220
8317 44000000000010000C10121 5 5220
8318 22000000C00000000000174 3 2121
8319 010000000000000C000023131 3112
8320 120000100C001000C022156 6 3222
8321 410000000000000000000123 6 4124
8322 0100000010000010CC22122 5 5225
 84 1 41000000011100000003013641 6210
 84 2 21100100010000000C02015271 7216
 84 3 01000001010000000002013511 5215
 84 4 41000000000000000000024751 6115
 84 5 41110100000000000C02215351 6116
 84 6 41000010000000000001055921 4114
 84 7 410000000000000C0000017141 5116
 91 1 41000000000000000000129 7 4210
 91 2 11000000000000000000136 7 4215
 91 3 21000000000000000000052331 4212
 91 4 21001000000000000C01114741 5210
 91 5 410000000000000000000175 2 2114
 91 6 11000010001000000131171 4 2112
 91 7 310000100C000000001062141 5114
 91 8 14000000000000000000174 2 2222
```

```
 91  9 21000000000000000000235 6 5152
 91 10 93000000000000000000244 3 4250
 91 11 21000000000000000000231 7 2210
 91 12 31000000000000000000262 4 2152
 91 13 24000000000000010011139 1 4225
 91 14 41000100000000000000526 7 4121
101  1 22000000000100001020158 6 7216
101  2 01101000000000001003336461 7116
101  3 41000000010100110004223051 7116
101  4 41100000010100110005013941 7210
101  5 01000000000000000000014171 5210
101  6 43001001001000010004026161 6115
101  7 35000001010100110005012521 5215
111  1 11010000000000000001112651 5214
111  2 31001000000000000001024641 4112
111  3 41000000010000100002113341 6210
111  4 21000000010000000001112641 4210
111  5 41000010010000000002214331 3215
111  6 45000000001000001002113141 6116
111  7 41000000000000000000055841 3116
112  1 11000010000000000010148 2 2122
112  2 21000000000000000000142 5 4220
112  3 11000000000000000000146 7 3124
112  4 41000000010000000001124621 2210
112  5 45000000000000000000247 2 2112
112  6 11000000000000000000229 2 4210
112  7 11000010000000000001022621 3114
113  1 21000000000000000000011911 3210
113  2 21000010000000000012014431 4212
113  3 21100000000000000113315521 2212
113  4 31000001000000000001123331 5112
113  5 01010010000000000002012231 4112
113  6 23000000000000000000025831 4112
113  7 11000000010000000102273721 4230
121  1 41000000000000000000126 6 4210
121  2 21000000000000000000015621 2210
121  3 21000001100000000022145 7 5210
121  4 13000010000000000011564 4 2112
121  5 91000010100000000021126 3 5110
121  6 21000010000000000001014741 2111
121  7 21000000000000000000054711 2212
122  1 31000010000000000001012041 4215
122  2 41000000000000000101024511 4250
122  3 21100000000000000011218 6 4210
122  4 25000000110000000002112131 5215
122  5 45000000000000000000121 2 5110
122  6 41111010110000000017414051 5115
122  7 11001000001000000021570 4 2113
122  8 31000000000000000000014411 2114
123  1 11000001000000000000010154 3 2112
123  2 21000000000000000000146 4 3210
123  3 21000010000000000001012731 4112
123  4 21000000000000000000000127 6 3210
123  5 21000000000000000000000118 5 3210
123  6 11000000000000000000183 2 1112
123  7 11000010000000000010275 3 2114
123  8 41000000000000000000523 1 3211
123  9 22000000000000000000017499 3216
123 10 14000010000000000011157 6 2114
123 11 21000001100000000022213011 3112
123 12 11000000010000000010525 6 3210
123 13 11000000110000000022155 5 3210
123 14 41000000000000010010127 7 4215
123 15 11001000000000000001013111 5110
123 16 41000001000000000010124 6 4110
123 17 01000010000000000010126 7 5210
123 18 31000010010000000002012531 4210
123 19 11000000000000000000237 6 2210
123 20 41000001010000000021131 7 5110
123 21 21100001111000000005414131 7120
123 22 24000000000000000000012241 4114
123 23 31000000008000000000053551 5116
131  1 12000000000000000000017399 2210
131  2 41000000000000000000022741 6116
131  3 41000000000000000000137 7 5210
131  4 41000100000000010010024151 4215
131  5 41000101110000000003313971 5210
131  6 21100000000010000021140 7 3113
131  7 21000001000000000001113341 4112
131  8 21000000000000000000014421 3210
131  9 21000010000000000010122 7 4212
131 10 21000000000000000000017421 2114
```

```
13111 210000000000000000112123021 6210
13112 210000100000000000011221  3 4112
13113 410000000000000001011267  3 2210
13114 410010100000000000020274  6 2112
13115 330000000000000000000248  6 3112
13116 310000000000000000000024741 3215
13117 410000000000000000111170  2 2114
13118 210000000000000000000015341 4210
13119 410001000000000000000025541 2214
13120 210000000000000000111158  7 4114
13121 310000100000000000011123  7 4114
13122 320000000000000000000247  3 2212
132  1 310010101000000000003324041 3112
132  2 010000000000000000000022141 2212
132  3 250010010000000011004222541 5114
132  4 310000100100000000002224041 4215
132  5 910000000000000000000274  3 1112
132  6 410001100000010000021230  6 2112
132  7 010000000000000000000023221 3210
132  8 220000000000000000000269  4 2210
132  9 310000000111001000004022741 6210
13210 050000000000000000000022521 4115
13211 010001100010000000020236  7 3114
13212 050000000001000000001023151 5115
```

# SPSS INSTALLATIONS
## JULY, 1970

The places listed have had experience with SPSS. For information, write to the SPSS Coordinator at any of these addresses.

## IBM 360 SYSTEMS

Alberta Department of Agriculture
10405 100th Avenue
Edmonton, Alberta, Canada

Allstate Insurance Company
Judson Branch Research Center
Menlo Park, Calif. 94025

American Medical Association
Department of Survey Research
535 North Dearborn
Chicago, Ill. 60610

Boston College
Institute of Human Sciences
Chestnut Hill, Mass. 02167

Boston University
Computing Center
Boston, Mass. 02215

Carnegie-Mellon University
Graduate School of Industrial Administration
Pittsburgh, Pa. 15213

Chicago Area Transportation Study
230 North Michigan
Chicago, Ill. 60601

Chicago Heart Association
Stroke Rehabilitation Project
22 West Madison
Chicago, Ill. 60602

Cologne University
Institut für Vergleichende
    Sozialforschung
Lindenburger Allee 15
5 Cologne-Lindenthal, Germany

Columbia University
Bureau of Applied Social Research
605 West 115th Street
New York, N.Y. 10025

Cornell University
Office of Computer Services
Ithaca, N.Y. 14850

Dart Industries, Inc.
Market Compilation and Research Division
North Hollywood, Calif. 91609

Harvard University
Computing Center
Cambridge, Mass. 02138

International Business Machines Corp.
Old Orchard Road
Armonk, N.Y. 10504

Los Angeles Community Analysis Bureau
316 West Second Street, Suite 800
Los Angeles, Calif. 90012

Massachusetts Institute of Technology
Department of Political Science
Cambridge, Mass. 02139

Northern Illinois University
Computer Services Department
DeKalb, Ill. 60115

Ontario Institute for Studies in Education
252 Bloor Street West
Toronto 5, Ontario, Canada

Pennsylvania State University
Computation Center
University Park, Pa. 16802

Princeton University
Office of Survey Research
Princeton, N.J. 08540

Queen's University
Computing Center
Kingston, Ontario, Canada

Rand Corporation
Santa Monica, California 90406

Rutgers University
Office of Political Science Research
New Brunswick, N.J. 08903

Stanford University
Institute of Political Studies
Stanford, Calif. 94305

Syracuse University
Computing Center
Syracuse, N.Y. 13210

Tufts University School of Medicine
Clinical Pharmacology Unit
400 Totten Pond Road
Waltham, Mass. 02154

U.S. Forest Service
Personnel Management Division
USDA-RPE
Washington, D.C. 20550

U.S. National Institute of Mental Health
Laboratory of Socio-Environmental Studies
Bethesda, Md. 20014

University of Alberta
Computing Center
Edmonton, Alberta, Canada

University of Calgary
Data Centre
Calgary, Alberta, Canada

University of California at Los Angeles
Campus Computing Network
Mathematics Sciences Addition
Los Angeles, Calif. 90024

University of California at Los Angeles
Survey Research Center
Los Angeles, Calif. 90024

University of California at Riverside
Department of Political Science
Riverside, Calif. 92502

University of California at Santa Barbara
Department of Sociology
Santa Barbara, Calif. 93107

University of Chicago
National Opinion Research Center
Chicago, Ill. 60637

University of Connecticut
Department of Sociology
Storrs, Conn. 06268

University of Delaware
Department of Political Science
Newark, Del. 19711

University of Edinburgh
Edinburgh Regional Computing Centre
Mayfield Road
Edinburgh 9, Scotland

University of Florida
Computing Center
Gainesville, Fla. 32601

University of Illinois–Chicago Circle
Computer Center
Chicago, Ill. 60680

University of Illinois
Survey Research Laboratory
Urbana, Ill. 61801

University of Iowa
Laboratory for Political Research
Iowa City, Iowa 52240

University of Leiden
Institute of Cultural Anthropology
Stationsplein 10
Leiden, The Netherlands

University of Missouri
Institute of Psychiatry
St. Louis, Mo. 63139

University of New Brunswick
Computing Centre
Fredericton, New Brunswick, Canada

University of North Carolina
Computing Center
Chapel Hill, N.C. 27514

University of Oregon
Computing Center
Eugene, Ore. 97403

University of Pittsburgh
Social Science Information Center
Pittsburgh, Pa. 15213

University of Rochester
Computing Center
River Campus Station
Rochester, N.Y. 14627

University of South Florida
Computing Research Center
Tampa, Fla. 33620

University of Southern California
Department of International Relations
Los Angeles, Calif. 90007

University of Tennessee
Department of Political Science
Knoxville, Tenn. 37916

University of Waterloo
Computing Centre
Waterloo, Ontario, Canada

Utah State University
Computer Center
Logan, Utah 84321

Wayne State University
Computing & Data Processing Center
Detroit, Mich. 48202

Yale University
Computer Center
New Haven, Conn. 06520

## CDC SYSTEMS.

Chicago Area Transportation Study
230 North Michigan
Chicago, Ill. 60601
(CDC 6400–Northwestern University)

Colorado State University
University Computer Center
Fort Collins, Col. 80521
(CDC 6400)

Northwestern University
Vogelback Computing Center
Evanston, Ill. 60201
(CDC 6400)

State University of New York
Survey Research Center
Amherst, N.Y. 14226
(CDC 6400)

University of Massachusetts
Research Computing Center
Amherst, Mass. 01002
(CDC 3600)

University of Texas
Department of Government
Austin, Tex. 78712
(CDC 6600)

University of Washington
Computer Center
Seattle, Wash. 98105
(CDC 6400)